Rick Steves'
EUROPE THROUGH THE BACK DOOR
1999

D1537319

John Muir Publications
Santa Fe, New Mexico

JMP travel guidebooks by Rick Steves
Asia Through the Back Door (with Bob Effertz)
Europe 101: History and Art for the Traveler (with Gene Openshaw)
Rick Steves' Mona Winks: Self-Guided Tours of Europe's Top Museums
(with Gene Openshaw)
Rick Steves' Postcards from Europe
Rick Steves' Best of Europe
Rick Steves' France, Belgium & the Netherlands (with Steve Smith)
Rick Steves' Germany, Austria & Switzerland
Rick Steves' Great Britain & Ireland
Rick Steves' Italy
Rick Steves' Russia & the Baltics (with Ian Watson)
Rick Steves' Scandinavia
Rick Steves' Spain & Portugal
Rick Steves' London
Rick Steves' Paris
Rick Steves' Phrase Books: German, Italian, French, Spanish/Portuguese, and
French/Italian/German

John Muir Publications, P.O. Box 613, Santa Fe, NM 87504
Copyright ©1998, 1997, 1996, 1995, 1994, 1993, 1992, 1990, 1988, 1987, 1986,
1985, 1984, 1982, 1981, 1980 by Rick Steves
Cover copyright ©1998 by John Muir Publications
All rights reserved.

Printed in the United States of America
Seventeenth edition. Second printing March 1999.

For the latest on Rick's lectures, guidebooks, tours, and public television series,
contact Europe Through the Back Door, Box 2009, Edmonds, WA 98020, tel.
425/771-8303, fax 425/771-0833, Web site: www.ricksteves.com, or e-mail:
rick@ricksteves.com.

ISSN 1096-794X
ISBN 1-56261-460-6

Europe Through the Back Door Editor Risa Laib
John Muir Publications Editors Krista Lyons-Gould, Dianna Delling
Graphics Editor Tom Gaukel
Production Janine Lehmann, Nikki Rooker
Interior Design Janine Lehmann
Cover Design Janine Lehmann
Illustrations Melissa Meier
Typesetting Marcie Pottern
Maps David C. Hoerlein
Printer Publishers Press
Cover Photo Rothenburg, Germany; Leo de Wys Inc./Steve Vidler
Photography Rick Steves (unless otherwise credited)

Distributed to the book trade by
Publishers Group West
Berkeley, California

To the People of Europe

Rich Sorensen

Acknowledgments

Danke to Risa Laib for her travel savvy and editing. *Dank u wel* to Gene Openshaw, Dave Hoerlein, Steve Smith, Rich Sorensen, and Brian Carr Smith for research assistance. And *grazie* to the following for help in their fields of travel expertise: Dave Hoerlein (his artful maps); Matthew Brumley (tours); Dale Torgrimson (travel agent, flights); Kevin Christian (travel insurance); Cathie Bachy and Wide World Books (guidebooks); Mary Carlson and the staff at RailEurope (train travel); Richard Walters (biking); Brooke Burdick (Cyberskills); Ruth "where are you" Kasarda, Suzanne Hogsett, Gail Morse, and Pam Negri (women traveling); Alan Spira, M.D., and Craig Karpilow, M.D. (health for travelers); Arlan Blodgett (photography); Ian Watson (Baltic States and Russia); Anne Steves (travel with kids); and Brian Carr Smith (traveling as a student). *Merci* for support from my entire well-traveled staff at ETBD and in particular to Anne Kirchner for keeping things in order while I'm both in and out. *Spasiba* also to Pat Larson, Sandie Nisbet, John Givens, and Dick Dahl at Small World Productions for introducing so many travelers to this book through our public television series, *Travels in Europe with Rick Steves*. Finally, *tusen takk* to my parents for dragging me to Europe when I didn't want to go and to my wife, Anne, for making home my favorite place to travel.

Contents

Preface

The average American traveler enters Europe through the front door. This Europe greets you with cash registers cocked, $5 cups of coffee, and service with a purchased smile.

To give your trip an extra, more real dimension, come with me through the back door. Through the back door a warm, relaxed, personable Europe welcomes us as friends, not as part of the economy.

Traveling this way, we become temporary Europeans, part of the family—approaching Europe on its level, accepting and enjoying its unique ways of life. We'll demand nothing, except that no fuss be made over us.

This "Back Door–style" travel is better because of—not in spite of—your budget. Spending money has little to do with enjoying your trip. In fact, spending less money brings you closer to Europe. A lot of money forces you through Europe's grand front entrance, where people in uniforms greet you with formal smiles. But the back door is what keeps me in my wonderful European rut.

Since 1973 I've spent a hundred days a year exploring Europe. For the first five trips I traveled purely for kicks. Then it became clear: Each trip was going smoother . . . I must be learning from my mistakes. And I saw people making the same mistakes I had made: mistakes costly in time, money, and experience. It occurred to me that if I could package the lessons I've learned into a class or book, others could learn from my mistakes rather than their own. I could help others enjoy a better, smoother trip. (And I'd have a good excuse to go back to Europe every summer to update my material.) Since 1978 I've been doing just that—traveling with my teaching in mind, making mistakes, taking careful notes, losing my traveler's checks just to see what will happen, ordering a margarita, and getting pizza. This book, which has evolved over 17 editions, is my report to you.

My readers (many of whose grandkids warned, "You shouldn't be doing this") are having great trips and coming home with money in the bank for next summer. I'm careful not to send people to Europe with too much confidence and not enough money, reservations, or skills. If I did, trips would suffer, and I'd hear about it. But judging from the happy gelato-stained postcards my road scholars send me, it's clear that those who equip themselves with good information and expect themselves to travel smart, do.

The first half of this book covers the skills of Back Door European travel—packing, planning an itinerary, finding good hotels, getting around, and so on. The second half gives you keys to my favorite discoveries, places I call "Back Doors," where you can dirty your fingers in pure Europe—feeling its fjords and caressing its castles. So raise your travel dreams to their upright and locked positions. Happy travels!

Rick Steves' Back Door Travel Philosophy

Travel is intensified living—maximum thrills per minute and one of the last great sources of legal adventure. Travel is freedom. It's recess, and we need it.

Experiencing the real Europe requires catching it by surprise; going casual . . . "Through the Back Door."

Affording travel is a matter of priorities. (Make do with the old car.) You can travel—simply, safely, and comfortably—anywhere in Europe for $60 a day plus transportation costs. In many ways, spending more money only builds a thicker wall between you and what you came to see. Europe is a cultural carnival, and time after time, you'll find that its best acts are free and the best seats are the cheap ones.

A tight budget forces you to travel close to the ground, meeting and communicating with the people. Never sacrifice sleep, nutrition, safety, or cleanliness in the name of budget. Simply enjoy the local-style alternatives to expensive hotels and restaurants.

Extroverts have more fun. If your trip is low on magic moments, kick yourself and make things happen. If you don't enjoy a place, maybe you don't know enough about it. Seek the truth. Recognize tourist traps. Give a culture the benefit of your open mind. See things as different, but not better or worse. Any culture has much to share.

Of course, travel, like the world, is a series of hills and valleys. Be fanatically positive and militantly optimistic. If something's not to your liking, change your liking.

Travel is addicting. It can make you a happier American, as well as a citizen of the world. Our Earth is home to nearly 6 billion equally important people. It's humbling to travel and find that people don't envy Americans. Europeans like us, but with all due respect, they wouldn't trade passports.

Globetrotting destroys ethnocentricity. It helps you understand and appreciate different cultures. Travel changes people. It broadens perspectives and teaches new ways to measure quality of life. Many travelers toss aside their hometown blinders. Their prized souvenirs are the strands of different cultures they decide to knit into their own character. The world is a cultural yarn shop, and Back Door Travelers are weaving the ultimate tapestry. Join in!

PART ONE
Travel Skills

Andrea Hagg

GETTING STARTED

1. Take a Tour or Be Your Own Guide?

A European adventure is a major investment of time and money. A well-planned trip is more fun, less expensive, and not necessarily more structured. Planning means understanding your alternatives and choosing what best fits your travel dreams. From the start you need to decide if you're taking a tour or going on your own.

Do you want the security of knowing that all your rooms are reserved and that a guide will take you smoothly from one hotel to the next? Do you require consistently good hotels and restaurant meals, but at the same time wish to be as economical as possible? Will you forgo adventure, independence, and the challenge of doing it on your own in order to take the worry and bother out of traveling? If you don't mind sitting on a bus with the same group of tourists and observing rather than experiencing, a tour may be the right way for you to scratch your travel bug bites. There's a tour for just about every travel dream. Your travel agent can help you.

For many people with limited time and money, tours are the most efficient way to see Europe. Without a tour, three restaurant meals a day and a big, modern hotel are very expensive. Large tour companies book thousands of rooms and meals year-round and can, with their tremendous economic clout, get prices that no individual tourist could even come close to getting. For instance, on a tour with Cosmos (one of the largest and cheapest tour companies in Europe), you'll get fine rooms (with private baths), three hot meals a day, bus transportation, and the services of a European guide—all for $100 a day. Considering that many of the hotel rooms alone cost $100, that all-inclusive tour price is great. Such comfort without a tour is expensive.

Efficient and "economical" as tours may be, the tour groups that unload on Europe's quaintest towns experience things differently. They are treated as an entity; a mob to be fed, shown around, profited from, and moved out. If money is saved, it's at the cost of real experience. For me, the best travel values in Europe are enjoyed not gazing through the tinted windows of a tour bus but by traveling independently.

This book focuses on the skills necessary for do-it-yourself European travel. If you're destined for a tour, read on anyway (especially Chapter 27: Bus Tour Self-Defense). Even on a bus with 50 other people, you can and should be in control, equipped with a guidebook, and thinking as an independent traveler. Your trip is too important for you to blindly trust an overworked and underpaid tour guide.

Eight and forty tourists baked in a bus

BEING YOUR OWN GUIDE

As this book has evolved with my experience as a tour guide, I find myself simply encouraging readers to travel with the same thoughtfulness and fore-sight. As a tour guide, I call ahead to reconfirm reservations, ask at hotel check-in if there's any folk entertainment tonight, and call restaurants to see if they're open before I cross town. A good guide reads ahead. Equip your-self with good information, use local entertainment periodicals, and talk to other travelers. Ask questions or miss the festival.

Putting together a dream trip requires skills. Consider this book a do-it-yourself manual.

TRAVELING ALONE

One of your first big decisions is whether to travel alone or with a friend. Consider the pros and cons of solo travel.

You have complete freedom and independence. You never have to wait for your partner to pack up; you never need to consider a partner's wishes when you decide what to see, where to go, how far to travel, how much to spend, or even when the day has been long enough. You go where you want to, when you want to, and you can get the heck out of that stuffy museum when all the Monets start to look alike.

You meet more people when you travel alone because you're more approachable in the eyes of a European, and loneliness will drive you to reach out and make friends. When you travel with someone, it's easy to focus on your partner and forget about meeting Europeans.

Solo travel is intensely personal. Without the comfortable crutch of a friend, you're more likely to know the joys of self-discovery and the pleasures found in the kindness of strangers. You'll be exploring yourself as well as a new city or country.

Traveling without a tour, you'll have the locals dancing with you—not for you.

But loneliness can turn hotel rooms into lifeless cells. And meals for one are often served in a puddle of silence. Big cities can be cold and ugly when the only person you have to talk to is yourself. Being sick and alone in a country where no one even knows you exist is, even in retrospect, a miserable experience.

Combating loneliness in Europe is easy. The Continent is full of lonely travelers and natural meeting places. You're likely to find vaga-buddies in hostels, in museums (offer to share your *Mona Winks* chapter), on one-day bus tours, and on trains. Eurailers buddy up on the trains. If you're carrying a Cook Train Timetable, leave it lying around, and you'll become the most popular kid on the train. Travel as a student, whatever your age: Students have more fun, make more friends, and spend less money than most travelers. Board the train with a little too much of a picnic—and share it with others. Be bold; if you're lonely, others are, too.

TRAVELING WITH A PARTNER

Having a buddy overcomes the disadvantages of solo travel. Shared experiences are more fun, and for the rest of your life, there will be a special bond between you and your partner. The confident, uninhibited extrovert is better at making things happen and is more likely to run into exciting and memorable events. When I travel with a partner, it's easier for me to be that kind of "wild-and-crazy guy."

Not all tours are as exciting as their brochures make them sound.

Traveling with a partner is cheaper. Rarely does a double room cost as much as two singles. If a single room costs $50, a double room will generally be around $60, a savings of $20 per night per person. Virtually everything is cheaper and easier when you share costs: picnicking, guidebooks, banking, maps, magazines, taxis, storage lockers, and much more. Besides expenses, partners can share the burden of time-consuming hassles, such as standing in lines at train stations, banks, and post offices.

Remember, traveling together greatly accelerates a relationship—especially a romantic one. You see each other constantly and make endless decisions. The niceties go out the window. Everything becomes very real; you're in an adventure, a struggle, a hot-air balloon for two. The experiences of years are jammed into one summer.

Try a trial weekend together before merging dream trips. A mutual travel experience is a good test of a relationship—often revealing its ultimate course. I'd highly recommend a little premarital travel.

You can get real close to traditional Europe—sometimes too close.

Your choice of a travel partner is critical. It can make or break a trip. Traveling with the wrong partner can be like a two-month computer date. I'd rather do it alone. Analyze your travel styles and goals for compatibility. One summer I went to Europe to dive into as many cultures and adventures as possible. I planned to rest when I got home. My partner wanted to slow life down, to get away from it all, relax, and escape the pressures of the business world. Our ideas of acceptable hotels and the purpose of eating were quite different. The trip was a near disaster.

Many people already have their partner—for better or for worse. In the case of married couples, minimize the stress of traveling together by recognizing each other's needs for independence. Too many people do Europe as a three-legged race, tied together from start to finish. Have an explicit understanding that there's absolutely nothing selfish, dangerous, insulting, or wrong with splitting up occasionally. This is a freedom too few travel partners allow themselves. Doing your own thing for a few hours or days breathes fresh air into your togetherness.

TRAVELING WITH THREE OR MORE COMPANIONS

Traveling in a threesome or foursome is usually troublesome. With all the exciting choices Europe has to offer, it's often hard for even a twosome to reach a consensus. Unless there's a clear group leader, the "split and be independent" strategy is particularly valuable.

To minimize travel partnership stress, go communal with your money. Separate checks, double bank charges, and long lists of petty IOUs in six different currencies are a pain. Pool your resources, noting how much each person contributes, and just assume everything equals out in the long run. Keep track of major individual expenses but don't worry who got an extra postcard or cappuccino. Enjoy treating each other to taxis and dinner out of your "kitty," and after the trip, divvy up the remains. If one person consumed $25 or $30 more, that's a small price to pay for the convenience and economy of communal money.

IF YOU'VE READ THIS FAR

. . . you've got what it takes intellectually to handle Europe on your own. If you're inclined to figure things out, you'll find Europe well organized and explained, usually in English. But some people are not inclined to figure things out. They figure things out to earn a living 50 weeks a year, and that's not their idea of a good vacation. These people should travel with a tour . . . or a spouse. But if you enjoy the challenge of tackling a great new continent, you can do it.

2. Gathering Information

Those who think of the planning stage as part of the experience invest wisely and enjoy tremendous returns. Study ahead. This kind of homework is fun. Take advantage of the wealth of material available: guidebooks, classes, videos, libraries, and tourist information offices.

GUIDEBOOKS

Guidebooks are $15 tools for $3,000 experiences. Many otherwise smart people base the trip of a lifetime on a borrowed copy of a three-year-old guidebook. The money they saved in the bookstore was wasted the first day of their trip, searching for hotels and restaurants long since closed. As a writer of guidebooks, I am a big fan of their worth. When I visit someplace as a rank beginner—a place like Belize or Sri Lanka—I equip myself with a good guidebook and expect myself to travel smart. I travel like an old pro, not because I'm a super traveler, but because I have good information and I use it. I'm a connoisseur of guidebooks. My trip is my child. I love her. And I give her the best tutors money can buy.

Too many people are penny-wise and pound-foolish when it comes to information. I see them every year, stranded on street corners in Paris— hemorrhaging money. It's flipping off of them in $20 bills. (Con artists smell the blood and circle anxiously.) These vacations are disasters. Tourists with no information run out of money, go home early, and hate the French. With a good guidebook you can come into Paris for your first time, go anywhere in town for a dollar on the subway, enjoy a memorable bistro lunch for $15, and pay just $50 for a double room in a friendly hotel (with a singing maid) on a pedestrian-only street in village Paris seven blocks from the Eiffel Tower. All you need is a good guidebook covering your destination.

Before buying a book, study it. How old is the information? The cheapest books are often the oldest—no bargain. Who wrote it? What's the author's experience? Does the book work for you—or the tourist industry? Does it specialize in hard opinions—or superlatives? For whom is it written? Is it readable? It should have personality without chattiness and information without fluff.

Don't believe everything you read. The power of the printed word is scary. Most books are peppered with information that is flat-out wrong. Incredibly enough, even this book may have an error. Many "writers" succumb to the temptation to write guidebooks based on hearsay, travel brochures, other books, and wishful thinking. A writer met at the airport by an official from the national tourist board learns tips handy only for others met at the airport by an official from the national tourist board. It can actually be dangerous for a travel writer to report that a particular town is "painfully in need of charm." (I know.)

Bookstores that specialize in travel books have knowledgeable salespeople and the best selection. If you have a focus, there's a book written just for you. There are books written for those traveling with toddlers, pets, grandparents, and wine snobs. There are books for vegetarians, galloping gluttons, hedonists, cranky teens, nudists, pilgrims, gays, bird-watchers, music lovers, campers, hikers, bikers, and motorcyclists. Some are for the rich and sophisticated, others are for the cheap and earthy.

While travel information is what keeps you afloat, too much information can sink the ship. I buy several guidebooks for each country I visit, rip them up, and staple the chapters together into my own personalized hybrid guidebook. To rip a book neatly, bend it over to break the spine, visualize your destination, and pull chapters out with the gummy edge intact (or just butcher and staple). Bring only the applicable pages. There's no point in carrying 120 pages of information on Scandinavia to dinner in Barcelona. When I finish seeing a country, I give my stapled-together chapter on that area to another traveler or leave it in my last hotel's lounge.

Here's a rundown of my favorite guidebooks.

Let's Go: Written for young train-travelers on tight budgets, Let's Go guidebooks include the huge *Let's Go: Europe* along with individual country guides. Covering big cities, small towns, and the countryside, Let's Go guides offer listings of budget accommodations and restaurants; information on public transportation; capsule social, political, and historical rundowns; and a refreshingly opinionated look at sights and tourist activities. Let's Go doesn't teach "Ugly Americanism," as do many prominent guidebooks.

Let's Go guides are updated annually (hit the bookstores in December) and sold in Europe for 50 percent more than U.S. prices. Always use the current edition. If you've got more money, stick to its higher-priced accommodations listings (although in many cities it lists only hostels and student hotels). With its hip student focus, Let's Go offers the best coverage on hosteling and the alternative nightlife scene.

Because of its wide scope, *Let's Go: Europe* is good only for the speedy, whirlwind-type itinerary. The book's drawback is that nearly every young North American traveler has it, and the flood of backpacker business it generates can overwhelm a formerly cozy village, hotel, or restaurant and give it a whopping Daytona Beach hangover.

Individual country guides in the series cover Britain/Ireland, France, Germany, Switzerland/Austria, Italy, Spain/Portugal, Eastern Europe, Greece/Turkey, and Israel/Egypt. With 10 times the information and one-tenth the readership of *Let's Go: Europe*, they don't have the negative impact that the big Europe book has on the featured sights.

Lonely Planet guidebooks: Published in Australia, these are the top independent budget travel guidebooks for most countries in Asia, Africa, and South America. Lonely Planet has successfully invaded Europe with brick-like Western, Central, Scandinavian, Mediterranean, and Eastern Europe editions and guidebooks to individual countries throughout Europe. The Lonely Planet guides offer no-nonsense facts and opinions without the narrow student focus of Let's Go.

Rough Guides: This fast-growing British series (formerly the Real Guides) includes books about every part of Europe as well as a fat all-Europe edition. They're a great source of hard-core go-local-on-a-vagabond's-budget information. While the hotel listings are skimpy and uninspired, these books are written by Europeans who understand the contemporary and social scene better than American writers. Rough Guides are particularly strong on Eastern European countries.

Frommer Guides: Arthur Frommer's classic guide, *Europe on $5 a Day*, is now *Europe from $50 a Day*. It's great for the 26 most important big cities but ignores everything else (and there's so much more!). It's full of reliable and handy listings of budget hotels, restaurants, and sightseeing ideas compiled by the father of budget independent travel himself. Every year I rip up an edition and take along chapters for supplemental information on the cities I plan to visit.

Frommer books on specific countries cover regions, towns, and villages as well as cities but are not as good as Frommer's Europe book. Arthur sold his name, and that's the only thing "Frommer" about these guides. Frommer guidebooks give good advice on which sites are essential when time is short. They are especially well-attuned to the needs of older travelers but handle many with unnecessary kid gloves.

Karen Brown's Country Inn series: These are great for people with extra bucks and an appetite for doilies under thatch. Her recommended routes are good, and her listings are excellent if you plan on spending $150 to $300 a night for your double rooms. My splurges are Karen's slums.

Michelin Green Guides: These famous tall green books, available in dryly translated English all over Europe, ignore hotels and restaurants but are a gold mine of solid, practical information on what to see. A French publisher, Michelin has English editions covering some regions of France and most countries of Europe. (English editions are available in Europe—especially in France—for lower prices than in the U.S.) French speakers will find more editions available. Each book includes small but encyclopedic chapters on history, lifestyles, art, culture, customs, and economy. These practical books are a tour guide's best friend. All over Europe tour leaders are wowing their bus loads by reading from their Green Guides. ("And these are fields of sugar beets. Three quarters of Austria's beet production lies along the banks of the Danube, which flows through 12 countries draining an area the size of the Sudan.") A wonderful and unique feature of the Green Guides is their handy "worth a journey/worth a detour" maps. The prominence of a listed place is determined by its importance to you, the traveler, rather than its population. This means that a cute visit-worthy village (like Rothenburg) appears bolder than a big, dull city (like Dortmund). These books are filled with fine city maps and are designed for drivers, ideally on Michelin tires.

The Michelin Red Guides are the hotel and restaurant connoisseur's bibles. But I don't travel with a poodle, and my taste buds weren't designed to appreciate $100 meals.

Blue Guides: The Blue Guides (which have nothing to do with European brothels) take a dry and scholarly approach to the countries of Europe. These guides are ideal if you want to learn as much about a country's history, art, architecture, and culture as you possibly can. With the *Blue Guide to Greece*, I had all the information I needed about any sight in Greece and never needed to hire a guide. Scholarly types actually find a faint but endearing personality hiding between the sheets of their Blue Guides.

City guides: Specializing in information overload, these guides can be great for travelers staying put for a week in a city. Let's Go, Lonely Planet, and Rough Guides all publish straightforward guides to Europe's grandest cities. The creatively crafted **Access Guides** offer the ultimate in-depth source of sightseeing information for London, Paris, Rome, and Florence/Venice/Milan. Two pricey series that also cover the biggies are **Knopf** and **Eyewitness** ($25 each; guides on Amsterdam, Paris, London, Rome, Venice, Florence/Tuscany, Prague, and more). These feature futuristic, high-tech, visually super, friendly layouts with appealing illustrations and tiny bullets of background text. Travelers love the Eyewitness format. Knopf is the more highbrow of the two. I don't travel with these, but if I ever need to locate, say, a Caravaggio painting in a church, I seek out a tourist with a copy and ask for a quick peek. **Fodor's City Guides** (Paris, London, Rome, Berlin, Prague), more portable and with fold-out maps, are also worth considering.

Cadogan guidebooks: Cadogan (rhymes with toboggan) guides are readable and thought-provoking, giving the curious traveler a cultural insight into many regions. The series, distributed by Globe Pequot Press, includes Scotland, France, Ireland, Italy, Italian islands, Umbria and Tuscany, Spain, Portugal, Morocco, Greek islands, Turkey, and more. They're good pretrip reading. If you're traveling alone and want to understand tomorrow's sightseeing, Cadogan gives you something productive to do in bed.

Overseas Work and Study: *Transitions Abroad* publishes the excellent, annual *Alternative Travel Directory: The Complete Guide to Work, Study, & Travel Overseas* ($23.95 postpaid) and *Work Abroad: The Complete Guide to Finding a Job Overseas* ($19.95 postpaid, tel. 800/293-0373). Vacation Work publishes Susan Griffith's *Work Your Way Around the World*, Lipinski's *Directory of Jobs & Careers Abroad*, and David Woodworth's *Overseas Summer Jobs*. Council Travel, the biggest and most energetic student service in the United States, offers free a *Student Travels* magazine (tel. 888/COUNCIL to request a copy).

RICK STEVES' GUIDEBOOKS

Country Guides: While *Europe Through the Back Door* covers travel skills, my country guides are blueprints for your actual trip. Annually updated, they weave together all my favorite sights, accommodations, and restaurants into trip strategies designed to give you the most value out of every day and every dollar. These books cut through the superlatives. Yes, I know "you can spend a lifetime in Florence." But you've got a day and a half, and I've got a great plan.

These guides are up-to-date. Of all of the 1999 guidebooks published, my 1999 country guides are the only ones that miss the 1998 Christmas sales season. That's expensive for the publisher but essential for the traveler. In order to experience the same Europe most of my readers do, I insist on doing my research in the peak tourist season. Also, my country guides are selective, covering fewer destinations within each country but covering each destination in more depth. My guidebooks will help you explore (and enjoy) Europe's big cities, small towns, and regions, mixing must-see sights with intimate Back Door nooks and offbeat crannies. *Rick Steves' Best of Europe*, twice the size of the others, covers Europe's top 30 destinations—including most of the Back Doors described in the last half of this book. If the

---

Rick Steves' Country Guidebooks

Rick Steves' Best of Europe
Rick Steves' France, Belgium & the Netherlands
Rick Steves' Germany, Austria & Switzerland
Rick Steves' Great Britain & Ireland
Rick Steves' Italy
Rick Steves' Russia & the Baltics
Rick Steves' Scandinavia
Rick Steves' Spain & Portugal
(John Muir Publications)

---

table of contents lists all your destinations, this book will serve your trip as well—and cheaper—than several individual country guides.

City Guides: My two new city guides are *Rick Steves' Paris* and *Rick Steves' London*. If you're staying a few days in either of these grand cities, you'll find this reliable, in-depth information invaluable. My guides also include fun-to-follow, self-guided tours of the top sights, emphasizing the great art with photos and commentary (available in Jan. 99).

Europe 101: History and Art for the Traveler is the only fun travelers' guide to Europe's history and art (by Rick Steves and Gene Openshaw, John Muir Publications, 1996). It's full of boiled-down, practical information to carbonate your sightseeing. Written for smart people who were sleeping in their art history classes before they knew they were going to Europe, *101* is the perfect companion to all the country guides. *Europe 101* is your passport to goosebumps in a practical and easy-to-read manual. After reading *Europe 101*, you can step into a Gothic cathedral, excitedly nudge your partner, and marvel, "Isn't this a great improvement over Romanesque!"

Rick Steves' Mona Winks: Self-Guided Tours of Europe's Top Museums gives you a breezy, step-by-step, painting-by-sculpture walk through the best two hours or so of Europe's 20 most overwhelming and exhausting museums and cultural obligations (by Gene Openshaw and Rick Steves, John Muir Publications, 1998). It covers the great museums of London, Paris, Venice, Florence, Rome, Amsterdam, and Madrid. Museums can ruin a good vacation . . . unless you're traveling with *Mona*. Don't assume you can buy good English guidebooks on the spot for Europe's sights and museums. Museum guidebooks available in Europe are

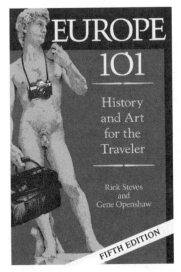

Rick Steves' art guides make your sightseeing more meaningful.

too big, too expensive, and so dry that if you read them out loud your lips would chap. If you're interested in art, you need *Mona.*

Rick Steves' Phrase Books for French, Italian, German, Spanish/Portuguese, and French/Italian/German (John Muir Publications) are the only phrase books on the market designed by a guy who speaks only English. That's why they're so good. They're based on more than 20 years of experience traveling with other phrase books. These are both fun and practical, with a meet-the-people and stretch-the-budget focus. Mr. Berlitz knew the languages, but he never stayed in a hotel where you need to ask, "At what time is the water hot?" *Rick Steves' Postcards from Europe*, my autobiographical new book, packs 20 years of travel anecdotes and insights into the ultimate 3,000-mile European adventure. While the Back Doors section of this book introduces you to my favorite European discoveries, "Postcards" introduces you to my favorite European friends. (See Back Door catalog.)

TRAVEL LITERATURE

Consider some trip-related recreational reading. A book on the court of Louis XIV brings Versailles to life. After reading Irving Stone's *The Agony and the Ecstasy*, you'll visit friends in Florence—who lived there 500 years ago. Books such as Michener's *Iberia* for Spain and Portugal, Stone's *The Greek Treasure* for Greece and Turkey, Wordsworth's poems for England's Lake District, and Uris' *Trinity* for Ireland are real trip bonuses. Your hometown library has a lifetime of valuable reading on European culture. Dewey gave Europe the number 914. Take your travel partner on a date to the library and start your trip early.

Paging through coffee-table books on places you'll be visiting (e.g., *Hill Towns of Tuscany*, *Castles of North Wales*) can give you some great, often untouristy, sightseeing ideas. If travel partners divide up their studying, they can take turns being "guide" and do a better job. Your local travel bookstore stocks good travel literature as well as guidebooks.

Rick Steves' phrase books: German, Italian, French, Spanish/Portuguese, French/Italian/German (not shown)

MAPS

Drivers need first-class maps. Excellent, up-to-date maps with the European place names spelled as you'll see them in your travels are on sale throughout Europe. While still at home, I buy the Michelin 970 Europe map for overall planning. I pick up the Michelin maps for each region (scale 1:200,000, $4 or $5 each) at gas stations, book shops, newsstands, and tourist shops as I go. Drivers should consider the popular and inexpensive road atlases for each country (1:200,000 with city maps and indexes).

Spend half a traffic jam learning the key. Handy sightseeing information such as scenic roads and towns, ruined castles, hostels, mountain huts, view points, and costs and opening schedules of remote roads can be found on good maps by good map readers.

By train, you can wing it with the map that comes free with your Eurailpass and the free (or cheap) little maps of each town that you can pick up at the local tourist offices as you go.

Maps can double as handy excuses to communicate with new friends. You can haul out the map and show them where you've been and where you're going.

TALK WITH OTHER TRAVELERS

Both in Europe and here at home, travelers love to share the lessons they've learned. Learn from other tourists. First-hand, fresh information can be good stuff. Keep in mind, however, that all assessments of a place's touristic merit are a product of that person's personality and time there. It could have rained, he could have shared an elevator with the town jerk, or she may have been sick in "that lousy, overrated city." Or he might have fallen in love in that "wonderful" village. Every year, I find travelers hell-bent on following miserable travel advice from friends at home. Except for those found in this book, treat opinions as opinions.

Take advantage of every opportunity (such as train or bus rides) to swap information with travelers you meet from other parts of the English-speaking world. This is particularly important when traveling beyond Western Europe.

CYBERSPACE

Cyberspace is filled with online travel talk these days. Anyone with access to the Internet can share travel information. Various online services offer global weather reports, news, visa information, flight and hotel reservations services, and travel advisory information, plus a travel forum where vagabonds hang out between trips. If you have a particular concern or need, you can get a world of advice through your computer modem. Many travel writers are getting involved with various forums and bulletin board systems. Be wary, however, of mainstream online services that sell information. These tend to be little more than infomercials from the tourist industry. Information from a front-door publisher, even from a snazzy online service, is still front door.

Easy-to-use search tools will help you find what you need. **AltaVista**, **Infoseek**, and the **Yahoo Travel Directory** will help you zero in on key travel resources. (Follow the search tips provided.)

Several Web sites pull up information according to destination and interest. **City.Net** and **Mapquest** feature travel tips, city and subway maps, and information on cultural sites for most European destinations. **Musi-Cal** and **Events Worldwide** make it easy to find live concerts, sporting events, and cultural happenings.

The **Tourism Offices Worldwide Directory** is a searchable directory of TI locations, phone numbers, and Web site addresses. The book *Net Travel: How Travelers Use the Internet* by Michael Shapiro includes information on how to stay online while on the road and excellent online travel planning tips and resources. If you're looking for a good guidebook, check out the wide selection at **Amazon.com.**

Get the latest exchange rates with the **Universal Currency Converter. Visa** and **MasterCard** have ATM Locators that will help you pinpoint Cirrus and Plus machines.

Good Sources for Travel Information Online

AltaVista
http://www.altavista.digital.com
City.Net
http://www.city.net
Council Travel
http://www.counciltravel.com
Deutsche Bahn
http://bahn.hafas.de/
Dan Youra's Ferry Guide
http://www.youra.com/ferry/intlferries.html
Europe Through the Back Door
http://www.ricksteves.com
European Railway Server
http://mercurio.iet.unipi.it
Eurotrip
http://www.eurotrip.com
Events Worldwide
http://www.eventsworldwide.com
The Hotel Guide
http://www.hotelguide.com
Infoseek
http://www.infoseek.com/Travel
Inter-Links
http://alabanza.com/kabacoff/Inter-Links/start.html
Internet Cafe Guide
http://www.netcafeguide.com
Internet Guide to Hostelling
http://www.hostels.com/
MailStart.com
http://www.mailstart.com
MapQuest
http://www.mapquest.com
MasterCard
http://www.mastercard.com/atm/
Motoeuropa
http://www.ideamerge.com/motoeuropa
Musi-Cal
http://concerts.calendar.com
TeleAdapt
http://www.teleadapt.com
Tourism Offices Worldwide Directory
http://www.mbnet.mb.ca/lucas/travel/
Universal Currency Converter
http://www.xe.net/currency/
Visa
http://www.visa.com
Yahoo Travel Directory
http://www.yahoo.com/Recreation/Travel

Current updates of these links can be found on my Web site at
http://www.ricksteves.com/tips/links.htm.

The Hotel Guide lists over 60,000 hotels, inns, and bed-and-breakfasts in Europe. You can search a destination, choose a hotel, and book your reservation online. For the traveler on a shoestring budget, **Eurotrip** and the **Internet Guide to Hostelling** offer cheap accommodations and transportation resources on the Internet. Find out about the International Student Identity Card and other student travel opportunities through **Council Travel**.

Looking for a cultural site, hotel, or restaurant that is off the beaten track? Use the many e-mail discussion lists and Usenet newsgroups to contact a European living in the area or a traveler who has just returned. Often travelers find a place to stay with European residents through these forums. **Inter-Links** has a searchable directory that will help you find the right forum. Use the keywords "travel" or "culture" and the name of your destination in your search.

Plan your train travel with the help of **Deutsche Bahn's** online timetable search service. The **European Railway Server** and **Dan Youra's Ferry Guide** will lead you to the Web sites of the European railway and ferry systems. Those traveling by car find **Motoeuropa** helpful.

International phone calls and postage rates from Europe are expensive. Stay in touch with home through cyber cafés—coffeehouses that offer Internet access and e-mail services. Send home an electronic postcard and plan the next leg of your trip while sipping a café latte. Check the **Internet Café Guide** for a listing of these plugged-in places. Many universities, schools, and libraries now offer e-mail services at little or no cost.

To send and receive e-mail in Europe, those without a laptop can use **MailStart.com** at any place with Web access. This free service allows you to access your current e-mail account via the Web. If you're traveling with a laptop, see if your Internet service offers global roaming services in Europe to access the Internet with a local phone call. **TeleAdapt** provides the know-how and adapters you need to connect your modem to the various telephone plugs throughout Europe.

Europe Through the Back Door's site at www.ricksteves.com is my effort at giving readers free access to the latest information for Back Door style travel. You can view (for no charge) my latest research notes, guidebook updates, country by country information, museum tours, travel articles, dispatches from Europe, and letters from readers. Be sure to drop by the Graffiti Wall, our message board where travelers share information. Get the latest on railpass prices through our Back Door Guide to European Railpasses, and sign up for our monthly e-mail newsletter. My e-mail address is rick@ricksteves.com. (For more on cyber-travel, see Chapter 20: Phones, E-mail, and Mail.)

TRAVEL MAGAZINES AND NEWSLETTERS

Transitions Abroad is the best travel periodical on work and study abroad and thoughtful, responsible travel (six issues a year, $24.95 subscription, tel. 800/293-0373, www.transabroad.com). *International Travel News*, on black and white newsprint, is packed with down-and-dirty travel news, industry announcements, reports from traveling readers, globetrotting personals, and advertisements from creative small-time travel operators (monthly, $18 subscription, tel. 800/486-4968). The intellectual *Consumer Reports Travel Letter* is a little too focused on the industry rather than independent travel, but does tedious, necessary studies and reports on the most confusing and expensive aspects of international travel (monthly, $39 subscription, tel. 800/234-1970).

At ETBD, we publish a free, 64-page quarterly newsletter filled with articles, book updates, letters from our "road scholars," and a complete rundown on our work (free copy, tel. 425/771-8303, www.ricksteves.com).

CLASSES

The more you understand a subject, the longer it stays interesting. Those with no background in medieval architecture are the first to get "cathedraled out." Whether you like it or not, you'll be spending lots of time browsing through historic buildings and museums. Those who read or take trip-related classes beforehand have more fun sightseeing in Europe.

There are plenty of worthwhile classes on many aspects of Europe. Although you can get by with English, a foreign language—even a few survival phrases—can only make Europe more fun. History tweaks Europe into life. A basic modern European history course makes a dull museum interesting. A class in Eastern European Studies will bring a little order to that demographic chaos.

Art history is probably the most valuable course for the prospective tourist. Don't go to Europe—especially Italy or Greece—without at least having read something on art and architecture.

Many universities have extension colleges that offer informal classes to the public on travel and foreign languages. I support a handful of "European travel resource centers" throughout the United States (listed in the ETBD newsletter) that give classes; do trip consulting; and have my latest class, research, and video material, just like my Resource Center in Seattle.

TRAVEL VIDEOS

The world is anxiously waiting for good travel videos. So far, most are uninspired destination picture books or cheesy promos sponsored by tourist boards or hotel groups. Most local TV travel shows shamelessly sell segments and are little more than disguised ads.

I'm doing my best to change this. My 52-week public television series, *Travels in Europe with Rick Steves*, which airs on more than 250 public television stations in the United States, is now available in 25 videos (55 to 80 minutes apiece; see Back Door Catalog at the end of this book).

All 24 hours of my slideshow/lectures are available on 12 simple but clean, information-packed videos. This includes my one-hour "How to Use Your Railpass" class, a four-hour "European Art for Travelers" video slideshow, and two-hour classes on each region of Europe. (See Back Door Catalog.)

TOURIST INFORMATION OFFICES

Tourism is an important part of Europe's economy. Virtually every European city has a tourist information office located downtown and loaded with maps and advice. This is my essential first stop upon arrival in a town. But you don't need to wait until you get to Europe. Each European country has a national tourist office in the United States with a healthy promotional budget. Switzerland, for instance, figures you'll be doing the Alps, but you've yet to decide if they'll be French, Swiss, or Austrian Alps. They are happy to send you a free package of promotional information to put you in a Swiss Alps frame of mind. Just send a postcard to the office of each country you plan to visit. Ask for specific information to get more than the general packet. If you want to sleep in a castle on the Rhine, river-raft in France, or hut-hop across Austria, there's a free brochure for you. Ask for an English-language schedule of upcoming events, and for maps of the country and various cities you'll be visiting. I find it's best to get answers to specific questions by telephone.

EUROPEAN NATIONAL TOURIST OFFICES IN THE U.S.

Austrian National Tourist Office: Box 1142, New York, NY 10108, tel. 212/944-6880, fax 212/730-4568, Web site: www.anto.com. Ask for their "Vacation Kit" map. Fine hikes and Vienna material.

Belgian National Tourist Office: 780 3rd Ave. #1501, New York, NY 10017, tel. 212/758-8130, fax 212/355-7675, Web site: www.visitbelgium.com. Good country map.

British Tourist Authority: 551 5th Ave., 7th floor, New York, NY 10176, tel. 800/462-2748 or 212/986-2200, Web site: www.visitbritain.com. Free maps of London and Britain. Meaty material, responsive to individual needs.

Czech Tourist Authority: 1109 Madison Ave., New York, NY 10028, tel. 212/288-0830, fax 212/288-0971, Web site: www.czech.cz/new_york. To get a weighty information package (1–2 lbs, no advertising), send a check for $3 to cover postage and specify places of interest.

Denmark (see Scandinavia)

Finland (see Scandinavia)

French Tourist Office: 444 Madison Ave., 16th floor, New York, NY 10022, Web site: www.francetourism.com; 676 N. Michigan Ave. #600, Chicago, IL 60611; 9454 Wilshire Blvd. #715, Beverly Hills, CA 90212. Their general information number (in Washington, D.C.) is 202/659-7779.

German National Tourist Office: 122 E. 42nd St., 52nd floor, New York, NY 10168, tel. 212/661-7200, fax 212/661-7174, Web site: www.germany-tourism.de. Maps, Rhine schedules, events; very helpful.

Greek National Tourist Organization: 645 5th Ave., 5th floor, New York, NY 10022, tel. 212/421-5777, fax 212/826-6940; 168 N. Michigan Ave., Chicago, IL 60601, tel. 312/782-1084, fax 312/782-1091; 611 W. 6th St. #2198, Los Angeles, CA 90017, tel. 213/626-6696, fax 213/489-9744. General how-to booklet, map of Athens, plenty on the islands. Web site on Greece generated in Canada: www.aei.ca/~gntomtl/.

Hungarian National Tourist Office: 150 E. 58th St., 33rd floor, New York, NY 10155, tel. 212/355-0240, fax 212/207-4103, Web site: www.hungarytourism.com.

Irish Tourist Board: 345 Park Ave., 17th floor, New York, NY 10154, tel. 800/223-6470 or 212/418-0800, fax 212/371-9052, Web site: www.ireland.travel.ie.

Italian Government Travel Office: 630 5th Ave. #1565, New York, NY 10111, tel. 212/245-4822, fax 212/586-9249; 401 N. Michigan Ave. #3030, Chicago, IL 60611, tel. 312/644-9448, fax 312/644-3019; 12400 Wilshire Blvd. #550, Los Angeles, CA 90025, tel. 310/820-0098, fax 310/820-6357.

Luxembourg National Tourist Office: 17 Beekman Pl., New York, NY 10022, tel. 212/935-8888, fax 212/935-5896, Web site: www.wwb.com /company/c006617.html.

Netherlands National Tourist Office: 225 N. Michigan Ave. #1854, Chicago, IL 60601, tel. 888/GO-HOLLAND (automated) or 312/819-1500 (live), fax 312/819-1740, Web site: www.goholland.com. Great country map.

Norway (see Scandinavia)

Polish National Tourist Office: 275 Madison Ave. #1711, New York, NY 10016, tel. 212/338-9412, fax 212/338-9283, Web site: www.polandtour.org.

Portuguese National Tourist Office: 590 5th Ave., 4th floor, New York, NY 10036, tel. 212/354-4403, fax 212/764-6137, Web site: www.portugal.org.
Scandinavian Tourism: P.O. Box 4649, Grand Central Station, New York, NY 10163-4649, tel. 212/885-9700, fax 212/885-9710, Web site: www.goscandinavia.com, e-mail: info@goscandinavia.com. Good general booklets on the Scandinavian countries; be sure to ask for city maps and specifics.
Spanish National Tourist Office: 666 5th Ave., 35th floor, New York, NY 10103, tel. 212/265-8822, fax 212/265-8864, Web site: www.okspain.org; 845 N. Michigan Ave., Chicago, IL 60611, tel. 312/642-1992, fax 312/642-9817; 1221 Breckell Ave., #1850, Miami, FL 33131, tel. 305/358-1992, fax 305/358-8223; San Vicente Plaza Bldg., 8383 Wilshire Blvd., #960, Beverly Hills, CA 90211, tel. 213/658-7188, fax 213/658-1061.
Sweden (see Scandinavia)
Swiss National Tourist Office: 608 5th Ave., New York, NY 10020, tel. 212/757-5944, fax 212/262-6116, Web site: www.switzerlandtourism.com; 222 N. Sepulveda Blvd., #1570, El Segundo, CA 90245, tel. 310/640-8900, fax 310/335-0131. Great maps, rail and hiking material.
Turkish Tourism Office: 821 United Nations Plaza, New York, NY 10017, tel. 212/687-2194, fax 212/599-7568, Web site: www.turkey.org/turkey, e-mail: tourny@soho.ios.com.

MIDDLE EASTERN AND NORTH AFRICAN TOURIST OFFICES IN THE U.S.
Egyptian Tourist Office: 630 5th Ave. #1706, New York, NY 10111, tel. 212/332-2570, fax 212/956-6439, Web site: http://touregypt.net.
Israel Government Tourist Office: 800 2nd Ave., New York, NY 10017, tel. 800/596-1199 or 212/499-5600, fax 212/499-5665, Web site: www.infotour.co.il. Good country map.
Moroccan National Tourist Office: 20 E. 46th St. #1201, New York, NY 10017, tel. 212/557-2520, fax 212/949-8148, Web site: www.kingdomofmorocco.com. Good country map.

3. Paper Chase
While going to Europe isn't all that complex, your trip will be smoother if you consider these documents and details well before your departure date.

PASSPORTS
In Western Europe, the only document a U.S. citizen needs is a passport. For most travelers, the only time any customs official will look at you seri-

ously is at the airport as you reenter the United States. Most European border crossings are a wave-through for U.S. citizens.

Passports, good for 10 years, cost $60 ($40 for a renewal). Minors under 16 pay $40 for a passport good for five years. Apply at the U.S. Passport Agency, any federal or state courthouse, or some post offices. You can telephone 800/688-9889 for complete details. Although they say applications take four to six weeks (and you should be prepared for delays), most passports are processed more quickly. If you can prove you're in an emergency situation, go in person and pay a $45 speed fee. They'll issue your new passport almost immediately.

As you travel, take good care of your passport. But Americans, notorious passport-grippers, need to relax when it comes to temporarily giving it up. As you cross some Eastern European borders by train, a usually unofficial-looking character will come down the aisle picking up all the passports. Relax, you'll get it back later. When you sleep in a *couchette* (night-train sleeping car) that crosses a border, the car attendant will take your passport so you won't be disturbed when the train crosses the border at 3:00 a.m. And hotels routinely take your passport "for the night" so they can register you with the police. This bookwork must be done for foreign guests throughout Europe. Receptionists like to gather passports and register them all at the same time when things are quiet. Although it's unreasonable to expect them to drop whatever they're doing to register me right now, I politely ask if I can pick up my passport in two hours. I just don't like my passport in the top drawer all night long.

A passport works well for collateral in cases when you don't have the cash right now (hefty deposits on bike rentals, hotels that don't trust you, etc.).

Losing your passport while traveling is a major headache. If you do, contact the police and the nearest U.S. consulate or embassy right away. You can get a short-term replacement, but you'll earn it. A photocopy of your passport can speed the replacement process.

VISAS

A visa is a stamp placed in your passport by a foreign government, allowing you to enter their country. Visas are not required for Americans traveling in Western Europe and most of the East.

Turkey requires a visa ($45), easy to get upon arrival at the border or airport. Travelers to Russia also need visas, which are best applied for in advance. (For specifics, see Chapter 56: Baltics and St. Petersburg.) For travel beyond Europe, get up-to-date information on visa requirements from your travel agent or the United States Department of State (http://travel.state.gov/foreignentryreqs.html).

If you do need a visa, it's usually best to get it at home before you leave. If you forget, virtually every country has an embassy or consulate (which can issue visas) in the capital of every other European country.

SHOTS

At this time, shots are not required for travel in Europe. But this can change, so check the inoculation requirements with your doctor or a travel medicine clinic before you leave home. Countries "require" shots in order to protect their citizens from you and "recommend" shots to protect you from them. If any shots are recommended, take that advice seriously. (For more information, see Chapter 21: Staying Healthy.)

STUDENT CARDS AND HOSTEL MEMBERSHIPS

The International Student Identity Card (ISIC), the only internationally recognized student ID card, gets you discounts on transportation, entertainment, and sightseeing throughout Europe, and even some medical insurance. If you are a full-time student or have been one in the last year (and can prove it), get one. The cost is $20 from Council Travel or from your university foreign study office. Teachers of any age may get similar student-type discounts with an ITIC (International Teacher Identification Card), but this is often not honored. Nonstudent travelers under age 26 can get a youth Go-25 card for similar discounts. (Council Travel offices sell all of these cards for $20 apiece; for the nearest of their 60 offices, call 800/2-COUNCIL, www.counciltravel.com).

If you plan to stay four or more nights at a hostel, a hostel membership will pay for itself. Before you leave, get a hostel membership card from your local hostel or Hostelling International at 800/444-6111 (for more information, see Chapter 15: Sleeping).

RAILPASSES AND CAR RENTAL

Most railpasses are not sold in Europe and must be purchased before you leave home. Car rental is usually cheaper when arranged before your trip through your hometown travel agent. For most, an international driver's license is not necessary (but if you're getting one, do it at AAA before your departure). For specifics on driving and train passes, see Chapters 9 through 12 on transportation and the "European Railpasses" guide in the Appendix.

TRAVEL INSURANCE—TO INSURE OR NOT TO INSURE?

Travel insurance is a way to buy off the considerable financial risks of traveling. These risks include accidents, illness, missed flights, canceled or interrupted tours, lost baggage, emergency evacuation, and getting your body home if you die. Each traveler's risk and potential loss varies, depending on how much of the trip is prepaid, the kind of air ticket purchased, your and your loved ones' health, value of your luggage, where you're traveling, what health coverage you already have, and the financial health of the tour company or airline. For some, insurance is a good deal; for others, it's not.

Travel agents recommend travel insurance because they make a commission on it, they can be held liable for your losses if they don't explain insurance options to you, and sometimes because it's right for you. But the final decision is yours. What are the chances of needing it, how able are you to take the risks, and what's peace of mind worth to you?

You can design your own coverage with à la carte policies from Access America or Mutual of Omaha. This insurance menu includes four sections: medical, baggage, trip cancellation, and flight insurance. Tailor it to your needs, then compare to the comprehensive travel insurance explained below.

Medical insurance generally covers only medical and dental emergencies. Check with your medical insurer—you might already be covered by your existing health plan. Find out about deductibles, if any, and the procedure for reimbursement of emergency expenses. Generally, your expenses are out-of-pocket, and you bring home documentation to be reimbursed. While most policies cover you overseas, Medicare does not. Emergency evacuation (e.g., nine first-class one-way seats to get your stretcher on the transatlantic plane) can be extremely expensive and is usually not covered by your regular medical insurance. Pre-existing conditions are now generally covered in medical and trip cancellation coverage, but check with your agent or insurer before you commit. The $20 ISIC student identity card includes basic travelers' health coverage.

Baggage insurance costs about $2 or $3 per day per $1,000 coverage (and doesn't cover items such as cash, eyewear, and photographic equipment). Homeowners' insurance (with the "floater" supplement, if necessary, to cover you out of the country) is cheaper, and you'll have coverage even after your trip. Travelers' baggage insurance will cover the deductibles and things excluded from your homeowners' policy. Double-check the particulars with your agent. If your policy doesn't cover railpasses, consider buying the $10 insurance deal sold with the pass.

Trip cancellation or interruption insurance covers the financial penalties or losses you incur when you cancel a prepaid tour or flight for an acceptable reason. These include if:

(1) you, your travel partner, or a family member cannot travel due to sickness or a list of other acceptable reasons;

(2) your tour company or airline goes out of business or can't perform as promised;

(3) a family member at home gets sick, causing you to cancel;

(4) for a good reason, you miss a flight or need an emergency flight.

In other words, if, on the day before your trip, you or your travel partner breaks a leg, you can both bail out (if you both have travel insurance), and neither of you will lose a penny. And if, one day into your tour, you have an accident, both of you will be flown home, and you'll be reimbursed for the emergency one-way return flight (which usually costs far more than your economy round-trip fare) and whatever portion of the tour you haven't used. People who aren't on a tour get coverage for their prepaid expenses (such as their flight and any nonrefundable hotel reservations). This insurance costs about 5.5 percent of the amount you want covered. For example, a $1,500 tour and $500 airfare can be insured for $116. (There are worst-case fly-home-in-a-hurry scenarios where you could need more coverage.) This is a good deal if you figure there's a better than 1-in-20 chance you'll need it. The rugged, healthy, unattached, and gung-ho traveler will probably skip this coverage. I have for more than 20 trips, and my number has yet to come up. If you're planning on taking an organized tour (which is expensive to cancel), if you have questionable health, or if you have a loved one at home in frail health, you should probably get this coverage.

Flight insurance (crash coverage) is a statistical rip-off that heirs love. More than 60,000 airplanes take off and land safely every day. The chances of being in an airplane crash are minuscule.

Comprehensive travel insurance, such as Travel Guard's, gives you everything but the kitchen sink for about 5.5 percent of your prepaid trip cost (airfare, car rental, tour cost, etc.). This can be a better deal for travelers with less of the trip prepaid (those without tours) because coverage is the same regardless of the premium you pay. This covers any deductible expense your existing medical insurance plan doesn't cover. For $6 extra per day you can get a supplemental collision damage waiver (CDW) on rental cars (see Chapter 11: Driving Europe Crazy).

Collision Damage Waiver (CDW) Insurance is a point of much confusion. When you rent a car, you are usually liable for the entire value of that car. Car rental agencies charge a rip-off $10 to $25 a day to buy this risk away. Travel Guard sells the same thing for $6 a day (tel. 800/826-1300). With some credit cards you are covered automatically when you rent the car using that card. (For details, see Chapter 11.)

Your travel agent has insurance brochures. Ask your agent which insurance he or she recommends for your travels and why. Study the brochures.

Consider how insurance fits your travel and personal needs, compare its cost to the likelihood of your using it and your potential loss—and then decide.

4. Pack Light Pack Light Pack Light

The importance of packing light cannot be overemphasized, but for your own good, I'll try. You'll never meet a traveler who, after five trips, brags, "Every year I pack heavier." The measure of a good traveler is how light she travels. You can't travel heavy, happy, and cheap. Pick two.

Limit yourself to 20 pounds in a carry-on-size bag. A 9" x 22" x 14" bag fits under most airplane seats. That's my self-imposed limit. At ETBD we've taken thousands of people of all ages and styles on tours through Europe. We allow only one carry-on bag. For many, this is a radical concept. "9 x 22 x 14 inches? That's my cosmetics kit!" But they manage and they're glad they did. And after you enjoy that sweet mobility and freedom, you'll never go any other way.

You'll walk with your luggage more than you think you will. Before leaving home, give yourself a test. Pack up completely, go into your hometown, and be a tourist for an hour. Fully loaded, you should enjoy window shopping. If you can't, stagger home and thin things out.

When you carry your own luggage, it's less likely to get lost, broken, or stolen. (Many travelers claim that airline employees rifle through checked luggage.) A small bag sits on your lap or under your seat on the bus,

Older travelers traveling like college kids—light, mobile, footloose and fancy-free, wearing their convertible suitcase rucksacks—have nothing to be ashamed of.

taxi, and airplane. You don't have to worry about it, and when you arrive, you can leave immediately. It's a good feeling. When I land in London, I'm on my way downtown while everyone else stares anxiously at the luggage carousel. When I fly home, I'm the first guy the dog sniffs.

Keep in mind that more and more airlines are limiting your carry-on luggage weight as well as size. Call your airline (or read the fine print on your ticket) to find out their policy. For example, British Air and SAS have a maximum of about 15 pounds. It's only worth fighting to carry on your bag if you have a tight connection.

Too much luggage marks you as a typical tourist. It slams the back door shut. Serendipity suffers. Changing locations becomes a major operation. Con artists figure you're helpless. Porters are a problem only to those who need them. With one bag hanging on your back, you're mobile and in control. Take this advice seriously.

BACKPACKADEMIA—WHAT TO BRING?

How do you fit a whole trip's worth of luggage into a small suitcase or rucksack? The answer is simple: Bring very little.

Spread out everything you think you might need on the living room floor. Pick up each item one at a time and scrutinize it. Ask yourself, "Will I really use this snorkel and these fins enough to justify carrying them around all summer?" Not "Will I use them?" but "Will I use them enough to feel good about carrying them over the Swiss Alps?" I would buy them in Greece and give them away before I would carry that extra weight over the Alps.

Don't pack for the worst scenerio. Risk shivering for a day rather than taking a heavy coat. Think in terms of what you can do without—not what will be handy on your trip. When in doubt, leave it out. I've seen people pack a whole summer's supply of deodorant, tampons, or razors, thinking they can't get them there. The world's getting awfully small; you can buy Dial soap, Colgate toothpaste, Tampax, Nivea cream, and Bic razors in Sicily. Tourist shops in major international hotels are a sure bet whenever you have difficulty finding some personal item. And if you can't find one of your "essentials," ask yourself how 250 million Europeans can live without it.

Whether you're traveling for three weeks or three months, you pack exactly the same. Rather than take a whole trip's supply of toiletries, take enough to get started and look forward to running out of toothpaste in Bulgaria. Then you have the perfect excuse to go into a Bulgarian department store, shop around, and pick up something you think might be toothpaste. . . .

RUCKSACK OR SUITCASE?

Whether you take a rucksack or a small soft-sided suitcase with a shoulder strap is up to you. Packing light applies equally to rucksack or suitcase travelers. Hard-sided suitcases with one-inch wheels are impractical. Bobbling down Europe's cobblestones, you'll know what I mean. (Those physically unable to lug a bag can manage best with the popular bags on wheels.)

Most young-at-heart travelers go the rucksack route. If you are a suitcase person who would like the ease of a rucksack without forgoing the "respectability" of a suitcase, try a convertible suitcase/rucksack with zip-away shoulder straps.

The same carry-on-the-plane-sized bag works as a suitcase or a rucksack.

These carry-on-size bags give you the best of both worlds. I live out of one of these for three months at a time. (See the Back Door Catalog at the end of this book.)

Unless you plan to camp or sleep out a lot, a sleeping bag is a bulky security blanket. Even on a low budget, bedding will be provided. (Hostels provide all bedding free or for a small fee and often don't allow sleeping bags.) Don't pack to camp unless you're going to camp. Without a sleeping bag, a medium-size rucksack is plenty big.

Pack your rucksack only two-thirds full to leave room for picnic food and souvenirs. Sturdy stitching, front and side pouches, padded shoulder straps, and a low-profile color are rucksack virtues. Many travelers figure an internal frame and a weight distribution hip belt are worth the extra money and get a more high-tech bag for around $120. Packing very light, I manage fine without the extra weight and expense of these fancier bags.

Entire books have been written on how to pack. It's really quite simple: Use stuff bags (one each for toiletries, underwear and socks, bigger clothing items and towel, camera gear and film, and miscellaneous stuff such as a first-aid kit, stationery, and sewing kit). Roll and rubber-band clothes, or zip-lock them in airless baggies to minimize wrinkles.

CLOTHING

The bulk of your luggage is clothing. Minimize by bringing less and washing more often. Every few nights you'll spend 10 minutes doing a little wash. This doesn't mean more washing, it just means doing it little by little as you go.

Be careful to choose dark clothes that dry quickly and either don't wrinkle or look good wrinkled. To see how wrinkled shirts will get, give everything a wet rehearsal by hand-washing and drying once at home. You should have no trouble drying clothing overnight in your hotel room. I know this sounds barbaric, but my body dries out a damp pair of socks or shirt in a jiffy. It's fun to buy clothes as you travel—another reason to start with less.

For winter travel, you can pack just about as light. Add a down or pile coat, long johns (quick-drying Capilene or super light silk), scarf, mittens, hat, and an extra pair of socks and underwear since things dry more slowly. Pack with the help of a climate chart (see the Appendix). Layer your clothing for warmth, and assume you'll be outside in the cold for hours at a time.

During the tourist season (April–September), the concert halls go casual. I have never felt out of place at symphonies, operas, or plays wearing a decent pair of slacks and a good-looking sweater. Pack with color-coordination in mind. Some cultural events require more formal attire, particularly outside of the tourist season, but the casual tourist rarely encounters these.

Many travelers are concerned about appropriate dress. European women wear dresses or skirts more often than pants. American women generally feel fine in pants, but in certain rural and traditional areas, they'll fit in better and may feel more comfortable in a skirt or dress. Women who prefer to wear slacks don't pack a dress and manage fine.

Your clothes will probably mark you as an American. Frankly, so what? Europeans will know anyway. I fit in and am culturally sensitive by watching my manners, not the cut of my pants.

Some sacred places, mostly in southern Europe (such as St. Peter's in Rome), have modest dress requirements for men and women: no shorts or bare shoulders. Although these dress codes deserve respect, they are often loosely enforced. If necessary, it's usually easy to improvise some modesty (a hairy-legged man can borrow a nearby tablecloth to wear as a kilt; a woman in a sleeveless blouse can wear maps on her shoulders). In southern cities—no matter how hot it is—men look goofy in shorts.

Go casual, simple, and very light. Remember, in your travels you'll meet two kinds of tourists—those who pack light and those who wish they had. Say it once out loud: "PACK LIGHT."

WHAT TO PACK

Indicates items available through Back Door Catalog at end of book.

Shirts. Bring up to five short-sleeved or long-sleeved shirts in a cotton/polyester blend. Arrange mix according to season.

Sweater. Warm and dark is best—for layering and dressing up. It never looks wrinkled and is always dark, no matter how dirty it is.

Pants. Bring two pairs: one lightweight cotton and another super-lightweight for hot and muggy big cities, and churches with modest dress codes. Jeans can be too hot for summer travel. Linen is great.

Shorts. Take a pair with plenty of pockets—doubles as a swimsuit for men.

Swimsuit. Especially for women.

Underwear and socks. Bring five sets (lighter dries quicker).

One pair of shoes. Take a well-used, light, and cool pair, with Vibram-type soles and good traction. I like Rockports or Easy Spirits. Sturdy, low profile–colored tennis shoes with a good tread are fine, too.

Jacket. Bring a light and water-resistant windbreaker with a hood. Gore-Tex is good if you expect rain. For summer travel, I wing it without rain gear but always pack for rain in Britain.

A tie or scarf. For instant respectability, bring anything lightweight that can break the monotony and make you look snazzy (cheap necklace, lime green socks, suspenders).

***Money belt.** It's essential for the peace of mind it brings. You could lose everything except your money belt, and the trip could still go on. Lightweight and low-profile beige is best.

Money. Bring your preferred mix of traveler's checks, a credit or debit card, an ATM card, a few personal checks, and some hard cash. Bring American dollars (Europeans get a kick out of seeing George Washington fold up into a mushroom) for situations when you want to change only a few bucks and not a whole traveler's check. I bring a few $1, $10, and $20 bills. And bring one foreign bill worth about $50 for each country you plan to visit, so you can function easily until you find a bank. (For details, see Chapter 13: Money.)

Documents and photocopies. Bring your passport, airline ticket, rail-pass or car rental voucher, driver's license, student ID, hostel card, and so on. Photocopies and a couple of passport-type photos can help you get replacements if the originals are lost or stolen. Carry photocopies separately in your luggage and keep the originals in your money belt.

***Small daypack.** A small nylon daypack is great for carrying your sweater, camera, literature, and picnic goodies while you leave your large bag at the hotel or train station. Fannypacks (small bags with thief-friendly zippers on a belt) are a popular alternative but should not be used as money belts.

Camera. Put a new battery in your camera before you go. Bring a protective and polarizing lens, midrange zoom lens, cleaning tissue, and a trip's worth of film. Store everything in a low-profile nylon stuff bag, not an expensive-looking camera bag.

Picnic supplies. Bring a small tablecloth to give your meal some extra class (and to wipe the knife on), salt and pepper, a cup, a damp facecloth in a baggie for cleaning up, and a Swiss Army–type knife with a corkscrew and can opener. A plastic plate is handy for picnic dinners in your hotel room.

Zip-lock baggies. Get a variety of sizes. They're great for packing out a little lunch from the breakfast buffet, leftover picnic food, containing wetness, and bagging potential leaks before they happen. The two-gallon jumbo size is handy for packing clothing.

Water bottle. The plastic half-liter mineral-water bottles sold throughout Europe are reusable and work great.

Wristwatch. A built-in alarm is handy. Otherwise, pack a small travel alarm clock.* Cheap hotel wake-up calls are unreliable.

*Earplugs. If night noises bother you, you'll love a good set of plugs such as those made by Sleep-well.

First-aid kit. See Chapter 21: Staying Healthy.

Medicine. Keep in original containers, if possible, with legible prescriptions.

Extra eyeglasses, contact lenses, and prescriptions. Many find their otherwise-comfortable contacts don't work in Europe. Bring your glasses just in case. Contact solutions are widely available in Europe.

*Toiletries kit. Sinks in cheap hotels come with meager countertop space and anonymous hairs. If you use a nylon toiletries kit that can hang on a hook or a towel bar, this is no problem. Put all squeeze bottles in zip-lock baggies, since pressure changes in flight cause even good bottles to leak. Consider a vacation from cosmetics. Bring a little toilet paper or tissue packets (sold at all newsstands in Europe). My Sonicare electric toothbrush holds a charge from home for one month of travel.

Soap. Not all hotels provide soap. A plastic squeeze bottle of concentrated, multipurpose, biodegradable liquid soap is handy for laundry and more.

*Clothesline. Hang it up in your hotel room to dry your clothes. The handy twist kind needs no clothespins.

Small towel. You'll find small bath towels at all moderate hotels and most cheap hotels. Although $30-a-day travelers will often need to bring their own towel, $60-a-day folks won't. I bring a thin hand towel for the occasional need. Face towels are rare in Europe. While I don't like them, many recommend the quick-drying "Sport Sponge" — a chamois in a plastic box.

Sewing kit. Clothes age rapidly while traveling. Your flight attendant may have a freebie for you. Add a few safety pins.

One carry-on-size bag?? Here's exactly what I traveled with for two months (photos taken naked in a Copenhagen hotel room): convertible 9" x 22" x 14" suitcase/rucksack; lightweight nylon day bag; ripped-up sections of three guidebooks, notes, maps, journal, tiny pocket notepad; wristwatch; tiny Swiss Army knife; pocket-sized radio with earplugs; money belt (with one credit card, driver's license, passport, plane ticket, train pass, cash, traveler's checks, sheet of phone numbers and addresses); toiletries stuff bag (with squeeze bottle of shampoo, soap in a plastic container, battery shaver, toothbrush and paste, comb, nail clippers, travel alarm clock, squeeze bottle of liquid soap for clothes); camera gear stuff bag (with camera, polarizer lens, cleaning tissues, film); miscellaneous bag with family photos, tiny odds and ends; Gore-Tex rain jacket in a stuff bag; long khaki cotton pants (button pockets, no wallet), super-light long pants, shorts, five pairs of socks, three underpants, long-sleeved shirt, two short-sleeved shirts, T-shirt; stuff bag with sweater, half a bath towel, plastic laundry bag; a light pair of shoes (Rockports).

Travel information (minimal). Rip out appropriate chapters from guide-books, staple them together, and store in a zip-lock baggie. When you're done, give them away.

*European map. Get a map best suited to your trip's overall needs and pick up maps for specific local areas as you go.

Address list. Use it to send post cards home and collect new addresses. Taking a whole address book is not packing light. Consider typing your mail list onto a sheet of gummed address labels before you leave. You'll know exactly who you've written to, and the labels will be perfectly legible.

Postcards or small picture book from your hometown, and family pictures. A zip-lock baggie of show-and-tell things is always a great conversation piece with Europeans you meet.

Journal. An empty book filled with the experiences of your trip will be your most treasured souvenir. Use a hardbound type designed to last a lifetime, rather than a spiral notebook. Attach a photocopied calendar page to visualize your itinerary and jot down reminders. Keep a traveler's check and expenses log in the appendix.

Small notepad and pen. A tiny notepad in your back pocket is a great organizer, reminder, and communication aid (for sale in European stationery stores).

OPTIONAL BRING-ALONGS

*Indicates items available through Back Door Catalog at end of book.

Skirt, sandals, robe, or nightshirt. Especially for women.

Sunglasses and sunscreen.

*Inflatable pillow (or "neck nest") for sun-snoozing.

Pillowcase. It's cleaner and possibly more comfortable to stuff your own.

Hairdryer. People with long or thick hair appreciate a travel hairdryer in the off-season, when hair takes a long time to dry and it's cold outside (see Electricity, below).

Light warm-up suit. Use for pajamas, evening lounge outfit, instant modest street wear, smuggling things, and going down the hall.

Teva-type sandals or thongs.

Leather-bottomed slippers. These are great for the flight and for getting cozy in your hotel room.

*Small flashlight. Handy for reading under the sheets after "lights out" in the hostel, late night trips down the hall, exploring castle dungeons, and hypnotizing street thieves.

Stronger light bulbs. You can buy these in Europe to give your cheap hotel room more brightness than the 25- to 40-watt norm.

Checklist of Essentials

- ❏ Carry-on-size bag or rucksack
- ❏ 5 shirts
- ❏ 1 sweater
- ❏ 2 pairs pants
- ❏ 1 pair shorts
- ❏ 1 swimsuit (women only)
- ❏ 5 pair underwear and socks
- ❏ 1 pair shoes
- ❏ 1 jacket
- ❏ Tie or scarf
- ❏ Money belt
- ❏ Money
  - ❏ Traveler's checks
  - ❏ Credit card or debit card
  - ❏ ATM card
  - ❏ A few personal checks
  - ❏ Hard cash
- ❏ Documents and photocopies
  - ❏ Passport
  - ❏ Airline ticket
  - ❏ Driver's license
  - ❏ Student ID and hostel card
  - ❏ Railpass/car rental voucher
  - ❏ Insurance details
- ❏ Daypack
- ❏ Picnic supplies
- ❏ Zip-lock baggies
- ❏ Camera, battery, film, lenses, stuff bag
- ❏ Water bottle
- ❏ Wristwatch and alarm clock
- ❏ Earplugs
- ❏ First-aid kit
- ❏ Medicine
- ❏ Extra glasses/contacts and prescriptions
- ❏ Toiletries kit
- ❏ Soap
- ❏ Laundry soap
- ❏ Clothesline
- ❏ Small towel
- ❏ Sewing kit
- ❏ Travel information
- ❏ European map
- ❏ Address list
- ❏ Postcards or photos from home
- ❏ Journal
- ❏ Notepad and pen

A good paperback. There's plenty of empty time on a trip to either be bored or enjoy some good reading.

Radio, Walkman, or recorder. Partners can bring a Y-jack for two sets of earphones. Some travelers use microcassette recorders to record pipe organs, tours, or journal entries. Some recorders have radios, adding a new dimension to your experience.

Collapsible cup.

Office supplies. Bring paper and an envelope of envelopes.

Packing Tips for Women

Thanks to Kendra Roth and Margaret Berger Cassady for the follow-ing tips:

Every piece of clothing packed should match at least two other items or have at least two uses (e.g., sandals double as slippers).

Tops: Bring two to three T-shirts and one to two short-sleeved blouses, plus one to two long-sleeved shirts. Long-sleeved shirts with sleeves that roll up and button can double as short-sleeved shirts. Look for a wrinkle-camouflaging pattern or fabrics that are supposed to look wrinkled. Silk dries quickly and is lightweight.

Pants and Shorts: Try the pants with the zip-off legs that convert to shorts. These are especially good in Italy, allowing you to cover up inside churches and stay cool outside. Patterned palazzo pants don't show dirt or wrinkles, and their elastic waistbands accommodate moneybelts and big Italian meals. Lightweight leggings can double as long johns or pajamas. You might feel more comfortable wearing a skirt or pants (not shorts) in Amsterdam, Paris, or Italian cities where the local women really dress up.

Skirts: Some women bring one to two skirts because they're as cool and breathable as shorts, but dressier. And skirts make life easier than pants when you're faced with a squat toilet! "Broomstick" skirts are lightweight, supposed to look wrinkled, pack compactly, and have a comfy elastic waistband. Tilley's makes expensive but great skirts (and other items) from blended fabric that feels like cotton (tel. 800/884-3797, www.tilley.com). You can wash them, wring them out, hang them to dry, and even stamp on them, and they still won't wrinkle. Denim or twill trouser skirts go with everything, and can easily be dressed up or down.

Shoes: Bring one pair of good comfortable walking shoes. Mephisto, Timberland, and Rykers look dressier and more European than sneak-ers but are still comfortable. For a second pair, consider sandals or Tevas in summer, or dark leather flats in winter (can be worn with tights and a skirt to dress up).

Socks, Underwear, and Swimsuit: *Cotton/nylon-blend socks dry faster than 100 percent cotton, which loses its softness when air-dried. Sports socks nicely cushion your feet. It's impossible to look stylish when wearing walking shoes and these little white socks, but comfort's more important. Try silk or stretch lace undies, which dry faster than all-cotton, but breathe more than nylon. Bring at least two bras (what if you leave one hanging over your shower rail by accident?). A sports bra doubles as a hiking/sunning top. You don't need a bikini to try sunbathing topless on European beaches. Local women with one-piece bathing suits just roll down the top.*

Jacket: *Neutral colors (black, beige, loden green) look more European than bright colors if you want to blend in. If your waterproof jacket doesn't have a hood, take a mini-umbrella or buy one in Europe. These are easy to find—vendors often appear as soon as the rain begins!*

Shoulder and Off-season Variations: *Silk long johns are great for layering, weigh next to nothing, and dry out quickly. Bring gloves and some kind of hat. Wear shoes that are water-resistant or waterproof.*

Toiletries: *All feminine products (even many of the same brands) are sold all over Europe, but it's easier to figure out how many tampons, pads, or panty shields you'll need and bring them with you rather than having to buy a large box in Europe. If you bring birth control pills (or any timed-dosage prescription), take the time difference into account. If you usually take a pill with breakfast, take it with lunch or dinner in Europe. Remember to bring the pills on the plane each way to take at your home-dosage time, too.*

Accessorize, accessorize: *A scarf can dress up your outfits, is lightweight, and can do double-duty as a belt, headband, or ponytail bow. Most women feel safe wearing engagement and wedding rings while traveling, but no other valuable jewelry. A few pairs of inexpensive earrings are fun to bring.*

Small roll of duct tape.
Collapsible umbrella.
*Tiny lock. Use it to lock your rucksack zippers shut.
Spot remover. Bring a dab of Goop in a film canister.
Bug juice. Especially for France and Italy.
Gifts. Local kids love T-shirts and baseball cards, and gardeners appreciate flower seeds.
Poncho. Hard-core vagabonds use a poncho as protection in a rainstorm, a ground cloth for sleeping, or a beach or picnic blanket.
*Hostel sheet. Hostels require one. Bring your own (sewn up like a sleeping bag), buy one, or rent a sheet at hostels (about $4 per stay). It doubles as a beach or picnic blanket, comes in handy on overnight train rides, shields you from dirty blankets in mountain huts, and will save you money in other dorm-type accommodations, which often charge extra for linen or don't provide it at all.

ELECTRICITY

Try to go without electrical gear. Travelers requiring electricity need a converter to let their American appliance work on the European current and an adapter to allow the American plug to fit into the European wall. Many travel accessories come with a built-in converter. Look for a small switch with voltages marked 120 (US) and 240 (Europe). Often, buying a new travel appliance with a built-in converter can be cheaper than buying a separate converter (often $20–$25) to use with your old appliance. Regardless, you'll still need an adapter.

British plugs have three big flat prongs, and Continental European plugs have two small round prongs. Many sockets in Europe are recessed into the wall. Your adapter should be small enough to fit into this hole in order for your prongs to connect. Cheap converters with built-in adapters have prongs that are the right size but are unable to connect.

Many budget hotel rooms have only one outlet, occupied by the lamp. Hardware stores in Europe sell cheap three-bangers that let you keep the lamp on and still plug in your toothbrush and Game Boy.

PLANNING YOUR ITINERARY

5. When to Go

In travel industry jargon, the year is divided into three seasons: peak season (late June, July, and August), shoulder season (May, early June, September, early October), and off-season (mid-October through April). Each has its pros and cons.

PEAK SEASON STRATEGIES

Except for the crowds, summer is a great time to travel. The sunny weather, long days, and exuberant nightlife turn Europe into a powerful magnet. Here are a few crowd-minimizing tips that I've learned over many peak seasons.

Arrange your trip with crowd control in mind. Consider, for instance, a six-week European trip beginning June 1, half with a Eurailpass to see the famous sights and half visiting relatives in Scotland. It would be wise to do the Eurail section first, enjoying those precious last three weeks of relatively uncrowded shoulder season, and then spend time with the family during the last half of your vacation, when Florence and Salzburg are teeming with tourists. Salzburg on June 10 and Salzburg on July 10 are two very different cities.

Seek out places with no promotional budgets. Keep in mind that accessibility and promotional budgets determine a place's fame and popularity just as much as its worthiness as a tourist attraction. For example, Zurich is big and famous—with nothing special to offer the visitor. The beaches of Greece's Peloponnesian Peninsula enjoy the same weather and water as the highly promoted isles of Mykonos and Ios but are out of the way, not promoted, and wonderfully deserted. If you're traveling by car or bike, take advantage of your mobility by leaving the well-worn tourist routes. The Europe away from the train tracks seems more peaceful and relaxed. Overlooked by the Eurail mobs, it's one step behind the modern parade.

Hit the back streets. So many people energetically jockey themselves into the most crowded square of the most crowded city in the most crowded month (St. Mark's Square, Venice, July) and complain about the crowds. You could be in Venice in July and walk six blocks behind St. Mark's Basilica, step into a café, and be greeted by Venetians who act as though they've never seen a tourist.

Spend the night. Popular day-trip destinations near big cities and

St. Mark's Square in July—no wonder Venice is sinking

resorts like Toledo (near Madrid), San Marino (near huge Italian beach resorts), and San Gimignano (near Florence) take on a more peaceful and enjoyable atmosphere at night, when the legions of day-trippers retreat to the predictable plumbing of their big-city hotels. Small towns normally lack hotels big enough for tour groups and are often inaccessible to large buses. So they will experience, at worst, midday crowds.

Be an early bird. Walk around Rothenburg's ancient wall before breakfast. Crack-of-dawn joggers and walkers enjoy a special look at wonderfully medieval cities as they yawn and stretch and prepare for the daily onslaught of the 20th century.

See how the locals live. Residential neighborhoods rarely see a tourist. Browse through a department store. Buy a copy of the local *Better Homes and Thatches* and use it to explore that particular culture. Dance with the locals. Play street soccer with the neighborhood gang.

Plan your museum sightseeing carefully. Avoid museums on their weekly free days, when they're most crowded. And because nearly all Parisian museums are closed on Tuesday, nearby Versailles, which is open, is predictably crowded—very crowded. And it follows that Parisian museums are especially crowded on Monday and Wednesday. While crowds at the Louvre can't be avoided altogether, some thought before you start your trip can help.

Arrive at the most popular sights early or late in the day to avoid tour groups. Germany's fairy-tale Neuschwanstein Castle is cool and easy with relaxed guides and no crowds at 8:30 or 9:00 in the morning. And very late in the day—when most tourists are long gone, exhausted in their rooms or searching for dinner—I linger alone, taking artistic liberties with Europe's greatest art in empty galleries.

Know the exceptions. Although the tourist crowds can generally be plotted on a bell-shaped curve peaking in July and August, there are

It's Tuesday at Versailles, and these people now have time to read their guidebooks, which warn: On Tuesday, most Paris museums are closed, and Versailles has very long lines.

odd glitches. For instance, Paris is empty and easy during its July and August holiday season, while a busy convention schedule packs the city full in June and September. And hotels in Scandinavia are cheapest in the summer, when travel—which, up there, is mostly business travel—is down.

In much of Europe (especially Italy and France), cities are partially shut down in July and August, when local urbanites take their beach break. You'll hear that these are terrible times to travel, but it's really no big deal. You can't get a dentist and many Laundromats are shut down, but tourists are basically unaffected by Europe's mass holidays unless they happen to be caught on the wrong road on the first or 15th of the month (when vacations often start or finish). Tourists can also count on being affected by mass holidays if they are crazy enough to compete with all of Europe for a piece of French Riviera beach.

SHOULDER SEASON

For many, "shoulder season"—May, early June, September, and early October—offers the best mix of peak-season and off-season pros and cons. In shoulder season you'll enjoy decent weather, long days, fewer crowds, and a local tourist industry that is still eager to please and entertain. Note that autumn in sunny Italy is still peak season.

OFF-SEASON EUROPE

Each summer, Europe greets a stampede of sightseers and shoppers with erect postcard racks. Before jumping into the peak-season pig-pile, consider an off-season trip.

The advantages of off-season travel are many. Off-season airfares are hundreds of dollars cheaper. With fewer crowds in Europe, you'll sleep cheaper. Many fine hotels drop their prices, and budget hotels will have plenty of vacancies. And, while many of the cheap alternatives to hotels will be closed, those still open are usually empty and therefore, more comfortable.

Off-season adventurers loiter all alone through Leonardo's home, ponder unpestered in Rome's Forum, kick up sand on virgin beaches, and chat with laid-back guards by log fires in French châteaus. In wintertime Venice you can be alone atop St. Marks' bell tower to watch the clouds of your breath roll over the Byzantine domes of the church to a horizon of cut-glass Alps. Below, on St. Mark's Square, pigeons fidget and wonder, "Where are the tourists?"

Off-season adventurers enjoy step-right-up service at banks and tourist offices and experience a more European Europe. Although many popular tourist-oriented parks, shows, and tours will be closed, off-season is in-season for the high culture: Vienna's Boys Choir, opera, and Spanish Riding School are in their crowd-pleasing glory.

But winter travel has its drawbacks. Because much of Europe is in upper latitudes, the days are short. It's dark by 5:00 p.m. The weather can be miserable—cold, windy, and drizzly—and then turn worse. But just as summer can be wet and gray, winter can be crisp and blue, and even into mid-November, hillsides blaze with colorful leaves.

Off-season hours are limited. Some sights close down entirely, and most operate on shorter schedules (such as 10:00 a.m.–5:00 p.m. rather than 9:00 a.m.–7:00 p.m.), with darkness often determining the closing time. Winter sightseeing is fine in big cities, which bustle year-round, but it's more frustrating in small tourist towns, which often shut down entirely. In December many beach resorts are shut up as tight as canned hams. While Europe's wonderful outdoor evening ambience survives year-round in the south, wintertime streets are empty in the north after dark. English-language tours, common in the summer, are rare during the off-season, when most visitors are natives. Tourist information offices normally stay open year-round but with shorter hours in the winter. A final disadvantage of winter travel is loneliness. The solo traveler won't have the built-in camaraderie of other travelers that she would find in peak season.

To thrive in the winter, you'll need to get the most out of your limited daylight hours. Start early and eat a quick lunch. Tourist offices close early, so call ahead to double-check hours and confirm your plans. Pack for the cold and wet—layers, rainproof parka, gloves, wool hat, long johns, waterproof shoes, and an umbrella. Remember, cold weather is colder when you're outdoors trying to enjoy yourself all day long. Use undershirts to limit the washing of slow-drying heavy shirts.

Empty beds abound in the off-season. I led an 18-day November tour of Germany, Italy, and France with 22 people and no room reservations. We'd amble into town around 5:00 p.m. and always found 22 beds with breakfast for our $25-per-bed budget. Dress warmly—cheap hotels are not always adequately heated in the off-season.

Most hotels charge less in the winter. To save some money, arrive late, notice how many empty rooms they have (keys on the rack), let them know you're a hosteler (student, senior, or whatever) with a particular price limit, and bargain from there. The opposite is true of big-city business centers (especially in Berlin, Brussels, and the Scandinavian capitals), which are busiest and most expensive off-season.

David C. Hoerlein

Regardless of when you go, if your objective is to "meet the people," you'll find Europe filled with them 365 days a year.

6. Itinerary Skills

If you have any goals at all for your trip, make an itinerary. I never start a trip without having every day planned out. Your reaction to an itinerary may be, "Hey, won't my spontaneity and freedom suffer?" Not necessarily. Although I always begin a trip with a well-thought-out plan, I maintain my flexibility and make plenty of changes. An itinerary forces you to see the consequences of any spontaneous change you make while in Europe. For instance, if you spend two extra days in the sunny Alps, you'll see that you won't make it to, say, the Greek Isles. With the help of an itinerary, you can lay out your goals, maximize their potential, avoid regrettable changes, and impress your friends.

ITINERARY CONSIDERATIONS

If you deal thoughtfully with issues like weather, culture shock, health maintenance, fatigue, and festivals, you'll travel happier.

Moderate the weather conditions you'll encounter. Match the coolest month of your trip with the warmest area, and vice versa. For a spring and early summer trip, enjoy comfortable temperatures throughout by starting in the southern countries and working your way north. If possible, avoid the midsummer Mediterranean heat. Spend those weeks in Scandinavia or the Alps. Scandinavia and Britain have miserable weather and none of the crowd problems that plague Italy and France. Ideally, forget crowd concerns and see them in the peak of summer. (See the Appendix for climate charts.)

Mix in cities and villages. Alternate intense big cities with villages and countryside. For example, break a tour of Venice, Florence, and Rome with an easygoing time in the hill towns or on the Italian Riviera. Judging Italy by Rome is like judging America by New York City.

Join the celebration. Hit as many festivals, national holidays, and arts seasons as you can. This takes some study. Ask the national tourist office of each country you'll visit for a calendar of events. An effort to hit the right places at the right time will drape your trip with festive tinsel.

Save your energy for the biggies. Don't overestimate your powers of absorption. Rare is the tourist who doesn't become somewhat jaded after several weeks of travel. At the start of my trip, I'll seek out every great painting and cathedral I can. After two months, I find myself "seeing" cathedrals with a sweep of my head from the doorway, and I probably wouldn't cross the street for a Rembrandt. Don't burn out on mediocre castles, palaces, and museums. Sightsee selectively.

Establish a logical flight plan. It's been years since I flew in and out of the same city. You can avoid needless travel time and expense by flying "open-jaws"—into one port and out of another. You usually pay just half the round-trip fare for each port. Even if your open-jaws flight plan is more expensive than the cheapest round-trip fare, it may save you lots of time and money when surface connections are figured in. For example, you could fly into London, travel east through whatever interests you in Europe, and fly home from Athens. This would eliminate the costly and time-consuming return to London. Your travel agent will know where flying open-jaws is economical.

See countries in order of cultural hairiness. If you plan to see Britain, the Alps, Greece, and Turkey, do it in that order so you'll grow steadily into the more intense and crazy travel. England, compared to any place but the United States, is pretty dull. Don't get me wrong—it's a great place to travel. But go there first, when cream teas and roundabouts will be exotic. And you're more likely to enjoy Turkey if you work gradually east.

Save your good health. Visit countries that may be hazardous to your health (North Africa or the Middle East) at the end of your trip, so you won't needlessly jeopardize your healthy enjoyment of the safer countries. If you're going to get sick, do it at the end of your trip so you can recover at home, missing more work—not vacation.

Minimize one-night stands. Even the speediest itinerary should be a series of two-night stands. I'd stretch every other day with long hours on the road or train and hurried sightseeing along the way in order to enjoy the sanity of two nights in the same bed. Minimizing hotel changes saves time and money and gives you the sensation of actually being comfortable in a town on the second night.

Leave some slack in your itinerary. Don't schedule yourself too tightly (a common tendency). Everyday chores, small business matters, transportation problems, constipation, and planning mistakes deserve about one day of slack per week in your itinerary.

Punctuate a long trip with rest periods. Constant sightseeing is grueling. Schedule a peaceful period every two weeks. If your trip is a long one, schedule a vacation from your vacation in the middle of it. Most people need several days in a place where they couldn't see a museum or take a tour even if they wanted to. A stop in the mountains or on an island, in a friendly rural town, or at the home of a relative is a great way to revitalize your tourist spirit.

Assume you will return. This Douglas MacArthur approach is a key to touristic happiness. You can't really see Europe in one trip. Don't even try. Enjoy what you're seeing. Forget what you won't get to on this trip. If you worry about things that are just out of reach, you won't appreciate what's in your hand. I'm planning my 26th three-month European vacation, and I still need more time. I'm happy about what I can't get to. It's a blessing that we can never see all of Europe.

YOUR BEST ITINERARY IN EIGHT STEPS

1. Read up on Europe and talk to travelers. Do some reading, get a guidebook or two, take a class, write to the tourist offices. You must have some friends who'd love to show you their slides. What you want to see is determined by what you know (or don't know). Identify your personal interests: World War II buffs study up on battle sites; McGregors locate their clan in Scotland. This is a time to grow a forest of ideas from which you'll harvest the dream trip.

2. Decide on the places you want to see. Start by listing everything you'd like to see. Circle your destinations on a map. Have a reason for every stop. Don't go to Casablanca just because it's famous.

Minimize redundancy. On a quick trip, focus on only one part of the Alps. England's two most well-known university towns, Oxford and Cambridge, are redundant. Choose one (Cambridge).

Example: Places I want to see:

London	*Alps*	*Bavaria*	*Florence*	*Amsterdam*
Paris	*Rhine*	*Rome*	*Venice*	*Greece*

3. Establish a route and timeline. Figure out a logical geographical order for your route. Decide on the length of your trip. Pin down any places that you have to be on a certain date (and ask yourself if it's really worth the stifle). Once you've settled on a list, be satisfied with your efficient plan, and focus any more study and preparation only on places that fall along your proposed route.

4. Decide on the cities you'll fly in and out of. If your route is linear (like London to Athens), fly open-jaws. If your route is circular, fly round-trip. Ask your travel agent about the cheapest and most convenient dates and ports.

Example: I can escape for 23 days.
Cheapest places to fly to: London, Frankfurt, Amsterdam.

5. Determine the mode of transportation. Do this not solely on economical terms but by analyzing what is best for the trip you envision.

Example: Since I'm traveling alone, going so many miles, and spending the majority of my time in big cities, I'd rather not mess with a car. I'll use a Eurailpass.

6. Rough in an itinerary. Write in the number of days you'd like to stay in each place. Carefully consider travel time. Driving, except on superfreeways, is slower than in the United States. Borrow a Thomas Cook Continental Train Timetable from your travel agent or library and get an idea of how long various train journeys will take. Learn which trains are fast, and avoid minor lines in southern countries. Eurailers often use night trains (NT) or boats (NB) to save time and money whenever possible.

Example: Logical order and desired time in each place:

Days

3	*London*
5	*Paris (NT)*
3	*Alps (NT)*
2	*Florence*
3	*Rome (NT)*
7	*Greece (NB)*
2	*Venice (NT)*
3	*Munich/Bavaria*
3	*Romantic Road/Rhine Cruise*
4	*Amsterdam*
35	*Notes: I have 23 days for my*

SAMPLE ITINERARY

vacation. If I eliminate Greece, I'll still need to cut five days. Open-jaws into London and out of Amsterdam is economical. "Logical" order may be affected by night-train possibilities.

7. Adjust by cutting, streamlining, or adding to fit your timeline or budget. Minimize travel time. When you must cut something, cut to save the most mileage. For instance, if Amsterdam and Berlin are equally important to you and you don't have time for both, cut the destination that saves the most miles (in this case, Berlin).

Minimize clutter. A so-so sight (San Sebastian) breaking a convenient night train (Paris–Madrid) into two half-day journeys is clutter.

Consider economizing on car rental or Eurailpass. For instance, try to manage a 23-day trip on a 15-day train pass by seeing London, Paris, and Amsterdam before or after you use the pass.

Example: Itinerary adjusted to time limitations:

Days
4   London
3   Paris (NT)
3   Alps (NT)
1   Florence
2   Rome (NT)
2   Venice (NT)
3   Munich/Bavaria
2   Romantic Road/Rhine Cruise
<u>3</u>   Amsterdam
23   *Twenty-three days with a 15-day Eurailpass (valid from last day in Paris until first day in Amsterdam).*

8. Fine tune. Study your guidebook. Maximize festival and market days. Be sure crucial sights are open the day you'll be in town. Remember that most cities close many of their major tourist attractions for one day dur-

SEPTEMBER

SUN.	MON.	TUE.	WED.	THUR.	FRI.	SAT.
			MOM'S BIRTHDAY! ☺			**1** USA TO → LONDON
2 ARRIVE LONDON /L	**3** LONDON /L	**4** LONDON, EVE TRAIN TO PARIS /P	**5** PARIS /P	**6** PARIS /P	**7** S.T. VERSAILLES, N.T. TO ALPS /N.T.	**8** ALPS /A
9 ALPS /A	**10** SWISS LAKES, N.T. TO FLORENCE /N.T.	**11** FLORENCE /F	**12** TO ROME /R	**13** ROME, N.T. TO VENICE /N.T.	**14** VENICE /V	**15** VENICE, N.T. TO MUNICH /N.T.
16 OKTOBERFEST! ☺ MUNICH /M	**17** DACHAU CLOSED S.T. NEUSCHWAN. CASTLE /M	**18** S.T. SALZBURG /M	**19** ROMANTIC ROAD BUS, TRAIN TO RHINE /RH	**20** RHINE BOAT CRUISE /RH	**21** TO AMST. /A	**22** AMSTERDAM /A
23 AMST. TO USA /	**24** BACK TO WORK ⌒ /	**25**	**26**	**27**	**28**	**29**

INITIAL IN THE BOTTOM RIGHT INDICATES WHERE TO SPEND EACH NIGHT.

N.T. = NIGHT TRAIN   **S.T.** = SIDE TRIP

ing the week. It would be a shame to be in Milan only on a Monday, for instance, when Leonardo da Vinci's *Last Supper* is out to lunch. In many cities, major tourist sights are closed on Monday including Brussels, Munich, Lisbon, Florence, Rome, and Naples. Paris closes the Louvre and many other sights on Tuesday. Write out a day-by-day itinerary.

Example: According to the guidebooks, I must keep these points in mind as I plan my trip. London: theaters closed on Sunday, Speaker's Corner is Sunday only. Paris: Most museums are closed on Tuesdays. Versailles and the Orsay Museum are closed on Monday. Florence: Museums are closed on Monday. Dachau: closed on Monday. Note that I'm choosing to pay a little extra on my flight to let my trip stretch over the weekends and minimize lost work time. Yes, I may be a zombie on that first Monday back, but hey, what's more important?

THE HOME BASE STRATEGY

The home base strategy is a clever way to make your trip itinerary smoother, simpler, and more efficient. Set yourself up in a central location and use that place as a base for day trips to nearby attractions.

The home base approach minimizes setup time (usually an hour). Searching for a good hotel can be exhausting, frustrating, and time-consuming. And hotels often give a better price, or at least more smiles, for longer stays. Many private homes don't accept those staying only one night.

You are freed from your luggage. Being able to leave your luggage in the hotel lets you travel freely and with the peace of mind that you are set up for the night.

You feel "at home" in your home base town. This comfortable feeling takes more than a day to get, and when you are changing locations every day or two, you may never enjoy this important rootedness. Home basing allows you to sense the rhythm of daily life.

Day-trip to a village, enjoy the nightlife in a city. The home base approach lets you spend the evening in a city, where there is some exciting nightlife. Most small countryside towns die after 9:00 p.m. If you're not dead by 9:00 p.m., you'll enjoy more action in a larger city.

Transportation is a snap. Europe's generally frequent and punctual train and bus systems (which often operate out of a hub anyway) make this home base strategy practical. With a train pass, trips are free; otherwise, the transportation is reasonable, often with reductions offered for round-trip tickets.

Resources: My country guidebooks are made to order for this home base approach. They give you the necessary step-by-step details for all of Europe's best home bases. The king of the day-trippers, Earl Steinbicker, has written an entire series of *Daytrips* books for Holland/Belgium/

My favorite home base cities and their best day trips:

Madrid: Toledo, Segovia, El Escorial, even Sevilla and Córdoba with the new AVE bullet trains

Amsterdam: Alkmaar, Arnhem's Folk Museum and Kröller-Müller Museum, Enkhuisen's Zuiderzee Museum, Scheveningen, Delft, most of the Netherlands

Copenhagen: Frederiksborg Castle, Roskilde, Helsingør, Odense

Paris: Reims, Versailles, Chartres, Fontainebleau, Chantilly, Giverny

London: Oxford, Stratford, Cambridge, Salisbury, Stonehenge, Bath, and many others

Avignon: Nîmes, Arles, the Rhône Valley, all of Provence

Florence: Pisa, Siena, San Gimignano, Arezzo, many small towns

Munich: Salzburg, Berchtesgaden, Augsburg, King Ludwig's castles (Neuschwanstein, Linderhof, and Chiemsee), Wies Church, Oberammergau and other small Bavarian towns

Sorrento: Naples, Capri, Pompeii, Herculaneum, Amalfi Coast, Paestum

Luxembourg, France, Italy, and Germany (published by Hastings House). For Ireland, try Patricia Preston's *Daytrips Ireland.*

HIGH-SPEED TOWN-HOPPING

When I tell people that I saw three or four towns in one day, many think, "Insane! Nobody can really see several towns in a day!" Of course, it's folly to go too fast, but many stop-worthy towns take only an hour or two to cover. Don't let feelings of guilt tell you to slow down and stay longer if you really are finished with a town. There's so much more to see in the rest of Europe! Going too slow is as bad as going too fast.

If you're efficient and use the high-speed town-hopping method, you'll amaze yourself at what you can see in a day. Let me explain with an example.

You wake up early in Town A. Checking out of your hotel, you have one sight to cover before your 10:00 a.m. train. (You checked the train schedule the night before.) After the sightseeing and before getting to the station, you visit the open-air market and buy the ingredients for your brunch and pick up a Town B map and tourist brochure at Town A's tourist office.

From 10:00 to 11:00 a.m. you travel by train to Town B. During that hour you'll have a restful brunch, enjoy the passing scenery, and prepare for Town B by reading your literature and deciding what you want to see. Just before your arrival, you put the items you need (camera, jacket, tourist information) into your small daypack and, upon arrival, check the rest of your luggage in a locker. Virtually every station has storage lockers or a baggage check desk.

Before leaving Town B's station, write down on a scrap of paper the departure times of the next few trains to Town C. Now you can sightsee as much or as little as you want and still know when to comfortably catch your train.

Town B is great. After a snack in the park, you catch the train at 2:30 p.m. By 3:00 p.m. you're in Town C, where you repeat the same procedure you followed in Town B. Town C just isn't what it was cracked up to be so, after a walk along the waterfront and a look at the church, you catch the first train out.

You arrive in Town D, the last town on the day's agenda, by 5:30 p.m. The man in the station directs you to a good budget pension two blocks down the street. You're checked in and unpacked in no time, and after a few moments of horizontal silence, it's time to find a good restaurant and eat dinner. After a meal and an evening stroll, you're ready to call it a day. Writing in your journal it occurs to you: This was one heck of a sightseeing day. You spent it high-speed town-hopping.

7. Sample Routes

After years of designing bus tours, brain-storming with my guides, and helping travelers plan their itineraries, I've come up with some fun and efficient three-week plans. These itineraries are the routes covered in my various country guidebooks. Each of these guidebooks gives you all the details you'll need for successful navigation.

This chapter also offers tips on crossing the Channel via Chunnel; traveling through Belgium, Germany, and Italy; and long-jumping to Greece.

"The Chunnel"—Getting from Great Britain to France

The fastest and most convenient way to travel between Big Ben and the Eiffel Tower is now by rail. Eurostar, a joint service of the Belgian, British, and French railways, is the speedy passenger train that zips you (and up to 800 others in 18 TGV-type cars) between downtown London and downtown Paris (nine trains/day, three-hour ride) or Brussels (five/day, three hours) faster and easier than flying. The train goes 100 mph in England and 160 mph on the Continent. The actual tunnel crossing is a 17-minute black, silent, 100 mph nonevent. Your ears won't even pop.

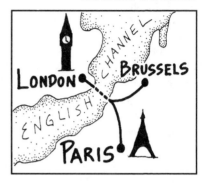

CROSSING THE ENGLISH CHANNEL

Chunnel fares are affordable—particularly the cheaper Leisure Tickets. You'll pay essentially the same whether your destination is Brussels, Paris, or London. These prices are for 1999. For the latest fares, call Rail Europe at 800/EUROSTAR.

First class: A regular first-class ticket costs $219 (including a meal on board—a dinner departure nets you more grub than breakfast). Tickets are fully refundable even after your departure date. You can save money by getting a first-class Leisure Ticket for $179, though it's only 50 percent refundable up to two days before departure. Unless you're Bill Gates, skip Premium First Class for $299 (Eurostar lounge privileges, exclusive compartment, taxi on arrival).

Second class: Second ("standard") class is $149 (fully refundable even after departure date) or only $109 for a Leisure Ticket (50 percent refundable up to two days before departure).

Discounts: Discounted fares are available for travelers holding railpasses that include France, Belgium, or Britain ($155 for first class, $95 for second); youths under 26 ($79 in second class); and children under 12 (about half fare). Seniors over 60 get a 25 percent discount off a regular first-class ticket.

Buying tickets: Cheaper seats can sell out. Ideally, buy a ticket before leaving home. When you're ready to commit to a date and time, book an "instant reservation" over the phone (800/EUROSTAR) or through your travel agent. Prices do not include FedEx ticket delivery. For maximum spontaneity, buy your tickets in Europe at any major train station.

Sailing across the Channel is more romantic but twice as complicated and time-consuming. Taking the bus rather than the train to the dock is cheapest, and round trips are a bargain. London to Paris by bus

THE BEST OF GREAT BRITAIN
in 22 days

Day 1 - Arrive in
London
Day 2 - London
Day 3 - London
Day 4 - Stonehenge,
Bath
Day 5 - Bath
Day 6 - Glastonbury,
Wells
Day 7 - South Wales,
Folk Museum
Day 8 - Cotswold
villages,
Blenheim
Day 9 - Stratford,
Warwick
Castle,
Coventry
Day 10 - Industrial
Revolution
Museum
Day 11 - North Wales,
Snowdonia,
Caenarfon
Castle, Medieval
Banquet
Day 12 - Blackpool
Day 13 - Lake District
Day 14 - Lake District
Day 15 - Scottish West Coast
Day 16 - Highlands, Loch Ness
Day 17 - Edinburgh
Day 18 - Edinburgh
Day 19 - Hadrian's Wall,
Durham Cathedral,
Beamish Folk Museum

Day 20 - Moors, York
Day 21 - York
Day 22 - Cambridge, back to
London

For all the specifics,
see *Rick Steves' Great Britain
& Ireland 1999.*

THE BEST OF FRANCE
in 22 days

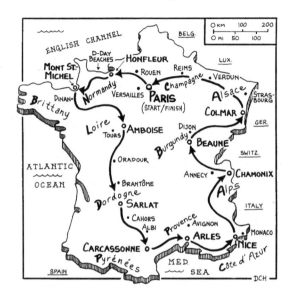

Day 1 - Arrive in Paris
Day 2 - Paris
Day 3 - Paris
Day 4 - Paris
Day 5 - Into Normandy
Day 6 - Bayeux, D-Day
beaches
Day 7 - Mont St. Michel,
Brittany, Loire
Valley
Day 8 - Château
hopping
Day 9 - Sarlat, Dordogne
Day 10 - Dordogne Valley
Day 11 - Albi and
Carcassonne
Day 12 - To Arles

Day 13 - Provence
Day 14 - To the Riviera
Day 15 - Beaches
Day 16 - To Alps
Day 17 - Alps admiration
Day 18 - Chamonix to
Chardonnay
Day 19 - A taste of Burgundy
Day 20 - To Alsace—Beaune
to Colmar via Dijon
Day 21 - The Route du Vin
Day 22 - Verdun, Reims, back
to Paris

For all the specifics, see *Rick
Steves' France, Belgium & the
Netherlands 1999.*

THE BEST OF SCANDINAVIA
in 22 days

Day 1 - Arrive in
Copenhagen
Day 2 - Copenhagen
Day 3 - Sightsee in
Copenhagen
Day 4 - Frederiksborg
Castle,
N. Zealand
Day 5 - Växjö, Kalmar,
glass country
Day 6 - To Stockholm
Day 7 - Stockholm
Day 8 - Stockholm,
evening cruise
Day 9 - Helsinki,
Finland

Day 10 - Stockholm, Uppsala, to Oslo
Day 11 - Oslo
Day 12 - Oslo
Day 13 - Peer Gynt country
Day 14 - Glacier hike, Sognefjord
Day 15 - Fjord cruise— "Norway in a Nutshell"
Day 16 - Bergen
Day 17 - To Setesdal Valley

Day 18 - Evening sail to Denmark
Day 19 - Jutland, Århus
Day 20 - Ærø Island
Day 21 - Ærø, Odense, Roskilde, Copenhagen
Day 22 - Fly home from Copenhagen

For all the specifics, see *Rick Steves' Scandinavia*.

and boat: $50 one-way, $75 round-trip, 10 hours, day or overnight, on Eurolines (tel. 0171/730–8235) or CitySprint (tel. 01304/240241). A seven-hour boat/train combination costs $60 one-way overnight or $90 if you travel during the day. To fly between London and Paris costs $140 regular, $70 student stand-by. Call in London for the latest on ticket availability.

THE BEST OF SPAIN & PORTUGAL
in 22 days

Day 1 - Arrive in
           Madrid
           and set up
Day 2 - Madrid
Day 3 - Madrid
Day 4 - Segovia
Day 5 - Salamanca
           to Coimbra,
           Portugal
Day 6 - Nazaré
Day 7 - Nazaré
Day 8 - Óbidos,
           Lisbon
Day 9 - Lisbon
Day 10 - Lisbon and
           nearby beach
           towns
Day 11 - Salema
Day 12 - Salema and beaches
Day 13 - Sevilla
Day 14 - Sevilla
Day 15 - Arcos, Tarifa
Day 16 - Tarifa
Day 17 - Morocco

Day 18 - Gibraltar
Day 19 - Costa del Sol
Day 20 - Granada and Moorish
           Alhambra
Day 21 - Toledo
Day 22 - Madrid

For all the specifics, see *Rick
Steves' Spain & Portugal 1999.*

Belgium

Anyone taking the six-hour train ride from Paris to Amsterdam will stop
in Brussels, but few even consider getting out. Each train stops in
Brussels, and there's always another train coming in an hour or so.
Leave an hour early, arrive an hour late, and give yourself two hours
in one of Europe's underrated cities. Luckily for the rushed tourist,
Brussels Central Station has easy money-changing and baggage storage
facilities and puts you two blocks (just walk downhill) from the local and
helpful tourist office, a colorful pedestrian-only city core, Europe's greatest city square (Grand Place), and its most overrated and tacky sight, the

THE BEST OF GERMANY, AUSTRIA & SWITZERLAND
in 22 days

Day 1 - Arrive Frankfurt, to Rothenburg

Day 2 - Rothenburg

Day 3 - Romantic Road to Tirol

Day 4 - Castle day

Day 5 - To Munich

Day 6 - Munich

Day 7 - To Salzburg

Day 8 - Hallstatt, Lakes District

Day 9 - To Vienna

Day 10 - Vienna

Day 11 - To Hall in Tirol

Day 12 - Into Switzerland

Day 13 - Interlaken and up into the Alps

Day 14 - Alps hiking day, Gimmelwald

Day 15 - French Switzerland

Day 16 - Chocolate and Mürten

Day 17 - Bern

Day 18 - Black Forest

Day 19 - Baden-Baden to the Rhineland

Day 20 - Rhine and castles

Day 21 - Mosel Valley, Köln

Day 22 - Berlin

For all the specifics, see *Rick Steves' Germany, Austria & Switzerland 1999.*

Mannekin Pis (a much-photographed statue of a little boy who thinks he's a fountain). Brussels has three stations: Nord, Midi, and Central. Ask if your train stops at Central (middle) Station. If you have to get off at Nord or Midi, there are local subway-like connecting trains every few minutes. You'll have no trouble finding English-speaking help.

The Best of Germany
The most interesting sightseeing route through Germany follows the most prosperous trade route of medieval Germany: down the Rhine, along the "Romantic Road" from Frankfurt to Munich, and through Bavaria near the Austrian border. Allow a week.

While many travelers spend too much time cruising the Rhine and not enough time in castles, I'd cruise just the best hour (St. Goar to Bacharach) and get some hands-on castle experience crawling through what was once the Rhine's mightiest fortress, Rheinfels (see Chapter 59).

From the end of this most impressive section of the Rhine, it's a short train ride to Frankfurt, the launching pad for a train or bus ride along the Romantic Road (Chapter 40) through Germany's medieval heartland. From there, the old trading route crossed the Alps (today's

THE BEST OF ITALY
in 22 days

Day 1 - Arrive in Milan
Day 2 - Sightsee in Milan
Day 3 - Train to Riviera
Day 4 - Cinque Terre
Day 5 - Pisa, Florence
Day 6 - Florence
Day 7 - Florence, Siena
Day 8 - Siena
Day 9 - Orvieto, Civita
Day 10 - To Rome
Day 11 - Rome
Day 12 - Rome
Day 13 - Rome
Day 14 - Naples, Sorrento
Day 15 - Amalfi, Paestum,
            night train
Day 16 - Venice
Day 17 - Venice, side trips
Day 18 - Dolomites
Day 19 - Dolomites
Day 20 - Dolomites to the lakes

Day 21 - Lake Como, Varenna
Day 22 - Return to Milan

For all the specifics, see
Rick Steves' Italy 1999.

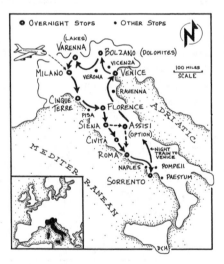

Brenner Pass) and headed into Italy, which makes sense for today's travelers as well.

How Much Italy?

Italy is Europe's richest cultural brew. Get out of the Venice-Florence-Rome crush and enjoy its hill towns and Riviera ports. Italy intensifies as you go south. If you like Italy as far south as Rome, go farther. It gets better. If Italy is getting on your nerves by the time you get to Rome, don't go farther south. It gets worse. For most first-timers, after a week in Italy, Switzerland starts looking really good. The travelers I respect most count Italy as one of their favorite countries.

By train, you might consider seeing everything except Venice on your way south. Enjoy a last romantic late evening in Rome before catching the midnight train north, arriving in Venice at 8:00 a.m., when it's easy to find a room.

Sailing from Italy to Greece

ITALY TO GREECE

Brindisi, the spur on the Italian boot, is at the end of a funnel where thousands of Eurailers, backpackers, and various other travelers fall out to catch the boat to Patras, Greece. Boats sail throughout the year. Two boats make the 18-hour crossing each day in the summer and on alternate days in the off-season. Boats depart in the evening; morning departures are also available in summer. Getting on the boat is no problem without reservations except at peak season (Italy to Greece from late July to mid-August; Greece to Italy from about August 11 to September 3), when it's a mob scene.

Making reservations at a travel agency in Italy or Greece: Prices for the Italy–Greece connection vary between the competing lines. The Eurailpass covers the trip on the Hellenic Mediterranean and Adriatica lines.

If you don't have a Eurailpass, compare prices before you sail; you may find it cheaper and easier to depart from Bari (90 minutes north of Brindisi by train). Brindisi–Patras tickets cost about $40 (low season) to $65 (high season) for basic deck class. On some ships "deck" is taken literally, and it's chilly at night, even in summer; vagabonds can spend the night in the bar, or in the restaurant after hours. On most boats you'll have access to a free

THE BEST OF EUROPE
in 22 days

Day 1 - Depart U.S. for Amsterdam
Day 2 - Arrive in Amsterdam
Day 3 - Amsterdam
Day 4 - To the Rhine
Day 5 - To Rothenburg
Day 6 - Rothenburg
Day 7 - Romantic Road, Dachau, Tirol
Day 8 - Bavaria and Castle Day
Day 9 - Over Alps to Venice
Day 10 - Venice
Day 11 - Florence
Day 12 - Rome
Day 13 - Rome
Day 14 - Italian hill towns
Day 15 - Italian Riviera
Day 16 - Cinque Terre beach
Day 17 - Drive to the Alps

Day 18 - Alps hike day, Gimmelwald
Day 19 - Alps to France
Day 20 - Colmar, Wine Road
Day 21 - Reims to Paris
Day 22 - Paris

For all the specifics, see *Rick Steves' Best of Europe 1999.*

airplane-type seat indoors. For more comfort, pay $40 for a bed in a four-person stateroom. During the mid-June to mid-September rush, crossing prices are $20 higher. Students under 30 and anyone under 26 save about $10. Cars cost $50 and bikes go for free.

A Eurailpass (or Europass) gives you free deck-class passage, but you'll have to pay a reservation fee, a $7 port tax, and, if traveling in the summer, a $15 peak-season supplement. You can get a stopover halfway on the lush and popular island of Corfu for the mere cost of two sets of port taxes ($14). Just get "S.O. Corfu" marked on your ticket when you buy it (particularly if you sail Adriatica).

For a summer crossing (particularly in August), make a reservation at least three days in advance from an Italian or Greek travel agency (easy but with varying service charges) or, ideally, go direct to an Adriatica or Hellenic office.

On arrival in Brindisi, follow the mob on the half-mile stampede from the train station down the city's main drag to the dock. You can walk, taxi, take a city bus, or see if you can hop a shuttle bus offered by the boat lines for ticket holders.

You'll see several agencies along the way that sell tickets and handle boat-related business such as reserving staterooms, collecting port taxes and Eurail supplements, and distributing boarding passes. Be wary of thieves. Expect con artists to tell you your Eurailpass doesn't work on today's boat or some similar nonsense. At the port, check in at the boat office two hours before departure or face the (slight) risk of being turned away. Then board your boat. The crossing from Patras to Brindisi features similar touts and headaches. Off-season, I'd go to the port and bargain. Student discounts are often given to anyone who asks for them.

The Patras-to-Athens connection is a five-hour train ride or a frightening three-hour bus ride. (The fear welds some special friendships on the bus.) Even with a railpass, I'd buy the $15 bus ticket with the boat ticket. Buses meet the boat—don't dally. Upon arrival in Athens, expect a welcoming committee of hotel runners and locals with rooms to rent. Consider putting off Athens and hooking south through the fascinating Peloponnesian Peninsula. Start with the hour-long bus ride (leaving Patras every two hours) to Olympia.

Brindisi is well connected by night trains from Rome, Milan, Florence (via Bologna), and Venice. Overnight trains arrive in Brindisi in the morning and the boats to Greece leave in the evening, so you'll likely have time to kill in Brindisi. Consider spending it in Lecce, a hot, noble, but sleepy city of lovely Baroque facades and Roman ruins; pick up a map of this confusing town at the three-star hotel in front of the Lecce train station. For one last Italian beach, try Apani (just 30 minutes north of town on the Adriatic coast). The beach is fair and the water is clean.

To Greece or Not to Greece?

Many itineraries are really stressed by people who underestimate the travel time involved and wrongly plug in Greece. By car or train, it takes two days of solid travel—if all goes well—to get from Rome to Athens, and two days to get back. If all you've got is a week for Greece, I question the sanity of traveling four days for a couple of days in huge, overrated, and polluted Athens and a quick trip to an island, especially when you consider that

ITINERARY PRIORITIES, COUNTRY BY COUNTRY

Use this chart to get ideas on how speedy travelers can prioritize limited sightseeing time in various countries. Add places from left to right as you build plans for the best of that country in three, five, seven, ten, or fourteen days. In some cases the plan assumes you'll take a night train. So, according to this chart, the best week in Britain would be spread between London, Bath, the Cotswolds, and York.

Country	3 days	5 days	7 days	10 days	14 days
Europe	Forget it	London, Paris	Amsterdam	Rhineland, Swiss Alps	Munich Venice
Austria	Salzburg Vienna	Hallstatt	Danube Valley	Prague	—
Britain	London Bath	Cotswolds	York	Edinburgh, Cambridge	N. Wales
France	Paris, Versailles	Loire, Chartres	Normandy	Provence, Nice, Riviera	Chamonix, Burgundy
Germany	Rhine Munich	Romantic Road, Rothenburg	Bavarian sights	Berlin	Black Forest, Mosel, Köln
Italy	Rome	Florence, Venice	Italian Riviera	Hill towns	Milan and Lake Como
Scandinavia	Copenhagen, Oslo, Stockholm	Bergen, "Norway in a Nutshell"	More time in capitals	Helsinki, Tallinn	Ærø, more fjords
Spain/ Portugal	Madrid, Toledo	Lisbon	Barcelona	Andalusia, Sevilla	Algarve
Switzerland	Bern and Berner Oberland	French Switzerland, Murten	Appenzell, Luzern	Zermatt	—
Turkey	Istanbul, Bosphorus	Ephesus, West Coast	Konya, Pamukkale	Cappadocia	Ankara, more Istanbul

500 years before Christ, southern Italy was called Magna Graecia (Greater Greece). You can find excellent Greek ruins at Paestum, just south of Naples. Greece is great, but it needs more time or an open-jaws plan that lets you fly out of Athens.

In the summer, Greece is the most touristed, least explored country in Europe. It seems that nearly all of its tourists are in a few places, while the rest of the country casually goes about its traditional business.

The Britain/Europe/Greece Plan
Here's an efficient overall plan for a six-week introduction to Europe: Fly into London and spend four days. Rent a car for a week in England (Bath, Cotswolds, Blenheim, Warwick, Ironbridge Gorge, North Wales). Drop it in North Wales. Boat to Dublin and take a look at West Ireland. Begin your 21-day Eurailpass to catch the discounted 20-hour boat ride from southeast Ireland to France. Spend three weeks touring central Europe (Paris, BeNeLux, Rhine, Romantic Road, Bavaria, Swiss Alps, Italy, boat to Athens, where train pass expires). Relax in the Greek Isles before flying home from Athens.

8. The Whirlwind Tour: Europe's Best Two-Month Trip

Let's assume you have two months, plenty of energy, and a desire to see as much of Europe as is reasonable. Fly into London and travel around Europe with a two-month Eurailpass. You'll spend two months on the Continent and use any remaining time in Great Britain, before or after you start your train pass (because Eurailpasses don't cover Great Britain). Budgeting for a $900 round-trip ticket to London, around $1,250 for a two-month first-class Eurailpass, and $70 a day for room, board, and sightseeing, the entire trip will cost about $6,500. It can be done. Rookies on a budget do it all the time—often for less.

If I were planning my first European trip and wanted to see as much as I comfortably could in two months (and I had the experience I now have to help me plan), this is the trip I'd take. I'll have to admit, I itch just thinking about this itinerary.

London and Side Trips—5 days
London is Europe's great entertainer; it's wonderfully historic. Mild compared to anything but the United States, it's the best starting point for a European adventure. The English speak English, but their accents will give you the sensation of understanding a foreign language.

Europe's Best Two-Month Trip

From London's airports, you'll find easy train or subway access to the hotels. Stay at the Aster House Hotel (hotelesque, tel. 0171/581-5888, e-mail: asterhouse@btinternet.com), Hotel Ravna Gora (funky, tel. 0171/727-7725), or the Vicarage House Bed and Breakfast (charming, tel. 0171/229-4030, Web site: www.londonvicaragehotel.com). To get your bearings, catch a "Round London" orientation bus tour (departs every 20 minutes) from the park in front of Victoria Station. Every day in London will be busy, and each night filled with a play and a pub.

Spend your remaining time in the English countryside: Bath (see Back Doors, Chapter 46), the Cotswolds (see Back Doors, Chapter 49), and the university city of Cambridge. But the Continent beckons. Paris is only three hours away by Eurostar train (9 trains/day). Cheaper seats can sell fast. To save money, order your tickets from home (tel. 800/EUROSTAR). If you'll be ending your trip in London, plan for your return: Reserve a good B&B and get tickets to a hot play.

Paris—3 days

Ascend the Eiffel Tower to survey a Paris studded with architectural gems and historical one-of-a-kinds. You'll recognize the Louvre, Notre-Dame, Arc de Triomphe, Sacré-Coeur, and much more.

Take a walk covering Paris' biggies. From the Latin Quarter, head to Notre-Dame, the Deportation Monument to Nazi victims, and St. Chapelle. Take the Pont-Neuf bridge over to the Samaritaine department store for a self-serve lunch. Walk by the Louvre, through the Tuileries Gardens, and up the Champs-Elysées to the Arc de Triomphe.

Be sure to visit Napoleon's Tomb, Les Invalides (Europe's best military museum), the Rodin Museum (*The Thinker* and *The Kiss*), the great Orsay Museum (Impressionism), a jazz club, and Latin Quarter nightlife. Spend an evening on Montmartre soaking in the spiritual waters of the Sacré-Coeur and browsing among the tacky shops and artists of the Place du Tertre. Pick up the *Pariscope* entertainment guide. Most museums are closed on Tuesday.

Learn the Paris subway—it's fast, easy, and cheap. Stay near the Eiffel Tower at Hotel Leveque (tel. 01-47-05-49-15) or in the Marais neighborhood at Hotel Jeanne-d'Arc (elegant, tel. 01-48-87-62-11) or Hotel Castex (cheap, friendly, tel. 01-42-72-31-52). Ask your hotelier to recommend a small family-owned restaurant for dinner.

Side-trip to Europe's greatest palace, Louis XIV's Versailles. Take the RER-C train to the end of the line, Versailles R.G. Another great side trip is the city of Chartres, with its great Gothic cathedral (lectures by Malcom Miller at noon and 2:45 p.m.).

Start your Eurailpass when you leave Paris. Take the overnight train to Madrid (6:00 p.m.–10:00 a.m.), or take a detour. . . .

Loire Valley—2 days

On the way to Spain, explore the dreamy châteaus of the Loire Valley. Make Amboise or Tours your headquarters. Consider an all-day bus tour of the châteaus. If you're not into châteaus, skip the Loire (and instead, try a 30-minute sidetrip from Paris to the epitome of a French château, Chantilly).

Madrid—2 days

On arrival, reserve your train out. Reservations on long trains are required in Spain (and Norway), even with Eurail.

Take a taxi or the subway to Puerto del Sol to find a central budget room. Try the Hotel Europa (most comfortable, just off Puerta del Sol, tel. 9152-12900), Hostel la Rosa (funky, 15 Plaza Santa Anna, tel.

9153-25805), Hostel Miami (cheap, at Gran Via 44, tel. 9152-11464), or Residencia Valencia (hotelesque, Gran Via 44, tel. 9152-21115).

Bullfights, shopping, and museums will fill your sunny days. Madrid's three essential sights are the Prado Museum (Goya, El Greco, Velázquez, Bosch), Reina Sofia (*Guernica*), and the Royal Palace (Europe's most lavish interior). Bullfights are on Sundays through the summer (check at hotel, buy tickets at arena). Tourists and thieves alike enjoy the sprawling El Rastro flea market every Sunday.

From Madrid, side-trip to Toledo (75-minute train ride).

Toledo—1 day
Save a day for this perfectly preserved historic capital, home of El Greco and his masterpieces. Back in Madrid, take the night train to Lisbon (11:30 p.m.–8:30 a.m.). Night travel is best in Iberia—long distances are boring and hot on crowded, slow day trains.

Lisbon—2 days
Lisbon, Portugal's friendly capital, can keep a visitor busy for days. Its highlight is the Alfama. This salty old sailors' quarter is a photographer's delight. You'll feel rich here in Europe's bargain basement, where a taxi ride is cheaper than a London bus ticket. (See Back Doors, Chapter 35: Lisbon.)

Take side trips to Sintra (ruined Moorish castle) and Estoril (casino nightlife). Circle south for a stop on Portugal's south coast, the Algarve (possible night train to Lagos, 11:00 p.m.–6:45 a.m.).

Algarve—2 days
Settle down in Salema, the best little beach village on the south coast of Portugal (see Back Doors, Chapter 36). Cross into Andalusia for flamenco, hill towns, and Sevilla.

Sevilla and Andalusia—3 days
After strolling the paseo of Sevilla, the city of flamenco, head for the hills and explore Andalusia's Route of the Whitewashed Hill Towns. Arcos de la Frontera is a good home base. Ride the speedy AVE train back to Madrid to catch the night train to Barcelona.

Barcelona—2 days
Tour the Picasso Museum, relax, shop, and explore the Gothic Quarter. Stay in Hotel Toledano (simple, top of Ramblas #138, tel. 9330-10872) or Catalunya Plaza (classy, Plaza Catalunya, tel. 9331-77171). Catch a night train to Arles, France (7:30 p.m.–7:00 a.m.).

Provence or French Riviera—2 days
Your best home base for Provence is Arles (Hotel Regence, tel. 04-90-96-39-85). Tour the Papal Palace in Avignon and ramble among Roman ruins in Nîmes and Arles.

Most of the Riviera is crowded, expensive, and stressful, but if you're set on a Riviera beach, Nice is where the jet set lies on rocks. Tour Nice's great Chagall Museum and stay at the Hotel Star (tel. 04-93-85-19-03). Then dive into intense Italy.

Cinque Terre—2 days
The Cinque Terre is the best of Italy's Riviera. You'll find pure Italy in these five sleepy, traffic-free villages between Genoa and Pisa. Unknown to most tourists, it's the ultimate Italian coastal paradise. (See Back Doors, Chapter 30.)

Florence—1 day
Florence is steeped in history and art. Europe's Renaissance art capital is packed in the summer but worth the headaches. Stay at Hotel La Scaletta (warm, friendly, tel. 055/283028) or Casa Rabatti (cheap, homey, near station, tel. 055/212393).

Hill Towns of Tuscany and Umbria—2 days
This is the most neglected and underrated side of Italy. Visit Siena and Civita di Bagnoregio. (See Back Doors, Chapters 31 and 32.)

Rome—3 days
Devote your first day to Classical Rome: Tour the Colosseum, Forum, Capitoline Hill (and its two museums), and Pantheon. Linger away the evening at Piazza Navona. *Tartufo* ice cream is mandatory.

For your second day, visit the Vatican and St. Peter's (climb the dome), and tour the Vatican Museum and Sistine Chapel (see *Rick Steves' Mona Winks* or rent a headphone guide). Take advantage of the Vatican's post office, much better than Italy's. Picnickers will find a great open-air produce market three blocks in front of the Vatican Museum entry.

Spend your third morning at Ostia Antica, Ancient Rome's seaport in the afternoon (like Pompeii, but just a subway ride away from Rome). In downtown Rome, visit Piazza Barberini for its Bernini fountain and Cappucin crypt (thousands of bones in the first church on Via Veneto). In the early evening, do the Dolce Vita stroll from Piazza del Popolo to Spanish Steps. Have dinner on Campo dei Fiori. Explore Trastevere, where old Rome is alive today.

Stay near the Vatican Museum at Pension Alimandi (Via Tunisi 8, 00192 Roma, tel. 06-39726300), near the train station at Hotel Nardizzi (Via Firenze 38, 00184 Roma, tel. 06-4880368), or even cheaper at Hotel Magic (Via Milazzo 20, 3rd floor, 00185 Roma, tel. & fax 06-4959880). Take a night train to Venice (11:30 p.m.–6:30 a.m.).

Venice—2 days
Cruise the colorful canals of Venice. Grab a front seat on boat #82 for an introductory tour down the Canale Grande. Stay at Albergo Guerrato (near Rialto Market at Calle drio la Scimia 240a, tel. 041-522-7131) or near the train station at Hotel Marin (San Croce 670b, tel. & fax 041-718022). The Accademia Gallery showcases the best Venetian art. Tour the Doges Palace, St. Mark's, and catch the view from the Campanile bell tower. Then wander, leave the tourists, and get as lost as possible. Don't worry, you're on an island and you can't get off. Catch the night train to Vienna (10:30 p.m.–6:30 a.m.).

Vienna—2 days
Savor the Old World elegance of Habsburg Vienna, Paris' eastern rival. This grand capital of the mighty Habsburg Empire is rich in art history, Old World charm, and elegance. You'll find a great tourist information office behind the impressive Opera (fine tours). Stay in the cheery home of friendly Budai Ildiko (7, Lindegasse 39/5, tel. & fax 01/526-2595) or the classier Pension Suzanne (near Opera, tel. 01/513-2507). Side-trip east for a look at Prague.

Prague—2 days
Prague, a magnificently preserved Baroque city, is a happening place. Visas are no longer required, and Prague is five hours from Vienna by train.

Salzburg—1 day
Mozart's gone but you'll find his chocolate balls everywhere. Baroque Salzburg, with its music festival and *Sound of Music* delights, is touristy in a way most love. Sleep cheap at Institute San Sebastian (Linzergasse 41, tel. 0662/871-386) or refined at Gasthaus Goldenen Ente (Goldgasse 10, tel. 0662/845-622).

Tirol and Bavaria—2 days
Tour "Mad" King Ludwig's fairy-tale castle at Neuschwanstein, and Bavaria's heavenly Wies Church. Visit the Tirolean town of Reutte and its forgotten—yet unforgettable—hill-crowning, ruined castle. Running

along the overgrown ramparts of the Ehrenberg ruins, your imagination works itself loose, and suddenly you're notching up your crossbow and ducking flaming arrows. (See Back Doors, Chapter 59.)

Switzerland—3 days

Pray for sun. For the best of the Swiss Alps, establish a home base in the rugged Berner Oberland, south of Interlaken. The traffic-free village of Gimmelwald in Lauterbrunnen Valley is everything an Alp-lover could possibly want. (See Back Doors, Chapter 43: Berner Oberland.)

Switzerland's best big city is Bern and best small town is Murten. Europe's most scenic train ride is across southern Switzerland from Chur to Martigny. Be careful: Mixing sunshine and a full dose of Alpine beauty can be intoxicating.

Munich—2 days

Munich, the capital of Bavaria, has a great palace, museums, and the world's best street singers. But they probably won't be good enough to keep you out of the beer halls. You'll find huge mugs of beer, bigger pretzels, and even bigger beermaids! The Hofbräuhaus is the most famous (near Marienplatz in the old town center). Hotel Utzelmann (elegant, near station, tel. 089/594889) and Hotel Münchner Kindl (simple, in old center, tel. 089/264-349) are good places to stay. The Romantic Road bus tour ($23 with a Eurailpass) is a handy day-long way to get from Munich to Frankfurt.

Romantic Road—1 day

The Romantic Road bus rolls through the heart of medieval Germany, stopping for visits at Dinkelsbühl and the always-popular queen of quaint German towns, Rothenburg (see Chapter 40). Consider an overnight stop in Rothenburg at the Hotel Goldener Rose (Spitalgasse 28, 91541 Rothenburg, tel. 09861/4638). Or head straight to the Rhine.

Rhine/Mosel River Valleys and Köln—2 days

Take a Rhine cruise (free with Eurail) from Bingen to Koblenz to enjoy a parade of old castles. The best hour of the cruise is from Bacharach to St. Goar. In St. Goar hike up to the Rheinfels castle. (See Chapter 59: Medieval Castle Experiences.) Stay in Bacharach at the Hotel Kranenturm (Langstrasse 30, 55422 Bacharach, tel. 06743/1308) or up at the Castle Youth Hostel (*Jugendherberge Stahleck*, tel. 06743/1266, $10 beds) with panoramic Rhine views.

Cruise along the sleepy Mosel Valley and tour Cochem's castle, Trier's Roman ruins, and the impressive medieval castle, Burg Eltz. From Köln, catch the night train (10:45 p.m.–7:00 a.m.) to Germany's capital, ever-vibrant Berlin.

Berlin—2 days
Berlin, capital of a united Germany, with its great art and Cold War remnants, is worth two busy days. Catch the night train from Berlin to Copenhagen (11:45 p.m.–8:30 a.m.). Stay at the classy Alpenland Hotel (Carmerstrasse 8, 10623 Berlin, tel. 030/312-3970) or at the homier Pension Peters (Kantstrasse 146, 10623 Berlin, tel. 030/3150-3944).

Copenhagen—1 day
Finish your Continental experience with a blitz tour of the capitals of Scandinavia: Copenhagen, Stockholm, and Oslo. To save money and time, sleep on trains. Scandinavia's capitals are a convenient 10 hours apart, the train rides are boring and sleepable, and hotels are expensive.

Leave your bags at the Copenhagen train station. Tour the city during the day and spend the evening at Tivoli, just across the street from the train station. Catch the night train to Stockholm (11:15 p.m.–7:30 a.m.). If you'd like to stay overnight in Copenhagen, try a comfortable B&B (Annette and Rudy Hollender's home, Wildersgade 19, 1408 Copenhagen, tel. 32-95-96-22).

Stockholm—2 days
With its ruddy mix of islands, canals, and wooded parks studded with fine sights such as the 350-year-old *Vasa* warship, Europe's best open-air folk museum at Skansen, and gas-lamped old town, Stockholm is a charmer. (See Chapter 54.) Catch an afternoon train to Oslo.

Oslo—1 day
After a busy day wandering through Viking ships, the *Kon-Tiki*, the Nazi Resistance Museum, and climbing the ski jump for a commanding view of the city and its fjord, you'll be famished. It's Rudolf with lingonberries for dinner! Sleep cozy near the palace at Ellingsen's Pensjonat (Holtegata 25, tel. 22 60 03 59), right downtown at the Rainbow Hotel Astoria (Dronningens gate 21, tel. 22 42 00 10), or cheap in the suburbs with the Casperi family's B&B (Heggelbakken 1, tel. 22 14 57 70).

Scenic Train, Fjord Country, and Bergen—2 days
For the best look at the mountainous fjord country of west Norway, do "Norway in a Nutshell," a combination of spectacular train, boat, and bus rides. Catch the morning train from Oslo over the spine of Norway to

Bergen. Stay overnight on the fjord near Flam in Aurland at the funky Aabelheim Pension or the basic Vangen Motel (same tel.: 57 63 35 80). Enjoy a day in salty Bergen. Stay downtown at the Heskja home (good budget beds, 17 Skivebakken, tel. 55 31 30 30) or catch the night train back to Oslo (11:00 p.m.–7:00 a.m.).

Oslo—1 day

Take a second day in Oslo. There's plenty to do. (See Chapter 53.) Hop a night train back to Copenhagen (10:45 p.m–8:30 a.m.).

Copenhagen—1 day

Another day in Copenhagen. Yes! Smörgåsbords, Viking *lur* horns, and healthy, smiling blondes are the memories you'll pack on the night train south to Amsterdam (10:00 p.m.–10:00 a.m.).

Amsterdam—2 days

The Dutch Golden Age sparkles in Amsterdam's museums, but the streets can be a bit seedy for many Americans' tastes. Consider day-tripping into Amsterdam from small-town Haarlem (Hotel Amadeus, Grote Markt 10, 2011 RD Haarlem, tel. 023/532 4530; or the homey bed and breakfast House de Kiefte, Coornhertstraat 3, 2013 EV Haarlem, tel. 023/532 2980, two-night minimum stay). You'll discover great side trips in all directions.

After touring crazy Amsterdam and biking through the tulips, sail for England (10:00 p.m.–9:00 a.m.). Or, to avoid a surface return to London, consider flying out of Amsterdam (arrange this open-jaws flight before you leave home).

EXCURSIONS YOU MAY WANT TO ADD

England—Oxford, Stratford, York
French Alps—Geneva, Chamonix, Aiguille du Midi, Aosta
Morocco and South Spain
South Italy or Greece
Finland or the Arctic
Eastern Europe or Russia
A day for showers and laundry
Visiting, resting, and a little necessary slack
Travel days to avoid sleeping on the train

This 61-day Whirlwind Tour is just a sampler. There's plenty more to see, but I can't imagine a better first two months in Europe. Use the train times only as a rough guide. The itinerary includes 14 nights on the train (saving about $450 in hotel costs), and 14 days for doing more interesting things than sitting on a train.

A Eurailpass is good for two calendar months (e.g., May 15 through midnight July 14). If you validate when you leave Paris and expire (the Eurailpass, not you) on arrival in Amsterdam, you'll spend 53 days, leaving eight days of railpass time to slow down or add options.

RECOMMENDED BOOKS FOR THE WHIRLWIND TOUR

My various country guides offer details on sights, hotels, and restaurants. See this book's "Part Two: Back Doors" for in-depth descriptions of some of the cities. For art history, read *Europe 101* before you go and take *Rick Steves' Mona Winks* for self-guided museum tours. My French/Italian/German and Spanish/Portuguese phrase books will help you leap over the language barrier. (All of my books are published by John Muir Publications.)

TRANSPORTATION

9. Travel Agents and Flights

The travel industry is considered the second biggest industry and employer on the planet (after armaments and the military). To travel, you need to deal with it, so it's good to know how, when, and where. Here are some ideas to help you consume with a little savvy.

OUR TRAVEL INDUSTRY

Travel is a huge business. Most of what the industry promotes is decadence: lie on the beach and be catered to; hedonize those precious two weeks to make up for the other 50; see if you can eat five meals a day and still snorkel when you get into port. That's where the money is, and that's where most of the interest is. The name of the game is to get people's money here for travel thrills over there. Independent travelers are a fringe that fits the industry like a snowshoe in Mazatlán.

Understand what shapes the information that shapes your travel dreams. As a newspaper travel columnist, I've learned that it takes a bold travel editor to run articles that may upset advertisers. Travel newspaper sections are possible only with the support of travel advertisers. And advertisers are more interested in filling cruise ships or tour buses than in turning people free to travel independently. In fact, when I first started running my weekly travel column, it was called "The Budget Traveler." Within a month of its appearance, that travel section's major advertisers met with the editor and explained they would no longer buy ads if he continued running a column with that name. Hastily, the editor and I found a new name. To save the column we called it "The Practical Traveler"—same subversive information but with a more palatable title.

Many travel agents don't understand travel "through the Back Door." The typical attitude I get when I hobnob with bigwigs from the industry in Hilton Hotel ballrooms is: "If you can't afford to go first-class, save up and go next year." I'll never forget the bewilderment I caused when I turned down a free room in Bangkok's most elegant Western-style hotel in favor of a cheap room in a simple Thai-style hotel.

Of course, these comments are generalizations. There are many great travelers in the travel industry. They understand my frustration because they've also dealt with it.

Travel can mean rich people flaunting their affluence, taking snapshots of black kids jumping off white ships for small change. Or it can promote understanding, bending out our hometown blinders and making our world more comfortable in its smallness. What the industry promotes is up to all of us—writers, editors, agents, and travelers.

YOU NEED A TRAVEL AGENT

I'm not "anti–travel agent." I *am* "anti–*bad* travel agent." My travel agent is my vital ally. I've never gone to Europe without her help. You don't need *my* agent, but you do need a good agent. Unfortunately, there are a lot of flat-out bad travel agents. As a tour organizer, it's frustrating when someone who wants to join one of my ETBD tours can't find an affordable airplane ticket. Many times, with customers from every part of the United States, I've said, "Don't give up. Let me see if I can find you something." And my Seattle travel agent beats their hometown agent's price by several hundred dollars (as could any good agent in their town).

Travel agency recommendations from other travelers provide excellent leads, but the right agency doesn't guarantee the right agent. You need a particular person—someone whose definition of "good travel" matches yours. Once you find the right agent, nurture your alliance. Be loyal. Travel with this expert on your side. Send her a postcard.

Travel agents save you money. These days it takes a full-time and aggressive travel professional to keep up with the constantly changing airline industry. I don't have time to sort through all the frustrating, generally too-good-to-be-true ads that fill the Sunday travel sections. I rely on the experience of an agent who specializes in budget European travel. And most agents charge you nothing. They make their money from commissions paid by the airlines, not by marking up your tickets. Take advantage of their expertise.

You can't save money by buying directly from the airlines. Most airline representatives barely know what they're charging, much less their competitors' rates and schedules. Only your agent would remind you that leaving two days earlier would get you in on the end of shoulder season—and save you $100.

A good agent can get you almost any ticket. Dumping your agent for a $30 savings from a discount agent down the street is a bad move. These days, many people milk good agents for all they're worth and then buy tickets from their sister's friend's agency around the corner. Because of this, it's tough to get good advice over the phone, and "browsers" usually get no respect. I enjoy the luxury of sitting down with my agent, explaining travel plans, getting a briefing on my options, and choosing the best flight.

Use your agent only for arranging transportation. Although many agents can give you tips on Irish B&Bs and sporadic advice on the best biking in Holland, assume you'll do better if you use your travel agent only to get you to your destination. After that, rely on a good guidebook. Travel agents handle their clients with kid gloves. Don't let their caution clamp a ball and chain onto your travel dreams. I use an agent for my plane ticket, train pass, or car rental, and nothing else.

Car rentals are cheaper when arranged before departure through your agent. Eurailpasses, and most country railpasses, must or should be purchased before you leave home. To get good service on small, tedious items like these, do all your trip business through the agent who made a healthy commission on your air ticket.

Students: check student travel agencies. Any city with a university probably has a student travel agency. Council Travel, with 60 offices in the United States, offers budget fares even to nonstudents (tel. 800/ 2-COUNCIL, www.counciltravel.com). Most big campuses also have a more independent agency that is a member of the University Student Travel Network (USTN). These agencies sell Council tickets as well as their own discounted tickets. If you're flexible enough to fly stand-by, consider Air-Tech, which offers unsold seats at bargain prices (tel. 800/575-TECH, Web site: www.airtech.com).

FLYING TO EUROPE

Flying to Europe is a great travel bargain—for the well-informed. The rules and regulations are confusing and always changing, but when you make the right choice, you get the right price.

Dollars saved = discomfort + restrictions + inflexibility. There is no great secret to getting to Europe for next to nothing. Assuming you know your options, you get what you pay for. There's no such thing as a free lunch in the airline industry. Regular fare is very expensive. You get the ultimate in flexibility, but I've never met anyone spending his or her own money who flew that way.

Rather than grab the cheapest ticket to Europe, go with your agent's recommendation for the best combination of reliability, economy, and flexibility for your travel needs. Buy your ticket when you're ready to firmly commit to flight dates and ports. As you delay, dates sell out.

Consider open-jaws. It's been 10 years since I flew into and out of the same European city. I fly "open-jaws": into one city and out of another. The fare is figured simply by taking half of the round-trip fare for each of those ports. I used to fly into Amsterdam, travel to Istanbul, and (having rejected the open-jaws plan because flying home from Istanbul costs $200 more than returning from Amsterdam) pay $200 to

ride the train for two days back to Amsterdam to catch my "cheap" return flight. Now I see the real economy in spending more for open-jaws. Open-jaws is cheapest when the same airline can cover each segment of the round-trip journey.

A good agent will check both consolidator and airline fares, then offer you the best deal. Consolidator tickets are generally cheapest, but fare wars can make an airline's prices unbeatable. Consolidators (or wholesalers) negotiate with airlines to get deeply discounted fares on a huge number of tickets; they offer these tickets to your travel agent, who then sells you a cheaper flight to Europe than the airline itself can. An airline's ticket prices, however, in a drawn-out fare war, can drop to bargain basement levels. A good travel agent will compare fares.

With consolidator tickets, you usually have seven to ten days to pay after booking, and credit cards normally aren't accepted. With airline tickets, you often just have a few days to pay up, and credit cards are accepted. If, after you buy an airline ticket, the airline's price drops yet again, you can exchange your ticket and save some money—if the discount is greater than the change fee. Consolidator tickets, however, won't get any cheaper; the price, once established, stays the same. Ask about cancellation policies: What is the fee? Will you receive a refund or credit?

Consolidator tickets often waive the normal advance-purchase and minimum- and maximum-stay requirements that come with other budget tickets. But remember the "dollars saved" equation. Consolidator tickets are cheap because they come with disadvantages: They are "nonendorsable," meaning that no other airline is required to honor that ticket if your airline is unable to get you home (though in practice, this is rarely a problem). You won't always get frequent-flier miles. And, if the airline drops its prices (which often happens), you are stuck with what was, but no longer is, a cheap fare.

Know Thy Travel Agent—A Quiz

One way to be sure your travel agent is properly suited to helping you with your trip is to ask him or her a few questions. Here's a little quiz—complete with answers.

1. **What is "open-jaws"?**
   a) Yet another shark movie sequel.
   b) A tourist in awe of the *Mannekin Pis*.
   c) A special-interest tour of Romania's dental clinics.
   d) An airline ticket that allows you to fly into one city and out of another.

2. **Which international boat rides are covered by the Eurailpass?**
   a) Poland to Switzerland.
   b) All of them.
   c) Ireland to France, Sweden to Finland, Italy to Greece, Germany to Denmark, and Sweden to Denmark.

3. **What's the age limit to sleep in a Youth Hostel?**
   a) Five.
   b) As high as 30 if you like rap music.
   c) There is none, except in Bavaria, where it's 26.

4. **What is the most economical way to get from London's Heathrow Airport into London?**
   a) Walk.
   b) In a youth hostel.
   c) Don't. Spend your whole vacation at Heathrow.
   d) By subway or airbus.

5. **What is an ISIC card?**
   a) A universal way to tell foreigners you're not feeling well.
   b) It beats three-of-a-kind.
   c) The International Student Identity Card, good for many discounts at sights and museums.

6. **Is there a problem getting a bed and breakfast in England's small towns without a reservation?**
   a) Not if you live there.
   b) Yes. Carry No-Doz in England.
   c) No.

7. **How much does a Hungarian visa cost?**
   a) "How much you have, comrade?"
   b) You can just charge it on your Visa card.
   c) More than a Grecian urn.
   d) It's not required.

Answers: The last answer to each question is the correct one.

Chartered flights can save you money. A charter company offers flights on certain days in and out of the same city. In return for fitting into their limits, you can fly cheaper than on scheduled airlines.

However, charter companies can cancel flights that don't fill. Anyone selling charters promotes an air of confidence, but at the last minute any flight can be "rescheduled" if it won't pay off. Those who "saved" by booking onto that charter are left all packed with nowhere to go. Get an explicit answer to what happens if the flight is canceled. "It won't be canceled" is not good enough. Some charter companies are reliable. Ask about their track record: How many flights did they cancel last year?

Scheduled airlines are most reliable. If for some reason (such as a strike) they can't fly you home, they find you a seat on another airline. You won't be stranded in Europe—unless you have a discounted ticket marked "nonendorsable."

Courier flights get some travelers to Europe for free. But for most, this is a pipe dream. You need to be very flexible and live in the right cities (such as New York or San Francisco). *Travel Unlimited* is a monthly newsletter which keeps flying cheapskates on top of the latest in courier and discount airfares ($25/year, $5/issue, Box 1058, Allston, MA 02134). Lately, courier services have found that they can get away with charging a percentage of the ticket value, making the whole notion less exciting.

Budget flights are restrictive. Most are nonchangeable and nonrefundable, but some offer changes on the return dates for a penalty of about $100 to $200. If you need to change your return date once you're in Europe, telephone your airline's European office. If that fails, I've found airlines become more lenient if you go to their office in person with a good reason for your need to change the return date. If you're dying to get home early, go to the airport. If you're standing at the airport and need to go home two days before your ticket says you can, they may have seats open on a flight. Regardless of the rules, they may figure that if they just let you fly, they can win a happy customer and gain two more days to try to sell an empty seat. Besides, at that point, it's the easiest way to get rid of you.

FLIGHTS WITHIN EUROPE

Europe is a small continent notorious for its big plane fares. But with recent deregulation, there are more budget airfares than ever before. These days, before buying any long train ticket, drop by a travel agency (either at home or in Europe) to check out budget airfares. A plane ticket can even be cheaper than the train. While your hometown travel agent may be able to get you a decent fare, the super-cheap fares for inter-

European flights can be purchased only in Europe. Some round-trip fares are cheaper than one way, but you won't be told unless you ask.

Extending your flight from the United States deeper into the Continent (without stopovers) can be very cheap. Explore your open-jaws possibilities before purchasing your ticket. Ask your agent if your airline offers "European passes" that allow you to travel inexpensively through Europe. Passes sell for about $300 to $400 and include three coupons good for that airline's routing through Europe (e.g., on a flight from Frankfurt to Istanbul, you might have to transfer in Copenhagen, taking extra time and two coupons). Your flights will likely take longer, but you'll save money. British Midland offers reasonable fares bookable in the United States for flights from Britain to the rest of Europe (about $120 per sector, tel. 800/788-0555 in the United States).

London, Amsterdam, Paris, and Athens have many "bucket shops." These agencies clear out plane tickets at super-discounted prices. If your travel plans fit the tickets available and you're flexible enough to absorb delays, these can be a great deal. Any cheap flight from London must be purchased from an agency in London. (This can be done by telephone and credit card from the U.S.) *Let's Go: Europe* lists a few of the bigger bucket shops. Your local library should have a London newspaper; look in the classifieds under "Travel" to see what's available. Tickets from London to the Mediterranean can be incredibly—and reliably—cheap. There are normally special deals on flights from London to Dublin, Paris, or Frankfurt that are as inexpensive as surface travel. Athens also has some great buys on tickets to London, Western Europe, and the Middle East. Aeroflot and other Eastern European airlines offer cheap flights, often on a roundabout route. On Aeroflot you may get a forced stopover in Moscow with a free hotel.

THE FEAR OF FLYING

Like many people, I'm afraid to fly. I always think of the little rubber wheels splashing down on a rain-soaked runway and then hydroplaning out of control. Or the spindly landing gear crumbling. Or if not that, then the plane tilting just a tad, catching a wing tip, and flipping into flames.

Despite my fears, I still fly. I remind myself that every day 60,000 planes take off and land safely in the United States alone. The pilot and crew fly daily, and they don't seem to be terrified. They let an important guy like Bill Clinton fly all over the place, and nothing has happened to him.

I guess it's a matter of aerodynamics. Air has mass, and the plane maneuvers itself through that mass. I can understand a boat coming into a dock—maneuvering through the water. That doesn't scare me. So I tell myself that a plane's a boat with an extra dimension to navigate, and its "water" is a lot thinner. Also, the pilot, who's still "flying" the plane after it lands, is as much in control on the ground as in the air. Only when he's good and ready does he allow gravity to take over.

Turbulence scares me, too. A United pilot once told me that he'd have bruises from his seat belt before turbulence really bothered him. Still, every time the plane comes in for a landing, I say a prayer, close my eyes, and take my pen out of my shirt pocket so it won't impale me if something goes wrong. And every time I stick my pen back in my shirt pocket, I feel thankful.

10. Train and Railpass Skills

The European train system makes life easy for the American visitor. The great trains of Europe shrink that already small continent, making the budget whirlwind or far-reaching tour a reasonable and exciting possibility for anyone.

Generally, European trains go where you need them to go and are fast, frequent, and inexpensive. (They're faster and more frequent in the north and less expensive but slower in the south.) You can easily have dinner in Paris, sleep on the train, and have breakfast in Rome, Munich, or Madrid.

You can buy train tickets as you travel or, depending on your trip, save money by buying a railpass.

RAILPASSES AND POINT-TO-POINT TICKETS

With a railpass, you can travel virtually anywhere, anytime without reservations. Just step on the proper train, sit in an unreserved seat, and when the uniformed conductor comes, flash your pass. More and more fast trains are requiring reservations, but despite that chore, a railpass is still a joy.

Choosing a pass used to be simple—it was just Eurail. Now, as train travel has gotten quite expensive, and shorter, focused trips are the trend, travelers can choose from a confusing multitude of passes. Many passes offer great discounts to youths (under 26), seniors, families, and even traveling twosomes.

Eurailpasses offer you unlimited first-class travel on all public railways in 17 European countries. These popular passes give you Western Europe (except Britain) by the tail. Choose between the consecutive-day pass (ranging from 15 days to three months) or the cheaper flexipass (any 10 or 15 individual days in two months). Travel partners (from two to five companions) save big with Eurail Saverpasses, available in consecutive-day and flexipass versions. Youths under 26 travel cheaper with second-class passes.

For the average independent first-timer planning to see lots of Europe (from Norway to Portugal to Italy, for instance), the Eurailpass is usually the best way to go. In a nutshell, you need to travel from Amsterdam to Rome to Madrid and back to Amsterdam to justify the purchase of a one-month Eurailpass. Two people on a three-week car trip (3,000 miles) and two people each using a three-week first-class Eurailpass will spend about the same, around $600 per person.

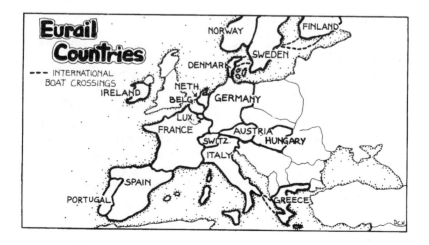

First class   *Second class*

First class costs 50 percent more than second.

Europasses are cheaper, mini-Eurail-type passes giving you from five to 15 "flexi" days in five core countries (France, Germany, Switzerland, Italy, and Spain). Neighboring regions can be added for an additional cost.

Country passes focus on a single country—virtually every European country has such a pass. If you're limiting your travels to one country, a country pass is your best bet. If you're planning on patching together several country passes, however, you're probably better off with a Eurailpass or Europass.

Rail and drive passes are popular varieties of many of these passes. Along with a railpass (Eurail, Euro, or country), you get vouchers for Hertz or Avis car rental days (billed at the economical weekly rate). These

---

EUROPEAN RAILPASSES GUIDE

Railpass details are confusing and tedious, but if you're planning to do Europe by rail on limited money, this book's "European Railpasses Guide" (in the Appendix) is very important. It's the only information source where you'll find rail deals available in the U.S.A. compared with rail deals available in Europe. My staff and I research and produce this guide annually. Our goal is to create smart consumers (as well as sell a few passes). It covers everything you need to know to order the best train pass for your trip; or to order nothing at all and save money by buying a pass or tickets in Europe. For our free updated 1999 Railpasses Guide, go to www.ricksteves.com or call 425/771-8303.

EUROPE BY RAIL: TIME AND COST

Connect the dots, add up the cost, and see if a railpass is right for your trip.

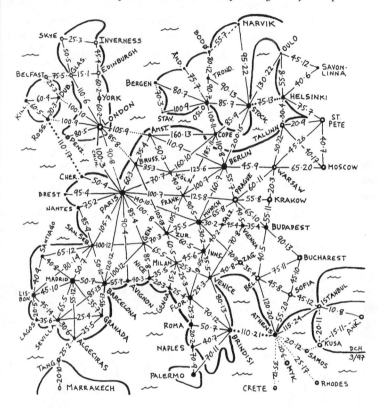

Map designed by Dave Hoerlein

The **first number** between cities = **cost** in $US for a 1-way, 2nd class ticket.

The **second number** = number of **hours** the trip takes.

- ● = Cities served by Eurailpass.
- ○ = Cities **not** served by Eurailpass (for example, if you want to go from Munich to Prague, you'll need to pay extra for the portion through the Czech Republic).
- ... = Boat crossings free or discounted with Eurailpass.
- .... = Boat crossings **not** included with Eurailpass.

Important: These fares and times are based on the Eurail Tariff Guide. Actual prices may vary due to currency fluctuations and local promotions. Local competition can cut the actual price of some boat crossings (from Italy to Greece, for example) by 50% or more. Ireland - France boat is half-price for Eurailpass holders. For approx. 1st class rail prices, multiply the prices shown by 1.5. In some cases faster trains (like the TGV in France) are available, cutting the hours indicated on the map. Travelers under age 26 can receive up to 1/3 off the 2nd class fares shown. Carefully read the railpass descriptions in the back of this book to see which countries are included.

allow travelers to do long trips by train and enjoy a car where they need the freedom to explore.

Point-to-point tickets can be your best budget bet. Many Eurail travelers would save lots of money by buying tickets as they go. While you can buy individual train tickets through your hometown travel agent, tickets are easy to buy—and cheaper—in Europe. You can buy tickets in train stations or, more comfortably, in the travel agency near your hotel. While most railpasses come only in first-class, travelers of any age can save 33 percent over first-class prices by purchasing second-class point-to-point tickets.

EUROPE'S TRAIN STATIONS
Train stations can be one of the independent traveler's best and most helpful friends. Take advantage of the assistance they can offer.

Train information: Every station has a train information office eager (or, at least, able) to help you with your scheduling. I usually consult the timetables myself first and write down my plan, then confirm this with the information desk. Written communication is easiest and safest. Computer terminals offering all the train schedules are now commonplace. They are multilingual and can be a real time-saver.

Eurail Freedom. My idea of good travel is being on this platform in Hamburg. In five minutes, the train on track 7 is going to Berlin. In six minutes, a train will leave from track 8 for Copenhagen. And I've yet to decide which train I'll be on.

Tourist information and room-finding services: These are usually either in the station (in the case of major tourist centers) or nearby. Pick up a map with sightseeing information and, if you need it, advice on where to find budget accommodations.

Money-changing: Often the station's money-changing office is open long after others have closed for the night (though the rates aren't great).

Lockers: Virtually every station has storage lockers and/or a luggage-checking service where, for about $5 a day, you can leave your luggage. People traveling light can fit two rucksacks into one storage locker, cutting their storage costs in half.

Waiting rooms: Most stations have comfortable waiting rooms. Those with fancy tickets often enjoy fancy lounges. The bigger stations are equipped with day hotels for those who want to shower, shave, rest, and so on. If, for one reason or another, you ever need a free, warm, and safe place to spend the night, a train station (or an airport) is my choice. Some stations boot everyone out from about midnight to 6:00 a.m. Ask before you bed down. Thieves work the stations in the wee hours. Be on guard.

Bus connections: Train stations are major bus stops, so connections from train to bus are generally no more difficult than crossing the street. Buses go from the stations to nearby towns that lack train service. If you have a bus to catch, be quick, since many are scheduled to connect with the train and leave promptly. If there's an airport nearby, you'll find bus or rail shuttle services (usually well-marked) at the train station.

GETTING ON THE RIGHT TRACK

Armed with a train pass or ticket, Europe becomes the independent traveler's playground. Most will master the system simply by diving in and learning from their mistakes. To learn quicker—from someone else's mistakes—here are a few tips:

Many cities have more than one train station. Paris has six, Brussels has three, and even Switzerland's little Interlaken has two. Be sure you know whether your train is leaving from Interlaken East or Interlaken West, even if that means asking what might seem like a stupid question. A city's stations are generally connected by train, subway, or bus. When arriving in a city (especially on a milk-run train), you may stop at several suburban stations with signs indicating your destination's name with the name of the neighborhood (e.g., Madrid Vallecas or Venezia Mestre). Don't jump out until you've reached the central station (Madrid Chamartin or Venezia S. Lucia). You can also avoid arrival frustrations by finding out if your train stops at a city's main station rather than a suburban one. For instance, half the trains from Rome to

"Florence" leave you at Florence's suburban station (Firenze Rifredi), where you'll be stranded without a hint of the Renaissance.

Ask for help and pay attention. Managing on the trains is largely a matter of asking questions, letting people help you, and assuming things are logical. I always ask someone on the platform if the train is going where I think it is. (Point to the train or track and ask, "Roma?") Uniformed train personnel can answer any question you can communicate. Speak slowly, clearly, and with caveman simplicity. Be observant. If the loudspeaker comes on, gauge by the reaction of those around you if the announcement concerns you. If, after the babble, everyone dashes over to track 15, assume your train is no longer arriving on track 7.

Scope out the train ahead of time. The configuration of many major trains is charted in little display cases on the platform next to where your train will arrive. As you wait, study the display to note where the first-class and sleeping cars are, whether there's a diner, and which cars are going where. Some train schedules will say, in the fine print, "Munich-bound cars in the front, Vienna-bound cars in the rear." Knowing which cars you're eligible for can be especially handy if you'll be competing with a mob for a seat. When expecting a real scramble, I stand on a bench at the far end of the track and study each car as the train rolls by, noting where the most empty places are. If there are several departures within an hour or so and the first train looks hopeless, I'll wait for the next.

This train started in Istanbul and will end in Wien Südbahnhof—Vienna's South Train Station.

Never assume the whole train is going where you are. Each car is labeled separately, because cars are usually added and dropped here and there along the journey. I'll never forget one hot afternoon in the middle of Spain. My train stopped in the middle of nowhere. There was some mechanical rattling. Then the train pulled away leaving me alone in my car . . . in La Mancha. Ten minutes later another train came along, picked up my car, and I was on my way. To survive all of this juggling easily, be sure that the city on your car's nameplate is your destination. The nameplate lists the final stop and some (but not all) of the stops in between.

Every car has plenty of room for luggage. In 20 years of train travel, I've never checked a bag. Simply carry it on and heave it up onto the racks above the seats. I've seen Turkish families moving all their worldly goods from Germany back to Turkey without checking a thing. They just loaded everything into the compartment and were on their way. People complain about the porters in the European train stations. I think they're great—I've never used one. People with more luggage than they can carry deserve porters.

Luggage is never completely safe. There is a thief on every train (union rules) planning to grab a bag (see Chapter 22: Outsmarting Thieves). Don't be careless. Before leaving my luggage in a compartment, I establish a relationship with everyone there. I'm safe leaving it among mutual guards.

Many train travelers are ripped off while they sleep. A $20 *couchette* (berth in a compartment, see below) is safer because the car attendant monitors who comes and goes. Those sleeping for free in regular cars should exercise extreme caution. Keep your valuables either in a money belt or at least securely attached to your body. For good measure, I clip and fasten my rucksack to the luggage rack. If one tug doesn't take the bag, a thief will usually leave it rather than ask, "*Scusi,* how is your luggage attached?" You'll hear stories of entire train cars being gassed and robbed in Italy and Spain. It happens—but I wouldn't lose sleep over it.

Women need to be careful on overnight rides. Women should use discretion when choosing a compartment. Sleeping in an empty compartment in southern Europe is an open invitation to your own private Casanova. Choose a room with a European granny or nun in it. That way you'll get a little peace, and he won't even try. A *couchette* (berth) is your best bet.

Use train time wisely. Train travelers, especially Eurailers, spend a lot of time on the train. This time can be dull and unproductive, or you can make a point to do whatever you can on the train to free up time off the train. It makes no sense to sit bored on the train and then, upon arrival, sit in the station for an hour reading your information and deciding where to go for hotels and what to do next.

Spend train time studying, reading, writing postcards or journal entries, eating, organizing, or cleaning. Talk to local people or other travelers. There is so much to be learned. Europeans are often less open and forward than Americans. You could sit across from a silent but fascinating and friendly European for an entire train ride, or you could break the ice by asking a question, quietly offering some candy or a cigarette (even if you don't smoke), or showing your Hometown, U.S. postcards. This can start the conversation flowing and the friendship growing.

TRAIN SCHEDULES—BREAKING THE CODE

Learning to decipher train schedules makes life on Europe's rails easier. These list all trains that come to and go from a particular station each day, and are clearly posted in two separate listings: departures (the ones we're concerned with, usually in yellow) and arrivals (normally in white).

You'll also find airport-type departure schedules that flip up and list the next eight or ten departures. These often befuddle travelers who don't realize that all over the world, the same four easy-to-identify columns are listed: destination, type of train, track number, and departure time. I don't care what language they're in, without much effort you can accurately guess which column is what.

Andrea Hagg

New train schedule computers (in most Italian stations and spreading quickly across Europe) will save you many long waits in station information lines. Use them to understand all your options. Indicate your language, departure and arrival points, and rough time of departure, and all workable connections will flash on the screen.

Learn to use the 24-hour clock used in European timetables. After 12:00 noon, the Europeans keep going—13:00, 14:00, and so on. To convert to the 12-hour clock, subtract 12 and add p.m. (16:00 is 4:00 p.m.). Train schedules are a great help to the traveler—if you can read them. Many rail travelers never take the time to figure them out. Here are a few pointers and a sample map and schedule to practice on. Understand it. You'll be glad you did.

The Thomas Cook Continental Timetable has become my itinerary-planning bible. Published several times a year, it contains nearly every European train schedule, complete with maps. (To order the up-to-date Cook Timetable, about $33 postpaid, call the Forsyth Travel Library, 800/FORSYTH.) I find that the schedules vary more with the season than with the year. I don't rely on them for the actual train I'll take, but I use an old one (which your travel agent might loan or give to you) at home before I leave to familiarize myself with how to read train schedules and to learn the frequency and duration of train trips I expect to take. Every station and most trains will be equipped with the same schedule, updated. Although I don't carry the bulky "Cook Book" with me, those who do find it handy.

Let's crack the code in the Cook Book. You'll find these confusing-looking charts (see example in this chapter) and maps in the Cook Timetable and in display cases in every station. Find the trip you want to take on the appropriate train map. Your route will be numbered, referring you to the proper timetable. That table is the schedule for the trains traveling along that line, in both directions (a. = arrivals, d. = departures).

As an example, let's go from Turin to Venice (the local spellings are always used, in this case, Torino and Venezia). This is #350 on the map (see next page). So refer to table 350. Locate your starting point, Torino. Reading from left to right, you will see that trains leave Torino for Venezia at 7:08, 9:06, 15:08, 15:50, and 22:50. Those trains arrive in Venezia at 11:55, 13:59, 19:55, 21:25, and 5:08, respectively. Note that Venezia has two stations (Mestre and the more central Santa Lucia). As you can see, not all Torino departures go all the way to Venezia. For example, the 8:50 train only goes to Milan, arriving at 10:40. From there, the 10:50 train will get you to Venezia SL by 13:59. This schedule shows an overnight train. You could leave Torino at 22:50 and arrive in Venezia by 5:08.

Table 350 — TORINO - MILANO - VENEZIA

km		IC 645	IR 2007	IR 2009	IC 649	IR 2097	E 351	IC 651	EC 39	IC 657	IR 2107	EC 13	IR 2019	IR 2031	E 869
0	Torino Porta Nuova 353 ...d.	0708	0750	(0850)	0906	...	...	1108	...	1508	...	...	1550	2150	2250
6	Torino Porta Susa 353 ...d.	0718	0800	0900	0915	...	...	1118	...	1518	...	...	1600	2200	2300
29	Chivasso 353 ...d.		0816	0916	0933	...	...		...		...	...	1616	2216	2316
60	Santhia ...d.		0834	0934		...	...		...		...	...	1634	2234	2334
79	Vercelli ...d.	0802	0846	0946	1002	...	...	1202	...	1602	...	...	1646	2246	2346
101	Novara ...d.	0818	0901	1001	1018	...	...	1218	...	1618	...	...	1701	2301	0001
153	Milano Centrale ...a.	0850	0940	(1040)	1050	...	...	1250	...	1650	...	...	1740	2340	0040
		IC 647									IR 2109				
153	Milano Centrale ...d.	0905	...	...	1105	1110	1210	..	(1305)	1705	1710	...	1810	...	0110
187	Treviglio ...d.		...	...		1135	1235	...			1735	...	1835	...	0150
236	Brescia ...d.	0952	...	...	1152	1206	1306	...	1352	1752	1806	...	1906	...	0239
263	Desenzano del Garda ...d.		...	...		1224	1324	...			1824	...	1924	...	0257
278	Peschiera del Garda ...d.		...	...		1235	1335	...			1835	...	1935	...	0309
300	Verona Porta Nuova ...d.	1027	...	...	1227	1254	1354	...	(1427)	1827	1854	(1910)	1954	...	0331
325	San Bonifacio ...d.		...	...		1311	1411	...			1911	...	2011	...	0347
351	Vicenza ...d.	1100	...	...	1300	1332	1432	...	1500	1900	1932	1945	2032	...	0410
382	Padova ...d.	1122	...	...	1323	1353	1453	...	1522	1922	1953	2004	2053	...	0433
411	Venezia Mestre ...a.	1140	...	...	1346	1413	1513	...	1540	1940	2013	2024	2113	...	0454
411	Venezia Mestre ...d.	1155	...	...	1349	1416	1516	...	1543	1955	2016	2026	2116	...	0459
420	Venezia Santa Lucia ...a.		...	...	1359	1425	1525	...	1552		2025	(2035)	2125	...	0508
	Trieste Centrale 376 ...a.	1345	...	...	...	...	...	...	2145		...	...	...	...	0910b

Train schedule and map from the Thomas Cook Timetable

Train schedules are helpful in planning your stopovers. For instance, this table shows a train leaving Torino at 8:50 and arriving in Milan at 10:40. You could spend two hours touring Milan's cathedral, catch the 13:05 train for Verona (arrive at 14:27, see the Roman Arena and Juliet's balcony), and hop on the 19:10 train to arrive in Venezia by 20:35.

Each table has three parts: a schedule for each direction and a section explaining the many exceptions to the rules. You never know when one of those confusing exceptions might affect your train. Schedule symbols

In this French train station, arrivals and departures are clearly listed. Who says you can't read French? The small schedule in the middle lists trains that are about to depart. The Tabac stand sells candy, phone cards, newspapers, and often subway and bus tickets.

also indicate problem-causing exceptions, such as which trains are first-class or sleepers only, or charge supplements. An X means you'll have to change trains, crossed hammers indicate the train goes only on work-days (daily except Sundays and holidays), a little bed means the train has sleeping compartments, an R in a box means reservations are required for that departure, and a cross means the train goes only on Sundays and holidays.

Remember that each table shows just some of the trains that travel along that track. Other tables feed onto the same line. To find out if you're on the right track . . .

Confirm your plans. The only person who knows everything is the one at the train station information window. Let that person help you. He can fix mistakes and save you many hours. Just show your plan on a scrap of paper (e.g., Torino→Milano, 8:50–10:40; Milano→Verona, 13:05–14:27) and ask, "OK?" If your plan is good, the information person will nod, direct you to your track, and you're on your way. If there's a problem, she'll solve it. Uniformed train employees on the platforms or on board the trains can also help.

HOW TO SLEEP ON THE TRAIN

The economy of night travel is tremendous. Sleeping while rolling down the tracks saves time and money, both of which, for most travelers, are limited resources. The first concern about night travel is usually, "Aren't you missing a lot of beautiful scenery? You just slept through half of Sweden!" The real question should be, "Did the missed scenery matter, since you gained an extra day for hiking the Alps, biking through tulips, or island-hopping in the Greek seas?" The answer: No. Maximize night trips.

Couchettes

To assure a safer and uninterrupted night's sleep, you can usually reserve a sleeping berth known as a *couchette* (koo-SHETT) at least a day in advance from a travel agency, at the station ticket counter, or, if there are any available, from the conductor on the train. For about the cost of a cheap hotel bed ($20), you'll get sheets, pillow, blankets, a fold-out bunk bed in a compartment with three to five other people, and, hopefully, a good night's sleep.

As you board, you'll give the attendant your *couchette* voucher, railpass or ticket, and passport. He deals with the conductors and customs officials and keeps the thieves out so you can sleep soundly and safely.

City Name Variations

American Name	European Name
Athens (Gre.)	Athinai
Bolzano (Italy)	Bozen in German
Bruges (Bel.)	Brugge
Brussels (Bel.)	Bruxelles
Cologne (Ger.)	Köln
Copenhagen (Den.)	København
Florence (Italy)	Firenze
Geneva (Switz.)	Genève
Genoa (Italy)	Genova (not Geneva)
Gothenburg (Swe.)	Göteborg
The Hague (Neth.)	Den Haag, S'Gravenhage
Helsinki (Fin.)	Helsingfors in Swedish
Lisbon (Port.)	Lisboa
London	Londres in French
Munich (Ger.)	München (in Italian, Monaco di Baviera)
Naples (Italy)	Napoli
Padua (Italy)	Padova
Pamplona (Spain)	Iruña in Basque
Paris (Fr.)	Parigi in Italian
Prague (Czech.)	Praha
Venice (Italy)	Venezia
Vienna (Aus.)	Wien
Warsaw (Pol.)	Warszawa

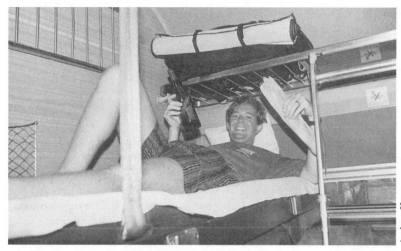

Andrea Hagg

For $20, you can rent a couchette *(bunk bed) on your overnight train. Top bunks give you a bit more room and safety—but BYOB.*

While some trains (especially in France) have cushier first-class *couchettes* (double rather than triple bunks for the same cost if you have a first-class ticket), most *couchettes* are the same for both classes. While the top bunk gives you more privacy and luggage space, it can be hotter and stuffier than lower bunks and a couple of inches shorter (a concern if you're 6'2" or taller). You can request smoking or nonsmoking, and top, middle, or bottom berths.

Sleeping Free in Compartments
Shoestring travelers avoid the $20 cost of a *couchette* and just sack out for free, draping their tired bodies over as many unoccupied seats as possible. But trying to sleep on an overnight train ride without a bed can be a waking nightmare.

One night of endless headbobbing, swollen toes, and a screaming tailbone, sitting up straight in a dark eternity of steel wheels crashing along rails, trying doggedly—yet hopelessly—to get comfortable, will teach you the importance of finding a spot to stretch out for the night. This is an art that vagabond night travelers cultivate. Those with the greatest skill at this game sleep. Those not so talented will spend the night gnashing their teeth and squirming for relief.

A traditional train car has about 10 compartments, each with six or eight seats (three or four facing three or four). Most have seats that pull out and armrests that lift, turning your compartment into a bed on wheels.

But this is possible only if you have more seats than people in your compartment. A compartment that seats six can sleep three. So if between 30 and 60 people choose your car, some will sleep and some will sit. Your fate depends on how good you are at encouraging people to sit elsewhere. There are many ways to play this game (which has few rules and encourages creativity). Here are my favorite techniques.

The Big Sleep: Arrive 30 minutes before your train leaves. Walk most of the length of the train but not to the last car. Choose a car that is going where you want to go, and find an empty compartment. Pull two seats out to make a bed, close the curtains, turn out the lights, and pretend you are sound asleep. It's amazing. At 9:00 p.m. everyone on that train is snoring away! The first 30 people to get on that car have room to sleep. Number 31 will go into any car with the lights on and people sitting up. The most convincing "sleepers" will be the last to be "woken up." (The real champs put a hand down their pants and smile peacefully.)

The Hare Krishna Approach: A more interesting way that works equally well and is more fun is to sit cross-legged on the floor and chant religious-sounding, exotically discordant harmonies, with a faraway look on your face. People will open the door, stare in for a few seconds, and leave, determined to sit in the aisle rather than share a compartment with the likes of you. You'll probably sleep alone, or end up chanting the night away with five other religious fanatics.

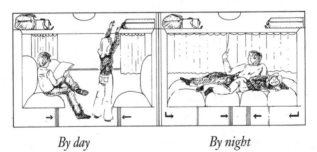

A Typical Train Compartment

By day   *By night*

For every night you spend on the train, you gain a day for sightseeing and avoid the cost of a hotel. If your compartment is not full, you can try sleeping for free by pulling out the seats to make a bed.

Car # 126 from Copenhagen to Paris' North Station is no smoking, second-class, and filled with bunk beds.

Using reservation cards to your advantage: Each compartment will have a reservation board outside the door. Never sit in a seat that is reserved because you'll be "bumped out" just before the train leaves. Few people realize that you can determine how far the people on a train will travel by reading their reservation tags. Each tag explains which segment of the journey that seat is reserved for. Find a compartment with three or four people traveling for just an hour or two, and for the rest of the night you will probably have that compartment to yourself.

Remember that trains add and lose cars throughout the night. A train could be packed with tourists heading for Milan, and at 1:00 a.m. an empty Milan-bound car could be added. The difference between being packed like sardines and stretching out in your own fishbowl could be as little as one car away.

These tricks work not to take advantage of others but to equal out the train load. When all compartments are lightly loaded and people continue to load in, let the air out of your inflatable travel partner and make room for your new roommates. To minimize the misery on a full train, sit opposite your partner, pull out the seats, and share a single bed (and the smell of your feet).

BUS VERSUS TRAIN

Except in Ireland, Greece, Turkey, Portugal, and Morocco, the trains are faster, more comfortable, and have more extensive schedules than buses. Bus trips are usually less expensive (especially in the British Isles) and are occasionally included on your train pass (where operated by the train companies, as many are in Germany, Switzerland, and Belgium).

There are some cheap, long-haul buses (often hippie-type "magic buses") from the hub cities of London, Munich, Amsterdam, and Athens. These can save you plenty over train fares. For example, Amsterdam to London costs $105 by train, $60 by bus; Amsterdam to Paris costs $95 by train, $50 by bus; and Amsterdam to Athens costs over $400 by train and about $250 by bus.

Use buses mainly to pick up where Europe's great train system leaves off. Buses fan out from the smallest train stations to places too small for the train to cover. For towns with train stations far from the center (e.g., hill towns), buses are often scheduled to meet each arrival and shuttle passengers to the main square (often for no extra cost). Many bus connections to nearby towns not served by train are timed to depart just after the train arrives.

11. Driving Europe Crazy

Behind the wheel you're totally free. You go where you want to, when you want to. You're not limited by tracks and schedules. And driving's great for those who don't believe in packing light . . . you can even rent a trailer.

Driving can be economical. Solo car travel is expensive, but three or four people sharing a rented car travel cheaper than three or four using train passes.

The super mobility of a car saves you time in locating budget accommodations in small towns and away from the train lines. This savings helps to rationalize the "splurge" of a car rental. You can also play it riskier in peak season, arriving in a town late with no reservation. If the hotels are full, you simply drive to the next town.

Every year, as train prices go up, car rental becomes a better option for budget travelers in Europe. While most travel dreams come with choo-choo noises, and most first trips are best by rail, you should at least consider the convenience of driving.

RENTING A CAR

Cars are economical when rented by the week with unlimited mileage through your travel agent or directly with the rental company in the

United States. (There are a few decent four-day deals.) There is no way to chart best car rental deals. Rates vary from company to company, month to month, and country to country. The cheapest company for rental in one country might be the most expensive in the next. After shopping for half an hour via the toll-free phone numbers listed below, you'll know who has the best deal for your travel plans. Rentals arranged from major companies in Europe are so expensive that you'd save money by having someone arrange your rental for you back in the United States.

In Europe cars are rented for a 24-hour day with a 59-minute grace period. Daily rates are ridiculously high. That's why the various rail 'n' drive passes are a good deal (see European Railpasses Guide in the Appendix). They basically allow you to rent a car one day at a time at one-seventh the cheap weekly rate.

While ages vary from country to country and company to company, those who are at least 23 years old should have no trouble renting a car. Only Ireland has a maximum age limit (75). If you're considered too young or too old, look into leasing (see below), which has less stringent age restrictions. Council Travel (800/2-COUNCIL) and car companies advertising in Let's Go guidebooks are seeking young renters.

Rental cars come with the necessary insurance and paperwork to cross borders effortlessly in all of Western Europe. Ask for specific limitations if you're driving through Eastern Europe. You are generally either penalized or not allowed to take your car from England to the Continent or

---

CAR OR TRAIN?

While you should travel the way you like, consider these variables when deciding if your European experience might be better by car or train:

Concern	By Car	By Train
• packing heavy?	• no problem	• must go light
• scouring one area	• best	• frustrating
• all over Europe	• too much driving	• great
• big cities	• expensive/worthless	• ideal
• camping	• perfect	• more like boot camp
• one or two people	• expensive	• probably cheaper
• three or more	• probably cheaper	• more expensive
• traveling with young kids	• survivable, given time	• miserable

Car vs. Train—
Rough Costs of Sample Trips per Person

Mode of Transportation	3 weeks 1,600 mi.	3 weeks 3,000 mi.	2 months 3,000 mi.	2 months 8,000 mi.
Eurailpass (first class)	$698*	$698*	$1,224*	$1,224*
Second-class individual train tickets	$350	$350	$550	$1,500
Subcompact car (two people)	$575	$670	$800	$1,200
Midsized car (four people)	$365	$410	$600	$800

Sample trips:
- Munich–Paris–Florence–Munich = 1,600 miles.
- Amsterdam–Munich–Rome–Barcelona–Paris = 3,000 miles.
- Amsterdam–Copenhagen–Stockholm–Oslo–Copenhagen– Berlin–Vienna–Athens–Rome–Nice–Madrid–Lisbon– Madrid–Paris–Amsterdam = 8,000 miles.

Train tickets cost about 18 cents per mile in the south and east, 25 cents per mile in the north. Car rates based on typical rentals or leases, including collision damage waiver (CDW) supplements and figuring $4 per gallon and 30 mpg. Rates vary wildly from company to company and from country to country.

* 1998 prices. Saverpass versions (for two or more travelers) are more than $100 cheaper.

COST OF CAR RENTAL: ABOUT $500 A WEEK

A rough estimate for weekly rental with unlimited mileage plus collision damage waiver (CDW) insurance. Two people in a car for three weeks pay around $575 each . . . about the cost of a three-week Eurail Saverpass.

Ford Fiesta:	$200–$300
Tax:	15–25 percent extra
CDW:	$10–$15/day
Gas:	$130/week ($4/gallon, 30 mpg, 140 miles/day)
Parking in big cities:	$20/day
Freeway tolls (France and Italy only):	$5/hour

to Ireland. Hertz, the exception, offers a "Le Swap" program—you get a round-trip Chunnel Passage and a right-hand car rental for Britain that's swapped for a left-hand rental on the Continent. Generally, the high ferry costs make renting two separate cars a better deal; two single weeks of car rental usually cost the same as two weeks in a row. Take advantage of open-jaws possibilities to save rental days and avoid big-city driving. You can normally pick up and drop off a car at any of your rental company's offices in one country. They don't care if you change your expected drop-off city. (Know where all the offices in a country are so you'll understand your options.) Some companies bring the car to your hotel for free. Others charge 10 percent or so for airport pick-ups, and there is usually about a $100 fee to drop in another country. (You'll find some happy and some outrageous exceptions. Ask or survey the lot to see if they have a car with your drop-off country's plates. You'll do them a favor and save yourself some money by driving this car "home" for them.)

Your American driver's license is all you need in most European countries. An international driver's license provides a translation of your American license—making it easier for the cop to write out the ticket.

Vanning through the windmills

Exactly where you need one depends on whom you talk to. People who sell them say you should have them almost everywhere. People who rent cars say you need them almost nowhere. Police can get mad (their concern is in finding the expiration date) and fine you if you don't have one. Those traveling in Portugal, Spain, Italy, Austria, Germany, Greece, and Eastern Europe probably should get an international driver's license. (They are easy to get at your local AAA office—$10 and two passport-type photos.)

COST OF CAR RENTAL
To really compare car costs with train costs, figure your weekly unlimited mileage rental rate plus:
- **Tax**, which is clear and consistent within each country, generally 18 to 25 percent (less in Spain, Germany, Ireland, and Luxembourg, and only 8 percent in Switzerland—but Swiss rental rates are that much higher)
- **CDW insurance supplement** (figure $10–25 a day, see below)
- **Gas** ($130 a week, giving you about 1,000 miles)
- **Tolls** for super-freeways in France and Italy (about $5 per hour), $30 for the highway permit decal as you enter Switzerland, $10 for Austria
- **Parking** ($20 a day in big cities, free otherwise)
- **Theft protection** (required in Italy, at about $12/day)

The Collision Damage Waiver (CDW) Racket
When you rent a car, you are generally liable for the entire value of that car. For peace of mind, get a collision damage waiver (CDW) supplement. This costs from $10 to $25 a day, depending on the country, the car, and the company. Figure roughly $150 a week for CDW. (Travel Guard sells CDW at a much better rate of $6 a day, tel. 800/826-1300.)

While some credit cards promise to give you free CDW coverage if you charge the rental on their card, you'll go without CDW as far as the rental company is concerned (and they'll often lie to you, saying your credit card coverage is no good). Check with your credit card company. Ask if the amount of coverage is limited to your credit limit on your card, and ask to have the worst-case scenario explained to you. Unscrupulous rental companies will put a hold on your credit card for the value of the car, which can cause problems. If you have an accident, you may have to settle with the rental company and then fight to get reimbursed by your credit card company when you get home. Also, many rental car companies have all-inclusive plans that include a more reasonable CDW. Ask your travel agent about this. Those renting a car for more than three

LEADING CAR RENTAL COMPANIES

Big companies (the first four listings below) offer more reliability and flexibility, but consolidators and wholesalers (the last five) can be cheaper. All can be arranged through your travel agent.

Hertz	800/654-3001
Avis	800/331-1084
Dollar	800/800-6000
Budget	800/472-3325
Kemwel	800/678-0678
Europcar	800/227-3876
Auto Europe	800/223-5555
Europe by Car	800/223-1516
DER Tours (best for German/Czech)	800/782-2424

Before you commit, ask about:
• weekly unlimited mileage rate
• age restrictions
• insurance cost
• CDW options
• theft insurance (particularly in Italy)
• cost of adding another driver
• drop-off costs within a country or in another country
• a listing of offices in the countries you're visiting (consider the most efficient pick-up and drop-off points)
• if there is a cheaper place to pick up a car (airport pick-ups can be more costly)
• if there is a covered trunk
• availability of automatics and car seats
• any restrictions on driving the car in all countries (particularly in Eastern Europe)
• any special "match the competition" deals for a better price
• any additional charges or local taxes such as VAT (value added tax)

Before you drive away, ask about:
• changing a tire
• how to use the radio, lights, etc.
• location of insurance green card
• if membership in local automobile clubs is included
• making repairs (e.g., Hertz has a handy service arrangement with Shell gas stations)

Luckily, he paid extra for full insurance.

weeks should ask their agent about leasing (see below), which skirts many tax and insurance costs. Big American-based companies are easier to work with if you have a problem.

CDW is most expensive when purchased at the car rental desk. If you do pay the car company, remember that the rental rates are so competitive that, to make a reasonable profit, these companies have had to make a killing on the CDW. If it's any consolation, think of your CDW fee as half for CDW and half money that you should have paid on the rental fee.

Regardless of how tough CDW is on the pocketbook, I get it for the peace of mind. It's much more fun to hold your own on the autobahn (German freeway) with Europe's skilled maniac drivers, knowing you can return your car in an unrecognizable shambles with an apologetic shrug and say, "S-s-s-sorry," and lose no money.

LEASING AND BUYING

Leasing (technically, buying the car and selling it back) gets around many tax and insurance costs and is a good deal for people needing a car for three weeks or more. Europe by Car now leases cars in France for as few as 17 days for $400. Lease prices include all taxes and CDW insurance. Germany, France, Belgium, and the Netherlands are also particularly good for leasing.

Although Americans rarely consider this budget option, Aussies and New Zealanders routinely buy used cars for their trips and sell them when they're done. The most popular places to buy cars are Amsterdam, Frankfurt, London, and U.S. military bases. Before your trip, or once in Europe, you can check the classified ads in the armed forces' *Stars and Stripes* newspaper. In London, check the used-car market on Market Road (Caledonian Road Tube) and look in London periodicals such as *TNT*, *Law*, and *New Zealand-UK News*, which list used cars as well as jobs, flats, cheap flights, and travel partners.

When buying or renting a vehicle, consider the advantage of a van or motor home, which gives you the flexibility to drive late and just pull over and camp for free. Campanje is a Dutch company that rents and sells used VW campers fully loaded for camping through Europe. Rates vary from $500 to $750 per week, including tax and insurance. (For a brochure, write P.O. Box 9332, 3506 GH Utrecht, Netherlands, tel. 31/30-244-7070, fax 31/30-242-0981, e-mail: campanje@xs4all.nl). In Copenhagen, Rafco rents cars (all sizes), station wagons, and fully equipped motorhomes for cheap. The manager, Ken, promises *ETBD* readers a 10 percent discount (Englandsvej 380, DK-2770 Kastrup, Denmark, tel. 45/32 51 15 00, fax 45/32 51 10 89, Web site: www.rafco.dk, e-mail: rafco@vip.cybercity.dk). For information on buying, renting, or leasing a vehicle to use for camping, including registration and insurance issues, see *Europe by Van and Motor Home* by David Shore and Patty Campbell (1999, 250 pages, $17 postpaid, 1842 Santa Margarita Dr., Fallbrook, CA 92028, tel. 800/659-5222, fax 760/723-6184, e-mail: shorecam@aol.com).

BEHIND THE EUROPEAN WHEEL

Horror stories about European traffic abound. They're fun to tell, but driving in Europe is really only a problem to those who make it one. Any good American driver can cope with European traffic.

Europe is a continent of frustrated race-car drivers. The most dangerous creature on the road is the timid American. Be aggressive, observe, fit in, avoid big-city driving when you can, wear your seat belt, and pay extra for CDW insurance.

Invest in an extra key. Most rental cars come with only one. That's needlessly risky. Besides, it's more convenient for two people to have access to the locked car. (Keep it to hang on your Christmas tree as a memento.) Some keys, though, now come with a computer chip that makes them impossible to duplicate.

Drive European. After a few minutes on the autobahn, you'll learn that you don't cruise in the passing lane. Cruise in the right-hand lane. In

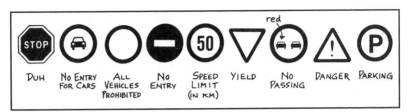

Don't even think of driving in Europe without knowing these standard signs.

Rome, my cabbie went through three red lights. White-knuckled, I asked, "*Scusi*, do you see red lights?"

He said, "When I come to light, I look. If no cars come, red light *stupido*, I go through. If policeman sees no cars—*no problema*—red light *stupido*."

Learn the signs. All of Europe uses the same simple set of road symbols. Just take a few minutes to learn them. Many major rest stops have free local driving almanacs (or cheap maps) explaining such signs, roadside facilities, and exits.

You can drive in and out of strange towns fairly smoothly by following a few basic signs. Most European towns have signs directing you to the "old town" or the center (such as *centrum, centro, centre ville, stadtmitte*). The tourist office, normally right downtown, will usually be clearly signposted (*i, turismo, VVV*, or various abbreviations that you'll learn in each country). The tallest church spire often marks the center of the old town. Park in its shadow and look for the information booth. To leave a city, look for freeway signs (distinctive green or blue, depending on the country) or "all directions" (*toutes directions*) signs. Avoid heavy traffic times. Big cities are great fun and nearly traffic-free for Sunday drives.

To save time, use the freeway. The shortest distance between any two European points is found on the autobahn/strada/route. Although tolls can be high in Italy and France ($30 to get from Paris to the Italian border), the gas and time saved on European super-freeways justifies the expense. Some prefer the more scenic and free national highway systems (*route nationale* in France). Small roads can be a breeze, or they can be dreadfully jammed up.

Passing is essential. Americans are timid about passing. Be bold but careful. On winding, narrow roads, you'll notice a turn-signal sign language from the slower car ahead of you indicating when it's OK to pass. This is used inconsistently. Don't rely on it blindly.

Don't use a car for city sightseeing. Park it and use public transportation (or taxis). City parking is a pain. Find a spot as close to the center as possible, grab it, and keep it. For overnight stops, it's crucial to choose a safe, well-traveled, and well-lit spot. Vandalism to a tourist's car parked overnight in a bad urban neighborhood is as certain as death and taxes. In cities where traffic is worst, look for huge government-sponsored (cheap) parking lots on the outskirts, where a bus or subway will zip you easily into the center. It's often worth parking in a garage ($10–30 a day). Ask your hotel receptionist for advice.

Go metric. On the Continent you'll be dealing with kilometers. To convert kilometers to miles, cut in half and add 10 percent (90 km/hr = 45 + 9 miles: 54 mph—not very fast in Europe). Britain uses miles instead of kilometers. Gas is sold by the liter (four to a gallon).

Explore Britain's round-abouts. Instead of intersections with stop lights, the British have roundabouts. These work wonderfully if you merge smoothly; yield to cars already inside the circle. Stopping needlessly before entering a roundabout ruins most of the efficiency and much of the fun. For many, roundabouts are high-pressure circles that require a snap decision about something you really don't completely understand—your exit. To replace the stress with levity, make it standard operating procedure to take a 360-degree case-out-your-options circuit, discuss the exits with your navigator, and then confidently wing off on the exit of your choice.

GAS

The cost of gas in Europe—$3 to $5 a gallon—sounds worse than it is. Distances are short, the petite puddle-jumpers get great mileage, and when compared to costly train tickets, expensive gas is less of a factor. You'll be impressed by how few miles you need to travel to enjoy diversity.

Pumping gas in Europe is as easy as finding a gas station ("self-service" is universal), sticking the nozzle in, and pulling the big trigger. Gas prices are listed by the liter (about a quart). Don't get confused: Gas is called *petrol* or *benzine*, while diesel is known as *gasoil*. Super is *super* and normal is *normal* (or *essence*) and increasingly rare. In Eastern Europe, use the highest octane available. Unleaded gas (look for the green pump) is standard throughout Western Europe. Freeway stations are more expensive than those in towns, but during siesta only freeway stations are open. Giant suburban supermarkets often offer the cheapest gas.

JOYRIDING

The British Isles are good for driving—reasonable rentals, no language barrier, exciting rural areas, and fine roads; and after one near head-on collision scares the bloody heck out of you, you'll have no trouble remembering which side of the road to drive on.

Other good driving areas are Scandinavia (call for free reservations to avoid long waits at ferry crossings); Belgium, Holland, and Luxembourg (yield to bikes—you're outnumbered); Germany, Switzerland, and Austria (driving down sunny Alpine valleys with yodeling on the tape deck is auto-ecstasy); and Spain and Portugal (with their exasperating public transportation system, I spell relief C-A-R). The whirlwind, see-Europe-from-top-to-bottom–type trip is best by train.

12. Biking, Hitching, Walking, and Hiking

BIKING IN EUROPE

Biking is big in Europe. Many cities such as Amsterdam, Copenhagen, and Munich are great by bike. Riverside bike paths from Salzburg, Luxor, and along the Rhine have left me with top-notch memories. Wherever it's worth biking, you'll find a bike rental shop.

Within cities, bikes cut transportation times in half, giving you more time to spend at the sites. Bikes are bargains at $10 to $15 a day, but a steal in Copenhagen, where you can borrow bikes for free from city bikestands by leaving a 20-kroner deposit.

Bikes are a fun change of pace if you're traveling by car or train. In many countries (especially France, Germany, Austria, Belgium, and the Netherlands), the train stations rent bikes (often with big percent discounts for those with train tickets or passes) and sometimes have easy "pick up here and drop off there" plans. For mixing train and bike travel, ask at stations for the *Fahrrad am Bahnhof* (German) or *Train + Velo* (French) booklet.

Guided bike tours, ranging from two to five hours, are becoming popular in Europe's cities (such as Amsterdam, Bruges, Munich, and Vienna). You'll get an entertaining, sometimes informative guide who will show you the back streets and treats of the city or countryside. Tours are fun, reasonable (about $15–30), good exercise, and an easy way to meet other travelers as well as get a fresh angle on an old city.

Some people travel almost exclusively by bike and wouldn't have it any other way. Rich Sorensen and Edwin McCain, who for years have gotten their travel thrills crisscrossing Europe by bike, helped me assemble the

Europe is made for biking.

following tips on bicycle touring in Europe.

Bicycle touring is cheap and rewarding. To see Europe on $20 a day, you don't need a time machine. What you need is a bike, farmers' markets, and campgrounds or hostels. Traveling this way, you'll not only save money and keep fit, but you'll experience a quieter side of Europe that travelers rarely see.

While bicycle touring is one of the cheapest ways to see Europe, most bikers choose to pedal for the sheer joy of it. Imagine low-gearing up a beautiful mountain road on a bike (smell the freshly mown hay), then picture an air-conditioned Mercedes with the windows closed and the stereo on (smell the upholstery). The driver might think, "Masochistic nut!" but he also might notice the biker's smiling face— the face of a traveler who can see clearly from mountain to village, smell the woods, hear the birds singing and the trees breezing, while anticipating a well-earned and glorious downhill run.

Determine if a bike is the right kind of transportation for your trip. Define what part of Europe you want to experience, and then ask yourself some basic questions to see whether your bicycle will be your key to freedom or an albatross around your neck. Remember that it takes an entire day to travel the same distance by bicycle that you could cover in a single hour by train or car. Sixty miles per day is a high average. With bakery stops, Rich averages about 40. For example, if you have the entire summer free, you and your bike can cover a lot of ground through, say, France, Germany, Benelux, Switzerland, and Italy. But if you have a month or less, will you be content to focus on a single country or region? Given what you want to see in the time you have, is the slow pace of bicycling a worthwhile trade-off for the benefits? And finally, do you want to spend much more of your time in rural and small-town Europe than in cities?

Read a biking guidebook. Consider *Europe by Bike*, by Karen and Terry Whitehill (Mountaineers); the various Mountaineers' country guides (*England by Bike, France by Bike,* and *Germany by Bike);* or *Cycling in the Netherlands, Belgium, and Luxembourg,* by Kathy and Jerry Widing.

Adventure Cycling Association's *Cyclists Yellow Pages* is a good resource directory and their *Cyclosource* catalog contains first-rate touring information and accessories (tel. 800/721-8719). **Take practice trips.** Make sure you really enjoy taking long rides weighed down with loaded panniers. Try some 60-mile-a-day rides (five hours at 12 mph) around home. If possible, take a weekend camping trip with everything you'll take to Europe. Know which tools to bring and learn basic repair work (like repairing flat tires, replacing broken spokes, and adjusting brakes and derailleurs). Ask about classes at your local bike shop.

Decide whether to go solo, with a partner, or with a tour. You can go it alone, with occasional pick-up pals on the way. As a loner, you'll go where, when, and as far and fast as you want. Traveling with a companion or two is more cost-effective, and can be more fun, but make sure your partner's cycling pace and temperament is compatible with yours. Organized tours, which usually have sag wagons to carry gear, average an easy 30 to 40 miles a day. For information, check out Europeds (tel. 800/321-9552), Euro-Bike Tours (tel. 800/321-6060), or the ads in *Bicycling* magazine.

When to go depends on where you go. Ideal biking temperatures are between 50 and 70 degrees Fahrenheit, so May is a good time to bike in the Mediterranean countries. Edwin started his five-week trip in Greece in May before it got too hot and then pedaled up through the Balkans to England. He had good temperatures all the way, but he also had headwinds (the prevailing westerlies). Rich and his wife, Risa, set out from Barcelona on a more leisurely spring-to-fall route that took them through France, England, Germany, Switzerland, Italy, and Greece, and they had not only ideal temperatures but also fewer headwinds.

Bring your bike from home. Although you can buy good touring bikes in Europe, they're no cheaper than here, and you're better off bringing a bike that you're sure is the right fit for you, your racks, and your panniers. The current debate among cyclists is whether to tour on a thick-tired mountain bike or a touring bike with skinnier tires. Mountain-bike tires are much more forgiving on the occasional cobblestone street, but they are more durable than necessary for most European roads and the chunky tread design will slow you down. In addition, straight mountain-bike handlebars will limit your hand positions, increasing fatigue on long riding days. If you already have a mountain bike, go ahead and take it, but add some bolt-on handlebar extensions.

Some airlines will ship your bike for free. To determine the airline's bike-checking policy, call the airline directly. Although some will charge a fee for your bike (more likely if there is a domestic leg to your flight), most airlines will fly it to Europe free, considering it to be one of your two allotted pieces of checked baggage. Most airlines require that bikes be partially disassembled and boxed. Get a box from your local bike shop or from Amtrak (which sells cavernous bike boxes). Reinforce your box with extra cardboard, and be sure to put a plastic spacer between your front forks (any bike shop will give you one). You can also toss in your panniers, tent, and so on for extra padding, as long as you stay under the airline's weight limit. Bring the tools you'll need to get your bike back into riding form, so you can ride straight out of your European airport.

Be prepared. Expect rain and bring good bikers' rain gear. A Gore-Tex raincoat can double as a cool-weather windbreaker. You'll also be exposed to the sun, so plan on using plenty of sunscreen. A bell is generally required by law in Europe, so you should have one on your bike—for giving a multilingual "Hi!" to other bikers as well as a "Look out, here I come!" Even if you never ride at night, you should at least bring a strobe-type taillight for the many long and unavoidable tunnels. Smaller Presta tire valves are standard in most of Europe, so if your bike has the automotive-type Shraeder valves, take along an adapter. To guard against unsightly road rash (and worse), always wear a helmet and biking gloves.

Obey Europe's traffic rules. Bikers generally follow the same rules as drivers. Some countries, such as the Netherlands, have rules and signs just for bikers: A bike in a blue circle indicates a bike route; a bike in a red circle indicates bikes are not allowed. Be alert, follow the blue bike signs, and these required bike paths will get you through even some of the most complicated highway interchanges. Beware of the silent biker who might be right behind you, and use hand signals before stopping or turning. Stay off the freeways. Little roads are nicer for biking, anyway.

Use good maps. Michelin's Europe and individual country maps are fine for overall planning. In Europe, use local maps for day-to-day navigation. Michelin and Die Generalkarte 1:200,000 maps reveal all the quiet back roads, and even the steepness of hills. Don't be obsessed with following a preplanned route. Delightful and spontaneous side trips are part of the spirit and joy of biking.

Taking your bike on a train greatly extends the reach of your trip. Every hour by rail saves a day that would have been spent in the saddle (and there's nothing so sweet as taking a train away from the rain and into a sunny place). To make sure you and your bike can travel on the same train, look for trains marked in timetables with little bicycle symbols, or ask at the station's information window.

Bike thieves abound in Europe. Use a good Kryptonite-style bike lock to secure your bike to something sturdy. Never leave your pump, water bottle, or computer on your bike when you can't see it. Keep your bike inside whenever possible. At hostels, ask if there is a locked bike room, and if not, ask or even plead for a place to put your bike inside overnight. Remember that hotels and many pensions don't really have rules against taking a bike up to your room. Just do it unobtrusively. You can even wheelie it into the elevator. Rich and Risa found campgrounds to be safe, but they always locked their bikes together.

Travel light . . . or camp. Unless you really love camping, staying in hostels or hotels makes more sense, since it frees you from lugging around a tent, sleeping bag, and cooking equipment. European campgrounds tend to be more crowded than American ones, so if you're willing to sacrifice privacy in order to mix with Europeans, camping can add a fun dimension to your trip.

A bike makes you more approachable. The most rewarding aspect of bicycling in Europe is meeting people. Europeans love bicycles, and they are often genuinely impressed when they encounter that rare American who rejects the view from the tour-bus window in favor of huffing and puffing through their country on two wheels. Your bike provides an instant conversation piece, the perfect bridge over a maze of cultural and language barriers.

HITCHHIKING—RULES OF THUMB

Hitching, sometimes called "auto-stop," is a popular and acceptable means of getting around in Europe. After picking up a Rhine riverboat captain in my rental car and running him back to his home port, I realized that hitchhiking doesn't wear the same hippie hat in Europe that it does in the United States.

Without a doubt, hitching is the cheapest means of transportation. It's also a great way to meet people. Most people who pick you up are genuinely interested in getting to know an American.

The farther you get from our culture's determination to be self-sufficient, the more volunteerism you'll encounter. Bumming a ride is a perfect example. In the Third World—rural Europe in the extreme—anything rolling with room will let you in. You don't hitch, you just flag the vehicle down.

Hitching is risky. Although hitching in Europe is safer than hitching in the United States, there is an ever-present danger any time you get into a stranger's car. That, coupled with the overabundance of lawyers in the United States, means I cannot recommend it. Personally, I don't hitchhike at home, and I wouldn't rely solely on my thumb to get me

Hitchhiking at the Bulgaria–Greece border, or wherever the train and bus schedules leave you stranded.

through Europe. But I never sit frustrated in a station for two hours because there isn't a bus or train to take me 15 miles down the road. Riding my thumb out of train and bus schedule problems, I can usually get to my destination in a friendly snap.

Hitching can be time-consuming. Some places have 20 or 30 people in a chorus line of thumbs, just waiting their turns. Once I said what I thought was goodbye forever to an Irishman after breakfast. He was heading north. We had dinner together that night, and I learned a lot about wasting a day on the side of a road. You'll find that Germany, Norway, Ireland, and Great Britain offer generally good hitchhiking, while southern countries are less reliable.

Learn the gestures. The hitchhiking gesture is not always the outstretched thumb. In some countries, you ring an imaginary bell. In others, you make a downward wave with your hand. Observe and learn.

Crank up your good judgment. Feel good about the situation before you commit yourself to it. Keep your luggage on your lap, or at least out of the trunk, so if things turn sour, you can excuse yourself quickly and easily. Women should not sit in the back seat of a two-door car. A fake wedding ring and modest dress are indications that you're interested only in transportation.

Consider your appearance. Look like the Cracker Jack boy or his sister—happy, wholesome, and a joy to have aboard. Establish eye contact. Charm the driver. Smile. Stand up. Don't walk and hitch. Pick a good spot on the road, giving the driver plenty of time to see you and a safe spot to pull over. Look respectable and a little gaunt. Arrange your luggage so it looks as small as possible. Those hitching with very little or no luggage enjoy a tremendous advantage.

A man and woman make the perfect combination. A single woman maximizes speed and risk. Two women travel more safely and nearly as fast. A single man with patience will do fine. Two guys go slow, and three or more should split up and rendezvous later. Single men and women are better off traveling together; these alliances are easily made at hostels. A man and a woman traveling together have it easy. If the woman hitches and the guy steps out of view around the corner or into a shop, they should both have a ride in a matter of minutes. (Dirty trick, but it works.)

Create pity. When I'm doing some serious hitching, I walk away from town and find a very lonely stretch of road. It seems that the sparser the traffic, the quicker I get a ride. On a busy road, people will assume that I'll manage without their ride. If only one car passes in five minutes, the driver senses that he may be my only chance.

Go the distance. To get the long ride, take a local bus out of town to the open country on the road to your destination. Make a cardboard sign with your destination printed big and bold in the local language, followed by the local "please." At borders, you might decide to choose only a ride which will take you entirely through that country. Use decals and license plates to determine where a car is from (and therefore likely heading). Every car has to have a large decal with a letter or two indicating in which country the car is registered. And in some countries (such as Germany and Italy), hometowns are indicated by the first few letters on the license plate.

Share-a-ride organizations match rides and riders. Look for Mitfahrzentralen in Germany and Allostop in France. You pay a small amount to join, and you help with gas expenses, but it works well and is much cheaper than train travel. Use student tourist information centers or big-city phone books. Informal ride services are on college and hostel bulletin boards all over Europe.

Try to meet the driver directly. Find a spot where cars stop, and you can encounter the driver face to thumb. A toll booth, border, gas station, or—best of all—a ferry ride gives you that chance to smile and convince him that he needs you in his car or truck. Although it's easy to zoom past a hitchhiker at 60 mph and not feel guilty, it's much more difficult to turn down an in-person request for a ride.

Hitching can become the destination. With the "hitch when you can't get a bus or train" approach, you'll find yourself walking down lovely rural roads and getting rides from safe and friendly small-town folk. I can recall some "it's great to be alive and on the road" days riding my thumb from tiny town to waterfall to desolate Celtic graveyard to coastal village and remembering each ride as much as the destinations. Especially in Ireland, I've found so much fun in the front seat that I've driven right by my planned destination to carry on with the conversation. In rural Ireland, I'd stand on the most desolate road in Connemara and hitch whichever way the car was coming. As I hopped in the driver would ask, "Where you goin'?" I'd say, "Ireland."

WALKING (AND DODGING)

You'll walk a lot in Europe. It's a great way to see cities, towns, and the countryside. Walking tours offer the most intimate look at a city or town. A walker complements the place she walks through by her interest and will be received warmly. Many areas, from the mountains to the beaches, are best seen on foot.

Be careful—walking can be dangerous. Pedestrians are run down every day. More than 300 pedestrians are run down annually on the streets of Paris. (And mom was worried about terrorism!) The drivers are crazy, and politeness has no place on the roads of Europe. Cross carefully, but if you wait for a break in the traffic, you may never get a chance to cross the street. Look for a pedestrian underpass or, when all else fails, find a heavy-set local person and just follow him like a shadow—one busy lane at a time—across that seemingly impassable street. Joggers have no problem finding good routes and can enjoy a good early morning tour as well as the exercise. Hotel receptionists usually know a good jogging route. Remember to carry identification and your hotel card with you.

Alpine trail signs show where you are, the altitude in meters, and how long in hours and minutes it takes to hike to nearby points.

HIKING

Imagine walking along a ridge high in the Swiss Alps. On one side of you, lakes stretch all the way to Germany. On the other sprawls the greatest mountain panorama in Europe—the Eiger, Monch, and Jungfrau. And then you hear the long legato tones of an alphorn,

A first-hand look at fairy-tale Alpine culture is just a hike away (Walderalm, above Hall in Tirol: See Part Two: Back Doors of Europe).

announcing that just ahead is a helicopter-stocked mountain hut, and the coffee schnapps is on.

Hiking in Europe is a joy. Travelers explore entire regions on foot. Switzerland's Jungfrau is an exciting sight from a hotel's terrace café, but those who hike the region enjoy nature's very own striptease as the mountain reveals herself in an endless string of powerful poses.

Romantics commune with nature from Norway's fjords to the English lakes to the Alps to the Riviera. Trails are generally well-kept and carefully marked. Very precise maps (scale 1:25,000) are readily available.

You could walk through the Alps for weeks—sleeping in mountain huts—and never come out of the mountains. You're never more than a day's hike from a mountain village, where you can replenish your food supply or enjoy a hotel and a restaurant meal. Most Alpine trails are free of snow by July, and lifts take less rugged visitors to the top in a sweat-free flash.

Throughout the Alps, trail markings are both handy and humiliating. Handy, because they show hours to hike rather than miles to walk to various destinations. Humiliating, because these times are clocked by local senior citizens. You'll know what I mean after your first hike.

Do some research before you leave. Buy the most appropriate hiking guidebook. Ask for maps and advice from the National Tourist Offices (for a list of tourist offices, see Chapter 2: Gathering Information).

MONEY AND YOUR BUDGET

13. Money

Years ago, it was just traveler's checks. Karl Malden warned sternly, "Don't leave home without them." Well, he's old hat and Europe is changing. Now ATM cards, credit cards, and debit cards compete with traveler's checks as the best way to change your dollars into European currency.

Smart budget travelers function in Europe with hard local cash. The big question is how to most conveniently and economically change your dollars into the European currencies. Banks make money from you in two ways: with fees and rates. There are two categories of rates: 1) lousy tourist rates—which are used for over-the-counter cash or traveler's checks exchanges and vary from mediocre at a good bank to criminal at some change desks; and 2) excellent "bank" rates—which banks give to each other and which you'll enjoy when you use a credit card, debit card, or ATM. Fees, charged for almost any money-changing transaction, vary enough to wipe out any gains you made by getting the right rate.

Those relying solely on credit cards and ATMs get the best rates but waste time looking for a bank or branch that speaks their electronic language. In a few years traveler's checks will not exist. But it's a little early to dump them entirely. Rely on a mix. Here's a review of your banking options.

TRAVELER'S CHECKS

Traveler's checks function almost like cash but are replaceable if lost or stolen. You need to choose the company, the currency, and a mix of denominations.

The company usually doesn't matter. Choose whichever big, well-known company (American Express, Cooks, Barclays, Visa) you can get for no fee. Ask around. There are plenty of ways to avoid that extra 1.5 percent charge. Any legitimate check is good at banks, but it's helpful when you're in a jam to have a well-known check that private parties and small shops will recognize and honor. In many cases traveler's checks get a better exchange rate than cash, so they can even save you money.

If you're traveling only in England, go with Barclays—a British bank with a branch in every town. They waive the $2- to $5-per-transaction service charge if you have their checks.

The American Express Company, or AmexCo, is popular for its centrally located "landmark" offices (listed at www.americanexpress.com on the Web), travel service, and clients' mail service. AmexCo checks (which normally come with a 1.5 percent charge) are free through AAA. While AmexCo offices offer mediocre exchange rates, they usually change their checks without the customary $2 to $5 fee. This fee relief can make up for their bad rates if you're exchanging less than several hundred dollars.

AmexCo has two helpful services for people planning long-term trips or carrying lots of money. You can keep your money belt thin by using their $500 or $1,000 checks, which can be broken free and fast into smaller checks (in dollars) at most AmexCo offices. Those with AmexCo cards can travel anywhere, buying traveler's checks as they go from AmexCo offices abroad, writing personal checks on their personal bank accounts (up to $10,000 per 21 days with a platinum card, $5,000 with a gold card, and $1,000 with their regular peasant's card). This method is particularly handy in Eastern Europe.

Understand the refund policy. Lost or stolen traveler's checks are replaceable only if you keep track of the serial numbers and know exactly which checks you've cashed and lost. Leave a photocopy of all your check numbers (along with photocopies of your passport, plane ticket, credit cards, and any other vital statistics) with someone at home, in your luggage, and in your wallet. Your original traveler's checks receipt is an important document. Keep it handy but separate from your checks (you may need to show it to cash a check). Use checks in numerical order and update your list regularly as you cash them. Do a complete inventory each week. Thieves may steal checks from the middle of your wad hoping the checks they swipe will go unnoticed. Get a police report after any theft. Report the loss to your issuing bank within 24 hours. (Travel with their emergency phone numbers.)

A traveler's check is a traveler's check. You'll hear many stories about slow or fast refunds. None of them matter. Extenuating circumstances— not the company—dictate the refund speed. If you keep your money belt tied around your waist and your brain tied to your head, you won't lose your checks.

For most trips, buy checks in U.S. dollars. Traveler's checks come in U.S. dollars, Swiss francs, British pounds, Deutsche marks, and even Japanese yen. When the dollar is shaky, many travelers consider bailing out early and buying traveler's checks in another, more stable, currency. You lose a couple of percent with this transaction, and then you lose 2 or 3 percent more when you change your "strong currency" into the local currency you need. The dollar does not drop drastically or predictably enough to merit this double loss. Get traveler's checks in U.S. dollars for this reason and because it's simpler. We think in dollars.

If your trip is mostly in one country, however, and the dollar is on a downward trend, you might buy checks in the currency of that country. But if you over-buy and have to trade them back to dollars, you've double changed with a double loss—expensive. If you bring home extra traveler's checks in dollars and have to change back, you lose nothing.

Get a mix of denominations. For $2,000 in checks, I would choose 13 $100, 10 $50, and 10 $20 checks. Large checks ($100, $500) save on signing and bulk. Since many banks (especially in Scandinavia) are charging their $2 to $4 fee per check rather than per transaction, large denominations can save money. Small checks ($20, $50) are more exact and, sometimes, easier to cash. If you're only passing through a country, you may want just $20. If you have only $100 checks, you'll have to change back $80. (You'll end up changing a total of $180 at that 2 or 3 percent loss with two bank fees to get $20. Ouch.) If you're out of cash and the banks are closed, it's easy to find a merchant or another traveler who will change a $20 check. Changing a large check in such a situation would be tough.

CASH MACHINES (ATMS)

Common in most of Europe, cash machines are quickly becoming the standard way for American travelers to change money. European ATMs work like your hometown machine and have English language instructions. An ATM withdrawal takes dollars directly from your bank account at home and gives you that country's cash. Your account is billed in dollars at the "wholesale" rate, which is always better than the traveler's checks' rate. Many travelers are doing entire trips on ATMs and give this method rave reviews—and never stand in a bank line.

Know your personal identification number (PIN) and confirm with your home bank that it will work in Europe. Ask exactly where, with which systems, what fees, and on what machines. (Tellers say, "It works everywhere: Bermuda, Canada, Virgin Islands, even Britain." But there's more to "Europe" than that.) Since European keypads have only numbers, you'll want a PIN with numbers and no letters (derive the numbers from your hometown bank's keypad). There are two dominant ATM systems: Plus and Cirrus. Those traveling with a credit card for each of these systems (you'll see the Plus or Cirrus logos on your Visa and MasterCard) double their cash advance options and avoid a little running around. Ask your banker how much you can withdraw per 24 hours and what the charge is for using a foreign ATM. For the location of Cirrus ATMs, call 800/424-7787 (www.mastercard.com); for Plus, go to www.visa.com. The glory days of the ATM may be numbered as bankers are learning they can add a 2 percent or so fee. Be sure to understand the latest fees.

CASH ADVANCES
Many fund their travels by relying solely on cash advances. They use their credit (or debit) card in banks all over Europe to change money quickly, easily, and at a good rate. Visa is the most commonly accepted card for cash advances.

The problem with using a credit card is that you are immediately into the 18 percent interest category with your new credit-card debt. (There's no one-month grace period on cash advances.) Avoid this by overpaying on your credit card before leaving home and drawing down on that amount. A debit card lets you avoid all interest concerns by drawing money from your existing bank account as if you were simply writing a personal check.

BUYING ON PLASTIC
Charge cards work fine throughout Europe (at hotels, gas stations, shops, fancy restaurants, travel agencies, and so on), although more and more merchants are establishing a $30 minimum. Visa and MasterCard are most widely accepted. American Express is much less widely accepted but popular for its extra services. Bring two cards in case one is demagnetized or eaten by a machine.

Plastic fans gloat that you get a better exchange rate by using your card. While it is true that plastic transactions are processed at the best possible exchange rate, card users are buying from businesses that have enough slack in their prices to absorb the bank's fee for the charge service. Those who travel on their plastic may be getting a better rate, but on a worse price. (As more and more consumers believe they are getting "free use of the bank's money," we're all absorbing the 4 percent the banks are making in higher purchase prices.)

Credit-card scams are commonplace, and many travelers are ripped off big-time. Know what you're signing, understand the numbers, and keep the receipts. Keep all bank cards safely in your money belt.

I use my charge card for cash advances, making hotel reservations by phone, major purchases (such as car rentals and plane tickets), car-rental security (usually required), and to avoid a trip to the bank when I'm low on cash at the end of my stay in a country. But a dependence on plastic reshapes the Europe you experience. Pedro's Pension, the guide at the cathedral, and the merchants in the market take only cash. Going through the back door requires hard local cash.

CHANGING MONEY AT BANKS
You'd be appalled if you knew how much money you'll lose in banks over the course of your trip. You can't avoid these losses, but you can minimize

them by understanding how the banks make their money. In spite of their ads, no bank really likes people. They like your money. Banks change money only to make money.

Look for fees and rates. Banks make money changing money in two ways: from fees and from rates. Banks with great rates have high fees. Others have lousy rates and no fees. Any place advertising "no fees" should complete the equation with "and lousy rates." For a small exchange, you don't care what the rate is, you want no fee. For a large exchange, the fee doesn't matter—you want a good rate. When I change $2,000 for one of my tours, I can save $50 in a few minutes by checking three banks and choosing the one whose strategy is to profit from its fees rather than its rates. These fees are often listed as a percentage with a fixed minimum.

Study this example: Krankenbank offers 1.55 DM per dollar and charges a small 1-DM fee. Alpenbank offers a better rate—1.60 DM per dollar—but charges a 4-DM fee. For $50 I'll get 76.50 DM at Krankenbank (50 x 1.55 less 1 DM) and only 76 DM at Alpenbank (50 x 1.6 less 4 DM). But if I change $500, I'll get 774 DM at Krankenbank (500 x 1.55 less 1 DM) and 796 DM at Alpenbank (500 x 1.60 less 4 DM). For a small exchange, Krankenbank gives me the most marks. For a $500 exchange, I get 22 DM extra at Alpenbank—$15 more.

Change only at places showing both rates. Every decent place that changes money displays both their buying and selling rates. The English

US DOLLAR	2.90
ENG. POND	4.30
BELG. FR.	5.35
DUITSE MK.	1.05
FR. FRANC	0.35
ZW. FRANC	1.30
ZW. KROON	0.35
ITAL. LIRE	18.00
CAN. DOLL.	2.20
SP. PESETA	1.85
OOST. SHILL	15.00
NOORSE KR.	0.37
DEENSE K.	0.29
FINSE MK	0.49
DRACHME	3.15
JAP. YEN	1.05
YOEG. DIN	3.00
IERS POND	3.40

*If they show you only one rate . . .
it's a bad one.*

bank in the photo is selling British pounds for $1.43 and buying them for $1.50 (third line up from bottom). After all the traveling I've done, I still can't conceptualize what's what here. Who's getting pounds? Who's giving dollars? It doesn't matter. We lose.

Here, all the cards are clearly on the table. This money changer is a pro, and you can see what he buys for and what he sells for. You don't need to shop around for the real rate. The true value of the local currency is halfway between what the pros buy and sell it for. In this case, a pound would be worth about $1.46. If I can establish a split of 5 percent (1.43 to 1.50 is the same as 95 to 100) and the fee is reasonable, it's fair. For maximum clarity when comparing banks, ask how much you'll get for $200 (or whatever) in traveler's checks. Tellers will quickly figure the fees and rates and give you a hard bottom line to compare with the next place.

Avoid "one-rate" exchange bureaus. Places that show only one rate are hiding something—an obscene profit margin. Check it out. Every rip-off exchange desk at every border crossing, casino, and nightclub in Europe shows only one rate . . . and it's a lousy one.

Minimize trips to the bank. It's expensive and time-consuming to change money. Bring your passport, find a decent bank, estimate carefully what you'll need, and get it all at once when you enter a new country. Rather than risk having to endure another round of bank hassles and expenses on your last day in a country, change a little more than you'll need. I leave most countries with a little extra paper money and economically flush all of those into the currency of the last country on my trip.

Most banks, especially in touristy places, levy a service fee for each transaction. This added charge is usually higher for checks than cash, but many banks give a slightly better exchange rate for checks than cash. (They prefer traveler's checks to cash for the same reason we do.) Clearly understand their extra-charge policy before you start signing checks.

CASH

Carry plenty of cash. Cash in your money belt comes in handy for emergencies, such as when banks go on strike. I've been in Greece and Ireland when every bank went on strike, shutting down without warning. Some places (such as Russia) make life with traveler's checks very difficult. But hard cash is cash. People always know roughly what a dollar, mark, or pound is worth, and you can always sell it.

On a short trip, you may want to leave home with a wad of $100 bills in your money belt. If you don't mind the risk, this can be the simplest way to fund your trip.

To save time and money, bring one day's budget in each country's currency with you from home. Your bank can sell you one bill worth around $50 from each country for a fair price. (You might compare those rates with AFEX in San Francisco, tel. 800/525-2339.) With six bills—for six countries—hidden safely in your money belt, you'll have enough money to get settled in each new country without worrying about banking. Arriving at night or when the banks are closed with $2,000 in your money belt but not enough local cash to catch a subway or make a phone call is maddening. After-hours exchange places come with long lines and terrible rates.

Use local money. Many Americans exclaim gleefully, "Gee, they accept dollars! There's no need to change money." Without knowing it, they're changing money—at a lousy rate—every time they buy something with their dollars. Many claim you get a better exchange rate by purchasing things directly with your credit card. This advice is only good for business travelers who eat and sleep at international-style places that always accept plastic but offer poor values. Anyone on a budget will stretch it by using hard local cash. Local hotels and small businesses, which suffer huge bank fees when they take your traveler's checks, prefer cash.

Figure out the money. To "ugly Americans," foreign money is "funny money." They never figure it out, get no respect from the locals, and are constantly ripped off. Local currencies are all logical. Each system is decimalized just like ours. There are a hundred "little ones" (cents, pence, centimes, pfennig, stotinki) in every "big one" (dollar, pound, franc, mark, leva). Only the names have been changed—to confuse the tourist. Get a good sampling of coins after you arrive, and in two minutes you'll be comfortable with the "nickels, dimes, and quarters" of each new currency. A currency-converting calculator isn't worth the trouble.

Very roughly, figure out what the unit of currency (franc, mark, krona, or whatever) is worth in American cents. For example, if there are 1.5 Deutsche marks in a dollar, each DM is a 70-cent piece. If a hot dog costs 5 marks, then it costs five 70-cent pieces or $3.50. Fifty little ones (pfennig) equals half a mark (35 cents). If mustard costs 10 pfennig (a tenth of a 70-cent piece), it costs the equivalent of 7 cents. Ten marks is $7, and 250 DM = $175 (250 x .7 or 250 less one-third). Quiz yourself. Soon it'll be second nature. Survival on a budget is easier when you're comfortable with the local currency.

Italian lire, around 1,600 to the dollar, drive visiting Yankees crazy. To translate, simply cover the last three digits with your finger and cut what's left by a third: 18,000 lire for dinner equals about $12; 75,000 lire for a hotel is about $50; 620,000 lire for a taxi ride is about . . . uh-oh.

Assume you'll be shortchanged. In banks, restaurants, at ticket booths, everywhere—assume you'll be shortchanged if you don't do your own figuring. People who spend their lives sitting in booths for eight hours a day taking money from strangers often have no problem stealing from dumb tourists who don't know the local currency. For 10 minutes I observed a man in the Rome metro shortchanging half of the tourists who went through his turnstile. Half of those shortchanged caught him and got their correct change with apologies. Overall, about 25 percent didn't notice and went home saying, "Boy, Italy is really expensive."

Paper money of any Western country is good at banks anywhere. Dollars are not sacred. If you leave Italy with paper money, that 10,000-lire note is just as convertible as dollars at any European bank or exchange office. Many people change excess local money back to dollars before they leave a country. Then they change those dollars into the next country's money. This double changing makes no sense and is expensive. It can be handy, however, to change your remaining local currency into the next country's currency before leaving a country. But changing dollars into, say, francs in Germany will send you through the bank expense wringer twice, since you'll actually be changing twice: from dollars to marks, and from marks to francs. Getting American cash from dollar traveler's checks is also expensive—you'll go through that same wringer twice.

There are 24-hour money munchers in big cities all over Europe. At midnight in Florence, you can push in a $20 bill (or any major European currency) and, assuming the president (or royalty) is on the right side, the correct value of local currency will tumble out. They are handy and open all the time, but rates can be bad. Use these only when decent rates and fees are clearly listed.

Coins are generally worthless outside their country. Since $3 coins are common in Europe, exporting a pocketful of change can be an expensive mistake. Spend them (postcards, newspaper, a quick phone call home, food or drink for the train ride), change them into paper before you cross the border, or give them away. Otherwise, you've just bought a bunch of souvenirs. The rare exceptions are border towns, which sometimes accept both currencies. For instance, waiters in Salzburg keep German money in one side of their coin bags, Austrian in the other.

Some Eastern European currencies are worthless outside their country. While paper money from any Western country is good at banks in every other country, some Eastern European currencies are still "soft"—kept at unrealistically high rates. You can't avoid buying this money when you're in Bulgaria, Romania, the Baltics, or Turkey. But it's worthless (or nearly so) in Western Europe. Until Eastern currency becomes hard, exchange it, spend it, buy candles in churches, ice cream cones for strangers: Give it away if you have to—but don't take it out of its country.

Getting back to dollars at the end of your trip. At your final European country, gather together all the small bills left over from your trip and change them into that final currency. It costs no more to change five different currencies into marks than one currency. If you have bills left over as you fly home, it's simplest to change them into dollars at your last European airport, but, remembering that banks only go from one currency to another via their own, you'll suffer double exchange losses. Your hometown bank will give you a few more dollars for that last smattering of foreign bills.

14. Your Budget

Many Americans are saying, "Europe's getting expensive!" Actually, it's staying about the same, and, in relative terms, we're getting poorer. Travelers from post-Reagan America, a debtor nation with a reshuffled social deck, are no longer as affluent as their European counterparts. This becomes painfully clear when you compare buying power with new European friends. Most of today's Europe is more expensive than the United States, and the sloppy traveler can blow a small fortune in a hurry. You can live well in Europe on a budget, but it will take some artistry, and if you travel like a big shot, you'd better be loaded.

I'm cautious about sending people to Europe without enough money and skills. The tips in this book are tried and tested in the worst circumstances every year. And my feedback from Back Door travelers bolsters my confidence. It can be done—by you.

TRIP COSTS

In 1999, you can travel comfortably for a month for around $3,500—not including your airfare ($700–1,000). If you have extra money, it's more fun to spend it in Europe.

Allow:

$800 for a one-month Eurailpass or split car rental
  600 for sightseeing
  300 for entertainment/shopping/miscellany
+1,800 for room and board ($60 a day)
$3,500

Students or rock-bottom budget travelers can enjoy a month of Europe at least as much for about a third less—$2,150 plus airfare.

Allow:

$600 for a one-month youth Eurailpass
  300 for sightseeing
  200 for entertainment/shopping/miscellany
+1,050 for room and board ($35 a day)*
$2,150

*$20 for a dorm bed or a bed in a private home with breakfast, $5 for a picnic lunch, $10 for dinner.

BUDGET BREAKDOWN

Airfare: Flying to Europe is a bargain. Get a good agent, understand all your options, and make the best choice. Traveling outside of peak season will save you several hundred dollars.

Surface Transportation: Transportation in Europe is reasonable if you take advantage of a Eurailpass or split a car rental between three or four people. Transportation expenses are generally fixed. People who spend $8,000 for their vacation spend about the same on transportation as do those whose trips cost half as much. Your budget should not dictate how freely you travel in Europe. If you want to go somewhere, do it, taking advantage of whatever money-saving options you can. You came to travel.

Sightseeing: Sightseeing costs have risen faster than anything else. Admissions to major attractions are now $5 to $10, smaller sights are $2 to $3. Don't skimp here. This category directly powers most of the experiences all the other expenses are designed to make possible.

Entertainment/Shopping/Miscellany: This part of the budget can vary from nearly nothing to a small fortune. Figure about $2 each for coffee, beer, ice cream, soft drink, and bus and subway ride, and $10 to $30 for evening entertainment. Good budget travelers find that this category has little to do with assembling a trip full of lifelong and wonderful memories.

Room and Board: The area that will make or break your budget—where you have the most control—is in your eating and sleeping expenses. In 1999, smart travelers can thrive on $60 a day (less if necessary) for room and board. Figure on $35 per person in a $70 hotel double with breakfast, $10 apiece for lunch, and $15 for dinner.

The key is finding budget alternatives to international-class hotels and restaurants, and consuming only what you want to consume. If you want real tablecloths and black-tie waiters, your tomato salad will cost 20 times what it costs in the market. If you want a private shower, toilet, room service, TV, and chocolate on your pillow, you'll pay in a day what many travelers pay in a week for a good, quiet eight hours of sleep.

My idea of "cheap" is simple but not sleazy. My budget morality is to never sacrifice safety, reasonable cleanliness, sleep, or nutrition to save money. I go to safe, central, friendly, local-style hotels, shunning TVs, swimming pools, people in uniforms, private plumbing, and transplanted American niceties in favor of an opportunity to travel as a temporary

European. Unfortunately, simple is subversive in the 1990s, and the system is bullying even cozy Scottish bed and breakfast places into more and more facilities, more and more debt, and higher and higher prices.

I traveled every summer for years on a part-time piano teacher's income (and, boy, was she upset). I ate and slept great by learning and using the skills in the following guidelines.

EATING AND SLEEPING ON A BUDGET

You can get eight good, safe hours of sleep and three square meals in Europe for $30 a day if your budget requires it. If your budget is tight, keep the following rules of thumb in your wallet.

Minimize the use of hotels and restaurants. Enjoying the sights and culture of Europe has nothing to do with how much you're spending to eat and sleep. Take advantage of each country's many alternatives to hotels and restaurants. If your budget dictated, you could have a great trip without hotels and restaurants—and probably learn, experience, and enjoy more than most tourists.

Budget for price variances. Prices as much as double from south to north. Budget more for the north and get by on less than your daily allowance in Spain, Portugal, and Greece. Exercise those budget alternatives where they'll save you the most money. A hostel saves $3 in Crete and $30 in Finland. In Scandinavia I picnic, walk, and sleep on trains, but I live like a king in southern Europe, where my splurge dollars go the farthest. And if your trip will last only as long as your money does, travel fast in the north and hang out in the south.

Swallow pride and save money. This is a personal matter, depending largely on how much pride and money you have. Many people cringe every time I use the word "cheap"; others appreciate the directness. I'm not talking about begging and groveling around Europe. I'm talking about choosing a room with no shower ($15 saved), drinking tap water ($3 saved), and lunching on uneaten portions from the cafeteria's dirty tray rack ($6 saved).

Find out the complete price before ordering anything, and say "no thanks" if the price isn't right. Expect equal and fair treatment as a tourist. When appropriate, fight the price, set a limit, and search on. Remember, even if the same thing would cost much more at home, the local rate should prevail. If you act like a rich fool, you're likely to be treated as one.

Avoid the tourist centers. The best values are not in the places that boast in neon: "We Speak English." Find places that earn a loyal local following. You'll get more for your money. If you do follow the tourists, follow the savvy Germans; never follow tour groups.

Adapt to European tastes. Most unhappy people I meet in my travels could find the source of their problems in their own stubborn desire to find the United States in Europe. If you accept and at least try doing things the European way, besides saving money you'll be happier and learn more on your trip. You cannot expect the local people to accept you warmly if you don't accept them. Things are different in Europe—that's why you go. European travel is a package deal. Accept the good with the "bad." If you require the comforts of home, that's where you'll be happiest.

Be a good guest. To Europeans, Americans occasionally act as though they "just got off the boat" (shoes on the train seats, grapes chilling in the bidet, talking loudly in restaurants, flash attachments and camcorders during Mass, wet clothes hanging out the window, and consuming energy like it's cheap and ours to waste). The Europeans you'll deal with can sour or sweeten your experience, depending on how they react to you. When you're in good favor with the receptionist or whomever, you can make things happen that people whose bucks talk can't.

Each year as I update my books, I hear over and over in my recommended hotels and private homes that my *Back Door* readers are the most considerate and fun-to-have guests. Thank you for traveling sensitive to the culture and as temporary locals. It's fun to follow you in my travels.

15. Sleeping

Hotels are the most expensive way to sleep and, of course, the most comfortable. With a reasonable budget, I spend most of my nights in hotels, but they can rip through a tight budget like a grenade in a dollhouse.

I always hear people complaining about that "$250 double in Frankfurt" or the "$200-a-night room in London." They come back from their vacations with bruised and battered pocketbooks, telling stories that scare their friends out of international travel and back to Florida or Hawaii one more time. True, you can spend $200 for a double, but I never have. That's four days' accommodations for me.

As far as I'm concerned, spending more for your hotel just builds a bigger wall between you and what you came to see. If you spend enough, you won't know where you are. Think about it. "In-ter-con-ti-nent-al." That means the same everywhere—designed for people who deep down inside wish they weren't traveling; people spending someone else's money; people who need a strap over the toilet telling them no one's sat there yet. It's uniform sterility, a lobby full of Stay-Press Americans with wheels on their suitcases, English menus, and lamps bolted to the tables.

Europe's small hotels and guest houses may have no room service and offer only a shower down the hall, but their staffs are more interested in seeing pictures of your children and helping you have a great time than in thinning out your wallet.

Europe is full of European hotels—dingy, old-fashioned, a bit rundown, central, friendly, safe, and government-regulated, offering good-enough-for-the-European-good-enough-for-me beds for $30 to $40 a night ($40–80 doubles). No matter what your favorite newspaper travel writer or travel agent says, this is hardcore Europe: fun, cheap, and easy to find.

WHAT'S A CHEAP ROOM?

In a typical budget European hotel, a double room costs an average of $50 a night. You'll pay about $40 at a pension in Madrid, $50 at a simple guest house in Germany or a one-star hotel in Paris, and $60 for a private room in a Stockholm home.

A typical room has a simple bed (occasionally a springy cot, so always check); a rickety, pre–World War II or new plastic chair and table; a free-standing closet; a small window; old wallpaper; a good sink under a neon light; a mysterious bidet; a view of another similar room across a tall, thin courtyard; peeling plaster; and a tiled or wood floor. The light fixtures are very simple, often with a weak and sometimes even bare and dangling ceiling light bulb. Some travelers BYOB when they travel. A higher wattage kills a lot of dinginess. Naked neon is common in the south. While Britain

Andrea Hagg

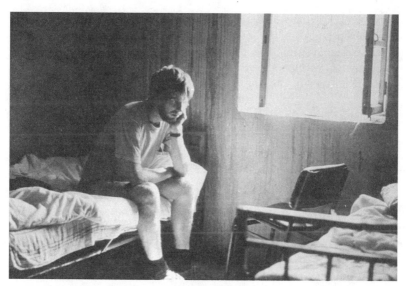

1977: It slowly dawns on Rick that cheap beds aren't always good beds.

has many smoke-free places, nearly all rooms on the Continent come with ashtrays. You won't have a TV or telephone, and, while more and more European hotels are squeezing boat-type prefab showers and toilets into their rooms, the cheapest rooms offer only a WC and shower or tub down the hall, which you share with a half-dozen other rooms.

Rooms often come with a continental breakfast (usually served from about 7:30 to 10:00 a.m. in the breakfast room near the front desk): coffee, tea, or hot chocolate, and a roll that's firmer than your mattress.

In the lobby there is nearly always a living room with a good TV, a couple of phone booths, and a person at the desk who is at your service and a good information source. You'll climb lots of stairs, as a hotel's lack of an elevator is often the only reason it can't raise its prices. You'll be given a front-door key because the desk is not staffed all night.

The bottom-of-the-line European hotel ($60 doubles in the north, $40 in the south) usually has clean enough but depressing shower rooms, with hot water normally free and constant (but occasionally available only through a coin-op meter or at certain hours). The WC, or toilet, is reliably clean and has toilet paper but is often missing its lid or has a cracked or broken plastic lid. In some hotels, you pay $2 to $5 for a towel and a key to the shower room. The cheapest hotels are run by and filled with people from the Two-thirds World.

I want to stress that there are places I find unacceptable. I don't mind dingy wallpaper, climbing stairs, and "going down the hall," but the place must be clean, central, friendly, safe, quiet enough for me to sleep well, and equipped with good beds.

The bottom-of-the-line hotel described above is appalling to many Americans; it's charming, colorful, or funky to others. To me, "funky" means spirited and full of character(s): a caged bird in the TV room, grandchildren in the backyard, a dog sleeping in the hall, no uniforms, singing maids, a night-shift man tearing breakfast napkins in two so they'll go farther, a handwritten neighborhood history lesson on the wall, different furniture in each room, and a willingness to buck the system when the local tourist board starts requiring shoeshine machines in the hallways. An extra $15 or $20 per night will buy you into cheerier wallpaper and less funkiness.

There is a real trend toward materialism throughout Europe. Land in big cities is so expensive that cheap hotels can't survive and are bought out, gutted, and turned into modern hotels. More and more Europeans are expecting what, until lately, have been considered American standards of plumbing and comfort. A great value is often a hardworking family-run place that structurally can't fit showers in every room and an elevator up its spiral staircase. Prices are regulated, and

Budget hotels can be comfortable, cheery, and friendly.

Rich Sorensen

In a Back Door–style hotel, you get more by spending less. Here, the shower's down the hall, and the Alps are in your lap.

regardless of how good it is, with no elevator and a lousy shower-to-room ratio, it's a cheap hotel.

MAKING RESERVATIONS

I used to travel with absolutely no reservations. A daily chore was checking out several hotels or pensions and choosing one. Europe was ramshackle, things were cheap, hotel listings were unreliable and unnecessary. Now, like hobos in a Jetson world, budget travelers need to think one step ahead.

Use a good guidebook. Choose a guidebook whose travel philosophy matches yours. These days, those who rely on the tourist office or go potluck are likely to spend $30 more than necessary and get a lousy room. That's why I give hotel listings a very high priority in researching and writing my eight country guidebooks.

Call ahead. My standard peak season room-finding tactic (assuming I know where I want to be) is to telephone in the morning to reserve my room for the night. I travel relaxed, knowing a good place is holding a room for me until late afternoon. A simple phone call a little in advance assures me a good-value room. Lately, I've been getting aced out by my own readers. So when I want to be certain to get my first choice, I call two or three days in advance.

Remember, a hotel prefers a cash deposit with a reservation unless there's not enough time to mail it in. In this case, most hotels will hold a room without a deposit if you promise to arrive early. The earlier you promise, the better your chances of being trusted. If you'll be a little late, call again to assure them you're coming. Also, cancel if you won't make it. If someone cancels after 5:00 p.m. and the room-finding service is closed, the room will probably go unfilled that night. When that happens too often, hotel managers start to get really surly and insist on cash deposits.

It's generally unnecessary to reserve long in advance. Reserving your hotels months in advance through your travel agent or room-booking agency is a needless and expensive security blanket. You won't know what you're getting. You'll destroy your itinerary flexibility. And you'll pay top dollar.

I make reservations from the United States only for my first night's accommodations, when huge crowds are anticipated, and in places in which I know for certain I want to stay and exactly when I'll be there.

Try to fax your long-distance reservations. Fax machines are standard now in European hotels, most pensions, and in many B&Bs. Photocopy and use the handy fax form included in this chapter. A typed fax in simple English communicates clearly, minimizes the language barrier (especially helpful in southern Europe, where, because of the language barrier, a phone call will accomplish little), and gives your hotel a quick and easy way to respond. If you don't get a response, assume the hotel received and understood your request and has no room available for you. You can also make a reservation by telephone (about $1 a minute from the U.S.).

In your fax, always list your dates (with date and expected time of arrival, number of nights you'll stay, and date of departure), your room needs (number of people, the facilities you require), and your budget concerns (of course, a trade-off with facilities), and ask for mercy on their deposit requirements (either by promising to telephone a day in advance to reconfirm or giving them your credit-card number with expiration date as security). Including your credit-card information avoids an extra volley of faxes. Request a written confirmation with the price quoted.

Ideally your credit-card number will be accepted as a deposit. If a cash deposit is required, you can mail a bank draft or, easier, a signed $50 traveler's check. (Leave the "pay to" line blank and encourage them to avoid bank fees by just holding the check as security until you arrive and can pay in cash.)

Don't panic. If, after several tries, it seems that every hotel in town is full, don't worry. Hotels take only so many long-distance advance reservations. They never know how long guests will stay and like to keep a few beds for their regulars. Call between 8:00 and 10:00 a.m. the morning you plan to arrive. This is when the receptionist knows exactly who's leaving and which rooms he needs to fill. He'll be eager to get a name for every available room. Those who are there in person are more likely to land a room. Many simple hotels don't bother with reservations more than a couple of weeks in advance, and some very cheap hotels take no reservations at all. Just show up and sleep with your money belt on.

BASIC BED-FINDING

In more than a thousand unreserved nights in Europe, I've been shut out three times. That's a 99.7 percent bedding average earned in peak

Faxing Your Hotel Reservation

Most hotel managers know basic "hotel English." Faxing is the preferred method for reserving a room. It's more accurate and cheaper than telephoning and much faster than writing a letter. Use this handy form for your fax. Photocopy and fax away.

One-Page Fax

To: _____ @ _____
          hotel   *fax*

From: _____ @ _____
            name   *fax*

Today's date: ____ / ____ / ____
                   day   month   year

Dear Hotel _____,
Please make this reservation for me:
Name: _____
Total # of people: _____   # of rooms: _____   # of nights: _____

Arriving: ____ / ____ / ____ My time of arrival (24-hr clock): _____
              day   month   year   (I will telephone if I will be late)
Departing: ____ / ____ / ____
                day   month   year

Room(s): Single___ Double___ Twin___ Triple___ Quad___
With: Toilet___ Shower___ Bath___ Sink only___
Special needs: View___ Quiet___ Cheapest Room___

Credit card: Visa___ MasterCard___ American Express___
Card #: _____ Exp. date: _____
Name on card: _____

You may charge me for the first night as a deposit. Please fax or mail me confirmation of my reservation, along with the type of room reserved, the price, and whether the price includes breakfast. Thank you.

_____
Signature

_____
Name

_____
Address

_____
City   *State*   *Zip Code*   *Country*

_____
E-mail address

season and very often in crowded, touristy, or festive places. What's so traumatic about a night without a bed anyway? My survey shows those who have the opportunity to be a refugee for a night have their perspectives broadened and actually enjoy the experience—in retrospect.

The cost of a wonderfully reservation-free trip is the remote chance you'll end up spending the night on a bench in the train station waiting room. Every year, I travel peak season (lately, with my wife and kids or a television film crew), arrive early or call a day or so in advance, and manage fine by using the few tricks listed here.

Travel with a good list of hotels. I spend more time in Europe finding and checking hotels (for my country guidebooks) than anything else. I can spend a day in Amsterdam, scaling the stairs and checking out the rooms of 20 different hotels, all offering double rooms from $50 to $100 a night. After doing the grand analysis, what's striking to me is how little correlation there is between what you pay and what you get. You are just as likely to spend $90 for a big impersonal place on a noisy highway as you are to spend $60 for a charming family-run guesthouse on a bikes-only stretch of canal.

These days, to sleep well and inexpensively on a big-city bed, you need a good guidebook's listing of hotels and budget alternatives. These lists are reliable and work well (but prices have likely gone up since the book was printed). Few guidebooks have the guts to list the very least expensive options. In the last few years, I've expanded my country guides to include all the room listings you'll need for the parts of Europe I cover.

Use room-finding services. Popular tourist cities usually have a room-finding service at the train station or tourist information office. They have a listing of that town's "acceptable" available accommodations. For a fee of a few dollars, they'll get you a room in the price range and neighborhood of your choice. Especially in a big city (if you don't have a guidebook's listings), their service can be worth the price when you consider the time and money saved by avoiding the search on foot.

I use room-finding services only when I have no listings or information of my own. Their hotel lists normally make no quality judgments, so what you get is potluck. The stakes are too high for this to be acceptable (especially when you consider how readily available good hotel listings are in guidebooks). Also, since many room-finding services profit from taking a "deposit" that they pocket, many managers of the best budget places tell the room-finding service they're full when they aren't. They know they'll fill up with travelers coming direct, allowing them to keep 100 percent of the room cost.

Recently some tourist information offices have lost their government funding and are now privately owned. This creates the absurdity of a profit-seeking tourist information "service." Their previously reliable advice is now colored with a need to make a kickback. Some room-finding services work for a group of supporting hotels. Room-finding services are not above pushing you into their "favored" hotels, and kickbacks are powerful motivators. Room-finding services give information on cheap sleep options—dormitory, hostel, and "sleep-in" (circus tents, gyms with mattresses on the floor, and other $10-a-night alternatives to the park or station)—only if you insist. And beware, many "tourist information offices" are just travel agencies and room-booking services in disguise.

Use the telephone. If you're looking on your own, telephone the places in your guidebook that sound best. Not only will it save the time and money involved in chasing down these places with the risk of finding them full, but you're beating all the other tourists—with the same guidebook—who may be hoofing it as you dial. It's rewarding to arrive at a hotel when people are being turned away and see your name on the reservation list because you called first. If the room or price isn't what you were led to believe it would be, you have every right to say, "No, thank you." If you like and trust the values of your guidebook's author, track down his recommendations by phone and use the tourist office only as a last resort.

Consider hotel runners. As you step off the bus or train, you'll sometimes be met by hotel runners wielding pictures of their rooms for rent. My gut reaction is to steer clear, but these people are usually just hardworking entrepreneurs who lack the location or write-up in a popular guidebook that can make life easy for a small hotel owner. If you like the guy and what he promises, and the hotel isn't too far away, follow him to his hotel. You are obliged only to inspect the hotel. If it's good, take it. If it's not, leave. You're probably near other budget hotels anyway. Establish the location very clearly, as many of these people have good places miserably located way out of town.

The early bird gets the room. If you anticipate crowds, go to great lengths to arrive in the morning when the most (and best) rooms are available. If the rooms aren't ready until noon, take one anyway; leave your luggage behind the desk; they'll move you in later and you're set up—free to relax and enjoy the city. I would leave Florence at 7:00 a.m. to arrive in Venice (a crowded city) early enough to get a decent choice of rooms. Consider the advantage of overnight train rides—you'll arrive, if not bright, at least early.

Your approach to room finding will be determined by the market situation—if it's a "buyer's market" or a "seller's market." Sometimes you can arrive late, be selective, and even talk down the price. Other times you'll grab anything with a pillow and a blanket. A person staying only

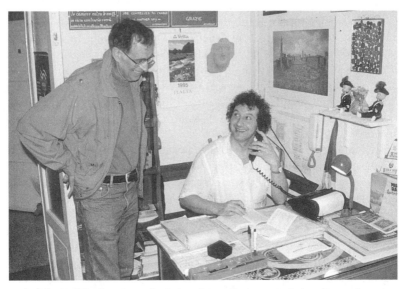

Ask your friend who runs today's hotel to call tomorrow's hotel to make you a reservation in the local language.

one night is bad news to a hotel. If, before telling you whether there's a vacancy, they ask you how long you're staying, be ambiguous.

Leave the trouble zone. If the room situation is impossible, don't struggle—just leave. An hour by car, train, or bus from the most miserable hotel situation anywhere in Europe is a town—Dullsdorf or Nothingston—that has the Dullsdorf Inn or the Nothingston Gasthaus just across the street from the station or right on the main square. It's not full—never has been, never will be. There's a guy sleeping behind the reception desk. Drop in at 11:00 p.m., ask for 14 beds, and he'll say, "Take the second and third floors, the keys are in the doors." It always works. Oktoberfest, Cannes Film Festival, St. Tropez Running of the Girls, Easter at Lourdes—your bed awaits you in nearby Dullsdorf. If you anticipate trouble, stay at the last train stop before the crowded city.

Follow taxi tips. A great way to find a place in a tough situation is to let a cabbie take you to his favorite hotel. They are experts. Cabs are also handy when you're driving lost in a big city. Many times I've hired a cab, showed him that elusive address, and followed him in my car to my hotel.

Let hotel managers help. Have your current manager call ahead to make a reservation at your next destination (offer to pay for the call). If you're in a town and having trouble finding a room, remember that nobody knows the hotel scene better than local hotel managers do. If one hotel is full, ask the manager for help. Often the manager has a list of neighborhood accommodations or will even telephone a friend's place that rarely fills up and is just around the corner. If the hotel is too expensive, there's nothing wrong with asking where you could find a "not so good place." The most expensive hotels have the

In France each hotel has a plaque next to the door telling you its category.

best city maps (free, often with other hotels listed) and an English-speaking staff that can give advice to the polite traveler in search of a cheap room. I find hotel receptionists understanding and helpful.

TO SAVE MONEY . . .

Think small. Large hotels, international chains, and big-city hotels are more expensive than their smaller counterparts.

Know the exceptions. Hotels in northern Europe are pricier than those in the south, but there are exceptions. In Scandinavia, Brussels, and Berlin, fancy "business hotels" are desperate for customers in the summer and on weekends, when their business customers stay away. They offer some amazing deals through the local tourist offices. The later your arrival, the better the discount.

Be a smart consumer—don't stray above your needs. Know the government ratings. A three-star hotel is not necessarily a bad value, but if I stay in a three-star hotel, I've spent $50 extra for things I don't need. You can get air conditioning, elevators, private showers, room service, a 24-hour reception desk, and people in uniforms to

Room prices vary within a hotel depending on the beds and plumbing. A price list hides near the check-in desk. Understand it. Use it.

Formule One is a French-style Motel 6. Fully automated, no-character $25 triples are at nearly every freeway off-ramp.

carry your bags. But each of those services adds $10 to your room cost, and before you know it, the simple $50 room is up to $100.

Avoid hotels that require you to buy meals. Many national governments regulate hotel prices according to class or rating. To overcome this price ceiling (especially at resorts in peak season, when demand exceeds supply), hotels often require that you buy dinner in their dining room. Breakfast normally comes with the room, but in some countries it's an expensive, kind-of-optional tack-on. One more meal (demi- or half-pension) or all three meals (full-pension) is usually uneconomical, since the hotel is skirting the governmental hotel price ceilings to maximize profit. I prefer the freedom to explore and sample the atmosphere of restaurants in other neighborhoods.

Shop around. When going door-to-door, rarely is the first place you check the best. It's worth 10 minutes of shopping around to find the going rate before you accept a room. You'll be surprised how prices vary as you walk farther from the station or down a street strewn with B&Bs. Never judge a hotel by its exterior or lobby. Lavish interiors with shabby exteriors (blame the landlord who's stuck with rent control, not the hotel) are a cultural trait of Europe. (If there are two of you, let one watch the bags over a cup of coffee while the other runs around.)

Check the prices on the room list to find the best value. Room prices vary tremendously within a hotel according to facilities provided. Most hotels have a room list clearly displayed, showing each room, its bed configuration, facilities, and maximum price for one and for two. Also read the breakfast, tax, and extra bed policies. By studying this list you'll see that, in many places, a shower is cheaper than a bath, and a double bed is cheaper than twins. In other words, a sloppy couple who prefer a shower and a double bed can pay $20 more for a bath and twins. In some cases, if you want any room for two and you say "double," they'll think you'll only take a double bed. To keep all my options open (twin and double) I ask for "a room for two people." Be snoopy. Hotels downplay their cheap rooms.

See if there's a discount for a longer stay. Some hotels offer a special price for a long stay. It doesn't hurt to ask. If you came direct and point out that the tourist office didn't get their 10 percent, you have a better chance of talking the price down.

If it's off-season, bargain. Prices usually rise with demand during festivals and in July and August. Off-season, try haggling. If the place is too expensive, tell them your limit; they might meet it.

Put more people in a room. Family rooms are common, and putting four in a quad is much cheaper than two doubles. Many doubles

Throughout southern Europe, even the cheapest hotel rooms come with a bidet. Europeans use them to stay clean without a daily shower.

come with a small double bed and a sliver single. A third person pays very little. A family with two small children can ask for triples and bring a sleeping bag for the stowaway.

Avoid doing outside business through your hotel. It's better style to go to the bullring and get the ticket yourself. You'll learn more and save money, and you won't sit with other tourists who drown your Spanish fire with Yankee-pankee. So often, tourists are herded together by a conspiracy of hotel managers and tour organizers and driven through gimmicky folk evenings featuring a medley of cheesy cultural clichés kept alive only for the tourists. You can't relive your precious Madrid nights. Do them right—on your own.

CHECK-IN PROCEDURE

Ask to see the room before accepting. Then the receptionist knows the room must pass your inspection. He'll have to earn your business. Notice the boy is given two keys. You asked for only one room. He's instructed to show the hard-to-sell room first. It's only natural for the hotel receptionist to try to unload the most difficult-to-sell room on the easiest-to-please traveler. Somebody has to sleep in it. If you ask to see both rooms, you'll get the better one. When you check out a room, point out anything that deserves displeasure. The price will come down, or they'll show you a better room. Think about heat and noise. I'll climb a few stairs to reach cheaper rooms higher off the noisy road. Some towns never quiet down. A room in back may lack a view, but it will also lack night noise.

Establish the complete and final price of a room before accepting. Know what's included and what taxes and services will be added. More than once I've been given a bill that was double what I expected. Dinners were required, and I was billed whether I ate them or not; so I was told—in very clear Italian.

When checking in, pick up the hotel's business card. In the most confusing cities, the cards come with a little map. Even the best pathfinders get lost in a big city, and not knowing where your hotel is can be scary. With the card, you can hop into a cab and be home in minutes.

If you need help, ask. Although you don't want to be a pest, remember, hotels are in the business of accommodating people. If you didn't get the kind of room you wanted, ask to switch when possible. If you need a different pillow, another blanket, mosquito netting, an electrical adapter, advice on a good restaurant or show, driving instructions for your departure, help telephoning your next hotel, and so on, be sure to ask.

When you pay is up to the hotel and you. Normally I pay upon departure. If they want prepayment, that's fine, but unless I'm absolutely

> **THE KEY TO KEYS**
> Tourists spend hours fumbling with old skeleton keys in rickety hotel doors. The haphazard, nothing-square construction of old hotels means the keys need babying. Don't push them in all the way. Pull the door in or up. Try a little in, quarter turn, and farther in for full turn. Always turn the top of the key away from the door to open it. Leave the key at the desk before leaving for the day. I've never had my room broken into in Europe. Confirm closing time. Some hotels lock up after their restaurant closes or after midnight and expect you to keep the key to the outside door with you in the evenings.

certain I'll be staying on, I pay one night at a time. Don't assume your room is yours once you're in. Make it clear when you check in how long you intend to stay, or you may get the boot.

BED-AND-BREAKFAST PLACES AND PENSIONS

Between hotels and hostels or campgrounds in price and style are a special class of accommodations. These are small, warm, and family-run, and offer a personal touch at a budget price. They are the next best thing to staying with a local family, and even if hotels weren't more expensive, I'd choose this budget alternative.

Each country has these friendly accommodations in varying degrees of abundance, facilities, and service. Some include breakfast; some don't. They have different names from country to country, but all have one thing in common: They satisfy the need for a place to stay that gives you the privacy of a hotel and the comforts of home at a price you can afford.

While information on some of the more established places is available in many budget travel guidebooks, the best information is often found locally, through tourist information offices, room-finding services, or even from the local man waiting for his bus or selling apples. Especially in the British Isles, each B&B host has a network of favorites and can happily set you up in a good B&B at your next stop.

Many times, the information is brought to you. I'll never forget struggling off the plane on my arrival in Santorini. Fifteen women were begging me to spend the night. Thrilled, I made a snap decision and followed the most attractive offer to a very nice budget accommodation.

The "part of the family" element of a B&B stay is determined entirely by you. Chatty friendliness is not forced on guests. Depending on my

SHOWERS

Showers are a Yankee fetish. A morning without a shower is traumatic to many of us: It can ruin a day. Get used to the idea that you won't have a shower every night. The real winners are those who manage with four showers a week and a few sponge baths tossed in when needed. Here are some tips on survival in a world that doesn't start and end with squeaky-clean hair.

Take quick showers. Americans are notorious (and embarrassing) energy gluttons—wasting hot water and leaving lights on as if electricity is cheap. Who besides us sings in the shower or would even dream of using a special nozzle to take a hot water massage? European electric rates are shocking, and some hotels have had to put meters in their showers to survive. Fifty cents buys about five minutes of hot water. It's a good idea to have an extra token handy to avoid that lathered look. A "navy shower," using the water only to soap up and rinse off, is a wonderfully conservative method, and those who follow you will more likely enjoy some *warm wasser*. (Although starting and stopping the water doesn't start and stop the meter.)

"C" can mean "hot." Half of all the cold showers Americans take in Europe are cold only because they don't know how to turn the hot on. Study the particular system, and before you shiver, ask the receptionist for help. There are some very peculiar tricks. In Italy and Spain, "C" is *caldo*, or hot. In many British places there's a "hot" switch at the base of the showerbox or even in the hallway. You'll find showers and baths of all kinds. The red knob is hot and the blue one is cold—or visa versa. Unusual showers normally have clear instructions posted.

If the water stays cold, ask, "When is the best time to take a hot shower?" Many cheap hotels have water pressure or hot water only during certain times. Other times, you'll get a shower—but no pressure or hot water. Hot water 24 hours a day is a luxury many of us take for granted.

Try a sponge bath. Nearly every hotel room in Europe comes with a sink and a bidet. Sponge baths are fast, easy, and European. A bidet is that

mood and workload, I am often very businesslike and private during my stay. On other occasions I join the children in the barn for the sheep-shearing festivities.

Don't confuse European bed-and-breakfasts with their rich cousins in America. B&Bs in the United States are usually doily-pretentious places, very cozy and colorful but as expensive as hotels. In a European B&B you don't get seven pillows and a basket of jams.

mysterious porcelain (or rickety plastic) thing that looks like an oversized bedpan. Tourists use them as anything from a laundromat to a vomitorium to a watermelon rind receptacle to a urinal. They are used by locals to clean the parts of the body that rub together when they walk—in lieu of a shower. Give it the old four Ss—straddle, squat, soap up, and swish off.

Bring soap. Many budget hotels and most dorm-style accommodations don't provide towels or soap. BYOS. Towels, like breakfast and people, get smaller as you go south. In simple places, you'll get no face towel, and bath towels are not replaced every day. Hang them up to dry.

Use the hall shower. The cheapest hotels rarely provide a shower or toilet in your room. Each floor shares a toilet and a shower "down the hall." To such a bathoholic people, this sounds terrible. Imagine the congestion in the morning when the entire floor tries to pile into that bathtub! Remember, only Americans "need" a shower every morning. Few Americans stay in these "local" hotels; therefore, you've got a private bath—down the hall. I spend 100 nights a year in Europe—probably shower 80 times—and I have to wait four or five times. That's the price I pay to take advantage of Europe's simple hotels.

In the last decade even the simplest places have added lots of private showers. For example, a hotel originally designed with 20 simple rooms sharing two showers will now be retrofitted with private showers in 14 of its rooms. That leaves a more reasonable six rooms rather than 20 to share the two public showers. Those willing to go down the hall for a shower enjoy the same substantial savings with much less inconvenience.

Try other places to shower. If you are vagabonding or sleeping several nights in transit, you can buy a shower in "day hotels" at major train stations and airports, at many freeway rest stops, in public baths or swimming pools, or even, if you don't mind asking, from hostels or small hotels. Most Mediterranean beaches have free, freshwater showers all the time. I have a theory that after four days without a shower, you don't get any worse, but that's another book.

Britain: Britain's B&Bs are the best of all. Very common throughout the British Isles, they are a boon to anyone touring England, Scotland, or Wales. As the name indicates, a breakfast comes with the bed, and (except in London) this is no ordinary breakfast. Most B&B owners take pride in their breakfasts. Their guests sit down to an elegant and very British table setting and feast on cereal, juice, bacon, sausages, eggs, broiled tomatoes, mushrooms, toast, marmalade, and coffee or tea. While you are finishing your coffee, the landlady (who by this time is probably on very friendly terms with you) may present you with her guest book, pointing out others from your state who have stayed in her house and inviting you to make an entry. Your hostess will sometimes cook you a simple dinner for a good price, and, if you have time to chat, you may get in on an evening social hour. When you bid her farewell and thank her for the good sleep and full stomach, it's often difficult to get away. Determined to fill you with as much information as food, she wants you to have the best day of sightseeing possible.

A special bonus when enjoying Britain's great bed-and-breakfasts: You get your own temporary local mother.

If you're going to the normal tourist stops, your guidebook will list some good B&Bs. If you're venturing off the beaten British path, you don't need (or want) a listing. The small towns and countryside are littered with places whose quality varies only in degrees of wonderful. I try not to take a B&B until I've checked out three. Styles and atmosphere vary from house to house, and besides, I enjoy looking through European homes.

The British Tourist Board's crown system rates, prices, and recommends places solely on their plumbing and appliances. Many small-time, easygoing proprietors have no choice but to go heavily into debt, gear up, and charge more. Mavericks don't play by the rules, don't get listed, and rely solely on their own followings. (Many—if not most—of my favorite British B&Bs do not play the rating game.) To try to measure coziness and friendliness, the British Tourist Board has added "commended" or "highly commended" to the otherwise-sterile crown system.

Ireland has essentially the same system of B&Bs. They are less expensive than England's and, if anything, even more "homely." With such a bleak economy, many Irish make ends meet by renting out rooms to travelers.

Germany, Austria, and Switzerland: Look for *Zimmer Frei* or *Privat Zimmer*. These are very common in areas popular with travelers (such as Austria's Salzkammergut Lakes District and Germany's Rhine,

Romantic Road, and southern Bavaria). Signs will clearly indicate whether they have available rooms (green) or not (orange). Especially in Austria, one-night stays are discouraged. Most *Zimmer* cost around $20 per person and include a hearty ontinental breakfast. *Pensionen* and *Gasthäuser* are similarly priced, small, family-run hotels. Switzerland has very few *Zimmer*. Don't confuse *Zimmer* with the German *Farienwohnung*, which is a self-catering apartment rented out by the week or fortnight.

France: The French have a growing network of *Chambre d'hôte* (CH) accommodations where locals, mainly in the coun-

Never judge a B&B by its name. Like many in Britain, this one is smoke-free and comes with numerous pleasant extras.

Bed-and-breakfast travelers scramble at the breakfast table.

tryside and in small towns, rent double rooms for about the price of a cheap hotel ($40) but include breakfast. Some CHs post *Chambre* signs in their windows, but most are listed only through local tourist offices. While your hosts will rarely speak English, they will almost always be enthusiastic and a delight to share a home with. For longer stays in the countryside, look into France's popular *Gîtes*. Pick up regional listings at local tourist offices.

Italy: Check out Italy's important alternatives to its expensive hotels: *albergo, locanda,* and *pensione.* (While these are technically all bunched together now in a hotel system with star ratings, you'll still find these traditional names, synonymous for simple budget beds.) Private rooms, called *camere libere* or *affitta camere,* are fairly common in Italy's small towns and touristy countryside. Small-town bars are plugged into the B&B grapevine. While breakfasts are rarely included, you'll sometimes get a kitchenette in the room.

Scandinavia: These usually luxurious B&Bs are called *rom, hus rum,* or, in Denmark, *værelser.* At $25 per bed, these are incredibly cheap (well, not so incredibly, when you figure it's a common way for the most heavily taxed people in Europe to make a little money under the table). Unfortunately many Scandinavian B&Bs are advertised only through the local tourist offices, which very often keep them a secret until all the hotels are full. In my *Rick Steves' Scandinavia* guidebook, I list plenty of wonderful money savers. An evening with a Scandinavian family offers a fascinating look at contemporary Nordic life. If they're serving breakfast, eat it. Even at $12, it's a deal by Nordic standards and can serve as your best big meal of the day. Some places leave a roll of foil on the table so you can pack out a sandwich for lunch.

Spain and Portugal: Travelers get an intimate peek into their small-town, whitewashed worlds by renting out *camas* and *casas particulares* in Spain and *quartos* in Portugal. In rural Iberia, where there's tourism, you'll find these budget accommodations. Breakfast is rarely included.

Greece: You'll find many $20-per-bed *dhomatia.* Especially in touristy coastal and island towns, hard-working entrepreneurs will meet planes, ferries, and buses as they come into town at any hour. In Greek villages with no hotels, ask for *dhomatia* at the town *taverna.* Forget breakfast.

Eastern Europe: This region has always had brave entrepreneurs running underground bed-and-breakfasts. Now, with the hard economic times; the freer atmosphere; and the overcrowded, overpriced, official hotels; you'll find more B&Bs in Eastern Europe than ever before. In Slovenia they're called *Sobe;* otherwise, they seem to go by the German

Country	Term for Private Rooms to Rent	Rough Cost per Bed
Great Britain	Bed-and-Breakfast	$25*
Norway/Sweden	Rom or Rum	$25
Denmark	Værelser	$25
Germany/Austria/ Switzerland	Zimmer	$20*
France	Chambre d'Hôte	$25
Italy	Affitta Camere	$25
Slovenia	Sobe	$20
Greece	Dhomatia	$20
Spain	Casa Particulare	$20
Portugal	Quarto	$20
Eastern Europe	All of the above, or "Rooms"	$15

includes breakfast

Zimmer. At train stations and around tourist offices, look for hustling housewives with rooms to rent. Many cities now have services that efficiently connect travelers with locals renting rooms. If you pay in hard Western currency, you'll make your host's day.

EUROPE'S 2,000 HOSTELS

Europe's cheapest beds are in hostels. Two thousand hostels provide beds throughout Europe for $10 to $20 per night. The buildings are usually in good, easily accessible locations.

As Europe has grown more affluent, hostels have been remodeled to provide more plumbing and smaller rooms. Still, hostels are not hotels—not by a long shot. Many people hate hostels. Others love them and will be hostelers all their lives, regardless of their budgets. Hosteling is a philosophy. A hosteler trades service and privacy for a chance to live simply and communally with people from around the world.

A youth hostel is not limited to young people. You may be ready to jump to the next section because, by every other standard, you're older than young. Well, many countries have dropped the word "youth" from "hostel," and a few years ago the Youth Hostel Association came out with a new card giving "youths" over the age of 54 a discount. People of any age can hostel anywhere in Europe (except for Germany's Bavaria, with a strictly enforced 26-year-old age limit). The average hosteler is 18 to 26, but every year there are more seniors and families hosteling. All you need is a hostel membership card ($25 a year, less for people under 18 and over 54, and families with kids under 15), available at your local student travel office, any hostel office, or Hostelling International (tel. 800/444-6111, www.hiayh.org). **Hostels provide "no frills" accommodations in clean dormitories.** The sexes are segregated, with four to 20 people packed in a room full of bunk beds. Pillows and blankets, but no sheets, are provided. You can bring a regular single bedsheet (sewn into a sack if you like), rent one at each hostel for about $4, or buy a regulation hostel sheet-sack at your first hostel (lightweight, ideal design at a bargain price). Many hostels have a few doubles for group leaders and couples, and rooms for families. Strong, hot showers (often with coin-op meters) are the norm, but simpler hostels have cold showers or even none at all. Hostels were originally for hikers and bikers, but that isn't the case these days. Still, give your car a low profile. Arriving by taxi is just plain bad taste.

Many hostels offer meals and meeting places. Hearty, super-cheap meals are served, often in family-style settings. A typical dinner is fish fingers and mashed potatoes seasoned by conversation with new friends from Norway to New Zealand. The self-service kitchen, complete with utensils, pots, and pans, is a great budget aid that comes with most

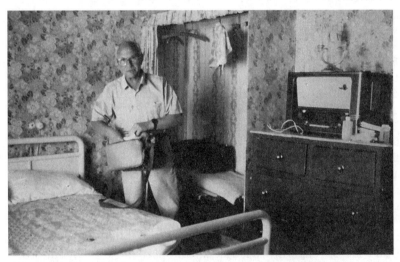

All over Europe, people rent spare bedrooms to budget travelers. Bed-and-breakfasts give you double the cultural experience for half the price of a hotel. In Scotland you may get a hot-water bottle. This Portuguese B&B came with a beach view and a bedpan.

One of Europe's 2,000 hostels—$10 a night, your own kitchen, a million-dollar view of the Jungfrau, and lots of friends. Note the worldwide triangular hostel symbol.

hostels. Larger hostels even have a small grocery store. Many international friendships rise with the bread in hostel kitchens.

The hostel's recreation and living rooms are my favorite. People gather, play games, tell stories, share information, marvel at American foreign policy, read, write, and team up for future travels. Solo travelers find a family in every hostel. Hostels are ideal meeting places for those in search of a travel partner. And those with partners do well to occasionally stay in a hostel to meet some new travelers.

Hostels are run by "wardens" or "house parents." They do their best to strictly enforce no-drinking rules, quiet hours, and other regulations. Some are loose and laid-back, others are like Marine drill sergeants, but all are hostel wardens for the noble purpose of enabling travelers to better appreciate and enjoy that town or region. While they are often overworked and harried, most wardens are great people who enjoy a quiet cup of coffee with an American and are happy to give you some local travel tips or recommend a special nearby hostel. Be sensitive to the many demands on their time, and never treat them like hotel servants.

Hostels have drawbacks. Many have strict rules. They lock up during the day (usually from 10:00 a.m. to 5:00 p.m.), and they have a curfew at night (10:00 p.m., 11:00 p.m., or midnight), when the doors are locked and those outside stay there. These curfews are for the greater good—not to make you miserable. In the mountains, the curfew is early because most people are early-rising hikers. In London the curfew is 11:45 p.m., giving you ample time to return from the theater. Amsterdam, where the sun shines at night, has a 1:45 a.m. curfew. The first half-hour after "lights out" reminds me of summer camp—giggles, burps, jokes, and strange noises in many languages. Snoring is permitted and practiced openly.

Hostel rooms can be large and packed. Many school groups (especially German) turn hostels upside down (typically weekends during the school year and weekdays in the summer). Try to be understanding (many groups are disadvantaged kids); we were all noisy kids at one time. Get to know the teacher and make it a "cultural experience."

Theft is a problem in hostels, but the answer is simple: Don't leave valuables lying around (no one's going to steal your tennis shoes or journal). Use the storage lockers that are available in most hostels.

Cooking in the hostel members' kitchen, this traveler lives in Europe on $15 a day for his bed plus the price of groceries.

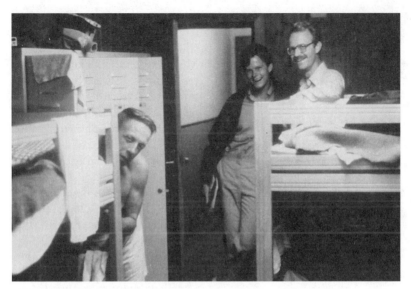

In a hostel, you'll have bunk beds and roommates.

In some hostels in Britain, hostelers are required to do chores (token duties that never take more than a few minutes). It used to be that every hosteler in Europe was assigned a chore. This custom has died out on the Continent, but lives on (barely) in Britain.

Hostel selectively. Hostels come in all shapes and sizes, and some are sightseeing ends in themselves. There are castles (Bacharach, Germany), cutter ships (Stockholm), Alpine chalets (Gimmelwald, Switzerland), huge modern buildings (Frankfurt), medieval manor houses (Wilderhope Manor, England), former choirboys' dorms (St. Paul's, London), and former royal residences (Holland Park, London). Survey other hostelers and hostel wardens for suggestions.

I hostel most in the north, where hostels are more comfortable and the savings over hotels more exciting. I rarely hostel in the south, where hostels are less common and two or three people can sleep just as cheaply in a budget hotel.

Big-city hostels are the most institutional and overrun by young backpackers. Rural hostels, far from train lines and famous sights, are usually quiet and frequented by a more mature crowd. If you have a car, use that mobility to leave the Eurail zone and enjoy some of Europe's overlooked hostels.

Getting a hostel bed in peak tourist season can be tricky. The

```
                    INFORMATION
   YOUNG     £3.50       SHEET    80 p
   JUNIOR    £4.40       SHOWERS  FREE
   SENIOR    £5.50

   DINNER          £3.00
   BREAKFAST       £2 30
   LUNCH PACK £ 1.60
   DOORS OPENED         7.30 AM
   RISING BELL & OFFICE OPEN 8.00
   BREAKFAST            8.30
   HOSTEL CLOSES        10.00
   HOSTEL REOPENS       5.00 PM
   DINNER              7.00
   HOSTEL CLOSES       11.00
   LIGHTS OUT          11.30
               WARDENS
     KEITH & JOAN BENNETT
   ASSISTANT WARDEN JAN VAN KAAM
  WE HOPE YOU ENJOY YOUR STAY AT
       STOW — ON — THE — OLD
```

most popular hostels fill up every day. Written reservations are possible, but I've never bothered. Most wardens will take telephone reservations. I always call ahead to try to reserve and at least check on the availability of beds. Don't rely solely on the phone, because hostels are required to hold some beds for drop-ins. Try to arrive early. If the hostel has a lockout period during the day, show up before the office closes in the morning; otherwise, line up with the scruffy gang for the 5:00 p.m. re-opening, when any remaining beds are doled out.

Thankfully, many hostels are putting out envelopes for each available bed, so you can drop by any time of day, pop your card into the reservation envelope and through the slot, and show up sometime that evening. Also, many German hostels have a new telex reservation system where, for a small fee, you can reserve and pay for your next hostel bed before you leave the last one.

You can book a European hostel from the U.S. (though I've never found it necessary) by calling Hostelling International at 800/444-6111 or 202/783-6161. For a $5 processing fee, they'll book you a dorm bed at many (but not all) of Europe's hostels. They need at least 10 days' notice, accept Visa or MasterCard, restrict their service to hostel members, and sell hostel membership cards.

Hostel bed availability is unpredictable. Some obscure hostels are booked out on certain days two months in advance. But I stumbled into Oberammergau one night during the jam-packed Passion Play festival and found beds for a group of eight.

Gung-ho hostelers can get a complete listing. Hostelling International publishes *Hostelling International: Europe* (annually, $14). This directory, available through Hostelling International, your local student travel office, or at any European hostel, lists each of Europe's 2,000 hostels with its number of beds, distance from the train station, directions, address, phone number, and day or season (if any) the hostel is closed. The book comes with a handy map of Europe locating all the hostels. Individual countries have a more accurate and informative directory or handbook (never expensive, usually free). England's is especially worthwhile. If you're sticking to the more popular destinations, the Let's Go guidebook (Europe, or individual countries) lists enough hostels to make the *Hostelling International* directory unnecessary.

UNOFFICIAL HOSTELS AND STUDENT HOTELS

There seem to be nearly as many unofficial or independent hostels as there are official ones. Many wardens and student groups prefer to run their own show and avoid the occasionally heavy-handed bureaucracy of the IYHF (International Youth Hostel Federation). Unofficial hostels are looser and more casual but not as clean or organized.

Ireland's Independent Hostel Owners (IHO) Association is a less institutional (fewer rules, no membership required) network of these maverick independent hostels. Pick up their booklet at any IHO hostel.

Many large cities have wild and cheap student-run hostels that are popular with wild and cheap student travelers. If these sound right for you, Let's Go has good listings.

CAMPING EUROPEAN-STYLE

Relatively few Americans take advantage of Europe's 10,000-plus campgrounds. Camping is the cheapest way to see Europe and the middle-class European family way to travel. Campers give it rave reviews.

"Camping" is the international word for campground. Every town has a camping with enough ground to pitch a tent or park a caravan (trailer), good showers and washing facilities, and often a grocery store and restaurant, all for just a few dollars per person per night. Unlike the picturesque, rustic American campground near a lake or forest, European camping is more functional, like spending the night in a park-and-ride. Campings forbid open fires, and you won't find a riverfront lot with a stove, table, and privacy. A camping is usually near or in the town—a place to sleep, eat, wash, and catch a bus downtown. They rarely fill up, and if they do, the "Full" sign usually refers to trailers (most Europeans are trailer campers). A small tent can almost always be squeezed in somewhere.

Europe's campgrounds mix well with just about any mode of transportation. And very light modern camp gear makes camping without a car easier than ever. Tent and train is a winning combination for many. Nearly every train station has a tourist office nearby. Stop by and pick up a map with campgrounds marked, local camping leaflets, and bus directions. In most cases, buses shuttle campers from station to campground with ease. Every station has lockers, in which those with limited energy can leave unneeded baggage.

Hitchhikers find camping just right for their tender budget. Many campgrounds are located near the major road out of town, where long rides are best snared. Any hitching camper with average social skills can find a friend driving his way with an empty seat. A note on the camp bulletin board can be very effective.

Tents and bikes also mix well. Bikers enjoy the same we-can-squeeze-one-more-in status as hikers and are rarely turned away.

Camping by car is my favorite combination. A car carries all your camp gear and gets you to any campground quickly and easily. Good road maps always pinpoint "campings," and when you're within a few blocks, the road signs take over. In big cities, the money you save on parking alone will pay for your camping. I usually take the bus downtown, leaving my camper van at the campground.

Learning about campgrounds: Each country's national tourist office in the United States can send you information on camping in its country. Consider getting the *Traveler's Guide to European Camping*, by Mike and Terri Church. The Let's Go guide gives good instructions on getting to and from the campgrounds. Campings are well posted, and local tourist information offices have guides and maps listing nearby campgrounds. Every country has good and bad campgrounds. Campgrounds mirror their surroundings. If the region is overcrowded, dusty, dirty, unkempt, and generally chaotic, you're unlikely to find an oasis behind the campground's gates. A sleepy Austrian valley will most likely offer a sleepy Austrian campground.

European sites called "weekend campings" are rented out on a yearly basis to local urbanites. Too often, weekend sites are full or don't allow what they call "stop-and-go" campers (you). Camping guidebooks indicate which places are the "weekend" types.

Prices: Prices vary according to facilities and style. Expect to spend around $5 per night per person. You'll often pay by the tent, so four people in one tent sleep cheaper than four individual campers. (Beware: Swiss and Italian campgrounds can be shockingly expensive.)

Registration and regulations: Camp registration is easy. As with most hotels, you show your passport, fill out a short form, and learn the rules. Checkout time is usually noon. English is the second language of campings throughout Europe, and most managers will understand the monoglot American.

Silence reigns in European campgrounds after the 10:00 or 11:00 p.m. curfew. Noisemakers are strictly dealt with. Many places close the gates to cars after 11:00 p.m. If you do arrive after the office closes, set up quietly and register in the morning.

Camping Carnet: The International Camping Carnet, or international campground membership card, is required at some sites, handy at others (when you're required to leave a picture I.D. at the campground office, it's less stressful to leave a carnet than a passport). You can buy a carnet at many European campgrounds or through the Family Campers and RVers Association ($35, 4804 Transit Road, Bldg. 2, Depew, NY 14043, tel. 800/245-9755, fax 716/668-6242; purchase includes membership in FCRV, which offers discounts at some American campgrounds). In Europe the carnet will get you an occasional discount or preferential treatment in a very crowded situation.

Campground services: European campgrounds have great, if sometimes crowded, showers and washing facilities. Hot water, as in many hostels and hotels, is metered, and you'll learn to carry coins and "douche" quickly. European tenters appreciate the in-camp grocery store, café, and restaurant. The store, while high-priced, stays open longer than most, offering latecomers a budget alternative to the restaurant. The restaurant or café is a likely camp hangout, and Americans enjoy mixing in this easy-going European social scene. I've scuttled many nights on the town so I wouldn't miss the fun with new friends right in the camp. Camping, like hosteling, is a great way to meet Europeans. If the campground doesn't have a place to eat, you'll find one nearby.

Camping with kids: A family sleeps in a tent a lot cheaper than in a hotel. There's plenty to occupy children's attention, including playgrounds that come fully equipped with European kids. As your kids make European friends, your campground social circle widens.

Safety: Campgrounds, unlike hostels, are remarkably theft-free. Campings are full of basically honest middle-class European families, and someone's at the gate all day. Most people just leave their gear zipped inside their tents.

Camping equipment: Your camping trip deserves first-class equipment. Spend some time and money outfitting yourself before your trip. There are plenty of stores with exciting new gear and expert salespeople to get you up-to-date in a hurry. European campers prefer a very lightweight "three-season" sleeping bag (consult a climate chart for your probable bedroom temperature) and a closed-cell ensolite pad to insulate and soften the ground. A camp stove is right for American-style camping but probably not your cup of tea in Europe. Start without a stove. If you figure you need one, buy one there. In Europe it's much easier to find fuel for a European camp stove than for its Yankee counterpart. (If you take one from home, it should be the butane *Gaz* variety.) I keep it simple, picnicking and enjoying food and fun in the campground restaurant. (For

Many campgrounds offer "bungalows" with kitchenettes and four to six beds.
Comfortable and cheaper than hotels, these are particularly popular in Scandinavia.

good catalogs full of camping gear, call REI at 800/426-4840, Campmor at 800/226-7667, or L.L. Bean at 800/226-7552.) Commit yourself to a camping trip or to a no-camping trip and pack accordingly. Don't carry a sleeping bag and a tent just in case.

Free camping: Informal camping, or "camping wild," is legal in most of Europe. Low-profile, pitch-the-tent-after-dark-and-move-on-first-thing-in-the-morning free camping is usually allowed even in countries where it is technically illegal. Use common sense, and don't pitch your tent informally in carefully controlled areas such as cities and resorts. It's a good idea to ask permission when possible. In the countryside, a landowner will rarely refuse a polite request to borrow a patch of land for the night. Formal camping is safer than free camping. Never leave your gear and tent unattended without the gates of a formal campground to discourage thieves.

HUT-HOPPING

Hundreds of Alpine huts exist to provide food and shelter for hikers. I know a family that hiked from France to Slovenia, spending every night along the way in a mountain hut. The huts are generally spaced four to six hours apart. Most serve hot meals and provide bunk-style lodging. Many Alpine huts (like unofficial hostels) require no linen and wash their blankets annually. I'll never forget getting cozy in my top bunk while a German with a "Rat Patrol" accent in the bottom bunk said, "You're climbing into the germs of centuries." Hut-hoppers hike with their own sheets.

In the Alps, look for the word *Lager*, which means they have a coed loft full of $10-a-night mattresses. If you plan to use the huts extensively, join an Alpine club. Membership in one of these European or American clubs entitles you to discounts on the cost of lodging and priority over nonmembers. The club can provide information about the trails and huts at which reservations are likely to be necessary. For specifics, ask your local travel bookstore about guidebooks on hiking in Europe.

SLEEPING FREE

There are still people traveling in Europe on $20 a day. The one thing they have in common (apart from B.O.) is that they sleep free. If even cheap pensions and hostels are too expensive for your budget, you too can sleep free. I once went 29 out of 30 nights without paying for a bed. It's not difficult, but it's not always comfortable, convenient, safe, or legal, either. This is not a vagabonding guide, but any traveler may have an occasional free night. Faking it until the sun returns can become, at least in the long run, a good memory.

Europe has plenty of places to roll out your sleeping bag. Some large cities, such as Amsterdam and Athens, are flooded with tourists during peak season, and many spend their nights dangerously in city parks. Some cities enforce their "no sleeping in the parks" laws only selectively. Big, crowded cities such as London, Paris, Munich, Venice, and Copenhagen run safe, legal, and nearly free "sleep-ins" (tents or huge dorms) during peak season. Away from the cities, in forests or on beaches, you can pretty well sleep where you like. I have found that summer nights in the Mediterranean part of Europe are mild enough that I am comfortable with just my jeans, sweater, and hostel sheet. I no longer lug a sleeping bag around, but if you'll be vagabonding a lot, bring a light bag.

Imaginative vagabonds see Europe as one big free hotel (barns, churches, buildings under construction, ruins, college dorms, etc.). Just keep your passport with you, attach your belongings to you so they don't get stolen, and use good judgment in your choice of a free bed.

Train stations: When you have no place to go for the night in a city, you can always retreat to the station for a free, warm, safe, and uncomfortable place to spend the night (assuming the station stays open all night). Most popular tourist cities in Europe have stations whose concrete floors are painted nightly with a long rainbow of sleepy vagabonds. This is allowed, but everyone is cleared out at dawn before the normal rush of travelers converges on the station. In some cases, you'll be asked to show a ticket. Any ticket or your Eurailpass entitles you to a free night in a station's waiting room: You are simply waiting for your early train. Whenever possible, avoid the second-class lounges; sleep with a better breed of hobo in first-class lounges. For safety, you can lock your pack in a locker.

Trains: Success hinges on getting enough room to stretch out, and that can be quite a trick (see Chapter 10: Train and Railpass Skills). It's tempting but quite risky to sleep in a train car that seems to be parked for the night in a station. No awakening is ruder than having your bedroom jolt into motion and roll toward God-knows-where. If you do find a parked train car to sleep in, check to see when it's scheduled to leave. Some Eurailers get a free if disjointed night by riding a train out for four hours and catching one back in for another four hours. Scandinavia, with Europe's most expensive hotels, offers *couchettes* for a reasonable $20. (Notice that its capital cities were each placed a very convenient overnight train ride apart.)

Airports: An airport is a large, posh version of a train station, offering a great opportunity to sleep free. After a late landing, I crash on a comfortable sofa rather than waste sleeping time looking for a place that will sell me a bed for the remainder of the night. Many cut-rate inter-European flights leave or arrive at ungodly hours. Frankfurt airport is served conveniently by the train and is great for sleeping free—even if you aren't flying anywhere. Some large airports have sterile womb-like "rest cabins" which rent for eight hours at the price of a cheap hotel room. (I routinely use the "cocoons" at the Paris and Copenhagen airports.)

FRIENDS AND RELATIVES

There is no better way to enjoy a new country than as the guest of a local family. And, of course, a night with a friend or relative stretches your budget (usually along with your belly). I've had nothing but good experiences (and good sleep) at my "addresses" in Europe. There are two kinds of addresses: European addresses brought from home and those you pick up while traveling.

Before you leave, do some research. Dig up some European relatives. No matter how far out on the family tree they are, unless you're a real jerk, they're tickled to have an American visitor in their nest. I send my relatives a card announcing my visit to their town and telling them when I'll arrive. They answer with "Please come visit us" or "Have a good trip." It is obvious from their letter (or lack of one) if I'm invited to stop by.

Follow the same procedure with indirect contacts. I have dear "parents away from home" in Austria and London. My Austrian "parents" are really the parents of my sister's ski instructor. In London they are the parents of a friend of my uncle. Neither relationship was terribly close—until I visited. Now we are friends for life. This is not cultural freeloading. Both parties benefit from such a visit. Never forget that a Greek family is just as curious and interested in you as you are in them (and the same old nightly family meals are probably pretty boring). Equipped with hometown postcards, pictures of my family, and a bag of goodies for the children, I make a point of giving as much from my culture as I am taking from the culture of my host. I insist on no special treatment, telling my host that I am most comfortable when treated simply as part of the family. I try to help with the chores, I don't wear out my welcome, and I follow up each visit with postcards to share the rest of my trip with my friends. I pay or reimburse my hosts for their hospitality only with a thank-you letter from home, possibly with color prints of all of us together.

The other kind of address is one you pick up during your travels. Exchanging addresses is almost as common as a handshake in Europe. If you have a business or personal card, bring a pile. When people meet, they invite each other to visit. I warn my friend that I may very well show up some day at his house, whether it's in Osaka, New Zealand, New Mexico, or Dublin. When I have, it's been a good experience.

SERVAS

Servas is a worldwide organization that connects travelers with host families with the noble goal of building world peace through international understanding. Travelers pay $65 to join. They can stay for two nights (more only if invited) in homes of other members around the world. Arrangements are made after an exchange of letters, and no money changes hands. This is not a crash-pad exchange. It's cultural sightseeing through a real live-in experience. Plan to hang around to talk and share and learn. Offer to cook a meal or help out around the house. Many travelers swear by Servas as the only way to really travel and build a truly global list of friends. Opening your own home to visitors is not required (but encouraged). For more information, write to Servas at 11 John St., #407, New York, NY 10038, tel. 212/267-0252, fax 212/267-0292, Web site: http://servas.org, e-mail: usservas@servas.org.

The Globetrotters Club (BCM/Roving, WC1N 3XX London) runs a similar network of hosts and travelers, and Friendship Force (57 Forsyth St. NW, #900, Atlanta, GA 30303, tel. 800/554-6715, www.friendship-force.org) offers cultural exchange tours for the purpose of promoting global goodwill.

The Europeans you visit don't need to be next-of-kin. This Tirolean is the father of my sister's ski teacher. That's close enough.

HOUSE SWAPPING
Many families enjoy a great budget option year after year. They trade houses (sometimes cars, too, but draw the line at pets) with someone at the destination of their choice. For information, contact Intervac Home Exchange (Box 590504, San Francisco, CA 94159, tel. 800/756-HOME), HomeLink (tel. 800/638-3841, www.swapnow.com), or Trading Homes International (tel. 800/877-TRADE, www.trading-homes.com). *Vacation Home Exchange and Hospitality Guide* (John Kimbrough) and *Home Exchanging Vacationing* (Bill and Mary Barbour) are two guidebooks on the subject.

16. Eating
Many vacations revolve around great restaurant meals, and for good reason. Europe serves some of the world's top cuisine at some of the world's top prices. I'm no gourmet, so most of my experience lies in eating well cheaply. Galloping gluttons thrive on $10 a day—by picnicking. Those with a more refined palate and a little more money can mix picnics with atmospheric and enjoyable restaurant meals and eat just fine for $30 a day.

This $30-a-day budget includes a $5 continental breakfast (usually figured into your hotel bill), a $5 picnic or fast-food lunch, a $15 good and filling restaurant dinner (more with wine or dessert), and $5 for your chocolate, cappuccino, or gelato fix. If your budget requires, you can find a satisfying dinner for $10 anywhere in Europe.

BREAKFAST

Only Britain, Scandinavia, and the Netherlands serve hearty breakfasts. In most of Europe, continental breakfasts are the norm. You'll get a roll with marmalade or jam, occasionally a slice of ham or cheese, and coffee or tea. Even the finest hotels serve the same thing—on better plates. It's the European way to start the day. (Sorry, no Mueslix.)

Supplement your breakfast with a piece of fruit and a wrapped chunk of cheese from your rucksack stash. Orange juice fans pick up liter boxes ($2) in the grocery store and start the day with a glass in their hotel room. If you're a coffee drinker, remember that breakfast is the only cheap time to caffeinate yourself. Some hotels will serve you a bottomless cup of a rich brew only with breakfast. After that, the cups acquire bottoms. Juice is often available, but you have to ask, and you might be charged.

Breakfast, normally "included" in your hotel bill, can sometimes be skipped and deducted from the price of your room. Ask what the breakfast includes and costs. You can usually save money and gain atmosphere by buying coffee and a roll or croissant at the café down the street or by brunching picnic-style in the park. I'm a big-breakfast person at home. When I feel the urge for a typical American breakfast in Europe, I beat it to death with a hard roll. You can find bacon, eggs, and orange juice, but it's nearly always overpriced and a disappointment.

Few hotel breakfasts are worth waiting around for. If you need to get an early start, skip it. Many places will fill your thermos with coffee before you go.

PICNICS—SPEND LIKE A PAUPER, EAT LIKE A PRINCE

There is only one way left to feast for $5 anywhere in Europe—picnic. You'll eat better while spending $15 to $20 a day less than those who eat exclusively in restaurants.

I am a picnic connoisseur. (After four months in Europe, the first thing I do when I get home is put some cheese on a hard roll.) While I'm the first to admit that restaurant meals are an important aspect of any culture, I picnic almost daily. This is not solely for budgetary reasons. It's fun to dive into a marketplace and actually get a chance to do business.

The continental breakfast—bread, jam, cheese, and coffee

Europe's colorful markets overflow with varied cheeses, meats, fresh fruits, vegetables, and still-warm-out-of-the-bakery-oven bread. Many of my favorite foods made their debut in a European picnic.

To busy sightseers, restaurants can be time-consuming and frustrating. After waiting to be served, tangling with a menu, and consuming a budget-threatening meal, you walk away feeling unsatisfied, knowing your money could have done much more for your stomach if you had invested it in a picnic. Nutritionally, a picnic is unbeatable. Consider this example: cheese, thinly-sliced ham, fresh bread, peaches, carrots, a cucumber, a half-liter of milk, and fruit yogurt for dessert.

To bolster your budget, I recommend picnic dinners every few nights. Save time and money by raiding the refrigerator for dinner, which, in Europe, is the corner deli or grocery store. There are plenty of tasty alternatives to sandwiches. Bakeries often sell little pizzas. Supermarkets, which hide out in the basements of big-city department stores, are getting very yuppie, offering salads, quiche, fried chicken, and fish, all "to go." "Microwave" is a universal word. When staying several nights, I "cozy up" a room by borrowing plates, glasses, and silverware from the hotel breakfast room and stocking the closet with my favorite groceries (juice, fruit and vegetables, cheese, and other munchies).

Picnic Shopping

Every town, large or small, has at least one colorful outdoor or indoor marketplace. Assemble your picnic here. Make an effort to communicate with the merchants. Most markets are not self-service: You point to what you want, and let the merchant bag it and weigh it for you. Know what you are buying and what you are spending. Whether you understand the prices or not, act like you do (observing the weighing process closely) and you're more likely to be treated fairly.

Learn the measurements. The unit of measure throughout the Continent is a kilo, or 2.2 pounds. A kilo has 1,000 grams. One hundred grams (a common unit of sale, in Italy called *un etto*) of cheese or meat tucked into a chunk of French bread gives you about a quarter-pounder.

Food can be priced by the kilo, 100-gram unit, or the piece. Watch the scale when your food is being weighed. It'll show grams and kilos. If dried apples are priced at 25 francs per kilo, that's $5 for 2.2 pounds, or $2.25 per pound. If the scale says 400 grams, that means 40 percent of 25 francs (or 10F), which is about $2.

Specialty foods are sometimes priced by 100 grams. If the *pâté* seems too cheap to be true, look at the sign closely. The posted price is probably followed by "100 gr." Chunky items like cucumbers will be priced by the piece (*Stück* in Germany or *pezzo* in Italy).

If no prices are posted, be wary. Tourists are routinely ripped off by market merchants in tourist centers. Find places that print the prices. Assume any market with no printed prices has a double price-standard: one for locals and a more expensive one for tourists.

I'll never forget a friend of mine who bought two bananas for our London picnic. He grabbed the fruit, held out a handful of change, and said, "How much?" The merchant took two pounds (worth $3). My friend turned to me and said, "Wow, London really is expensive." Anytime you hold out a handful of money to a banana salesman, you're just asking for trouble.

If you want only a small amount . . . You'll likely want only one or two pieces of fruit, and many merchants refuse to deal in small quantities. The way to get what you want and no more is to estimate about what it would cost if the merchant were to weigh it and then just hold out a coin worth about that much in one hand and the apple, or whatever, in the other. Have a look on your face that says, "If you take this coin, I'll go away." Rarely will he refuse the deal.

In supermarkets, it's a cinch to buy a tiny amount of fruit or vegetables. Most have an easy push-button pricing system: Put the banana on the scale, push the picture of a banana (or the banana bin number), and a sticky price tag prints out. You could weigh and sticker a single grape.

Picnic Drinks

There are plenty of cheap ways to wash down a picnic. Milk is always cheap, available in quarter-, half-, or whole liters. Be sure it's normal drinking milk. Strange white liquid dairy products in look-alike milk cartons abound (and careless tourists ruin their milk-and-cookie dreams). Look for local words for whole or light, such as *voll* or *lett*. Nutritionally, half a liter provides about 25 percent of your daily protein needs. Get refrigerated, fresh milk. You will often find a "longlife" kind of milk that needs no refrigeration. This milk will never go bad—or taste good.

European yogurt is delicious and can usually be drunk right out of its container. Fruit juice comes in handy liter boxes (look for "100% juice, no sugar" to avoid Kool-Aid clones). Buy cheap by the liter, and use a reusable half-liter plastic mineral-water bottle (sold next to the Coke all over) to store what you can't comfortably drink in one sitting. Liter bottles of Coke are cheap, as is wine in most countries. Local wine gives your picnic a nice touch. Any place that serves coffee has free boiling water. Those who have more nerve than pride get their plastic water bottle (a sturdy plastic bottle will not melt) filled with free boiling water at a café, then add their own instant coffee or tea bag later. Many hotels or cafés will fill a thermos with coffee for about the price of two cups.

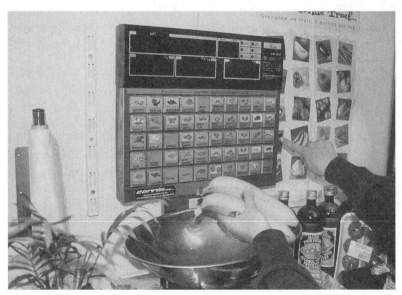

Put your banana in the bin, push the banana button, rip off the price sticker, and stick it on your banana.

Picnic on the train—quick, hearty, scenic

Picnic Atmosphere

There is nothing second-class about a picnic. A few special touches will even make your budget meal a first-class affair. Proper site selection can make the difference between just another meal and *le piquenique extraordinaire*. Since you've decided to skip the restaurant, it's up to you to create the atmosphere.

Try to incorporate a picnic brunch, lunch, or dinner into the day's sightseeing plans. For example, I start the day by scouring the thriving market with my senses and my camera. Then I fill up my shopping bag and have breakfast on a riverbank. After sightseeing, I combine lunch and a siesta in a cool park to fill my stomach, rest my body, and escape the early afternoon heat. It's fun to eat dinner on a castle wall enjoying a commanding view and the setting sun. Some of my all-time best picnics have been lazy dinners accompanied by medieval fantasies in the quiet of after-hours Europe.

Mountain hikes are punctuated nicely by picnics. Food tastes even better on top of a mountain. Europeans are great picnickers. Many picnics become potlucks, resulting in new friends as well as full stomachs.

Table Scraps and Tips

Bring picnic supplies. Pack Zip-lock baggies (large and small) and a good knife with a can opener. In addition to being a handy plate, fan, and lousy Frisbee, a plastic coffee can lid makes an easy-to-clean cutting board with a juice-containing lip. A dishtowel doubles as a small table-cloth. And a fancy hotel shower cap contains messy food nicely on your picnic cloth. Bring an airline-type coffee cup and spoon for cereal, and a fork for take-out salad and chicken. Some travelers get immersion heaters (buy in Europe for a compatible plug) to make hot drinks to go with munchies in their hotel room.

Stretch your money. Bread has always been cheap in Europe. (Leaders have learned from history that when stomachs rumble, so do the mobs in the streets.) Cheese is a specialty nearly everywhere and is, along with milk, one of the Continent's cheapest sources of protein. The stan-dard low-risk option anywhere in Europe is Emmentaler cheese (the kind with holes that we call "Swiss"). In season, tomatoes, cucumbers, and watermelons are good deals in Italy. Eastern Europe has some of the best and cheapest ice cream anywhere. Ice cream is costly in Scandinavia (what isn't?), and wine is a best buy in France. Anything American is usually expensive and rarely satisfying.

Make your big meal of the day a picnic lunch or dinner. Only a glutton can spend more than $10 for a picnic feast. In a park in Paris, on a Norwegian ferry, high in the Alps, on your dashboard at an autobahn rest stop, on your convent rooftop, or in your hotel room, picnicking is the budget traveler's key to cheap and good eating.

A picnic of Franciscan splendor, overlooking Assisi

FAST FOOD, CAFETERIAS, AND MENSAS

McEurope: Fast-food places are everywhere. Yes, the hamburgerization of the world is a shame, but face it—the busiest and biggest McDonald's in the world are in Tokyo, Rome, and Moscow. The burger has become a global thing. You'll find Big Macs in every language—not exciting (and more than the American price), but at least at McDonald's you know exactly what you're getting, and it's fast. A hamburger, fries, and shake are fun halfway through your trip.

American fast-food joints are kid-friendly and satisfy the need for a cheap salad bar and a tall orange juice. They've grabbed prime bits of real estate in every big European city. Since there's no cover, this is an opportunity to savor a low-class paper cup of coffee while enjoying some high-class people-watching.

Each country has its equivalent of the hamburger stand (I saw a "McCheaper" in Switzerland). Whatever their origin, they're a hit with the young locals and a handy place for a quick, cheap bite.

Cafeterias: "Self-service" is an international word. You'll find self-service restaurants in big cities everywhere, offering low-price, low-risk, low-stress, what-you-see-is-what-you-get meals. A sure value for your dollar, franc, or schilling is a department store cafeteria. These places are designed for the shopping housewife who has a sharp eye for a good value. At a salad bar, grab the small (cheap) plate and stack it like the locals—high.

When exhaustion hits, munch a light dinner in your hotel room.

A quick dashboard picnic halfway through a busy day of sightseeing

Mensas: If your wallet is as empty as your stomach, find a "mensa." Mensa is the pan-European word for a government-subsidized institutional (university, fire station, union of gondoliers, etc.) cafeteria. If the place welcomes tourists, you can fill yourself with a plate of dull but nourishing food for an unbeatable price in the company of local students or workers.

University cafeterias (often closed during summer holidays) offer a surefire way to meet educated English-speaking young locals with open and stimulating minds. They're often eager to practice their politics and economics, as well as their English, on a foreign friend. This is especially handy as you travel beyond Europe.

CAFÉS AND BARS
From top to bottom, Europe is into café-sitting, coffee, and people-watching. Tourists are often stung by not understanding the rules of the game. You'll pay less to stand and more to sit. In general, if you simply want to slam down a cup of coffee, order and drink it at the bar. If you want to sit awhile and absorb that last museum while checking out the two-legged art, grab a table with a view, and a waiter will take your order. This will cost you about double. If you're on a budget, always confirm the price for a sit-down drink. While it's never high profile, there's always a

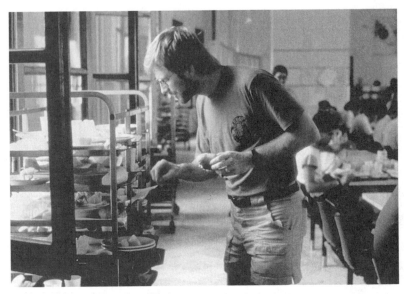

Cafeteria leftovers: even cheaper than picnics . . .

price list posted somewhere inside with the two-tiered price system clearly labeled (e.g., at the bar, 5 francs; at the table, 8 francs). If you pay for a seat in a café with a more expensive drink, that seat's yours for the entire afternoon if you like.

In some coffee bars (especially in Italy), you pay for your drink (or whatever) at the cash register, then take your receipt to the bar, where you'll be served.

RESTAURANTS

Restaurants are the most expensive way to eat. They can pillage and plunder a tight budget, but it would be criminal to pass through Europe without sampling the local specialties served in good restaurants. A country's high cuisine is just as culturally important as its museums. Experience it.

European restaurant meals are about as expensive as those in the United States. The cost of eating is determined not by the local standard but by your personal standard. Many Americans can't find an edible meal for less than $20 in their hometown. Their neighbors enjoy eating out for half that. If you can enjoy a $10 meal in Boston, Detroit, or Seattle, you'll eat well in London, Rome, or Helsinki for the same price. Last year I ate 100 dinners in Europe. My budget target was $5 to $10 for a simple, fill-the-tank meal; $15 for a memorable restaurant dinner; and $20 to $25 for a splurge meal. Forget the scare stories. People who spend $50 for a dinner in Dublin and then complain either enjoy complaining or are fools. Let me fill you in on filling up in Europe.

In European cafés, menus are two-tiered: cheaper at the bar, more at a table.

Average tourists are attracted—like flies to cow pies—to the biggest neon sign that boasts, "We speak English and accept credit cards." Wrong! The key to finding a good meal is to find a restaurant filled with loyal, local customers enjoying themselves. Be snoopy. Look at what people are eating—just don't ask for a taste. After a few days in Europe, you'll have no trouble telling a local hangout from a tourist trap.

Restaurants listed in your guidebook are usually fine, but too often when a place becomes famous this way, it goes downhill. You don't need those listings to find your own good restaurant. Leave the tourist center and stroll around until you find a restaurant with a happy crowd of locals. Ask your hotel receptionist, or even someone on the street, for a good place—not a good place for tourists, but a place they'd take a local guest.

Deciphering the Menu
European restaurants post their menus outside. Check the price and selection before entering. If the menu's not posted, ask to see one.

Finding the right restaurant is only half the battle. Then you need to order a good meal. Ordering in a foreign language can be fun, or it can be an ordeal. Ask for an English menu—if nothing else, you might get the waiter who speaks the *goodest* English. Most waiters can give at least a very basic translation—"cheekin, bunny, zuppa, green salat," and so on. A phrase book or menu reader (especially one of Altar Publishing's handy little *Marling Menu Masters*) is very helpful for those who want to avoid ordering sheep stomach when all they want is a lamb chop.

If you don't know what to order, go with the waiter's recommendation or look for your dream meal on another table and order by pointing. People are usually helpful and understanding to the poor and hungry

A promising menu: hand-written in only the local language, with a limited selection. For 90 francs you'll get a three-course meal with these choices.

monoglot tourist. If they aren't, you probably picked a place that sees too many of them. Europeans with the most patience with tourists are the ones who rarely deal with them.

People who agonize over each word on the menu season the whole experience with stress. If you're in a good place, the food's good. Get a basic idea of what's cooking, have some fun with the waiter, be loose and adventurous, and just order something.

To max out culturally, my partner and I order two different meals: one high-risk and one low-risk. We share, sampling twice as many dishes. At worst, we learn what we don't like and split the chicken and fries. My groups cut every dish into bits, and our table becomes a lazy Susan. If anything, the waiters are impressed by our interest in their food, and very often they'll run over with a special treat for all of us to sample—like squid eggs.

Common in Italy and France, the "tourist menu" or "menu of the day" is very popular and normally a good value. Look for the posted *menù turistica* or *menù del giorno* in Italy, or the *menu touristique* in France. For a set price, you get the "special of the day," a multicourse meal complete with bread, service, and sometimes, wine. Often you can choose from several appetizers and entrées. When I'm lazy and the price is right, I go for it, and it usually turns out OK. But you'll notice that people in the know (locals) order à la carte.

The best values in entrées are usually fish, veal, and chicken. In Italy, ordering pasta as an entrée saves money. Drinks (except for wine in France and Italy) and desserts are the worst value. Skipping those, you can enjoy some surprisingly classy $15 meals.

Restaurant Drinks

In restaurants, Europeans drink bottled water (for taste, not health). Tap water is normally not served (except in France). You can get free tap water, but you may need to be polite, patient, inventive, and know the correct phrase. There's nothing wrong with ordering tap water, and wait-

Young taste buds having their horizons stretched

ers are accustomed to this American request. But it is a special favor, and while your glass or carafe of tap water is normally served politely, occasionally it just isn't worth the trouble, and it's best to just put up with the bottle of Perrier or order a drink from the menu.

Bottled water is served crisp and cold, either with or without carbonation, usually by happier waiters. Most tourists don't like the bubbly stuff. Learn the phrase–*con/avec/mit/*with gas or *senza/sans/ohne/*without gas (in Italian, French and German, respectively), and you will get the message across. Acquire a taste for *acqua con gas*. It's a lot more fun (and read on the label what it'll do for your rheumatism).

If your budget is tight and you want to save $5 to $10 a day, never buy a restaurant drink. Scoff if you have the money, but drinks can sink a budget. Water is jokingly called the "American champagne" by the waiters of Europe.

Drink like a European. Cold milk, ice cubes, and coffee with (rather than after) your meal are American habits. Insisting on any of these in Europe will get you nothing but strange looks and a reputation as the ugly—if not downright crazy—American. Order local drinks, not just to save money but to experience the culture and to get the best quality and service. The timid can order the "American waters" (Coke, Fanta, and 7-Up), sold everywhere.

Buying local alcohol is cheaper than your favorite import. A shot of the local hard drink in Portugal will cost a dollar, while an American drink would cost at least the American price. Drink the local stuff with local people in local bars; a better experience than a gin and tonic in your hotel with a guy from Los Angeles. Drink wine in wine countries and beer in beer countries. Sample the regional specialties. Let a local person order you her favorite. You may hate it, but you'll never forget it.

Getting the Bill

A Continental meal is a leisurely experience, the focus of the evening. At good restaurants, service will seem slow. Meals won't always come simultaneously—it's fine to eat when served. A European meal is an end in itself. Europeans will spend at least two hours enjoying a good dinner, and for the full experience, so should you. Fast service is rude service. If you need to eat and run, make your time limits very clear as you order.

To get the bill, you'll have to ask for it (catch the waiter's eye and, with raised hands, scribble with an imaginary pencil on your palm). Before it comes, make a mental tally of roughly how much your meal should cost. The bill should vaguely resemble the figure you expected. It should have

A fun neighborhood restaurant: no English menus, no credit cards, but good food, good prices, and a friendly chef.

European pubs don't serve minors beer—but many locals do.

the same number of digits. If the total is a surprise, ask to have it itemized and explained. Some waiters make the same "innocent" mistakes repeatedly, knowing most tourists are so befuddled by the money and menu that they'll pay whatever number lies at the bottom of the bill.

Tipping
Tipping is a minuscule concern of mine during a European trip. Front-door travel agents advise going to Europe armed with dollar bills for tipping. They'll advise putting five bucks under your pillow to get extra towels from the maids. (Instead, I leave a small chocolate on the pillows when departing for the day.)

When traveling through the Back Door the only tipping you'll do is in the rare restaurant where service isn't included, rounding the taxi bill up, or when someone assists you in seeing a sight and is paid no other way (such as the man who shows people an Etruscan tomb that just happens to be in his backyard).

In restaurants, a service charge of about 15 percent is almost always included in the menu price or added automatically to your bill. If service is not included, the menu will say so (*service non compris* or *s.n.c.*). Tipping (as opposed to "service") is another matter and is not expected.

Leaving the coins or rounding up the bill is a nice touch for especially good service. Overtipping is Ugly American. In the days of the big buck, Americans shaped an image that Yankees today are having a hard time living down. If your bucks talk at home, muzzle them in Europe. As a matter of principle, if not economy, the local price should prevail.

Vegetarians

Vegetarians find life a little frustrating in Europe. Very often, Europeans think "vegetarian" means "no red meat" or "not much meat." If you are a strict vegetarian, you'll have to make things very clear. Write the appropriate phrase below, keep it handy, and show it to each waiter before ordering your meal:

German: *Wir sind (Ich bin) Vegetarier. Wir essen (Ich esse) kein Fleisch, Fisch oder Geflügel. Eier und Käse OK.*

French: *Nous sommes (Je suis) vegetarien. Nous ne mangons (Je ne mange) pas de viande, poisson, ou poulet. Oeufs et fromage OK.*

Italian: *Siamo vegetariani (Sono vegetariano/a). Non mangiamo (mangio) nè carne, nè pesce, nè polli. Uova e formaggio OK.*

Dutch: We are (I am) vegetarian. We (I) do not eat meat, fish, or chicken. Eggs and cheese are OK. (Most Dutch speak English.)

Vegetarians have no problem with continental breakfasts, which are normally meatless anyway. Meat-free picnic lunches are delicious, since bread, cheese, and yogurt are wonderful throughout Europe. It's in restaurants that your patience may be minced. Big-city tourist offices list restaurants by category. In any language, look under "V." Italy seems to sprinkle a little meat in just about everything. German cooking normally keeps the meat separate from the vegetables. Hearty German salads, with beets, cheese, and eggs, are a vegetarian's delight.

Tap Water in Five Languages

Italian–*acqua del rubinetto*
French–*l'eau du robinet*
German–*Leitungswasser*
Spanish–*agua del grifo*
Portuguese–*agua a torneira*

In all other languages, just do the international charade: hold imaginary glass in left hand, turn on tap with right, make sound of faucet. Stop it with a click and drink it with a smile.

For restaurant food at halfway-to-picnic prices, visit the local rosticceria *or take-out deli.*

Vegetarians enjoy salad bars, Third World cuisine, and ethnic restaurants throughout Europe.

LOCAL SPECIALTIES, ONE COUNTRY AT A TIME

Eating in Europe is sightseeing for your taste buds. Every country has local specialties that are good, memorable, or both. Seek out and eat or drink, at least once, the notorious "gross" specialties: ouzo, horse meat, snails, raw herring, and so on (but not *lutefisk*). All your life you'll hear references to them, and you'll have actually experienced what everyone's talking about. Here are some tips to help you eat, drink, and be merry in Europe.

Belgium

Belgians boast that they eat as heartily as the Germans and as well as the French. This tiny country is into big steaks and designer chocolates. While Godiva's chocolate is considered the finest, most locals will enjoy triple the dose for the same investment by getting their fix at Leonidas. Belgian beer is tops. Connoisseurs arrive with a checklist, hoping to hop from Kriek (a cherry-flavored beer) to Dentergems (with coriander and orange peel) to Trappist (a dark, monk-made brew). The French fries even taste good dunked in mayonnaise (local-style). Don't miss mussels in Brussels.

Britain and Ireland

Rather than looking for fine cuisine in Britain and Ireland, settle for decent cuisine in great atmosphere. I'm a sucker for pub grub. The days of starchy microwaved meat pies and mushy peas are over, and pubs actually turn out good, filling, hot meals with crispy fresh vegetables for $8. Locals seem to take great care in keeping up-to-date on which pubs do the best meals. Stow your guidebook and go with the local favorite. Beer snobs appreciate England's ales and bitters. If you're just looking for a cold Bud, ask for a lager. For a change of pace, try Indian food—as popular in Britain as hamburgers are in America.

France

France is famous for its cuisine—and rightly so. Dining in France can be surprisingly easy on a budget, especially in the countryside. Small restaurants throughout the country love their regional cuisine and take great pride in serving it.

The *plat du jour* (daily special) or *menu* (fixed-price, three- to six-course meal) are often good deals. To get a complete list of what's cooking, ask for the *carte* (not the *menu*). The cheese boards that come with multicourse meals offer the average American a new adventure in eating. When it comes, ask for "a little of each, please" (*un peu de chaque, s'il vous plaît*). Wine is the cheapest drink, and every region has its own wine and cheese. Order the house wine (*vin du pays*). Classy restaurants are easiest to afford at lunchtime, when meal prices are reduced. France is known for particularly slow (as in polite) service. If you need to eat and run, make it clear from the start. Bars serve reasonable omelets, salads, and the *croque monsieur*—your standard grilled cheese and ham sandwich.

Degustation gratuite is not a laxative but an invitation to sample the wine. You'll find D/G signs throughout France's wine-growing regions. When buying cheese, be sure to ask for samples of the local specialties. Croissants are served warm with breakfast, and baguettes (long, skinny loaves of French bread) are great for budget munching.

Regardless of your budget, picnic for a royal tour of French delicacies. Make a point of visiting the small specialty shops and picking up the finest (most expensive) *pâtés*, cheeses, and hors d'oeuvres. As you spread out your tablecloth, every passerby will wish you a cheery "*Bon appétit!*"

Germany

Germany is ideal for the "meat-and-potatoes" person. With straightforward, no-nonsense food at budget prices, I eat very well in Deutschland.

Andrea Hagg

Ein Beer, ein Pretzel, und thou

Small-town restaurants serve up wonderful plates of hearty local specialties for $10. The *Würst* is the best anywhere, and *Kraut* is not as *sauer* as the stuff you hate at home. Eat ugly things whenever possible. So many tasty European specialties come in gross packages.

Drink beer in Bavaria and wine on the Rhine, choosing the most atmospheric *Bräuhaus* or *Weinstube* possible.

Browse through supermarkets and see what Germany eats when there's no more beer and pretzels. Try Gummi Bears, the bear-shaped jelly bean with a cult following, and Nutella, a sensuous choco-nut spread that turns anything into a first-class dessert. Fast-food stands are called *Schnell Imbiss.* For budget relief in big-city Germany, find a Greek, Turkish, or Italian restaurant.

Greece

While the menus are all Greek to most tourists, it's common and acceptable to go into the kitchen and point to the dish you want. This is a good way to make some friends, sample from each kettle, get what you want (or at least know what you're getting), and have a memorable meal. (The same is true in Turkey.) Be brave. My favorite Greek snack is a tasty shish kebab wrapped in flat bread—called a souvlaki pita.

Souvlaki stands, offering $1 take-out pita sandwiches, are all over Greece. On the islands, eat fresh seafood and dunk bread into *tzatziki*, a refreshing cucumber and yogurt dip. Don't miss the creamy yogurt with honey. The feta (goat) cheese salads and the flaky nut 'n' honey dessert called baklava are two other tasty treats. If possible, go to a wine festival. Retsina is a pine resin–flavored wine that is a dangerous taste to acquire. For American-style coffee, order "Nescafe," but try the potent, grainy Greek coffee for a real kick. Eat when the locals do—late.

Italy

Italians eat huge meals consisting of a first course of pasta, a second plate of meat, plus a salad, fruit, and wine. The pasta course alone is usually enough to fill the average tourist. Some restaurants won't serve just pasta; find one that will, and you'll enjoy a reasonably priced meal of lasagna or minestrone and a salad. Also know that anytime you eat or drink at a table, you'll be charged a cover (*coperto*) of a dollar or two. That, plus service (*servizio*), makes even a cheap, one-course restaurant meal cost $10.

For inexpensive Italian eateries, look for the term *osteria, tavola calda, rosticceria, trattoria, pizzeria,* or "self-service." A big pizza (sold everywhere for under $7) and a cold beer is my idea of a good, fast,

The best snack deal in Europe—a Greek souvlaki

Pizza: the cheapest meal in Italy. Note on this menu the cover and service charge or the cheaper "exportation" option.

cheap Italian meal. For a stand-up super bargain meal, look for a Pizza Rustica, which sells pizza by weight. Just point to the best-looking pizza and tell them how much you want (200 grams is a filling meal). They weigh, you pay. They heat it, you eat it.

The *menù del giorno* (menu of the day, usually a good deal), *pane e coperto* (charge for bread and cover), and *servizio compreso* (service included) are three important phrases to know. But the most important word in your Italian vocabulary is *gelato*—probably the best ice cream you'll ever taste. A big cone or cup containing a variety of flavors costs about $2.

Cappuccino, rich coffee with a frothy head of steamed milk, is very popular, and it should be. Tiny coffee shops are tucked away on just about every street. All have a price list, and most require you to pay the cashier first and then take the receipt to the man who makes the drinks. Experiment. Try coffee or tea *freddo* (cold) or a *frappe* (blended ice). Discover a new specialty each day. Bars sell large bottles of cold mineral water, with or without gas, for about $1. *Panini* (sandwiches) are cheap and widely available.

Bar-hopping is fun. A carafe of house wine serves four or five people for $4. Many bars have delicious *cicchetti* (cheh-KAY-tee), local toothpick munchies. A *cicchetteria* is a great place for an entire meal of these pint-sized taste treats.

The Netherlands

My favorite Dutch food is Indonesian. Indonesia, a former colony of the Netherlands, fled the nest, leaving behind plenty of great Indonesian restaurants. The cheapest meals, as well as some of the best splurges, are found in these "Chinese-Indisch" restaurants. The famous *rijsttafel* (rice table) is the ultimate Indonesian meal, with as many as 36 delightfully exotic courses, all eaten with rice. One meal is plenty for two, so order carefully. In a small-town restaurant, a *rijsttafel* can be a great bargain—two can split 12 exotic courses with rice for $14. *Bami* or *nasi goreng* are smaller and cheaper but still filling versions of *rijsttafel*.

Other Dutch treats include *nieuwe haring* (raw herring) and *siroopwafels*—a syrup-filled cookie that's best eaten warm from the bakery.

Portugal

Portugal has some of the most enjoyable and cheapest eating I've found in Europe. Find a local sailors' hangout and fill up on fresh seafood, especially clams and cockles. While Portuguese restaurants are not expensive, food stands in the fairs and amusement parks are even cheaper. The young *vinho verde* is an addictive local specialty and a favorite of visiting wine buffs.

Scandinavia

Most Scandinavians avoid their highly taxed and very expensive restaurants. The cost of alcohol alone is a sobering experience. The key to budget eat-

Two fine reasons to savor Italy: gelato *and the Riviera*

Rich Sorensen

Enough food to sink a Viking ship: Smörgåsbord

ing in Nordic Europe is to take advantage of the smörgåsbord. For about $15 (cheap in Scandinavia), breakfast smörgåsbords will fill you with plenty of hearty food. You won't get a doggie bag, but I have noticed empty rucksacks (or zip-lock baggies) filling out as fast as their owners. Since both meals are, by definition, all-you-can-eat, I opt for the budget breakfast meal over the fancier and more expensive ($25) *middag*, or midday, smörgåsbords. Many train stations and ferries serve smörgåsbords.

For a budget lunch in Denmark, find a *smörrebröd* (open-face sandwich) shop. These places make artistic and delicious sandwich picnics to go.

All over Scandinavia, keep your eyes peeled for daily lunch specials called *dagens rett*. You can normally have all the vegetables (usually potatoes) you want when you order a restaurant's entrée. Just ask for seconds. Many Scandinavian pizzerias offer amazing all-you-can-eat deals and hearty salad bars. (Your bill will double if you order a beer.) The cheapest cafeterias often close around 5:00 or 6:00 p.m. Fresh produce, colorful markets, and efficient supermarkets abound in Europe's most expensive corner. Save money and get some fresh air—picnic.

Spain

The greatest pleasure in Spanish eating is the price tag. Take advantage of the house wine. Fit the local schedule: Lunch is late (1:00–3:00 p.m.), and dinner is later (8:30–11:30 p.m.). Restaurants are generally closed except at mealtimes. *Platos combinados* (combination plates of three or more items) are a reasonable way to sample Spanish cuisine. At other times, bars and coffee spots serve snacks of *bocadillos* (sandwiches), *tortillas* (omelets, great in a bar for a cheap and hearty breakfast), and *tapas* (hors d'oeuvres). On my last trip, I ate at least one easy, quick, and very cheap tapas meal a day. It seems that the most popular local bars are the ones with the most litter on the floor.

Switzerland

Swiss restaurant prices will ruin your appetite and send you running to a grocery store. Even locals find their restaurants expensive. The Migros and Co-op grocery stores sell groceries for about the same price as you'd find in American stores—cheap by European standards. Hostels usually serve large family-style dinners at a low price. *Rösti* (a hash-browns-with-onions dish) is a good, hearty standby. *Raclette* (melted cheese, potatoes, and pickles) is also popular. Split a cheese fondue with your hiking partner before filling up on Swiss chocolate. The remote mountain huts offer more than shelter. Many have provisions helicoptered in, are reasonably priced, and bubble with Alpine atmosphere. The Swiss wine, *Fendant*, is expensive (sold by the deciliter) but worth every franc. Local beer is cheap by Swiss standards and good.

Turkey

Bring an appetite and order high on the menu in nice restaurants. Eating's cheap in Turkey. The typical eatery is a user-friendly cafeteria with giant bins of lots of delicacies you always thought were Greek. *Kebabs* are a standard meaty snack. *Pide*, fresh out of the oven, is Turkish pizza. *Sutlac* (rice pudding) and *baklava* will satisfy your sweet tooth. Munch pistachios by the pocketful. Tea in tiny hourglass-shaped glasses is served constantly everywhere. A refreshing milky yogurt drink called *ayran*, cheap boxes of cherry juice, and fresh-squeezed orange juice make it fun to quench your Turkish thirst. Or try the *raki* (Turkish ouzo). Let a local show you how to carefully create a two-layered *raki* drink by adding water. For breakfast, get ready for cucumbers, olives, tomatoes, and lots of goat cheese and bread.

17. Shopping

Gift shopping is getting very expensive. I remember buying a cuckoo clock 15 years ago for $5. Now a "Happy Meal" at the Munich McDonald's costs that much.

SOUVENIR STRATEGIES

Shop in countries where your dollar stretches farthest. Shop in Turkey, Morocco, Portugal, Spain, and Greece. For the price of a four-inch pewter Viking ship in Norway, you can buy a real boat in Turkey.

Shop at flea markets. The most colorful shopping in Europe is at its flea markets. Among the best are Amsterdam's Waterlooplein (Saturday), London's Bermondsey (early Friday) and Portobello Market (Saturday), Madrid's El Rastro (Sunday), and Paris' Porte de Clignancourt (best on Sunday; also on Saturday and Monday). Flea markets anywhere have soft prices. Bargain like mad. Pickpockets love flea markets—wear your money belt and watch your day bag.

Check out large department stores. These often have a souvenir section with standard local knickknacks and postcards at prices way below the cute little tourist shops'.

Stay in control. Shopping is an important part of the average person's trip, but all too often, slick marketing and cutesy, romantic window displays can succeed in shifting the entire focus of your vacation toward things in the tourist shops. (It's a lucrative business. Many souvenir merchants in Italy work through the tourist season, then retire for the rest of the year.) This sort of tourist brainwashing can turn you into one of the many people who set out to see and experience Europe but find themselves wandering in a trancelike search for signs announcing Duty-Free Shopping. I've seen half the members of a British Halls of Parliament guided tour skip out to survey an enticing display of plastic "bobby" hats and Union Jack panties. Even if the sign says, "Keep Italy green, spend dollars," don't let your trip degenerate into a glorified shopping spree.

Ask yourself if your enthusiasm is merited. More often than not, you can pick up a very similar item of better quality for a cheaper price at home. Unless you're a real romantic, the thrill of where you bought something fades long before the item's usefulness. My life has more room for a functional souvenir than for a useless symbol of a place I visited. Even thoughtful shoppers go overboard. I have several large boxes in my attic labeled "great souvenirs."

Try to restrict your shopping to a stipulated time. Most people have an idea of what they want to buy in each country. Set aside one day to shop in each country, and stick to it. This way you avoid drifting through your trip thinking only of souvenirs.

To pack light, shop at the end of your trip. Ideally, end your trip in a cheap country, do all of your shopping, then fly home. One summer I had a 16-pound rucksack and nothing more until the last week of my trip

Boxloads of Davids *await busloads of tourists.*

when, in Spain and Morocco, I managed to accumulate two medieval chairs, two sets of bongos, a camel-hair coat, swords, a mace, and a lace tablecloth.

Good souvenirs: My favorites are books (a great value all over Europe, with many impossible-to-find-in-the-U.S. editions), local crafts (well-explained in guidebooks, such as hand-knit sweaters in Portugal or Ireland, glass in Sweden, lace in Belgium), strange stuffed animals (at flea markets), cassettes of music I heard live, posters (one sturdy tube stores eight or ten posters safely), clothing, photographs I've taken, and memories whittled carefully into my journal.

VALUE-ADDED TAX (VAT) REFUNDS

Local European sales taxes vary from 15 to 25 percent. Tourists who buy something new (and expensive) and carry it with them out of the country can often get this tax refunded. And each year more than half a billion dollars of refundable taxes are left unclaimed. Yes, that is exciting. But VAT refunds are generally not worth the trouble.

Each country sets a different limit for the minimum amount you must buy in a store to qualify for a refund. Generally if you're buying something worth over $100 in a country with high taxes (Britain and most of northern Europe), ask about a VAT refund.

Getting a refund: If you shop at a store that participates in the Tax-free Program (look for the sticker in the window or ask a clerk), you'll get a Tax-free Shopping Cheque after you make a major purchase. Get the cheque validated at customs in the airport (when you leave Europe), and then claim your refund at the nearby "Tax-free Refund" booth. You can request cash, check, or charge-card credit. Save up your cheques from various European countries and process them all when you leave Europe. Be prepared to show your purchased goods to customs officials.

Ideally you'll talk your merchants into deducting the VAT from your purchase price and let them process the refund. When VAT refunds are worthwhile, merchants use them in their sales pitch. Local merchants know the VAT ropes and are the best VAT information source for their country.

CUSTOMS FOR AMERICAN SHOPPERS

You are allowed to take $400 of souvenirs home duty-free. The next $1,000 is dutied at a flat 10 percent. After that, you pay the individual item's duty rate. You can also bring in a liter of alcohol duty-free and more tobacco and cigarettes than you'd ever want.

You can mail one package per person per day worth up to $50 duty-free from Europe to the United States. Mark it "Unsolicited Gift." You'll need to fill out a customs form at the post office. (For details, see Chapter 20: Phones, e-mail, and Mail.)

SUCCESSFUL BARGAINING

In much of the world, the price tag is only an excuse to argue. Bargaining is the accepted and expected method of finding a compromise between the wishful thinking of the merchant and the tourist. Prices are "soft" in much of the Mediterranean world. In Europe bargaining is common only in the south, but you can fight prices at flea markets and with street vendors anywhere.

While bargaining is good for your budget, it can also become an enjoyable game. Many travelers are addicted hagglers who would gladly skip a tour of a Portuguese palace to get the price down on the black-clad lady's handmade tablecloth.

The Ten Commandments of the Successful Haggler

1. Determine if bargaining is appropriate. It's bad shopping etiquette to "make an offer" for a tweed hat in a London department store. It's foolish not to at a Greek outdoor market. To learn if a price is fixed, show some interest in an item but say, "It's just too much money." You've put the merchant in a position to make the first offer. If he comes down even 2 percent, there's nothing sacred about the price tag. Haggle away.

2. Shop around, and find out what locals pay. Prices can vary drastically among vendors at the same flea market, and even at the same stall. If prices aren't posted, assume there's a double price-standard: one for locals and one for you. If only tourists buy the item you're pricing, see what an Arab, Spanish, or Italian tourist would be charged. I remember thinking I did well in Istanbul's Grand Bazaar, until I learned my Spanish friend bought the same shirt for 30 percent less. Merchants assume American tourists are rich. And they know what we pay for things at home.

3. Determine what the item is worth to you. Price tags can be meaningless and serve to distort your idea of an item's true worth. The merchant is playing a psychological game. Many tourists think that if they can cut the price by 50 percent they are doing great. So the merchant quadruples his prices and the tourist happily pays double the fair value. The best way to deal with crazy price tags is to ignore them. Before you even see the price tag, determine the item's value to you, considering the hassles involved in packing it or shipping it home.

4. Determine the merchant's lowest price. Many merchants will settle for a nickel profit rather than lose the sale entirely. Promise yourself that no matter how exciting the price becomes, you won't buy. Then work the cost down to rock bottom. When it seems to have fallen to a record low, walk away. That last price he hollers out as you turn the corner is often the best price you'll get. If the price is right, go back and buy.

5. Look indifferent. As soon as the merchant perceives the "I gotta have that!" in you, you'll never get the best price. He knows Americans have the money to buy what they really want.

6. Employ a third person. Use your friend who is worried about the ever-dwindling budget or who doesn't like the price or who is bored and wants to return to the hotel. This trick may work to bring the price down faster.

7. Impress the merchant with your knowledge—real or otherwise. He'll respect you, and you'll be more likely to get good quality. Istanbul has very good leather coats for a fraction of the U.S. cost. Before my trip I talked to some leather-coat sellers and was much better prepared to confidently pick out a good coat in Istanbul for $100.

8. Obey the rules. Don't hurry. Bargaining is rarely rushed. Get to know the shopkeeper. Accept his offer for tea, talk with him. He'll know you are serious. Dealing with the owner (no salesman's commission) can lower the price. Bid carefully. If a merchant accepts your price (or vice versa), you must buy the item.

9. Show the merchant your money. Physically hold out your money and offer him "all you have" to pay for whatever you are bickering over. He'll be tempted to just grab your money and say, "Oh, OK."

10. If the price is too much, leave. Never worry about having taken too much of the merchant's time and tea. They are experts at making the tourist feel guilty for not buying. It's all part of the game. Most merchants, by local standards, are financially well-off.

Remember, you can generally find the same souvenirs in large department stores at fair and firm prices. Department store shopping is quicker, easier, often cheaper—but not nearly as much fun.

CITY SKILLS

18. Getting Oriented

Many Americans are overwhelmed by European big-city shock. Struggling with the Chicagos, New Yorks, and L.A.s of Europe is easier if you take advantage of the local tourist information office, catch some kind of orientation tour, and take advantage of the public transportation system. You can't Magoo Europe's large cities. Plan ahead. Have a directory-type guidebook for wherever you're traveling. Spend the last hour as you approach by train or bus reading and planning. Know what you want to see. To save time and energy, plan your sightseeing strategy to cover the city systematically and efficiently, one neighborhood at a time.

TOURIST INFORMATION OFFICES

No matter how well I know a town, my first stop is the tourist information office. Any place with a tourist industry has an information service for visitors located on the central square, in city hall, at the train station, or at the freeway entrance. You don't need the address—just follow the signs. An often-hectic but normally friendly and multilingual staff will give out sightseeing information, reserve hotel rooms, sell concert or play tickets, and answer questions.

Prepare a list of questions ahead of time. Write up a proposed sightseeing schedule. Find out if it's workable or if you've left out any important sights. Confirm closed days and free-admission days.

Ask for a city map, public transit information, and a list of sights with current hours. Find out about special events and pick up any local periodical entertainment guide. See if walking tours or self-guided walking tour brochures are available. Check on any miscellaneous concerns (such as safety, laundry, bike rental, parking, camping, transportation tips for your departure, maps of nearby towns, or help with booking a room for your next destination).

Europe is amazingly well-organized. For instance, many tourist offices in major cities sell a "tourist card" for about $15, which includes 24 hours of free entrance to all the sights; free use of all the subways, buses, and boats; a booklet explaining everything; and a map. It's all very straightforward and usually in English.

If necessary, get ideas on where to eat and sleep. But remember, tourist information offices don't volunteer information on cheap alternatives to hotels, and they pocket any "deposits" collected.

Your first stop in a new town—the tourist information office

If you'll be arriving late, call ahead before the tourist office closes. Good information (in English) is worth a long-distance phone call. Guidebooks list the phone numbers.

MORE INFORMATION SOURCES

Big-hotel information desks, hostel wardens, other travelers, and guidebooks are helpful. To find guidebooks in English, check newsstands and English sections in large bookstores. All big cities have English bookstores (particularly in Great Britain), and most general bookstores have local guidebooks in several languages. If you find yourself in a town with no information and the tourist office is closed, a glance through a postcard rack will quickly show you the town's most famous sights.

Youth Centers: Many cities, especially in the north, have industrious youth travel-aid offices. The Scandinavian capitals' Interpoint centers offer comfortable lounges, showers, free luggage storage, discounts at local restaurants, and city information. Copenhagen has a great youth center called Use It, and several cities publish very practical youth-oriented budget travel magazines (available at the tourist office).

Entertainment Guides: Big European cities bubble with entertainment, festivities, and nightlife. But they won't come to you. New in town and unable to speak the local language, it's easy to be oblivious to a once-in-a-lifetime event erupting just across the bridge. A periodical entertainment guide is the ticket. Every big city has one, either in English (such as *This Week in Oslo*) or in the local language but easy to decipher (such as the *Pariscope* weekly). Buy one at a newsstand (if it's not free from the tourist office). In Venice, Florence, and Rome, the best guides are published monthly by the big, fancy hotels and are available for free at their desks. (Leave your rucksack outside.) Ask at your hotel about entertainment. Events are posted on city walls everywhere. Read posters. They are in a foreign language, but that really doesn't matter when it reads: Weinfest, Musica Folklorico, 9 Juni, 21:00, Piazza Major, Entre Libre, and so on. Figure out the signs—or miss the party.

MAPS

The best and cheapest map is often the public transit map. Try to get one that shows bus lines, subway stops, and major sights. Many tourist offices and big-city hotels (along with the McDonald's in Paris and Rome) give out free city maps. Study the map to understand the city's layout. Relate the location of landmarks—your hotel, major sights, the river, main streets, and station—to each other. Use any viewpoint—such as a church spire, tower, top story of a skyscraper, or hilltop—to look over the city.

At the Oslo tourist office, you can pick up a monthly entertainment guide, list of sights, 24-hour bus pass, telephone card, and city map.

Retrace where you've been, see where you're going. Back on the ground, you won't be in such constant need of your map.

WALKING TOURS AND LOCAL GUIDES

Walking tours are my favorite introduction to a city. Since they focus on just a small part of a city, generally the old town center, they are thorough. The tours are usually conducted in English by well-trained local people who are sharing their town for the noble purpose of giving you an appreciation of the city's history, people, and culture—not to make a lot of money. Walking tours are personal, inexpensive, and a valuable education. I can't recall a bad one. Many local tourist offices organize the tours or provide a do-it-yourself walking tour leaflet. The avid walking tourist should consider purchasing one of the many "turn-right-at-the-fountain"–type guidebooks which are carefully written collections of self-guided walks through major cities.

For the price of three seats on a forgettable quadralingual tape-recorded city bus tour, you can often hire your own private guide through the tourist office for a personalized city tour (most cost-effective if you're traveling with a group). Hiring a private guide is especially easy, cheap, and helpful in Eastern Europe and Russia. The best guides are often those whose tours you can pick up at the specific sight. These guides usually really know their museum, castle, or whatever.

BUS ORIENTATION TOURS

Many cities have fast-orientation bus tours like London's famous "Round London" tour. You'll see major sights (from the bus window) and get a feel for the urban lay of the land. They cost around $20, and if you've got the money and not much time, they provide a good orientation. If I had only one day in a big city, I might spend half of it on one of these bus tours.

As a popular trend, many cities now offer a public bus (e.g., Berlin's bus #100) or boat route (e.g., Amsterdam's museum boat) that connects all of the city's major sightseeing attractions, often with printed, recorded, or live narration en route. Tourists buy the one-day pass and make the circuit at their leisure.

Bus tours can be worthwhile solely for the ride. Some sights are awkward to reach by public transportation, such as the châteaus of France's Loire, King Ludwig's castles in Bavaria, and the stave church and Grieg's home outside Bergen, Norway. An organized tour not only whisks you effortlessly from one hard-to-reach-without-a-car sight to the next, but gives you lots of information as you go.

If you're about to spend $40 anyway for a train ticket, let's say from London to Bath, why not take a $40 one-day tour from London that visits Stonehenge and Bath? You can leave the tour in Bath before it returns to London and enjoy a day of transportation, admissions, and information for the price of a two-hour train ticket.

Fancy coach tours—the kind that leave from the big international hotels—are expensive. Some are great. Others are boring and so depersonalized, sometimes to the point of multilingual taped messages, that you may find the Chinese soundtrack more interesting than the English. These tours can, however, be of value to the budget-minded do-it-yourselfer. Pick up the brochure for a well-thought-out tour itinerary and do it on your own. Take local buses at your own pace and tour every sight for a fraction of the cost.

PUBLIC TRANSPORTATION

When you master a city's subway or bus system, you've got it by the tail. Europe's public transit systems are so good that many Europeans choose not to own a car. Their wheels are trains, buses, and subways.

Save time, money, and energy. Too many timid tourists avoid buses or subways and use up their energy walking or their money on taxis. Subways are speedy and comfortable, never slowed by traffic jams.

Get a transit map. With a map, anyone can decipher the code to cheap and easy urban transportation. Paris and London have the most extensive—and the most needed—subway systems. Both cities are covered with subway maps and expert subway tutors. Paris even has maps that plan your route for you. Just push your destination's button, and the proper route lights up.

Find out about specials. Some cities offer deals such as discounted packets of subway tickets (in Paris) or tourist tickets allowing unlimited travel on all public transport for a day or several days (in London and elsewhere). These "go as you please" passes may seem expensive, but if you do any amount of running around, they can be a convenient money-saver. And remember, they are more than economical. With a transit pass you'll avoid the often-long ticket lines.

Ask for help. Buses and subways are run by people who are happy to help lost tourists locate themselves. Confirm with a local that you're at the right platform or bus stop. If a ticket seems expensive, ask what it covers—two dollars may seem like a lot until you learn it's good for a round trip, two hours, or several transfers. And if you tell them where you're going, bus drivers and passengers sitting around you will gladly tell you where to get off.

Be cautious. While public transportation feels safe, be constantly on guard. Wear your money belt. Thieves thrive underground. Buses that are particularly popular with tourists are equally popular with pickpockets.

TAXIS

Taxis are often a reasonable option and are especially cheap in southern countries. While expensive for the lone budget traveler, a group of three or four people can frequently travel cheaper by taxi than by buying three or four bus tickets. (You can go anywhere in downtown Athens for $3.) Don't be bullied by cabbie con men (common in the south and east). Insist on the meter, agree on a rate, or know the going rate. Taxi drivers intimidate too many tourists. If I'm charged a ridiculous price for a ride, I put a reasonable sum on the seat and say good-bye. But don't be too mistrusting. Many tourists wrongly accuse their cabbies of taking the long way around or adding unfair extras. Cabbies are generally honest. There are lots of legitimate supplements (nights, weekends, baggage, extra person, airport ride, etc.), and winding through medieval street plans is rarely even close to direct.

You or your hotel receptionist can always call for a cab, but the meter may be well under way by the time you get in. It's cheaper and easier just to flag one down or ask a local to direct you to the nearest taxi stand.

TRAVELER'S TOILET TRAUMA

Every traveler has one or two great toilet stories. Foreign toilets can be traumatic, but they are one of those little things that make travel so much more interesting than staying home. If you plan to venture away from the international-style hotels in your Mediterranean travels and become a temporary resident, "going local" may take on a very real meaning.

Most European toilets are reasonably similar to our own, but some consist simply of porcelain footprints and a squat-and-aim hole. Those of us who need a throne to sit on are in the minority. Most humans sit on their haunches and nothing more. When many Asian refugees are de-Oriented in the United States, they have to be taught not to stand on the rims.

Toilet paper (like a spoon or a fork) is another Western "essential" that most people on our planet do not use. What they use varies. I won't get too graphic here, but remember that a billion people in south Asia never eat with their left hand. Some countries, such as Turkey, have very frail plumbing, and toilet paper will jam up the WCs. If wastebaskets are full of dirty paper, leave yours there, too.

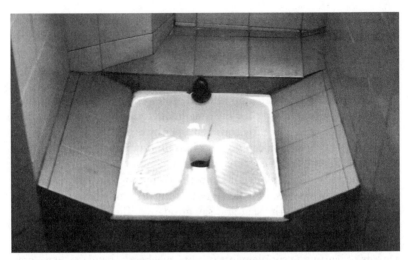

One of Europe's many unforgettable experiences, the squat-and-aim toilet

The TP scene has improved markedly in western Europe the last few years, and while you'll still find some strange stuff worth taking home to show your friends, there is no longer any need to BYOTP.

FINDING A TOILET

Finding a decent public toilet can be frustrating. I once dropped a group off in a town for a potty stop, and when I picked them up 20 minutes later, none had found relief. Most countries have few public restrooms. Learn to sniff out a biffy in a jiffy.

Restaurants: Any place that serves food or drinks has a restroom. No restauranteur would label his WC so those on the street can see, but you can walk into nearly any restaurant or café, politely and confidently, and find a bathroom. Assume it's somewhere in the back, upstairs or downstairs. It's easiest in large places that have outdoor seating, because waiters will think you're a customer just making a quick trip inside. Some call it rude—I call it survival. If you feel like it, ask permission. Just smile, "Toilet?" I'm rarely turned down. Timid people buy a drink they don't want in order to lose one. That's unnecessary. American-type fast-food places are very common these days and always have a decent and fairly "public" restroom.

Public buildings: When nature beckons and there's no restaurant or bar handy, look in train stations, government buildings, and upper floors of department stores. Parks often have restrooms, sometimes of the gag-a-maggot variety. Never leave a museum without taking ad⸱·antage of its restrooms—free, clean, and decorated with artistic graffiti. Large, classy, old hotel lobbies are as impressive as many palaces you'll pay to see. You can always find a royal retreat here and plenty of soft TP.

Coin-op toilets on the street: Many cities, such as Paris, London, and Amsterdam, are dotted with coin-operated telephone booth–type WCs on street corners. You simply insert a coin, the door opens, and you have 15 minutes of toilet accompanied by Sinatra Muzak. When you leave, it even disinfects itself.

Trains: Use the free toilets on the train rather than in the station to save time and money. Toilets on first-class cars are a cut above second-class toilets. I go first class even with a second-class ticket. Train toilets are located on the ends of cars, where it's most jiggly. A trip to the train's john always reminds me of the rodeo. Never use a train WC while stopped in a station (unless you didn't like that particular town). Toilets empty directly on the tracks. Train WC cleanliness deteriorates as the journey progresses.

The flush: After you've found and used a toilet, you're down to your last challenge—flushing it. Rarely will you find a familiar handle. Find some protuberance and push, pull, twist, squeeze, step on, or pray to it until the waterfall starts. Electric-eye sinks and urinals are increasingly common.

The tip: Paying to use a public WC is a European custom that irks many Americans. But isn't it really worth a quarter, considering the cost of water, maintenance, and cleanliness? And you're probably in no state to argue, anyway. Sometimes the toilet is free, but the woman in the corner sells sheets of toilet paper. Most common is the tip dish by the entry. The local equivalent of about 25 cents is plenty. Caution: Many attendant ladies leave only bills and too-big coins in the tray to bewilder the full-bladdered tourist. The keepers of Europe's public toilets have earned a reputation for crabbiness. You'd be crabby, too, if you lived under the street in a room full of public toilets. Humor them, understand them, and leave them a coin or two.

Men: The women who seem to inhabit Europe's WCs are a popular topic of conversation among Yankee males. Sooner or later you'll be minding your own business at the urinal and the lady will bring you your change or sweep under your feet. Yes, it is distracting, but you'll just have to get used to it—she has.

Getting comfortable in foreign restrooms takes a little adjusting, but that's travel. When in Rome, do as the Romans do—and before you know it . . . Euro-peein'.

TRAVEL LAUNDRY

I met a woman in Italy who wore her T-shirt frontward, backward, inside-out frontward, and inside-out backward to delay the laundry day. A guy in Germany showed me his take-it-into-the-tub-with-you-and-make-waves method of washing his troublesome jeans. And some travelers just ignore their laundry needs and stink.

One of my domestic chores while on the road is washing my laundry in the hotel room sink. I bring a quick-dry travel wardrobe that either looks OK wrinkled or doesn't wrinkle. I test wash and dry my shirts in the sink at home once before I let them come to Europe with me. Some shirts are fine, others prune up.

Pack a self-service laundry kit. Bring a stretchable "travel clothesline." These are twisted, so clothespins are unnecessary. Stretch it over your bathtub or across the back of your car, and you're on the road to dry clothes. Pack a concentrated liquid detergent in a small, sturdy, plastic squeeze bottle wrapped in a zip-lock baggie to contain leakage. A large plastic bag with a drawstring is handy for dirty laundry.

Wash clothes in the sink in your room. Every real hotel room in Europe has a sink, usually equipped with a multilingual "no washing clothes in the room" sign. This (after "eat your peas") may be the most ignored rule on earth. Interpret this as an "I-have-lots-of-good-furniture-and-a-fine-carpet-in-this-room-and-I-don't-want-your-drippy-laundry-ruining-things" order. In other words, you can wash clothes carefully, wring them nearly dry, and hang them in a low-profile, nondestructive way. Don't hang it out the window. The maid hardly notices my laundry. It's hanging quietly in the bathroom or shuffled among my dry clothes in the closet. Occasionally a hotel will keep the stoppers in an attempt to discourage washing. You can try using a wadded-up sock or a film canister cap, or line the sink with your plastic laundry bag and wash in it. Some create their own washing machine with a large two gallon zip-lock baggie: soak sudsy an hour, agitate, drain, rinse.

Wring wet laundry as dry as possible. Rolling it in a towel and twisting or stomping on it can be helpful, but most places don't provide new towels everyday. Always separate the back and front of hanging clothes to speed drying. Some travelers pack an inflatable hanger. Laid-back hotels will let your laundry join theirs on the lines out back or on the rooftop.

Smooth out your wet clothes, button shirts, set collars, and "hand iron" to encourage wrinkle-free drying. If your shirt or dress dries wrinkled, hang it in a steamy bathroom. A piece of tape is a good ad-lib lint brush. In very hot climates, I wash my shirt several times a day, wring it, and put it on wet. It's clean and refreshing, and in 15 minutes it's dry.

Whistler's laundry

Use a Laundromat occasionally. For a thorough washing, ask your hotel to direct you to the nearest Laundromat. Nearly every neighborhood has one. It takes about $8 and an hour if there's no line. (Many hostels have coin-op washers and dryers or heated drying rooms.) Better Laundromats have coin-op soap dispensers, change machines, and helpful attendants. Others can be very frustrating. Use the time to catch up on postcards and your journal or chat with the local crowd. Laundromats throughout the world seem to give people the gift of gab. Full-service places are quicker—just drop it off and come back in the afternoon—but much more expensive. Still, every time I slip into a fresh pair of jeans, I figure it was worth the hassle and expense.

19. Hurdling the Language Barrier

CONFESSIONS OF A MONOGLOT

That notorious language barrier is about two feet tall. It keeps many people out of Europe, but with a few communication tricks and a polite approach, you can step right over it.

While it's nothing to brag about, I speak only English. Of course, if I spoke more languages, I could enjoy a much deeper understanding of the people and cultures I visit, but even with English-only I have no problems getting transportation, rooms, eating, and seeing the sights. While you can manage fine with the blunt weapon of English, you'll get along with Europe better if you learn and use a few basic phrases and polite words.

Having an interest in the local language wins the respect of those you'll meet. Get an English-German (or whatever) phrase book and start your practical vocabulary growing right off the bat. You're surrounded by expert, native-speaking tutors in every country. Let them teach you. Spend bus and train rides learning. Start learning the language when you arrive. Psychologically, it's hard to start later because you'll be leaving so soon. I try to learn five new words a day. You'd be surprised how handy a working vocabulary of 50 words is. A phrase book with a dictionary is ideal; a two-language dictionary is cheap and easy to find.

While Americans are notorious monoglots, Europeans are very good with languages. Make your communicating job easier by choosing a multilingual person to speak with. Business people, urbanites, young well-dressed people, students, and anyone in the tourist trade are most likely to speak English. Most Swiss grow up trilingual. Many young North Europeans speak several languages. People speaking minor languages (Dutch, Belgians, Scandinavians) have more reason to learn German,

Europe is multilingual where necessary. At Croatian truck stops, the packet says "sugar" in five languages.

French, or English since their linguistic world is so small. Scandinavian students of our language actually decide between English and "American." My Norwegian cousin speaks with a touch of Texas and knows more slang than I do.

We English speakers are the one linguistic group that can afford to be lazy. English is the world's linguistic common denominator. When a Greek meets a Norwegian, they speak English. You'd be hard-pressed to find a Greek speaking Norwegian.

Imagine if each of our states spoke its own language. That's the European situation. They've done a great job of minimizing the communication problems you'd expect to find in a small continent with such a Babel of tongues. Most signs that the traveler must understand (such as road signs, menus, telephone instructions, and safety warnings) are printed either in several languages or in universal symbols. Europe's uniform road sign system enables drivers to roll right over the language barrier. And rest assured that any place trying to separate tourists from their money will explain how to spend it in whatever languages are necessary. English always makes it.

Start every conversation by politely asking, "Do you speak English?", *"Parlez-vous anglais?"*, *"Sprechen Sie Englisch?"*, or whatever. If they say "No," then I do the best I can in their language. Normally, after a few sentences they'll say, "Actually, I do speak some English." One thing Americans do well linguistically is put others at ease with their linguistic shortcomings. Your European friend is doing you a favor by speaking your language. The least we can do is make our English simple and clear.

USING SIMPLE ENGLISH

English may be Europe's lingua franca, but communicating does require some skill. If you have a trip coming up and don't speak French yet, forget it. It's hopeless. Rather than learning a few more French verbs, the best way to increase your ability to communicate is to master what the Voice of America calls "simple English."

Speak slowly, clearly, and with carefully chosen words. Assume you're dealing with someone who learned English out of a book, reading British words, not hearing American ones. They are reading your lips, wishing it was written down, hoping to see every letter as it tumbles out of your mouth. Choose easy words and clearly pronounce each letter. (Crispy po-ta-to chips.) Use no contractions. When they aren't understood, many Americans speak louder and toss in a few extra words. Listen to other tourists, and you'll hear your own shortcomings. If you want to be understood, talk like a Dick and Jane primer. For several months out of every year, I speak with simple words, pronouncing every letter. When I return home, my friends say (very deliberately), "Rick, you can relax now, we speak English."

Can the slang. Our American dialect has become a super-deluxe slang pizza not found on any European menu. The sentence "Can the slang," for example, would baffle the average European. If you learned English in school for two years, how would you respond to the American who exclaims, "What a day!" or asks, "Howzit goin'?"

Keep your messages grunt simple. Make single nouns work as entire sentences. When asking for something, a one-word question ("Photo?") is more effective than an attempt at something more grammatically correct. ("May I take your picture, sir?") Be a Neanderthal. Strip your message naked and drag it by the hair into the other person's mind. But even Neandertourists will find things go easier if they begin each request with the local "please" (e.g., "*Bitte*, toilet?").

Use internationally understood words. Some spend an entire trip telling people they're on *vacation*, draw only blank stares, and slowly find themselves in a soundproof, culture-resistant cell. The sensitive communicator notices that Europeans understand the word *holiday* (probably because that's what the English say), plugs that word into her simple English vocabulary, is understood, and enjoys a much closer contact with Europe. If you say restroom or bathroom, you'll get no room. *Toilet* is direct, simple, and understood. If my car is broken in Portugal, I don't say "Excuse me, my car is broken." I point to the vehicle and say, "Auto kaput."

TIPS ON CREATIVE COMMUNICATION

Even if you have no real language in common, you can have some fun communicating. Consider this profound conversation I had with a cobbler in Sicily:

"Spaghetti," I said, with a very saucy Italian accent.

"Beel Cleenton," was the old man's reply.

"*Mama mia, magnifico!*" I said, tossing my hands and head into the air.

"Yes, no, one, two, tree," he returned, slowly and proudly. By now we'd grown fond of each other, and I whispered, secretively, "*Molto buono*, ravioli."

He spat, "Be sexy, drink Pepsi!"

Waving goodbye, I hollered "*Huevos rancheros, amigos.*"

"*Ciao*," he said, smiling.

Risk looking goofy. Even with no common language, rudimentary communication is easy. Butcher the language if you must, but commu-

International Words

As our world shrinks, more and more words leap their linguistic boundaries and become international. Sensitive travelers develop a knack for choosing words most likely to be universally understood ("auto" instead of "car," "kaput" rather than "broken," "photo," not "picture"). They also internationalize their pronunciation. "University," if you play around with its sound (oo-nee-vehr-see-tay) can be understood anywhere. The average American is a real flunky in this area. Be creative.

Analogy communication is effective. Anywhere in Europe, "Attila" means "crude bully." When a bulky Italian crowds in front of you, say, "*Scusi*, Ah-tee-la" and retake your place. If you like your haircut and want to compliment your Venetian barber, put your hand sensually on your hair and say "Casanova." Nickname the hairstylist "Michelangelo" or "Rambo."

Here are a few internationally understood words. Remember, cut out the Yankee accent and give each word a pan-European sound.

Stop	Kaput	Vino
Restaurant	Ciao	Bank
Hotel	Bye-bye	Rock 'n' roll
Post	Camping	OK
Auto	Picnic	Amigo
Autobus (booos)	Nuclear	English (Engleesh)
Yankee, Americano	Tourist	Mama mia
Michelangelo (artistic)	Beer	Oo la la
Casanova (romantic)	Coffee	Moment
Disneyland (wonderland)	Tea	Hercules (strong)
Coke, Coca-Cola	No problem	Attila (mean, crude)
Sexy	Europa	Self-service
Toilet	Police	Super
Taxi	Telephone	Photo
Photocopy	Central	Information
Mañana	University	Passport
Chocolate	Pardon	Fascist
Rambo	Communist	Hello
America's favorite four-letter words	No	Elephante (a big clod)
	Bon voyage	

nicate. I'll never forget the lady in the French post office who flapped her arms and asked, "Tweet, tweet, tweet?" I understood immediately, answered with a nod, and she gave me the airmail stamps I needed. At the risk of getting birdseed, I communicated successfully. If you're hungry, clutch your stomach and growl. If you want milk, "moo" and pull two imaginary udders. If the liquor was too strong, simulate an atomic explosion starting from your stomach and mushrooming to your head. If you're attracted to someone, pant.

Be melodramatic. Exaggerate the local accent. In France communicate more effectively (and have more fun) by sounding like Maurice Chevalier or Inspector Clousseau. The locals won't be insulted; they'll be impressed. Use whatever French you know. But even English, spoken with a sexy French accent, makes more sense to the French ear. In Italy be melodic, exuberant, and wave those hands. Go ahead, try it: *Mama mia!* No. Do it again. *MAMA MIA!* You've got to be uninhibited. Self-consciousness kills communication.

Hurdle the language barrier by thinking of things as multiple-choice questions and making educated guesses. This is a sign on a shop in Germany. It lists open times. Hours can only be open or closed. I'd guess it lists hours open from (vom = from, if it rhymes, I go for it) the Fourth of July. Those six words on the left, most of which end in tag, *must be days of the week. Things are open from 9:00 to 11:00 and from 16:00 to 18:00 (24-hour clock). On Mittwoch (midweek) afternoon, something different happens. Since it can only be open or closed, and everything else is open, you can guess that on Wednesdays, nach Mittag, this shop is geschlossen!*

Figure things out. Most major European languages are related, coming from Latin. Knowing that, words become meaningful. The French word for Monday (our "day of the moon") is *lundi* (lunar day). The Germans say the same thing—*Montag*. *Sonne* is sun, so *Sonntag* is Sunday. If *buon giorno* means good day, *zuppa del giorno* is soup of the day. If *Tiergarten* is zoo (literally "animal garden") in German, then *Stinktier* is skunk and *Kindergarten* is children's garden. Think of *Vater, Mutter, trink, gross, gut, nacht, rapide, grand, economico, delicioso,* and you can *comprende mucho.*

Make an educated guess and go for it. Can you read the Danish: "Sentral Syke Haus"? Too many Americans would bleed to death on the street corner looking for the word "hospital."

Many letters travel predictable courses (determined by the physical way a sound is made) as related languages drift apart over the centuries. For instance, *p* often becomes *v* or *b* in the next language. Italian menus always have a charge for *coperto*—a "cover" charge.

Practice your understanding. Read time schedules, posters, multilingual signs (and graffiti) in bathrooms, and newspaper headlines. Develop your ear for foreign languages by tuning in to the other languages on a multilingual tour. It's a puzzle. The more you play, the better you get.

A notepad works wonders. The written word or number is understood much easier than when it's spoken—and mispronounced. (My backpocket notepad is my constant travel buddy.) To repeatedly communicate something difficult and important (such as medical instructions, "I'm a strict vegetarian," "boiled water," "well-done meat," "your finest ice cream," or "Yes, I am rich and single"), have it written in the local language on your notepad.

Assume you understand and go with your educated guess. My master key to communication is to see most communication problems as multiple-choice questions, make an educated guess at the meaning of a message (verbal or written), and proceed confidently as if I understood it correctly. This applies to rudimentary things like instructions on customs forms, museum hours, menus, questions the hotel maid asks you, and so on. With this approach I find that 80 percent of the time I'm correct. Half the time I'm wrong I never know it, so it doesn't really matter. So 10 percent of the time I really blow it. My trip becomes easier—and occasionally much more interesting.

Let's take a border crossing as an example. I speak no Bulgarian. At the border a uniformed guard struts up to my car and asks a question. Not understanding a word he said, but guessing what the average border guard would ask the average tourist, I look at him and answer with a solid "*Nyet.*" He steps back, swings his arm open like a gate, and says, "OK." I'm on my way, quick and easy. I could have gotten out of the car, struggled with the phrase book, and made a big deal out of it, but I'd rather fake it, assuming he was asking if I'm smuggling anything in, and keep things simple. It works.

POLITE PARIS

The "mean Parisian" problem is a holdover from de Gaulle days. It's definitely fading, but France's lingering reputation of rudeness creates a self-fullfilling expectation. You can enjoy the French. Make it your goal.

The French, as a culture, are pouting. They used to be the *crème de la crème*, the definition of high class. Their language was the lingua franca—everyone wanted to speak French. There was a time when the czar of Russia and his family actually spoke better French than

Enjoy the French

Russian. Your passport even has French on it—leftovers from those French glory days.

Modern French culture is reeling—humiliated by two world wars, lashed by Levi's, and crushed by the Big Mac of American culture. And our two cultures aren't natural buddies. The French enjoy subtleties and sophistication. American culture sneers at these fine points. We're proud, brash, and like to think we're rugged individualists. We are a smiley-face culture whose bank tellers are fined if they forget to say, "Have a nice day." The French don't find slap-on-the-back niceness terribly sincere.

Typically, Americans evaluate the French by the Parisians they meet. Big cities are colder than small towns. And remember, most of us see Paris at the height of the hot, busy summer, when those Parisians who can't escape on vacation see their hometown flooded with insensitive foreigners who butcher their language and put ketchup on their meat. That's tough to take smiling and, if you're looking for coldness, this is a good place to start.

To make the Parisians suddenly 40 percent friendlier, learn and liberally use these four phrases: *bonjour, s'il vous plaît, merci,* and *pardon.*

Tongue Twisters

These are a great way to practice a language—and break the ice with the Europeans you meet. Here are some that are sure to challenge you and amuse your new friends.

German	**Fischer's Fritze fischt frische Fische, frische Fische fischt Fischer's Fritze.**	Fritz Fischer catches fresh fish, fresh fish Fritz Fischer catches.
	Ich komme über Oberammergau, oder komme ich über Unterammergau?	I am coming via Oberammergau, or am I coming via Unterammergau?
Italian	**Sopra la panca la capra canta, sotto la panca la capra crepa.**	On the bench the goat sings, under the bench the goat dies.
	Chi fù quel barbaro barbiere che barberò così barbaramente a Piazza Barberini quel povero barbaro di Barbarossa?	Who was that barbarian barber in Barberini Square who shaved that poor barbarian Barbarossa?
French	**Si ces saucissons-ci sont six sous, ces six saucissons-ci sont trop chers.**	If these sausages are six cents, these six sausages are too expensive.
	Ce sont seize cents sèches dans seize cent sachets secs.	There are 600 dry hyacinths in 600 dry sachets.
Spanish	**Un tigre, dos tigres, tres tigres comían trigo en un trigal. Un tigre, dos tigres, tres tigres.**	One tiger, two tigers, three tigers ate wheat in a wheatfield. One tiger, two tigers, three tigers.
	Pablito clavó un clavito. ¿Qué clavito clavó Pablito?	Paul stuck in a stick. What stick did Paul stick in?
Portuguese	**O rato roeu a roupa do rei de Roma.**	The mouse nibbled the clothes of the king of Rome.
	Se cá nevasse fazia-se cá ski, mas como cá não neva não se faz cá ski.	If the snow would fall, we'd ski, but since it doesn't, we don't.

Excerpted from Rick Steves' phrase books—full of practical phrases, spiked with humor, and designed for budget travelers who like to connect with locals.

HAPPY TALK

English	French	Italian	German	Spanish
Good day.	Bonjour.	Buon giorno.	Guten Tag.	Buenos días.
How are you?	Comment allez-vous?	Come sta?	Wie geht's?	¿Cómo está?
Very good.	Très bien.	Molto bene.	Sehr gut.	Muy bien.
Thank you.	Merci.	Grazie.	Danke.	Gracias.
Please.	S'il vous plaît.	Per favore.	Bitte.	Por favor.
Do you speak English?	Parlez-vous anglais?	Parla inglese?	Sprechen Sie Englisch?	¿Habla usted inglés?
Yes. / No.	Oui. / Non.	Sì. / No.	Ja. / Nein.	Sí. / No.
My name is...	Je m'appelle....	Mi chiamo...	Ich heiße....	Me llamo....
What's your name?	Quel est votre nom?	Come si chiama?	Wie heißen Sie?	¿Cómo se llama?
See you later.	À bientôt.	A più tardi.	Bis später.	Hasta luego.
Goodbye.	Au revoir.	Arrivederci.	Auf Wiedersehen.	Adiós.
Good luck!	Bonne chance!	Buona fortuna!	Viel Glück!	¡Buena suerte!
Have a good trip!	Bon voyage!	Buon viaggio!	Gute Reise!	¡Buen viaje!
OK.	D'accord.	Va bene.	O.K.	De acuerdo.
No problem.	Pas de problème.	Non c'è problema.	Kein Problem.	No hay problema.
Everything was great.	C'était super.	Tutto magnifico.	Alles war gut.	Todo estuvo muy bien.
Enjoy your meal!	Bon appétit!	Buon appetito!	Guten Appetit!	¡Qué aproveche!
Delicious!	Délicieux!	Delizioso!	Lecker!	¡Delicioso!
Magnificent!	Magnifique!	Magnifico!	Wunderbar!	¡Magnífico!
Bless you! (after sneeze)	À vos souhaits!	Salute!	Gesundheit!	¡Salud!
You are very kind.	Vous êtes très gentil.	Lei è molto gentile.	Sie sind sehr freundlich.	Usted es muy amable.
Cheers!	Santé!	Salute!	Prost!	¡Salud!
I love you.	Je t'aime.	Ti amo.	Ich liebe dich.	Te quiero.

And to really revel in French friendliness, visit an untouristy part of the countryside and use those four phrases. Oh, and *vive la différence.*

EUROPEAN GESTURES

In Europe, gestures can contribute to the language barrier. Here are a few common gestures, their meanings, and where you are likely to see them:

Fingertips kiss: Gently bring the fingers and thumb of your right hand together, raise to your lips, kiss lightly, and joyfully toss your fingers and thumb into the air. Be careful, tourists look silly when they overemphasize this subtle action. This gesture is used commonly in France, Spain, Greece, and Germany as a form of praise. It can mean sexy, delicious, divine, or wonderful.

Hand purse: Straighten the fingers and thumb of one hand, bringing them all together making an upward point about a foot in front of your face. Your hand can be held still or moved a little up and down at the wrist. This is a common and very Italian gesture for a query. It is used to say "What do you want?" or "What are you doing?" or "What is it?" or "What's new?" It can also be used as an insult to say "You fool." The hand purse can also mean "fear" (France), "a lot" (Spain), and "good" (Greece and Turkey).

Cheek screw: Make a fist, stick out your forefinger, and (without piercing the skin) screw it into your cheek. The cheek screw is used widely and almost exclusively in Italy to mean good, lovely, beautiful. Many Italians also use it to mean clever. Be careful—in Southern Spain the cheek screw is used to call a man effeminate.

Eyelid pull: Place your extended forefinger below the center of your eye and pull the skin downward. In France and Greece this means "I am alert. I'm looking. You can't fool me." In Italy and Spain it is a friendlier warning, meaning "Be alert, that guy is clever."

Forearm jerk: Clench your right fist and jerk your forearm up as you slap your right bicep with your left palm. This is a rude phallic gesture that men throughout southern Europe often use the way many Americans "give someone the finger." This jumbo version of "flipping the bird" says "I'm superior" (it's an action some monkeys actually do with their penises to insult their peers). This "get lost" or "up yours" gesture is occasionally used in Britain and Germany as more of an "I want you" gesture about (but never to) a sexy woman.

Chin flick: Tilt your head back slightly and flick the back of your fingers forward in an arc from under your chin. In Italy and France this means "I'm not interested, you bore me," or "You bother me." In Southern Italy it can mean "No."

"Thumbs up," "V for Victory," and more: The "thumbs up" sign popular in the United States is used widely in France and Germany to say "OK." The "V for victory" sign is used in most of Europe as in the United States (Beware, the V with your palm toward you is the rudest of gestures in England.) "Expensive" is often shown by shaking your hand and sucking in like you just burned yourself. In Greece and Turkey you signal "no" by jerking your eyebrows and head upward. In Bulgaria and Albania "OK" is indicated by happily bouncing your head back and forth as if you were one of those Asian dolls with a spring neck and someone slapped you.

To beckon someone, remember that in northern Europe you bring your palm up, and in the south you wave it down. While most people greet each other by waving with their palm out, you'll find many Italians wave "at themselves" as infants do, with their palm towards their face. *Ciao-ciao.*

EUROPEAN NUMBERS AND STUMBLERS

Europeans do many things different from the way we do. Simple as these things are, they can be frustrating barriers and cause needless, occasionally serious problems.

Numbers: A European's handwritten numbers look different from ours. The ones have an upswing (1). Fours often look like short lightning bolts (4). If you don't cross your 7 (7) it may be mistaken as a sloppy 1 and you could miss your train (and be mad at the French for "refusing to speak English"). Avoid using "#" for "number"—it's not common in Europe and can look like a currency symbol.

Counting: When counting with your fingers, start with your thumb. If you hold up your first finger, you'll probably get two; and making a "peace" sign to indicate the number 2 may get you a punch in the nose in parts of Britain, where it's an obscene gesture.

Dates and Decimals: Europeans reverse the day and month in numbered dates. Christmas is 25-12-99 instead of 12-25-99, as we would write it. Commas are decimal points and decimals commas, so a dollar and a half is 1,50 and there are 5.280 feet in a mile.

Time: The 24-hour clock is used in any official timetable. This includes bus, train, and tour schedules. Learn to use it quickly and easily. Everything is the same until 12:00 noon. Then, instead of starting over again at 1:00 p.m., the Europeans keep on going—13:00, 14:00, and so on. 18:00 is 6:00 p.m. (subtract 12 and add p.m.).

Metric: European countries (except Great Britain) use kilometers instead of miles. A kilometer is six-tenths of a mile. To quickly translate kilometers to miles, cut the kilometer figure in half and add 10 percent of the original figure (e.g., 420 km = 210 + 42 = 252 miles). Quick, what's 360 km? (180 + 36 = 216 miles) "36-26-36" means nothing to a European (or metric) girl-watcher. But a "90-60-90" is a real *pistachio*.

Temperatures: Europeans measure temperatures in degrees Celsius. Zero degrees C = 32 degrees Fahrenheit (C x 9/5 + 32 = F); or, easier and nearly as accurate, double the Celsius temperature and add 30. A memory aid: 281° C = 821° F—darn hot.

Addresses: House numbers often have no correlation to what's across the street. While odd is normally on one side and even is on the other, #27 may be directly across from #2.

Floors: Floors of buildings are numbered differently. The bottom floor is called the ground floor. What we would call the second floor is a

This is Danish for "tour bus." These days most come with air conditioning.

European's first floor. So if your room is on the second floor (European), bad news—you're on the third floor (American). On the elevator, push whatever's below "1" to get to the ground floor. On an escalator, keep the left lane open for passing. Stand to the right.

A YANKEE-ENGLISH PHRASE BOOK

Oscar Wilde said, "The English have everything in common with the Americans—except, of course, language." On your first trip to England you'll find plenty of linguistic surprises. I'll never forget checking into a small-town bed-and-breakfast, a teenager on my first solo European adventure. The landlady cheerily asked me, "And what time would you like to be knocked up in the morning?" I looked over at her husband, who winked, "Would a fry at half-eight be suitable?" The next morning I got a rap on the door at 8:00 and a huge British breakfast a half-hour later.

Traveling through England is an adventure in accents and idioms. Every day you'll see babies in prams, sucking dummies as mothers change wet nappies. Soon the kids can trade in their nappies for smalls and spend a penny on their own. "Spend a penny" is British for a visit to the loo (bathroom). Older British kids enjoy candy floss (cotton candy), naughts and crosses (tic-tac-toe), big dippers (roller coasters), and iced lollies (popsicles), and are constantly in need of an elastoplast (Band-Aid).

It's fun to browse through an ironmonger's (hardware store), chemist's shop (pharmacy), or Woolworth's and notice the many familiar items with unfamiliar names. The school supplies section includes sticking plaster (adhesive tape), rubbers (erasers), and scribbling blocks (scratch pads). Those with green fingers (a green thumb) might pick up some courgette (zucchini), swede (rutabaga), or aubergine (eggplant) seeds.

In England, chips are fries and crisps are potato chips. A hamburger is a bomb (success) on a toasted bap. Wipe your fingers with a serviette— never a napkin.

The English have a great way with names. You'll find towns with names like Upper and Lower Piddle, Once Brewed, and Itching Field. This cute coziness comes through in their language as well. Your car is built with a bonnet and a boot rather than a hood and trunk. You drive on motorways, and when the freeway divides, it becomes a dual carriageway. And never go anticlockwise (counterclockwise) in a roundabout. Gas is petrol, a truck is a lorry, and when you hit a traffic jam, don't get your knickers in a twist (make a fuss), just queue up (line up) and study your American-English phrase book.

A two-week vacation in England is unheard of, but many locals holiday for a fortnight in a homely (pleasant) rural cottage, possibly on the

Continent (continental Europe). They'll pack a face flannel (washcloth), torch (flashlight), hoover (vacuum cleaner), and hair grips (bobby pins) before leaving their flat (apartment). You can post letters in the pillar box and give your bird (girlfriend) a trunk (long distance) call. If you reverse the charges (call collect), she'll say you're tight as a fish's bum. If she witters on (gabs and gabs), tell her you're knackered (exhausted) and it's been donkey's years (ages) since you've slept. On a cold evening it's best to pick up a pimp (bundle of kindling) and make a fire or take a walk wearing the warmest mackintosh (raincoat) you can find or an anorak (parka) with press studs (snaps). After washing up (doing the dishes), you can go up to the first floor (second floor) with a neat (straight) Scotch and a plate of biscuits (sweet cookies) and get goose pimples (goose bumps) just enjoying the view. Too much of that Scotch will get you sloshed, paralytic, bevvied, wellied, popped up, ratted, or even pissed as a newt.

All across the British Isles, you'll find new words, crazy local humor, and colorful accents. Pubs are colloquial treasure chests. Church services, sporting events, the House of Parliament, live plays featuring local comedy, the streets of Liverpool, the docks of London, and children in parks are playgrounds for the American ear. One of the beauties of touring the British Isles is the illusion of hearing a foreign language and actually understanding it—most of the time.

20. Phones, E-mail, and Mail

Communication for travelers in Europe has never been easier. Not only are more and more people speaking English, but telephoning (local, long distance, and home to the U.S.) is a cinch. Most hotels have fax machines, many are able to take reservations online, and cyber cafés are catching on fast. Oh yes, and each country still has a postal system.

SMART TRAVELERS USE THE TELEPHONE

The only way to travel smoothly is to use the telephone. Call tourist offices to check sightseeing plans, train stations to check travel plans, museums to see if an English tour is scheduled, restaurants to see if they're open, hotels to confirm reservations, and so on.

I get earnest letters from readers asking me to drop a hotel from my listings because they made a reservation, got a written confirmation, and still arrived to find no room available. Hotels make mistakes. Call a day in advance to double-check reservations. As we were filming my public television show in Ireland, I took a minute to call Avis in England to reconfirm our car pick-up the next day at the ferry dock in

Most European phone booths use phone cards rather than coins.

North Wales. The man at Avis said, "Right-tee-o, Mr. Steves, we'll have your car waiting for you, noon tomorrow, at Heathrow Airport." No, at North Wales! "Oh, sorry, Mr. Steves. It's good you called ahead." I didn't think, "Boy, Avis sure screwed up." I thought, "You can't travel smart without double-checking things by telephone." The more I travel, the more I use the telephone.

Each country's phone system is different, but each one works—logically. The key to figuring out a foreign phone is to approach it without comparing it to yours back home. It works for the locals, and it can work for you. Many people flee in terror when a British phone starts its infamous "rapid pips." (That's just the British way of telling you to pop in a few coins.)

Each country has phone booths with multilingual instructions. If you follow these step by step, the phone will work—usually. Operators generally speak some English and are helpful. International codes, instructions, and international assistance numbers are usually on the wall (printed in several languages) or in the front of the phone book. If I can't manage in a strange phone booth, I ask a nearby local person for help.

PHONE CARDS AND COIN-OP PHONES
The first step is to find the right phone. The increasingly rare coin-op phones are being replaced by more convenient and vandal-resistant

phones that accept only phone cards. If you spend time looking for coin-operated phones in Europe, you're still traveling in the '80s. The first thing I purchase upon arrival in a new country is a phone card.

Phone cards: European telephone cards (not to be confused with American phone credit cards) are common throughout Europe. They're easy to use and sold conveniently at newsstands, street kiosks, tobacco shops, and post offices. You just slide your card into a slot in the phone and dial any local or international number. The phone reads your card's magnetic strip, and a readout tells you how much money is remaining on your card. The only drawback is that the cheapest cards can cost $5, more phone time than you may need in that country. If you're as frugal as me, you'll lay awake at night wondering how to productively use it up before you cross the next border—a worthwhile exercise. You can always blow the remaining telephone time by calling home.

Coin-operated phones: For coin-op phones, have enough small coins to complete your call. The instructions may say the local minimum, your credit total is generally shown, and only entirely unused coins will be returned. Many phones allow run-on calls, so you won't lose your big-coin credit (if you need to make another call). Look for this (usually black) button and push it rather than hanging up. In countries such as Britain, where you hear tourists in phone booths yelling, "Hello . . . Hello . . . HELLO," your voice won't be heard until you push a button to engage the call.

DIALING DIRECT

You'll save money if you learn to dial direct. Prefixes are a common source of phone booth frustration. They are usually listed by city on the wall of the phone booth or in the phone book.

There are three types of prefixes, dialed in this order:
- international access code (of the country you're calling from; it's usually 00)
- country code (of the country you're calling to)
- city code

Nearly any call out of town will require a city code. Most city codes start with zero. The zero is dropped in international calls but included in long-distance calls within a country.

To make international calls: First dial the international access code, then the country code, then the city code (if it starts with zero, drop the zero), and finally the local number.

To make long-distance calls within a European country: Dial the city code (if it starts with zero, include the zero), then the local number.

Example: Britain's international access code is 00. Germany's country code is 49, Munich's city code is 089. My favorite Munich hotel's telephone number is 264-349. To call that hotel within Munich, dial 264-349. To call it from Frankfurt, dial 089-264-34. To call it from Britain, dial 00-49-89-264-349. From the U.S.A., dial 011-49-89-264-349 (011 is the U.S.'s international access code).

Major Exceptions: Italy, France, Spain, Denmark, and Norway don't use city codes at all. To make an international call to Italy, Spain, Denmark, or Norway, dial the international access code of the country you're calling from, then the country code of the country you're calling, then the local number. Of course there's an exception to this exception. To make an international call to France, dial the international access code, France's country code (33), then the local number *without its initial zero*. Calling within any of these countries (whether across the country or across town), just dial the local number in its entirety.

Italy and Spain just changed to a codeless system. Their new numbers consist of their old city codes plus the local number. If you're using an old guidebook and you're trying to reach, say, a hotel in Madrid, dial the entire city code plus the local number (even if you're *in* Madrid).

Communication tips: Once you've made the connection, the real challenge begins. With no visual aids, getting the message across in a language you don't speak requires some artistry. Speak slowly and clearly, pronouncing every letter. Keep it very simple—don't clutter your message with anything less than essential. Don't overcommunicate—many things are already understood and don't need to be said (those last six words didn't need to be written). Use international or carefully chosen English words. When all else fails, let a local person on your end (such as a hotel receptionist) do the talking after you explain to him, with visual help, the message. My Rick Steves' Phrase Books predict conversations you'll need to make on the phone and provide the necessary foreign language templates with various options you may need to fill in the blanks.

CALLING HOME

You can call the United States directly from Europe (and say a few things very quickly) for as little as 50 cents—half the cost of a postcard stamp. Rather than write postcards, just call in your "scenery's here, wish you were beautiful" messages.

Phone booths: I normally just get a phone card or a pile of coins, find a phone booth, dial direct, and keep it short and sweet. Nearly all European countries have "dial direct to anywhere" phone booths. Calls to the United

Phone Codes

INTERNATIONAL ACCESS CODES
When dialing direct, first dial the international access code of the country you're calling from.

Austria:	00	Latvia:	00
Belgium:	00	Lithuania:	810
Britain:	00	Netherlands:	00
Czech Rep:	00	Norway:	00
Denmark:	00	Portugal:	00
Estonia:	800	Russia:	810
Finland:	990	Spain:	00
France:	00	Sweden:	009
Germany:	00	Switzerland:	00
Ireland:	00	USA/Canada:	011
Italy:	00		

COUNTRY CODES
After you've dialed the international access code, then dial the code of the country you're calling.

Austria:	43	Latvia:	371
Belgium:	32	Lithuania:	370
Britain:	44	Netherlands:	31
Czech Rep:	420	Norway:	47
Denmark:	45	Portugal:	351
Estonia:	372	Russia:	7
Finland:	358	Spain:	34
France:	33	Sweden:	46
Germany:	49	Switzerland:	41
Ireland:	353	USA/Canada:	1
Italy:	39		

States cost less than $1 per minute. Talk as short or long as you want. First dial the international access code of the country you're calling from (wait for tone), then the country code of the U.S.A. (1), then the area code and the seven-digit number. To call me from France, put in two francs (40 cents), dial 00-1-425-771-8303, and talk fast. Every country has its quirks. Try

Desperate Telephone Communication

Let me illustrate with a hypothetical telephone conversation. I'm calling a hotel in Barcelona from a phone booth in the train station. I just arrived, read my guidebook's list of budget accommodations, and I like Pedro's Hotel. Here's what happens:

Pedro answers, "Hotel Pedro, grabdaboodogalaysk."

I ask, "Hotel Pedro?" (Question marks are created melodically.)

He affirms, already a bit impatient, "*Si*, Hotel Pedro."

I ask, "*Habla* Eng-leesh?"

He says, "No, dees ees Ehspain." (Actually, he probably would speak a little English or would say "moment" and get someone who did. But we'll make this particularly challenging. Not only does he not speak English—he doesn't want to . . . for patriotic reasons.)

Remembering not to overcommunicate, you don't need to tell him you're a tourist looking for a bed. Who else calls a hotel speaking in a foreign language? Also, you can assume he's got a room available. If he's full, he's very busy and he'd say "complete" or "no hotel" and hang up. If he's still talking to you, he wants your business. Now you must communicate just a few things, like how many beds you need and who you are.

I say, "OK." (OK is international for, "Roger, prepare for the next transmission.") "Two people"—he doesn't understand. I get fancy, "*Dos* people"—he still doesn't get it. Internationalize, "*Dos* pehr-son"—no comprende. "*Dos* hombre"—nope. Digging deep into my bag of international linguistic tricks, I say, "*Dos* Yankees."

"OK!" He understands, you want beds for two Americans. He says, "*Si*," and I say, "Very good" or "*Muy bueno*."

Now I need to tell him who I am. If I say, "My name is Mr. Steves and I'll be over promptly," I'll lose him. I say, "My name Ricardo (Ree-KAR-do)." In Italy I say, "My name Luigi." Your name really doesn't matter; you're communicating just a password so you can identify yourself when you walk through the door. Say anything to be understood.

He says, "OK."

You repeat slowly, "Hotel, *dos* Yankees, Ricardo, coming *pronto*, OK?"

He says, "OK."

You say, "*Gracias, ciao!*"

Twenty minutes later you walk up to the reception desk, and Pedro greets you with a robust, "Eh, Ricardo!"

pausing between codes if you're having trouble, or dial the English-speaking international operator for help. Off-hours calls are cheaper.

At coin-op phones, I start with a small coin worth 25 to 50 cents to be sure I get the person I need or can say, "I'm calling back in five minutes, so wake him up." (Remember, it's about six hours earlier in New York and nine hours earlier in California.) Then I plug in the larger coins. I keep one last sign-off coin ready. When my time is done, I pop it in and say good-bye. The digital meter warns you when you're about to be cut off.

Calling collect is sometimes more complicated and always more expensive. It's cheaper (about $1 a minute—and the other end pays) and easier if you have your friend call you back, dialing direct from the States. Call cheap and fast from a phone booth and ask your friend to call you at your hotel (in 10 minutes or so).

Metered phones: Some post offices have metered phone booths. The person who sells stamps will plug you in, assign you a booth, and help you with your long-distance prefixes. You sit in your private sweat-box, make the call, and pay the bill when you're done (same cost as a public phone). Beware of a popular new rip-off: small businesses on main tourist streets that look like telephone company long-distance services but actually charge like hotels. Ask the price per minute (or per unit on the clicking meter) before you take a metered phone booth.

Hotel phones: Telephoning through your hotel's phone system is fine for local calls or toll-free USA Direct calls (see below) but an almost-criminal rip-off for long-distance calls. I do this only when I'm feeling flush and lazy for a quick "Call me in Stockholm at this number" message.

USA Direct: USA Direct service offered by Sprint, AT&T, and MCI are handy and popular. Each company has a toll-free access number in every European country (listed on the info that comes with your card and included most days in the European editon of the *International Herald Tribune*). Cardholders dial the English-speaking operator, give their card number, and are put through immediately. The rates—while decent—are no longer any better than the direct dial phone booth rates from Europe. And for short calls the rates are much worse. You'll pay about $3 for the first minute and $1.30 per additional minute, plus a $2.50 service fee for the call. Calling an answering machine can be expensive. As soon as you connect, you're billed for the full first minute plus the service fee—$5.50). For less than 25 cents, call first with a coin or European phone card to see if the answering machine is off or if the right person's at home. It's ridiculously expensive to use USA Direct to call from one European country to another. When you're in Europe—calling anywhere, it's far cheaper to simply dial direct using a European phone card.

E-MAIL

Cyber cafés and e-mail: On the road, stop by a cyber café. Found in major European cities, these cafés are a great way to stay in touch through the Internet and World Wide Web. Over coffee, use a rentable computer to send and pick up your e-mail. For the latest listing, search the Web for "cyber cafe" or direct your modem to the Internet Cafe Guide (www. netcafeguide.com). In Europe, any local computer store or tourist office in a major city can steer you to the nearest cyber café. (For more information, see Chapter 2: Gathering Information.)

MAIL

Receiving mail: Minimize mail pick-ups to maximize your flexibility. Arrange your mail stops before you leave. Most American Express offices (listed on the Web at: www.americanexpress.com) offer a free clients' mail service for those who have an American Express card or traveler's checks (even just one). Have mail marked "Clients' Mail." They'll hold it for 30 days unless the envelope instructs otherwise.

Every city has a general delivery service. Pick a small town where there is only one post office and no crowds. Have letters sent to you in care of "Poste Restante." Tell your friends to print your last name in capitals, underline it, and omit your middle name. If possible, avoid the Italian male, I mean mail.

Friends or relatives in Europe are fine for mail stops. Or, to a void mail pick-up commitments on a long trip, have mail sent to a friend or relative at home. When you know where you'll be, you can telephone them from Europe with instructions on where to mail or FedEx your letters. Second-day services are reliable and reasonable. With the ease of phoning these days, I've dispensed with mail pick-ups altogether.

Sending packages home: Shoppers lighten their load by sending packages home by surface mail. Postage is expensive. A box the size of a small fruit crate costs about $40 by slow boat. Books are much cheaper if they are sent separately.

Customs regulations amount to 10 or 15 frustrating minutes of filling out forms with the normally unhelpful postal clerk's semi-assistance. Be realistic in your service expectations. Remember, European postal clerks are every bit as friendly, speedy, and multilingual as ours in the United States.

You can mail one package per person per day worth up to $50 duty-free from Europe to the United States. Mark it "Unsolicited Gift." When you fill out the customs form, keep it simple (contents: clothing, carving, gifts, poster, value $50). You can mail home all the "American Goods Returned" you like with no customs concerns.

Post offices usually provide boxes and string or tape for about $2. Service is best north of the Alps and in France. Small-town post offices can be less crowded and more user-friendly. Every box I've ever mailed has arrived—bruised and battered but all there—within six weeks.

21. Staying Healthy

GET A CHECKUP

Just as you'd give your car a good checkup before a long journey, it's smart to meet with your doctor before your trip. Get a general checkup and ask for advice on maintaining your health.

At the time of this printing, no shots are required for basic European travel, but it's always best to check. Obtain recommended immunizations and discuss proper care for any pre-existing medical conditions while on the road. Bring along a letter from your doctor describing any special health problems and a copy of any pertinent prescriptions.

Travel medicine specialists: While I consider Europe as safe as the United States, those traveling to more exotic destinations should consult a travel medicine physician. Only these specialists keep entirely up-to-date on health conditions for travelers around the world. Tell the doctor about every place you plan to visit and anyplace you may go. Then you can have the flexibility to take that impulsive swing through Turkey or Morocco knowing that you're prepared medically and have the required shots. Ask the doctor about Havrix (a new vaccine that protects against hepatitis A), antidiarrheal medicines, and any extra precautions. The Centers for Disease Control offers (and can fax you) updated information on every country (24-hour hotline: tel. 404/332-4559; info by fax: 888/232-3299; info by recorded voice: 888/232-3228; Web site: www.cdc.gov/travel/travel.html).

Dental checkup: Get a dental checkup before you go. Emergency dental care during your trip is time- and money-consuming, and can be hazardous and painful. I was once crowned by a German dentist who knew only one word in English, which he used in question form—"Pain?"

JET LAG AND THE FIRST DAY OF YOUR TRIP

Anyone who flies through time zones has to grapple with the biorhythmic confusion known as jet lag. When you switch your wristwatch six to nine hours forward, your body says, "Hey, what's going on?" Body clocks don't reset so easily. All your life you've done things on a 24-hour cycle.

Jet lag hits even the very young.

Now, after crossing the Atlantic, your body wants to eat when you tell it to sleep and sleep when you tell it to enjoy a museum.

Too many people assume their first day will be made worthless by jet lag. Don't prematurely condemn yourself to zombiedom. Most people I've traveled with, of all ages, have enjoyed productive—even hyper—first days. You can't avoid jet lag, but with a few tips you can minimize the symptoms.

Leave home well-rested. Flying halfway around the world is stressful. If you leave frazzled after a hectic last night and a wild bon voyage party, there's a good chance you won't be healthy for the first part of your trip. An early-trip cold used to be a regular part of my vacation until I learned a very important trick. Plan from the start as if you're leaving two days before you really are. Keep that last 48-hour period sacred, even if it means being hectic before your false departure date. Then you have two orderly, peaceful days after you've packed so that you are physically ready to fly. Mentally, you'll be comfortable about leaving home and starting this adventure. You'll fly away well-rested and 100 percent capable of enjoying the bombardment of your senses that will follow.

On the flight, drink plenty of liquids, eat lightly, and rest. Long flights are dehydrating. I ask for "two orange juices with no ice" every chance I get. Help yourself to the juice pitchers in the galley area. Eat lightly and have no coffee and only minimal sugar until the flight's almost over. Alcohol will stress your body and aggravate jet lag. The in-flight movie is good for one thing—nap time. With three hours' sleep during the transatlantic flight, you will be functional the day you land.

Reset your mind to local time. When the pilot announces the local European time, reset your mind along with your wristwatch. Don't prolong jet lag by reminding yourself what time it is back home. Be in Europe.

On arrival, stay awake until an early local bedtime. If you doze off at 4:00 p.m. and wake up at midnight, you've accomplished nothing. Plan a good walk until early evening. Jet lag hates fresh air, daylight, and exercise. Your body may beg for sleep but stand firm: Refuse. Force your body's transition to the local time. You'll probably awaken very early on your first morning. Trying to sleep later is normally futile. Get out and enjoy a "pinch me, I'm in Europe" walk, as merchants set up in the marketplace and the town slowly comes to life. This will probably be the only sunrise you'll see in Europe.

You'll read about many jet lag "cures." Most are worse than the disease. Just leave unfrazzled, minimize jet lag's symptoms, force yourself into European time, and give yourself a chance to enjoy your trip from the moment you step off the plane.

TRAVELING HEALTHY

Europe is generally safe. All the talk of treating water with purification tablets is applicable only south and east of Europe. Many may disagree with me but, with discretion and common sense, I eat and drink whatever I like in Europe. If any area deserves a little extra caution, it is rural areas in Spain, Portugal, Italy, and Greece. As our world becomes more chemical, reasons for concern and caution will increase on both sides of the Atlantic.

I was able to stay healthy throughout a six-week trip traveling from Europe to India. By following these basic guidelines, I never once suffered from Tehran Tummy, Delhi Belly, or the Tegucigallop.

Eat nutritiously. The longer your trip, the more you'll be affected by an inadequate diet. Budget travelers often eat more carbohydrates and less protein to stretch their travel dollar. This is the root of many nutritional problems. Protein helps you resist infection and rebuilds muscles. Get the most nutritional mileage from your protein by eating it with the day's largest meal (in the presence of all those "essential" amino acids). Supplemental super-vitamins, taken regularly, help me to at least feel healthy. If you have a serious dietary restriction, have a multilingual friend write it in the local language on the back of a business card and use it to order in restaurants.

Use good judgment. Avoid unhealthy-looking restaurants. Meat should be well-cooked and in some places avoided altogether. Have "well-done" written on a piece of paper in the local language and use it when ordering. Pre-prepared foods gather germs (a common cause of diarrhea). Outside of Europe, be especially cautious. Peel all fruit. When in serious doubt, eat only thick-skinned fruit.

Keep clean. Wash your hands often, keep your nails clean, and never touch your fingers to your mouth.

Practice safe sex. Sexually transmitted diseases are widespread. Obviously, the best way to prevent acquiring an STD is to avoid exposure. Condoms (readily available in restroom vending machines) are fairly effective in preventing transmission. (Cleaning with soap and water before and after exposure is also helpful, if not downright pleasurable.) AIDS is also a risk; according to CNN, more than 60 percent of the prostitutes in Amsterdam are HIV-positive.

Exercise. Physically, travel is great living—healthy food, lots of activity, fresh air, and all those stairs! Still, you may want to work out during your trip. Jogging, while not as widespread in Europe as it is in the United States, is nothing weird. Traveling joggers can enjoy Europe from a special perspective—at dawn. Swimmers will find that Europe has plenty of good, inexpensive public swimming pools. Whatever your racket, if you want to badly enough, you'll find ways to keep in practice as you travel. Most big-city private tennis and swim clubs welcome foreign guests for a small fee. This is a good way to make friends as well as stay fit.

If you're a couch potato, try to get in shape before your trip by taking long walks. You'll be less likely to strain your muscles in Europe.

Give yourself psychological pep talks. Europe can do to certain travelers what south France did to van Gogh. Romantics can get the sensory bends, patriots can get their flags burned, and anyone can suffer from culture shock.

Europe is crowded, smoky, and not particularly impressed by America or Americans. It will challenge givens that you always assumed were above the test of reason, and most of Europe on the street doesn't really care that much about what you, the historical and cultural pilgrim, have waited so long to see.

A break—a long, dark, air-conditioned trip back to California in a movie theater; a pleasant sit in an American embassy reading room surrounded by eagles, photos of presidents, *Time* magazines, and other Yankees; or a visit to the lobby of a world-class hotel, where any hint of the local culture has been lost under a big-business bucket of intercontinental whitewash—can do wonders for the struggling traveler's spirit.

EUROPEAN WATER

I drink European tap water and any water served in restaurants. Read signs carefully, however, because some taps, like those on trains, are not for drinking. If there's any hint of nonpotability—a decal showing a glass with a red "X" over it, or a skull and crossbones—don't drink it.

The water (or, just as likely, the general stress of travel on your immune system) may, sooner or later, make you sick. It's not necessarily dirty. The bacteria in European water is different from that in American water. Our bodily systems—raised proudly on bread that rips in a straight line—are the most pampered on earth. We are capable of handling American bacteria with no problem at all, but some people can go to London and get sick. Some French people visit Boston and get sick. Some Americans travel around the world, eating and drinking everything in sight, and don't get sick, while others spend weeks on the toilet. It all depends on the person.

East of Bulgaria and south of the Mediterranean, do not drink untreated water. Water can be treated by boiling it for 10 minutes or by using purifying tablets or a filter. Bottled water, beer, wine, boiled coffee and tea, and bottled soft drinks are safe as long as you skip the ice cubes. Coca-Cola products are as safe in Syria as they are at home.

TRAVELER'S FIRST-AID KIT

You can buy anything you need in Europe, but it's handy to bring along:
- Band-Aids
- soap or alcohol preps (antiseptic Handiwipes)
- moleskin
- tweezers
- thermometer in a hard case
- Tylenol (or any nonaspirin pain reliever)
- medication for colds and diarrhea
- prescriptions and medications (in labeled, original containers)

Particularly if you'll be hiking in isolated areas, bring a first-aid booklet, Ace bandage, space blanket, and tape and bandages.

For eye care: Those with corrected vision should carry the lens prescription as well as extra glasses in a solid protective case. Contact lenses are used all over Europe, and the required solutions for their care are easy to find. Soft lenses can be boiled like eggs. (Remind your helpful landlady to leave them in their case.) Do not assume that you can wear your contacts as comfortably in Europe as you can at home. I find that the hot, dusty cities and my style of travel make contacts difficult. Every summer I end up wearing my glasses and carrying my contacts.

BASIC FIRST AID

Travel is a package deal. You will probably get sick in Europe. If you stay healthy, feel lucky.

Headaches and other aches: Tylenol (or any other nonaspirin pain reliever) soothes headaches, sore feet, sprains, bruises, Italian traffic, hangovers, and many other minor problems.

Abrasions: Clean abrasions thoroughly with soap to prevent or control infection. Bandages help keep wounds clean but are not a substitute for cleaning. A piece of clean cloth can be sterilized by boiling for 10 minutes or by scorching with a match.

Blisters: Moleskin, bandages, tape, or two pairs of socks can prevent or retard problems with your feet. Cover any irritated area before it blisters.

Motion sickness: To be effective, medication for motion sickness (Bonine or Dramamine) should be taken several hours before you think you'll need it. This medication can also serve as a mild sleeping pill.

Swelling: Often accompanying a physical injury, swelling is painful and delays healing. Ice and elevate any sprain periodically for 48 hours. A package of frozen veggies works as a cheap ice pack. Use an Ace bandage to immobilize, stop swelling, and, later, provide support. It is not helpful to "work out" a sprain.

Fever: A high fever merits medical attention. To convert from Celsius to Fahrenheit, use the formula $F = (C \times 9/5) + 32$. A temperature of 101 degrees Fahrenheit equals 38.3 degrees Celsius.

Colds: Haste can make waste when it comes to gathering travel memories. Keep yourself healthy and hygienic. If you're feeling run-down, check into a good hotel, sleep well, and force fluids. Stock each place you stay with boxes of juice upon arrival. Sudafed (pseudoephedrine) and other cold capsules are available near cemeteries everywhere.

Diarrhea: Get used to the fact that you might have diarrhea for a day. (Practice that thought in front of the mirror tonight.) If you get the runs, take it in stride. It's simply not worth taking eight Pepto Bismol tablets a day or brushing your teeth in Coca-Cola all summer long to avoid a day of the runs. I take my health seriously, and for me, traveling in India or Mexico is a major health concern. But I find Europe very mild.

Every year I take a group of 24 Americans through Turkey for two weeks. With adequate discretion, we eat everything in sight. At the end of the trip, my loose-stool survey typically shows that five or six travelers coped with a day of the Big D and one person was stuck with an extended week-long bout.

To avoid getting diarrhea, eat yogurt. Its helpful enzymes ease your system into the local cuisine.

If you get diarrhea, it will run its course. Revise your diet, don't panic, and take it easy for a day. Make your diet as bland and boring as possible for a day or so (bread, rice, boiled potatoes, clear soup, weak tea). Keep telling yourself that tomorrow you'll feel much better. You will. Most conditions are self-limiting.

If loose stools persist, replenish lost liquids and minerals. Bananas are effective in replacing potassium, which is lost during a bout with diarrhea.

Do not take antidiarrheals if you have blood in your stools or a fever greater than 101 degrees F (38.3 degrees C). You need a doctor's exam and antibiotics. A child (especially an infant) who suffers a prolonged case of diarrhea also needs prompt medical attention.

I visited the Red Cross in Athens after a miserable three-week tour of the toilets of Syria and Jordan. My intestinal commotion was finally stilled by its recommended strict diet of boiled rice and plain tea. As a matter of fact, after five days on that dull diet, I was constipated.

Constipation: With all the bread you'll be eating, constipation, the other side of the intestinal pendulum, is (according to my surveys) as prevalent as diarrhea. Get exercise, eat lots of roughage—raw fruits, leafy vegetables, prunes, or bran tablets from home—and everything will come out all right in the end.

PHARMACIES AND DOCTORS

Throughout Europe, people with a health problem go first to the local pharmacy, not to their doctor. European pharmacists diagnose and prescribe remedies for most simple problems. They are usually friendly and speak English. If necessary, they'll send you to a doctor.

Serious medical treatment in Europe is generally of high quality. To facilitate smooth communication, it's best to find an English-speaking doctor. Before your trip you can get a list of English-speaking doctors in member countries who provide services at special rates and offer travel medicine advice. Join IAMAT, the International Association for Medical Assistance to Travelers (free but donation requested, 417 Center St., Lewiston, NY 14092, tel. 716/754-4883, www .sentex.net/~iamat). In Europe get a referral from agencies that deal with Americans (such as embassies, consulates, American Express companies, large hotels, and tourist information offices).

Most hotels generally can get an English-speaking doctor to stop by within the same day. As a tour guide I've been impressed with the quality of "house call" care and the reasonable fees ($50 per visit). You're diagnosed, billed, and you pay on the spot. You'll generally head off to the nearest 24-hour pharmacy with a prescription, and by the next day you're back in sightseeing business.

22. Outsmarting Thieves

Europe is safe when it comes to violent crime. But it's a very dangerous place—if you're an American—from a petty purse-snatching, pickpocketing point of view. Thieves target Americans: not because they're mean but because they're smart. Loaded down with valuables in a strange new environment, we stick out like jeweled thumbs. If I were a European street thief, I'd specialize in Americans. My card would say "Yanks Я Us." Americans are the ones with all the good stuff in their bags and wallets. Last year I met an American woman whose purse was stolen, and in her purse was her moneybelt. That juicy little anecdote was featured in every street-thief newsletter.

If you're not constantly on guard, you'll have something stolen. One summer, four out of five of my traveling companions lost cameras in one way or another. (Don't look at me.) In more than 20 summers of travel, I've been mugged once (in a part of London where only fools and thieves tread), had my car broken into six times (broken locks and shattered wing windows, lots of nonessential stuff taken), and had my car hot-wired once (it was abandoned a few blocks away after the thief found nothing to take). But I've never had my room rifled and never had any moneybelt-worthy valuables stolen.

Remember, nearly all crimes suffered by tourists are nonviolent and avoidable. Be aware of the pitfalls of traveling but relax and have fun. Limit your vulnerability rather than your travels. Most people in every country are on your side. If you exercise adequate discretion, aren't overly trusting, and don't put yourself into risky situations, your travels should be about as dangerous as hometown grocery shopping. Don't travel afraid—travel carefully.

MONEY BELTS

Money belts are your key to peace of mind. I never travel without one. A money belt is a small, nylon-zippered pouch that ties around the waist under your pants or skirt. You wear it completely hidden from sight, tucked in like a shirttail (over your shirt and under your pants). It costs only $8 (see Back Door Catalog) to protect your fortune.

Tour of a Moneybelt. Packing light applies to your moneybelt as well as your suitcase. Here's what to pack in your moneybelt:

Passport. You're legally supposed to have it with you at all times.

Plane ticket. Put essential pages in your moneybelt, non-essential pages in your luggage.

Railpass. This is as valuable as cash.

Driver's license. This works just about anywhere in Europe, and is necessary if you want to rent a car on the spur of the moment.

Credit card. These are required for car rental and handy to have if your cash runs lows.

ATM card. A Visa debit card is by far the most reliable for ATMs (cheaper than a credit-card cash advance).

Cash. Keep only major bills in your moneybelt.

Traveler's checks. Keep receipt and up-to-date log (necessary for replacement if lost) and a few checks in your moneybelt. Keep bulk of checks (they're replaceable) in your luggage.

Plastic sheath. Moneybelts easily get slimy and sweaty. Damp traveler's checks, railpasses, and plane tickets are disgusting and sometimes worthless. Even a plain old baggie helps keep things dry.

Address list. Print small, and include every number of importance in your life.

With a money belt, all your essential documents are on you as securely and thoughtlessly as your underpants. Have you ever thought about that? Every morning you put on your underpants. You don't even think about them all day long. And every night when you undress, sure enough, there they are, exactly where you put them. When I travel, my valuables are just as securely out of sight and out of mind, around my waist in a money belt. It's luxurious peace of mind. I'm uncomfortable only when I'm not wearing it.

Operate with a day's spending money in your pocket. You don't need to get at your money belt for every nickel, dime, and quarter. Your money belt is your deep storage—for select deposits and withdrawals. Lately, I haven't even carried a wallet. A few bills in my shirt pocket—no keys, no wallet—I'm on vacation!

Precautions: Never leave a money belt "hidden" on the beach while you swim. It's safer left in your hotel room. You can shower with your money belt (hang it—maybe in a plastic bag—from the nozzle) in sleazy hotel or dorm situations where it shouldn't be left alone in your room. Keep your money belt contents dry and unsweaty with a zip-lock baggie. Damp traveler's checks can be hard to cash.

Purses and wallets are handy for odds and ends and a day's spending money, but plan on losing them. A Velcro strip sewn into your front or back pocket slows down fast fingers. Those with nothing worth stealing (cars, video cameras, jewelry, and so on) except what's in their money belt can travel virtually invulnerably.

TIPS ON AVOIDING THEFT

Thieves thrive on confusion, crowds, and other tourist traps. Here's some advice given to me by a thief who won the lotto.

Keep a low profile. Never leave your camera lying around where hotel workers and others can see it and be tempted. Keep it either around your neck or zipped safely out of sight. Luxurious luggage lures thieves. The thief chooses the most impressive suitcase in the pile—never mine. Thieves assume that anyone leaving a bank with their luggage just changed money. Bags are much safer in your room than with you on the streets. Hotels are a relative haven from thieves and a good resource for advice on personal safety.

On trains and at the station: When sleeping on a train (or at an airport or anywhere in public), clip or fasten your pack or suitcase to the chair, luggage rack, or to yourself. Even the slight inconvenience of undoing a clip foils most thieves. Women probably shouldn't sleep in an empty train compartment. You're safer sharing a compartment with a family or a couple of nuns. Be on guard in train stations, especially upon arrival, when you may be overburdened by luggage and overwhelmed by a new location. If you check your luggage at a train station, keep the claim ticket or key in your money belt. Thieves know just where to go if they get one of these.

Tourists are often the targets of thieves at major sights in Italy, especially around Rome's Forum and the Florence train station. Some will pose as beggars—using babies or newpapers to distract you while they rip you off.

The Métro, subway, and flea markets: Crowding through the Paris Métro turnstiles is a popular way to rip off the unsuspecting tourist. Imaginative artful-dodger thief teams create a fight or commotion to distract their victims. Crowded flea markets and city buses that cover the tourist sights (like Rome's notorious #64) are also happy hunting grounds. Thief teams will often block a bus or subway entry, causing the person behind you to "bump" into you. While I don't lock my zippers, most zippers are lockable, and even a wire twisty or keyring is helpful to keep your bag zipped up tight. Thieves assume your daypack is where you keep your goodies.

Your rental car: Thieves target tourists' cars—especially at night. Don't leave anything even hinting of value in view in your parked car. Put anything worth stealing in the trunk. Leave your glove compartment open so the thief can look in without breaking in. Choose your parking place carefully. (Your hotel receptionist knows what's safe and what precautions are necessary.)

Make your car look local. Take off or cover the rental company decals. Leave no tourist information laying around. Leave a local

newspaper in the back. More than half of the work that European automobile glass shops get is repairing wings broken by thieves. Before I
choose where to park my car, I check if the parking lot's asphalt glitters.
If you have a hatchback, leave the trunk covered during the day. At night
take the cover off the trunk and lay it on the back seat so the thief thinks
you're savvy and can see there's nothing stored in the back of your car.
Many police advise leaving your car unlocked at night. Worthless but irre-
placeable things are stolen only if left in a bag. Lay these things loose in
the trunk. In major cities in Spain, crude thieves reach into windows or
even smash the windows of occupied cars at stoplights to grab a purse or
camera. In Rome my favorite pension is next to a large police station—a
safe place to park, if you're legal.

SCAMS

Many of the most successful scams require a naive and trusting tourist. Be
wary of any unusual contact or commotion in crowded public (especially
touristic) places. If you're alert and aren't overly trusting, you should have
no problem. Here are a few clever ways European thieves bolster their cash
flow:

Slow count: Cashiers who deal with lots of tourists (especially in
Italian tourist spots) thrive on the "slow count." Even in banks, they'll
count your change back with odd pauses in hopes the rushed tourist will
gather up the lire early and say "*Grazie.*" Also be careful when you pay
with too large a bill. Waiters have a tough time keeping track of 10,000
and 100,000 lire notes. Take time to give accurate coins to minimize the
complexity of the deal (e.g., give 50,300 lire for a 10,300-lire bill and wait
for 40,000 in change).

Oops!: You're jostled in a crowd as someone spills mustard, ketchup,
or fake pigeon poop on your shirt. The thief offers greedy apologies while
dabbing it up—and pawing your pockets. The latest variation: someone
throws a baby into your arms as your pockets are picked.

The "helpful" local: Thieves posing as concerned locals will warn
you to store your wallet safely—and then steal it after they see where
you stash it. Some thieves put out tacks and ambush drivers with their
"assistance" in changing the tire. Others hang out at subway ticket
machines eager to "help you" the bewildered tourist, buy tickets with
a pile of your quickly disappearing foreign cash. If using a station
locker, beware the "hood samaritan" who may have his own key to a
locker he'd like you to use.

Fake police: Two thieves in uniform—posing as "Tourist Police"—
stop you on the street, flash their badges, and ask to check your wallet

for counterfeit bills. You won't even notice some bills are missing until they leave. Never give your wallet to anyone.

Young thief gangs: These are common throughout urban southern Europe, especially in the touristed areas of Milan, Florence, and Rome. Groups of youngsters with big eyes, troubled expressions, and colorful dresses play a game where they politely mob the unsuspecting tourist, beggar-style. As their pleading eyes grab yours and they hold up their pathetic message scrawled on cardboard, you're fooled into thinking that they're beggars. All the while, your purse, fanny-bag, or rucksack is being expertly rifled. If you're wearing a money belt and you understand what's going on here, there's nothing to fear. In fact, having a street thief's hand in your pocket becomes just one more interesting cultural experience.

IF YOU'RE RIPPED OFF . . .

Even the most careful traveler can get ripped off. If it happens, don't let it ruin your trip. (If you'll be making an insurance claim, get a police report immediately. Traveler's check thefts must be reported within 24 hours.) Many trips start with a major rip-off, recover, and with the right attitude and very light bags, finish wonderfully.

Before you leave on your trip, make photocopies of your valuable documents and tickets. It's easier to replace a lost or stolen plane ticket, passport, Eurailpass, or car rental voucher if you have a photocopy proving that you really owned what you lost.

American embassies or consulates are located in major European cities. They're there to help American citizens in trouble but don't fancy themselves as travelers' aid offices. They will inform those at home that you need help, assist in replacing lost or stolen passports, and arrange for emergency funds to be sent from home (or, in rare cases, loan it to you directly).

23. Museum Strategies

CULTURE BEYOND THE PETRI DISH

Europe is a treasure chest of great art. You'll see many of the world's greatest museums. Here are a few hints on how to get the most out of them.

Learn about art. If the art's not fun, you don't know enough about it. I remember touring the National Museum of Archaeology in Athens as an obligation. My mom said it would be a crime to miss it. It was boring. I was convinced that those who looked like they were enjoying it were actually just faking it—trying to look sophisticated. Two years later, after a class

A victim of the Louvre

in ancient art history, that same museum was a fascinating trip into the world of Pericles and Socrates, all because of some background knowledge. Some pretrip study makes the art more fun.

Be selective. A common misconception is that a great museum has only great art. A museum like the Louvre in Paris is so big (the building itself was, at one time, the largest in Europe), you can't possibly cover everything—so don't try. Only a fraction of a museum's pieces are really "greats." It's best, with the help of a guide or guidebook, to focus on just the museum's top two hours. Some of Europe's great museums provide brief pamphlets recommending the best basic visit. With this selective strategy, you'll appreciate the highlights when you're fresh. If you still have any energy left, you can explore other areas of specific interest to you. For me, museum-going is the hardest work I do in Europe, and I'm rarely good for more than two or three hours at a time. If you're determined to cover a large museum thoroughly, try to tackle one section a day for several days.

Get a guidebook. Readable English guidebooks are rare. To get the most out of your trip, consider getting my art guidebook, *Rick Steves' Mona Winks: Self-Guided Tours of Europe's Top Museums* (co-authored with Gene Openshaw, John Muir Publications, 1998; see Back Door Catalog).

This book is a fun collection of take-you-by-the-hand two-hour tours of Europe's 20 most important (and exhausting) museums and sights. It's just us together with the greatest art of our civilization. Of all of my guide-books, *Mona Winks* sells the least and has the most devoted following. If you decide to travel without *Mona*, try to make friends and tag along with someone in the big museums who's got it.

Try to get a tour. Phone ahead. Some museums offer regularly scheduled tours in English. If the tour is in French or German only, politely let the guide know at the beginning that there are several English-speaking people in the group who'd love some information.

Eavesdrop. If you are especially interested in one piece of art, spend half an hour studying it and listening to each passing tour guide tell his or her story about *David* or the *Mona Lisa* or whatever. They each do their own research and come up with different information to share. Much of it is true. There's nothing wrong with this sort of tour freeloading. Just don't stand in the front and ask a lot of questions.

Make sure you don't miss your favorites. On arrival, look through the museum's guidebook index or the gift shop's postcards to make sure you won't miss anything of importance to you. For instance, I love Salvador Dalí's work. One time I thought I was finished with a museum, but as I browsed through the postcards . . . Hello, Dalí. A museum guide

A local guide brings the castle to life.

was happy to show me where this Dalí painting was hiding. I saved myself the disappointment of discovering too late that I'd missed it.

Know the museum's schedule. Most museums are closed one day during the week (usually Monday or Tuesday). Your guidebook or a tourist information office has that information. Many museums also stop selling tickets and start shutting down rooms 30 to 60 minutes before closing. Free admission days are usually the most crowded. In many cases it's worth the entrance fee to avoid the crowds. My favorite time in museums is the cool, lazy, last hour. But I'm careful to get to the far end early, see the rooms that are first to shut down, and work my way back toward the entry.

Miscellaneous tips: Particularly at huge museums, ask if your ticket allows in-and-out privileges. Check the museum map or brochure at the entrance for the location of particular kinds of art, the café, and bathrooms (usually free and clean). Also, note any special early closings of rooms or wings. Get comfortable—check your bag. (If you want to try to keep your bag with you, carry it low like a purse, not on your back.) Cameras are often allowed if you don't use a flash or tripod. Look for signs or ask. More and more museums offer a greatest-hits plan or brochure. Some (like London's National Gallery) even have a computer study room where you can input your interests and print out a tailored museum tour.

OPEN-AIR FOLK MUSEUMS

Many people travel in search of the old life and traditional culture in action. While we book a round-trip ticket into the romantic past, those we photograph with the Old World balanced on their heads are struggling to dump that load and climb into our modern world. In Europe, most are succeeding.

The easiest way and, more than ever, the only way to see the "real local culture" is by exploring the open-air folk museums. True, it's culture on a lazy Susan, but the future is becoming the past faster and faster, and in many places it's the only "Old World" you're going to find for miles around.

An open-air folk museum is a collection of traditional buildings from every corner of a country or region carefully reassembled in a park, usually near the capital or major city. These sprawling museums are the best bet for the hurried (or tired) tourist craving a magic carpet ride through that country's past. Log cabins, thatched cottages, mills, old schoolhouses, shops, and farms come complete with original furnishings and usually a local person dressed in the traditional costume who's happy to answer any of your questions about life then and there.

To get the most out of your visit, start by picking up a list of that day's special exhibits, events, and activities at the information center, and take

SOME OF EUROPE'S BEST OPEN-AIR FOLK MUSEUMS

Benelux
- Zaanse Schaans near Zaandijk, 30 miles north of Amsterdam. *Windmills, wooden shoes, etc.*
- De Zeven Marken Open-Air Museum, in Schoonoord, Netherlands.
- Zuiderzee Open-Air Museum, in Enkhuisen, Netherlands. *Lively setting, lots of craftspeople.*
- Bokrijk Open-Air Museum, between Hasselt and Genk, in Belgium. *Old Flemish buildings and culture in a natural setting.*

Denmark
- Funen Village (Den Fynske Landsby), just south of Odense.
- Old Town, Arhus. *Sixty houses and shops show Danish town life from 1580 to 1850.*
- Lyngby Park, north of Copenhagen.

Finland
- Seurasaari Island, near Helsinki. *Reconstructed buildings from all over Finland.*
- Handicraft Museum, Turku. *The life and work of 19th-century craftspeople.*

Germany
- Cloppenburg Open-Air Museum, southwest of Bremen. *Traditional life in Lower Saxony, 17th and 18th centuries.*

Great Britain
- Blists Hill Open-Air Museum, near Coalport. *Shows life from the early days of the Industrial Revolution.*
- Beamish Open-Air Museum, northwest of Durham. *Life in northeast England in 1900.*
- Welsh Folk Museum, at St. Fagans, near Cardiff. *Old buildings and craftspeople illustrate traditional Welsh ways.*

Ireland
- Bunratty Folk Park, near Limerick. *Buildings from the Shannon area and artisans at work.*
- Irish Open-Air Folk Museum, at Cultra near Belfast. *Traditional Irish lifestyles and buildings from all over Ireland.*
- Glencolumbcille Folk Museum, Donegal. *Thatched cottages show life from 1700 to 1900. A Gaelic-speaking cooperative runs the folk village and a traditional crafts industry.*

Norway
- Norwegian Folk Museum, at Bygdøy near Oslo. *Norway's first, with 150 old buildings from all over Norway and a 12th-century stave church.*
- Maihaugen Folk Museum, at Lillehammer. *Folk culture of the Gubrandsdalen. Norway's best.*

Sweden
- Skansen, Stockholm. *One of the best museums, with more than 100 buildings from all over Sweden, craftspeople at work, live entertainment, and a Lapp camp with reindeer.*
- Kulteren, Lund. *Features southern Sweden and Viking exhibits.*

Switzerland
- Ballenberg Swiss Open-Air Museum, just northeast of Lake Brienz. *A fine collection of old Swiss buildings with furnished interiors.*

Traditional culture is kept alive in Europe's open-air folk museums. At Stockholm's you may be entertained by this rare band of left-handed fiddlers.

advantage of any walking tours. In the summer, folk museums buzz with colorful folk dances, live music performances, and young craftspeople specializing in old crafts. Many traditional arts and crafts are dying, and these artisans do what they can to keep the cuckoo clock from going the way of the dodo bird. Some of my favorite souvenirs are those I watched being dyed, woven, or carved by folk-museum artists.

Popularized in Scandinavia, these sightseeing centers of the future are now found all over the world. The best folk museums are still in the Nordic capitals. Oslo's, with 150 historic buildings and a 12th-century stave church, is just a boat ride across the harbor from the city hall. Skansen, in Stockholm, gets my first-place ribbon for its guided tours, feisty folk entertainment, and Lapp camp complete with reindeer.

Switzerland's Ballenberg Open-Air Museum, near Interlaken, is a good alternative when the Alps hide behind clouds.

The British Isles have no shortage of folk museums. For an unrivaled look at the Industrial Revolution, spend a day at the Blists Hill Open-Air Museum in the Ironbridge Gorge, northwest of Stratford. You can cross the world's first iron bridge to see the factories that lit the fuse of our modern age.

Every year new folk museums open. Before your trip, send a card to each country's national tourist office (addresses are listed in Chapter 2: Gathering Information) requesting, among other things, a list of open-air folk museums. As you travel, use a current guidebook and local tourist information centers.

Folk museums teach traditional lifestyles better than any other kind of museum. As our world hurtles past 100 billion McDonald's hamburgers served, these museums will become even more important. Of course, they're as realistic as Santa's Village, but how else will you see the elves?

24. Travel Photography

If my hotel were burning down and I could grab just one thing, it would be my exposed film. Every year I ask myself whether it's worth the worry and expense of mixing photography with my travels. After my film is developed and I relive my trip through those pictures, the answer is always "Yes!" Here are some tips and lessons that I've learned from the photographic school of hard knocks.

BUYING A CAMERA

Good shots are made by the photographer, not the camera. For most people, a very expensive camera is a bad idea. Your camera is more likely to be lost, broken, or stolen than anything else you'll travel with. An expensive model may not be worth the risks and headaches that accompany it.

A good eye is more important than an extra lens.

A basic 35 mm point-and-shoot or single-lens reflex (SLR) can provide most people with everything they need. When buying a camera, get one that will do what you want and a little bit more. You're buying a camera not only for the trip but also for use later.

Visit your local camera shops, ask questions, and ask your friends and neighbors what they use. Be careful of what the salespeople try to sell. They make more money if they can sell you the camera that is being promoted for the month, but it may not be what you need. Get a camera built by a well-known company.

Don't buy a camera a day or two before you fly. Not every camera works perfectly right out of the box. Shoot a roll of 24-exposure film, indoors (with flash) and outdoors, before you leave. Check your pictures for a good exposure and sharp focus. If they're not right, take it back. Do the same checks with the replacement camera. Do your learning on Main Street rather than Piazza San Marco.

TYPES OF CAMERAS

Disposables: The simple choice for an amateur photographer (lacking an environmental conscience) is a disposable or "single-use" camera. These disposables cost as little as $7 ($10 with flash) for 24 exposures of 400-speed film. A cheap panorama camera, with a very wide-angle lens for 180-degree shots, is a fun supplement.

Focus-free: The compact little "focus-free" cameras ($25–50) give you very little creative control but are almost foolproof in getting a decent picture. They're fragile and, when broken, usually just tossed out.

Point-and-shoot: Moving up in cost, point-and-shoot cameras ($50–100) are auto-focus but have a wide-angle 38 mm lens. Models over $100 come with small zoom (adjustable) lenses of 38 to 70 mm and a few helpful bells and whistles. The best units have a zoom lens from about 28 to 105 mm. These can cost more than a low-end single-lens reflex. If you spend less than $100, you'll get a cheap camera that might not last much longer than the trip. Point-and-shoot cameras should be used only with color print film. Their shutters are set to overexpose about a half-stop, which gives the best prints from negative film (but not for slides). Some of the latest point-and-shoot cameras can be reprogrammed for use with slide film.

Single lens reflex (SLR): Those shooting slides should stick with a good SLR. Regardless of advertising claims, there's no real difference between the mind of Minolta and the mind of Pentax, Nikon, or Canon. The trend in SLRs is toward auto-focus lenses, but most of these units have a manual focus-override switch. There aren't many non-auto-focus

SLRs still being made. For traveling, the quick and accurate auto-focus is handy, but creative photographers will also want the manual capabilities. Be sure to leave home with a fresh battery.

LENSES, FILTERS, AND FILM

Lenses: Your best all-around lens is an f/3.5 28–70 mm or 80 mm "mid-range" zoom lens. No, it's not as fast as an f/1.7, but with the fine-grain ASA-400 films on the market today, it's almost like having an f/1.7 lens.

Filters: Make sure all your lenses have a haze or UV filter on them. It's better to bang and smudge up your filter than your lens. The only other filter you might use is a polarizer, which eliminates reflections and enhances color separation, but you can lose up to two stops in speed with it. Never use more than one filter at a time.

Film: When choosing film, I go with 400-speed film in 36-exposure rolls. Print films are all about the same. You'll see more difference between the print processors than between the films. With slide film, stick with the films that are known as E-6 developing (Ektachrome, Fujichrome, and so on). They can be developed overnight in most large cities and usually cost less, too. Kodak film is cheapest in the United States. In Europe buy film in department stores or camera shops rather than for rip-off prices at the sights. Fuji and Konica are reasonable in Europe.

A GALAXY OF GADGETS

Like many hobbies, photography is one that allows you to spend endless amounts of money on accessories. The following are particularly useful to the traveling photographer:

Gadget bag: The most functional and economical is simply a small nylon stuff bag made for hikers. When I'm taking a lot of pictures, I like to wear a nylon belt pouch (designed to carry a canteen). This is a handy way to have your different lenses and filters readily accessible, allowing you to make necessary changes quickly and easily. A formal camera bag is unnecessary and attracts thieves.

Mini C-clamp/tripod: About five inches high, this great little gadget screws into most cameras, sprouts three legs, and holds the camera perfectly still for slow shutter speeds, timed exposures, and automatic shutter release shots. (It looks like a small lunar landing module.) The C-clamp works where the tripod won't, such as on a fence or handrail. A conventional tripod is too large to lug around Europe. Those without a minitripod use a tiny beanbag (or sock filled with rice) or get good at balancing their camera on anything solid and adjusting the tilt with the lens cap or strap.

Tissue, cleaner, and lens cap: A lens-cleaning tissue and a small bottle of cleaning solution are wise additions to any gadget bag. I leave my protective camera case at home and protect my lens with a cap that dangles on its string when I'm shooting. Carrying film in a lead-lined bag is unnecessary since European airport X-rays these days really are "film safe."

TRICKS FOR A GOOD SHOT

Most people are limited by their skills, not by their camera. Understand your camera. Devour the manual. Shoot experimental shots, take notes, and see what happens. You might have to put a lot of expense and energy into your travel photography. If you don't understand f-stops or depth of field, find a photography class or book and learn. Camera stores sell good books on photography in general and travel photography in particular. I shutter to think how many people are underexposed and lacking depth in this field.

A sharp eye connected to a wild imagination will be your most valuable piece of equipment. Develop a knack for what will look good and be interesting after the trip. The skilled photographer's eye sees striking light, shade, form, lines, patterns, texture, and colors. Weed out dull shots before you take them, not after you get them home. It's cheaper.

Look for a new slant to an old sight. Postcard-type shots are boring. Everyone knows what the Eiffel Tower looks like. Find a unique or different approach to sights that everyone has seen. Shoot the bell tower through the horse's legs or lay your camera on the floor to shoot the Gothic ceiling.

Capture the personal and intimate details of your trip. Show how you lived, who you met, and what made each day an adventure (a close-up of the remains of a picnic, your leech bite, laundry day, or a local schoolboy playing games with his nose).

Vary your perspective. Shoot close, far, low, high, during the day and at night. Don't fall into the rut of always centering a shot. Use foregrounds to add color, depth, and interest to landscapes.

Be bold and break rules. For instance, we are told never to shoot into the sun. But some into-the-sun shots bring surprising results. Try to use bad weather to your advantage. Experiment with strange or difficult light situations. Buy a handbook on shooting photos in existing light.

Maximize good lighting. Real photographers get single-minded at the magic hours—early morning and late afternoon, when the sun is very low and the colors glow. Plan for these times. Grab bright colors.

Get close. Notice details. Get closer, real close. Eliminate distractions. Get so close that you show only one thing. Don't try to show it all in one shot. For any potentially great shot, I invest two or three exposures.

People are the most interesting subjects. It takes nerve to walk up to people and take their picture. It can be difficult, but if you want some great shots, be nervy. Ask for permission. The way to do this in any language is to point at your camera and ask, "Photo?" Your subject will probably be delighted. Try to show action. A candid is better than a posed shot. Even a posed candid is better than a posed shot. Give your subject something to do. Challenge the lady in the market to juggle her kiwis. Many photographers take a second shot immediately after the first portrait to capture a looser, warmer subject. If the portrait isn't good, you probably weren't close enough. My best portraits are so close that the entire head can't fit into the frame.

Buildings, in general, are not interesting. It doesn't matter if Karl Marx or Beethoven was born there, a house is as dead as its former resident. As travel photographers gain experience, they take more people shots and fewer buildings or general landscapes.

Be able to take a quick shot. If you're shooting manually, practice setting it. Understand depth of field and metering. In a marketplace situation, where speed is crucial, I preset my camera. I set the meter on the sunlit ground and focus at, let's say, 12 feet. Now I know that, with my depth of field, anything from about 10 to 15 feet will be in focus and, if it's in the sunshine, properly exposed. I can take a perfect picture in an instant, provided my subject meets these preset requirements. It's possible to get some good shots by presetting the camera and shooting from the waist. Ideally, I get eye contact while I shoot from the hip.

Expose for your subject. Even if your camera is automatic, your subject can turn out a silhouette. Meter without the sky. Get those faces in the sun, or lit from the side. For slides, you'll get richer tones if you underexpose just a bit. Expose for the highlights.

Don't be afraid to hand-hold a slow shot. You'll hear that the focal length of your lens dictates the slowest safe hand-held shutter speed you can use. For instance, a 50 mm lens should shoot no slower than 1/50th of a second. That rule is too conservative. You can get decent shots out of a 50 mm lens at 1/30th of a second, even 1/15th. Do what you can to make your camera steady. If you can lean against a wall, for instance, you become a tripod instead of a bipod. If you have a self-timer, it can click the shutter more smoothly than your finger can. Using these tricks, I get good pictures inside a museum at 1/30th of a second. With ASA-400 film, I manage indoors without a flash. Most museums allow photography without a flash or tripod. A flash ages a painting the equivalent of three days of sunshine. (If your camera has an automatic flash, know how to suppress it.) A tripod enables professional (profitable) shots that could compete with the museum gift shop's. Nearly every important museum has a good selection of top-quality slides, cards, and prints at reasonable prices.

Bracket shots when the lighting is tricky. A lot of time-exposure photography is guesswork. The best way to get good shots in difficult lighting situations is to bracket your shots by trying several different exposures of the same scene. You'll have to throw out a few slides that way, but one good shot is worth several in the garbage can. Automatic cameras usually meter properly up to eight or ten seconds, making night shots easy, but bracketing may still be necessary.

Limit your scrapbook or slideshow. Nothing is worse than suffering through an endless parade of lackluster and look-alike shots. If putting together a slideshow, set a limit (maximum two carousels of 140 slides each) and prune your show down until it bleeds. Keep it tight. Keep it moving. Leave the audience crying for more . . . or at least awake.

TRAVELING WITH A VIDEO CAMERA

With video cameras getting better, smaller, and more affordable, more and more Americans are compromising a potentially footloose and fancy-free vacation to get a memory on videotape. To me, a still camera is trouble enough. But thousands of amateur videographers happily seeing Europe through their viewfinders can't all be wrong. Charging your video camera's batteries will be easy, but if your camera doesn't have a built-in converter, you'll have to get one. And remember, European sockets are different (usually two round holes rather than two flat ones). Adapters, which can be tough to find in Europe, are available at your hometown travel accessories or electronics store.

STOW THAT CAMERA!

When not using your camera or camcorder, stow it in your day bag. Many go through their entire trip with a camera bouncing on their belly. That's a tourist's badge that puts a psychological wall between you and Europe. To locals, it screams, "Yodel."

SPECIAL CONCERNS

25. The Woman Traveling Alone

In my classes, women often ask, "Is it safe for a woman to travel alone in Europe?" This is a question best answered by a woman. Europe Through the Back Door tour guide and researcher Risa Laib wrote this chapter based on her solo experience and tips gleaned from other travelers: Gail Morse, Peggy Roberts, Suzanne Hogsett, Bharti Kirchner, and Kendra Roth. Collectively, these women have more than three years of solo travel experience in over 30 countries.

Every year, thousands of women, young and old, travel to Europe on their own. You're part of a grand group of adventurers. Traveling alone, you'll have the chance to make your own discoveries and the freedom to do what you like. It becomes habit-forming.

As a solo woman, you're more approachable than a couple or a solo man. You'll make friends from all over the world, and you'll have experiences that others can only envy. When you travel with a partner, your focus narrows and doors close. When you're on your own, you're utterly open to the moment.

Solo travel is fun, challenging, vivid, and exhilarating. It's a gift from you to you. Prepared with good information and a positive attitude, you'll dance through Europe. And you'll come home stronger and more confident than ever before. Here's how to make it happen.

GETTING INSPIRED

Read exciting books written by solo women travelers about their experiences (try Dervla Murphy's outrageous adventures). For practical advice, read "how-to" travel guidebooks written by and for women.

Seek out other women travelers. Invite them out for dinner and pepper them with questions.

Take classes. A foreign language course is ideal. Consider a class in European history, art history, or travel skills.

Keep up on international news so you can discuss local politics. Study a map of Europe—get to know your neighbors.

Pretend you're traveling alone before you ever leave America. Practice reaching out. Strike up conversations with people in the grocery line. Consciously become more adaptable. If it rains, marvel at the miracle.

Think hard about what you want to see and do. Create the trip of your dreams.

FACING THE CHALLENGES

These are probably your biggest fears: vulnerability to theft, harassment, and loneliness. Take heart. You can tackle each of these concerns head-on. If you've traveled alone in America, you're more than prepared for Europe. In America theft and harassment are especially scary because of their connection with violence. In Europe you'll rarely, if ever, hear of violence. Theft is past tense (as in, "Where did my wallet go?"). As for experiencing harassment, you're far more likely to think, "I'm going to ditch this guy A.S.A.P.," rather than "This guy is going to hurt me."

Loneliness is often the most common fear. But remember, if you get lonely, you can do something about it.

TRAVELING ALONE WITHOUT FEELING LONELY

Here are some tips on meeting people, eating out, and enjoying your nights.

Meeting people: Stay in hostels and you'll have a built-in family (hostels are open to all ages, except in Bavaria, where the age limit is 26). Or choose small pensions and B&Bs, where the owners have time to talk with you. Join Servas (see Chapter 15: Sleeping) and stay with local families. Camping is also a good, safe way to meet Europeans.

At most tourist sites you'll meet more people in an hour than you would at home in a day. If you're feeling shy, cameras are good icebreakers; offer to take someone's picture with their camera.

Talk to other solo women travelers and share advice.

Take your laundry and a deck of cards to a Laundromat and turn solitaire into gin rummy. You'll end up with a stack of clean clothes and conversations.

Stop by any American Express office.

Take a walking tour of a city (ask at the tourist information office). You'll learn about the town and meet other travelers, too.

It's easy to meet local people on buses and trains. You're always welcome at a church service; stay for the coffee hour. When you meet locals who speak English, find out what they think—about anything.

Play with kids. Bring along a puppet or a ball-toss game. Learn how to say "pretty baby" in the local language. If you play peek-a-boo with a baby or fold an origami bird for a kid, you'll make friends with the parents.

Call the English department at a university. See if they have an English conversation club you can visit. Or ask if you can hire a student to be your guide (you'll see the city from a local's perspective, give a student a job, and possibly make a friend).

Try pairing up with another solo traveler. Or return to a city you enjoyed. The locals will remember you, you'll know the neighborhood, and it'll feel like home.

Eating out: Consider quick and cheap alternatives to formal dining. Try a self-service café, a local fast-food restaurant, or a small ethnic eatery. Visit a supermarket deli and get a picnic to eat in the square or a park (local families often frequent parks). Get a slice of pizza from a takeout shop, and munch it as you walk along, people-watching and window-shopping. Eat in the members' kitchen of a hostel; you'll always have companions. Make it a potluck.

A restaurant feels cheerier at noon than at night. Have lunch as your main meal. If you like company, eat in places so crowded and popular that you have to share a table. Or ask other single travelers if they'd like to join you.

If you eat alone, be busy. Use the time to learn more of the language. Practice with the waiter or waitress (when I asked a French waiter if he had kids, he proudly showed me a picture of his twin girls). Read your mail, a guidebook, a novel, or the *International Herald Tribune*. Do trip planning, write or draw in your journal, or scrawl a few postcards.

Most countries have a type of dish or restaurant that's fun to experience with a group. When you run into tourists during the day, make plans for dinner. Invite them to join you for, say, a *rijsttafel* dinner in the Netherlands, a smörgåsbord in Scandinavia, a fondue in Switzerland, a paella feast in Spain, or a spaghetti feed in an Italian trattoria.

At night: Experience the magic of European cities at night. Go for a walk along well-lit streets. With *gelato* in hand, enjoy the parade of people, busy shops, and illuminated monuments. Night or day, you're invariably safe when lots of people are around. Take advantage of the wealth of evening entertainment: concerts, movies, puppet shows, and folk dancing. Some cities offer tours after dark; you can see Paris by night on a river cruise.

If you like to stay in at night, get a room with a balcony overlooking a square. You'll have a front-row seat to the best show in town. Bring along a radio to brighten your room; pull in local music, a friendly voice, maybe even the BBC. Call home, a friend, your family. With a calling card, it's easier than ever. Read novels set in the country you're visiting. Learn to treasure solitude. Go early to bed, be early to rise. Shop at a lively morning market for fresh rolls and join the locals for coffee.

PROTECTING YOURSELF FROM THEFT

As a woman, you're often perceived as being more vulnerable to theft than a man. Here are tips that'll help keep you safe:

Carry a daypack instead of a purse. Leave expensive-looking jewelry at home. Keep your valuables in your money belt and tuck your wallet (containing only a day's worth of cash) in your front pocket. Keep your camera zipped up in your daypack. In crowded places (buses, subways, street markets), carry your daypack over your chest, straps looped over one shoulder. Ask at your hotel or the tourist office if there's a neighborhood you should avoid, and mark it on your map.

Avoid tempting people into theft. Make sure any valuables in your hotel room are kept out of sight. Wear your money belt when you sleep in hostels. When you're sightseeing, never set down anything of value (such as a camera or wallet). Either have it in your hand or keep it hidden. If you're sitting and resting, loop a strap of your daypack around your arm, leg, or chair leg. Remember, you're unlikely ever to be hurt by thieves. They want to separate you from your valuables painlessly.

DEALING WITH MEN

In small towns in Continental Europe, men are often more likely to speak English than women. If you never talk to men, you could miss out on a chance to learn about the country. So by all means, talk to men. Just choose the men and choose the setting.

In northern Europe, you won't draw any more attention from men than you do in America. In southern Europe, particularly in Italy, you'll get more attention than you're used to, but it's nothing you can't handle.

Be aware of cultural differences. In Italy, when you smile and look a man in the eyes, it's considered an invitation. If you wear dark sunglasses, no one can see your eyes. And you can stare all you want.

Dress modestly to minimize attention from men. Take your cue from what the local women wear. In Italy slacks and skirts (even short ones) are considered more proper than shorts.

Wear a real or fake wedding ring and carry a picture of a real or fake husband. There's no need to tell men that you're traveling alone. Lie unhesitatingly. You're traveling with your husband. He's waiting for you at the hotel. He's a professional wrestler who retired from the sport for psychological reasons.

If you'd like to date a local man, meet him at a public place. Tell him you're staying at a hostel—you have a 10:00 p.m. curfew and 29 room-mates. Better yet, bring a couple of your roommates along to meet him. After the introductions, let everyone know where you're going and when you'll return.

HANDLING HARASSMENT

The way you handle harassment at home works in Europe, too.

In southern Europe men may think that if you're alone, you're available. If a man comes too close to you, say "no" firmly in the local

In Europe, sometimes blondes have more trouble.

language. That's usually all it takes. Tell a slow learner that you want to be alone. Then ignore him.

If he's obnoxious, solicit the help of others. Ask people at a café or on the beach if you can join them for a while.

If he's well-meaning but too persistent, talk openly to him. Turn him into an ally. If he's a northern Italian, ask him about southern Italian men. Get advice from him on how you can avoid harassment when you travel farther south. After you elicit his "help," he'll be more like a brother than a bother.

Usually men are just seeing if you're interested. Only a few are difficult. If a man makes a lewd gesture, look away and leave the scene.

Harassers don't want public attention drawn to their behavior. I went out for a walk in Madrid one evening, and a man came up much too close to me, scaring me. I shouted, "Get!" And he was gone. I think I scared him as much as he scared me. Ask a local woman for just the right thing to say to embarrass jerks. Learn how to say it, loudly.

If you feel the need to carry Mace, take a self-defense class instead. Mace can be confiscated at the airport, but knowledge and confidence are yours to keep. And remember, the best self-defense is common sense.

TRAVELING SMART

Create conditions that are likely to turn out in your favor. By following these tips, you'll have a safer, smoother, more enjoyable trip.

Have a little local cash with you when you enter a country, and change money before you run low. Bank holidays strike without warning throughout Europe.

Be self-reliant, so that you don't need to depend on anybody unless you want to. Always carry food, water, a map, a guidebook, and a phrase book. When you need help, ask another woman or a family.

Walk purposefully. Look like you know where you're going. Use landmarks (such as church steeples) to navigate. If you get lost in an unfriendly neighborhood, go into a restaurant or store to ask for directions or to look at your map.

Learn enough of the language to get by. With a few hours' work you'll know more than most tourists and be better prepared to deal with whatever situation arises. At a bus station in Turkey, I witnessed a female tourist repeatedly asking in English, louder and louder, "When does the bus leave?" The frustrated ticket clerk kept answering her in Turkish, "Now, now, now!" If you know even just a little of the language, you'll make it much easier on yourself and those around you.

Before you leave a city, visit the train or bus station you're going to leave from, so you can learn where it is, how long it takes to reach it, and what services it has. Reconfirm your departure time.

On a bus, if you're faced with a choice between an empty double seat and a seat next to a woman, sit with the woman. You've selected your seat partner. Ask her (or the driver) for help if you need it. They will make sure you get off at the right stop.

If you have to hitchhike, choose people to ask, instead of being chosen. Try your luck at a gas station, restaurant, or the parking lot of a tourist attraction. If possible, pair up with another traveler. (Though I wouldn't recommend hitchhiking alone, I've found it necessary on rare occasions and have hitched without hassles.)

When taking the train, avoid staying in empty compartments. Share a compartment with women, a couple, a mixed group, or a family. Rent a *couchette* for overnight trains. Ask for a compartment for women (available in Spain and some other countries). For about $20, you'll stay with like-minded roommates in a compartment you can lock, in a car monitored by an attendant. You'll wake reasonably rested with your belongings intact.

Try to arrive at your destination during the day. Daylight feels safer than night. For peace of mind, consider reserving a room. If you can't avoid a late-night arrival or departure, use the waiting room of the train station or airport as your hotel for the night.

If you're not fluent in the language, accept the fact that you won't always know what's going on. There's a reason why the Greek bus driver drops you off in the middle of nowhere. It's a transfer point, and another bus will come along in a few minutes. You'll discover that often the locals are looking out for you.

The same good judgment you use at home applies to Europe. Start out cautious and figure out as you travel what feels safe to you.

Treat yourself right—get enough rest, food, and exercise. Walking is a great way to combine exercise and sightseeing. I've jogged alone in cities and parks throughout Europe without any problems. If a neighborhood looks seedy, head off in another direction.

Relax. There are other trains, other buses, other cities, other people. If one thing doesn't work out, something else will. Thrive on optimism.

Have a grand adventure!

RESOURCES

Here are a few books you'll find in travel bookstores: *A Journey of One's Own: Uncommon Advice for the Independent Woman Traveler* and *Adventures*

in Good Company, both by Thalia Zepatos; *A Woman's World* and *Gutsy Women: Travel Tips and Wisdom for the Road*, both by Marybeth Bond; *Handbook for Women Travellers*, by Maggie and Gemma Moss; *More Women Travel*, published by Rough Guide; and *A Foxy Old Woman's Guide to Traveling Alone Around Town and Around the World* (Jay Ben-Lesser, Crossing Press). Journeywoman shares travel tips through its Web site: www.journeywoman.com. For a list of books by and about women travelers, check the Globe Corner Bookstore's Web site: www .globecorner.com.

26. Families, Seniors, and Disabled Travelers

TRAVELS WITH BABY ANDY—LEASHES AND VALIUM?

My wife (Anne), seven-year-old (Andy), and VW van (Vinnie) have spent seven one-month trips with me traveling from Norway to Naples and Dublin to Dubrovnik. It's not hell, but it's not terrific travel, either. Still, when he was younger, we'd have rather changed diapers in Paris than in Seattle.

Young European families, like their American counterparts, are traveling, babies and all. You'll find more and more kids' menus, hotel playrooms, and kids-go-crazy zones at freeway rest stops all over Europe. And Europeans love babies. You'll also find that babies are great icebreakers—socially and in the Arctic.

An international adventure is a great foundation for a mountain of family memories. Here are some of the lessons we've learned whining and giggling through Europe with baby, toddler, and now little boy, Andy.

BABY GEAR

Since a happy baby on the road requires a lot of gear, a key to survival with a baby in Europe is to have a rental car or stay in one place. Of course, pack as light as you can, but if you figure you'll need it, trust your judgment.

Bring a car seat, buy one in Europe, or see if your car rental company can provide one. If you're visiting friends, with enough notice they can often borrow a car seat and a stroller for you. If you'll be driving long hours while the baby sleeps, try to get a car seat that reclines.

A stroller is essential. Umbrella models are lightest, but we found a heavy-duty model with reclining back worth bringing for the baby. Andy could nap in it, and it served as a luggage cart for the Bataan Death March parts of our trip when we had to use public transportation. Carry the stroller onto the plane—you'll need it in the airport. Big wheels handle cobblestones best.

A small travel crib was a godsend. No matter what kind of hotel, pension, or hostel we ended up in, as long as we could clear a four-by-four-

Siena? We love Siena!

foot space on the floor, we'd have a safe, clean, and familiar home for
Andy to sleep and play in. During the day we'd salvage a little space by
flipping it up on its side and shoving it against the wall.

If a baby backpack works for you at home, bring it to Europe. (I just
use my shoulders.) Rucksacks in general are great for parents who wish
they had the hands of an octopus. Prepare to tote more than a tot. A
combo purse/diaper bag with shoulder straps is ideal. Be on guard: Purse-
snatchers target mothers (especially while busy and off-guard, as when
changing diapers). Remember, in most of Europe a mother with a small
child is given great respect. You'll generally be offered a seat on crowded
buses and allowed to go to the front of the line at museums.

There's lots more to pack. Encourage bonding to a blanket or stuffed
critter and take it along. We used a lot of Heinz dehydrated food dumped
into zip-lock baggies. Tiny Tupperware containers with lids were great for
crackers, raisins, and snacks. You'll find plenty of disposable diapers, wipes,
baby food, and so on in Europe, so don't take the whole works from home.
Before you fly away, be sure you've packed ipecac, a decongestant, aceta-
minophen, and a thermometer. For a toddler, bring a few favorite books
and a soft (easy on hotel rooms) ball, and buy little European toys as you go.
As Andy got older, activity books and a Sega Game Gear kept him occupied
for what might have been countless boring hours. Also, a daily holiday

---

RESOURCES FOR TRAVELING WITH KIDS IN EUROPE

Common sense and lessons learned from day trips at home are your best sources of information. *Take Your Kids to Europe* (by Cynthia Harriman, Globe Pequot Press, 1997, 320 pages, $16.95 plus $3.95 shipping, tel. 800/243-0495) is full of practical, concrete lessons from first-hand family travel experience, and the only good book I've seen for those traveling with kids ages 6 to 16. The best book we found on traveling with infants was Maureen Wheeler's *Travel with Children* (Lonely Planet Publications). Though designed for Asian travel, it's good advice for Europe-bound parents. For a catalog full of family travel guides, send $1 (or a long SASE with 32 cents postage) to Carousel Press, Box 6038, Berkeley, CA 94706, tel. 510/527-5849.

---

allowance as a reward for assembling a first-class daily picture journal gave our seven-year-old reasons to be enthusiastic about every travel day. (As an older child, his journal project has grown.)

PARENTING AT 32,000 FEET

Gurgling junior might become an airborne Antichrist as soon as the seat belt light goes off. You'll pay 10 percent of the ticket cost to take a child under the age of two on an international flight. The child doesn't get a seat, but many airlines have flying baby perks for moms and dads who ask for them in advance—roomier bulkhead seats, hang-from-the-ceiling bassinets, and baby meals. After age two, a toddler's ticket costs 70 to 90 percent of the adult fare—a major financial owie. From age 12 on, kids pay full fare. (Rail passes and train tickets are free for kids under age four. Those under 12 ride the rails for half price.)

Ask your pediatrician about sedating your baby for a 10-hour intercontinental flight. We think it's only merciful (for the entire family). Dimetapp, Tylenol, or Pediacare have also worked well for us.

Prepare to be 100 percent self-sufficient throughout the flight. Expect cramped seating and busy attendants. Bring extra clothes (for you and the baby), special toys, and familiar food. Those colored links are handy for attaching toys to the seat, crib, highchairs, jail cells, and so on. The in-flight headphones are great entertainment for flying toddlers.

Landings and takeoffs can be painful for ears of all ages. A bottle, a pacifier, or anything to suck helps equalize the baby's middle-ear pressure. For this reason, nursing moms will be glad they do when it comes to flying. If your kid cries, remember: Crying is a great pressure equalizer.

Once on foreign soil, you'll find that your footloose and see-it-all days of travel are over for a while. Go easy. Traveling with a tyke is tiring, wet, sticky, and smelly. Your mobility plummets.

Be warned—jet lag is nursery purgatory. On his first night in Europe, baby Andy was furious that darkness had bullied daylight out of his up-'til-then reliable 24-hour body clock cycle. Luckily, we were settled in a good hotel (and most of the guests were able to stay elsewhere).

SHELTER

We slept in rooms of all kinds, from hostels (many have family rooms) to hotels. Until he was five, we were never charged for Andy, and while we always use our own bedding, many doubles have a sofa or extra bed that can be barricaded with chairs and used instead of the crib.

Childproof the room immediately on arrival. A roll of masking tape makes quick work of electrical outlets. Anything breakable goes on top of the free-standing closet. Proprietors are generally helpful to considerate and undemanding parents. We'd often store our bottles and milk cartons in their fridge, ask (and pay) for babysitting, and so on.

Every room had a sink where baby Andy could pose for cute pictures, have a little fun, make smelly bubbles, and get clean. With a toddler, budget extra to get a bath in your room—a practical need and a fun diversion. (Many showers have a six-inch-tall "drain extension," enabling you to create a bathing puddle.) Toddlers and campgrounds—with swings, slides, and plenty of friends—mix wonderfully.

Self-catering flats rented by the week or two-week period, such as *gîtes* in France and villas in Italy, give a family a home on the road. Many families prefer settling down this way and side-tripping from a home base.

FOOD

We found European restaurants and their customers cool to noisy babies. Highchairs are rare. We ate happiest at places with outdoor seating; at the many McDonald's-type, baby-friendly fast-food places; or picnicking. In restaurants (or anywhere), if your infant is making a disruptive fuss, apologetically say the local word for "teeth" (*dientes*-Spanish, *dents*-French, *denti*-Italian, *Zahn*-German), and annoyed locals will become sympathetic.

Nursing babies are easiest to feed and travel with. Remember, some cultures are uncomfortable with public breastfeeding. Be sensitive.

We stocked up on munchies (fruit, pretzels, and tiny boxes of juice—which double as squirt guns). A 7:00 a.m. banana worked wonders, and a

Families bathe together at Disneyland Paris.

5:00 p.m. snack made late European dinners workable. In restaurants we ordered an extra plate for Andy, who just nibbled from our meals. We'd order "fizzy" (but not sticky) mineral water, call it "pop," and the many spills were no problem. With all the candy and sweet temptations at toddler eye level in Europe, you can forget a low-sugar diet. While *gelati* and pastries are expensive, Andy's favorite suckers; Popsicles; and hollow, chocolate, toy-filled eggs were cheap and available everywhere.

Plan to spend more money. Use taxis rather than buses and subways. Hotels can get babysitters, usually from professional agencies. The service is expensive but worth the splurge when you crave a leisurely, peaceful evening *sans* bibs and cribs.

With a baby, we arranged our schedule around naps and sleep time. A well-rested child is worth the limitation. Driving while Andy siestaed worked well. As a toddler, however, Andy was up very late, playing soccer with his new Italian friends on the piazza or eating huge ice creams in the hotel kitchen with the manager's kids. We gave up on a rigid naptime or bedtime, and we enjoyed Europe's evening ambience as a family.

OK, you're there—watered, fed, and only a little bleary. Europe is your cultural playpen, a living fairy tale, a sandbox of family fun and adventure. Grab your kid and dive in.

Family update and warning: Now, with little sister Jackie, our family travels mean double the dribbles. While Andy is more fun and less trouble than ever, traveling with two small kids is more complicated and limiting than with one. This chapter will grow with our family.

GLOBETROTTING FOR SENIORS

More people than ever are hocking their rockers and buying plane tickets. Many senior adventurers are proclaiming, "Age matters only if you're a cheese." Travel is their fountain of youth.

I spent three weeks last summer in Europe with a group that made my parents look young. They taught me many terrific things, including the fact that it's never too late to have a happy childhood. The special discounts that exist in much of the world should encourage older travelers.

I spend a lot of time meeting with retired couples who fly off to Europe with Eurailpasses, carry-on suitcases that convert into rucksacks, and $60 a day. Most of them are on their second or third retirement trip, and each time they walk out my door I think, "Wow, I've got a good 30 years of travel ahead of me."

Gertrude and Vernon Johnson, both 68, are in Europe now. Nobody knows where. Before they left, I quizzed them on geriatric globetrotting.

Was this your first major trip abroad? "Last year's trip was our first trip anywhere! We spent six weeks with a train pass and $150 a day for the both of us. Out of that $150, we spent $100 on room and board, going the B&B way, and $50 a day covered everything else, including transportation, admissions, little souvenirs, and even a weekly call home to the kids."

Their fountain of youth is Europe!

Were you hesitant at first? "Yes, indeed. I remember climbing into that airplane thinking I might be making a big mistake. But when we got over there and tackled problem after problem successfully, our confidence soared. Friendly people were always coming out of the woodwork to help us when we needed it."

What about theft and physical safety for a couple of retired people like yourselves running around Europe independently? "As far as retired people go, we never felt like we were 'retired.' I never felt any different from anyone else, and people accepted us as just two more travelers."

Gertrude added, "Later on, as we remembered our trip, we thought maybe people treated us 'gray-haired rucksackers' a little kinder because of our age. We never had a bit of a problem with theft or safety. Of course, we'd wear our money belts every day and choose our neighborhoods carefully. It's pretty obvious when you're getting into a bad neighborhood. We never felt that Ugly American problem. People treated us very well. If anything, there was more help for seniors in public in Europe than we find at home."

Were the Europeans impressed by a retired couple with such an independent travel style? "I'd say they were," said Vernon. "In fact, at one place, Rick, we were sitting down and . . ."

The table jolted as Gertrude grabbed Vernon's knee, saying, "Nothin' doing! That's too good a story." She plans on becoming a travel writer—so we'll just have to wait for the rest of that adventure.

Do you speak any languages? "No, but we worked on a Berlitz French record for three weeks, and that was helpful. We found the best way to get along with the locals was to try to speak their language. They'd laugh a lot, but they appreciated our effort and would bend over backward to help us. They could usually speak enough English to help us out."

Did you have trouble finding rooms? "No. We traveled from May 1 to June 15 without reservations. Arthur Frommer's guide was handy, and, of course, we got help from the tourist offices and people in the towns. We had no problems. Decent budget hotels are close to the station, and that made setting up a snap.

"We always planned to arrive early. The overnight trains were ideal because they arrived first thing in the morning. We took our

Frommer's guide into the tourist office, which was always in or near the station, and they'd call the hotel for us. A few times they charged extra for their service, but it was always very convenient. For older people, I would insist on arriving early in the day, having local money with you when you arrive, and remembering that Europe is less exhausting away from the heat and crowds of peak season."

How much did you pack? "Our luggage weighed a total of 25 pounds. Gertrude carried 11, and I packed 14. We just packed a few easy-wash and fast-dry clothes. Before our first trip you told us to bring nothing electrical. We didn't listen, and we almost burned down our hotel in Paris." (The table jolted again.) "So this time we're bringing nothing electrical."

What was the most important lesson you learned on your first trip? "Pack even less. When you pack light, you're younger—footloose and fancy-free. And that's the way we like to be." Sound familiar?

Elderhostel, which offers study programs around the world for those over 55, will send you a free catalog listing their educational tours, varying in length from one to four weeks (tel. 617/426-8056, 75 Federal St., Boston, MA 02110, Web site: www.elderhostel.org).

THE DISABLED TRAVELER
Thanks to Susan Sygall from Mobility International for this article.

More and more people with disabilities are heading to Europe and more of us are looking for the Back Door routes so we can get off the tourist track and still stay

*within a budget. Yes, that includes those of us who use wheelchairs. I've been trav-
eling the "Rick Steves' way" since about 1973—and here are some of my best tips.*

*I use a manual lightweight wheelchair with pop-off tires. I take a backpack
that fits on the back of my chair and store my daypack underneath my chair in a
net bag. If I can't carry it myself (since I usually travel alone), I don't take it. I
keep a bungee cord with me for the times I can't get my chair into a car or when
I need to secure it on a train. I always insist on having MY OWN wheelchair to
the airline gate and when I transfer planes I insist again that I get my own chair.*

*Bathrooms are always a hassle so I have learned to use creative ways to trans-
fer into narrow bathrooms (or use a belt to narrow my wheelchair width). To be
blatantly honest, when there are no accessible bathrooms in sight I have found ways
to pee discreetly just about anywhere (outside the Eiffel Tower—or on a glacier
in a national park). You gotta do what you gotta do and hopefully one day the access
will improve, but in the meantime—there is a world out there to be discovered.
Bring along an extra pair of pants and a great sense of humor.*

*I always try to learn some of the language of the country I'm in, because it
cuts through the barriers when people stare at you (and they will) and also comes
in handy when you need assistance in going up a curb or a flight of steps. Don't
accept other people's notions of what is possible—I have climbed Masada in Israel
and made it to the top of the Acropolis in Greece.*

*If a museum lacks elevators for visitors, be sure to ask about freight eleva-
tors because almost all have them somewhere and that can be your ticket to seeing a world-class treasure.*

*I always get information about disability groups where I am going—they will
have the best access information and many times they will become your new traveling partners and friends. They can show you the best spots. Remember that you
are part of a global family of disabled people.*

*Each person with a disability has her/his own unique needs and interests, and
many of my friends use power wheelchairs, or are blind, or deaf, or have other disabilities—and have their own travel tips. People who don't walk long distances
might want to think of taking or borrowing a sports wheelchair when needed.
Whether you travel alone, with friends, or with an assistant, you're in for a great
adventure.*

*Don't confuse being flexible and having a positive attitude with settling for
less than your rights. I expect equal access and constantly let people know about the
possibility of providing access through ramps or other modifications. When I believe
my rights have been violated, I do whatever is necessary to remedy the situation so
the next traveler, or disabled people in that country, won't have the same frustrations. Know your rights as a traveler with a disability. For information on your
rights regarding travel on U.S. airlines, get the free book* The Air Carriers Act:
Make It Work For You *free from the Paralyzed Veterans of America (tel.*

*888/860-7244). If, under the Americans with Disabilities Act or Air Carriers
Act, you feel you have been discriminated against (such as not being allowed on a
U.S. tour company's tour of Europe), contact the Disability Rights Education and
Defense Fund (tel. 800/466-4232 voice and TDD).*

*If you are interested in work, study, research, or volunteering abroad, contact
the Clearinghouse on Disability and Exchange at Mobility International USA
(tel. 541/343-1284 voice and TDD e-mail: clearinghouse@miusa.org). Check
out the Web and do some investigating. Search for "travel" and "disability."*

*Hopefully more books like Rick's will include basic access information—which
will allow everyone to see Europe through the Back Door. Let's work toward making that door accessible so we can all be there together.*

ADDITIONAL RESOURCES

The U.S.A. office of Mobility International (a nonprofit organization with
branches around the world) sponsors international exchange programs for
the disabled, publishes a quarterly newsletter ($25/year, available on
audio-cassette), and sells a handy book entitled *A World of Options: A Guide
to International Educational Exchange, Community Service, and Travel for
Persons with Disabilities* (600 pages, $35 ppd., P.O. Box 10767, Eugene, OR
97440, tel. 541/343-1284 voice and TDD, info@ miusa.org).

The Society for the Advancement of Travel for the Handicapped
(SATH), a nonprofit membership organization, publishes a travel magazine and offers travel advice ($45 membership, $30 for students and
seniors, includes magazine; $13 for magazine subscription only;
tel. 212/447-SATH, fax 212/725-8253, e-mail sathtravel@aol.com).

Travelin' Talk, a network for disabled travelers, hooks you up with
members in other states and countries. It focuses on America but is
gradually going global (P.O. Box 3534, Clarksville, TN 37043, tel.
931/552-6670, online at trvlntlk@aol.com).

If you're interested in a tour, these companies offer international
travel for the disabled: Accessible Journeys (35 W. Sellers Ave., Ridley
Park, PA 19078, tel. 800/846-4537) and Flying Wheels Travel (P.O. Box
382, Owatonna, MN 55060, tel. 800/535-6790).

Access to the Skies Quarterly newsletter offers useful information on
accessible airline travel (free from Paralyzed Veterans Association, 801
18th St. NW, Washington, D.C. 20006, tel. 202/872-1300 ext. 709).

Servas, an organization that enables travelers to stay with families
in other countries, welcomes disabled travelers. Some European Servas
branches list accessibility, or contact your host in advance ($65/year
membership, 11 John St., #407, New York, NY 10038, tel. 212/267-
0252, fax 212/267-0292, Web site: http://servas.org).

Hostelling International indicates in its guides which hostels are accessible (tel. 800/444-6111).

27. Bus Tour Self-Defense

Average American tourists see Europe on an organized bus tour and don't even consider using a guidebook. They pay a guide to show them around.

I'm going to lambast big bus tours here for a few pages. But first I want to mention that there are cute little tour companies (like mine) that have a passion for a particular angle on European travel. By effectively tapping into the efficiency and economy of group travel, they put together a package that is both profitable to them and a good value to the right customer.

But I want to discuss your typical, impossibly cheap, 48-persons-on-a-48-seat-bus tours that are heavily advertised and sold by travel agents for a 15 percent commission. These can be a good value, but only if you know how they work.

By understanding the tour business, you can take advantage of a big bus tour and it won't take advantage of you. Many savvy travelers take escorted coach tours year after year only for the hotels, meals, and transportation provided. Every day they do their own sightseeing, simply applying the skills of independent travel to the efficient, economical trip shell an organized coach tour provides. You can take a tour, and to a limited degree, still go "on your own."

A typical big bus tour has a professional multilingual European guide and 40 to 50 people on board. The tour company is probably very big, booking rooms by the thousand and often even owning the hotels it uses. Typically, the bus is a luxurious, fairly new 48-seater with a high, quiet ride, comfy seats, air conditioning, and a toilet on board.

The hotels will fit American standards—large, not too personal, and offering mass-produced comfort, good plumbing, and only double rooms. Your hotel's location can make the difference between a fair trip and a great trip. Beware if the tour brochure says you'll be sleeping in the "Florence area"—you may be stuck in the middle of nowhere halfway to Bologna. If this is important to you, get explicit locations in writing before your trip. Most meals are included, generally unmemorable buffets that hotel restaurants serve large groups. The prices are driven to almost inedible lows by the tour company. A common complaint among tourists is that hotel meals don't match the local cuisine.

As long as people on board don't think too much or try to deviate from the plan, things go smoothly and reliably, and you really do see a lot of Europe. Note I said "see" rather than "experience." If you like the

Many who take an organized bus tour could have managed fine on their own.

itinerary, guide, and people on your bus, a tour can be a good, easy, and inexpensive way to go.

Having escorted several large European coach tours and now owning and operating a tour company of my own, I've learned that you must understand tour guides and their position. Leading a tour is a demanding job with lots of responsibility, paperwork, babysitting, and miserable hours. Very often, guides are tired. They're away from homes and families, often for months on end, and are surrounded by foreigners having an extended party that they're probably not in the mood for. Most guides treasure their time alone and, except for romantic sidetrips, keep their distance from the group socially. Each tourist has personal demands, and a group of 48 can often amount to one big pain in the bus for the guide.

To most guides, the best group is one that lets her do the thinking, is happy to be herded around, and enjoys being spoon-fed Europe. The guide's base salary is normally low (about $70 a day), but an experienced guide makes $300 to $400 a day when the wage is supplemented by a percentage of the optional excursions, kickbacks from merchants that the group patronizes, and the trip-end tips from the busload.

The best-selling tours are the ones that promise you the most in the time you have available. But no tour can give you more than 24 hours in a day or seven days in a week. What the "blitz" tour can do is give you more hours on the bus. Choose carefully among the itineraries available. Do you really want a series of one-night stands? Bus drivers call tours with ridiculous itineraries "pajama tours." You're in the bus from 8:00 a.m. until after dark, so why even get dressed?

HOW TO ENJOY A BUS TOUR

Keep your guide happy. Independent-type tourists tend to threaten guides. It's important to be independent without alienating them. Don't insist on individual attention when the guide is hounded by 47 others. Wait for the quiet moment to ask for advice. If a guide wants to, he can give his entire group a lot of unrequired extras—but only if he wants to. Your objective, which requires some artistry, is to keep the guide on your side without letting him take advantage of you.

Discriminate among options. While some sightseeing is included, each day one or two special excursions or evening activities, called "options," are offered for $30 to $100 apiece. Each person decides which options to take and pay for. Since budget tours are so competitive, the profit margin on their base price is very thin. The tour company assesses the work of a guide not by how much fun the trip was, but by how many options were sold. Guides sell these options aggressively, discouraging people from going off on their own and even withholding information.

Dishonest tour guides pad their income by cleverly cutting out excursions that the tour company includes (e.g., pocketing $150 by showing a group the windmills but not taking them inside) or by doing "black excursions," where she'll charge for a visit that is supposed to be free (such as to Dachau) and not report the income to the tour company.

Some options are great; others are not worth the time or money. In general, the half-day city sightseeing tours are a good value. A local guide will usually show you her city much more thoroughly than you could do on your own, given the time limitations of a "pajama tour." Illuminated night tours of Rome and Paris can be marvelous. I'd skip most other illuminated tours and "nights on the town." On a typical big-bus tour evening, several bus tours come together for the "evening of local color." Three hundred Australian, Japanese, and American tourists drinking sangria and watching flamenco dancing onstage to the rhythm of their automatic rewinds isn't exactly local.

Maintain your independence. Your guide may pressure you into taking the options. Stand firm. You are capable of doing plenty on your own. Get maps and tourist information from your (or another) hotel desk or a tourist information office. Tour hotels are often located

A well-chosen tour can be a fine value, giving you a great trip and a busload of new friends.

outside the city, where they cost the tour company less and where they figure you are more likely to book the options just to get into town. Some tours promise to take you downtown if the hotel is outside the city limits. Ask the person behind the desk how to get downtown using public transportation. Taxis are always a possibility; with three or four people sharing, they're affordable. Team up with others on your tour to explore on your own. No city is dead after the shops are closed. Go downtown and stroll.

Don't let your guide intimidate you. In Amsterdam guides are instructed to spend two hours in the diamond polishing place and not to visit the Van Gogh Museum (no kickbacks on van Gogh). If you want to skip out, your guide will warn you that you'll get lost and the bus won't wait. Keep your travel spirit off its leash and the hotel address in your money belt.

Do your own research. Know what you want to see. Tour guides hate guidebooks. They call the dreaded tourist with a guidebook an "informed passenger." But a guidebook is *your* key to travel freedom. Your guide will be happy to spoon-feed Europe to you, but it will be from his or her menu. This often distorts the importance of the sights you'll see. Many tours seem to make a big deal out of a statue in Luzern called the *Dying Lion*, and obedient tourists are impressed on command. The guide declares that this mediocre-at-best sight is great, and that's how it's perceived. What makes it "great" for the guide is that Luzern (which has a hotel the tour company owns but not a lot of interesting sights) was given too much time in the itinerary, and the *Dying Lion* has easy tour bus parking. Leonardo da Vinci's *The Last Supper*, however, is often passed over, as bus tours skirt Milan. It's an inconvenient sight.

Remember, you can't take 40 people into a "cozy" pub and be cozy. A good stop for a guide is one with great freeway accessibility and bus parking; where guides and drivers are buttered up with free coffee and cakes; where they serve bottomless cups of American-style coffee, speak English, accept bank cards, and will mail souvenirs home; and where 30 people can go to the bathroom at the same time. *Arrivederci, Roma.*

If you shop, shop around. Many people make their European holiday one long shopping spree. This suits your guide and the local tourist industry just fine. Guides are quick to say, "If you haven't bought a Rolex, you haven't really been to Switzerland," or "You can't say you've experienced Florence if you haven't bargained for and bought a leather coat." In Venice, as I orient my groups, merchants are tugging at my arm and whispering, "Bring your groups to *our* glassworks next time. We'll give you 15 percent back on whatever they spend—and a free glass horse!"

Cruise ships don't pay for their Turkish guides. Cruise companies rent their groups out to the local guide who bids the most. That "scholar" who meets you at the dock is actually a carpet salesman in disguise. He'll take you to the obligatory ancient site and then to the carpet shop.

Every tour guide in Europe knows just where to park the bus in Luzern for Swiss clocks. The guide will get $40 and a bottle of champagne as soon as the bus parks, and 45 minutes later, she steps into the back room and gets 15 percent of whatever went into the till. That's good business. And any tour guide in Europe knows that if she's got Americans on board, she's carting around a busload of stark raving shoppers.

Don't necessarily reject your guide's shopping tips; just keep in mind that the prices you see often include a 15 percent kickback. Never swallow the line, "This is a special price available only to your tour, but you must buy now." The sellers who prey on tour buses are smooth. They zero in on the gullible group member who has no idea what a good buy is.

Create a group "kitty." It's fun, as well as economical, to create a kitty for communal niceties. If each person contributes $10, the "kitty-keeper" can augment dry continental breakfasts with fresh fruit, provide snacks and drinks at rest stops, get stamps for postcards, and so on.

Seek out locals who never deal with tourists. Most tour groups see only a thin slice of people—not real locals but hardened business people who know how to make money off tour groups. If you go through Italy in a flock of 48 Americans following your tour guide's umbrella, these are the only Italians you'll meet. Break away. One summer night in Regensburg, I skipped out. While my tour was still piling off the bus, I enjoyed a beer overlooking the Danube and under shooting stars with the great-great-great-grandson of the astronomer Johannes Kepler.

PERSPECTIVES

28. Political Unrest

An awareness of current social and political problems is as vital to smart travel as a listing of top sights. While some popular tourist destinations are entertaining tourists with "sound and light" shows in the old town, they're quelling terrorist and separatist movements in the new. Countries from England to Italy are dealing with serious or potentially serious internal threats.

Newspaper headlines shape many trips. Many people skip Northern Ireland because of "the troubles," avoid Spain in fear of the militant Basques, and refuse to fly out of Athens or Frankfurt because of a bomb attack years ago. This is like avoiding a particular mall in the United States because it had a robbery last month. Don't let these problems dictate your itinerary. Stay up on the news and exercise common sense (don't sing Catholic songs in Ulster pubs). You can travel safely and still experience first-hand the demographic chaos that explains much of what fills the front pages of our newspapers.

Travel broadens your perspective, enabling you to rise above the 6:00 p.m. entertainment we call news and see things as a citizen of our world. While monuments from the past are worthy of your sightseeing energy, travel can also plug you directly into the present.

There are many peoples fighting the same thrilling battles we Americans won 200 years ago, and while your globe may paint Turkey orange and Iran green, racial, linguistic, and religious groups rarely color within the lines.

Look beyond the beaches and hotels in your tourist brochures for background on how your vacation target's cultural, racial, and religious makeup is causing problems today or may bring grief tomorrow. With this foundation and awareness, you can enjoy the nearly unavoidable opportunities to talk with involved locals about complex current situations. If you're looking to talk politics, you must be approachable—on your own or away from your tour.

Like it or not, people around the world look at "capitalist Americans" as the kingpins of a global game of Monopoly. Make this a political sightseeing plus by striking up conversations. Young, well-dressed people are most likely to speak (and want to speak) English. Universities are the perfect place to solve the world's problems in English with a liberal, open-minded foreigner over a government-subsidized cafeteria lunch.

Understand a country's linguistic divisions. It's next to impossible to keep everyone happy in a multilingual country. Switzerland has four languages, but *Deutsch ist über alles*. In Belgium there's tension between the Dutch- and French-speaking halves. Like many French Canadians, Europe's linguistic underdogs will tell you their language receives equal treatment only on cornflakes boxes, and many are working on adjustments.

In Ireland "the troubles" are kept at least simmering. At any pub in the Emerald Isle, you'll get an earful of someone's passionate feelings. In Russia and Eastern Europe, whenever you want some political or economic gossip, sit alone in a café. After a few minutes and some eye contact, you'll have company and a thrilling chat with a resident malcontent.

After your smashingly successful European adventure, you'll graduate to more distant cultural nooks and geographic crannies. If you mistakenly refer to a Persian or Iranian as Arabic, you'll get a stern education on the distinction; and in eastern Turkey you'll learn more about that fiercely nationalistic group of people called Kurds, who won't rest until that orange and green on the globe is divided by a hunk of land called Kurdistan.

TERRORISM

I'd rather not discuss terrorism. But I'm concerned that people are planning their trips thinking they can slip over there and back while there's a lull in the action. There's always been terrorism, and there always will

be terrorism. It's in your interest, psychologically, to plan your trip assuming there will be a terrorist event sometime between now and your departure date—most likely in the city into which you're flying. Because, sure enough, as soon as you buy your plane ticket to London, the IRA's going to blow up another pub, and your loved ones will leap into action (as if they've already had a meeting) trying to get you to cancel your trip.

The real enemy: loved ones and the TV. Your loved ones' hearts are in the right place. But their minds aren't. Your trip's too important for sensationalism and hysteria to get in the way. Understand the risk of terrorism in a cold, logical, statistical way. (You take many greater risks without even considering them when you travel.) If you want to take that risk, travel in a way that minimizes that tiny threat. Let me explain.

Terrorism is tailor-made for TV—quick, emotional, and gruesome 90-second spots. Consider the emotional style in which terrorism is covered and how expertly terrorists are milking that, even providing TV news broadcasts with video footage. It's quaint to think that our news media is interested in anything other than ratings and selling advertising. Terrorism sells ads big time. TV news—with the least sophisticated and most lucrative audience—is worst.

Loved ones often take TV news to heart, lack a broad understanding of the world, and may stand between us and our travel dreams—begging and even bribing us not to go. If I'm in Europe and there's a boat hijacked or a train wreck in Italy, I always call to let my mother know I survived. Assure those who'll worry about you that you'll call home every few days. If you're a teenager with worrying parents, hit them up for a $1 per 30-second "I'm doing fine" call, and call home regularly.

Traveling safely. Talking to people about local problems is fine. Dodging bullets isn't. Even in areas that aren't "hot spots," it's wise to be up on the news. English newspapers and broadcasts are available in most of the world. Other tourists can be valuable links with the outside world as well. Most importantly, the nearest American or British consulate can advise you on problems that merit concern.

Take your government's travel advice seriously but don't trust it blindly. I try to weed through State Department travel advisories. While I travel right through advisories designed to stoke domestic hysteria to build support for a presidential adventure (generally terrorist-related), others (such as warnings about civil unrest in a country that's falling apart) are grounds to scrub my mission. For the latest U.S. Department of State travel advisories online, check the Web site: http://travel.state.gov/travel_warnings.html.

I can't remember ever hearing a gun or a bomb in my Mediterranean travels. Many times, however, I've had the thrill of a first-hand experience merely by talking with people who were personally involved. Your tour memories can include lunching with a group of Palestinian college students, walking through Moscow with a diehard Communist, listening to the Voice of America with curious Bulgarians in a Black Sea coast campground, and learning why the Swiss aren't completely comfortable with a unified Europe. Or your travel memories can be built on the blare of your tour guide's bullhorn as he tells you who did the stucco in empty Gothic cathedrals and polished palaces.

Certainly we need to consider the real risk of terrorism, evaluate it, and then travel in a way that minimizes the risk. If you can't accept the risk, settle for a lifetime of *National Geographic* specials.

Comparing risks. Travel is accelerated living and comes with many risks. But statistically, the risk of terrorism is much smaller than the chances tourists have always taken without a second thought. Let's look at it in cold unemotional statistics. In 1985, we let terrorism change our way of looking at the world; 28 Americans, out of 25 million who traveled, were killed by terrorists. Sure, that's a risk, but in the same year, 8,000 Americans were killed by handguns on our own streets. Europeans laugh out loud when they read of Americans staying home so they won't be murdered. Statistically, even in the worst times of terrorism, you're much safer in Europe.

Flying is also risky. But in the United States alone, more than 60,000 planes take off and land safely every day. There's a one-in-6-million chance that the plane I board will crash and someone will die. I take the risk and travel. Every year, several hundred pedestrians are run down on the streets of Paris—not glamorous enough for headlines, but dead is dead. By the way, according to our State Department, more Americans were killed by terrorists in 1974 than in 1985, but the media didn't pick up on it, and we tourists didn't notice.

The stealth tourist. Terrorist targets are predictable. They lash out at the high-profile symbols of our powerful and wealthy society—airplanes, luxury cruise ships, elegant high-rise hotels, posh restaurants, military and diplomatic locations. When you travel through the Back Door, you're melting into Europe, keeping the lowest possible profile. You're staying in simple, local-style places—like Pedro's Pension. Terrorists don't bomb Pedro's Pension. That's where they sleep. And if you just really hate terrorism, the most effective way for you to fight it is to travel a lot, learn about the world, come home, and help our country fit better into this ever-smaller planet.

CALMING LOVED ONES WITH STATISTICS AS YOU TRAVEL IN AN AGE OF TERROR

From 1980 to 1990, Americans made about 130 million trips overseas. During that time (according to Bruce Hoffman, a specialist in international security at the Rand Corporation), less than 300 Americans were killed by terrorists. Most of those were victims of the Lockerbie crash in 1988.

Chance of an American overseas or in the air being killed by a terrorist: 1 in 650,000

Chance of being hit by lightning this year in the U.S.: 1 in 600,000

Chance you'll be killed by a fire in your home this year: 1 in 50,000

Chance you'll be murdered this year if you live in a small American town: 1 in 12,000; in a city of over 250,000 people: 1 in 2,000

Deaths per year in the U.S.:
50,000 in car accidents

8,000 by handguns (vs. less than 100 a year in Britain, France, or Germany)

2,500 choking on food

28 Americans killed by terrorists in 1985 (the scariest year yet)

300 pedestrians a year killed by drivers on the streets of Paris

(Most of these statistics are from *What Are the Chances: Risks and Odds in Everyday Life*, by Bernard Siskin, 1989.)

29. Attitude Adjustment

THE UGLY AMERICAN

Many Americans' trips suffer because they are treated like Ugly Americans. Those who are treated like Ugly Americans are treated that way because they *are* Ugly Americans. They aren't bad people, just ethnocentric.

Even if you believe American ways are better, your trip will go better if you don't compare. Enjoy doing things the European way during your trip, and you'll experience a more welcoming Europe.

Europe sees two kinds of travelers: those who view Europe through air-conditioned bus windows, socializing with their noisy American friends; and those who are taking a vacation from America, immersing themselves in different cultures, experiencing different people and lifestyles, and broadening their perspectives.

Europeans judge you as an individual, not by your government. A Greek fisherman once told me, "For me, Reagan is big problem—but I like you." I have never been treated like the Ugly American. I've been proud to wear our flag on my lapel. My Americanness in Europe, if anything, has been an asset.

You'll see plenty of Ugly Americans slogging through a sour Europe, mired in a swamp of complaints. Ugly Americanism is a disease, but fortunately there is a cure: a change in attitude. The best over-the-counter medicine is a mirror. Here are the symptoms. The Ugly American:

• criticizes "strange" customs and cultural differences. She doesn't try to understand that only a Hindu knows the value of India's sacred cows, and only a devout Spanish Catholic appreciates the true worth of his town's patron saint.

• demands to find America in Europe. He insists on orange juice and eggs (sunny-side up) for breakfast, long beds, English menus, punctuality in Italy, and cold beer in England. He measures Europe with an American yardstick.

• invades a country while making no effort to communicate with the "natives." Traveling in packs, he talks at and about Europeans in a condescending manner. He sees the world as a pyramid, with the United States on top and the "less developed" world trying to get there.

THE THOUGHTFUL AMERICAN

The Thoughtful American celebrates the similarities and differences in cultures. You:

• seek out European styles of living. You are genuinely interested in the people and cultures you visit.

• want to learn by trying things. You forget your discomfort if you're the only one in a group who feels it.

• accept and try to understand differences. Paying for your Italian coffee at one counter, then picking it up at another may seem inefficient, until you realize it's more sanitary: The person handling the food handles no money.

• are observant and sensitive. If 60 people are eating quietly with hushed conversation in a Belgian restaurant, you know it's not the place to yuk it up.

• maintain humility and don't flash signs of affluence. You don't joke about the local money or overtip. Your bucks don't talk.

Thank You

Arabic	*shukran*	Greek	*efharisto*
Bulgarian	*blagodarya*	Iraqi	*shukran*
Danish	*tak*	Italian	*grazie*
Dutch	*dank u wel*	Portuguese	*obrigado*
English	*thank you*	Russian	*spasiba*
Finnish	*kiitos*	Serbo-Croatian	*hvala*
French	*merci*	Spanish	*gracias*
German	*danke*	Turkish	*teşekkurler*

• are positive and optimistic in the extreme. You discipline yourself to focus on the good points of each country. You don't dwell on problems or compare things to "back home."

• make an effort to bridge that flimsy language barrier. Rudimentary communication in any language is fun and simple with a few basic words. On the train to Budapest, you might think that a debate with a Hungarian over the merits of a common European currency would be frustrating with a 20-word vocabulary; but you'll surprise yourself at how well you communicate by just breaking the ice and trying. Don't worry about making mistakes—communicate!

I've been accepted as an American friend throughout Europe, Russia, the Middle East, and North Africa. I've been hugged by Bulgarian workers on a Balkan mountaintop; discussed the Olympics over dinner in the home of a Greek family; explained to a young, frustrated Irishman that California girls take their pants off one leg at a time, just like the rest of us; and hiked through the Alps with a Swiss schoolteacher, learning German and teaching English.

Go as a guest; act like one, and you'll be treated like one. In travel, too, you reap what you sow.

RESPONSIBLE TOURISM

As we learn more about the problems that confront the earth and humankind, more and more people are recognizing the need for the world's industries, such as tourism, to function as tools for peace. Tourism is a $2 trillion industry that employs more than 60 million people. As travelers become more sophisticated and gain a global perspective, the demand for socially, environmentally, and economically responsible means of travel will grow. Peace is more than the absence of war, and if

---

RESOURCES FOR SOCIALLY RESPONSIBLE EUROPEAN TRAVEL

Global Volunteers, a nonprofit organization, offers useful "travel with a purpose" trips throughout the world (375 E. Little Canada Rd., St. Paul, MN 55117-1628, tel. 800/398-8787, fax 612/482-0915, www.globalvolunteers.org). The work varies per country, but if Europe's your goal, you'll likely teach conversational English in Italy, Spain, Poland, Turkey, or Ukraine. Ask about peace reconciliation programs in Northern Ireland.

Co-op America Travel-Links, a great source of information, can arrange socially responsible travel options (120 Beacon St., Somerville, MA 02143-4369, tel. 800/648-2667).

If you'd like to help the homeless, watch whales, or dig up old bones, send $18.95 (ppd.) to Chicago Review (814 N. Franklin, Chicago, IL 60610, tel. 800/888-4741, fax 312/337-5985) for *Volunteer Vacations*, which lists 500 options for one- to six-week domestic and foreign volunteer programs.

Other resources are *International Directory of Voluntary Work* (Peterson's) and *Volunteer Vacations: Short Term Adventures That Will Benefit You and Others* (Bill McMillon).

---

we are to enjoy the good things of life—such as travel—into the next century, the serious issues that confront humankind must be addressed now.

Although the most obvious problems relate specifically to travel in the Third World, European travel also offers some exciting socially responsible opportunities. Above are a few sources of information for the budding "green" traveler.

Consume responsibly in your travels. Understand your power to shape the marketplace by what you decide to buy (whether in the grocery store, in the movie theater, or in your choice of hotels). Do your part to conserve energy.

In my travels (and in my writing), whenever possible, I patronize and support small, family-run, locally owned businesses (hotels, restaurants, shops, tour guides). I choose people who invest their creativity and resources in giving me simple, friendly, sustainable, and honest travel experiences—people with ideals. Back Door places don't rely on slick advertising and marketing gimmicks, and they don't target the created needs of people whose values are shaped by capitalism gone wild.

Consuming responsibly means buying as if your choice is a vote for the kind of world we could have.

MAKING THE MOST OF YOUR TRIP

Accept that today's Europe is changing. Among the palaces, quaint folk dancers, and museums, you'll find a living civilization grasping for the future while we romantic tourists grope for its past. This presents us with a sometimes painful dose of truth.

Today's Europe is a complex, mixed bag of tricks. It can rudely slap you in the face if you aren't prepared to accept it with open eyes and an open mind. Europe is getting crowded, tense, seedy, polluted, industrialized, hamburgerized, and far from the everything-in-its-place fairy-tale land I'm sure it used to be.

If you're not mentally braced for some shocks, local trends can tinge your travels. Hans Christian Andersen's statue has four-letter words scrawled across its base. Amsterdam's sex shops and McDonald's share the same streetlamp. In Paris a Sudanese salesman baits tourists at Notre-Dame with ivory bracelets and crocodile purses. Many a Mediterranean hotelkeeper would consider himself a disgrace to his sex if he didn't follow a single woman to her room. Drunk punks do their best to repulse you as you climb to St. Patrick's grave in Ireland, and Greek ferryboats dump mountains of trash into their dying Aegean Sea. An eight-year-old boy in Denmark smokes a cigarette like he was born with it in his mouth, and in a Munich beer hall, an old drunk spits *Sieg heils* all over you. The Barcelona shoeshine man will triple-charge you, and people everywhere eat strange and wondrous things. They eat next to nothing for breakfast, mud for coffee, mussels in Brussels, and snails in Paris; and dinner's at 10:00 p.m. in Spain. Beer is warm here, flat there, coffee isn't served with dinner, and ice cubes can only be dreamed of. Roman cars stay in their lanes like rocks in an avalanche, and beermaids with huge pretzels pull mustard packets from their cleavage.

Contemporary Europe is alive and groping. Today's problems will fill tomorrow's museums. Feel privileged to walk the vibrant streets of Europe as a sponge—not a judge. Be open-minded. Absorb, accept, and learn.

Don't be a creative worrier. Travelers tend to sit at home before their trip—all alone, just thinking of reasons to be stressed. Travel problems are always there; you just notice them when they're yours. Every year there are air-controller strikes, train wrecks, terrorist attacks, new problems, and deciduous problems sprouting new leaves.

Travel is ad-libbing; incurring and conquering surprise challenges. Make an art out of taking the unexpected in stride. Relax; you're on the other side of the world playing games in a continental backyard. Be a good sport, enjoy the uncertainty, and frolic in the pits.

Many of my readers' richest travel experiences were the result of seemingly terrible mishaps: the lost passport in Slovenia, having to find a doctor in Ireland, the blowout in Portugal, or the moped accident on Corfu.

Expect problems, tackle them creatively. You'll miss a museum or two and maybe blow your budget for the week. But you'll make some local friends and stack up some memories. And this is the essence of travel that you'll enjoy long after the journal is shelved and your trip is stored neatly in the slide carousel of your mind.

KISS: "Keep it simple, stupid!" Don't complicate your trip. Simplify! Travelers get stressed and cluttered over the silliest things, which, in their nibbly ways, can suffocate a happy holiday: registering your camera with customs before leaving home, spending too much time trying to phone home on a sunny day in the Alps, worrying about the correct answers to meaningless bureaucratic forms, making a long-distance hotel reservation in a strange language and then trying to settle on what's served for breakfast, having a picnic in pants that worry about grass stains, sending away for Swedish hotel vouchers.

People can complicate their trips with video cameras, lead-lined film bags, special tickets for free entry to all the sights they won't see in England, inflatable hangers, immersion heaters, instant coffee, 65 Handiwipes, and a special calculator that figures the value of the franc to the third decimal. They ask for a toilet in 17 words or more, steal Sweet 'n' Low and plastic silverware off the plane, and take notes on facts that don't matter. Travel more like Gandhi—with simple clothes, open eyes, and an uncluttered mind.

Ask questions. If you're too proud to ask questions, your trip will be dignified but dull. Many tourists are actually afraid or too timid to ask questions. The meek may inherit the earth, but they make lousy travelers. Local sources are a wealth of information. People are happy to help a traveler. Hurdle the language barrier. Use a paper and pencil, charades, or whatever it takes to be understood. Don't be afraid to butcher the language.

Ask questions—or be lost. If you're lost, take out a map and look lost. You'll get help. If lonely or in need of contact with a local person, take out a map and look lost again. Perceive friendliness and you'll find it.

Be militantly humble—Attila had a lousy trip. All summer long I'm pushing for a bargain, often for groups. It's the hottest, toughest time of year. Tourists and locals clash. Many tourists leave soured.

When I catch a Spanish merchant shortchanging me, I correct the bill and smile, "*Adios.*" When a French hotel owner blows up at me for no

Put yourself where you become the oddity. If people stare, sing to them.

legitimate reason, I wait, smile, and try again. I usually see the irate ranter come to his senses, forget the problem, and work things out.

"Turn the other cheek" applies perfectly to those riding Europe's magic carousel. If you fight the slaps, the ride is over. The militantly humble can spin forever.

Make yourself an extrovert, even if you're not. Be a catalyst for adventure and excitement. Meet people. Make things happen or often they won't. The American casual and friendly social style is charming to Europeans who are raised to respect social formalities. While our "slap-on-the-back" friendliness can be overplayed and obnoxious, it can also be a great asset for the American interested in meeting Europeans. Consider that cultural trait a plus. Enjoy it. Take advantage of it.

I'm not naturally a wild-and-crazy kind of guy. But when I'm shy and quiet, things don't happen, and that's a bad rut to travel in. It's not easy, but this special awareness can really pay off. Let me describe the same evening twice—first, with the mild-and-lazy me, and then, with the wild-and-crazy me.

The traffic held me up, so by the time I got to that great historical building I've always wanted to see, it was six minutes before closing. No one was allowed to enter. Disappointed, I walked to a restaurant and couldn't make heads or tails out of the menu. I recognized "steak-frites" and settled for a meat patty and french fries. On the way home I looked into a colorful local pub but didn't see any tourists, so I walked on. A couple waved at me from their balcony, but I didn't know what to say, so I ignored them. I returned to my room and did some laundry.

That's not a night to be proud of. A better traveler's journal entry would read like this:

I got to the museum only six minutes before closing. The guard said no one could go in now, but I begged, joked, and pleaded with him. I had traveled all the way to see this place and I would be leaving early in the morning. I assured him that I'd be out by six o'clock, and he gave me a glorious six minutes in that building. You can do a lot with a Botticelli in six minutes when that's all you've got. Across the street at a restaurant that the same guard recommended, I couldn't

Extroverts have more fun. If you see four cute men on a bench, ask them to scoot over.

make heads or tails out of the menu. Inviting myself into the kitchen, I met the cooks and got a first-hand look at "what's cookin'." Now I could order an exciting local dish and know just what I was getting. It was delicious! On the way home, I passed a lively local pub, and while it seemed dark and uninviting, I stepped in and was met by the only guy in the place who spoke any English. He proudly befriended me and told me, in very broken English, of his salty past and his six kids, while treating me to his favorite local drink. As I headed home, a couple waved at me from their balcony, and I waved back, saying "Buon giorno!" I knew it didn't mean "Good evening," but they understood. They invited me up to their apartment. We joked around—not understanding a lot of what we were saying to each other—and they invited me to their summer cottage tomorrow. What a lucky break! There's no better way to learn about this country than to spend an afternoon with a local family. And to think that I could be back in my room doing the laundry.

Pledge every morning to do something entirely different today. Create adventure—or bring home a boring journal.

BECOMING A TEMPORARY EUROPEAN

Most travelers tramp through Europe like they're visiting the cultural zoo. "Ooo, that guy in lederhosen yodeled! Excuse me, could you do that again in the sunshine with my wife next to you so I can take a snapshot?" This is fun. It's a part of travel. But a camera bouncing on your belly tells locals you're hunting cultural peacocks. When I'm in Europe, I'm the best German or Spaniard or Italian I can be. While I never drink tea at home, after a long day of sightseeing in England, "a spot of tea" really does feel right. I drink wine in France and beer in Germany. In Italy I eat small breakfasts. Find ways to really be there. Consider these:

Go to church. Many regular churchgoers never even consider a European worship service. Any church would welcome a traveling American. And an hour in a small-town church provides an unbeatable peek into the local community, especially if you join them for coffee and cookies afterwards. I'll never forget going to a small church on the south coast of Portugal one Easter. A tourist stood at the door videotaping the "colorful natives" (including me) shaking hands with the priest after the service. You can experience St. Peter's by taking photographs . . . or by taking communion (daily 5:00 p.m. Mass).

Root for your team. For many Europeans, the top religion is soccer. Getting caught up in a sporting event is going local. Whether enjoying soccer in small-town Italy, greyhound racing in Scotland, or hurling in Ireland, you'll be surrounded by a stadium crammed with devout locals.

Play where the locals play. A city's popular fairgrounds and parks are filled with local families, lovers, and old-timers enjoying a cheap afternoon or evening out. European communities provide their heavily taxed citizens with wonderful athletic facilities. Check out a swimming center, called a "leisure center" in Britain. While tourists outnumber locals five to one at the world-famous Tivoli Gardens, Copenhagen's other amusement park, Bakken, is enjoyed purely by Danes. Disneyland Paris is great. But Paris' Asterix Park is more French.

Experiment. Some cafés in the Netherlands (those with plants in the windows or Rastafarian colors on the wall) have menus that look like a drug bust. Marijuana is less controversial in Holland than tobacco is these days in the United States. For a casual toke of local life without the risk that comes with smoking in the United States, drop into one of these cafés and roll a joint. If you have no political aspirations, inhale.

Take a stroll. Across southern Europe, communities *paseo*, or stroll, in the early evening. Stroll along. Join a *Volksmarch* in Bavaria to spend a day on the trails with people singing "I love to go a-wandering" in its original language. Remember, hostels are the American target, while mountain huts and "nature's friends huts" across Europe are filled mostly with local hikers. Most hiking centers have Alpine clubs that welcome foreigners and offer organized hikes.

Get off the tourist track. Choose destinations busy with local holiday-goers but not on the international tourist map. Campgrounds are filled with Europeans in the mood to toss a Frisbee with a new American friend (bring a nylon "whoosh" Frisbee). Be accessible. Accept invitations. Assume you're interesting and do Europeans a favor by finding ways to get invitations.

Challenge a local to the national pastime. In Greece or Turkey drop into a local teahouse or *taverna* and challenge a local to a game of backgammon. You're instantly a part (even a star) of the local café or bar scene. Normally the gang will gather around, and what starts out as a simple game becomes a fun duel of international significance.

Contact the local version of your club. If you're a member of a service club, bridge club, professional association, or international organization, make a point to connect with your foreign mates.

Search out residential neighborhoods. Ride a city bus or subway into the suburbs. Wander through a neighborhood to see how the locals live when they're not wearing lederhosen and yodeling. Visit a supermarket. Make friends at the Laundromat.

Drop by a school or university. Mill around a university and check out the announcement boards. Eat at the school cafeteria. Ask at the

Connect with the locals. Greeks and Turks love a revealing game of backgammon.

English language department if there's a student learning English whom you could hire to be your private guide. Be alert and even a little bit snoopy. You may stumble onto a grade-school talent show.

Join in. When you visit the town market in the morning, you're just another local, picking up your daily produce. You can take photos of the pilgrims at Lourdes—or volunteer to help wheel the chairs of those who've come in hope of a cure. Traveling through the wine country of France during harvest time, you can be a tourist taking photos—or you can pitch in and become a local grape-picker. Get more than a photo op. Get dirty. That night at the festival, it's just grape-pickers dancing (and some of them are tourists).

If you're hunting cultural peacocks, remember they spread their tails best for people . . . not cameras. When you take Europe out of your viewfinder, you're more likely to find it in your lap.

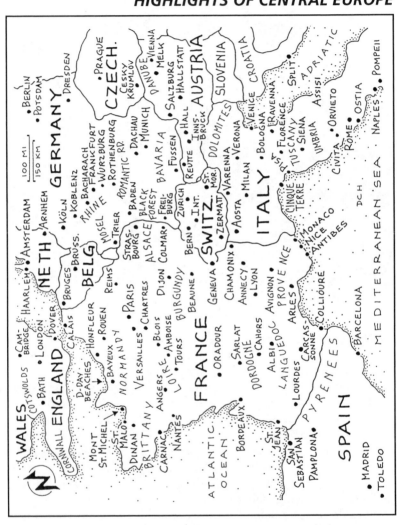

PART TWO

Back Doors of Europe

Europe, here you come

Contents

EUROPE'S BACK DOORS

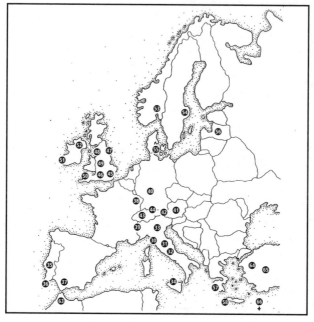

What Is a Back Door, and How Can I Find One of My Own?

The travel skills covered in the first half of this book enable you to open doors most travelers don't even know exist. Now I'd like you to meet my "Back Doors." This is a chance for you and the travel bug to get intimate. By traveling vicariously with me through these chapters, you'll get a peek at my favorite places. And just as important, by internalizing the lifetime of little travel moments that I've enjoyed and compiled here, you'll develop a knack for finding your own.

Europe is a bubbling multicultural fondue. A Back Door is a steaming forkful. It could be an all-day Alpine ridge walk, a friendly swing with a church spire bell-ringer, a sword-fern fantasy in a ruined castle, uncovering the village warmth of a big cold city, or jamming your camera with Turkish delights. By learning where to jab your fork, you'll put together a travel feast exceeding your wildest dreams.

Some of my Back Doors are undiscovered towns that have, for various reasons, missed the modern parade. With no promotional budgets to attract travelers, they're ignored as they quietly make their traditional way through just another century. Many of these places won't hit you with their cultural razzle-dazzle. Their charms are too subtle to be enjoyed by the tour-bus crowd. But, learning from the experiences described in the last half of this book, Back Door travelers will make their own fun.

We'll also explore natural nooks and undeveloped crannies. These are rare opportunities to enjoy Europe's sun, beaches, mountains, and natural wonders without the glitz. While Europeans love nature and are fanatic sun-worshipers, they have an impressive knack for enjoying themselves in hellish crowds. Our goal is to experience Europe's quiet alternatives: forgotten stone circles, desolate castles, breezy bike rides, and snippets of the Riviera not snapped up by entrepreneurs.

With a Back Door angle on a big city, you can slip your fingers under its staged culture and actually find a pulse. Even London has a warm underbelly, where you'll rumble with a heart that's been beating for more than 2,000 years.

And finally, to squeeze the most travel experience out of every mile, minute, and dollar, look beyond Europe. Europe is exciting, but a dip into Turkey, Morocco, or Egypt is well worth the diarrhea.

The promotion of a tender place that has so far avoided the tourist industry reminds me of the whaler who screams, "Quick, harpoon it before it's extinct!" These places are this Europhile's cupids. Publicizing them gnaws at what makes them so great. But what kind of a travel writer can keep his favorite discoveries under wraps? Great finds are too hard to come by to just sit on. I keep no secrets.

With ever-more-sophisticated travelers armed with ever-better guidebooks, places I "discovered" eight or ten years ago are undeveloped and uncommercial only in a relative sense. And certain places that I really rave about suffer from Back Door congestion. At least, from my experience, Back Door readers are pleasant people to share Europe with.

People recommended in this book tell me that Back Door readers are good guests who undo the "ugly" image created by the more demanding and ethnocentric American tourists. By traveling sensitively, you're doing yourself a favor as well as those you'll deal with, travelers who'll follow . . . and me. Thank you.

These Back Doors combine to give you a chorus line of travel thrills. While the Appendix lists nitty-gritty information and the best accommodations for each Back Door, I've written these chapters to give you the flavor of the place, not to navigate by. A "take-along" guidebook (like one of my eight country guides) will give you the details necessary to splice your chosen Back Doors into a smooth trip. *Bon voyage!*

Italy

30. Cinque Terre: Italy's Traffic-free Riviera

"A sleepy, romantic, and inexpensive town on the Riviera without a tourist in sight." That's the mirage travelers chase around busy Nice and Cannes. Pssst! Paradise sleeps just across the border in Italy's Cinque Terre.

The Cinque Terre, meaning "five lands," is five pastel villages clinging to the most inaccessible bit of coast on the Italian Riviera. Established centuries ago by locals hiding out from pirates, the towns are still hideaways, virtually inaccessible by car.

The Cinque Terre, between Pisa and Genova, was too rugged to develop. And now, as locals sense a possible tourist boom, the government protects these well-preserved villages, and new building is not allowed. The villagers have almost no choice but to go about their business as if the surrounding vineyards are the very edges of the earth.

Each town is a character. Monterosso al Mare, happy to be appreciated, boasts the area's only sandy beach, plenty of fine hotels, restaurants, and rentable paddle boats. Its four little sisters frolic overlooked—forgotten behind battered breakwaters. (Since my mind usually goes on vacation with the rest of me when I'm here, I think of the towns by number for easy orientation. They go—east to west—from one to five. Number five, Monterosso, is the resort.)

The first town of the Cinque Terre, Riomaggiore (#1), is a beauty that has seduced famed artists into becoming residents. The most substantial non–resort town of the group, Riomaggiore is a disappointment from the station. But walk through the tunnel next to the train tracks, and you land in a fascinating tangle of pastel homes leaning on each other as if someone stole their crutches. There's homemade *gelati* at the Bar Central. Mama Rosa's ramshackle hostel, a block from the train station, offers the looniest budget beds in the area and an instant family of fellow backpackers.

The Via dell' Amore (walkway of love) leads from Riomaggiore to Manarola (#2). This is a film-gobbling 15-minute promenade wide enough for baby strollers. There's no beach here, but stairways lead to remote rocks for sunbathing. Uppity little Manarola rules its ravine and drinks its wine while its sun-bleached walls slumber on.

Corniglia (#3) sits smugly on its hilltop, a proudly victorious king of the mountain. Most visitors—lured to Corniglia by its scrawny, stony beach and the Cinque Terre's best swimming—never tackle the winding stairs to the actual town. Those who make the Corniglian climb are rewarded by the Cinque Terre's finest wine and most staggering view. Corniglia has a windy belvedere, a few restaurants, and a handful of often-empty private rooms for rent. With each visit I find myself ducking into a cellar with a grape-stained local, dipping long straws into heavy, dark kegs.

As I step off the train in Vernazza (#4), I know my race is run. With the closest thing to a natural harbor, overseen by a ruined castle and an old church, Vernazza is my 5-Terre home base. Its one street connects the harbor with the train station before melting into the vineyards. Like veins on a grape leaf, paths and stairways connect this watercolor huddle of houses with Main Street. Every day is a rerun in this hive of lazy human activity. A rainbow of laundry flaps as if to keep the flies off the old men who man the bench. Like fat barnacles filling ancient doorways, local grandmothers watch life drift by. Little varnished boats are piled peely everywhere, and sailors suckle at salty taverns. The sun sets unnoticed—except by tourists.

The Cinque Terre is best seen on foot. A fragrant trail leads you through sunny vistas from Riomaggiore to Monterosso. The

Vernazza, on Italy's Riviera

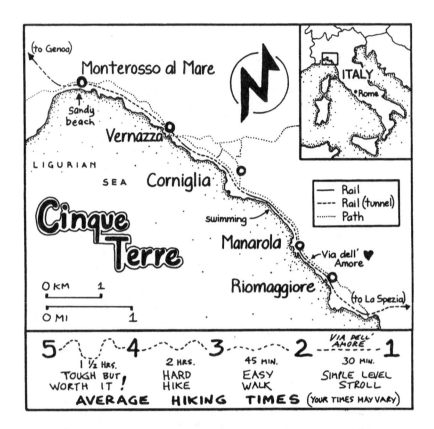

Vernazza–Monterosso trail is as rugged as the people who've worked the terraced vineyards that blanket the region. Flowers and an ever-changing view entertain you at every step. As you make your sweaty way high above the glistening beaches and approach each time-steeped village, you'll ponder paying for your trip with the photos you've shot.

When you run out of time or energy, simply catch a train back to your home base. While these towns are barely accessible by car, a tunnel-train blinks open at each village and provides a quick and easy way to explore the region. Milk-run trains connect all five towns for $1. A ferry carries people scenically from Vernazza to Monterosso al Mare. And those in search of no-tan-line coves, refreshing waterfalls, and natural high dives find them tucked away along the coast between these two towns.

For a great day in the Cinque Terre, start by walking the Via dell' Amore from Riomaggiore to Manarola. Buy a picnic in Manarola and walk to the Corniglia beach. Swim, enjoy the shady bar, shower, picnic, and take the train to Monterosso al Mare for a look at the local big town. Enjoy its sandy beach before hiking home to Vernazza. Vernazza's best bar is the umbrella-shaded balcony halfway between the castle and the surf. Climb its rope railing for a glass of *vino de la Cinque Terre* or the local, sweet sherry-like wine, *Sciachetra* (worth the extra lire). Peek inside at the photo (above the door) of giant winter waves crashing over Vernazza's harbor.

While the Cinque Terre is unknown to the international mobs that ravage the Spanish and French coasts, plenty of Italians and my readers come here, so getting a room can be tough. August and weekends are bad. Weekends in August are worst. Off-season is easy.

Paint a dream in vineyard greens and Mediterranean blues. Italy's Cinque Terre—five towns and a rocky surf—can make it come true.

See the Appendix (Recommended Accommodations) for more information.

31. The Hill Towns of Tuscany and Umbria

Too many people connect Venice, Florence, and Rome with straight lines. Break out of this syndrome, and you'll lick a little Italy that the

San Marino, just another magic Italian hill town (only this one's an independent country).

splash of Venice, the finesse of Florence, and the grandeur of Rome were built on.

The hill towns of Tuscany and Umbria hold their crumbling heads proudly above the noisy flood of the 20th century and offer a peaceful taste of what eludes so many tourists. Sitting on a timeless rampart high above the traffic and trains, hearing only children in the market and the rustling wind aging the weary red-tile patchwork that surrounds me, I find the essence of Italy.

Hill towns, like Greek islands, come in two basic varieties—touristy and untouristy. There are a dozen great touristed towns and countless ignored communities casually doing time and drinking wine. See some of each.

San Gimignano bristles with towers and bustles with tourists. A thrilling silhouette from a distance, Italy's best-preserved medieval skyline gets better as you approach. Sunset's the right time to conquer the castle. Climb high above the crowds, sit on the castle's summit, and imagine the battles Tuscany's armadillo has endured.

Siena, unlike its rival, Florence, is a city to be seen as a whole rather than as a collection of sights. Climb to the dizzy top of the bell tower and reign over urban harmony at its best. While memories of Florence consist of dodging Vespas between oppressive museums,

So often photography—and a little wine—brings out the warmth in Italian women.

HILL TOWNS OF CENTRAL ITALY

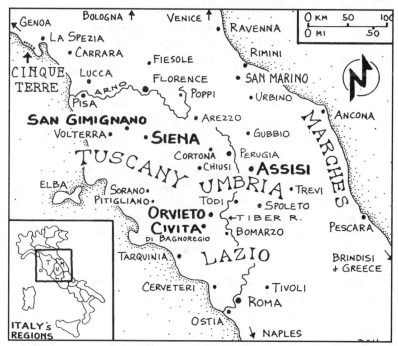

Siena has an easy-to-enjoy, well-pickled Gothic soul: Courtyards sport flower-decked wells, churches modestly hoard their art, and alleys dead-end into red-tiled rooftop panoramas. At twilight, first-time poets savor that magic moment when the sky is a rich blue dome no brighter than the medieval towers that hold it high.

Assisi, a worthy hometown for St. Francis, is battling a commercial cancer of tourist clutter (and recovering from 1997 earthquakes). In the summer the town bursts with splash-in-the-pan Francis fans and monastic knick-knacks. Those able to see past the tacky monk mementos can actually have a "travel on purpose" experience. With a quiet hour in the awesome Basilica of St. Francis, some reflective reading (there's a great bookstore below the church), and a meditative stroll through the back streets, you can dissolve the tour buses and melt into the magic of Assisi. St. Francis would recognize Assisi best after dark.

Orvieto, the tourist's token hill town, sits majestically on its tufa throne, offering those on the train or *autostrada* to Rome its impressive hill-capping profile. Its cathedral, with some fascinating Signorelli frescoes, is surrounded by an excellent tourist information office, a fine Etruscan museum, a world-class *gelato* shop, and Italy's most pleasant public toilet. Buses go regularly from Orvieto to the queen of hill towns, Civita di Bagnoregio (see next chapter).

Any guidebook lists these popular hill towns. But if you want to dance at noon with a toothless lady while your pizza cooks, press a good-luck coin into the moldy ceiling of an Etruscan wine cellar, or be introduced to a mediocre altarpiece as proudly as if it were a Michelangelo, stow your guidebook, buy the best local map you can find, and explore.

Perfect Back Door villages, like hidden pharaohs' tombs, await discovery. Photographers delight in Italian hill towns. Their pictorial collections (such as *Italian Hill Towns*, by Norman Carver) are a fine source of information. Study these, circling the most intriguing towns on your map. Talk to travelers who have studied or lived in Italy. Ask locals for their favorites. Scan the horizon for fortified towers. Drive down dead-end roads.

Gubbio, Volterra, Cortona, and Arezzo are discovered but rarely visited. Civita di Bagnoregio, Sorano, Pitigliano, Trevi, Poppi, Orte (just north of Rome off the freeway), and Bagnaia (near Viterbo) are virgin hill towns. The difference between "discovered" and "virgin," touristically speaking, is that "discovered" towns know what tourism is and have an appetite for the money that comes with it. "Virgin" towns are simply pleased that you dropped in.

Hill towns are a vital slice of the Italian pizza—crumbly crust with a thick gooey culture. Leave the train lines. Take the bus, hitch, or rent a car for a few days. (Many hill towns have a train station nearby. A bus shuttle begins its winding climb shortly after your train arrives.) If you're using a rail-and-drive pass, this is car country. Don't just chase down my favorites or your guidebook's recommendations. Somewhere in the social slumber of Umbria and the human texture of Tuscany, the ultimate hill town awaits your visit.

See the Appendix (Recommended Accommodations) for more information.

32. Civita di Bagnoregio

People who've been there say "Civita" (chee-vee-tah) with warmth and love. This precious chip of Italy, a traffic-free community with a grow-it-in-the-valley economy, has so far escaped the ravages of modernity.

Please approach it with the same respect and sensitivity you would a dying relative, because—in a sense—that's Civita.

Fifteen people still live here. There's no car traffic. A man with a donkey works all day ferrying the town's goods across the long umbilical bridge that connects the town with a small distant parking lot and the rest of Italy. Rome, just 60 miles to the south, might as well be on the other side of the moon.

Civita is a man-gripped pinnacle in a vast canyon. Wind and erosion rule the valley, but Civita persists. Its charms are subtle, and many tourists wouldn't know what to do in a town without arcade tourism. No English menus, lists of attractions, orientation tours, or museum hours. Just Italy.

Sit in the piazza. Smile and nod at each local who passes by. It's a social jigsaw puzzle, and each person fits. The old woman hanging out the window monitors gossip. A tiny hunchback lady is everyone's daughter. And cats, the only growing segment of the population, scratch an itch on ancient pillars that stick up like bar stools in front of the church. Two thousand five hundred years ago these graced the facade of an Etruscan temple.

Civita's population is revised downward with each edition of this book. As old people get frail, they move into apartments in nearby Bagnoregio. Most of the young people are gone, lured away by the dazzle of today to grab their place in Italy's cosmopolitan parade.

The perfect hill town, Civita di Bagnoregio

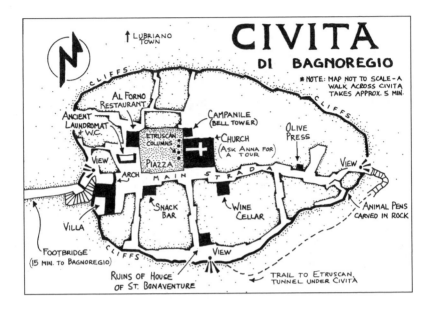

Today Civita's social pie has three slices: the aging, full-time resident community; the rich Italians from Rome and Milan who are slowly buying up the place for their country escape (the Ferrari family owns the house next to the town gate—and Civita's only Jacuzzi); and a small University of Washington architecture program headed by Professor Astra Zarina, who owns a villa in Civita. When in session, 10 to 20 UW students live and study here. Over the years, alumni and their families have made Civita their Italian retreat, and you'll often find a Seattle-ite or two enjoying *il dolce far niente* (the sweetness of doing nothing).

Explore Civita. Maria introduces you to a baby donkey as if it were her child. Anna is the keeper of the church. The heartbeat and pride of the village, this is where festivals and processions start, visitors are escorted, and the town's past is honored. Enjoy paintings by students of famous artists; relics of the hometown boy-made-saint, Bonaventure; a dried floral decoration spread across the floor; and a cool, quiet moment in a pew.

Just around the corner from the church is the village cantina. Pull up a stump and enjoy a glass of very local wine. The white has a taste reminiscent of dirty socks; the red tastes cleaner. But it's made right here. That donkey brought up the grapes. Climb down into the ancient cellar. Grab the stick and thunk on the kegs to measure their fullness. Even on a blistering day, those caves are always cool—they have been since Etruscan times. In them, an endless supply of local Civita wine is kept chilled, awaiting future fun.

Victoria, numb to her eye-boggling view of the valley, showed me the latest in a 2,000-year line of olive presses that have filled her ancient Etruscan cave. She'll exact a small fee for her talk (in fluent Italian). The few residents of Civita are adept at making a little lire from tourists.

Victoria's grandchildren, in the local equivalent of a lemonade stand, sell *bruschetta* to visitors. Bread toasted on an open fire, drizzled with the finest oil and rubbed with garlic, these edible souvenirs stay on your breath for hours and in your memory forever.

Civita has one restaurant. You can see its red door and handmade sign from the piazza. At Antico Forno (the antique oven), you eat what's cooking. Mom and Pop slice and quarter happily through the day. Spaghetti, salad, and wine on the Antico Forno patio, cuddled by Civita—I wouldn't trade it for all-you-can-eat at Maxim's.

Spend the evening. Sit on the church steps with people who've done exactly that for 60 years. Antico Forno serves late in the summer. Children play on the piazza until midnight. As you walk back to your car—that scourge of the modern world that enabled you to get here—stop under a lamp on the donkey path, listen to the canyon . . . distant voices . . . fortissimo crickets.

Civita is an artist's dream, a town in the nude. Each lane and footpath holds a surprise. Horses pose, the warm stone walls glow, each stairway is dessert to a sketch pad or camera, and the Grand Canyon moat does its best to keep things that way. It's changing, however, as the persistent battering ram of our modern world pounds on these rare strongholds of the past. With recent exposure in German and French travel magazines, Civita sees up to 200 tourists a day on summer weekends. Civita will be great for years but never as great as today.

You won't find Civita on your map. Take the train to Orvieto and catch a bus to Bagnoregio. From Bagnoregio, walk 20 minutes to Civita. Civita has a few rooms (run by English-speaking Franco at Antico Forno, tel. 0761-760-016, cell phone 0347-6115426) and Bagnoregio has two hotels. Orvieto, a 30-minute bus ride away, has plenty in every price range.

The more colorful of Bagnoregio's hotels is Al Boschetto, a 20-minute walk out of town (Strada Monterado, Bagnoregio, Viterbo, Italy, tel. 0761-792-369). This family-run place serves traditional food. Descend into the fragrant bowels of their wine cellar as if it were a Venus flytrap. There are no rules unless female participants set them. Music and vino kill the language barrier in la cantina, where the theme song is, "Trinka, Trinka, Trinka."

See the Appendix (Recommended Accommodations) for more information.

33. North Italy Choices: Milan, Lakes, or Mountains

Italy: Venice, Florence, Rome, hill towns, and the Riviera . . . Yes, those are the first targets, but there's much more. My favorite European country is a grab bag of cultural, artistic, edible, and natural thrills. Pull off the tourist *autostrada*, grab a *gelato*, and explore more of this intriguing country.

Italy intensifies as you plunge deeper. If you like it as far south as Rome, go farther—it gets better. But, for many travelers, after seven days of "*buon giorno*" and "*grazie*," Switzerland starts looking better and better. If you've yet to satisfy your appetite for cappuccino, *gelato*, and people-watching, but Italy's starting to grab you the wrong way, you'll find a milder Italy in the North.

North Italy's charms come in three packages: urban Milan, romantic lakes, and Alpine Dolomites. All are within three hours of Venice, Florence, and each other.

Milan is the Italy of the '90s. The economic success of modern Italy (which now has a higher per-capita income than Britain) can be blamed on cities like Milan. As the saying goes, for every church in Rome, there's a bank in Milan. Italy's second city, Milan has a hard-working, fashion-conscious population of 2 million. From publicists to pasta power lunches, this is Italy's industrial, banking, TV, publishing, and convention capital.

Much of Milan is ugly, with a recently bombed-out feeling (WWII). Its huge financial buildings are as manicured as its parks are shaggy. As if to make up for its harsh concrete shell, its people and windows are works of art. Milan is an international fashion capital. Cigarettes are still chic, and even the cheese is gift-wrapped.

Milan's cathedral, the city's centerpiece, is the third-largest church in Europe. At 480 feet long and 280 feet wide, forested with 52 150-foot-tall sequoia pillars and more than 2,000 statues, the place can seat 10,000 worshipers. Hike up to the rooftop, a fancy crown of spires with great views of the city, the square, and, on clear days, the Swiss Alps.

The cathedral square, Piazza Duomo, is a classic European scene. Professionals scurry, label-conscious kids loiter, young thieves peruse.

NORTH ITALY

Facing the square, the Galleria Vittorio Emanuele, Milan's great four-story-high, glass-domed arcade, invites you in to shop or enjoy a café. This is the place to turn a too-expensive cup of coffee into a good value with some of Europe's hottest people-watching. For good luck, locals step on the testicles of the mosaic Taurus on the floor's zodiac design. Two local girls explained that it works better if you actually give a twirl.

La Scala, possibly the world's most prestigious opera house, is just a holler away. While tickets are as hard to get as they are expensive, anyone can peek into the theater from the museum. Opera buffs will love the museum's extensive collection of things that would mean absolutely nothing to the MTV crowd: Verdi's top hat, Rossini's eye-glasses, Toscanini's baton, Fettucini's pesto, and the original scores, busts, portraits, and death masks of great composers and musicians.

The Brera Art Gallery, Milan's top collection of paintings, is world-class. But you'll see better in Rome and Florence. The immense Sforza Castle, Milan's much-bombed and rebuilt brick fortress, is overwhelming at first sight. But its courtyard has a great lawn for picnics and siestas. Its free museum features interesting medieval armor, furniture, Lombard art, and a Michelangelo statue with no crowds—his unfinished *Rondanini Pietà*.

Leonardo da Vinci's ill-fated *Last Supper* is flecking off the refectory wall of the nearby church of Santa Maria delle Grazie. The fresco suffers from Leonardo's experimental use of oil. Decay began within six years of its completion. It's undergone more restoration work than Liz Taylor, and that work continues. Most of the original paint is gone, but tourists are still encouraged to pay $8 to see what's left.

More of Leonardo's spirit survives in Italy's answer to the Smithsonian, the National Leonardo da Vinci Science and Technology Museum. While most tourists visit for the hall of Leonardo designs illustrated in wooden models, the rest of this immense collection of industrial cleverness is just as fascinating. There is plenty of push-button action displaying the development of trains, the evolution of radios, old musical instruments, computers, batteries, telephones, and chunks of the first transatlantic cable. Unfortunately, English descriptions are rare.

The Italian Lakes, at the base of Italy's Alps, are a romantic and popular destination for Italians and their European neighbors. The million-lire question is: "Which lake?" For the best mix of handiness, scenery, and offbeatness, giving you a complete dose of Italian-lakes wonder and aristocratic old-days romance, visit Lake Como.

Lined with elegant 19th-century villas, crowned by snow-capped mountains, buzzing with ferries, hydrofoils, and little passenger ships,

On Lake Como, ferries hop from town to town.

this is a good place to take a break from the intensity and obligatory turnstile culture of central Italy. Lake Como is Italy for beginners. It seems half the travelers you'll meet on Lago di Como have tossed their itineraries overboard and are actually relaxing. The area's isolation and flat economy have left it pretty much the way the 19th-century romantic poets described it.

While you can easily drive around the lake, the road is narrow, congested, and lined by privacy-seeking walls, hedges, and tall fences. This is train-and-boat country. Regular train departures whisk you from intense Milan into the serenity of Lago di Como in an hour. The lake is well-served by pricey little boats. When you consider the included scenery, the $3-per-one-stop hop isn't quite so expensive.

The town of Bellagio, "the Pearl of the Lake," is a classy combination of tidiness and Old World elegance. If you don't mind that tramp-in-a-palace feeling, it's a fine place to surround yourself with the more adventurous of the soft travelers and shop for umbrellas and ties. The heavy curtains between the arcades keep the tourists and their poodles from sweating.

One hop away by ferry, the town of Varenna offers the best of all lake worlds. On the less driven side of the lake, with a romantic promenade, a tiny harbor, narrow lanes, and its own villa, Varenna is the right place to savor a cappuccino and ponder the place where Italy is welded to the Alps. Listen to the volume go down with the sun. The town is quiet at night. After dark, the *passerella* (lakeside walk) is adorned with caryatid lovers pressing silently against each other in the shadows.

Menaggio, directly across the lake from Varenna and just 8 miles from Lugano in Switzerland, feels more like a real town than its neighbors. Since the lake is too dirty for swimming, consider its fine public pool.

Finding a room on Lake Como is tight in August, snug in July, and wide-open most of the rest of the year. Varenna's Albergo Olivedo is a neat old hotel (lumpy beds and glorious little lake-view balconies overlooking the ferry dock, tel. & fax 0341-830115, $75–95 doubles; half-pension, reqired at times, costs extra). Albergo Milano—more comfortable and right in the old town, with a magnificent breakfast terrace—is your best Varenna splurge (tel. & fax 0341-830298, $120 doubles).

Menaggio's La Primula Youth Hostel is a rare hostel. Family-run for ten years by Ty and Paola, it caters to a quiet, savor-the-lakes crowd and offers the only cheap beds in the region. Located just south of the Menaggio dock, it has a view terrace, lots of games, a members' kitchen, washing machine, bike rentals, easy parking, and a creative, hardworking staff. Ty and Paola print a newsletter to advertise their activities programs: inexpensive 14-day Italian language courses, three- to seven-day hikes, bike trips, and cooking classes. (Ostello "La Primula," $12 per night in four- to six-bed rooms, with sheets, break- fast, and a souvenir cookbook; hearty $12 dinners with wine and flair, 22017 Menaggio, tel. & fax 0344-32356.)

The Dolomites, Italy's dramatic limestone rooftop, combine Alpine thrills with Italian sunshine. The famous valleys and towns of the well-developed Dolomites suffer from an après-ski fever, but the bold snow-flecked mountains and green meadows offer great hikes. The cost for reliably good weather is a drained-reservoir feeling. Lovers of the Alps may miss the lushness that comes with the unpre- dictable weather farther north.

A hard-fought history has left this part of Italy bicultural and bilin- gual with *der* emphasis on the *Deutsche*. Locals speak German first, and some wish they were still Austrian. In the Middle Ages the region faced north, part of the Holy Roman Empire. Later it was firmly in the Austrian Hapsburg realm. After Austria lost World War I, its South Tirol became Italy's Alto Adige. Mussolini did what he could to Italianize the region, including giving each town an Italian name. The government has wooed cranky German-speaking locals with economic breaks that make this one of Italy's richest areas (as local prices attest).

Don't forget Italy's Alps, the Dolomites.

Today signs and literature in the autonomous province of Süd Tirol/Alto Adige are in both languages.

In spite of all the glamorous ski resorts and busy construction cranes, local color survives in a warm, blue-aproned, ruddy-faced, long-white-bearded way. There's yogurt and yodeling for breakfast. Culturally, as much as geographically, the area feels Austrian. (The western part of Austria is named after Tirol, a village that is now actually in Italy.)

Lifts, good trails, outdoor activity–oriented tourist offices, and a decent bus system make the region especially accessible. But things are expensive. Most towns have no alternative to $60 doubles in hotels, or $50 doubles in private homes. Beds usually come with a hearty breakfast. If you're low on both money and scruples, Süd Tirolean breakfasts are the only ones in Italy big enough to steal lunch from.

The seasons are brutal. Everything is open, booming, full-price, and crowded from mid-July through September. After a dreary November, the snow hits and it's busy again until April. May and early June are dead. The most exciting trails are still under snow, and the mountain lifts are shut down. Most huts and budget accommodations are closed, as locals are more concerned with preparing for another boom season than catering to the stray off-season tourist.

With limited time and no car, maximize mountain thrills and minimize transportation headaches by taking the train to Bolzano and the public bus from there into the mountains.

By car, circle north from Venice and drive the breathtaking Great Dolomite Road (130 miles: Belluno–Cortina–Pordoi Pass–Sella Pass–Val di Fassa–Bolzano). In the spring and early summer, passes labeled "Closed" are often bare, dry, and, as far as local drivers are concerned, wide-open. Conveniently for local tour operators, no direct public transportation route covers the Great Dolomite Road.

If Bolzano, (*Bozen*, to its German-speaking locals) weren't so sunny, you could be in Innsbruck. This arcaded old town of 100,000, with a great open-air market on Piazza Erbe, is worth a Tirolean stroll and a stop at its Dolomite information center.

Tourist offices in any Dolomite town are a wealth of information. Before choosing a hike, get their advice. Ideally, pick a hike with an overnight in a hut and make a telephone reservation. Most huts, called *refugios*, offer reasonable doubles, cheaper dorm (*Lager*) beds, and good inexpensive meals.

Many are tempted to wimp out on the Dolomites and admire the spires from a distance. They take the cable car into the hills above

Bolzano to the cute but very touristy village of Oberbozan. Don't. Bus into the Dolomites instead. Three great destinations, just an hour or two from Bolzano, are the Val di Fassa, Val Gardena, and, best of all, the Alpe di Suisi.

The Alpe di Suisi, Europe's largest Alpine meadow, is a car-free natural preserve, with a park bus service and well-marked trails fanning out below the ultimate Dolomite peaks, Sassolunga and the Sella range.

The town of Castelrotto (or, in German, Kastelruth), with good bus connections and more village character than any town around, makes a charming home base. Gasthof zum Turm (tel. 0471-706349, $80–90 doubles) and the fancier Gasthof zum Wolf (tel. 0471-706332, $110–150 doubles) are each a few cobbles from the church.

Castelrotto/Kastelruth: your home base in the Dolomites

At Europe Through the Back Door, where I work, Italy is considered the greatest country in Europe. If all you have is ten days, then do Venice, Florence, Rome, the hill towns, and the Riviera. If you have more time and seek intensity, head south. But to round out your itinerary with all the best of Italy and none of the chaos, splice in a little of the Dolomites, the lakes, and Milan.

See the Appendix (Recommended Accommodations) for more information.

34. Palermo: Sicily's Urban Carnival

It took me seven trips to get down past Italy's "boot." The Sicilians (along with the Irish and except for the street thieves) are the warmest and friendliest Europeans I've met.

Palermo is intense—Italy in the extreme—with lots of purse-snatchers, lousy showers, and grueling heat. It's generally run-down and chaotic, but if you want exotic, urban Italian thrills, Italy's football is a kick. The overnight train ride south from Rome or Naples drops you right into this rich culture, which lives in peaceful oblivion to the touristic bustle that takes such a toll on Venice, Florence, and Rome.

Eating and sleeping stylishly and affordably with no reservations is easy. From the Palermo train station, walk straight down Via Roma for your choice of many hotels.

Eating in Palermo is a treat. Colorful street markets make shopping for picnics a joy. Pizzeria Bellini on Piazza Bellini, near the landmark "four corners" in downtown Palermo, was my dinnertime hangout. Over the course of several meals, I ate my way through their menu, discovering for myself why Italians like to eat. Their fanciest pizza, *Quatro Gusti con Fungi*, rates as the best $7 I've ever spent in Italy.

One reason Palermo lacks tourist crowds is that it has very few tourist sights, as such. It does have a way of life that, in its own way, offers the tourist more than any monument or museum ever could. Don't tour Palermo—live in it.

Thriving marketplaces abound in nearly every neighborhood. If you've ever wondered what it would be like to be a celebrity, go on a photo safari through the urban jungles of Palermo. The warmth and excitement will give you smile wrinkles. Scores of merchants, house-wives, and children compete for your attention. Cries of "Photo?" come from all corners as you venture down busy alleys.

Visit a vertical neighborhood. Small apartments stack high above

Rich Sorensen

the side streets. If you stop to chat, six floors of balconies will fill up, each with its own wav-ing family. I found a wobbly stack of tenements facing one another, a faded rainbow with lots of laundry and people hanging out. One wave worked wonders. Walking around, craning my neck upward, I felt like a victorious politician among hordes of supporters. They called out for pictures and wouldn't let me go until I had filmed each window and balcony full of people: Mothers held up babies; sisters posed arm-in-arm; a wild pregnant woman stood on a fruit crate holding her bulging stomach; and an old, wrinkled woman filled her paint-starved window frame with a toothy grin. I was showered with scraps of paper, each with an address on it. A contagious energy filled the air. It hurt to say *ciao*.

For a strange journey through an eerie cellar of the dead, visit the Catacombs of the Capuchin Monks (Convento di Cappuccini). This dark and dreary basement is decorated with the skeletal remains of 8,000 monks, many clothed and hanging on its walls. With their strange but meaningful habit, this order of monks reminds us that in the middle of our busy vacation or workaday scramble, in a cosmic heartbeat, none of our earthly concerns may matter.

While you're there, notice how much the monks (those still alive) look like that wonderful cup of cappuccino with which you start your Italian day. Their rich brown cowls with the frothy white tops gave the coffee its name.

For a more typical tourist attraction and a respite from Palermo's swelter-skelter, bus inland to the soothing mountain town of Monreale.

Portugal and Spain

35. Lisbon's Gold Still Shines

Barely elegant outdoor cafés, glittering art, and the saltiest sailors'
quarter in Europe, all at bargain basement prices, make Lisbon an
Iberian highlight. Portugal's capital is a wonderful mix of now and
then. Old wooden trolleys shiver up its hills, bird-stained statues guard
grand squares, and people sip coffee in Art Nouveau cafés.

Present-day Lisbon is explained by its past. Her glory days were the
15th and 16th centuries, when explorers like Vasco da Gama opened up
new trade routes, making Lisbon the queen of Europe. Later, the riches
of Brazil boosted Lisbon even higher. Then, in 1755, an earthquake lev-
eled the city, killing more than 20 percent of its people.

Lisbon was rebuilt on a strict grid plan, symmetrically, with broad
boulevards and square squares. The grandeur of pre-earthquake Lisbon
survives only in Belem, the Alfama, and the Bairro Alto districts.

Fish market in Lisbon's Alfama

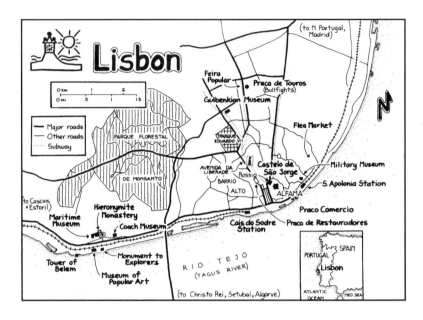

While the earthquake flattened a lot of buildings, and its colonial empire is long gone, Lisbon's heritage survives. Follow me through a day in Lisbon.

After breakfast, taxi to the Alfama, the city's colorful sailors' quarter. This was the center of Visigothic Lisbon, a rich district during the Arabic period and now the shiver-me-timbers home of Lisbon's fisherfolk. One of the few areas to survive the 1755 earthquake, the Alfama is a cobbled cornucopia of Old World color. Visit during the busy midmorning market time or in the late afternoon and early evening, when the streets chatter with activity.

Wander deep. This urban jungle's roads are squeezed into tangled stairways and confused alleys. Bent houses comfort each other in their romantic shabbiness, and the air drips with laundry and the smell of clams and raw fish. Get lost. Poke aimlessly, sample ample grapes, avoid rabid-looking dogs, peek through windows. Make a friend, pet a chicken. Taste the *blanco seco*—the local dry wine.

Gradually zigzag your way up the castle-crowned hill until you reach a little green square called Maradouro de Santa Luzia. Rest here and enjoy the lovely view of the Alfama below you. By now it's noon, and you should be quite hungry (unless you accumulated more than photos in the Alfama market). A block behind Maradouro de Santa Luzia is Largo Rodrigues Freitas, a square with several scruffy, cheap, very local eateries.

Treat yourself to the local special—a plate of boiled clams and cockles.

If you climb a few more blocks to the top of the hill, you'll find the ruins of Castelo de São Jorge. From this fortress, which has dominated the city for more than 1,000 years, enjoy a commanding view of Portugal's capital city.

After lunch, grab a tram or taxi to Torre de Belem (the Belem Tower). The Belem District, 4 miles from downtown, is a pincushion of important sights from Portugal's Golden Age, when Vasco da Gama and company made her Europe's richest power.

The Belem Tower, built in Manueline style (ornate Portuguese Renaissance) has guarded Lisbon's harbor since 1555. Today it symbolizes the voyages that made her powerful. This was the last sight sailors saw as they left and the first one they'd see when they returned, loaded down with gold, diamonds, and venereal diseases.

Nearby, the giant Monument to the Discoverers honors Portugal's King Henry the Navigator and the country's leading explorers. Across the street, the Monastery of Jeronimos is Portugal's most exciting building—my favorite cloister in Europe. The Manueline style of this giant church and cloister combines Gothic and Renaissance features with motifs from the sea—the source of the wealth that made this art possible.

Spend the evening at a Portuguese bullfight. It's a brutal sport, but the bull lives through it and so will you. The fight starts with an equestrian duel—fast bull against graceful horse and rider. Then the fun starts. A colorfully clad eight-man team enters the ring strung out in a line as if to play leapfrog. The leader taunts El Toro noisily and, with testosterone sloshing everywhere, the bull and the man charge each other. The speeding bull plows into the leader head-on. Then—thud, thud, thud—the raging bull picks up the entire charging crew. The horns are wrapped so no one gets gored—just mashed.

The crew wrestles the bull to a standstill, and one man grabs the bull's tail. Victory is complete when the team leaps off the bull and the man still hanging onto the tail "waterskis" behind it. This thrilling display of insanity is repeated with six bulls. After each round, the bruised and battered leader limps a victory lap around the ring. Portugal's top bullring is Lisbon's Campo Pequeno (fights on Thursday, mid-June through September; other arenas advertise fights most Sundays from Easter to October).

These are the usual sights; cultural cancans you can find in any guidebook. But with some imagination, your sightseeing can also include Portugal in action.

Go into a bar as if your poetry teacher sent you there on assignment. Observe, write, talk, try to understand and appreciate; send your senses on a scavenger hunt. The eating, drinking, and socializing rituals are fascinating.

My favorite Lisbon evening was at the Feira Popular, which rages nightly until 1:00 a.m. from May through September (on Ave. da Republica at the Entrecampos metro stop). This popular fair bustles with Portuguese families at play. I ate dinner surrounded by chattering Portuguese families and ignoring the ever-present TVs, while great platters of fish, meat, fries, salad, and lots of wine paraded frantically in every direction. A seven-year-old boy stood on a chair and sang hauntingly emotional folk songs. With his own dogged clapping, he dragged applause out of the less-than-interested crowd and then passed his shabby hat. All the while, fried ducks drip, barbecues spit, dogs squirt the legs of chairs, and somehow local lovers ignore everything but each other's eyes.

See the Appendix (Recommended Accommodations) for more information.

36. Salema, on Portugal's Sunny South Coast

Any place famous as a "last undiscovered tourist frontier" no longer is. Many travelers come to the Algarve, Portugal's south coast, looking for

Salema. Catch the Algarve before it's gone.

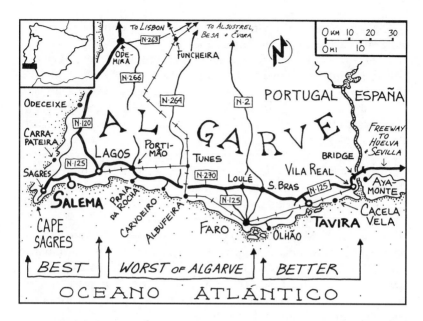

fun in the sun on undeveloped beaches . . . and find sunburned tourists simmering in carbon monoxide and traffic noise.

But the lucky, persistent, or savvy traveler can find a number of places that lack fame, crowds, condos, and concrete. There are a few towns where colorful boats share the beach with a colony of sun-worshipers who relax far from the tacky souvenir racks and package-tour rat race.

The Algarve of your dreams survives—just barely. To catch it before it goes, find a fringe. It took me three tries. West of Lagos, I tried Lux and Burgano, both offering only a corpse of a fishing village, bikini-strangled and Nivea-creamed. Then, just as darkness turned couples into peaceful silhouettes, I found Salema.

Any Algarve town with a beach will have tourism, but few mix tourism and realism as well as little Salema. Tucked away where a dirt road hits the beach between Lagos and Cape Sagres on Portugal's southwestern tip, Salema is an easy 15-mile bus ride or hitch from the closest train station in Lagos. Don't let the ladies hawking rooms in Lagos waylay you into staying in their city by telling you Salema is full.

Salema has a split personality. Half is a whitewashed old town of scruffy dogs, wide-eyed kids, and fishermen who've seen it all. The other half was built for tourists. The parking lot that separates the jog-ging shorts from the black shawls becomes a morning market with the horn-tooting arrival of the trucks: a fruit-and-veggies mobile, a rolling meat-and-cheese shop, and the clothing van.

The two worlds pursue a policy of peaceful coexistence. Tractors pull in and push out the fishing boats, two-year-olds toddle in the waves, topless women read German fashion mags, and old men really do mend the nets. Tourists laze in the sun, while locals grab the shade. Dogs roam like they own the place, and a dark, withered granny shells almonds with a railroad spike.

Salema is my kind of beach resort—four restaurants specializing in fresh fish and *vinho verde* (green wine), three hotels, lots of *quartos* (Portuguese bed and breakfasts), and an inviting beach. It's being quietly discovered by British, German, and Back Door connoisseurs of lethargy.

Those in need of activity can hire a local for a three-hour fishing-boat trip from Salema to Sagres and back, with possible swimming stops at desolate beaches along the way (ask John at Pension Mare for specifics). Or, for the best secluded beach in the region, drive to Praia do Castelo, just north of Cape Sagres (from Vila do Bispo, turn inland and follow the signs for 15 minutes).

So often tourism chases quaint folksiness. And the quaint folks can survive only with the help of tourist dollars. One way a fishing family boosts its income is to rent out a spare bedroom to the ever-growing stream of tan fans from the drizzly north. I arrived at 7 p.m. with a group of nine people and saw no "B&B" signs anywhere. I asked some locals, "*Quarto?*" Eyes perked, heads nodded, and I got ten beds in three homes at $10 per person. Quartos line the lane running left from the village center as you face the beach. Our rooms were simple, with showers, springy beds, and glorious views of pure paradise. Friendly local smiles assured us that this was the place to be.

As the sun sets, a man catches short fish with a long pole. Behind him is Cape Sagres—the edge of the world 500 years ago. As far as the gang sipping port and piling olive pits in the beachside bar is concerned, it still is.

See the Appendix (Recommended Accommodations) for more information.

37. Southern Spain's Pueblos Blancos: Andalusia's Route of the White Villages

When tourists head south from Madrid, it's generally with Granada, Córdoba, Sevilla, or the Costa del Sol in mind. The big cities have their

Estepa, southern Spain

urban charms, but the Costa del Sol is a concrete nightmare, worthwhile only as a bad example. The most Spanish thing about the south coast is the sunshine—but that's everywhere. For something different and more authentic, try exploring the interior of Andalusia along the "route of the white villages."

Make this an exercise in going where no tourist has gone before. If you don't know where you are, you've arrived. I spent several days driving aimlessly from town to village on the back roads of southern Spain, enjoying untouched Spanish culture.

Ronda, straddling an impressive gorge while cradling lots of history, is an entertaining starting point. Nearby you'll find the prehistoric Pileta Caves (open daily 10:00 a.m.–1:00 p.m. and 4:00–5:00 p.m., a rocky drive or a two-hour uphill hike from the nearest train station). Follow signs to the caves past groves of cork trees to the desolate parking lot. If no one's there, a sign says (in four languages) to "call." Holler down into the valley, and the old man will mosey up, unlock the caves, light the lanterns, and take you on a memorable, hour-long, half-mile journey. He ably hurdles the language barrier, and you'll get a good look at countless natural formations and paintings done by prehistoric hombres 25,000 years ago. (That's five times as old as the oldest

SOUTHERN SPAIN

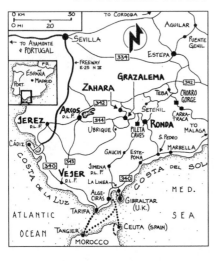

Egyptian pyramid.) These are crude and faint, but since the Altamira caves are closed, these are the best original neolithic paintings in Spain.

From Ronda, the road to Arcos de la Frontera is a charm bracelet of whitewashed villages. In Zahara, climb the ruined castle for a view that would knock Sancho Panza off his ass. Grazalema is ideal for a picnic on its Grand Canyon balcony.

Arcos de la Frontera is a more substantial town with a labyrinthine Old Quarter overlooking a vast plain. Driving through Arcos is about as easy as threading a needle while giggling. Spend the night. Climb the church bell tower (possibly with a picnic for the summit). You'll walk right through the caretaker's living room, get the key, leave a tip, and climb to the top. Cover your ears when the giant old clappers whip into action.

Estepa was my Spanish treasure chest. Below a hill crowned with a castle and convent spreads a freshly washed and very happy town that fit my dreams of southern Spain.

Situated halfway between Córdoba and Málaga (a seven-mile hitch from the La Roda train station), but light years away from either, Estepa hugs a small hill. Atop the hill is the convent of Santa Clara, worth three stars in any guidebook but found in none. Enjoy the territorial view from the summit, then step into the quiet, spiritual perfection of the church. (If it's locked, find someone with a key.)

The evening is prime time in Estepa. The promenade begins as everyone gravitates to the central square. The spotless streets are polished nightly by the feet of ice cream–licking strollers. The whole town strolls—it's like "cruising" without cars. Buy an ice cream *bocadillo* and join in. The town barber, whose shop faces the square, is an artist.

Good information on small-town Andalusia is rare. Little is written on the Pueblos Blancos. The Michelin Guide, usually invaluable, skips the Andalusian countryside. This area is unvisited, so tourist facilities are limited. Get the best map you can find, ask locals for tips on hotels and touring suggestions, and pick up the *Route of the White Towns* booklet in Sevilla or at any major Spanish tourist office.

This Andalusian adventure is best by car. Hitching is dreary, and public transportation is pretty bad. Hit the back roads and find that perfect village.

See the Appendix (Recommended Accommodations) for more information.

France

38. Alsace and Colmar

The French province of Alsace stands like a flower-child referee between Germany and France. Bounded by the Rhine River on the east and the well-worn Vosges Mountains on the west, this is a lush land of villages, vineyards, ruined castles, 20th-century war memorials, and an almost naive cheeriness.

Because of its location, natural wealth, naked vulnerability, and the fact that Germany thinks the mountains are the natural border and France thinks the Rhine River is, nearly every Alsatian generation has weathered an invasion. Centuries as a political pawn between Germany and France has given the Alsace a hybrid culture. Alsatian French is peppered with German words. On doorways of homes, you'll see names like Jacques Schmidt or Dietrich Le Beau. Most locals can swear bilingually. Half-timbered restaurants serve sauerkraut and escargot.

Wine is the primary industry, topic of conversation, dominant mouthwash, perfect excuse for countless festivals, and a tradition providing the foundation for Alsatian folk culture.

Alsace's wine road, the Route du Vin, is an asphalt ribbon tying 90 miles of vineyards, villages, and feudal fortresses into an understandably popular tourist package. The dry and sunny climate has produced good wine and happy tourists since Roman days.

During the October harvest season, all Alsace erupts into a carnival of colorful folk costumes, traditional good-time music, and Dionysian smiles. I felt as welcome as a local grape-picker, and my tight sightseeing plans became as hard to follow as a straight line.

If you can pick grapes, you might land a job in October. For a hard day in the vineyards you'll get room and board, $30, and an intimate Alsatian social experience lubricated liberally, logically, by plenty of local wine.

Winetasting is popular throughout the year. Roadside *dégustation* signs invite you into wine "caves," where a local producer will serve you all seven Alsatian wines from dry to sweet, with educational commentary (probably in French) if requested. Try Cremant, the Alsatian champagne. Cave-hopping is a great way to spend an afternoon on the Route du Vin. With free tasting and fine $5 bottles, French winetasting can be an affordable sport.

The small caves are fun, but be sure to tour a larger wine co-op. Beer-drinking Germans completely flattened many Alsatian towns in

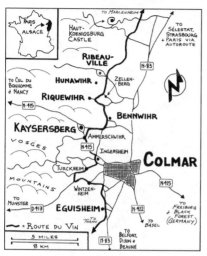

COLMAR AREA

1944. The small family-run vineyards of these villages sprang back as large, modern, and efficient cooperatives. In the village of Bennwihr, a co-op of 211 people is proud to show you its facilities, which can crush 600 tons of grapes a day and turn out 14,000 bottles an hour. No tour ends without taking full advantage of the tasting room. Bennwihr has a wine tradition going back to Roman times. Its name is from the Latin *Benonis Villare*, or "Beno's estate"—and Beno served up a great Riesling.

There's more to Alsace than meets the palate. Centuries of successful wine production built prosperous, colorful villages. Countless castles capped hilltops to defend the much-invaded plain, and wine wasn't the only art form loved and patronized by local connoisseurs.

Alsatian towns are historic mosaics of gables, fountains, medieval bell towers and gateways, ancient ramparts, churches, and cheery old inns. More than anywhere in France, you'll find plenty of budget beds in private homes ($35 doubles, ask at village TIs or look for *Chambre d'Hôte* signs). While Colmar is the best home-base city, petite Eguisheim, with plenty of small hotels, minimum tour crowds, and maximum village charm, is the ideal small-town home. Nearby Riquewihr and Kaysersberg are two more crackerjack villages. A scenic path—one of countless in the Alsace—connects these two towns. Take a hike or rent a bike. Drop by a castle or two. Climb the tallest tower and survey Alsace, looking as it has for centuries—a valley of endless vineyards along the Route du Vin.

COLMAR

Colmar, my favorite city in Alsace, sees few American tourists but is popular with Germans and the French. This well-preserved old town of 70,000 is a handy springboard for Alsatian explorations.

Historic beauty, usually a poor excuse to be spared the ravages of World War II, saved Colmar. The American and British military were careful not to bomb the burghers' old half-timbered houses,

COLMAR

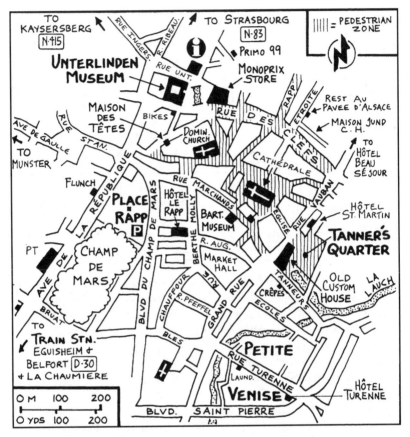

characteristic red- and green-tiled roofs, and the cobbled lanes of Alsace's most beautiful city.

Today Colmar not only survives, it thrives—with historic buildings, impressive art treasures, and a cuisine that attracts eager taste buds from all over Europe. And Colmar has that special French talent of being great but cozy at the same time. Antique shops welcome browsers, and hotel managers run down the sleepy streets to pick up fresh croissants in time for breakfast. Schoolgirls park their rickety horse-drawn carriages in front of the city hall, ready to give visitors a $4 clip-clop tour of the old town.

Colmar offers heavyweight sights in a warm, small-town package. By the end of the Middle Ages, the walled town was a thriving trade center filled with rich old houses. The wonderfully restored tanners' quarters is a quiver of tall, narrow, half-timbered buildings. Its confused rooftops struggle erratically to get enough sun to dry their animal skins. Nearby you'll find "La Petite Venise," complete with canals and a pizzeria.

Colmar combines its abundance of art with a knack for showing it off. The artistic geniuses Grunewald, Schongauer, and Bartholdi all called Colmar home.

Frederic Bartholdi, who created our Statue of Liberty a century ago, adorned his hometown with many fine, if smaller, statues. Don't miss the little Bartholdi museum, offering a good look at the artist's life and some fun Statue of Liberty trivia.

Four hundred years earlier, Martin Schongauer was the leading local artist. His *Virgin of the Rose Garden* could give a state trooper goose bumps. Looking fresh and crisp, it's set magnificently in a Gothic Dominican church. I sat with a dozen people, silently, as if at a symphony, as Schongauer's Madonna performed solo on center stage. Lit by 14th-century stained glass, its richness and tenderness cradled me in a Gothic sweetness that no textbook could explain. Even if you become so jaded that you "never want to see another Madonna and Child," give this one a chance.

The Unterlinden Museum, one of my favorite small museums, is housed in a 750-year-old convent next to the tourist office. It has the best collection anywhere of Alsatian folk art and art exhibits ranging from Neolithic and Gallo-Roman archaeological collections to works by Monet, Renoir, Braque, and Picasso. It's a medieval and Renaissance "home show." You can lose yourself in a 17th-century Alsatian wine cellar complete with presses, barrels, tools, and aromas.

The highlight of the museum (and for me, the city) is Grunewald's gripping Isenheim Altarpiece. This is actually a series of paintings on hinges that pivot like shutters. Designed to help people in a hospital—long before the age of painkillers—suffer through their horrible skin diseases, it's one of the most powerful paintings ever. Stand petrified in front of it and let the agony and suffering of the Crucifixion drag its fingers down your face. Just as you're about to break down and sob with those in the painting, turn to the happy ending—a psychedelic explosion of Resurrection happiness. It's like jumping from the dentist's chair directly into a Jacuzzi. We know very little about Grunewald except that his work has played tetherball with human emotions for 500 years.

Colmar's tourist information office provides city maps, guides, and a room-finding service. They can also suggest side trips around

Alsace's wine road, into Germany's Black Forest and nearby Freiburg, or a tour of the Maginot Line.

I sleep at the magnificent half-timbered Maison Jund. This B&B, a medieval tree house soaked in wine and filled with flowers, is warmly run in the center of Colmar ($40 doubles, 12 rue de l'Ange, tel. 03 89 41 58 72, fax 03 89 23 15 83).

For maximum local fun, remember that Colmar goes crazy during its winefest (August) and Sauerkraut Days (two weekends in September). You'll enjoy plenty of revelry—feasting, dancing, music, and wine—Alsatian-style.

See the Appendix (Recommended Accommodations) for more information.

39. From France to Italy over Mont Blanc

Europe's ultimate mountain lift towers high above the tourist-choked French resort town of Chamonix. Ride the Aiguille du Midi *téléphérique* (gondola) to the dizzy 12,600-foot-high tip of a rock needle. As you get in, remind yourself that this thing has been going back and forth now since 1954; surely it'll make it one more time. Chamonix shrinks as trees fly by, soon replaced by whizzing rocks, ice, and snow until you reach the top. Up there, even sunshine is cold. The

Alps from atop the Aiguille du Midi, 12,600 feet up

ALPINE CROSSING FROM FRANCE TO ITALY

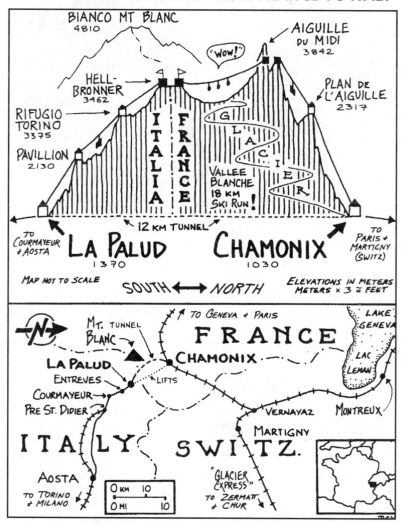

air is thin. People are giddy. Fun things can happen if you're not too winded to join locals in the Halfway-to-Heaven tango.

Before you spread the Alps. In the distance is the bent little Matterhorn. You can almost reach out and pat the head of Mont Blanc, at 15,781 feet, the Continent's highest point.

Next, for Europe's most exciting border crossing, get into the tiny red gondola and head south. Dangle silently for 40 minutes as you

Andrea Hagg

Dangle silently for 40 minutes as you glide over the glacier from France to Italy.

glide over the glacier to Italy. Squeeze out your porthole, exploring every corner of your view. You're sailing a new sea.

Show your passport at Hellbronner Point (11,000 feet) and descend into the remote Italian Valle d'Aosta. It's a whole different world.

Your starting point for this adventure is Chamonix, a convenient overnight train ride from Paris or Nice. Chamonix is a resort town—packed in August but surprisingly easy and affordable the rest of the year. Like Interlaken, it's a springboard for mountain-worshipers. The town has an efficient tourist information center and plenty of reasonable accommodations, including chalets offering $15 dorm beds.

From Chamonix, there are days of hikes and cable car rides. The best hikes are opposite the most staggering peaks on the Gran Balcon Sud, a world of pristine lakes, great Mont Blanc range views, and para-sailers lunging off the cliff from the Brévent lift station. Watching these daredevils fill the valley like spaced-out butterflies is a thrilling spectator sport. Probably the best easy hike—two hours each way—is from the top of the Flégère lift to Lac Blanc.

For the ultimate ride, take that *téléphérique* to the Aiguille du Midi. This lift ($40 round-trip, daily, 7:00 a.m.–5:00 p.m. in the summer, shorter hours off-season) is Europe's highest and most spectacular. If the weather is good, forget your budget. (The hostel gives 25 percent discount coupons.) Afternoons are most likely clouded and crowded. In August ride very early to avoid miserable delays. If you plan to dilly-dally, ride directly to your farthest point and linger on your return.

To both save a little money and enjoy a hike, buy a ticket to the top of Aiguille du Midi, but only halfway back down. This gives you a chance to look down at the Alps and over at the summit of Mont Blanc from your lofty 12,600-foot lookout. Then you descend to the halfway point, where you're free to frolic in the glaciers and hike to Mer de Glace, where you can catch a train back to Chamonix.

From the top of Aiguille du Midi, you can continue (weather permitting) over the mountain to Italy. It's a long trip; the last departure is at about 4:00 p.m. The descent from Hellbronner Point (about $18) takes you into the remote Italian Valle d'Aosta, where a dash of France and a splash of Switzerland blend with the already rich Italian flavor and countless castles to give you an easy-to-like first taste of Italy.

The town of Aosta, your best valley home base, is a two-hour bus ride (hourly departures, change in Courmayeur) from the base of the lift in La Palud. If a fellow cable-car passenger has a car parked in La Palud, charm yourself a ride to Aosta.

"The Rome of the Alps," as Aosta is called, has many Roman ruins and offers a great introduction to the fine points of Italian life: cappuccino, *gelati*, and a busy evening stroll, or *passeggiata*. The popular and inexpensive Ulisse Restaurant at Via Ed. Aubert 58 has great pizza. An evening here is a fine way to ease into *la dolce vita*.

Chamonix, Aiguille du Midi, and the Valle d'Aosta—surely a high point in anyone's European vacation.

See the Appendix (Recommended Accommodations) for more information.

Germany, Austria, and Switzerland

40. Rothenburg and the Romantic Road: From the Rhine to Bavaria Through Germany's Medieval Heartland

Connect the castles of the Rhine and the lederhosen charm of Bavaria by traveling Germany's "Romantische Strasse." Along the Romantic Road (and especially just off it, where no unfamiliar car passes unnoticed and flower boxes decorate the unseen sides of barns), visitors find the Germany most come to see. Church-steeple masts sail seas of rich, rolling farmland, and fragrant villages invite you to slow down. At each village, ignore the signposts and ask an old woman for directions to the next town—just to hear her voice and enjoy the energy in her eyes. Thousands of tourists pass through. Few stop to chat.

The Romantic Road, peppered with pretty towns today because it was such an important and prosperous trade route 600 years ago, is no secret. But even with its crowds, it's a must.

A car or bike gives you complete freedom to explore Germany's medieval heartland—just follow the green Romantische Strasse signs. The most scenic sections are from Bad Mergentheim to Rothenburg (in the north) and from Landsberg to Füssen (in the south). Those without wheels can take the train or the convenient Europabus tour. From April through October, Romantic Road buses run daily between Frankfurt and Munich, and Frankfurt and Füssen. Eurailers, who get a 75 percent discount, pay only about $23 (including the registration fee) for the ride. Otherwise, the bus from Munich to Frankfurt costs about $60 (the same as a second-class train ticket). The main advantage of the bus is that it stops at sights not served by the train line, such as Dinklesbühl and the Wies Church. The disadvantages are that no picnicking is allowed on the bus and the length of stops may be arbitrarily shortened by arbitrary tour guides. The trip takes 11 hours, including two to three hours off the bus to explore the fairy-tale towns of Rothenburg and Dinkelsbühl. Bus reservations are free, easy, and highly recommended (call Munich's Euraide office at least one day in advance, tel. 089/593-889, fax 089/550-3965). You can break your journey anywhere along the road and catch the same bus the next day—but you'll be guaranteed a seat only if you reserve each segment. If you're going only to Rothenburg, take the train.

GERMANY'S ROMANTIC ROAD

ROTHENBURG

Of the many lovable little towns along the Romantic Road, Rothenburg is the most lovable. This is probably the most touristy town in Germany, but it's your best-possible look at a medieval town. In the Middle Ages, when Frankfurt and Munich were just wide spots in the road, Rothenburg was Germany's second-largest city, with a whopping population of 6,000. Today it's her best-preserved medieval walled town, enjoying tremendous tourist popularity without losing its charm.

Romantic Road bus-tourists get only a short break to roam. Here's Rothenburg's best 90 minutes: The bus drops you at the train station, a few blocks outside the wall. The street from the station leads to the nearest town gate, Rödertor. Climb Rödertor for a fine town view and an interesting display of World War II damage. From there, follow the cobbles to the Market Square (tourist information office). Continue straight down Herrengasse (lined with the mansions of the richest townsmen, or *Herren*) to the Castle Garden for fine views of the "Tauber Riviera." You may have a few minutes left to see the Riemenschneider altarpiece in St. Jacob's Church, visit the town history museum under the tower just off the Market Square, or shop.

By this time, any normal person will have decided that, when it comes to Germany's many cute small towns, monogamy is the best policy. Forget the bus or train, spend the night and love only Rothenburg.

Those spending the night in Europe's most exciting medieval town enjoy Rothenburg without its daily hordes of big city day-trippers and risk actually hearing the sounds of the Thirty Years' War still echoing through its turrets and clock towers.

Too often, Rothenburg brings out the shopper in visitors before they've had a chance to appreciate the historic city. True, this is a great place to do your German shopping (visit friendly Anneliese Friese's shop, two doors left of the tourist office—10 percent discount with this book and the best money exchange rates in town), but see the town first.

The tourist information office on the Market Square offers guided tours in English (each afternoon at 2:00 p.m. and with the more colorful night watchman evenings at 8:00 p.m., about $4). A local historian, usually an intriguing character, brings the ramparts alive. A thousand years of history are packed between the cobbles.

After your walking-tour orientation, you'll have plenty of sightseeing ideas. The mile-and-a-half walk around Rothenburg's medieval wall offers great views—especially before breakfast or at sunset. For the best view of the town and surrounding countryside, make the rigorous but rewarding climb to the top of the Town Hall Tower. The friendly ticket-taker on top speaks more Japanese than English, an interesting sign of the touristic times.

Rothenburg's fascinating Medieval Crime and Punishment Museum is full of legal bits and diabolical pieces, instruments of punishment and torture, and even an iron cage—complete with a metal nag gag—all unusually well-explained in English.

St. Jacob's Church contains the one must-see art treasure in Rothenburg, a glorious 500-year-old altarpiece by Riemenschneider, the Michelangelo of German woodcarvers. Pick up the free brochure

that explains the church's art treasures and head upstairs behind the organ for Germany's greatest piece of woodcarving.

To hear the birds and smell the cows, take a walk through the Tauber Valley. The trail leads downhill from Rothenburg's idyllic castle gardens to a cute, skinny 600-year-old castle, the summer home of Mayor Toppler. It's intimately furnished and well-worth a look. On the top floor, notice the photo of bombed-out 1945 Rothenburg. From here, walk past the covered bridge and trout-filled Tauber to the sleepy village of Detwang, which is actually older than Rothenburg and has a church with another impressive Riemenschneider altarpiece.

Rothenburg's well-preserved medieval sister is Dinkelsbühl, an hour to the south. Old walls, towers, gateways, and the peaceful green waters of the moat defend its medieval architecture from the 20th century. The Romantic Road bus also makes a short stop here to grab a quick bite or to explore, camera in hand, the old cobbled streets. Dinkelsbühl celebrates its colorfully medieval Kinderfest (Children's Festival) in mid-July (from the weekend before the third Monday through the weekend after).

The Romantic Road has much more. If you order now, you'll get Würzburg, with its fine Baroque Prince Bishop's Residenz—the Versailles of Franconia—and its oh-wow Baroque chapel. You can see another lovely carved altarpiece by Riemenschneider (with the unique thimble museum across the street) a mile from Creglingen. To the south is the flamboyant Wies Church, near Oberammergau, and Mad King Ludwig's Disneyesque Neuschwanstein Castle near Füssen.

The Romantic Road—a quick, comfortable, and inexpensive way to see two of Germany's most beautiful towns—is the best way to connect the Rhine and Bavaria.

See the Appendix (Recommended Accommodations) for more information.

41. Hallstatt, in Austria's Commune-with-Nature Lakes District

With the longest life span and one of the shortest work weeks in Europe, Austrians are experts at good living. They focus their free time on the fine points of life: music, a stroll, pastry, and a good cup of coffee. The uniquely Austrian *gemütlichkeit* (as difficult to translate as it is to pronounce, meaning something like a warm, cozy, friendly, focus-on-the-moment feeling) is something even whirlwind tourists pick up in the Salzkammergut Lakes District, where big-city Austrians go to relax.

Far from the urban rat race, though just two hours by train from Salzburg, this is the perfect place to commune with nature, Austrian-style. The Salzkammergut is a lushly forested playground dotted with

Hallstatt, in Austria's Salzkammergut Lakes District

David C. Hoerlein

AUSTRIA'S SALZKAMMERGUT LAKES DISTRICT

cottages. Trains, buses, or boats lead the traveler through gentle mountains and shy lakes, winding from relaxed village to relaxed village.

The Salzkammergut's pride and joy is the town of Hallstatt. The minute it popped into view, I knew Hallstatt was my Alpine Oz. It's just the right size (1,200 people), wonderfully remote, and almost traffic-free. A tiny ferry takes you from the nearest train station across the fjord-like lake and drops you off on the town's storybook square.

Bullied onto its lakeside ledge by a selfish mountain, Hallstatt seems tinier than it is. Its pint-sized square is surrounded by ivy-covered guest houses and cobbled lanes. It's a toy town. You can tour it on foot in about 10 minutes.

Except in August, when tourist crowds trample most of Hallstatt's charm, there's no shortage of pleasant $20-per-person *Zimmer* (bed-and-breakfast places). I splurge for a creaky old hotel, spending $70 for a double with breakfast in the Gasthof Simony (tel. 06134/8231). This hotel separates the square from the lake, with balconies overlooking each. One rustic room has hardwood floors, rag rugs, an antique wooden bed with a matching free-standing closet, grandmother lamps, and a lakeside, flower-decked balcony.

Three thousand years ago this area was the salt-mining capital of Europe. An economic and cultural boom put it on the map back in Flintstone times. In fact, an entire 1,000-year chapter in the story of Europe is called "The Hallstatt Period." A humble museum next to the tourist office shows off Hallstatt's salty past. For a better look, you can tour the world's first salt mine, located a thrilling funicular ride above downtown Hallstatt. You'll dress up in an old miner's outfit, ride trains into the mountain where the salt was mined, cruise subterranean lakes, scream down long sliver-free banisters, and read brief and dry English explanations while entertaining guides tell the fascinating story in German.

Hallstatt outgrew its little ledge, and many of its buildings climb the mountainside, with street level on one side being three floors above street level on the other. Land is limited—so limited that, in the church cemetery, bones received only 12 years of peaceful subterranean darkness before making way for those of the newly dead. The result is a fascinating chapel of decorated bones. Each skull is lovingly named, dated, and decorated, with the men getting ivy and the women getting rose motifs. This practice was stopped in the 1960s, about when the Catholic Church began permitting cremation.

Passing time in and around Hallstatt is easy. The little tourist office will recommend a hike—the 9,000-foot Mt. Dachstein looms overhead—or a peaceful cruise in a rented canoe. Most people go to Hallstatt simply to relax, eat, shop, and stroll. To cloak yourself in the *gemütlichkeit*, flowers, and cobblestones of Austria's Salzkammergut Lakes District, visit Hallstatt.

See the Appendix (Recommended Accommodations) for more information.

42. Hall, in the Shadow of Innsbruck

It's a brisk mountain morning in the Tirolean town of Hall. Merchants in aprons hustle, and roses, peppers, and pears fill their tidy street-side stalls, competing for my photograph. There's not a tourist in sight. They're all five miles up the river, in Innsbruck. Just as Hallstatt is the small-town escape from Salzburg, Hall is the place to go if you want the natural surroundings of Innsbruck without the big city. Vagabuddies, who enjoy the cheap accommodations in Innsbruck, do Hall as a day trip.

Hall was a rich salt-mining center when Innsbruck was just a humble bridge (*Brücke*) town on the Inn River. Sprawling Innsbruck's tourist industry crowds into its tiny medieval town center. Hall, a diminutive village in comparison, actually has a bigger old center. Its rich bundle of pastel buildings and cobbled streets feels refreshingly real—too real if you're trying to accomplish anything more than a leisurely lunch between noon and 2:00 p.m., when everything closes.

The tourist office organizes daily walking tours—in English, when necessary. The luxurious Tirolean Baroque church, the elegant architecture lining the streets, and 500-year-old mint (which lets visitors make a coin the traditional way) combine to make it clear that in its day, Hall was a local powerhouse.

The village of Hall near Innsbruck

INNSBRUCK AND HALL

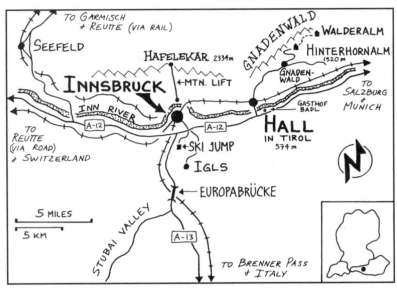

Back when salt was money, Hall was loaded. You can tour salt mines near Hall in places like Hallein and Hallstatt (*Hall* was an ancient word for salt). Salt mine tours are fun but cost about $10 and can be crowded with long lines. While they are the major reason to go through a turnstile in this area, I find them marginally worth the money, time, and trouble. Hall has a quicker, cheaper, and easier alternative—its Bergbaumuseum. Tours are given daily of the town's reconstructed salt mine, complete with pits, shafts, drills, tools, and—the climax of any salt mine tour—the slippery wooden slide. It feels like a real mine.

Give your trip a memorable splash by spending a sunny afternoon at Hall's magnificent Freischwimmbad. This huge outdoor swimming pool has four diving boards, a giant lap pool, and a kiddies' pool bigger than anything in my hometown, bordered by a lush garden, a sauna, a minigolf course, and lounging locals.

The same mountains that put Innsbruck on the vacation map surround Hall. For a lazy look at life in the high Alps, drive up to 5,000-foot Hinterhornalm and walk to a remote working farm.

Begin your ascent in Gnadenwald, a chalet-filled village sandwiched between Hall and its Alps. Pay $6 and pick up a brochure at the toll hut. Then wind your way upward, marveling at the crazy amount of energy put into this remote road, to a parking lot at the rustic Hinterhornalm Berg restaurant. This place serves hearty food and a cliffhanger of a view (tel. 06641/211-2745, crowded on summer weekends, closed by avalanches from November to April). Hinterhornalm is a hang-gliding springboard. On sunny days it's a butterfly nest of thrill-seekers ready to fly.

It's a level 20-minute stroll from the restaurant to the Walderalm farm (see photo in Chapter 12), where you are welcome to wander around a working dairy farm that shares its meadow with the clouds. Cows ramble along ridgetop lanes surrounded by cut-glass peaks. The lady of the farm serves hot soup, Alpine snacks, and drinks (very fresh milk in the afternoon) on rough plank tables. In the distance below you can almost see the Inn River Valley autobahn bringing all the tour buses into Innsbruck.

See the Appendix (Recommended Accommodations) for more information.

43. The Berner Oberland: The Alps in Your Lap

Switzerland offers Europe's most spectacular mountain scenery. The only thing higher than those Alpine peaks is the prices you'll pay to see them. Switzerland is one of Europe's most expensive destinations. But with good weather, a guidebook's help, and the right itinerary, it's worth the financial pain. While you can't control the clouds, you can visit the right region, and that's the Berner Oberland. Sleep in

Thrill-seeking hang gliders are a common sight on Alpine peaks. Here, an absent-minded hang glider prepares for his last takeoff.

THE BERNER OBERLAND

Gimmelwald, and ride the lifts and hike around Kleine Scheidegg and the Schilthorn.

KLEINE SCHEIDEGG—THE MONA LISA OF MOUNTAIN VIEWS

I had always considered Interlaken overrated. Now I understand that Interlaken is only a jumping-off point—the gateway to the Alps. Stop in Interlaken for shopping, banking, post, and telephone chores, and to pick up information on the region. Then head south, into the Berner Oberland.

You have several options. Vagabonds who just dropped in on the overnight train (ideal from Paris) can do a loop trip, going down Grindelwald Valley, over the Kleine Scheidegg ridge, and then into our target, Lauterbrunnen. From there, you can head on out by returning to Interlaken or settle into Gimmelwald for the Alpine cuddle after the climax. Those with more time and less energy will set up in Gimmelwald and ride up to Kleine Scheidegg from Lauterbrunnen, skipping Grindelwald.

Loop trippers should get an early start and catch the private train from the Interlaken East Station (discounted with a Eurail or Europass) to Grindelwald. Don't sleep in heavily touristed Grindelwald. Take advantage of its well-informed tourist information office. Browse through the pricey tourist shops and buy a first-class mountain picnic at the co-op grocery store. Then ascend by train into a wonderland of powerful white peaks to Kleine Scheidegg, or even higher by gondola to Männlichen (discounted with Eurail). It's an easy one-hour walk from Männlichen down to Kleine Scheidegg.

Now you have successfully run the gauntlet of tourist traps and reached the ultimate. Before you towers Switzerland's mightiest mountain panorama. The Jungfrau, the Mönch, and the Eiger boldly proclaim that they are the greatest. You won't argue.

Like a saddle on the ridge, Kleine Scheidegg gives people something to hang onto. It has a lodge (with $25 dorm bunks) and an outdoor restaurant. People gather here to marvel at tiny rock climbers—many of them quite dead—dangling by ropes halfway up the icy Eiger. You can splurge for the expensive ride from here to the towering Jungfraujoch ($80 round-trip from Kleine Scheidegg; early and late rides are discounted; expect crowd-control problems on sunny summer days, especially after a stretch of bad weather). The ride's impressive, but I couldn't have asked for more than the *Mona Lisa* of mountain views that I enjoyed from Kleine Scheidegg.

From Kleine Scheidegg, start your hike into the less touristed Lauterbrunnen Valley. The hike is not difficult. My gear consisted only of shorts (watch the mountain sun), tennis shoes, a tourist brochure map, and a bib to catch the drool.

It's lunchtime as you hike into your own peaceful mountain world. Find a grassy perch, and your picnic will have an Alpine ambience that no restaurant could match. Continuing downhill, you may well be all alone and singing to the rhythm of your happy footsteps. The gravelly walk is steep in places, and you can abbreviate it by catching the train at one of two stations you'll pass along the way. As the scenery changes, new mountains replace the ones you've already seen. After two hours you enter the traffic-free town of Wengen. Avoid the steep, dull hike from Wengen to Lauterbrunnen by taking the $5 train down to the valley floor, where you can continue by bus and gondola or funicular and train to the village of Gimmelwald. This is the scenic but very roundabout way to Gimmelwald. For a much more direct route, take the train from Interlaken-East to Lauterbrunnen.

Once you're set up, Gimmelwald becomes your springboard for Alpine fun. Back Door Explorers: If you discover that one "Gimmelwald" isn't enough, Switzerland has others tucked away. Seek out Bosco Gurin, Corippo Sognogno (Larentezzo), Valle de Verzasca, Vallais, Val d'Herens, Les Handeres, and La Forclaz.

GIMMELWALD—WHERE HEIDI LIVES
The traffic-free village of Gimmelwald hangs nonchalantly on the edge of a cliff high above the floor of the Lauterbrunnen Valley, 30 minutes by car or train south of Interlaken. It's a sleepy village with more cows ringing bells than people. Small avalanches on the almost-touchable mountain wall across the valley look and sound like distant waterfalls. The songs of birds and brooks, and the crunchy march of happy hikers constantly remind you why so many travelers say, "If Heaven isn't what it's cracked up to be, send me back to Gimmelwald."

When told you're visiting Gimmelwald, Swiss people assume you mean the famous resort in the next valley, Grindelwald. When assured that Gimmelwald is your target, they lean forward, widen their eyes, and ask, "*Und* how do you know about Gimmelvald?"

"If heaven isn't what it's cracked up to be, send me back to Gimmelwald."

The village of Gimmelwald, an ignored station on the spectacular Schilthorn gondola (of James Bond fame), should be built to the hilt. But it's classified "avalanche zone"—too dangerous for serious building projects. So while developers gnash their teeth, sturdy peasants continue milking cows and making hay, surviving in a modern world only by the grace of a government that subsidizes such poor traditional industries. Those who brave the possible avalanches (or visit in the summer when there's no snow) enjoy the Alps in their laps in a Swiss world that looks and lives the way every traveler dreams it might.

Since it allows no cars, there are only two ways to get to Gimmelwald. Drivers can park in Stechelberg at the far end of Lauterbrunnen Valley and catch the $5 gondola. Others can catch the bus from Lauterbrunnen to Stechelberg (best choice in the rain). The more scenic but complicated option is to take the Lauterbrunnen–Grutschalp funicular (a small train) up the steep wall and catch the scenic train (called the *Panorama Fahrt* in German) to the resort town of Mürren. From Mürren, Gimmelwald is a pleasant, ambling, 30-minute downhill walk.

Sleep in Gimmelwald's very rugged youth hostel ($10/bed) or at the storybook chalet called Hotel Mittaghorn ($50/double with breakfast).

Gimmelwald's shacky hostel is the loosest and friendliest hostel I've ever fallen in love with. Every day its Alps-happy family of hostelers adopts newcomers, filling them with spaghetti and mountain stories. High in the Alps, this relaxed hostel barely survives. Please treat it with loving care, respect its rules, and leave it cleaner than when you found it (tel. & fax 033/855-1704). Since Gimmelwald has no grocery store, you may want to pack in food.

Up the hill is the treasure of Gimmelwald. Walter Mittler, the perfect Swiss gentleman, runs a creaky chalet called Hotel Mittaghorn. It's a classic Alpine-style place with a million-dollar view of the Jungfrau Alps. Walter is careful not to let his place get too hectic or big and enjoys sensitive Back Door travelers. He runs his hotel alone, keeping it simple but with class. Since he's often booked up, call Walter well in advance at 033/855-1658. Hotel Mittaghorn is about the last building at the top of the town on the service road to Mürren.

Evening fun in Gimmelwald is found in the hostel (lots of young Alp-aholic hikers and a good chance to share information on the surrounding mountains) and, depending on Walter's mood, at Hotel Mittaghorn. If you're staying at Walter's, don't miss his simple supper or his coffee schnapps. Then sit on the porch and watch the sun lick the mountaintops to bed as the moon rises over the Jungfrau.

From Gimmelwald, ride the gondola up the Schilthorn ($55 round-trip, early birds get discounts), a 10,000-foot peak capped by Piz Gloria, a revolving restaurant. After watching clips from *On Her Majesty's Secret Service*, showing Piz Gloria getting blown up (free, in the theater below the restaurant), go outside for the real thrills. Frolic on the ridge. If you want to hike down, the first 300 yards are the most difficult. The easiest descent is just to the right of the cable car as you face down. The three-hour hike drops 5,000 feet. If this is too thrilling, ride the gondola back down to Birg (the midway station) and enjoy an easier (but still steep) hike from Birg back to Gimmelwald via Wasenegg Ridge. To leave this Alpine wonderland, take the lift back down to Stechelberg and then catch a bus to Interlaken.

If you're interested in the Alpine cream of Switzerland, it's best seen from Kleine Scheidegg. If you're looking for Heidi and an orchestra of cowbells in a Switzerland that most people think exists only in storybooks—take off your boots in Gimmelwald.

See the Appendix (Recommended Accommodations) for more information.

44. Offbeat Alps

Even those who know a Rocky Mountain high find something special about the Alps. In the Alps nature and civilization mix it up comfortably, as if man and mountain shared the same crib. You can hike from France to Slovenia, finding a hut or remote village for each overnight, and never come out of the mountains. Many times, you'll walk to the haunting accompaniment of long, legato alphorns. And often, just when you need it most, there will be a mechanical lift to whisk you silently and effortlessly—if not cheaply—to the top of that staggering ridge or peak, where your partner can snap a photo of you looking ruggedly triumphant. You'll pass happy yodelers, sturdy grannies, and ponytailed, dirndl-skirted, singing families. The consistently cheery greetings make passing hikers a fun part of any trek.

While the most famous corners are now solidly in the domain of tour groups, much of the best Alpine charm is folded away in no-name valleys, often just over the ridge from the Holiday Inns and the canned culture on stage.

Here are a few places and activities that will make your Alpine adventures more than a lovely hike.

Extremely remote but accessible by car (barely) is the village of **Taveyanne**, in the French-speaking part of Switzerland, two miles off the road from Col de la Croix to Villars (or take the footpath from Villars). It's just a jumble of log cabins and snoozing cows stranded all alone at 5,000 feet. The only business in town is the Refuge de Taveyanne, where the Siebenthal family serves hearty meals—great fondue and a delicious *croute au fromage avec oeuf* for $8—in a prize-winning, rustic setting. There's no electricity, low-beamed ceilings, a huge charred fireplace with a cannibal-sized caldron, a prehistoric cash register, and well-hung ornamental cowbells. For a memorable experience (and the only rentable beds in the village), consider sleeping in their primitive loft—never full, five mattresses, accessible by a ladder outside, urinate with the cows ($6, May–October, tel. 024/498-1947).

In western Austria, south of Reutte, lies a treat for those who suspect they may have been Kit Carson in a previous life. **Fallerschein** is an isolated log-cabin village, smothered in Alpine goodness. Drop into its flower-speckled world of serene slopes, lazy cows, and musical breezes. Thunderstorms roll down this valley like it's God's bowling alley, but the blissfully simple pint-sized church on the high ground seems to promise that this huddle of houses will remain standing. The people sitting on benches are Austrian vacationers or clandestine lovers who've rented cabins. Fallerschein is notorious as a hideaway for those having affairs. For a rugged chunk of local Alpine peace, spend a night in the local Matratzen *Lager* (simple dorm loft), Almwirtscheft

There's more than one way to get down an Alp.

Fallerschein (open mid-May through October, $12 per night with breakfast, 27 beds and one outhouse, edible meals, tel. 05678/5142). Fallerschein is 4,000 feet high at the end of a miserable 1-mile fit-for-jeep-or-rental-car-only gravel road near Namlos on the Berwang road south of Reutte in Austria's Tirol.

The **Sommerrodelbahn** is one of the great Alpine experiences. Several Alpine ski slopes are outfitted with concrete bobsled courses. Local speed demons spend entire summer days riding chairlifts up to "luge" down on oversized skateboards. You sit with a brake stick between your legs. Push to go fast. Pull to stop. There's a Sommerrodelbahn at Chamonix in France, one south of Salzburg, and several in Tirol—one near Neuschwanstein and two off the Fernpass road: one halfway between Reutte and Lermoos, the other just past Biberwier, in the shadow of the gray and powerful Zugspitze (Germany's tallest mountain). Luge courses are normally open daily in the summer from 8:30 a.m. to 5:00 p.m., unless it's wet. The Biberwier luge is the longest in Austria—4,000 feet. The concrete course banks on the corners, and even a first-timer can go very, very fast. Most are careful their first run and really rip on their second. To avoid a slow-healing souvenir, keep both hands on your stick. You'll rumble, windblown and smile-creased, across the finish line with one thought on your mind—"Do it again!"

A Swiss cliffhanger of a hideaway: Berggasthaus Ascher on Ebenalp

For a slower but just as invigorating activity, join the people of **Bern** for a midday float through their city on the Aare River. The lunchtime float is a popular tradition in the Swiss capital. Local merchants, legislators, publishers, and students, proud of their clean river and their basic ruddiness, grab every hot summer opportunity to enjoy this wet and refreshing *paseo*. Join the locals in the ritual 20-minute hike upstream from the Swiss National Parliament building, then float playfully or sleepily back down to the excellent and free riverside baths and pool (Aarebad). If the river is a bit much, spectating is fun, and you're welcome to enjoy just the pool.

Switzerland's Appenzell is a region whose forte is cow culture rather than staggering peaks. It has one famous mountain, the 8,200-foot-high Säntis Peak. For a fun angle on Alpine culture, go five miles south of Appenzell town to Wasserauen, and ride the lift to the top of nearby **Ebenalp** ($12 round-trip). From its summit, enjoy a sweeping view of a major chunk of Switzerland. Then hike down about 15 minutes to a prehistoric cave home (its tiny museum is always open). Wander in and through until you reach a narrow, sunny ledge. Perched here is the Wildkirchli, a 400-year-old cave church that housed hermit monks from 1658 to 1853, and a guest house, Berggasthaus Ascher, clinging precariously to the cliffside. This rugged guest house was originally built to accommodate those who came here to pray with the hermit monk.

Rather than sleep in the unmemorable town of Appenzell, stay in the Berggasthaus Ascher ($10 per dorm bed, blankets but no sheets required or provided, $6 breakfast, Family Knechtle-Wyss, 9057 Weissbad, 12 minutes by steep trail below top of lift, open May–October, tel. 071/799-1142). This old house has only rainwater and no shower. The goats live in a neighboring hut. The Berggasthaus is often festive (locals party until the wee hours on weekends) and often quiet. While it can—and on Saturday, often does—sleep 40 people (four hikers to three mattresses on a crowded night), you'll normally get a small woody dorm to yourself. The hut is actually built onto the cliffside; the back wall is the rock. Study the Alpine architecture from the toilet. Sip your coffee on the deck, behind a fairy's curtain of water dripping from the gnarly overhang a hundred yards above. Leave me a note in the guest book, which goes back 50 years.

From this perch you can almost hear the cows munching on the far side of the valley. In the distance, below Säntis, an hour's walk away, is your destination, the Seealpsee (lake) and Wasserauen. Only the parasailers, like neon jellyfish, tag your world 20th-century.

Along with staggering mountains, Switzerland is loved for its delicious chocolates. All day long, rivers of molten chocolate work their
way through factories into small foil packages. While **Swiss chocolate
factories** generally give tours only to business clients or visiting groups,
many have "museums," showrooms, video presentations, and free tasting rooms where individuals are welcome. With a little creative persis-
tence, you may be able to telephone and latch onto a scheduled group
visit. Try the Caillers Chocolate factory in Broc, just north of
Lausanne, in French Switzerland (open Monday–Friday, April–June,
August–mid-November; tel. 026/921-5151; call one day in advance to
reserve).

The **Bunker Furigen, Museum of War History** (Festung
Furigen das Museum zur Wehrgeschichte) offers a rare glimpse into
Swiss military preparedness. To protect its people in case of attack, this
little country has built 20,000 bunkers into the sides of the Alps. The
Festung Furigen, built during WWII, is the only bunker open to the
public. Tour the kitchen, hospital, dorms, and machine-gun nests (open
daily except Monday, April–October, 11:00 a.m.–5:00 p.m., tel.
041/610-9525). It's in Stansstad on Lake Luzern, a 10-minute train ride
from Luzern.

Imagine a fine Bavarian Baroque church at a monastery that serves
hearty food and the best beer in Germany in a carnival setting full of
partying locals. That's the **Andechs monastery**, hiding happily
between two lakes at the foot of the Alps, just south of Munich. Come
with an appetite because the food is great and served in medieval pro-
portions: chunks of tender pork chainsawed especially for you, huge
and soft pretzels (the best I've had), spiraled white radishes, savory
sauerkraut, and Andecher beer that lives up to its reputation.

My favorite map hangs as an eight-foot-by-two-foot poster in my
office. It's a pictorial view of the Alps, looking south from an imaginary
perch high above Germany, arcing from Vienna to Marseilles. As I gaze
at it, I can almost see, hear, feel, and taste the endless natural and cultural charms that can be called Alpine.

British Isles

45. London: A Warm Look at a Cold City

I've spent more time in London than in any other European city. It lacks the grandeur of Rome, the warmth of Munich, the coffee of Seattle, and the elegance of Paris, but its history, traditions, people, markets, museums, and entertainment keep drawing me back.

London Town has changed dramatically in recent years, and many visitors are surprised to find how "un-English" it is. Whites are a minority in major parts of a city that once symbolized white imperialism. Arabs have nearly bought out the area north of Hyde Park. Chinese takeouts outnumber fish-and-chips shops. Many hotels are run by people with foreign accents, while outlying suburbs are home to huge communities of Indians and Pakistanis. London is learning—sometimes fitfully—to live as a microcosm of its former worldwide empire.

An urban jungle sprawling over 600 square miles with 7 million struggling people, a world in itself, a barrage on all the senses, and a first stop for many travelers, London can be overwhelming. On my first visit I felt very, very small. Here are a few ideas to soften and warm this hard and cold city.

Get oriented by taking the 90-minute London Sightseeing Tour—the best possible fast and cheap introduction to London. Buses leave regularly from Piccadilly Circus, Marble Arch, and Victoria Station. Every other bus comes with a live guide . . . worth waiting for. This $20 open-top double-decker bus tour shows you most of the major landmarks and gives you a feel for the city. While several companies claim to be the "original," it's very competitive, and they're all about the same.

On your first evening in London, give yourself a brief "London-by-night" walking tour. If you just flew in, this is an ideal way to fight jet lag. Catch a bus to the first stop across (east of) Westminster Bridge. Walk downstream along the Jubilee Promenade for a capital view. Then, for that "Wow, I'm really in London!" feeling, cross the bridge to view the floodlit Houses of Parliament and Big Ben up close.

To thrill your loved ones (or stoke their envy), call home from a pay phone near Big Ben at about three minutes before the hour. As Big Ben chimes, stick the receiver outside the booth and prove you're in London: ding dong ding dong . . . dong ding ding dong.

Then cross Whitehall, noticing the Churchill statue in the park.

Have you tried London lately?

(He's electrified to avoid the pigeon problem that stains so many other great statues.) Walk up Whitehall toward Trafalgar Square. Stop at the barricaded and guarded little Downing Street to see #10, home of the British prime minister. Chat with the bored bobby. From Trafalgar, walk to pop-hopping Leicester Square and continue to youth-on-the-rampage Piccadilly, through safely sleazy Soho (north of Shaftesbury Avenue) up to Oxford Street. From Piccadilly or Oxford Circus you can taxi, bus, or subway home.

To grasp the city comfortably, see it as the old town without the modern, congested, and seemingly endless sprawl. After all, most of the visitors' London lies between the Tower of London and Hyde Park—about a three-mile walk.

Nibble on London one historic snack at a time by taking any of a series of focused, two-hour walking tours of the city. For about $8, local historians take small groups for a good look at one page of the London story. You can choose from topics such as London's plague, Dickens' London, Roman Londinium, Legal London, the Beatles in London, or Jack the Ripper's London (which, even though guides admit is a lousy walk, is the most popular). Pub Crawl walks are also a hit. Some walks focus on the various "villages" of London, such as trendy Chelsea and stately, impressed-with-itself Belgravia.

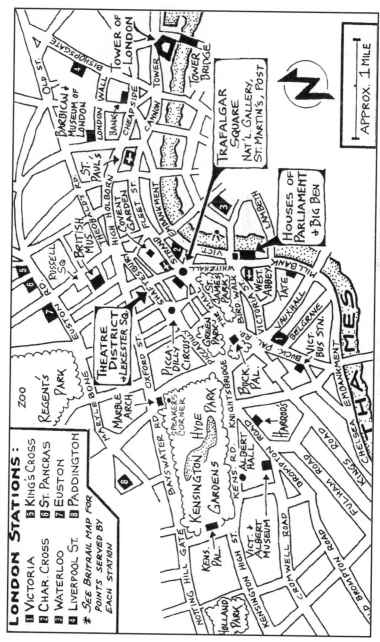

CENTRAL LONDON

LONDON STATIONS:

1 VICTORIA   5 KING'S CROSS
2 CHAR. CROSS   6 ST. PANCRAS
3 WATERLOO   7 EUSTON
4 LIVERPOOL ST.   8 PADDINGTON

* SEE BRITRAIL MAP FOR
  POINTS SERVED BY
  EACH STATION

APPROX. 1 MILE

TRAFALGAR SQUARE
NAT'L. GALLERY,
ST. MARTIN'S, POST

HOUSES OF
PARLIAMENT
+ BIG BEN

THEATRE
DISTRICT
+LEICESTER SQ.

The most central square mile of London—and all of Britain—is "The City." This is London's Wall Street. Nearby, traditional British justice is on display at the Central Criminal Courts, nicknamed Old Bailey. Powdered wigs, black capes, and age-old courtesies, my Lord, make the public trials quite entertaining. While churning with briskly walking black-suited people with tightly wrapped umbrellas during the business day, almost nobody actually lives in "The City." It's a desolate ghost town on Saturdays and Sundays.

The newly renovated National Gallery, showing off Britain's top collection of European paintings by masters such as Leonardo, Botticelli, Velazquez, Rembrandt, Turner, the Impressionists, and van Gogh, is now one of Europe's classiest galleries. Don't miss the "Micro Gallery," a high-tech computer room even your low-tech dad could enjoy. You can study any artist, style, or topic in the museum and even print out a museum tour map tailor-made to your interests. The National Portrait Gallery, just around the corner, is about as exciting as somebody else's yearbook.

The Tate Gallery, with its wonderful collection of British art (particularly works by Blake, Turner, and the pre-Raphaelites), Impressionists, and off-the-wall modern art, is a must. Sophisticated art historians patiently take rank beginners by the hand on free tours throughout the day.

History buffs enjoy the Museum of London. It offers a well-organized trip through time—from the swords of Roman Londinium to the bombs of World War II. For more on the war, Churchill's underground headquarters, the Cabinet War Rooms, about two blocks from Big Ben, give you a feel for London's darkest days and finest hour.

For megatons of things military, the impressive Imperial War Museum covers the wars of this century. You'll see heavy weaponry, love notes, Varga Girls, Monty's Africa campaign tank, and Schwartzkopf's Desert Storm uniform. Trace the development of the machine gun, push a computer button to watch footage of the first tank battles, and hold your breath through the gruesome "WWI trench experience." You can even buy WWII-era toys. The museum doesn't glorify war but chronicles the sweeping effects of humanity's most destructive century.

London's latest blockbuster museum, the Museum of the Moving Image, is just down the road. This high-tech, interactive, hands-on museum traces the story of moving images, from the caveman whirling a flaming stick to modern TV. Watch great footage of the earliest movies and TV shows. Turn-of-the-century-clad staff speak as if silent films are the latest marvel.

The British love their gardens, especially the peaceful and relaxing Kew Gardens. Cruise down the Thames or take the subway to Kew for plants galore, a respite from the city, and a good look at the British people. Don't miss the famous Palm House, built of glass and filled with exotic tropical plant life. A walk through this hothouse is a veritable swing through the tropics—in London.

Nearly every morning you can find a thriving market. There are markets for fish, fruit, used cars, antiques, clothing, and plenty of other things. Portobello Road (antiques on Saturday mornings) and Camden Lock (hip crafts and miscellany, Saturday and Sunday 9:00 a.m. to 6:00 p.m.) are just two of the many colorful markets that offer you great browsing. Don't expect great prices. These days, the only people getting a steal at London's markets are the pickpockets.

On Sunday enjoy an hour of craziness at Speaker's Corner in Hyde Park. By noon there are usually several soapbox speakers, screamers, singers, Communists, or comics performing to the crowd of onlookers. If you catch the London double-decker bus tour from Speaker's Corner Sunday at 10:00 a.m., you'll return at noon for the prime-time action. Sundays are otherwise frustrating sightseeing days in London, as most major museums are open only from 2:00 p.m. to 5:00 p.m.

No visit to London is complete without spending some time in one of its woody, smoky pubs. They are an integral part of the English culture. You'll find all kinds of pubs, each with its own personality. Taste the different beers. If you don't know what to order, ask the bartender for a half-pint of his or her favorite. Real ale, pumped by hand from the basement (look for the longest handles on the bar), is every connoisseur's choice. For a basic American-type beer, ask for a lager. Children are welcome in most pubs but will not be served alcohol until they are 18. Order some "pub grub" and talk to the people—enjoy a public house.

London's great theater is as good as (and cheaper than) New York's Broadway. Choose from the Royal Shakespeare Company, top musicals, comedy, thrillers, sex farces, and more. Over the years I've enjoyed *Harvey,* starring James Stewart, *The King and I,* with Yul Brynner, *My Fair Lady, A Chorus Line, Cats, Starlight Express,* and *Les Miserables.* Performances are nightly except Sunday, usually with one matinee a week. Matinees are cheaper and rarely sell out. Tickets range from about $12 to $40. Most theaters are marked on the tourist maps and cluster in the Piccadilly-Trafalgar area.

Unless you want this year's smash hit, getting a ticket is easy. The "Theater Guide" (free at any hotel or tourist office) lists everything in town. Once you've decided on a show, call the theater directly, ask about seat availability and prices, and book a ticket using your credit card. Pick up your ticket 20 minutes before show time. You can even book tickets from the U.S. before your trip. Call the British Tourist Authority (tel. 800/462-2748) for the schedule or photocopy it from the London newspaper at your library.

Ticket agencies, which charge a standard 20 to 25 percent booking fee, are scalpers with an address. Agencies are worthwhile only if a show you've just got to see is sold out at the box office. Various ticket agencies scarf up hot tickets, planning to make a killing after the show is otherwise sold out. U.S.A. booking agencies get their tickets from another agency, adding to your expense by involving yet another middleman.

Cheap theater tricks: Most theaters offer cheap returned tickets, matinees, standing room, and senior or student standby deals. Picking up a late return can get you a great seat at a cheap price. Standing room costs only a few pounds. If a show's "sold out," there's usually a way to get a seat. Call the theater and ask how. The famous "half-price booth" in Leicester (pronounced "lester") Square sells cheap day-of-the-show tickets to a very limited number of shows on the push list (2:30–6:30 p.m., Monday–Saturday, no phone). I usually buy the second-cheapest tickets directly from the theater box office. Many theaters are so small that there's hardly a bad seat. "Scooting up" later on is less than a capital offense. (Shakespeare did it.)

See the Appendix (Recommended Accommodations) for more information.

46. Bath: England at Its Elegant and Frivolous Best

Two hundred years ago, this city of 80,000 was the Hollywood of Britain. Today the former trendsetter of Georgian England invites you to take the 90-minute train ride from London and sample its aristocratic charms. Enjoy violins with your tea, discover the antique of your dreams, and trade your jungle of stress for a stroll through the garden.

If ever a city enjoyed looking in the mirror, Bath's the one. It has more government-protected buildings per capita than any town in England. The entire city is built of a warm-tone limestone it calls "Bath stone." The use of normal bricks is forbidden, and Bath beams in its cover-girl complexion.

In Bath, even the street musicians play a Georgian beat.

Bath is an architectural chorus line. It's a triumph of the Georgian style (British for neoclassical), with buildings as competitively elegant as the society they housed. If you look carefully, you'll see false windows built in the name of balance (but not used, in the name of tax avoidance) and classical columns that supported only Georgian egos. Two centuries ago, rich women wore feathered hats atop three-foot hairdos. The very rich stretched their doors and ground floors to accommodate this high fashion. And today, many families have a tough time affording the cost of peeling the soot of the last century from these tall walls.

Few towns combine beauty and hospitality as well as Bath. If you don't visit the tourist office, it'll visit you. A tourist board crew, wearing red, white, and blue "visitor carer" T-shirts, roams the streets in search of tourists to help.

Bath's town square, a quick walk from the bus and train station, is a bouquet of tourist landmarks, including the Abbey, the Roman and medieval baths, the royal "Pump Room," and a Georgian flute player complete with powdered wig.

Experience the elegance of Bath by staying in one of its top bed and breakfasts. My favorite is Brock's Guest House. This $40-per-person splurge will be the rubber ducky of your Bath time. Marian Dodd, who can say "right-o" and sound natural, just redid her 1765 home. It's quiet and friendly and couldn't be better located, at 32 Brock Street, just between the Royal Crescent and the Circus (tel. 01225/338374, fax 01225/334245).

A good day in Bath starts with a tour of the historic baths. Even in Roman times, when the town was called Aquae Sulis, the hot mineral water attracted society's elite. The town's importance peaked in 973, when the first king of England, Edgar, was crowned in Bath's Anglo-Saxon Abbey. Bath reached a low ebb in the mid-1600s, when the town was just a huddle of huts around the Abbey and a hot springs with 3,000 residents oblivious to the Roman ruins 18 feet below their dirt floors. Then, in 1687, Queen Mary, fighting infertility, bathed here. Within 10 months she gave birth to a son . . . and a new age of popularity for Bath. The town boomed as a spa resort. Ninety percent of the buildings you see today are from the 18th century. Local architect John Wood was inspired by the Italian architect Palladio to build a "new Rome." The town bloomed in the neoclassical style, and streets were lined with wide "parades" rather than scrawny sidewalks, upon which the women in their stylishly wide dresses could spread their fashionable tails.

For a taste of aristocracy, enjoy tea and scones with live classical music in the nearby Pump Room. For the authentic, if repulsive, finale, have a sip of the awfully curative Bath water from the elegant fountain. To make as much sense as possible of all this fanciness, catch the free city walking tour that leaves from just outside the Pump Room door. Bath's volunteer guides are as much a part of Bath as its architecture. A walking tour gives your visit a little more intimacy, and you'll feel like you actually have a friend in Bath.

In the afternoon, stroll through three centuries of fashion in the Costume Museum. Follow the evolution of clothing styles, one decade at a time, from the first Elizabeth in the 16th century to the second Elizabeth today. The guided tour is excellent—full of fun facts and fascinating trivia. Haven't you always wondered what the line, "Stuck a feather in his cap and called it macaroni," from "Yankee Doodle" means? You'll find the answer (and a lot more) in Bath—the town whose narcissism is justified.

See the Appendix (Recommended Accommodations) for more information.

47. York: Vikings to Dickens

Historians run around York like kids in a candy shop. But the city is so fascinating that even nonhistorians find themselves exploring the past with the same delight they'd give a hall of fun-house mirrors.

Old World main street, York's Castle Museum

York is 200 miles north of London, only 90 minutes on British Rail. Start your visit by taking one of the entertaining and informative guided walking tours. These free walks, leaving morning, afternoon, and summer evenings from the tourist office, offer a practical introduction to the city. To keep the day open for museums and shopping and enjoy a quieter tour (with a splash of ghostly gore), take the evening walk. The excellent guides are likably chatty and opinionated. By the end of the walk, you'll know the latest York city gossip, several ghost stories, and which "monstrosity" the "insensitive" city planners are about to inflict on the public.

With this introductory tour under your belt, you're getting the hang of York and its history. Just as a Boy Scout counts the rings in a tree, you can count the ages of York by the different bricks in the city wall: Roman on the bottom, then Danish, Norman, and the "new" addition—from the 14th century.

The pride of the half-timbered town center is the medieval butcher's street called the Shambles, with its rusty old hooks hiding under the eaves. Six hundred years ago, bloody hunks of meat hung here, dripping into the gutter that still marks the middle of the lane. This slaughterhouse of commercial activity gave our language a new word. What was once a "shambles" is now ye olde tourist shopping mall.

York's four major sights—the York Castle Museum, the Jorvik Viking Museum, the best-in-Europe National Railway Museum, and the huge and historic York Minster church—can keep a speedy sightseer busy for two days.

York's Castle Museum is a walk with Charles Dickens. The England of the 18th and 19th centuries is cleverly saved and displayed in a huge collection of craft shops, old stores, living rooms, and other intimate glimpses of those bygone days.

As towns were being modernized in the 1930s, the museum's founder, Dr. Kirk, collected whole shops intact and reassembled them here. On Kirkgate, the museum's most popular section, you can wander through a Lincolnshire butcher's shop, Bath bakery, coppersmith's shop, toy shop, and barbershop.

The shops are actually stocked with the merchandise of the day. Eavesdrop on English grannies as they reminisce their way through the museum's displays. The general store is loaded with groceries and candy, and the sports shop has everything you'd need for a game of 19th-century archery, cricket, skittles, or tennis. Anyone for "whiff-whaff" (Ping-Pong)? In the confectionery, Dr. Kirk beams you into a mouth-watering world of "spice pigs," "togo bullets," "hum bugs," and "conversation lozenges."

In the period rooms, three centuries of Yorkshire living rooms and clothing fashions paint a cozy picture of life centered around the hearth. Ah, a peat fire warming a huge brass kettle and the aroma of fresh baked bread soaking into the heavy, open-beamed ceilings. After walking through the evolution of romantic valentines and unromantic billy clubs, you can trace the development of early home lighting—from simple waxy sticks into the age of electricity. An early electric heater has a small plaque explaining, "How to light an electric fire: Switch it on!"

Dr. Kirk's "memorable collection of bygones" is the closest thing in Europe to a time-tunnel experience, except perhaps for the Jorvik Viking Exhibit just down the street.

A thousand years ago, York was a thriving Viking settlement called Jorvik. While only traces are left of most Viking settlements, Jorvik is an archaeologist's bonanza, the best-preserved Viking city ever excavated.

Sail the "Pirates of the Caribbean" north and back in time 800 years, and you get Jorvik. More a ride than a museum, this exhibit drapes the abundant harvest of this dig in Disney cleverness. Rolling backward in a little train car for two, you descend a thousand years in time: past the ghosts and cobwebs of 50 generations. Cromwell . . .

Shakespeare . . . Anne Boleyn . . . William the Conqueror . . . and your car flips around. It's A.D. 995. You're in Jorvik.

Slowly you glide through the reconstructed village. Everything—sights, sounds, even smells—has been carefully re-created. You experience a Viking village.

Then your time-traveling train car rolls you into the excavation site, past the actual remains of the reconstructed village you just saw. Stubs of buildings, piles of charred wood, broken pottery—a time-crushed echo of a thriving town.

Your ride ends at the museum filled with artifacts from every aspect of Viking life: clothing, cooking, weapons, clever locks, jewelry, even children's games. The gift shop—the traditional finale of any English museum—has capitalized nicely on my newly developed fascination with Vikings in England.

In summer Jorvik's midday lines are more than an hour long. But early or late visitors (last entrance in summer is 7:00 p.m.) usually walk right in. Jorvik's commercial success has spawned a series of similar historic rides that take you into Britain's burly wax-peopled past. While innovative 10 years ago, Jorvik and its cousins seem tired and gimmicky today. For straightforward Viking artifacts, beautifully explained and set in historical context with no crowds at all, tour the nearby Yorkshire Museum.

York's thunderous National Railway Museum shows 150 fascinating years of British railroad history. Fanning out from a grand round-house is an array of historic cars and engines, including Queen Victoria's lavish royal car and the very first "stagecoaches on rails." Even spouses of train buffs will find the exhibits on dining cars, post cars, Pullman cars, and vintage train posters interesting.

York's minster, or cathedral, is the largest Gothic church in Britain. Henry VIII, in his self-serving religious fervor, destroyed nearly everything that was Catholic—except the great York Minster. Henry needed a northern capital for his Anglican church.

The minster is a brilliant example of how the high Middle Ages were far from dark. The east window, the largest medieval glass window in existence, is just one of the art treasures explained in the free hour-long tours given throughout the day. The church's undercroft gives you a chance to climb down, archaeologically and physically, through the centuries to see the roots of the much smaller but still huge Norman church (built in A.D. 1100) that stood on this spot and, below that, the Roman excavations. Constantine was proclaimed Roman emperor here in A.D. 306. The undercroft also gives you a look at the modern concrete and stainless steel save-the-church foundations.

To fully experience the cathedral, go for an evensong service. (No offering plates, no sermon; 5:00 p.m. almost nightly, 4 p.m. on Saturday and Sunday; usually spoken, not sung, on Wednesday and Saturday.) Arrive early and ask to be seated in the choir. You're in the middle of a spiritual Oz as 40 boys sing psalms—a red-and-white-robed pillow of praise, raised up by the powerful pipe organ. You've got elephant-sized ears as the beautifully carved choir stalls, functioning as giant sound scoops, magnify the grunting and trumpeting pipes. If you're lucky the organist will run a spiritual musical victory lap as the congregation breaks up. Thank God for York. Amen.

See the Appendix (Recommended Accommodations) for more information.

48. Blackpool: Britain's Coney Island

Blackpool, England's tacky glittering city of fun, with a six-mile beach promenade, is ignored by American guidebooks. Located on the coast north of Liverpool, it's the private playground of North England's Anne and Andy Capps.

When I told Brits I was Blackpool-bound, their expressions soured and they asked, "Oh, God, why?" Because it's the ears-pierced-while-you-wait, tipsy-toupee place that local widows and workers go to year after year to escape. Tacky, yes. Lowbrow, OK. But it's as English as can be, and that's what I'm after. Give yourself a vacation from your sightseeing vacation. Spend a day just "muckin' about" in Blackpool.

Blackpool is dominated by the Blackpool Tower—a giant fun center that seems to grunt, "have fun." You pay about $10 to get in, and after that the fun is free. Work your way up from the bottom through layer after layer of noisy entertainment: circus, bug zone, space world, dinosaur center, aquarium, and the silly house of horrors. Have a coffee break in the elegant ballroom festooned with golden oldies barely dancing to barely live music. The finale at the tip of this 500-foot-tall symbol of Blackpool is a smashing view, especially at sunset. The Tower, a stubby version of its more famous Parisian cousin, was painted gold in 1994 to celebrate its 100th birthday.

Hop a vintage trolley car to survey Blackpool's beach promenade. The cars, which rattle constantly up and down the waterfront, are more fun than driving. Each of the three amusement piers has its own personality. Are you feeling sedate (north pier), young and frisky (central pier), or like a cowboy dragging a wagon full of children (south pier)?

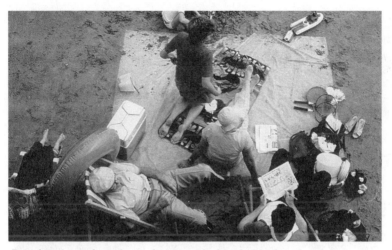

British trying to have fun in the sun at the beach, Blackpool

Stroll the Promenade. A million greedy doors try every trick to get you inside. Huge arcade halls advertise free toilets and broadcast bingo numbers into the streets. The wind machine under a wax Marilyn Monroe blows at a steady gale, and the smell of fries, tobacco, and sugared popcorn billows everywhere. Milk comes in raspberry or banana in this land where people under incredibly bad wigs look normal. I was told I mustn't leave without having my fortune told by a Gypsy-type spiritualist, but at $4 per palm, I'll read them myself.

Don't miss an evening at an old-time variety show. Blackpool always has a few razzle-dazzle music, dancing girl, racy humor, magic, and tumbling shows ($7 to $15 tickets at the door). I enjoy the "old-time music hall" shows. The shows are corny—neither hip nor polished—but it's fascinating to be surrounded by hundreds of partying British seniors, swooning again and waving their hankies to the predictable beat. Busloads of happy widows come from all corners of North England to giggle at jokes I'd never tell my grandma.

Blackpool's "Illuminations" are the talk of England every late September and October. Blackpool (the first city in England to "go electric") stretches its season by illuminating its six-mile waterfront with countless blinking and twinkling lights. The American inside me kept saying, "I've seen bigger and I've seen better," but I stuffed him with cotton candy and just had some simple fun like everyone else on my specially decorated tram.

For a fun forest of amusements, "Pleasure Beach" is tops. These 42 acres of rides (more than 80, including "the best selection of white-knuckle rides in Europe"), ice-skating shows, cabarets, and amusements attract 6 million people a year, making Pleasure Beach England's most popular single attraction. Their new roller coaster is the world's highest (235 feet), fastest (85 mph), and least likely to have me on board.

For me, Blackpool's top sight is its people. You'll see England here like nowhere else. Grab someone's hand and a big stick of candy floss (cotton candy) and stroll. Ponder the thought that legions of English dream of actually retiring here to spend their last years, day after day, dog-paddling through this urban cesspool of fun, wearing hats with built-in ponytails.

Blackpool is in the business of accommodating the English who can't afford to go to Spain. Its 140,000 residents provide 120,000 beds in 3,500 mostly dumpy, cheap, nondescript hotels and B&Bs. Almost all have the same design—minimal character, maximum number of springy beds—and charge $15 to $20 per person, including "a plate of cardiac arrest" for breakfast.

Blackpool is a scary thing to recommend. Maybe I overrate it. Many people (ignoring the "50 million flies can't all be wrong" logic) think I do. If you're not into kitsch and greasy spoons (especially if you're a nature lover and the weather happens to be good), skip

Blackpool and spend more time in nearby North Wales or England's Lake District. But if you're traveling with kids—or still are one yourself—visit Blackpool, Britain's fun puddle where every Englishman goes, but none will admit it.

See the Appendix (Recommended Accommodations) for more information.

49. The Cotswold Villages: Inventors of Quaint

The Cotswold region, a 25-by-50-mile chunk of Gloucestershire, is a sightseeing treat: crisscrossed with hedgerows, raisined with storybook villages, and sprinkled with sheep.

As with many fairy-tale regions of Europe, the present-day beauty of the Cotswolds was the result of an economic disaster. Wool was a huge industry in medieval England, and the Cotswold sheep grew it best. Wool money built lovely towns and houses as the region prospered. Local "wool" churches are called "cathedrals" for their scale and wealth. A typical prayer etched into their stained glass reads, "I thank my God and ever shall, it is the sheep hath paid for all."

With the rise of cotton and the Industrial Revolution, the woolen industry collapsed, mothballing the Cotswold towns into a depressed

Cotswold village signpost

THE COTSWOLDS

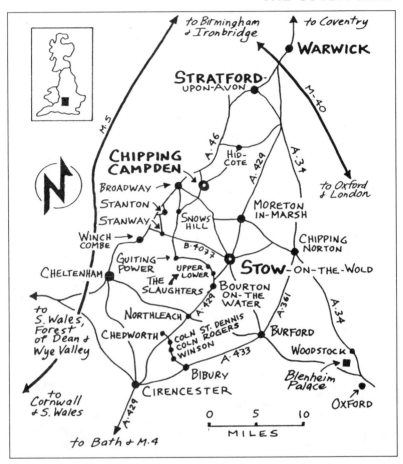

time warp. The villages were so poor that nobody even bothered to knock them down. Today visitors enjoy a harmonious blend of humanity and nature—the most pristine of English countrysides decorated with time-passed villages, rich wool churches, tell-me-a-story stone fences, "kissing gates" you wouldn't want to experience alone, and the gracefully dilapidated homes of an impoverished nobility. Appreciated by hordes of 20th-century romantics (in spite of local moaning about "the recession"), the Cotswolds are enjoying new prosperity.

The area is provincial. Chatty locals, while ever so polite, commonly rescue themselves from a gossipy tangent by saying, "It's all very . . . ummm . . . yyya." Rich people open their gardens to support their favorite charities, while the less couth enjoy "badger baiting" (a gambling cousin of cock fighting where a badger, with its teeth and claws taken out, is mangled by right-wing dogs).

The north Cotswolds are best. Moreton-in-Marsh, a workaday village, is the public transportation gateway to the region. Two of the region's coziest towns, Stow-on-the-Wold and Chipping Campden, are four and eight miles respectively from Moreton. Any of these three towns makes a fine home base for your exploration of the thatch-happiest of Cotswold villages and walks. Stanway, Stanton, and Snowshill, between Stow and Chipping Campden, are my nominations for the cutest Cotswold villages. Like marshmallows in hot chocolate, they nestle side by side—awaiting your arrival.

Stow-on-the-Wold—Eight roads converge on Stow-on-the-Wold, but none interrupts the peaceful main square. Stow has become a crowded tourist town, but most visitors are day-trippers, so even summer nights are lazy and quiet. The town has no real sights other than itself, some good pubs, cutesy shops, and art galleries draped seductively around a big town square. The tourist office sells a handy 25p walking tour brochure called "Town Trail." A visit to Stow is not complete until you've locked your partner in the stocks on the green.

Imprisoned by the charm of the Cotswolds

Chipping Campden—Ten miles north of Stow and less touristy, Chipping Campden is a working market town, home of some proudly thatched roofs and the richest Cotswold wool merchants. Both the great British historian Trevelyan and I call Chipping Campden's High Street the finest in England.

Walk the full length of High Street (like most market towns, wide enough for plenty of sheep business on market days). Near the south end you'll find the best thatched homes. Walking north on High Street, you'll pass the Market Hall (1627), the wavy roof of the first great wool mansion, a fine and free memorial garden, and, finally, the town's famous 15th-century Gothic "wool" church.

Chipping Campden's comically pathetic tourist office (which will send you to the post office to buy a photocopied town map) bounces here and there along High Street as it endures the wrath of frustrated local B&B owners and lost tourists.

Moreton-in-Marsh—A fine home base for those without a car, Moreton is a Chipping Campden without the touristic sugar. Rather than gift and antique stores, you'll find streets lined with real shops. Ironmongers sell cottage nameplates, and carpet shops are strewn with the remarkable patterns that decorate B&B floors. A traditional market filling High Street with 260 stalls gets the whole town shin-kicking each Tuesday. There is an economy outside of tourism in the Cotswolds, and you'll feel it in Moreton.

Stanway—While not much of a village, Stanway is notable for its manor house. Lord Neidpath, whose family tree charts relatives back to 1270, opens his melancholy home—Stanway House—to visitors (2:00–5:00 p.m. Tuesday and Thursday, June–September, other times by appointment, $6, tel. 01386/584469).

While his bitchin' 14th-century Tithe Barn is no longer used to greet motley peasants with their feudal "rents," the lord still collects rents from his vast land holdings. But the place feels poor, his children live in London, and those invited to his parties don't even RSVP.

Guests loiter in his office—littered with bills—and rummage through centuries of oil on canvas, black and white, and Kodak moments. There's a likable Old World elegance about the place. While the manor dogs have their own cutely painted "family tree," Lord Neidpath admits that his current dog is "all character and no breeding."

The place has a story to tell. And so do the docents (modern-day peasants who, even without family trees, probably have relatives going back just as far in this village) stationed in each room. Talk to these people. Probe. That's what they're there for. Learn what you can about this side of England.

Stanway and neighboring Stanton are separated by a great oak forest and grazing land with parallel waves echoing the furrows plowed by medieval farmers. Let someone else drive so you can pop out of the sunroof like a balloon—under an oak canopy, past stone walls and sheep—to Stanton.

Stanton—Flowers trumpet, knockers shine, and slate shingles clap—a rooting section cheering visitors up Stanton's main street. The church, which dates to the ninth century, betrays a pagan past. Stanton is at the intersection of two lines (called ley lines) connecting prehistoric sights. Churches like Stanton's, built on a pagan holy ground, are dedicated to St. Michael. You'll see his well-worn figure above the door as you enter. Inside, above the capitals in the nave, find the pagan symbols for the moon and the sun. But it's Son-worship that's long-established, and the list of rectors goes back to 1269. Finger the back pew grooves, worn away by sheepdog leashes. A man's sheepdog accompanied him everywhere. The popular Mount Pub is just up the hill (easy parking, indoor/outdoor seating, decent lunches, real ale).

Snowshill—Another nearly edible little bundle of cuteness, Snowshill village has a photogenic triangular square with a fine pub at its base. The Snowshill Manor is a dark and mysterious old palace filled with the lifetime collection of Charles Paget Wade (who looks eerily like the tragic young Lord Neidpath of Stanway House). It's one big musty celebration of craftsmanship, from finely carved spinning wheels to frightening Samurai armor to tiny elaborate figurines carved by long-forgotten prisoners from the bones of meat served at dinner. Taking seriously his family motto, "Let Nothing Perish," he dedicated his life and fortune to preserving things finely crafted. The house (whose management made me promise not to promote it as an eccentric collector's pile of curiosities) really shows off Mr. Wade's ability to recognize and acquire fine examples of craftsmanship. It's all very . . . ummm . . . yyya.

The Cotswolds are walker country. The English love to walk the peaceful footpaths that shepherds walked back when "polyester" meant two girls. They vigorously defend their age-old right to free passage. Once a year the "Rambling Society" organizes a "Mass Trespass," when each of England's 50,000 miles of public footpaths is walked. By assuring each path is used at least once a year, they frustrate fence-happy landlords. Most of the land is privately owned and fenced in, but you're welcome (and legally entitled) to pass through, using the various sheep-stopping steps, gates, and turnstiles provided at each stone wall.

After a well-planned visit, you'll remember everything about the Cotswolds—the walks, churches, pubs, B&Bs, thatched roofs, gates, tourist offices, and even the sheep—as quaint.

See the Appendix (Recommended Accommodations) for more information.

50. Mysterious Britain

Stonehenge, Holy Grail, Avalon, Loch Ness . . . there's a mysterious side of Britain steeped in lies, legends, and at least a little truth. Haunted ghost walks and Nessie the Monster stories are profitable tourist gimmicks. But the cultural soil that gives us *Beowulf*, Shakespeare, and "God Save the Queen" is fertilized with a murky story that goes back to 3000 B.C., predating Egypt's first pyramids.

As today's sightseers zip from castle to pub, they pass countless stone circles, forgotten tombs, manmade hills, and figures carved into hillsides whose stories will never be fully understood. Of course, certain traveling Druids skip the Beefeater tours and zero right in on this side of Britain. But with a little background on this slice of the British pie, even the complete skeptic or novice can appreciate Britain's historic aura.

Britain is crisscrossed by lines connecting prehistoric Stonehenge-type sights. Apparently prehistoric tribes intentionally built sites along this huge network of lines, called ley lines, which may somehow have functioned together as a cosmic relay or circuit.

Glastonbury, two hours west of London and located on England's most powerful ley line, gurgles with a thought-provoking mix of history and mystery. As you climb the legend-soaked, conical hill called Glastonbury Tor, notice the remains of the labyrinth that made the hill a challenge to climb 5,000 years ago.

In A.D. 37, Joseph of Arimathea brought vessels containing the blood and sweat of Jesus to Glastonbury and, with that, Christianity to England. While this is "proven" by fourth-century writings and accepted by the Church, the Holy Grail legend which sprang from this in the Middle Ages isn't.

In the 12th century, England needed a morale-boosting folk hero to inspire its people during a war with France. The ruins of a fifth-century Celtic timber fort at Glastonbury were considered proof of the greatness of that century's obscure warlord Arthur. After his supposed remains were found buried in the abbey, Glastonbury became linked

MYSTERIOUS BRITAIN

with King Arthur and his knights. Arthur's search for the Holy Grail, the chalice used at the Last Supper, could be mere legend. But many people think the Grail trail ends at the bottom of the "Chalice Well," a natural spring at the base of Glastonbury Tor.

In the 16th century, Henry VIII recognized the powerful Glastonbury Abbey as a bastion of the church he fought, so he destroyed it. For emphasis he hung and quartered the abbot, sending the parts of his body to four different towns. While that was it for the abbot, two centuries later Glastonbury rebounded. In an 18th-century tourism campaign, thousands signed affidavits stating that water from the Chalice Well healed them, and once again Glastonbury was on the tourist map.

Today Glastonbury and its Tor are a center for searchers, too creepy for the mainstream church but just right for those looking for a place to recharge their crystals. Since the society that built the labyrinth worshipped a mother goddess, the hill, or Tor, is seen by many today as a Mother Goddess symbol.

After climbing the Tor (great view, easy parking, always open), visit the Chalice Well at its base. Then tour the evocative ruins of the abbey, with its informative visitor's center and a model of the church before Henry got to it. Don't leave without a browse through the town. The Rainbow's End Café (two minutes from the abbey on High Street) is a fine place for salads and New Age people-watching. Read the notice board for the latest on midwives and male bonding.

From Glastonbury, as you drive across southern England, you'll see giant figures carved on hillsides. The white chalk cliffs of Dover stretch across the south of England, and almost anywhere you dig you hit chalk. While most of the giant figures are creations of 18th- and 19th-century humanists reacting against the coldness of the industrial age, three Celtic figures (the Long Man of Willmington, the White Horse of Uffington, and the Cerne Abbas Giant) have, as far as history is concerned, always been there.

The Cerne Abbas Giant is armed with a big club and an erection. For centuries, people fighting infertility would sleep on Cerne Abbas. And, as my English friend explained, "maidens can still be seen leaping over his willy."

Stonehenge is surrounded by barbed wire. This is as close as you'll get.

Stonehenge, England's most famous stone circle, is an hour's drive from Glastonbury. Built between 3100 and 1100 B.C. with huge stones brought all the way from Wales or Ireland, it still functions as a remarkably accurate celestial calendar. A recent study of more than 300 similar circles in Britain found that each was designed to calculate the movement of the sun, moon, and stars, and even to predict eclipses in order to help these early societies know when to plant, harvest, and party. Even today, as the summer solstice sun sets in just the right slot at Stonehenge, pagans boogie. Modern-day tourists and Druids are kept at a distance by a fence, but if you're driving, Stonehenge is just off the highway and worth a stop ($5). Even a free look from the road is impressive.

Why didn't the builders of Stonehenge use what seem like perfectly adequate stones nearby? There's no doubt that the particular "blue stones" used in parts of Stonehenge were found only in (and therefore brought from) Wales or Ireland. Think about the ley lines. Ponder the fact that many experts accept none of the explanations of how these giant stones were transported. Then imagine congregations gathering here 4,000 years ago, raising thought levels, creating a powerful life force transmitted along the ley lines. Maybe a particular kind of stone was essential for maximum energy transmission. Maybe the stones were levitated here. Maybe psychics really do create powerful vibes. Maybe not. It's as unbelievable as electricity used to be.

The nearby stone circle at **Avebury**, 16 times the size of Stonehenge, is one-sixteenth as touristy. You're free to wander among a hundred stones, ditches, mounds, and curious patterns from the past, as well as the village of Avebury, which grew up in the middle of this 1,400-foot-wide neolithic circle.

Spend some time at Avebury. Take the mile-long walk around the circle. Visit the fine little archaeology museum and pleasant Stones Café next to the National Trust store. The Red Lion Pub (also within the circle) has good, inexpensive pub grub. As you leave, notice the pyramid-shaped Silbury Hill. This manmade mound, nearly 5,000 years old, is a reminder that you've only scratched the surface of Britain's fascinating prehistoric and religious landscape.

A fine way to mix neolithic wonders and nature is to explore one of England's many turnstile-free moors. You can get lost in these stark and sparsely populated time-passed commons, which have changed over the centuries about as much as the longhaired sheep that seem to gnaw on moss in their sleep. Directions are difficult to keep. It's cold and gloomy, as nature rises like a slow tide against human constructions. A crumpled castle loses itself in lush overgrowth. A church grows shorter as tall weeds eat at the stone crosses and bent tombstones.

Dartmoor is the wildest moor—a wonderland of green and powerfully quiet rolling hills in the southwest near the tourist centers of Devon and Cornwall. Crossed by only two or three main roads, most of the area is either unused or shared by its 30,000 villagers as a common grazing land—a tradition since feudal days. Dartmoor is best toured by car, but it can be explored by bike, rental horse, thumb, or foot. Bus service is meager. Several national park centers provide maps and information. Settle into a small-town B&B or hostel. This is one of England's most remote corners—and it feels that way.

Dartmoor, with more Bronze Age stone circles and huts than any other chunk of England, is perfect for those who dream of enjoying their own private Stonehenge sans barbed wire, policemen, parking lots, tourists, and port-a-loos (English sani-cans). The local Ordnance Survey maps show the moor peppered with bits of England's mysterious past. Hator Down and Gidleigh are especially thought-provoking.

Word of the wonders lurking just a bit deeper into the moors tempted me away from my Gidleigh B&B. Venturing in, I sank into the powerful, mystical moorland. Climbing over a hill, surrounded by hateful but sleeping towers of ragged granite, I was swallowed up. Hills followed hills followed hills—green, growing gray in the murk.

Where was that 4,000-year-old circle of stone? I wandered in a world of greenery, eerie wind, white rocks, and birds singing but unseen. Then the stones appeared, frozen in a forever game of statue-maker. For endless centuries they had waited, patiently, for me to come. Still and silent, they entertained.

I sat on a fallen stone, holding the leash as my imagination ran wild, pondering the people who roamed England so long before written history documented their story. Grabbing the moment to write, I took out my journal. The moor, the distant town, the chill, this circle of stones. I dipped my pen into the cry of the birds and wrote.

51. Dingle Peninsula: A Gaelic Bike Ride

Be forewarned, Ireland is seductive. In many areas, traditions are strong and stress is a foreign word. I fell in love with the friendliest land this side of Sicily. It all happened in a Gaeltacht.

Gaeltachts are national parks for culture, where the government protects the old Irish ways. Shaded green on many maps, these regions brighten the west coast of the Emerald Isle. "Gaeltacht" means a place where Gaelic (or Irish) is spoken. The Gaelic culture is more than just the old language. You'll find it tilling the rocky fields, singing in the pubs, and lingering in the pride of the small town preschool that brags "all Irish."

Ireland's top attraction—the friendliest people in Europe

DINGLE PENINSULA

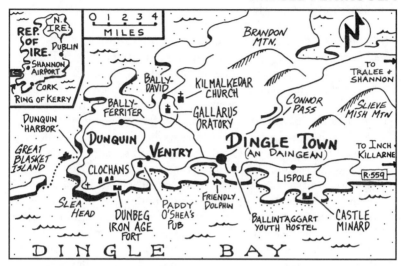

Many signposts are in Gaelic only, with the old Irish lettering. If your map is in English . . . good luck. The old-timers are a proud bunch. Often, when the signposts are in both English and Gaelic, the English is spraypainted out. And Irish yuppies report that in the 1990s, Gaelic is cool and on the rise.

Dingle Peninsula—green, rugged, and untouched—is my favorite Gaeltacht. While the big tour buses clog the neighboring Ring of Kerry before heading east to kiss the Blarney Stone, in Dingle it still feels like the fish and the farm actually matter. Fifty fishing boats sail from Dingle. And a nostalgic whiff of peat continues to fill its nighttime streets, offering visitors an escape into pure Ireland. For 15 years my Irish dreams have been set here, on this sparse but lush peninsula where locals are fond of saying, "the next parish is Boston."

Of the peninsula's 10,000 residents, 1,300 live in Dingle town. Its few streets, lined with ramshackle but gaily painted shops and pubs, run up from a rain-stung harbor. During the day, kids—already working on ruddy beer-glow cheeks—roll kegs up the streets and into the pubs in preparation for another tin whistle night.

Fishing once dominated Dingle, and the town's only visitors were students of old Irish ways. Then, in 1970, the movie *Ryan's Daughter* introduced the world to Dingle. The trickle of its fans has grown to a flood in the 1990s, as word has spread of its musical, historical, gastronomical, and scenic charms—not to mention the friendly dolphin who hangs out in the harbor.

THE DINGLE PENINSULA CIRCLE—BY BIKE OR CAR
The Dingle Peninsula is 10 miles wide and runs 40 miles from Tralee to Slea Head. The top of its mountainous spine is Mount Brandon—at 3,300 feet, the second tallest mountain in Ireland. While only tiny villages lie west of Dingle town, the peninsula is home to half a million sheep. The weather on this distant tip of Ireland is often misty, foggy, and rainy. But don't complain—as locals will explain, there is no bad weather . . . only inappropriate clothing. Good and bad weather blow by in a steady meteorological parade. With stops, the 30-mile circuit (go with the traffic—clockwise) takes five hours by bike or three hours by car.

Leaving Dingle town, it becomes clear that the peninsula is an open-air museum. It's littered with monuments reminding visitors that the town has been the choice of Bronze Age settlers, Dark Age monks, English landlords, and Hollywood directors. The Milestone B&B decorates its front yard not with a pink flamingo, but with a pillar stone—one of more than 2,000 stony pieces in the puzzle of prehistoric life here.

Across the bay, the manor house of Lord Ventry is surrounded by palms, magnolias, fuchsias, and fancy flora introduced to Dingle by the Englishman who once owned the peninsula. His legacy—thanks only to the mild Gulf Stream–protected weather—is the festival of fuchsias that lines the peninsula roads. And just down the street, locals point to the little blue house which kept Tom Cruise and Nicole Kiddman cozy during the filming of *Far and Away*.

Near a yellow schoolhouse, a Gaelic street sign warns, "Taisteaal go Mall"—slow down. Near the playground, students hide out in circular remains of a late Stone Age ring fort. In 500 B.C. it was a petty Celtic chieftain's headquarters, a stone and earth stockade filled with little stone houses. So many of these ring forts survived the centuries because of superstitious beliefs that they were "fairy forts."

In the little town of Ventry, talk with the chatty Irish you'll meet along the roadside. An elfish, black-clad Gaelic man might point out a landmark or sing you a song. When I asked if he were born here, he breathed deeply and said, "No, 'twas about six miles down the road." When I told him where I was from, a faraway smile filled his eyes as he looked out to sea and sighed, "Ah, the shores of Americay."

The wet sod of Dingle is soaked with medieval history. In the darkest depths of the Dark Ages, when literate life almost died in

Europe, peace-loving, bookwormish monks fled the chaos of the Continent and its barbarian raids. They sailed to this drizzly fringe of the known world and lived their monastic lives in lonely stone igloos or "beehive huts," which you'll see dotting the landscape.

Several groups of these mysterious huts, called *clochans*, line the road. Built without mortar by seventh-century monks, these huts take you back. Climb into one. You're all alone, surrounded by dank mist and the realization that it was these monks who kept literacy alive in Europe. To give you an idea of their importance, Charlemagne, who ruled much of Europe in the year 800, imported Irish monks to be his scribes.

It was from this peninsula that Saint Brandon, the semi-mythical priest-explorer, is said to have set sail in the sixth century in search of a legendary western paradise. Some think he beat Columbus to North America . . . by nearly a thousand years!

Rounding Slea Head, the point in Europe closest to America, the rugged coastline offers smashing views of deadly black-rock cliffs and the distant Blasket Islands. The crashing surf "races in like white horses," while long-haired sheep—bored with the weather, distant boats, and the lush countryside—couldn't care less.

Just off the road you'll see the scant remains of the scant home that was burned by the movie-star equivalent of Lord Ventry as he evicted his potato-eating tenants in the movie *Far and Away*.

Even without Hollywood, this is a bleak and godforsaken place. Ragged patches of reclaimed land climb the hillsides. Rocks were moved and piled into fences. Sand and seaweed heaped on the clay eventually became soil. The created land was marginal, just barely growing potatoes.

Study the highest fields, untouched since the planting of 1845, when the potatoes rotted in the ground. The vertical ridges of the potato beds can still be seen—a reminder of that year's great famine, which, through starvation or emigration, nearly halved Ireland's population.

The Gallarus Oratory, circa A.D. 800, is the sightseeing highlight of your peninsula tour. One of Ireland's best-preserved early Christian churches, its shape is reminiscent of an upturned boat. Take shelter within its watertight dry-stone walls as travelers and pilgrims have for 1,200 years.

From the Oratory, continue up the rugged one-lane road to the crest of the hill, then coast back into Dingle—hungry, thirsty, and ready for . . .

DINGLE PUBS

With 50 pubs for its 1,500 people, Dingle is a pub crawl waiting to happen. Even if you're not into pubs, give these a whirl. The town is renowned among traditional musicians as a place to get work ("£30 a day, tax-free, plus drink"). There's music every night ($2 beers and never a cover charge). The scene is a decent mix of locals, Americans, and Germans. While two pubs, the Small Bridge Bar and O'Flaherty's, are the most famous for their good beer and folk music, make a point to wander the town and follow your ear.

When you say "a beer, please" in an Irish pub, you'll get a pint of "the black beauty with a blonde head"—Guinness. If you want a small beer, ask for a half-pint. Never rush your bartender when he's pouring a Guinness. It takes time—almost sacred time. If you don't like Guinness, try it in Ireland. It doesn't travel well and is better in its homeland. Murphy's is a very good Guinness-like stout but a bit smoother and milder.

In an Irish pub, you're a guest on your first night; after that, you're a regular. Women traveling alone need not worry—you'll become part of the pub family in no time.

It's a tradition to buy your table a round, and then for each person to reciprocate. If an Irishman buys you a drink, thank him by saying, "*Guh rev mah a gut.*" Offer him a toast in Irish—"*Slahn-chuh!*" A good excuse for a conversation is to ask to be taught a few words of Gaelic. You've got a room full of Gaelic speakers who will remind you that every year five languages go extinct. They'd love to teach you a few words of their favorite language.

Craic (crack) is the art of conversation—the sport that accompanies drinking in a pub. People are there to talk. Join in. Here's a goofy excuse for some *craic*: Ireland—small as it is—has many dialects. People from Cork (the big city of Ireland's south coast) are famous for talking very fast (and in a squeaky voice). So fast that some even talk in letters alone. "ABCD fish?" (Anybody see the fish?) "DRO fish." (There are no fish.) "DR fish." (There are fish.) "CDBD Is." (See the beady eyes?) "OIBJ DR fish." (Oh aye, be Jeeze, there are fish.) For a possibly more appropriate spin, replace "fish" with "bird" (girl). This is obscure, but your pub neighbor may understand and enjoy hearing it. If nothing else, you won't seem so intimidating to him anymore.

Also, you might ask if the people of one county are any smarter than the next. Kerry people are famous for being a bit out of it. It's said that when the stupidest man in county Cork moved to county Kerry, it raised the cumulative IQ in each area.

TRADITIONAL IRISH MUSIC

Traditional music is alive and popular in pubs throughout Ireland. "Sessions" (musical evenings) may be planned and advertised or impromptu. Traditionally, musicians just congregate and jam. There will generally be a fiddler, flute or tin whistle, guitar, bodhran (goat skin drum), and maybe an accordion. Things usually get going around 9:30 or 10:00 p.m. "Last call" (last chance to order a drink before closing) is around "half eleven" (11:30 p.m.).

The bodhran is played with two hands: one wielding a small two-headed club and the other stretching the skin to change the tone and pitch. The wind and string instruments embellish melody lines with lots of improvised ornamentation. Occasionally the fast-paced music will stop, and one person will sing an a cappella lament. This is the one time when the entire pub will stop to listen, as sad lyrics fill the smoke-stained room. Stories—ranging from struggles against English rule to love songs—are always heartfelt. Spend a lament enjoying the faces in the crowd.

The music comes in sets of three songs. Whoever happens to be leading determines the next song, only as the song the group is playing is about to be finished. If he wants to pass on the decision, it's done with eye contact and a nod.

A session can be magic, or it may be lifeless. If the chemistry is right, it's one of the great Irish experiences. The music churns intensely while the group casually enjoys exploring each others' musical styles. The drummer dodges the fiddler's playful bow, with his cigarette sticking half-ash straight from the middle of his mouth. Sipping their pints, a faint but steady buzz is skillfully maintained. The floor on the musicians' platform is stomped paint-free, and barmaids scurry artfully through the commotion, gathering towers of empty cream-crusted glasses. With knees up and heads down, the music goes round and round. Make yourself perfectly at home, drumming the table or playing the 10-pence coins.

GREAT BLASKET AND THE ARAN ISLANDS

Great Blasket

Great Blasket, a rugged uninhabited island off the tip of Dingle Peninsula, seems particularly close to the soul of Ireland. Its population, home to as many as 160 people, dwindled until the last handful of residents were moved by the government to the mainland in 1953. These people were the most traditional Irish community of the 20th

Ghost town on Blasket Island

century—the symbol of antique Gaelic culture. They had a special closeness to their island, combined with a knack for vivid storytelling. From this poor, primitive but proud fishing and farming community came three writers of international repute whose Gaelic work—basically tales of life on Great Blasket—is translated into many languages. In shops all over the peninsula you'll find *Peig* (by Peig Sayers), *Twenty Years a-Growing* (Maurice O'Sullivan), and *The Islander* (Thomas O'Crohan).

Today Great Blasket is a grassy three-mile poem, overrun with memories. With fat rabbits, ruffled sheep, abandoned stone homes, and a handful of seals, it's ideal for wind-blown but thoughtful walks.

An irregular ferry service shuttles visitors from a desperate wad of concrete called "Dunquin Harbor" to Great Blasket. The schedule is dictated by demand and weather.

The state-of-the-art Blasket and Gaelic Heritage Center (on Dingle Peninsula facing the islands) creatively gives visitors the best possible look at the language, literature, life, and times of the Blasket Islanders. See the fine video, hear the sounds, read the poems, browse through old photos, and then gaze out the big windows at those rugged islands and imagine. Even if you never got past limericks, the poetry of these people—so pure and close to each other and nature—is an inspiration.

The Aran Islands

Another Gaelic treat along Ireland's west coast is the Aran Islands. The three islands are a 20-minute flight or two-hour boat ride from Galway, the only sizable town in western Ireland. The largest island, Inishmor, is eight miles long, with one sleepy town, a few farming hamlets, and a blustery charm.

As in Dingle, local homes rent rooms inexpensively. Rent a bike or hire a horse and buggy, and explore. Like the rest of Ireland, the Aran Islands have a deep and mysterious history.

The island's famous Iron Age fortress, Dun Aengus, is the most impressive of its kind in all of Europe. For 20 centuries angry waves have battered away at its black foundation, 300 feet straight down. Even with nothing to guard, it still stands strong, overlooking the sea from a cliff-edge perch. While Inishmor's 900 residents are outnumbered by day-tripping tourists on some summer days, if you arrive early or late, you can be completely alone in Dun Aengus. Spread-eagled on the slate, beak in the wind, gawking straight down at the point where Europe crashes like an egg into the Atlantic, you become part bird.

Stacks of history can be read into the stones of Inishmor. This tiny island, which looks like alligator skin from the air, is a maze of stone fences. Poor people cleared the stony land to make it arable. With unrivaled colonial finesse, the British required Irish families to divide their land among all heirs. This doomed even the largest estates to fragmentation, shrinking lots to sizes just large enough to starve a family. Ultimately, of course, the land ended up in the possession of British absentee landlords. The tiny rock-fenced lots that carve up the treeless landscape remind the farmers of the structural poverty that shaped their history. And weary farmers have never bothered with gates. Even today they take a hunk of wall down, let their sheep pass, and stack the rocks again.

Imagine Ireland back in its heyday, before the Protestants came, before the potato famine, and before so many of its best and brightest emigrated to America. The population of this island was 8 million. During the Great Hunger of 1845–1848, a million people starved, and more left in "coffin ships," so called because many departed so weak from hunger that they died en route. Today Ireland's population is only 5 million. It's been a struggle. Ireland is called the Terrible Beauty. And through all its hard times, the people of this "island of saints and scholars" remain its most endearing attraction.

See the Appendix (Recommended Accommodations) for more information.

With this Union Jack bulldog street mural, a Belfast Protestant neighborhood makes its Unionist feelings pitbull-clear.

52. Northern Ireland and Belfast

Ireland is a split island still struggling with questions left over from its stint as a British colony. While the island won its independence back in the 1920s, the predominantly Protestant northern section opted to stick with its pope-ophobic partners in London. While somewhere between a headache and a tragedy for locals, this adds up to some fascinating travel opportunities for you and me. And lately there are some good, solid reasons to be hopeful.

With so many people working so hard to bring Ireland together, a browse through Belfast will give you more faith in people than despair over headlines. There's a guarded optimism as creative grassroots efforts to grow peace are taking hold.

Make your visit to Ireland complete by including Northern Ireland. This is a British-controlled six-county section of a nine-county area called Ulster. It offers the tourist a very different and still very Irish world. The British-ruled counties of Northern Ireland, long a secret enjoyed and toured mainly by its own inhabitants, are finally being recognized by international travelers.

Of course, people are being killed in Northern Ireland—but not as many as in New York City. Car accidents kill more Northern Irish than do bombs or guns. With common sense, travel in this area is safe.

No American has ever been injured by "the Troubles," and travelers give Northern Ireland rave reviews.

Include Belfast in your Irish travel plans. Here's an itinerary that will introduce you to a capital city of 400,000 and Ireland's best open-air folk museum. At the same time, you'll meet some of the friendliest people on Earth and learn first-hand about their struggle.

BELFAST

Seventeenth-century Belfast was only a village. With the resettlement, or "plantation," of Scottish and English settlers and the success of the local linen, rope-making, and ship-building industries, Belfast boomed. The Industrial Revolution took root with a vengeance. While the rest of Ireland remained rural and agricultural, Belfast earned its nickname, "Old Smoke," when many of the brick buildings you'll see today were built. The year 1888 marked the birth of modern Belfast. Queen Victoria gave the boom town of 300,000 city status. Its citizens then built the city's centerpiece, City Hall.

Belfast is the birthplace of the *Titanic* (and many ships that didn't sink). The two huge mustard-colored cranes (the biggest in the world, nicknamed Samson and Goliath) rise like skyscrapers above the harbor, as if declaring this town's ship-building might. It feels like a new morning in Belfast. Security checks, once a tiresome daily routine, are now rare. What was the traffic-free security zone has shed its grey skin and has become a bright and bustling pedestrian zone. On my last visit, the children dancing in the street were both Catholic and Protestant—part of a community summer camp program giving kids from both communities reason to live together rather than apart.

Still, it's a fragile peace and a tenuous hope. The pointedly Protestant billboards and the helicopter that still hovers over the Catholic end of town remain a reminder that the island is split, and about a million Protestants like it that way.

A visit to Belfast is actually easy from Dublin. Consider this plan for the most interesting Dublin day trip: With the handy 90-minute Dublin–Belfast train ($24 "cheap day-return" tickets), you can leave Dublin early and catch the Belfast City Hall tour at 10:30 a.m. After browsing through the pedestrian zone, ride a shared cab through the Falls Road neighborhood. At 2:30 p.m. head out to the Cultra Folk and Transport Museum. Picnic on the evening train back to Dublin.

The well-organized day-tripper will get a taste of both Belfast's Industrial Age glory and the present (and related) troubles. It will be a happy day when the sectarian neighborhoods of Belfast have nothing to be sectarian about. For a look at what was one of the home bases for the Troubles, explore the working class Catholic Falls Road neighborhood.

A few blocks from City Hall you'll find a square filled with old black cabs—and the only Gaelic-language signs in downtown Belfast. These shared black cabs efficiently shuttle residents from outlying neighborhoods up and down Falls Road and to the city center. All cabs go up Falls Road and past Sinn Fein (the IRA's political wing) headquarters and lots of murals to the Milltown Cemetery. Sit in front and talk to the cabbie. Easy-to-flag-down cabs run every minute or so in each direction on Falls Road. They do one-hour tours for about $20 (cheap for a small group of travelers).

At the Milltown Cemetery you'll be directed past all the Gaelic crosses down to the IRA "Roll of Honor"—set apart from the thousands of other graves by little green railings. They are treated like fallen soldiers. You'll see a memorial to Bobby Sands and the 11 other hunger strikers who starved in support of a united Ireland in 1981.

The Sinn Fein headquarters is on Falls Road (look for the protective boulders on the sidewalk and the Irish Republic flag on the roof). The adjacent bookstore is worth a look. Page through books featuring color photos of the political murals that decorate the local buildings. Money raised here supports families of imprisoned IRA members.

A sad corrugated wall called the "Peace Line" runs a block or so north of Falls Road, separating the Catholics from the Protestants in the Shankill Road area.

While you can ride a shared black cab up Shankill Road, the easiest way to get a dose of the Unionist side is to walk Sandy Row—a working class Protestant street behind the Hotel Europa (Europe's most bombed hotel). You'll see a few murals filled with Unionist symbolism. The mural of William of Orange's victory over the Catholic King James II (Battle of the Boyne, 1690) stirs Unionist hearts.

Most of Ireland has grown disillusioned by the violence wrought by the Irish Republican Army (IRA) and the Protestants' Ulster Volunteer Force (UVF), which are now seen by many as rival groups of terrorists who actually work together in Mafia style to run free and wild in their established territories. Maybe the solution can be found in the mellowness of Ulster retirement homes, where old "Papishes" with their rosaries and old "Prods" with their prayer books sit side by side talking to the same heavenly father. But that kind of peace is elusive. An Ulster Protestant on holiday in England once told me with a weary sigh, "Tomorrow I go back to my tribe."

For a trip into a cozier age, take the eight-mile bus or train ride to the Ulster Folk and Transport Museum. The Folk Museum is an open-air collection of 30 reconstructed buildings from all over the nine counties of Ulster, designed to showcase the region's traditional lifestyles. After wandering through the old town site (church, print shop, schoolhouse, humble Belfast row home, and so on), you'll head into the country to nip into cottages, farmhouses, and mills. Each house is warmed by a peat fire and a friendly attendant. The museum can be dull or vibrant, depending upon your ability to chat with the people staffing each building. Drop a peat brick into a fire.

The adjacent Transport Museum traces the evolution of trans-portion from its beginning 7,500 years ago, when someone first decided to load an ox, and continues to the present, with particularly interesting sections on the local Gypsy (traveler) culture and the sinking of the Belfast-made *Titanic*. In the next two buildings, you roll through the history of bikes, cars, and trains. The car section goes from the first car in Ireland (an 1898 Benz), through the "Cortina Culture" of the 1960s, to the local adventures of John De Lorean with a 1981 model of his car.

Speeding on the train back to Dublin, gazing at the peaceful and lush Irish countryside while pondering De Lorean, the *Titanic*, and the Troubles, your delusions of a fairy-tale Europe have been muddled. Belfast is a bracing dose of reality.

See the Appendix (Recommended Accommodations) for more information.

Scandinavia and the Baltics

53. Oslo

On May 17, Norway's national holiday, Oslo bursts with flags, bands, and parades. Blond toddlers are dressed up in colorful ribbons, traditional pewter buckles, and wool. But Oslo has plenty to offer the visitor, even without its annual patriotic bash. Oslo is fresh, not too big, surrounded by forests, near mountains, and on a fjord. And Oslo's charm doesn't stop there. Norway's largest city, capital, and cultural hub is a smörgåsbord of history, sights, art, and Nordic fun.

An exciting cluster of sights is just a ten-minute ferry ride from the city hall. The Bygdøy area reflects the Norwegian mastery of the sea. Some of Scandinavia's best-preserved Viking ships are on display here. Rape, pillage, and—ya sure you betcha—plunder was the rage 1,000 years ago in Norway. There was a time when much of a frightened Western Europe closed every prayer with, "And deliver us from the Vikings, amen." Gazing up at the prow of one of those sleek, time-stained vessels, you can almost hear the shrieks and smell the armpits of those redheads on the rampage.

Nearby, Thor Heyerdahl's balsa raft, *Kon-Tiki*, and the polar ship *Fram* illustrate Viking energy channeled in more productive directions. The *Fram*, serving both Nansen and Amundsen, ventured farther north and south than any other ship.

Just a harpoon-toss away is Oslo's open-air folk museum. The Scandinavians were leaders in the development of these cultural parks that are now so popular around Europe. More than 150 historic log cabins and buildings from every corner of the country are gathered together in this huge folk museum. Inside each house, a person in local dress is happy to answer questions about tradi-

Oslo on Parade—May 17th, Norway's Independence Day

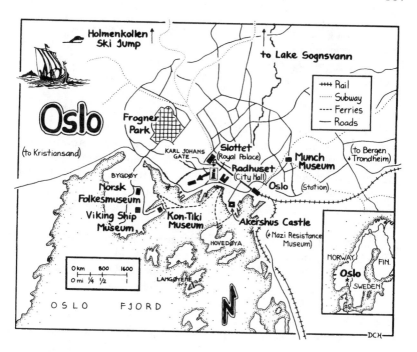

tional life in that part of Norway. Don't miss the thousand-year-old wooden stave church.

Oslo's avant-garde city hall, built 40 years ago, was a communal effort of Norway's greatest artists and designers. Tour the interior. More than 2,000 square yards of bold, colorful murals are a journey through the collective mind of modern Norway.

Norway has given the world two outstanding modern artists: Edvard Munch and Gustav Vigeland. After visiting Oslo, many tourists become Vigeland fans—or even "Munchies." Frogner Park, behind the royal palace, features 150 bronze and granite sculptures representing 30 years of Vigeland creativity. The centerpiece is the impressive 60-foot-tall totem pole of bodies known as the *Monolith of Life*. This, along with the neighboring Vigeland Museum, is a must on any list of Oslo sights.

Oslo's Munch Museum is a joy. It's small, displaying an impressive collection of one man's work, rather than stoning your powers of absorption with art by countless artists from countless periods. You leave the Munch Museum with a smile, feeling like you've learned something about one artist, his culture, and his particular artistic "ism"—expressionism. Don't miss *The Scream*, which captures the exasperation many feel as our human "race" does just that.

You can explore Oslo's 700-year-old Akershus Castle. Its Freedom Museum, a fascinating Nazi-resistance museum, shows how one country's spirit cannot be crushed, regardless of how thoroughly it's occupied by a foreign power. The castle itself is interesting only with a guided tour.

Oslo has been called Europe's most expensive city. I'll buy that. Without local relatives, life on a budget is possible only if you have a good guidebook and take advantage of money-saving options. Remember: Budget tricks like picnicking and sleeping in private homes offer the most exciting savings in the most expensive cities.

If you opt for hotels, you have no choice but to rent rooms that are efficient, clean, and pleasant. It's a kind of forced luxury. Know your budget alternatives, bring a little extra money, and enjoy it.

Language problems are few. The Norwegians speak better English than any people on the Continent. My cousin attends the University of Oslo. In her language studies she had to stipulate English or American. She learned American—and can slang me under the table.

ONE DAY FOR THE FJORDS?

If you go to Oslo and don't get out to the fjords, you should have your passport revoked. Norway's greatest claim to scenic fame is her deep and lush fjords. "Norway in a Nutshell," a series of well-organized

Norway's Sognefjord

NORWAY IN A NUTSHELL

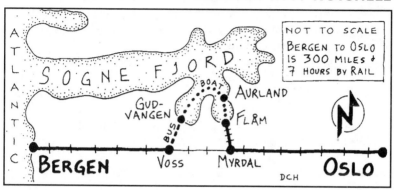

train, ferry, and bus connections, lays this most beautiful fjord country spread-eagle on a scenic platter.

Every morning, northern Europe's most spectacular train ride leaves Oslo (at 7:30 a.m.) for Bergen. Cameras smoke as this super-scenic railroad roars over Norway's mountainous spine. The barren, windswept heaths, glaciers, deep forests, countless lakes, and a few rugged ski resorts create a harsh beauty. The railroad is an amazing engineering feat. Completed in 1909, it's 300 miles long and peaks at 4,266 feet (which, at this Alaskan latitude, is far above the tree line). You'll go under 18 miles of snow sheds, over 300 bridges, and through 200 tunnels in just under seven hours ($70, or free with railpass).

At Myrdal, a 12-mile spur line ($8 supplement for Eurailpass holders) drops you 2,800 breathtaking feet in 50 minutes to the village of Flåm for Norway's ultimate natural thrill, Sognefjord. This is a party train. The conductor even stops the train for photographs at a particularly picturesque waterfall.

From Flåm, take the most scenic of fjord cruises. Sightseeing boats leave throughout the day ($15, half off with a train pass, student card, or full-fare spouse). These boats get you right into the mist of the many fjord waterfalls and close to the goats, sheep, and awesome cliffs. For 90 minutes, camera-clicking tourists scurry on the drool-stained deck like nervous roosters, scratching fitfully for a photo to catch the magic. Waterfalls turn the black-rock cliffs into a bridal fair. You can nearly reach out and touch the sheer towering walls. The ride is one of those fine times, like being high on the tip of an Alp, when a warm camaraderie spontaneously combusts between the strangers who came together for the experience. The boat takes you up one narrow arm

(Aurlandsfjord) and down the next (Nærøyfjord) to the nothing-to-stop-for town of Gudvangen, where waiting buses ($10) shuttle you back to the main train line at Voss. From Voss, return to Oslo or carry on into Bergen for the evening.

Bergen, Norway's second city and historic capital, is an entertaining place in which to finish the day and enjoy an evening before catching the overnight train back to Oslo. As you yawn and stretch and rummage around for a cup of morning coffee back in Oslo's station, it'll hit you: You were gone for 24 hours, spent very little, experienced the fjord wonder of Europe, and saw Bergen to boot.

See the Appendix (Recommended Accommodations) for more information.

54. Stalking Stockholm

If I had to call one European city home, it would be Stockholm. Green, clean, efficient, and surrounded by as much water as land, Sweden's stunning capital is underrated by most tourists, ranking just above Bordeaux, Brussels, and Bucharest on their checklists.

While progressive and sleek, Stockholm respects its heritage. Every day, mounted bands strut through the heart of town to the royal palace, announcing the changing of the guard and turning even the most dignified tourist into a scampering kid. The Gamla Stan (Old Town) celebrates the Midsummer Festivities (June 21–22) with the down-home vigor of a rural village, forgetting that it's the core of a gleaming 20th-century metropolis.

Start your visit with a stop at Europe's most energetic tourist information office, the Sweden House (Sverigehuset), 3 blocks from the station. This organization will do everything short of whipping you with birch twigs in the sauna. They have an English library and reading room, free pamphlets on every aspect of Swedish culture, and daily walking tours through the Old Town. Pick up the usual lists of sights and maps as well as the handy *This Week in Stockholm*, a periodical entertainment guide in English.

Stockholm is a place to "do" as well as see. The culture and vitality of Sweden is best felt at Skansen. On a wooded island near the town center, this is a huge park of traditional and historic houses, schools, and churches transplanted from all over Sweden. Skansen entertains with live folk music, dancing, pop concerts, a zoo, restaurants, peasant-craft workshops, and endless amusements. It's a cultural treat enjoyed by tourists and locals alike.

Nearby is the *Vasa*, the royal flagship that sank just minutes into her maiden voyage 350 years ago. While not a good example of Viking seaworthiness, the *Vasa* is incredibly intact in her state-of-the-art display house and a highlight on any sailor's itinerary.

The Carl Milles Garden is filled with the work of Sweden's favorite sculptor. Strong, pure, expressive, and Nordic, Milles' individual style takes even the most uninterested by surprise. Hanging on a cliff overlooking the city, this sculpture park is perfect for a picnic.

A sauna, Sweden's answer to support hose and a facelift, is as important as a smörgåsbord in your Swedish experience. "Simmer down" with the local students, retired folks, and busy executives. Try cooking as calmly as the Swedes. Just before you become edible, go into the shower room. There's no "luke-cold," only one button, bringing a Niagara of liquid ice. Suddenly your shower stall becomes the Cape Canaveral launch pad, and your body scatters to every corner of the universe. A moment later you're back together, rejoining the Swedes in the slow cooker, this time with their relaxed confidence and a small but knowing smile. More exhilaration is just around the corner. Only rarely will you feel so good.

Stockholm is notoriously expensive, but with a few tips you can manage fine on a budget. Land a budget bed by calling ahead or arriving

Stockholm's floating youth hostel, the af Chapman

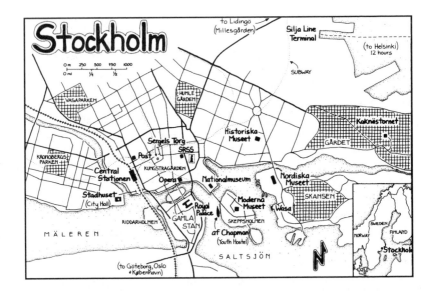

in the morning. Train travelers coming from Oslo or Copenhagen should take an overnight train and rent a *couchette*. Scandinavia, always thinking ahead, located its capitals convenient ten-hour train rides apart. Scandinavian *couchettes*, at $20, are a great deal.

Take advantage of your guidebook's listing of budget accommodations. Stockholm's *af Chapman* youth hostel is a classic "cutter ship" permanently moored five minutes from downtown. The *af Chapman*, with $16 bunks, is one of Europe's most popular hostels. It holds 30 beds every morning for drop-ins, and these are usually taken by mid-morning (tel. 08/679-5015). For a good, basic, and friendly hotel a 15-minute walk from the train station, I stay at the Queen's Hotel near the center (Drottninggatan 71A, tel. 08/249460).

Finally, take advantage of $10-a-day tourist transportation passes that give you free run of Stockholm's excellent bus and subway system as well as unlimited entrance to Skansen. A more expensive 24-hour pass, allowing you entrance to all the sights and free use of public transit, pays for itself as soon as you tour Skansen (and its aquarium), the *Vasa* warship, and Carl Milles Garden.

While most visitors side-trip to cute Sigtuna, a quick visit to Helsinki is more exciting. Finland's capital, just an overnight boat ride away, is Scandinavian only by geography. Its language is completely unrelated, and culturally, there's nothing "ya sure you betcha" about Finland.

Getting to Helsinki is a joy. The daily or nightly ships (as little as $110 round-trip with smörgåsbord breakfast, dinner, and a stateroom bed each way; dicounts with a Eurail or ScanRail pass) feature lavish buffets, dancing, duty-free bingeing, gambling, and the most enchanting island scenery in Europe. A 36-hour "minicruise" gives you a day to tour Helsinki and two nights on Scandinavia's biggest "luxury hotel."

See the Appendix (Recommended Accommodations) for more information.

55. Ærø: Denmark's Ship-in-a-Bottle Island

Few visitors to Scandinavia even notice Ærø, a sleepy, 6-by-22-mile island on the south edge of Denmark. Ærø has a salty charm. Its tombstones say things like, "Here lies Christian Hansen at anchor with his wife. He'll not weigh until he stands before God." It's a peaceful and homey island, where baskets of new potatoes sit in front of farmhouses—for sale on the honor system.

Ærø's capital, Ærøskøbing, makes a fine home base. Temple Fielding said it's "one of five places in the world that you must see." Many Danes agree, washing up the cobbled main drag in waves with the landing of each ferry. In fact, this is the only town in Denmark that is entirely protected and preserved by law.

Ærøskøbing is a town-in-a-bottle kind of place. Wander down lanes right out of the 1680s, when the town was the wealthy home port

A warm and traditional welcome awaits you at an old-fashioned Danish country inn.

to more than 100 windjammers. The post office dates to 1749, and cast-iron gaslights still shine each evening. Windjammers gone, the harbor now caters to German and Danish holiday yachts. On midnight low tides you can almost hear the crabs playing cards.

The Hammerich House, full of old junk, is a turn-of-the-century garage sale open daily in summer. The "Bottle Peter" museum on Smedegade is a fascinating house with a fleet of 750 different bottled ships. Old Peter Jacobsen died in 1960 (probably buried in a glass bottle), leaving a lifetime of his tedious little creations for visitors to squint and marvel at.

Touring Ærø by car is like sampling chocolates with a snow shovel. Enjoy a breezy 18-mile tour of Ærø's subtle charms by bike. Borrow a bike from your hotel or rent one from the Esso station on the road behind the tourist office. On Ærø, there are no deposits and no locks. If you start in the morning, you'll be home in time for a hearty lunch.

Ready? Leave Ærøskøbing west on the road to Vra past many U-shaped farms, typical of this island. The three sides block the wind and are used for storing cows, hay, and people. *Gaard* (meaning "farm") shows up in many local names. Bike along the coast in the protection of the dike, which turned the once-salty swampland to your left into farmable land. Pedal past a sleek modern windmill and Borgnæs, a pleasant cluster of mostly modern summer cottages. (At this point, bikers with one-speeds can shortcut directly to Vindeballe.)

Main Street, Ærøskøbing

DENMARK'S ÆRØ ISLAND BIKE RIDE

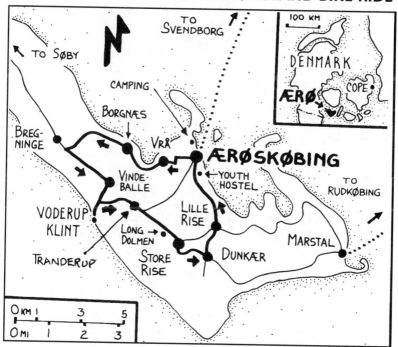

After passing a secluded beach, climb uphill over the island's summit to Bregninge. Unless you're tired of thatched and half-timbered cottages, turn right and roll through Denmark's "second longest village" to the church. Peek inside. Then roll back through Bregninge, head a mile down the main road to Vindeballe and take the Vodrup exit.

A straight road leads you to an ancient site on a rugged bluff called Vodrup Klint. If I were a pagan, I'd stop here to worship. Savor the sea, the wind, and the chilling view.

Pedal to Tranderup, past the old farm with the cows with the green hearing aids, a lovely pond, and a row of wind-bent stumps. At the old town of Olde, you'll hit the main road. Turn right toward Store Rise—marked by its church spire in the distance. Just behind the church is a 5,000-year-old neolithic burial place, the Langdysse (Long Dolmen) Tingstedet. Hunker down. Ærø had more than 100 of these. Few survive.

Inside the Store Rise church, notice the little boats hanging in the nave, the fine altarpiece, and Martin Luther in the stern making sure everything's theologically shipshape.

Continue down the main road, with the hopeful forest of modern windmills whirring on your right, until you get to Dunkær.

For the homestretch, take the small road past the topless windmill. Except for "Lille Rise," it's all downhill as you coast home past great sea views to Ærøskøbing.

After a power tour of big-city Scandinavia, Ærø offers a perfect time-passed island in which to wind down, enjoy the seagulls, and pedal a bike into the essence of Denmark. Take a break in a cobbled world of sailors who, after someone connected a steam engine to a propeller, decided, "maybe building ships in bottles is more our style."

See the Appendix (Recommended Accommodations) for more information.

56. The Baltics and St. Petersburg: Scandinavia's Rough-and-Tumble Backyard

The Baltics and St. Petersburg, an easier-than-ever boat ride away from Helsinki or Stockholm, offer a tremendous load of travel thrills. A swing through a couple of Baltic capitals to spice up your Scandinavian adventure is globetrotting kid stuff. Including Russia ups the ante and, for many, is plenty rewarding. Luckily, with dollars, you're powerful, and with information, you can travel smart. Good guidebooks give you the step-by-step. Here's a brief intro to the four most accessible and comfortable cities in what was the Soviet Union.

ST. PETERSBURG, RUSSIA

Once an imperial showpiece of aristocratic opulence, now draped in the grimy cobwebs of socialism, St. Petersburg is Russia's most tourist-worthy city. Standing on Palace Square, you'll shiver and think, "The Russian revolution started here." (You may also shiver and think, "I'm as far north as Alaska.") Romanov palaces, statue-maker gardens, and arched bridges over graceful canals bring back the time of the czars. The cultural cherry on top is the Hermitage Palace. Filled with the czars' art collection, this is one of the world's finest art galleries.

St. Petersburg's artistic and historical splendor is soaked in the sweet-and-sour sauce of modern Russia, with its streets of legless beggars, Mafia-controlled kiosks, wheezing buses, shabby bread stores, broken signs, exhaust-stained façades, and pornography dealers. Hammers and sickles teeter tentatively on Stalin-gothic buildings.

From comrades to Cokes

Compared to Moscow, St. Petersburg is compact, walkable, friendly, manageable, and architecturally intact. Save a sunny day just to walk. Keep your head up: Ugly Soviet shops mar the first floor of nearly every building, but the upper façades have managed to stay above the squalor.

Nevsky Prospekt, St. Petersburg's main drag, with the most commerce, most landmarks, and safest feeling, is the natural walk. But make a point to explore the back streets along the canals. Take a Romanov stroll through the Summer Gardens. Climb St. Isaac's Cathedral to count the tired smokestacks through the urban haze.

While the subway is a fire hose of a people-mover, the easiest way to get around downtown is by taxi. Two dollars turns nearly any car into a taxi. Just point to the asphalt and within a few seconds a car will stop. Tell him where you want to go (you might have a postcard to point to), let him know you have two dollars for the fare, and you're on your way.

Ready for some culture beyond what was growing on your lunch? How about arguably the best ballet on earth? In St. Petersburg, as in Moscow, tourists can get $10 tickets from scalpers on the sidewalk a few minutes before each performance. Inside the theater, the browbeaten despair and dog-eared chaos of today's Russia fades, as the cultural spirit of old Russia swirls around the chandeliers. First World–by-the-tail tourists suddenly become gawking bumpkins as babushkas in gowns heap bouquets on the conductor who stands tall in Rimsky-Korsakov's place.

Ushers sell naive western tourists surplus programs to long-finished performances and prepare tiny two-for-a-dollar black-caviar sandwiches. As the faded red stage curtain is pulled aside, the riches of Russia are resurrected in music and dance.

Down the street, well-scrubbed agents of the latest revolution—with fast-food arches rather than the hammer and sickle on their caps—eagerly raise their hands, calling customers over to order. Attendants stand guard with mops. Shadowy managers patrol the gleaming quarters enforcing a radical new notion—the customers are king. Serve them fast and serve them with a smile. Yuppie locals (car radios safely at their side) video each other munching hot apple turnovers and slurping shakes. You can get a cheeseburger, fries, and tea for $4—a day's wages for the babushka perusing garbage cans across the street. Downstairs are the best toilets in Russia—actually a joy.

The Bolshoi and begging, Mafia and burgers, hope and despair—nobody knows where Russia's going. But now, anyone can visit.

BALTICS AND WESTERN RUSSIA

TALLINN, ESTONIA

Visiting Tallinn fills us with hope for the future of the ex–Soviet Union. Tallinners, after years of watching Finnish television beamed across the gulf from Helsinki, knew exactly what a Western economy should look like. Since 1991 they've been putting one together with unprecedented speed.

Tallinn, with 29 pointy-roofed medieval towers ringing its easy-to-fortify castle-crowned hill, is a toy city. It feels strangely Scandinavian but ramshackle and cheap.

Tallinn has real grocery stores now, where you pick food off the shelves yourself instead of asking clerks behind a counter to do it. Estonian design has recovered from Sovietism: Colorful, simple, Scandinavian-type layout is showing up in yogurt packaging, monthly bus-pass design, and window displays. Estonia is producing goods that actually look competitive on the world market. Uppity Tallinn food stores (whose Moscow counterparts would snort at carrying Russian-made products) are proud to carry Estonian butter and cheese. Pharmacies stock attractively presented, Estonian-made toothpaste alongside the imported tubes of Colgate.

Tallinn looks a little dilapidated but perfectly normal if you come on the boat from Helsinki. Arriving in Tallinn from Russia or one of the other Baltic capitals, its success is shinier. Do Tallinn last.

Estonians consider their country a Nordic nation of solid, hard-working Protestant folk like those who made Scandinavia a showcase of order, propriety, and comfort. They're quick to point out that Finland and Estonia both gained independence from Russia after World War I and that as late as 1938, Estonia's living standard was equal to Finland's. Estonians would have kept pace had it not been for a couple hundred Russian tanks.

RIGA, LATVIA

Tall 19th- and 20th-century buildings give Riga a cosmopolitan feel and a vertical accent unique among the Baltic capitals. Riga has always been the Baltics' closest thing to a metropolis. German merchants and Teutonic knights made Riga the center of Baltic Christianization, commercialization, and colonization in the Middle Ages. Under the czars, the city was the Russian Empire's busiest commercial port. Under Soviet rule, Riga became first an important military center and later, because of its high standard of living, one of the favored places for high-ranking military officers to retire. (They could choose any-where in the U.S.S.R. except Moscow, Kiev, and Leningrad.)

Riga's old town is about to wake up. When it does it will have as much medieval ambience as any old-town center in northern Europe. It's got the requisite gas lamps and cobbles—now all it needs is customers. It's a construction zone by day and a trendy café and bar scene by night.

In the heart and soul of the Old Town, you'll find Latvia's Freedom Monument. Dedicated in 1935, it was strangely left standing by the Soviets, though KGB agents apprehended anyone who tried to come near it. Now locals lay flowers on its foundation. Riga's most beloved landmark, the symbol of an independent Latvia, stands proud and tall as an exclamation point.

VILNIUS, LITHUANIA

Sprawling and disorganized, a Catholic church on every corner, Vilnius is the homiest and coziest of the three Baltic capitals, and also the most unsophisticated and run-down. A restful, horizontal city, Vilnius' one- and two-story buildings and its arches and courtyards are more reminiscent of a friendly Polish provincial capital than of the tall, German-influenced architecture in Riga or the Hanseatic frosting-cake feel of Tallinn.

Vilnius' old town, dating largely from the 17th and 18th centuries, is huge and amazingly dilapidated. Burned-out windows, crumbling wooden shutters, cracked plaster, and patchwork roofs cry out for millions of dollars' worth of restoration work, while Soviet "improvements," like the central telephone office, beg for the wrecking ball.

The fact that Vilnius is falling apart gives the visitor a heightened sense of possibility. Every paneless window and paintless shutter makes you think of what could be there: a family, a shop, a sewing machine, candles on the table.

Vilnius' ramshackle desolation challenges you to explore. The old town is full of cozy cafés and fascinating galleries and shops. Many of them don't have any signs; you have to duck through archways into courtyards, open gates and doors, and slowly learn your way from nook to cranny. Otherwise the city may seem so dead you'll wonder if it weren't the accidental target of a Soviet neutron bomb.

The city museums have more babushka guards than visitors. Apparently labor is cheaper than a light bulb, so the exhibit rooms are kept dark, and you walk through the museum with your own personal light switcher.

As the only inland Baltic capital, Vilnius was always politically and economically closer to its Slavic neighbors (Russia and Poland) than to

Scandinavia. This survives: As in Russia, politicians are comic, bombastic, and bumpkinesque. And Lithuania's economy lags behind that of Estonia and Latvia. The country can still seem like a part of the Soviet Union, not so much in the way the harsh, urban Sovietism still survives in Riga, but in the provincial inertia that nevertheless makes Vilnius endearing.

GETTING YOUR VISA

You can visit Latvia, Estonia, and Lithuania without a visa. Just your passport will do.

Russian visas are more difficult. The St. Petersburg Youth Hostel is the most simple and reliable option. Nobody else in Russia is so well set up and capable of combining a low per-night price with efficient visa support (English always spoken, tel. 7/812/329-8018, fax 7/812/329-8019, Web site: www.spb.su/ryh, e-mail: ryh@ryh.spb.su). The cost of obtaining a visa through the St. Petersburg Youth Hostel is $54 (includes a $25 visa service fee, $10 fax fee, and $19 for the first night's stay in the hostel).

For much more information, *Rick Steves' Russia & the Baltics* (with Ian Watson, John Muir Publications) offers the most up-to-date rundown on budget independent travel in the Baltics, St. Petersburg, and Moscow.

See the Appendix (Recommended Accommodations) for more information.

Greece

57. Peloponnesian Highlights: Overlooked Greece

The Peloponnesian Peninsula stretches south from Athens. This antiquity-studded land of ancient Olympia, Corinth, and Sparta offers plenty of fun in the eternal Greek sun, with pleasant fishing villages, sandy beaches, bathtub-warm water, and none of the tourist crowds that plague the much-scrambled-after Greek Isles.

The Peloponnesian port town of Nafplion, two hours southwest of Athens by car or bus, is small, cozy, and strollable. It's a welcome relief after the black-hanky intensity of smoggy Athens. Not only is Nafplion itself fun, but it's a handy home base for exploring two of Greece's greatest ancient sights—Epidavros and Mycenae.

Nafplion's harbor is guarded by two castles, one on a small island and the other capping the hill above the town. Both are wonderfully floodlit at night. Just looking from the town up to its castle makes you need a tall iced tea.

But this old Venetian outpost, built in the days when Venice was the economic ruler of Europe, is the best-preserved castle of its kind in Greece and well worth the 999-step climb. From the highest ramparts you'll see several Aegean islands (great day trips by boat from Nafplion)

Epidavros' state-of-the-art acoustics

and look deep into the mountainous interior of the Peloponnesian Peninsula. Below you lies an enticing beach.

Nafplion has plenty of hotels, and its harbor is lined with restaurants specializing in fresh seafood. An octopus dinner cost me $8—succulent!

The infamous resin-flavored *retsina* wine is a drink you'll want to experience—once. Maybe with octopus. The first glass is like drinking wood. The third glass is dangerous: It starts to taste good. If you drink any more, you'll smell like it the entire next day.

On another night I left Nafplion's popular waterfront district and had a memorable meal in a hole-in-the-wall joint. There was no menu, just an entertaining local crowd and a nearsighted man who, in a relaxed frenzy, ran the whole show. He scurried about, greeting eaters, slicing, dicing, laughing, singing to himself, cooking, serving, and billing. Potato stew, meatballs, a plate of about 30 tiny fried fish with lime, and unlimited wine cost $20 for two—and could have fed four.

Epidavros, 18 miles northeast of Nafplion, is the best-preserved ancient Greek theater. It was built 2,500 years ago to seat 14,000. Today it's kept busy reviving the greatest plays of antiquity. You can catch performances of ancient Greek comedies and tragedies on week-ends from mid-June through September. Try to see Epidavros either early or late in the day. The theater's marvelous acoustics are best enjoyed in near-solitude. Sitting in the most distant seat as your partner stands on the stage, you can practically hear the *retsina* rumbling in her stomach.

Thirty minutes in the other direction from Nafplion are the ruins of Mycenae. This was the capital of the Mycenaeans, who won the Trojan War and dominated Greece 1,000 years before Socrates.

As you tour this fascinating fortified citadel, remember that these people were as awesome to the ancient Greeks of Socrates' day as those Greeks are to us. The classical Greeks marveled at the huge stones and workmanship of the Mycenaean ruins. They figured that only a race of giant Cyclopes could build with such colossal rocks and called it "Cyclopean" architecture.

Visitors today can gape at the Lion's Gate, climb deep into a cool, ancient cistern, and explore the giant *tholos* tombs. The tombs, built in 1500 B.C., stand like huge stone igloos, with smooth subterranean domes 40 feet wide and 40 feet tall. The most important Mycenaean artifacts, like the golden "Mask of Agamemnon," are in the National Museum in Athens.

FINIKOUNDAS

The prize-winning Peloponnesian hideaway is the remote village of Finikoundas. Located on the southwest tip of the peninsula between the twin Venetian fortress towns of Koroni and Methoni (two hours by public bus from Kalamata), Finikoundas is big enough to have a good selection of restaurants, pensions, and a few shops, but it's small enough to escape the typical resort traffic, crowds, and noise. It's just right for a sleepy Greek sabbatical.

Finikoundas has plenty of private rooms, or *dhomatia*, for rent. Plan to spend $20 for a simple double a few steps from the beach. The little bay just east of the rock breakwater was the best beach I found, and the swimming was fine—even in October.

After a little Apollo-worshipping, I wandered through town in search of Dionysus at just the right waterfront restaurant. The place I found couldn't have been more "waterfront." Since the fishing village had no dock, its Lilliputian fishing boats were actually anchored to the restaurant. I settled my chair comfortably into the sand and the salty atmosphere, as weak wavelets licked my table's legs. I dined amid rusty four-hooker anchors, honorably retired old ropes, and peely dinghies. A naked 20-watt bulb dangled from the straw roof, which rotted unnoticed by Greeks and a few perpetually off-season Germans who seemed to be regulars.

Cuisine in a village like this is predictable. I enjoyed fresh seafood, Greek salad, and local wine. After a few days in Greece you become a connoisseur of the salad, appreciating the wonderful tomatoes, rich feta cheese, and even the olive-oil drenching.

Almost within splashing distance of my table, young Greek men in swimsuits not much bigger than a rat's hammock gathered around a bucketful of just-caught octopi. They were tenderizing the poor things to death by whipping them like wet rags over and over on a big flat rock. They'd be featured momentarily on someone's dinner plate—someone else's.

Evening is a predictable but pleasant routine of strolling and socializing. The streets buzz with take-it-easy action. Dice chatter on dozens of backgammon boards, entrepreneurial dogs and goal-oriented children busy themselves as a tethered goat chews on something inedible in its low-profile corner. From the other end of town comes the happy music of a christening party. Dancing women fill the

You can be a guest of honor at a Greek wedding festival.

building, while their children mimic them in the street. Farther down, two elderly, black-clad women sit like tired dogs on the curb.

Succumbing to the lure of the pastry shop, I sat down for my day-end ritual, honey-soaked baklava. I told the cook I was American. "Oh," he said, shaking his head with sadness and pity. "You work too hard."

I answered, "Right. But not today."

See the Appendix (Recommended Accommodations) for more information.

58. Crete's Gorge of Samaria

Swarms of tourists flock to the Greek island of Crete. Many leave, disappointed by the crowds. Try to avoid peak season and the crowded cities. Hike through the rugged interior instead and find a remote corner of the south coast. While ridiculously congested in the height of summer, the 10-mile hike through the Gorge of Samaria can be a Cretan highlight.

Your home base for this loop trip is Hania, a city on Crete's north coast serviced frequently by the overnight boat from Athens. Catch the earliest bus from Hania to Xyloskalo to beat the heat and midday crowds. After a scenic 25-mile bus ride, you'll be standing high above the wild

Don McCort

Gorge of Samaria. Xyloskalo is a small lodge, the end of the road, and the beginning of the trail. The bus will be full of hikers; no one else would come here at this hour. The air is crisp, the fresh blue sky is cool, and most of the gorge has yet to see the sun. Before you lies a 10-mile downhill trek, dropping 5,000 feet through some of the most spectacular scenery anywhere in Greece to a black-sand beach on the south coast. (The hike takes four to six hours; the gorge is open from May through October and costs about $5 to enter.)

Pack light but bring a hearty picnic lunch, a water bottle, and extra film. Food can't be bought

CRETE

in this wonderfully wild gorge, and things get pretty dry and dusty in the summer. There are several springs, and you follow a pure mountain stream through much of the gorge. Wear light clothes but bring a jacket for the cool morning at the top. Come prepared to swim in one of the stream's many refreshing swimming holes.

Descend to the floor of the gorge down an hour of steep switchbacks, where you'll reach the stream, a great place for your picnic brunch. A leisurely meal here will bolster your energy, lighten your load, and bring you peace, as this break will let most of the other hikers get ahead of you. If the crowds just won't let up, find solitude by following a stream up a side gorge.

Between you and the Libyan Sea on Crete's southern shore are about eight miles of gently sloping downhill trails. Hiking along the cool creek, you'll pass an occasional deserted farmhouse, lazy goats, and a small ghost town with a well. In the middle of the hike, you'll come to the narrowest (and most photographed) point in the gorge, where only three yards separate the 1,000-foot-high cliffs. Keep your eyes peeled for the nimble, cliff-climbing *agrimi*, the wild Cretan mountain goats.

Finally, by midafternoon, signs of Greek civilization begin peeking through the bushes. An oleander chorus cheers you along the last leg of your hike to the coast. You'll find a tiny community with a small restaurant and a few cheap places to stay. The town, Agia Roumeli, is accessible only by foot or boat. Three to six times a day, a small boat picks up the hikers and ferries them to Chora Sfakion (last ride is usually around 6:00 p.m.). Before you begin your hike, confirm when the last boat leaves so you can pace yourself.

While you're waiting for the boat (after you buy your ticket), take a dip in the bathtub-warm, crystal-clear waters of the Libyan Sea. Africa is out there somewhere. The black-sand beach absorbs the heat, so wear your shoes right to the water's edge. A free shower is available on the beach.

The hour-long boat ride (or eight-hour hike) to Chora Sfakion passes some of Crete's best beaches and stops briefly at the pleasant fishing village of Loutro (with several pensions). Buses meet each boat at Chora Sfakion to return you to Hania. The untouristy village of Paleohora (west of Agia Roumeli) has great beaches and a bus connection to Hania. In crossing the island of Crete, the bus goes through some dramatic scenery and several untouched villages inhabited by high-booted, long-mustachioed, espresso-drinking Cretans.

Throughout Europe

59. Dungeons and Dragons: Europe's Nine Most Medieval Castle Experiences

Castles excite Americans. Medieval fortresses are rotting away on hilltops from Ireland to Israel, from Sweden to Spain, lining the Loire and guarding harbors throughout the Mediterranean. From the west coast of Portugal to the crusader city of Rhodes, you'll find castle thrills lurking in every direction.

Most of Europe's castles have been discovered, but some are forgotten, unblemished by turnstiles, postcard racks, and coffee shops, and ignored by guidebooks. Since they're free, nobody promotes them. The aggressive traveler finds them by tapping local sources, like the town tourist office and the friendly manager of your hotel or pension.

Here are nine medieval castles, some forgotten, some discovered, where the winds of the past really howl.

CARCASSONNE, FRANCE

Before me lies Carcassonne, the perfect medieval city. Like a fish that everyone thought was extinct, Europe's greatest Romanesque fortress-city has somehow survived the centuries.

I was supposed to be gone yesterday, but here I sit—imprisoned by choice—curled in a cranny on top of the wall. The moat is one foot

Europe is full of fortified fantasies. One of Sweden's best is Kalmar Castle.

EUROPE'S NINE BEST CASTLES

over and 100 feet down. Small plants and moss upholster my throne. The wind blows away much of the sounds of today, and my imagination "medievals" me.

Twelve hundred years ago, Charlemagne stood below with his troops—besieging the town for several years. Just as food was running out, a cunning townsperson had a great idea. She fed the town's last bits of grain to the last pig and tossed him over the wall. Splat. Charlemagne's restless forces, amazed that the town still had enough food to throw fat party pigs over the wall, decided they'd never succeed in starving the people out. They ended the siege, and the city was saved. Today the walls that stopped Charlemagne open wide for visitors.

Located in southwest France, Carcassonne is a medieval fantasy of towers, turrets, and cobbled alleys. It's a castle and a walled city rolled into one—and a refreshing break after the touristic merry-go-round of the French Riviera and Paris.

WARWICK CASTLE, ENGLAND

From Land's End to John O'Groats, I searched for the best castle in Britain. I found it. Warwick Castle is a medieval festival wrapped in a fairy-tale exterior. Even with its crowds of modern-day barbarians and its robber-baron entry fee, it's worthwhile.

Like nearby Stratford, Warwick is "upon the Avon" (which is Celtic for "river"—any river). Once past its moat, now a lush green park, Warwick (war-ick) will entertain you from lookout to dungeon. Knaves, nobles, jesters, and damsels will all find something interesting: a fine and educational armory, a terrible torture chamber, a knight in shining armor on a horse, a Madame Tussaud re-creation of a royal weekend party (an 1898 game of statue-maker), and a garden park patrolled by peacocks who welcome picnickers.

ELTZ CASTLE, GERMANY

Germany's best medieval castle experience is the Eltz Castle, above the Mosel River between Cochem and Koblenz. One of the very few Rhine/Mosel–area castles to escape destruction under the French, Burg Eltz is incredibly well preserved and elegantly furnished. The approach to it is part of the thrill. From the car park, you'll hike through a mysterious forest long enough to get you into a medieval mood, and then

Eltz Castle, near Cochem on Germany's Mosel River

all of a sudden it appears, all alone—the past engulfed in nature—Burg Eltz. It's an hour's steep hike from the nearest train station (and boat dock), Moselkern. Drivers, following a roundabout road leaving the Mosel at Hatzenport, can get within a 15-minute walk or quick shuttle-bus ride of the castle. Call and ask if there's a scheduled English tour that you can join (tel. 02672/1300). Here you'll learn how the lives of even the Middle Ages' rich and famous were "nasty, brutish, and short."

RHEINFELS CASTLE, GERMANY'S RHINELAND

Once the mightiest of the Rhine castles, today Rheinfels is an intriguing ruin overlooking the medieval town of St. Goar. Study the English information sheet and map before diving in. Check out the classic dungeon with its ceiling-only access. The well (tour guides report) was dug by death-row-type prisoners who were promised freedom if they hit water. They spent months toiling at the dark bottom of the hole. When they finally succeeded and were lifted, wet and happy, up into the daylight, they were immediately blinded by the bright sunlight. Ponder life in the Middle Ages as you enjoy a glorious Rhine view from the tallest turret.

A flashlight is handy if you want to explore some of Rheinfels' several miles of spooky tunnels. The museum has a reconstruction of the castle showing how it looked before the French flattened it. Louis XIV destroyed all but one of the castles that line Germany's Rhine. (That castle is Marksburg, which is great, but it lies on the inconvenient side of the river and requires visitors to take a guided tour offered only in German.)

Germany's Rhine River is filled with castle-crowned hills. There's even a castle built in the middle of the river (called Pfalz, accessible by tiny ferry but not worth touring). These can be enjoyed conveniently by train, car, or boat. The best 50-mile stretch is between Koblenz and Mainz. The best one-hour cruise is from St. Goar to Bacharach.

CHÂTEAU CHILLON, SWITZERLAND

Set romantically at the edge of Lake Geneva near Montreux, this wonderfully preserved 13th-century castle is worth a side trip from anywhere in southwest Switzerland. Follow the English brochure, which takes you on a self-guided tour from tingly perch-on-the-medieval-windowsill views through fascinatingly furnished rooms. The dank dungeon, mean weapons, and 700-year-old toilets will excite even the dullest travel partner. A handy but too-close-to-the-train-tracks youth

Run with the winds of the past in Europe's countless ruined castles. Here, with a little imagination, you're under attack a thousand years ago in Portugal.

hostel, Haut Lac, is a 10-minute stroll down the lakeside promenade toward Montreux (tel. 021/963-4934). Attack or escape the castle by ferry (free with your train pass).

MOORISH RUINS OF SINTRA, PORTUGAL
The desolate ruins of an 800-year-old Moorish castle overlook the sea and the town of Sintra, just west of Lisbon. Ignored by most of the tourists who flock to the glitzy Pena Palace (a castle capping a neighboring hilltop), the ruins of Sintra offer scramble-up-and-down-the-ramparts fun, atmospheric picnic perches, views, and an enchanted forest. With a little imagination, it's 1,000 years ago, and you're under attack.

REIFENSTEIN CASTLE, ITALY
For an incredibly medieval kick in the pants, get off the autobahn one hour south of Innsbruck at the Italian town of Vipiteno (called "Sterzing" by residents who prefer German). With her time-pocked sister just opposite, Reifenstein bottled up this strategic valley leading to the easiest way to cross the Alps. It offers castle connoisseurs the best-preserved original medieval castle interior I've ever seen. The lady who lives in Reifenstein Castle takes groups through in Italian, German, and *un poco* English (tours normally at 9:30 a.m., 10:30 a.m., 2:00 p.m., and 3:00 p.m., closed Friday; tel. 0472-765879 in Italy, 0039-472-765879 from Austria). You'll discover the mossy past as she explains how the cistern collected water, how drunken lords managed to get their keys into the keyholes, and how prisoners were left to rot in the dungeon (you'll look down the typical only-way-out hole in the ceiling). In the only surviving original knights' sleeping quarters (rough-hewn plank boxes lined with hay), you'll see how knights spent their nights. Lancelot would cry a lot.

The amazing little fortified town of Glurns hunkers down about an hour west of Reifenstein Castle (on the high road to Lake Como).

Glurns still lives within its square wall on the Adige River, with a church bell tower that has a thing about ringing, and real farms, rather than boutiques, filling the town courtyards. You can sleep with the family Hofer near the church, just outside of town (tel. 0473-831597).

CASTLE DAY: NEUSCHWANSTEIN (BAVARIA) AND THE EHRENBERG RUINS (REUTTE IN TIROL)

Three of my favorite castles—two famous, one unknown—can be seen in one busy day. "Castle Day" takes you to Germany's Disney-like Neuschwanstein Castle, the more stately Hohenschwangau Castle at its foot, and the much older Ehrenberg Ruins across the Austrian border in Reutte.

Home base is the small Austrian town of Reutte (just over the German border, three Alp-happy hours by train west of Innsbruck). Reutte has a helpful tourist information office with a room-finding service that can set you up in a private home "any day of the year" for $25 (open until 5:00 p.m., tel. 05672/62336).

From Reutte, catch the early bus across the border to touristy Füssen, the German town nearest Neuschwanstein. (Planning ahead, note times buses return to Reutte.) From Füssen, you can walk, pedal a rented bike, or ride a local bus to Neuschwanstein.

Neuschwanstein is the greatest of King Ludwig II's fairy-tale castles. His extravagance and romanticism earned this Bavarian king the title "Mad King Ludwig" (and an early death). His castle is one of Europe's most popular attractions. Get there early. The doors open at 8:30 a.m., an hour before the tour groups from Munich attack.

Take the fascinating (and required) English tour. This castle, which is about as old as the Eiffel Tower, is a textbook example of 19th-century romanticism. After the Middle Ages ended, people disparagingly named that era "Gothic," or barbarian. Then, all of a sudden, in the 1800s, it was hip to be square, and neo-Gothic became the rage. Throughout Europe, old castles were restored and new ones built—wallpapered with chivalry. King Ludwig II put his medieval fantasy on the hilltop, not for defensive reasons, but simply because he liked the view.

The lavish interior, covered with damsels in distress, dragons, and knights in gleaming armor, is enchanting. (A little knowledge of Wagner's operas goes a long way in bringing these stories to life.) Ludwig had great taste—for a mad king. Read up on this political misfit—a poet, hippie king in the "realpolitik" age of Bismarck. He was found dead in a lake under suspicious circumstances, never to enjoy his medieval fantasy come true. After the tour, climb farther up the hill to

HIGHLIGHTS OF
SOUTHERN BAVARIA
AND TIROL

Mary's Bridge for the best view of this crazy yet elegant castle.

Ludwig's boyhood home, the Hohenschwangau Castle at the foot of the hill, offers a better look at Ludwig's life and far fewer crowds. Like its more famous neighbor, it costs about $7 and takes an hour to tour.

This is a busy day. By lunchtime, catch the bus back to Reutte and get ready for a completely different castle experience.

Pack a picnic and your camera, and with the help of some local directions, walk 30 minutes out of town to the brooding Ehrenberg Ruins. You'll see a small hill crowned by a ruined castle.

The Kleine Schloss ("small castle") is really ruined but wonderfully free of anything from the 20th century—except for a fine view of Reutte sleeping peacefully in the valley below.

"Mad" King Ludwig's Neuschwanstein Castle

You have your own castle. When cloaked in a cloud shroud, you can peer into the spooky mist and almost see medieval knights in distress and damsels in shining armor. Grab a sword fern, lower your hair, and unfetter that imagination.

Back in the 20th century, you'll find Ehrenberg's castle reconstructed on Reutte's restaurant walls. Ask at your hotel where you can find a folk evening full of slap-dancing and yodel foolery. A hot, hearty dinner and an evening of local Tirolean entertainment is a fitting way to raise the drawbridge on your memorable "Castle Day."

See the Appendix (Recommended Accommodations) for more information.

60. Sobering Sights of Nazi Europe

Fondue, nutcrackers, Monet, Big Ben . . . gas chambers. A trip to once-upon-a-time Europe can be a fairy tale. It can also help tell the story of Europe's 20th-century fascist nightmare. While few travelers go to Europe to dwell on the horrors of Nazism, most value visiting the memorials of fascism's reign of terror and honoring the wish of its survivors—"Forgive but never forget."

Of the countless concentration camps, **Dachau**, just outside of Munich, is most visited. While some visitors complain that it's too "prettied-up," it gives a powerful look at how these camps worked. Built in 1933, this first Nazi concentration camp offers a compelling voice from our recent, grisly past, warning and pleading "Never Again"—the memorial's theme. On arrival, pick up the miniguide and check when the next documentary film in English will be shown. The museum, the movie, the chilling camp-inspired art, the reconstructed barracks, the gas chambers (never used), the cremation ovens, and the memorial shrines will chisel into you the hidden meaning of fascism. (Dachau is free, open Tuesday–Sunday 9:00 a.m.–5:00 p.m., and closed Monday.)

Auschwitz (or Oswiecim), near Krakow in Poland, and **Mäthausen**, near Linz on the Danube in Austria, are more powerful and less touristed. While many camps were slave-labor camps, Auschwitz, the dreaded destination of the Polish Jews such as those on Schindler's list, was built to exterminate. View the horrifying film shot by the Russians who liberated the camp in early 1945. Don't miss the museum. The simple yet emotionally powerful display of prisoners' shoes, hairbrushes, and suitcases puts lumps in even the most stoic throats. Allow plenty of time to wander and ponder.

A second Auschwitz camp, **Birkenau**, is two miles away. This bleak ghost camp, an orderly pile of abandoned barracks and watch-towers overlooking an ash-gray lake, is left as if no one after the war had the nerve to even enter the place. Today, pilgrims do. Auschwitz is just 90 minutes by train from the wonder of Krakow, Poland's best-preserved medieval city.

Mäthausen town sits cute and prim on the romantic Danube at the start of the very scenic trip downstream to Vienna. But nearby, atop a now-still quarry, linger the memories of a horrible slave-labor camp. Less tourist-oriented than Dachau, Mäthausen is a solemn place of meditation and continuous mourning. Fresh flowers adorn yellowed photos of lost loved ones. The home country of each victim has erected a gripping monument. You'll find yourself in an artistic gallery of grief, resting on a foundation of Never Forget. Mäthausen (open 8:00 a.m. to 5:00 p.m. daily) offers an English booklet, a free English Walkman tour, an English movie, and a painful but necessary museum.

Paris and Amsterdam also have their Nazi sights: the **Memorial de la Deportation** in Paris and **Anne Frank's house** in Amsterdam. To commemorate the 200,000 French victims of Hitler's camps, Paris built an evocative memorial on the tip of the Île de la Cité, just behind Notre-Dame. A visit to this memorial is like entering a work of art. Walk down the claustrophobic stairs into a world of concrete, iron

Memorial at the Dachau concentration camp

NAZI SIGHTS

bars, water, and sky. Inside the structure, the 200,000 crystals—one for each lost person—eternal flame, triangular niches containing soil from various concentration camps, and powerful quotes will etch the message into your mind.

Anne Frank's house, made famous by her diary, gives the cold, mind-boggling statistics of fascism the all-important intimacy of a young girl who lived through it and died from it. Even bah-humbug types, who are dragged in because it's raining and their spouses read the diary, find themselves caught up.

Before you leave Anne's beyond-the-hidden-staircase world, you'll get an update on fascism in Europe today. The committed volunteers at the Anne Frank house know that the only way fascism will emerge from its loony fringe is if we get complacent and think it could never happen again.

While Hitler controlled Europe, each country had a courageous, if small, resistance movement. All over Europe you'll find streets and squares named after the martyrs of the resistance. Any history buff or champion of the underdog will be thrilled by the patriotism documented in the **Oslo and Copenhagen Nazi resistance museums.**

Since destruction and death are fascist fortes, only relatively insignificant bits and pieces of Hitler's Germany survive. **Berlin**, now that its Wall is history, is giving its Nazi chapter a little more attention. There are several new Nazi-related museums, memorials, and guided walks. You might visit Berlin's Great Synagogue (which was burned on Kristallnacht in 1938), the site of Hitler's bunker (where he committed suicide in the last days of the war), the Topography of Terror exhibit (near what was Checkpoint Charlie, illustrating SS tactics), and the adjacent four small "mountains" made from the rubble of the bombed-out city. The gripping **Käthe Kollwitz Museum** is filled with art inspired by the horrors of Berlin's Nazi experience.

Munich's most Hitleresque building is the stony, bold **Haus der Kunst.** Hitler's house of art is now filled with the stuff he hated most . . . modern art. Dali. Picasso. Kandinsky. Take that!

In **Nuremberg** the ghosts of Hitler's showy propaganda rallies still rustle in the Rally Grounds (now Dutzendteich Park), down the Great Road, and through the New Congress Hall. The local tourist office has a handy booklet entitled *Nuremberg 1933 to 1945*.

The town of **Berchtesgaden**, near the Austrian border, is any German's choice for a great mountain hideaway—including Hitler's. The remains of Hitler's Obersalzburg headquarters, with its extensive tunnel system, thrill some World War II buffs but are so scant that most visitors are impressed only by the view.

Knowing you can't take on the world without great freeways, Hitler started Germany's autobahn system. **Hitler's first autobahn rest stop** is on the lake called Herrenchiemsee, between Munich and Salzburg. Now a lakeside hotel for U.S. military personnel, it's still frescoed with "*Deutschland über alles*" themes. Take the Feldon exit and politely wander around the hotel. The dining room has the best "love-your-Aryan-heritage-and-work-hard-for-the-state" art.

Your greatest opportunity to experience fascist architecture is in Rome, where you can wander through Mussolini's futuristic suburb called **E.U.R.** and the bold pink houses of fascist Italy's Olympic Village. South of Rome, on the coastal road to Naples, are several towns built in the Mussolini era (such as Latina, Sabaudia, Pontinia, and Aprilia), which are interesting for their stocky colonnades and the intentional sterility of their piazzas.

After completing his "final solution," Hitler had hoped to build a grand museum of the "decadent" Jewish culture in **Prague**. Today Prague's State Jewish Museum (Statni Zidovske Muzeum), in a complex of old synagogues, contains artifacts the Nazis assembled from that city's once-thriving Jewish community.

Just outside of Prague is the **Terezin concentration camp**. This particularly insidious place was dolled up as a model camp for Red Cross inspection purposes. Displays show how the inmates had their own newspaper and how the children put on cute plays. But after the camp passed its inspection, life returned to slave labor and death. Ponder the touching collection of Jewish children's art.

Possibly the most moving sight of all is the martyred village of **Oradour-sur-Glane,** in central France. This town, 15 miles northwest of Limoges, was machine-gunned and burned in 1944 by Nazi SS troops. Seeking revenge for the killing of one of their officers, they left 642 townspeople dead in a blackened crust of a town under a silent blanket of ashes. The poignant ruins of Oradour-sur-Glane—scorched sewing machines, pots, pans, bikes, and cars—have been preserved as an eternal reminder of the reality of war. When you visit you'll see the simple sign that greets every pilgrim who enters: "*Souviens-toi . . .* remember."

61. Europe's Best-Preserved Little Towns

Every once in a while as you travel, you stumble onto a town that somehow missed the 20th-century bus. Ironically, many of these wonderfully preserved towns are so full of Old World charm because, for various reasons, their economies failed. The towns became so poor that no one even bothered to tear them down to build more modern towns. The Cotswolds lost their export market. Bruges' harbor silted up. Stranded-in-the-past Dutch fishing towns were left high and dry as the sea around them was reclaimed. Toledo lost its position as Spain's capital city.

Today many of these towns enjoy a renewed prosperity as "tourist dreams come true." Others slumber on, quietly keeping their secrets. When the Old World is not performing on big-city stages, it huddles in the pubs and gossips in the markets of Europe's villages. Here are a few of my favorites.

Óbidos, Portugal's medieval walled gem, is a short drive north of Lisbon. Its city wall circles a clutter of cobbled paths, alleys, flower-decked homes, and a castle, now one of Portugal's popular *pousadas* (historic government-run hotels). While several queens used the town as a dowry, today's Óbidos is promoted by the Portuguese tourist board to lure visitors. Like a glazed tile, it's beautiful but dead.

Toledo, so historic and well-preserved that the entire city is protected as a national monument, is Spain's historic, artistic, and spiritual capital. Toledo is filled with tourists day-tripping from Madrid, 90 minutes to the north. Miss the bus and spend the night! After dark, Toledo is much more medieval—almost haunted in some corners. Explore its back streets and marvel at the great cathedral with a sacristy full of El Greco masterpieces. Munch on communion wafer-like cookies the size of paper plates. End your day with a feast of roast suckling pig somewhere in the dark tangle of nighttime Toledo.

The small resorts of the French Riviera line the beach like prostitutes on bar stools, promising tourists a good time. But **Collioure**, just before the Spanish border, aims its charms at its own people and a few savvy passersby. And while most of France's Mediterranean coast is condo city, the stretch just south of Perpignon is more like camping village. Collioure offers an ideal small-town-without-the-glitz alternative to condo-city Riviera. Like an ice cream shop, it offers 31 flavors of pastel houses and six petite scooped-out beaches—sprinkled lightly with beachgoers. This sweet scene, capped by Collioure's winking lighthouse, sits under a once-mighty castle in the shade of the Pyrenees. It's no wonder painters and local families feel no need to struggle with the Cannes-fusion that grabs the typical Riviera-bound visitor. In a district called Catalane, flying a flag looking just like Barcelona's over its tiny bullring, and greeting you with its own accent, in some ways Collioure has turned its cobbled back on France. But the ambience of Collioure is what was so charming about the Côte d'Azur back before the introduction of the paid vacation made the Riviera France's holiday beach. Collioure is about two hours by car or train from Avignon, Carcassonne, and Barcelona. And by car, you're an hour's climb to Peyrepertuse, the most impressive castle ruins of the many that dot the Pyrenees. For cheap, airy, and comfortable rooms a block past the streamed in the old town, call "Chambres," 20 rue Pasteur, tel. 04 68 82 15 31.

Bruges, (BROOZH, in French) or Brugge (Broo-guh, in Flemish), is Belgium's medieval wonderland. Bruges has enough art to make a big city proud. Let a local guide show you the town's treasures: fun modern art, an impressive collection of Flemish paintings, a leaning tower, and the only finished Michelangelo statue in Northern Europe. Like so many small-town wonders, Bruges is well-pickled because its economy went sour. Formerly a textiles trading center riding high on the prosperity of the Northern Renaissance, its harbor silted up, the shipping was lost, and Bruges was forgotten—until rediscovered by modern-day tourists. Once again, Bruges thrives. Just 15 minutes from Oostende, where boats dock from Dover, Bruges makes a fine first night on the Continent for travelers coming over from England.

The Netherlands will tempt you with splashy tourist towns— communities of clichés where women with the ruddiest cheeks are paid to stand on doorsteps wearing wooden shoes, lace aprons, and smiles. A local boy peels eels, there's enough cheese to make another moon, and some kid somewhere must have his finger in a dike. These towns (such as Volendam, Monnickendam, and Marken) are designed to be fun, and they are. But make an effort to find a purely Dutch town that is true to itself, not to tourism. Rent a bike and enjoy exploring this tiny, flat country with your own wheels. In Holland you can rent a bike at one train station and leave it at nearly any other. My favorite village is little **Hindeloopen** (near Sneek). Silent behind its dike, it's right out of a Vermeer painting—hardcore Holland. The towns of Haarlem, Delft, and Edam are pleasant bases for day-tripping into often-sleazy Amsterdam.

England loves quaintness. Every year she holds most-beautiful-town contests, and all over the country cobbles are scrubbed, flowers are planted, and hedges shaved. With such spirit, it's not surprising that England is freckled with more small-town cuteness than any country in Europe. The "ye olde" pubs and markets, combined with townspeople who happily eat, breathe, and sleep their history, make any rural part of England a fine setting to enjoy tea and scones or a pint of beer.

While you're likely to find a small, prize-winning town just about anywhere in England, the **Cotswold Hills** and the southeast coast tuck away some of the best. Both regions were once rich, but shifting seas and industrial low tides left them high and dry. Today their chief export is coziness with a British accent. The southeast coast has five former ports—the "Cinque Ports"—that now harbor tourists for a living. One of them, Rye, is commonly overrated as England's most photogenic village. England's many moors hide away time-passed villages that have refused to join the modern parade. **Staithes**, Captain Cook's boyhood town, just north of Whitby near the York Moors, is a salty jumble of ancient buildings bunny-hopping down a ravine to a cramped little harbor.

Europe has become a scavenger hunt for tourists, and most of the prizes have been found. But there are many towns that time forgot and tourists neglect. Passau in Germany, Hall in Tirol, Rouen in France, Sighisoara in Romania, and Erice in Sicily are just a few. Even with tourist crowds, which are now a standard feature in the summer months, the smaller towns of Europe give the traveler the best look at Europe's old culture.

See the Appendix (Recommended Accommodations) for more information.

62. Bad Towns and Tourist Traps

It's generally not considered "in good taste" to write negatively about tourist destinations. But since I'm the kind of tour guide who burps with the mike on, I'd like to give you my opinion on Europe's dullest places. Chances are that you have too many stops on your trip wish list and not enough time. To make your planning a little easier, take my advice and skip the places described here.

Zurich and Geneva are two of Switzerland's largest and most sterile cities. Both are pleasantly situated on a lake—like Buffalo and

Cleveland. And both are famous, but name familiarity is a rotten reason to go somewhere. If you want a Swiss city, see Bern. But it's almost criminal to spend a sunny Swiss day anywhere but high in the Alps.

Bordeaux must mean "boredom" in some ancient language. If I were offered a free trip to that town, I'd stay home and clean the fridge. Connoisseurs visit for the wine, but Bordeaux wine country and Bordeaux city are as different as night and night soil. There's a wine-tourist information bureau in Bordeaux which, for a price, will bus you out of town into the more interesting wine country nearby.

Andorra, a small country in the Pyrenees between France and Spain, is as scenic as any other chunk of those mountains. People from all over Europe flock to Andorra to take advantage of its famous duty-free shopping. As far as Americans are concerned, Andorra is just a big Spanish-speaking Radio Shack. There are no bargains here that you can't get at home. Enjoy the Pyrenees with less traffic elsewhere.

Germany's famous Black Forest disappoints more people than it excites. If that's all Germany offered, it would be worth seeing. For Europeans, any large forest is a popular attraction. But I'd say the average American visitor who's seen more than three trees in one place would prefer Germany's Romantic Road and Bavaria to the east, the Rhine and Mosel country to the north, the Swiss Alps to the south, and France's Alsace region to the west—all high points that cut the Black Forest down to stumps.

Norway's Stavanger, famous for nearby fjords and its status as an oil-boom town, is a large port that's about as exciting as, well, put it this way . . . emigrants left it in droves to move to the wilds of Minnesota. Time in western Norway is better spent in and around Bergen.

Bucharest, the capital of Romania, has little to offer. Its top-selling postcard is of the Intercontinental Hotel.

If you're heading from eastern Europe to Greece, skip Thessaloníki, which deserves its place in the Bible but doesn't belong in travel guidebooks.

Athens, while worth visiting, is probably the most overrated city in Europe. A century ago Athens was a sleepy town of 8,000 people with a pile of ruins in its backyard. Today it's a giant mix of concrete, smog, noise, tourists, and 4 million Greeks. See the four major attractions (the Acropolis, the Agora, the Plaka, and the great National Archaeological Museum) and get out to the islands or countryside.

Extra caution is merited in southwest England, a minefield of tourist traps. The British are masters at milking every conceivable tourist attraction for all it's worth. Here are some booby traps worth avoiding if you're traveling on limited time or money:

Cornwall, England's southernmost region, has more than its share of cotton-candy touristic fluff. I'll never forget driving past signs prepping me for the "Devil's Toenail." "Only five miles—The Devil's Toenail." Then, "The Devil's Toenail—next left!" Well, I figured I'd better check it out. I pulled into the parking lot. Paid to park. Paid again to pass through the turnstile. Walked to the bottom of the ravine. And there was a watermelon-sized rock that looked just like . . . a toenail. Disappointed and a bit embarrassed, I took a quick picture and hiked back to my car, vowing never again to fall for such a sly snare.

Predictably, Land's End, the far southwest tip of England, is geared up to attract hordes of tourists. You pay to park, pay to enter, walk to the point for a photo to prove you were there, grab a postcard, and leave.

On the north Cornwall coast, above Land's End, are two more tourist magnets. Tintagel's famous castle is the legendary birthplace of King Arthur. Its exciting windswept and wave-beaten ruins are well worth exploring. Meanwhile, the town does everything in its power to exploit the profitable Arthurian legend, even with the Excali Bar pub.

Just up the coast is Clovelly. I had it circled in my guidebook years before I ever got there. It sounded so cute—"daintily clinging to the rocky coast, desperately trying not to plunge into the wicked seas." But when you arrive, reality rules. You'll pay to park your car 100 yards away and join the crowds funneling into the little town's one street. You can shop your way down one side to the waterfront and up the other side past cute knickknack shops, all selling just about the same goodies—like "clotted cream that you can mail home." Don't let tourist traps get between you and the real beauties of England.

The towns and places I've mentioned here are worth skipping only because they're surrounded by so many places much more worthy of the average traveler's limited vacation time. If you have a villa in Andorra or a cuckoo-clock shop in the Black Forest, no offense is meant. Just remember to distinguish carefully between entrepreneurial ventures and legitimate sightseeing attractions.

Beyond Europe

63. Morocco: Plunge Deep

Walking through the various souks of the labyrinthine medina, I found sights you could only dream of in America. Dodging blind men and clubfeet, I was stoned by smells, sounds, sights, and feelings. People came in all colors, sizes, temperaments, and varieties of deformities. Milky eyes, charismatic beggars, stumps of limbs, sticks of children, tattooed women, walking mummies, grabbing salesmen, teasing crafts-men, seductive scents, half-bald dogs, and little boys on rooftops were reaching out from all directions.

Ooo! Morocco! Slices of Morocco make the *Star Wars* bar scene look bland. And it's just a quick cruise from Spain. You can't, however, experience Morocco in a day trip from the Costa del Sol. Plunge deep and your journal will read like a Dalí painting. While Morocco is not easy traveling, it gets rave reviews from those who plug this Islamic detour into their European vacation.

In Spain catch a boat to Tangier from Algeciras or the more pleas-ant town of Tarifa. Don't linger in Tangier and Tetuan, the Moroccan Tijuanas of the north coast. Tangier is not really Morocco—it's a city full of con men who thrive on green tourists. Find the quickest con-nections south to Rabat. Power your way off the boat, then shove through the shysters to the nearby train station. They'll tell you there's no train until tomorrow, or "Rabat is closed on Thursdays," anything to get you to stay in Tangier. Believe nothing. Be rude if you have to. Tangier can give you only grief, while the real Morocco lies to the south. Try to make friends with a Moroccan traveler on the boat, who won't be a con man and who'll usually be happy to help you slip through his embarrassingly stressful port of entry.

Rabat, Morocco's capital, is a good first stop. This comfortable most-European city in Morocco lacks the high-pressure tourism of the towns on the north coast. Or, for a pleasant break on the beach and a relaxing way to break into Morocco, spend a day at Asilah, between Tangier and Larache.

Taxis are cheap and a real bargain when you consider the comfort, speed, and convenience they provide in these hot, dusty, and confusing cities. Eat and drink carefully in Morocco. Bottled water and bottled soft drinks are safe. The extra cautious might have "well-cooked" writ-ten in Arabic on a scrap of paper and flash it when you order meat. I found the couscous, *tajine*, and omelets uniformly good. The Arabs use

MOROCCO

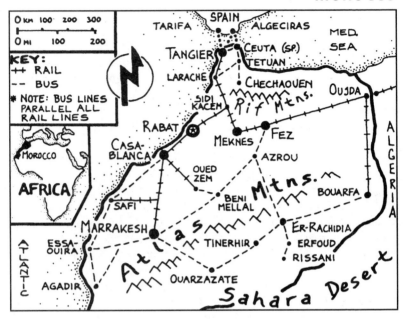

different number symbols. Learn them. You can practice on license plates, which list the number twice. Morocco was a French colony, so French is more widely understood than English. A French phrase book is handy. Travel very light in Morocco. You can leave most of your luggage at your last Spanish hotel for free if you plan to spend a night there on your return from Africa.

After Rabat, pass through Casablanca (great movie, dull city) and catch the Marrakech Express south. You'll hang your head out the window of that romantic old train and sing to the passing desert.

Marrakech is the epitome of exotic. Take a horse-drawn carriage from the station to downtown and find a hotel near the Djemaa el Fna, the central square of Marrakech, where the action is. Desert musicians, magicians, storytellers, acrobats, snake charmers, gamblers, and tricksters gather crowds of tribespeople who have come to Marrakech to do their market chores. As a tourist, you'll fit in like a clown at a funeral. Be very careful, don't gamble, and hang onto your wallet. You're in another world, and you're not clever here. Spend an entire day in the colorful medina wandering aimlessly from souk to souk. There's a souk for each trade, such as the dyers' souk, the leather souk, and the carpet souk.

Moroccan road sign: Beware of toboggans

In the medina, you'll be badgered—or "guided"—by small boys all claiming to be "a friend who wants to practice English." They are after money, nothing else. If you don't want their services, make two things crystal clear: You have no money for them, and you want no guide. Then completely ignore them. Remember that while you're with a guide, he'll get commissions for anything you buy. Throughout Morocco you'll be pestered by these obnoxious hustler-guides.

I often hire a young and easy-to-control boy who speaks enough English to serve as my interpreter. It seems that if I'm "taken," the other guides leave me alone. And that in itself is worth the small price of a guide.

The market is a shopper's delight. Bargain hard, shop around, and you'll come home with some great souvenirs. Government emporiums usually have the same items you find in the market, but priced fairly. If you get sick of souks, shop there and you'll get the fair price—haggle-free.

From Marrakech, consider getting to Fez indirectly by taking an exciting seven-day loop to the south. While buses are reliable and efficient throughout Morocco, this tour is best by car, and it's easy to rent a car in Marrakech and drop it off in Fez. (Car rentals are cheaper when arranged from the U.S.A.)

Drive or catch the bus south over the rugged Atlas Mountains to Saharan Morocco. Explore the isolated oasis towns of Ouarzazate, Tinerhir, and Er-Rachidia. If time permits, the trip from Ouarzazate to Zagora is an exotic mud-brick pie. These towns each have a weekly "market day," when the tribespeople gather to do their shopping. This is your chance to stock up on honeydew melons and goats' heads. Stay in Tinerhir's Hotel du Todra and climb to the roof for a great view of the busy marketplace below.

Venture out of town into the lush fields, where you'll tumble into an almost Biblical world. Sit on a rock and dissect the silence. A weary donkey carrying a bearded old man in a white robe and turban clip-clops slowly past you. Suddenly, six Botticelli maidens flit like watercolor confetti across your trail and giggle out of sight. Stay tuned. The show goes on.

Bus rides in this part of Morocco are intriguing. I could write pages about experiences I've had on Moroccan buses—good and bad—but I don't want to spoil the surprise. Just ride them with a spirit of adventure, fingers crossed, and keep your bag off the rooftop.

SAHARAN ADVENTURE

Heading south from Er-Rachidia, a series of mud-brick villages bunny-hop down a lush river valley and into the Sahara. Finally the road melts into the sand, and the next stop is, literally, Timbuktu.

The strangeness of this Alice in a sandy Wonderland world, untempered, can be overwhelming—even frightening. The finest hotel in Erfoud, the region's major town, will provide a much-needed refuge, keeping out the sand, heat waves, and street kids and providing safe-to-eat and tasty local food, reliable information, and a good and affordable bed.

But the hotel is only your canteen and springboard. Explore! If you plan to go deep into the desert, hire a guide. Choose one you can understand and tolerate, set a price for his services, and before dawn, head for the dunes.

You'll drive to the last town, Rissani (market days are Tuesday, Thursday, Sunday), and then farther south over 15 miles of natural asphalt to the oasis village of Merzouga. There's plenty of tourist traffic at sunrise and in the early evening, so hitching is fairly easy. A couple of places in Merzouga rent spots on their terrace for those who spend the night. If a civil war is still smoldering in the desert, you may have to show your passport.

Leave Europe and a warm Islamic welcome awaits.

Before you glows a chain of sand-dune mountains. Climb one. It's not easy. I seemed to slide farther backward with each step. Hike along a cool and crusty ridge. Observe bugs and their tracks. Watch small sand avalanches you started all by yourself. From the great virgin summit, savor the Sahara view orchestrated by a powerful silence. Your life sticks out like a lone star in a black sky. Tumble, roll, and slosh down your dune. Look back and see the temporary damage one person can inflict on that formerly perfect slope. Then get back in your car before the summer sun turns the sand into a steaming griddle and you into an omelet. Off-season, the midday desert sun is surprisingly mild.

Merzouga is full of very poor people. The village children hang out at the ruins of an old palace. A ragtag percussion group gave us an impromptu concert. The children gathered around us tighter and tighter, as the musicians picked up the tempo. We shared smiles, warmth, and sadness. A little Moroccan Judy Garland saw out of one eye, the other cloudy as rice pudding. One gleaming six-year-old carried a tiny brother slung, sleeping, on her back. His crusty little fly-covered face was too tired to flinch. We had a bag of candy to share and tried to get 40 kids into an orderly line to march past one by one. Impossible. The line degenerated into a free-for-all, and our bag became a piñata.

Only through the mercy of our guide did we find our way back to Rissani. Camels loitered nonchalantly, looking very lost and not caring.

Cool lakes flirted, a distant mirage, and the black hardpan road stretched endlessly in all directions.

Then, with a sigh, we were back in Rissani, where the road starts up again. For us, it was breakfast time, and Rissani offered little more than some very thought-provoking irony. My friends and I could find no "acceptable" place to eat. Awkwardly, we drank germ-free Cokes with pursed lips, balanced bread on upturned bottle caps, and swatted laughing legions of flies. We were by far the wealthiest people in the valley—and the only ones unable to enjoy an abundant variety of good but strange food.

Observing the scene from our humble rusted table, we saw a busy girl rhythmically smashing date seeds; three stoic, robed elders with horseshoe beards; and a prophet wandering through with a message for all that he was telling to nobody.

Our Er-Rachidia hotel was Western-style—as dull and comforting as home. We shared the Walkman and enjoyed the pool, resting and recharging before our next Saharan plunge.

SAHARAN NIGHTLIFE

Desert dwellers and smart tourists know the value of a siesta during the hottest part of the day. But a Saharan evening is the perfect time for a traveler to get out and experience the vibrancy of North African village life. We drove 10 miles north of Erfoud to a fortified mud-brick oasis village. There were no paint, no electricity, no cars—only people, adobe walls, and palm trees. Absolutely nothing other than the nearby two-lane highway hinted of the 20th century.

We entered like Lewis and Clark without Sacajawea, knowing instantly we were in for a rich experience. A wedding feast was erupting, and the whole town buzzed with excitement, all decked out in colorful robes and their best smiles. We felt very welcome.

The teeming street emptied through the medieval gate onto the field, where a band was playing squawky oboe-like instruments and drums. A circle of 20 ornately dressed women made siren noises with tongues flapping like party favors. Rising dust diffused the lantern light, giving everything the grainy feel of an old photo. The darkness focused our attention on a relay of seductively beautiful, snake-thin dancers. A flirtatious atmosphere raged, cloaked safely in the impossibility of anything transpiring beyond coy smiles and teasing twists.

Then the village's leading family summoned us for dinner. Pillows, blankets, a lantern, and a large round filigreed table turned a stone cave into a warm lounge. The men of this family had traveled to Europe and spoke some English. For more than two hours, the women prepared dinner and the men proudly entertained their First World guests. First was the ritualistic tea ceremony. Like a mad chemist, the tea specialist mixed it just right. With a thirsty gleam in his eye and a large spike in his hand, he hacked off a chunk of sugar from a coffee can–sized lump and watched it melt into Morocco's basic beverage. He sipped it, as if testing a fine wine, added more sugar, and offered me a taste. When no more sugar could be absorbed, we drank it with cookies and dates. Then, with the fanfare of a pack of Juicy Fruit, the men passed around a hashish pipe. Our shocked look was curious to them. Next, a tape deck brought a tiny clutter of music, from Arab and tribal Berber music to James Brown, reggae, and twangy Moroccan pop. The men danced splendidly.

Finally the meal came. Fourteen people sat on the floor, circling two round tables. Nearby, a child silently waved a palm branch fan, keeping the flies away. A portable washbasin and towel were passed around to start and finish the meal. With our fingers and gravy-soaked slabs of bread, we grabbed spicy meat and vegetables. Everyone dipped eagerly into the delicious central bowl of couscous.

So far, the Moroccan men dominated. Young girls took turns peeking around the corner and dashing off—much like teeny-boppers anywhere. Two older women in striking, black-jeweled outfits were squatting attentively in the corner, keeping their distance and a very low profile. Then one pointed to me and motioned in charades, indicating long hair, a backpack, and a smaller partner. I had been in this same village in the '70s. I had longer hair and a backpack and was traveling with a short partner. Did she remember us? I scribbled "1978" on a scrap of paper. She scratched it out and wrote "1979." Wow! She remembered my 20-minute stay so long ago! People in remote lands enjoy a visiting tourist and find the occasion at least as memorable as we do. So many more doors open to the traveler who knocks.

After a proud tour of their schoolhouse, we were escorted across the field back to our car, which had been guarded by a silent, white-robed man. We drove away, reeling with the feeling that the memories of this evening would be the prize souvenir of our trip.

64. Turkey's Hot

Turkey is a proud new country. It was born in 1923, when Ataturk, the father of modern Turkey, rescued it from the buffet line of European colonialism. He divided church and state, liberated women (at least on paper), replaced the Arabic script with Europe's alphabet, and gave the battle-torn, corrupt, and demoralized remnants of the Ottoman Empire the foundation of a modern nation. Because of Ataturk, today's 60 million Turks have a flag—and reason to wave it. For a generation, many young Turkish women actually worried that they'd never be able to really love a man because of their love for the father of their country.

At the same time, Turkey is a musty archeological attic, with dusty civilization stacked upon civilization. The more they dig, the more they learn that Turkey, not Mesopotamia, is the cradle of Western civilization.

I find Turkey even tastier, friendlier, cheaper, and richer in culture and history than Greece. But the average Turk looks like a character the average American mother would tell her child to run from. Dark and unshaven . . . Turks can't help it if they look like someone who could assassinate the pope. It's important that we see past our visual hangups and recognize Turks as the sincere and friendly people they are.

Those who haven't been to Turkey wonder why anyone would choose to go there. Those who've been dream of returning. Turkey is being discovered. Tourists are learning that the image of the terrible Turk is false, created to a great degree by its unfriendly neighbors. Turks are quick to remind visitors that, surrounded by Syria, Iraq, Iran, Armenia, Georgia, Bulgaria, and Greece, they're not living in Mr. Rogers' neighborhood.

Many Americans know Turkey only from the thrilling but unrealistic movie *Midnight Express*. The movie was paid for, produced, and performed by Armenians and Greeks (historically unfriendly neighbors). It says nothing about the Turks or Turkey today. Also, many visitors are put off by Turkey's "rifles on every corner" image. Turkey is not a police state. Its NATO commitment is to maintain nearly a million-man army. Except in the far east, where this million-man army is dealing with the Kurds and Iraq, these soldiers have little to do but "patrol" and "guard"—basically, loiter in uniform.

Today Turkey is on the move. It's looking West and getting there. You can travel throughout the country on Turkey's great bus system. Telephones work. Hotels have fax machines. I had a forgotten plane ticket expressed across the country in 24 hours for $3. Fifty percent of Turkey's 42,000 villages had electricity in 1980. Now all do. Does all this modernization threaten the beautiful things that make Turkish culture so Turkish? An old village woman assured me, "We can survive TV and tourism because we have deep and strong cultural roots."

English is more widely spoken, and tourism is booming. Business everywhere seems brisk, but inflation is so bad that most hotels list their prices in deutsche Marks or dollars. With thousands of Turkish liras to the dollar, shoppers carry calculators to count the zeros.

Travel in Turkey is cheap. Good, comfortable, double rooms with private showers cost $30. Vagabonds order high on menus. And buses, which offer none of the romantic chaos of earlier years, take travelers anywhere in the country nearly any time for about $2 an hour.

Turkey knows it's on the fence between the rising wealth and power of a soon-to-be-united Europe and a forever-fragile-and-messy Middle East. Turks know the threat of the rising tide of Islamic fundamentalism and, while the country is 98 percent Muslim, they want nothing of the Khomeni-style rule that steadily blows the dust of religious discontent over their border. But fundamentalists are making inroads. As they walk by, veiled women in tow, modern-minded Turks grumble—a bit nervously. On Ataturk Day, stadiums around the country are filled with students shouting in thunderous unison, "We are a secular nation."

Two months after the Gulf War, I enjoyed my ninth trip through Turkey, this time with 22 travel partners and a Turkish co-guide. We had a life-changing 15 days together, enjoyed a level-headed look at Islam, took a peek at a hardworking, developing country with its act impressively together, and learned how our mass media can wrongly shape America's assessment of faraway lands. No survey was necessary to know that we all brought home a better understanding of our world. But a survey did show that 14 people bought carpets (mostly under $1,000, one for $3,000), eight people had diarrhea (seven for less than two days, one for six days), and nine of us learned to play backgammon well enough to actually beat a Turk in a smoky teahouse. For $5 you can buy tea for 20 new friends, play backgammon until the smoke doesn't bother you, and rock to the pulse of Turkey. Oh, those tiny handmade dice . . . cockeyed dots in a land where time is not money.

Turkey reshuffles your cards. A beautiful girl is called a *pistachio*. A person with a beautiful heart but an ugly face is called a Maltese plum—the ugliest fruit you'll ever enjoy. Industrious boys break large chocolate bars into small pieces to sell for a profit. For $2 a Gypsy's bear will do a show called "your mother-in-law dancing in a Turkish bath."

Much of Turkey is scrambling into the modern Western world, but the Turkish way of life is painted onto this land with an indelible cultural ink. If you're able to put your guidebook aside and follow your wanderlust, you'll still find sleepy goats playing Bambi on rocks overlooking a nomad's black tent. High above on the hillside, the lone but happy song of the goatherd's flute plays golden oldies. The mother bakes bread and minds the children, knowing her man is near.

Riding the waves of Turkey is like abstract art, a riveting movie without a plot, a melody of people, culture, and landscape that you just can't seem to stop whistling.

GÜZELYURT—CAPPADOCIA WITHOUT TOURISTS

Cappadocia is rightly famous as the most bizarre and fascinating bit of central Turkey that accepts bank cards. The most exciting discovery I made on my last trip was a town on the edge of Cappadocia called Güzelyurt.

Güzelyurt means "beautiful land." It's best known in Turkey as the town where historic enemies—Greeks, Turks, Kurds, and Bulgarians—live in peace. The town is a harmony of cultures, history, architecture, and religions. Walk down streets that residents from 3,000 years ago might recognize, past homes carved into the rocks, enjoying friendly greetings of *merhaba*. Scowling sheepdogs, caged behind 10-foot-high troglodyte rockeries, give the scene just enough tension.

Walk to a viewpoint at the far side of town (above the Sivisli church), toward the snowy slopes of the Fuji-like volcano that rules the horizon. Before you is a lush and living gorge. The cliff rising from the gorge is stacked with building styles: Upon the 1,600-year-old church sit troglodyte caves, Selcuk arches, and Ottoman facades. And on the horizon gleams the tin dome of the 20th-century mosque, with its twin minarets giving you a constant visual call to prayer. The honey that holds this architectural baklava together is people.

Put your camera away, shut your mouth, and sit silently in the sounds of 1000 B.C. Children play, birds chirp, roosters crow, shepherds chase goats, and mothers cackle. (Ignore that distant motorbike.)

Traditional lifestyles survive in Turkey.

Below you, sleeping in the greens and wet browns of this tidepool of simple living, is the church of St. Gregorius. Built in 385, it's thought by Gregorian fans to be the birthplace of church music, specifically the Gregorian chant. Its single minaret indicates that it's preserved as a mosque today in a valley where people call god Allah.

Who needs three-star sights and tourist information offices? In Güzelyurt, we dropped by the city hall. The mayor scampered across town to arrange a lunch for us in his home. He welcomed us Christians, explaining, "We believe in the four books"—the local way of saying, "It doesn't matter what you call Him, as long as you call Him." He showed us the names of his Greek Christian friends, kept as safe and sacred as good friends could be in his most precious and holy possession, the family Koran bag.

The lady of the house made tea. Overlapping carpets gave the place a cozy bug-in-a-rug feeling. As the lady cranked up the music, we all began to dance like charmed snakes. It was very safe sex until our fingers could snap no more. A small girl showed me a handful of almonds and said, "Buy dem." *Badam* is Turkish for almond, and this was her gift to me. Enjoying her munchies, I reciprocated with a handful of Pop Rocks. As the tiny candies exploded in her mouth, her surprised eyes became even more beautiful.

The town's name is spelled proudly across its volcanic backdrop. The black bust of Ataturk seems to loom just as high over the small modern market square. The streets are alive with the relaxed click of victorious *tavla* (backgammon) pieces. The men of the town, who seem to be enjoying one eternal cigarette break, proudly make a point not to stare at the stare-worthy American visitors searching for postcards in a town with no tourism.

Güzelyurt, in central Turkey, is 35 miles from Nevsehir and a short bus ride from Aksaray. It's near the Peristrema Valley, famous for its seven-mile hike through a lush valley of poplar groves, eagles, vultures, and early Christian churches. The town has one rustic but classy hotel (Hotel Karballa, Güzelyurt, Aksaray, $50 doubles with dinner and breakfast, tel. 382/451-2103, fax 382/451-2107) and one pension (Pansion Gelveri, run by Kadir Gok, who speaks German, one block off the town square, $15 for bed and a great local-style breakfast, tel. 382/451-2166).

Belisirma, a village near Güzelyurt, is even more remote. With a population of "100 homes," Belisirma zigzags down to its river, which rushes through a poplar forest past the tiny Belisirma Walley Wellkome Camping (one bungalow). A group of bangled women in lush purple wash their laundry in the river under the watchful eyes of men who seem to have only a ceremonial function. Children on donkeys offer to show off the troglodyte church carved into the hill just past the long, narrow farm plots. A lady, face framed in the dangling jewelry of her shawl, her net worth hanging in gold around her neck, points to my postcard, a picture of a little girl holding a baby sheep. The girl is her niece. They call the card "Two Lambs."

14 DAYS IN TURKEY

Turkey offers the most enjoyable culture shock within striking distance of Europe. But it's a rich brew, and for most, two weeks is enough. Here's my recommendation for the best two-week look at Turkey.

Flying to Istanbul is about as tough as flying to Paris. For instance, if you fly SAS, both are about a two-hour flight from your Copenhagen hub. When planning your trip, remember that flying "open-jaws" into Istanbul and home from Athens is about $50 cheaper than flying in and out of Istanbul . . . and makes for a more diverse and efficient itinerary.

Spend your first two days in Istanbul. Take the taxi ($12) from the airport to the Hippodrome, near the Blue Mosque, where you'll find several decent small hotels and pensions. My choice would be the Turkoman Hotel ($80 doubles, Asmali Cesme Sokak #2, 34400

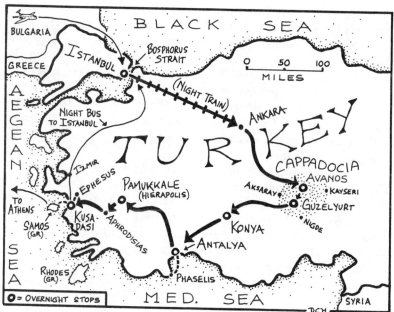

Two weeks of Turkey

Sultanahmet, tel. 212/516-2956, fax 212/516-2957). Cheaper and also good in the neighborhood is the Hotel Best Hipodrom (very simple, $25 doubles, Ucler Sokak #9, Sultanahmet, tel. 212/516-0902, fax 212/518-1251).

For an easygoing first evening, walk over to the Blue Mosque and enjoy the free sound and light show in the park. Spend the next day doing the historic biggies: Topkapi Palace, Blue Mosque, and the Aya Sofya church. The latter was built in 537, when Istanbul was called Constantinople and was the leading city in Christendom. It was the largest domed building in Europe until Brunelleschi built Florence's great dome in the Renaissance, nearly a thousand years later.

Bone up on Anatolian folk life in the Islamic Arts Center (just off the old Roman racetrack called the Hippodrome), then taxi to the modern center of bustling Istanbul for dinner in the "Flower Passage," where Istanbul's beautiful people and tourists alike enjoy the funky elegance. If you like baklava, stroll the city's main drag, Istiklal Street, in search of a pastry shop. From the heartbeat of Istanbul, Taksim Square, catch a cab home. Less touristy dinner options include Kumkapi, a fishermen's wharf district teeming with seafood restaurants and happy locals (a pleasant walk from the Hippodrome), and the more romantic Ortakoy district (in the shadow of the Bosphorus bridge).

The next morning, browse the bizarre Grand Bazaar and Egyptian Spice Market. After lunch take an intercontinental cruise up the Bosphorus. If you disembark in Asian Istanbul, you can taxi quickly to the station to catch your overnight train to Ankara.

This, the only reliable train in Asian Turkey, gets you to the country's capital by 8:00 a.m. As you munch feta cheese, olives, tomatoes, and cucumbers for breakfast in the dining car, it dawns on you that you're far from home.

Ankara has two blockbuster sights. The Museum of Anatolian Civilizations is a prerequisite for meaningful explorations of the ancient ruins that litter the Turkish countryside. The Ataturk Mausoleum shines a light on the recent and dramatic birth of modern Turkey and gives you an appreciation of that country's love of its George Washington. For a happening scene, a great view, and a look at modern Turkey, ride to the top of the Ankara tower.

From Ankara, it's a four-hour bus ride to exotic and evocative Cappadocia, an eroded wonderland of cave dwellings that go back to the early Christian days, when the faithful fled persecution by hiding in Cappadocian caves. Cappadocia gives you a time-tunnel experience, with its horse carts, troglodytes, strangely eroded mini-Matterhorns called "fairy chimneys," traditional crafts, and labyrinthine underground cities. Don't miss the Back Door town of Güzelyurt (see above).

Exotic terrain, ornery transport . . . Cappadocia

From mysterious Cappadocia, cross the Anatolian Plateau to Konya, the most conservative and orthodox Muslim city in Turkey, home of the Mevlana order and the Whirling Dervishes. The dance of the dervish connects a giving god with our world. One hand is gracefully raised, the other is a loving spout as he whirls faster and faster in a trance the modern American attention span would be hard-pressed to understand.

Then follow the steps of St. Paul over the Taurus Mountains to the Mediterranean resort of Antalya. You can hire a yacht to sail the Mediterranean coast to your choice of several beachside ruins. After a free day on the beach, travel inland to explore the ruins of Aphrodisias and its excellent museum.

Nearby is Pamukkale, a touristy village and Turkey's premier mineral spa. Soak among broken ancient columns in a mineral spring and wander the acres and acres of terraced steamy mineral pools. Hop like a frisky sparrow through a kaleidoscope of white birdbaths.

For the final leg of your two-week swing through Turkey, head west to the coastal resort of Kusadasi. Nearby is my favorite ancient site, the ruins of Ephesus. For a relaxing finale, take a Turkish *hamam* (bath with massage) in Kusadasi before catching the daily boat to the entertaining island of Samos in Greece (see below). Boats and planes take travelers from Samos to other Greek islands and on to Athens.

SOME HINTS TO MAKE TURKEY EASIER

Good information is rare here, especially in the east. Bring a guidebook from home. Take advantage of Tom Brosnahan's guidebook to Turkey (Lonely Planet). Maps are easy to get in Turkey.

Eat carefully. Find a cafeteria-style restaurant and point. Choose your food personally by tasting and pointing to what you like. Joke around with the cooks. They'll love you for it. The bottled water, soft drinks, *chai* (tea), and coffee are cheap and generally safe. Watermelons are a great source of safe liquid. If you order a glass of tea, your waiter will be happy to "process" your melon, giving it to you peeled and in little chunks on a big plate.

Learn to play backgammon before you visit Turkey. Backgammon, the local pastime, is played by all the men in this part of the world. Join in. It's a great way to instantly become a contributing member of the local teahouse scene.

Really get away from it all. Catch a *dolmus* (shared taxi) into the middle of nowhere. Get off at a small village. If the bus driver thinks you must be mistaken or lost to be getting off there, you've found the right place. Explore the town, befriend the children, trade national dance lessons. Act like an old friend returning after a 10-year absence, and you'll be treated like one.

You'll be stared at all day long. Preserve your sanity with a sense of humor. Joke with the Turks. Talk to them, even if there's no hope of communication. One afternoon, in the town of Ercis, I was waiting for a bus and writing in my journal. A dozen people gathered around me, staring with intense curiosity. I felt that they needed entertainment. I sang the Hoagy Carmichael classic, "Huggin' and a-Chalkin'." When the bus came, my friend and I danced our way on board, waving good-bye to the cheering fans. From then on my singing entertained most of eastern Turkey.

Make invitations happen and accept them boldly. While exploring villages with no tourism, I loiter near the property of a large family. Very often the patriarch, proud to have a foreign visitor, will invite me to join him cross-legged on his large, bright carpet in the shade. The women of the household bring tea, then peer at us from around a distant corner. Shake hands, jabber away in English, play show and tell, pass around photos from home, take photos of the family, and get their addresses so you can mail them copies. They'll always remember your visit. And so will you.

ISLAM IN A PISTACHIO SHELL

Five times a day, God enjoys a global wave as the call to prayer sweeps at the speed of the sun from the Philippines to Morocco. The muezzin chants, "There is only one God, and Mohammed is one of his prophets."

Islam is the fastest-growing religion on earth. Unbiased listings place Mohammed above Jesus on *Guinness*-type rankings of all-time most influential people. For us to understand Islam by studying Khadafy and Hussein would be like a Turk understanding capitalism and Christianity by studying Hitler and Reagan.

Your journeying may give you the opportunity to travel in, and therefore to better understand, Islam. Just as it helps to know about spires, feudalism, and the saints to comprehend your European sightseeing, a few basics on Islam help make your sightseeing in Moslem countries more meaningful. Here they are.

The Islamic equivalent of the Christian bell tower is a minaret, which the muezzin climbs to chant the call to prayer. In a kind of architectural Darwinism, the minarets have shrunken as calls to prayer have been electronically amplified; their height is no longer necessary

Greek and Turkish travel agencies are more helpful than they look.

or worth the expense. Many small modern mosques have one tin mini-minaret about as awesome as your little toe.

Worshipers pray toward Mecca, which, from Turkey, is about in the same direction as Jerusalem but not quite. In Istanbul, Aya Sofya was built 1,400 years ago as a church, its altar niche facing Jerusalem. Since it became an out-of-sync-with-Mecca mosque, the Moslem focus-of-prayers niche is to the side of what was the altar.

Ah, the smell of socks. A mosque is a shoes-off place. Westerners are welcome to drop in. The small stairway that seems to go nowhere is symbolic of the growth of Islam. Mohammed had to stand higher and higher to talk to his growing following. Today every mosque will have one of these as a kind of pulpit. No priest ever stands on the top stair. That is symbolically reserved for Mohammed.

The "five pillars" of Islam are basic to an understanding of a religious force that is bound to fill our headlines for years to come. Followers of Islam should:

1. Say and believe, "There is only one God, and Mohammed is one of his prophets."

2. Visit Mecca. This is interpreted by some Muslims as a command to travel. Mohammed said, "Don't tell me how educated you are, tell me how much you've traveled."

3. Give to the poor (one-fortieth of your wealth, if you are not in debt).

4. Fast during daylight hours through the month of Ramadan. Fasting is a great social equalizer and helps everyone to feel the hunger of the poor.

5. Pray five times a day. Modern Muslims explain that it's important to wash, exercise, stretch, and think of God. The ritual of Muslim prayer works this into every day—five times.

You'll notice women worship in back of the mosque. For the same reason I find it hard to concentrate on God at aerobics classes, Muslim men decided prayer would go better without the enjoyable but problematic distraction of bent-over women between them and Mecca.

How Muslims can have more than one wife is a bigamistry to many. While polygamy is illegal in Turkey, Islam does allow a man to have as many wives (up to four) as he can love and care for equally. This originated as Mohammed's pragmatic answer to the problem of too many unattached women caused by the death of so many men in the frequent wars of his day. Religious wars have been as common in Islam as they have been in Christendom.

These basics are a simplistic but honest attempt by a non-Muslim to help travelers from the Christian West understand an often-misunderstood but very rich culture worthy of our respect. And these days, when those who profit from arms sales are so clever at riding the bloody coattails of religious conflict, we need all the understanding we can muster.

THE BEST WAY FROM ATHENS TO TURKEY

The best thing about Athens is the boat to Turkey. Athens is a crowded, overrated, and polluted tourist trap. See what's important (Acropolis, Agora, Plaka, and National Museum) and leave! Catch a boat ($30 for deck class, $45–55 for cabin,, 12 hours) or plane ($70, one hour) to Samos, Rhodes, or Kos. Each of these islands is connected daily by boat ($40, two hours) to Turkey. This short boat ride gives you more of a cultural change than the flight from the United States to Athens.

Leaving Greece via Samos offers a look at one of my favorite Greek islands and drops you in Kusadasi, a pleasant place to enter Turkey and a 20-minute drive from Ephesus.

Samos—green, mountainous, diverse, and friendly—has tourist crowds but not as bad as other Greek islands. Bus transportation on the island is fine. And for $12 a day you can crisscross Samos on your own moped. Pounding over potholes, dodging trucks, and stopping to dream across the sea at the hills of Turkey, spanked happily by the

prickly wind and Greek sun, a moped ride around Samos is my annual jackhammer of youth.

The tourist map shows plenty of obscure sights on Samos. Gambling that the Spiliani monastery was worth the detour, I traded potholes for gravel and wound up the hill. The road ended at a tiny church overlooking the sunburnt island.

Behind the church was the mouth of a cave, with whitewashed columns carved like teeth into the rock. I wandered into the drippy, dank darkness, cool and quiet as another world. Sitting still, I could almost hear the drip-by-drip growth of the stalagmites and the purr of my brain. The only motion was the slight flicker of slender candles. I was ready to venture out of Christendom and into Islam.

See the Appendix (Recommended Accommodations) for more information.

65. Eastern Turkey

Istanbul and the western Turkish coast, while still fascinating, cheap, and eager to please, are moving toward European-style mainstream tourism. For the most cultural thrills, head east. Tour inland Anatolia with abandon, using Ankara as a springboard. From here, buses transport you to the region, culture, and era of your choice.

Find a town that has yet to master the business of tourism, like Kastamonu (five hours northeast of Ankara). Business hotels are comfortable ($15 doubles) but not slick. I handed a postcard to the boy at the desk, hoping he could mail it for me. He looked it over a couple of times on both sides, complimented me, and politely handed it back. As I left, he raised his right hand like a cigar-store Indian and said, "Hello." While changing money, I was spotted by the bank manager, who invited me into his office for tea. I was his first American customer.

Wandering in and out of small crafts shops, I met an 85-year-old white-bearded wood-carver who bragged that his work decorated prayer niches in mosques all over Iran. As he sized up just the right chunk of wood, he held up his chisel and said with a twinkle in his eye, "*This* is the greatest factory in the world." A few minutes and a pile of wood shavings later, the man gave me a carved floral decoration with his signature in swirling Arabic. When I offered to pay, he refused. At his age, he explained, if I appreciated his art, that was all he needed.

Outside, a gaggle of men wearing grays, blacks, and browns were shuffling quietly down the street. A casket floated over them as each man jostled to the front to pay his respects by "giving it a shoulder."

Turkey is a land of ceremonies. Rather than relying on a list of festivals, travel with sharp eyes, flexibility, and some knowledge of the folk culture. Local life here is punctuated with colorful, meaningful events. As the dust from the funeral procession clears, you may see a proud eight-year-old boy dressed like a prince or a sultan. He's celebrating his circumcision, a rite of passage that some claim is an echo from the days of matriarchal Amazon rule, when entry into the priesthood required c-c-c-castration. This is a great day for the boy and his family. Turks like to call it the "happiest wedding," because there are no in-laws.

Having an interpreter helps you explore and mingle with meaning, but it's not required. Many older Turks speak German. The friendliness of Turkey is legendary among those who have traveled beyond the cruise ports. While relatively few small-town Turks speak English, their eagerness to help makes the language barrier an often enjoyable headache.

In Turkey, you don't need museums; they're living in the streets.

Enjoy jabbering with the people you meet. If Turkish sounds tough to you, remember, it's the same in reverse. Certain sounds, like our "th," are tricky. My friend Ruth was entertained by the tortured attempts Turks made at pronouncing her name. Any English-speaking Turk can remember spending long hours looking into the mirror, slowly enunciating: "This and these are hard to say. I think about them every day. My mouth and my teeth, I think you see, help me say them easily."

Throughout Turkey, travelers often lament over the ugly, unfinished construction that scars nearly every town with rusty tangles of steel rebar waiting to reinforce future concrete walls. But in Turkey, unfinished buildings are family savings accounts. Inflation here is ruinous. Any local in need of a hedge against inflation keeps a building under construction. Whenever there's a little extra cash, rather than watch it evaporate in the bank, Ahmed will invest in the next stage of construction. It's the goal of any Turkish parent to provide each child with a house or apartment with which to start adult life. A popular saying is, "Rebar holds the family together."

If you're looking for a rain forest in Turkey, go to the northeast, along the Black Sea coast, where it rains 320 days a year. This is the world's top hazelnut-producing region, and home of the Laz people. A highlight of one tour (which I led through Eastern Turkey with 22 American travelers and a Turkish co-guide) was spending an evening and a night with a Laz family. Actually the families of three brothers, they all live in one large three-layered house provided them by their now-elderly parents.

Our group was the first Americans that the 16 people who lived there had ever seen. We were treated to a feast. In Turkey it's next to impossible to turn down this kind of hospitality. As we praised the stuffed peppers, members of our group discreetly passed Pepto Bismol tablets around under the table. (The pouring tea didn't quite mask the sound of ripping cellophane.)

After dinner we paid our respects to the grandma. Looking like a veiled angel in white, she and her family knew she would soon succumb to her cancer. But for now she was overjoyed to see such a happy evening filling her family's home.

When we wondered about having an extended family under one roof, the sons assured us, "If a day goes by when we don't see each other, we are very sad." To assure harmony in the family, the three brothers married three sisters from another family. They also assured us that entertaining our group of 22 was no problem. If we weren't there, they'd have had as many of their neighbors in.

No Turkish gathering is complete without dancing, and anyone who can snap her fingers and swing a Hula-Hoop can be comfortable on the living room dance floor of new Turkish friends. Two aunts, deaf and mute from meningitis, brought the house down with their shoulders fluttering like butterflies. We danced and talked with four generations until after midnight.

Stepping into the late-night breeze, I noticed what had seemed to be a forested hillside was now a spangled banner of lights shining through windows, each representing a "Third World" home filled with as many "family values" as the one we were a part of that night. So much for my stereotypical image of fanatical Muslim hordes. Before leaving the next morning, our friends tossed a gunnysack of hazelnuts into our bus.

For decades this eastern end of Turkey's Black Sea coast was a dead-end butting up against the closed border of Soviet Georgia. But today the former U.S.S.R. is ringed by sprawling "Russian markets" rather than foreboding guard posts.

From Finland to Turkey we found boxy Lada automobiles overloaded with the lowest class of garage-sale junk, careening toward the nearest border on a desperate mission to scrape together a little hard cash. In the Turkish coastal town of Trabzon, 300 yards of motley tarps and blankets displayed grandpa's tools, pink and yellow *"champagnski"*

($1.50 a bottle), Caspian caviar (the blue lid is best, $3), battered samovars, fur hats, and nightmarish Rube Goldbergian electrical gadgetry. A Georgian babushka lady with a linebacker build, caked-on makeup, and bleached blonde hair offered us a wide selection of Soviet pins, garish plastic flowers, and now-worthless ruble coins.

To satisfy my group's strange appetite for godforsaken border crossings, we drove out to the Georgian border. No one knew if we could cross or not. As far as the Turkish official was concerned, "No problem." We were escorted through the mud, past pushcarts bound for flea markets and huge mired-in-red-tape trucks. In this strange economic no man's land, the relative prosperity of Muslim Turkey was clear. Just a prayer call away from Georgia, a sharp little Turkish mosque with an exclamation-point minaret seemed to holler, "You sorry losers, let us help you onto our boat." Young Georgian soldiers with hardly a button on their uniforms checked identity cards, as those who qualified squeezed past the barbed wire and through the barely open gate. A soldier told us we couldn't pass. In search of a second opinion, we fetched an officer who said, "Visa no, problem"—a negative that, for a second, I misinterpreted as a positive.

Driving inland from the Black Sea under 10,000-foot peaks, our bus crawled up onto the burnt, barren, 5,000-foot-high Anatolian plateau to Erzurum, the main city of Eastern Turkey (24 hours by bus from Istanbul). Life is hard here. Blood feuds, a holdover from feudal justice under the Ottomans, are a leading cause of imprisonment. Winters are below-zero killers. Villages spread out onto the plateau like brown weeds, each with the same economy: ducks, dung, and hay. But Allah has given this land some pleasant surprises. The parched plain hides lush valleys where rooftops sport colorful patches of sun-dried apricots, where shepherd children still play the flute, and where teenage boys prefer girls who dress modestly. And you can crack the sweet, thin-skinned hazelnuts with your teeth.

Entering a village, we passed under a banner announcing, "No love is better than the love for your land and your nation." Another hay, duck, and dung town, it took us warmly into its callused hands. Each house wore a tall hat of hay—food for the cattle and insulation for the winter. Mountains of cow pies were neatly stacked promises of warmth and cooking fuel for six months of snowed-in winter that was on its way. A man with a donkey cart wheeled us through town. Veiled mothers strained to look through our video camera's viewfinder to see their children's mugging faces. The town's annually elected policeman bragged that he keeps the place safe from terrorists. Children scampered around women beating raw wool with sticks—a rainbow of browns that would one day be woven into a carpet to soften a stone sofa, warm up a mud-brick wall, or serve as a daughter's dowry.

Driving east from Erzurum, we set our sights on 18,000-foot Mount Ararat. Villages growing between ancient rivers of lava expertly milk the land for a subsistence living. After a quick reread of the flood story in Genesis, I couldn't help but think that this powerful, sun-drenched, windswept land had changed little since Noah docked.

Turkey is in the middle of a small war in the east. Forty thousand Kurdish guerrillas ("terrorists" or "freedom fighters," depending on your politics) are "in the mountains," while 10 million Turkish Kurds, leading more normal lives, help provide their base of support. The guerrillas have not targeted tourists, perhaps because of the American relief for their beleaguered comrades in nearby Iraq, or because their quarrel is with the Turkish army, not with visitors. On a ridge high above our bus, I could make out the figure of a lone man silhouetted against a bright blue sky, waving to us as we rolled by.

When I got up early the next morning to see the sunrise over Mount Ararat, I could make out a long convoy of Turkish army vehicles. It reminded me that these days it takes more than 40 days of rain to fix things. Our world is a complicated place in which the nightly news is just a shadow play of reality. To give it depth, you need to travel.

66. The Treasures of Luxor, Egypt

With my travel spirit flapping happily in the breeze, I pedal through Luxor on my rented one-speed, catching the cool shade and leaving the stifling heat with the pesky baksheesh-beggar kids in the dusty distance.

Choosing the "local ferry" over the "tourist ferry," I'm surrounded by farmers rather than sightseers. As the sun rises, reddening the tomb-filled mountains, I pedal south along the West Bank of the Nile. The noisy crush of tourists is gone. The strip of riverbank hotels back in Luxor is faint and silent. I'm alone in Egypt: a lush brown and green world of reeds, sugarcane, date palms, mud huts, and a village world amazingly apart from what the average tourist sees.

An irrigation ditch leads me into the village of Elbairat. Here, I am truly big news on two wheels. People scurry, grabbing their families to see the American who chose them over Tut. I'm sure, somewhere in the Egyptian babble, were the words, "My house is your house." They would have given me the Key to the Village, but there were no locks.

Elbairat is a poor village with a thriving but extremely simple farm economy. A little girl balances a headful of grass—heading home with a salad for the family water buffalo. A proud woman takes me on a tour of her mudbrick home complete with the no-fly pantry filled with chicken and pigeons.

This is the real Egypt . . . how the majority of Egypt's 60 million people live. So close to all the tourists, and rarely seen.

Start your Egyptian experience in the urban jungle of Cairo. It has a chaotic charm. With each visit, I stay at the Hotel Windsor. Stepping into the ramshackle elevator, I asked the boy who ran it if he spoke English. He said, "Up and down." I said, "Up." He babied the collapsing door to close it, turned the brass crank to send us up, and expertly stopped us within an inch of the well-worn second floor lobby where even people who don't write feel like writers. I kept looking for the English Patient.

Across the street, the neighborhood gang sat in robes sucking lazy waterpipes called sheeshaws (a.k.a. hookas or hubbly-bubblies). With everyone wearing what looked like hospital robes, playing backgammon and dominoes with pipes stuck in their mouths like IVs and clearly going nowhere in a hurry, it seemed like some strange outdoor hospital gameroom. For about U.S. $.25 the smoke boy brought me one of the big free-standing pipes and fired up some apple-flavored tobacco.

For a sensuous immersion in this cultural blast furnace, hire a taxi and cruise through the teeming poor neighborhood called "old Cairo." Roll down the windows, crank up the Egyptian pop on the radio, lean out, and give pedestrian's high fives as you glide by.

Then head for Luxor. The overnight train ride from Cairo to Luxor is posh and scenic a fun experience itself. A second-class air-conditioned sleeping car provides comfortable two-bed compartments, fresh linen, a wash basin, dinner, and a wake-up service.

I spent more time in and around Luxor than in any European small town, and I could have stayed longer. On top of the "village-by-bike" thrills, there are tremendous ancient ruins. The East Bank offers two famous sites: Karnak (with the Temples of Amun, Mut, and Khonsu, one mile north of Luxor), and the Temple of Luxor, which dominates Luxor town.

To the ancient Egyptian, the world was a lush green ribbon cutting north and south through the desert. It was only logical to live on the East Bank, where the sun rises, and bury your dead on the West Bank, where the sun is buried each evening. Therefore, all the tombs, pyramids, and funerary art in Egypt is on the West Bank.

Directly across the Nile from Luxor is the Temple of Queen Hatshepsut, Deir el-Medina, Ramseseum, Colossi of Memnon, and the Valleys of the Kings, Queens, and Nobles. Be selective. You'll become jaded sooner than you think. Just because something's B.C. doesn't mean it's got to be seen. Skip anything mediocre.

Luxor town itself has plenty to offer. Explore the market. You can get an inexpensive custom-made caftan with your name sewn on in arty Arabic. I found the merchants who pester the tourists at the tombs across the Nile had the best prices on handicrafts and instant antiques. A trip out to the camel market is always fun (and you can pick up a camel for half the U.S. price). For me, five days in a small town is asking for boredom. But Luxor fills five days like no town its size.

FIVE DAYS IN LUXOR

Day 1. Your overnight train from Cairo arrives around 5:00 a.m. If it's too early to check in, leave your bags at a hotel, telling them you'll return later to inspect the room. Hop a horse carriage to be at the temples at Karnak when they open, while it's still cool. These comfortable early hours should never be wasted. Check into a hotel by midmorning. Explore Luxor town. Enjoy a felucca ride on the Nile at sunset.

Day 2. Cross the Nile and rent a taxi for the day. It's easy to gather other tourists and split the transportation costs. If you're selective and start early, you'll be able to see the best sites and finish by noon. That's a lot of work, and you'll enjoy a quiet afternoon back in Luxor.

Day 3. Through your hotel, arrange an all-day minibus trip to visit Aswan, the Aswan Dam, and the important temples (especially Edfu) south of Luxor. With six or eight tourists filling the minibus, this day should not cost more than $15 per person.

Day 4. Rent bikes and explore the time-passed villages on the west side of the Nile. Bring water, your camera, and a bold spirit of adventure. This was my best Egyptian day.

Day 5. Tour the excellent Luxor museum. Enjoy Luxor town and take advantage of the great shopping opportunities. Catch the quick flight or overnight train back to Cairo.

Egypt seems distant and, to many, frightening. The constant hustle ruins the experience for some softer tourists. But once you learn the local ropes, that's less of a problem, and there's a reasonable chance you'll survive and even enjoy your visit.

In the cool months (peak season), it's wise to make hotel reservations. Off-season, in the sweltering summer heat, plenty of rooms lie vacant. Air conditioning is found in moderately-priced hotels. Budget

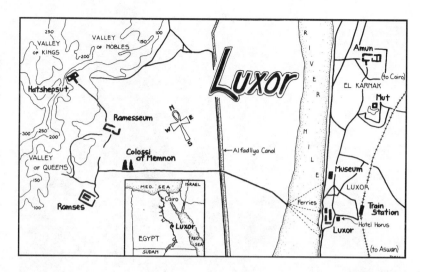

hotels with a private shower, fan, and balcony offer doubles for around $20. (Consider Hotel Horus, Karnak Temple St., tel. 095/372-165, fax 095/373-447.) A cot in the youth hostel costs $2. But Egypt is not a place where you should save money at the expense of comfort and health. For $100 you'll get a double room with a buffet breakfast in a First World resort-type hotel with an elitist pool and a pharoah's complement of servants. (Consider the riverside Sofitel Hotel Winter Palace; the new section is less atmospheric but half the price of the historic old palace, tel. 095/380-422, fax 095/374-087.)

Eat well and carefully. With the terrible heat, your body requires lots of liquid. Bottled water is cheap and plentiful as are soft drinks. Watermelons are thirst-quenching. Cool your melon in your hotel's refrigerator. Choose a clean restaurant. Hotels generally have restaurants comparable to their class and price range.

To survive the summer heat, limit your sightseeing day to 5:00 a.m. until noon. The summer heat, which they say can melt car tires to the asphalt, is unbearable and dangerous after noon. Those early hours are prime time: the temperature is comfortable, the light is crisp and fresh, and the Egyptian tourist hustlers are still sleeping. Spend afternoons in the shade. Carry water and wear a white hat (on sale there). An Egypt guidebook (I'd use one by Moon or Lonely Planet) is a shield proving to unwanted human guides that you need no help.

Stay on the budgetary defense. No tip will ever be enough. Tip what you believe is fair by local standards and ignore the inevitable

One of the most interesting ways to see Egypt

plea for more. Unfortunately, if you ever leave them satisfied, you were ripped off. Consider carrying candies or little gifts for the myriad children constantly screaming "Baksheesh!" ("Give me a gift!") Hoard small change in a special pocket so you'll have tip money readily available. Getting change back from your large bill is tough.

Transportation in and around Luxor is a treat. The local taxis are horse-drawn carriages. These are a delight but drive a hard bargain and settle on a price before departing. The locals' ferry crosses the Nile from dawn until late at night and costs only pennies.

Travel on the West Bank by donkey, bike, or automobile taxi. You can rent donkeys for the romantic approach to the tombs and temples of West Thebes. Sun melts the romance fast. Bikes work for the cheap and hardy. A taxi is the quickest and most comfortable way to explore. When split among four, a taxi for the "day" (6:00 a.m. until noon) is reasonable. Save money by assembling a tour group at your hotel. You'll enjoy the quick meet-you-at-the-ferry-landing service and adequately cover Luxor's West Bank sights.

Cruise on the Nile in a *felucca*, the traditional sailboat, for just a few dollars an hour. Lounging like Cleopatra in the cool beauty of a Nile sunset is a romantic way to end the day and start the night.

Send Me a Postcard—Drop Me a Line

If you enjoyed a successful trip with the help of this book and would like to share your discoveries, please fill out the Road Scholar Feedback survey (see next page) and send it to me at Europe Through the Back Door, Box 2009, Edmonds, WA 98020. I personally read and value all feedback. Thanks in advance—it helps a lot—and I'll send you my Back Door quarterly newsletter free for one year.

For our latest travel information, tap into our ETBD Web site: www.ricksteves.com. My e-mail address is rick@ricksteves.com. Anyone is welcome to request a free issue of our newsletter (425/771-8303).

Travel in Europe with Rick Steves

Join me for 52 shows of my favorite places—from the Nile to Norway. Call your local public television station or the Travel Channel to ask when *Travels in Europe with Rick Steves* airs in your neighborhood. For information on the series, go to www.ricksteves.com or travelsmallworld.com. For home videos (each containing two to three *Travels in Europe* shows), see our catalog page at the back of this book.

Road Scholar Feedback for
Europe Through the Back Door 1999

We're all in the same travelers' school of hard knocks. Your feedback helps me improve this book for future travelers. Please fill this out (attach more info if you'd like) and send it to me. As thanks for your help, I'll send you my quarterly travel newsletter free for one year. Thanks! **Rick**

Favorite tips from this book:

_____

_____

Least useful (even misleading) tips:

_____

_____

Tips you'd like me to add to the book:

_____

_____

Do you have a Back Door discovery to share?

_____

_____

Best ways to improve this book:

_____

_____

I'd like a free newsletter subscription:

___ Yes ___ No ___ Already on list

_____

Name

_____

Address

_____

City, State, Zip

_____

E-mail address

Please send to:
ETBD
Box 2009, Edmonds, WA 98020

A New Enlightenment Through Travel

Thomas Jefferson said, "Travel makes you wiser but less happy." "Less happy" is a good thing. It's the growing pains of a broadening perspective. After viewing our culture from a coffeehouse in Vienna or a village in Tuscany, I've found truths that didn't match those I always assumed were "self-evident" and "God-given." And flying home gives me a healthy dose of culture shock in reverse. You know how I love Europe. But I haven't told you about my most prized souvenir—a new way of thinking.

The "land of the free" has a powerful religion—materialism. Its sophisticated priesthood (business, media, military, and political leaders) worships unsustainable growth. Contentment and simplicity are sins. Mellow is yellow. And evil is anything steering you away from being a good producer/consumer.

Yes, greater wealth could be wonderful. But for whom? The gap between rich and poor—both within our society and among humankind in general—is growing. Regulatory tax and spending policies in the United States since 1982 have caused the greatest trickle-up of wealth in our nation's history. And globally, the richest 358 people now own as much as the poorest 45 percent of humanity put together. Designer fortifications protect the wealthy in much of the world. In the U.S.A. two kinds of communities are the rage: "gated communities" and prisons. The victims are the politically meek—those who don't or can't vote: the young, the poor, the environment, and the future. More and more Americans have lost hope. And when "freedom" grows at hope's expense, your children will ponder their blessings behind deadbolts.

Whoa! What happened to me? The young Republican traveled. I saw countries less wealthy than ours (but with bigger governments), where everyone had a home, enough food, and healthcare. And, like the early astronauts, I saw a planet with no boundaries—a single, tender organism painted with the faces of 6 billion equally precious people. I unpack my rucksack marveling at how politically active American Christians can believe that we're all children of God—while fighting aid for the hungry and homeless.

A new Enlightenment is needed. Just as the French "Enlightenment" led us into the modern age of science and democracy, this new Enlightenment will teach us the necessity of sustainable affluence, peaceful coexistence with other economic models, "controlling" nature by obeying her, and measuring prosperity by something more human than material consumption.

I hope your travels will give you a fun and relaxing vacation or adventure. I also hope they'll make you an active patriot of our planet and a voice for people in our country who will never see their names on a plane ticket.

Appendix

Back Doors: Recommended Accommodations

This book is not written as a directory-type guidebook. Nonetheless, here are a few specific recommendations to help you plug the 37 Back Doors featured in this book into your trip. While many travelers rip out this Appendix section and use it to navigate by, I have covered virtually all of the Back Doors much more thoroughly in my various country guidebooks. For a complete rundown on good places to eat and sleep (including more details on those listed here, plus others), please navigate by one of my eight country guidebooks (published by John Muir Publications). In this Appendix I've listed only prices for double rooms; most places have singles and triples. Prices may vary with plumbing and season. In the interest of brevity, I've been lean with descriptions here. Assume you get what you pay for.

Sleep code: D = Double, Db = Double with private bath, CC = Credit cards accepted.

CINQUE TERRE: ITALY'S TRAFFIC-FREE RIVIERA (CH. 30)
(1,600 lire = about $1)

I sleep in **Vernazza** (zip code: 19018): **Trattoria Gianni** rents 14 small, simple, comfortable doubles near the castle with sea views (D-L85,000, Db-L100,000; CC; Piazza Marconi 5, tel. 0187-821-003, tel. & fax 0187-812-228). No reply to your fax means they don't want you to make a reservation. Ideally, telephone three days in advance and leave your first name and time of arrival. **Pension Sorriso** offers basic rooms and serves small portions (with obligatory breakfast and dinner, D-L75,000 per person, Db-L90,000 per person, 50 yards uphill from the train station, tel. 0187-812-224). **Barbara** is run by kindly Giuseppe and his Swiss wife Patricia (10 harborfront rooms, tiny loft D-L70,000, bigger D-L80,000 Piazza Marconi 21, tel. 0187-812-398. **Affitta Camere:** Vernazza is honeycombed with private rooms and apartments for rent. Most work with one of the eateries or shops on the main street. They are reluctant to reserve rooms in advance. To minimize frustration, call just a day or two in advance or simply show up in the morning and look around. All are comfortable and inexpensive; some are lavish with killer views. The cost is roughly L30,000 to L40,000 per person depending on the view. **Affitta Camere da Nicolina** has great views, right over the harbor but close to the noisy church bell tower (ask at the harborside Vulnetia restaurant/pizzeria, tel. 0187-821-193). **Affitta Camere da Filippo** has no views but less noise (Via A. Del Santo 62 or ask at Blue Marlin bar, tel. 0187-812-244). The lady at the grocery store across from the gelateria has a line on rooms at **Affitta Camere da Giuseppina Villa** (Via S. Giovanni Battista 5, tel. 0187-812-026). Or ask about rooms at the **Gambero Rosso** restaurant (tel. 0187/812-265) or **Trattoria Il Baretto** (tel. 0187-812-381, Francesca). Friendly English-speaking Monica doesn't rent rooms, but she runs a great restaurant–**Castello's** (tel. 0187-812-296).

Riomaggiore: Youth Hostel **Mama Rosa** is run with a splash of John Belushi by Rosa Ricci (an almost-too-effervescent and friendly character who welcomes backpackers at the train station), her husband, Carmine, and their English-speaking son, Silvio. The only cheap dorm in Riomaggiore, this unique comedy of errors creates a special bond among the young, rugged, and poor who sleep here. Many consider it a slum. It's chaotic, with the ambience of a YMCA locker room filled with bunk beds (L25,000 beds; no curfew; Piazza Unita 2 in front of the station, tel. 0187-920-050 is rarely answered, just show up without a reservation).

THE HILL TOWNS OF TUSCANY AND UMBRIA (CH. 31)
(1,600 lire = about $1)

Siena (zip code: 53100): **Locanda Garibaldi** has seven doubles above a fine little family-run restaurant (D-L75,000, half a block downhill off the Campo at Via Giovanni Dupre 18; disdains taking reservations, call only a few days in advance; tel. 0577-284-204, fax . . . what's that?). **Hotel Duomo** is the best in-the-old-town splurge, a truly classy place with spacious, elegant rooms (Db-L200,000; CC; Via Stalloreggi 38, tel. 0577-289-088, fax 0577-43043). **Albergo Bernini** is the place to stay if you want to join a Sienese family in a modest, clean home (D-L100,000, Db-L120,000, prices drop for drop-ins; on the main San Domenico-Il Campo drag at Via Sapienza 15, tel. & fax 0577-289-047). **Alma Domus** is ideal, unless nuns make you nervous. This quasi-hotel (not a convent) is run by firm but angelic sisters who offer clean, quiet, cheap rooms and save the best views for the foreigners (Db-L90,000; near San Domenico at Via Camporegio 37, tel. 0577-44177, fax 0577-47601).

Assisi (zip code: 06081): **Albergo Italia** is clean and simple with great beds and delightful owners (D-L50,000, Db-L70,000; CC; on the town square at Vicolo della Fortezza, tel. 075-812-625, fax 075-804-3749). **Hotel Belvedere** offers comfortable rooms, good views, and is run by friendly, English-speaking Enrico and his American wife, Mary (D-L70,000, Db-L100,000; two blocks past St. Clare's church at Via Borgo Aretino 13, tel. 075-812-460, fax 075-816-812). **Camere Annalisa Martini** is a cheery home swimming in vines, roses, and bricks in the town's medieval core (Db-L60,000; Via S. Gregorio 6, tel. 075-813-536).

Orvieto (zip code: 05018): **Hotel Corso** is small, clean, and friendly, with comfy modern rooms (Db-L135,000; CC; Via Cavour 339, tel. & fax 0763-342-020). **Hotel Duomo**, with not-quite-clean rooms and a great location, is a funky, brightly colored, Old World place (D-L60,000, Db-L85,000; Via di Maurizio 7, tel. 0763-341-887). **Albergo Posta** is big, old, formerly elegant, but well-cared-for-in-its-decline with a grand old lobby and spacious, clean, plain rooms with vintage rickety furniture and springy beds (D-L68,000, Db-L88,000; Via Luca Signorelli 18, tel. 0763-341-909). **Hotel Picchio** is a shiny, modern, concrete and marble place, handy and comfy but with less character in the lower part of town near the train station (D-L50,000, Db-L70,000; Via G. Salvatori 17, 05019 Orvieto Scalo, tel. 0763-301-144 or 0763-90246).

CIVITA DI BAGNOREGIO (CH. 32)
(1,600 lire = about $1)

Bagnoregio has no private rooms but two good hotels: **Al Boschetto** is a family circus of Italian culture (D-L90,000, Db-L95,000; Strada Monterado, Bagnoregio/Viterbo, tel. 0761-792-369). **Hotel Fidanza** is modern, comfortable, normal, and right in town (Db-L90,000; Via Fidanza 25, Bagnoregio/Viterbo, tel. & fax 0761-793-444). Rooms 206 and 207 have views of Civita.

NORTH ITALY CHOICES: MILANO, LAKES, OR MOUNTAINS (CH. 33)
(1,600 lire = about $1)
Milan: Hotel Speronari is ideally located on a pedestrian street one block off the Piazza Duomo (D-L90,000, Db-L130,000; CC; Via Speronari 4, 20123 Milano, tel. 02-864-61125, fax 02-720-03178). **Hotel Gritti**, your best splurge near the Duomo, is a bright classy three-star hotel (Db-L220,000; CC; Piazza. S. Maria Beltrade 4, 20123 Milano, tel. 02-801-056, fax 02-890-10999, e-mail hotel.gritti@iol.it). **"The Best" Hotel** actually *is* the best in its price range near the station (Db-L120,000; Via B. Marcello 83, 20124 Milano, tel. 02-294-04757, fax 201966).

Varenna (zip code: 22050): **Albergo Olivedo**, facing the ferry dock, is a neat and tidy old hotel. Each room has squeaky hardwood floors, World War II furniture, and Art Nouveau mattresses (prices vary with season and views: D-L80,000 to L110,000, Db-L100,000 to L135,000; tel. & fax 0341-830-115; Laura speaks English and serves great meals). **Albergo Milano**, in the old town, is your best splurge (Db-L170,000, a little more in July and August, discounted for three nights in off-season or with a side view; CC; Via XX Settembre 29, tel. & fax 0341-830-298). This place whispers *luna di miele* (honeymoon).

Menaggio (zip code: 22017): **La Primula Youth Hostel** is a rare hostel. Family-run for 10 years by Ty and Paola (and their Australian sidekick, Paul), it caters to a quiet, savor-the-lakes crowd and offers the only cheap beds in the area. Located just south of the Menaggio dock (you'll see the sign from the boat), it has a view terrace; lots of games, a members' kitchen, a washing machine, bike, canoe, and kayak rentals, and a creative and hardworking staff (L17,000 per night in four-to six-bed room with sheets and breakfast, L19,000 with private plumbing, fine dinners L15,000; Ostello La Primula, Via IV Novembre 86, tel. & fax 0344-32356).

Castelrotto/Kastelruth (zip code: 39040): **Gasthof Zum Turm/Albergo Torre** is simple, clean, and traditional with great beds and modern bathrooms (Db-L112,000–L130,000; CC; Kofelgasse 8, tel. 0471-706-349, fax 0471-707-268). **Gasthof Zum Wolf** is a newly remodeled Tirolean mod with all the comforts (Db-L160,000–L210,000, depending on the season; Wolkensteinstrasse 5, tel. 0471-706-332, fax 0471-707-030). In the town center, **Haus Harderer** rents out three rooms (Db-84,000 with breakfast, minimum two nights; Plattenstrasse 20, tel. 0471-706-702). **Tirler Hof**, the storybook Jaider family farm, has 35 cows, one friendly hound, four Old World–comfy guest rooms, and a great mountain view (D-L70,000; practical only for drivers; out of town on the road to St. Michael, Paniderstrasse 44, tel. 0471-706-017).

LISBON'S GOLD STILL SHINES (CH. 35)
(170$ = about $1)
Lisboa e Tejo is a good splurge, newly and tastefully refurbished, with comfortable rooms and a welcoming staff (Db-12,000$ to 15,000$; CC; one block off Praça da Figueira on Rua do Poço do Borratém 4, 1100 Lisbon, tel. 01-886-6182, fax 01-886-5163). **Pensão Residencial Gerês**, your best budget bet downtown, has clean, cozy rooms worth reserving in advance (D-6,000$, Db-7,000$; CC; one block off Rossio square at Calçada do Garcia 6, 1100 Lisbon, tel. 01-888-2039, fax 888-2006). **Albergaria Residencial Insulana**, on a pedestrian street, is professional, with 32 quiet and comfortable, if a bit smoky, rooms (Db-8,

500$; CC; Rua da Assuncao 52, 1100 Lisbon, tel. 01-342-3131, fax 01-342-3131). **Residencial Duas Nações** is a hard-working old hotel in the heart of Rossio on a pedestrian street (D-4,500$, Db-7,500$; CC; Rua Augusta e Rua da Vitoria 41, 1100 Lisbon, tel. 01-346-0710, fax 01-347-0206). **Hotel Suisso Atlantico** is formal, hotelish, and a bit stuffy, with lots of tour groups and drab carpets throughout and a practical location (Db-9,500$; CC; Rua da Gloria 3-19, 1200 Lisbon, on a quiet street one block off Praça dos Restauradores, tel. 01-346-1713, fax 01-346-9013). **Pensão Residencial 13 da Sorte**, a cheery, homey place, has 24 bright and well-tiled rooms (Db-6,000$ to 7,500$; CC; 10-minute walk from downtown, Rua do Salitre 13, 1200 Lisbon, tel. 01-353-9746, fax 01-353-1851).

SALEMA, ON PORTUGAL'S SUNNY SOUTH COAST (CH. 36)
(170$ = about $1)

For maximum comfort, there's no need to look beyond John's Pensión Mare (see below). For maximum economy and experience, go for the *quartos* (rooms rented out of private homes). The **Boto family** rents two simple rooms (D-2,500$ to 3,000$) and a spacious apartment with kitchenette and a view (Db-6,000$ to 7,000$; at the top of *quartos* street at 4 Rua dos Pescadores, tel. 082-695265). **Ercilia Viegas** rents seven doubles; none have sinks, but there are three bathrooms, plus a communal kitchenette on the pleasant sun terrace (D-2,500$ to 3,000$, #64 on the *quartos* street, tel. 082-695128). At the friendly **Acacios**, the two adjoining upstairs rooms are best, with kitchenette, balcony, and a great ocean view (Db-5,000$ to 6,000$; on the *quartos* street at #91, tel. 082-695473). **Casa Duarte** has five pleasant rooms (four with views), two terraces, and a communal kitchenette (D-3,000$ to 5,500$; on a side alley closer to the water at #7, tel. 082-695181 or 082-695307). **Pensión Mare**, a blue and white building looking over the village above the main road into town, is the best normal hotel value in Salema (Db-6,500$ to 9,000$; CC; Praia de Salema, Vila do Bispo 8650, Algarve, tel. 082-695165; run by an easygoing Englishman, John). **Hotel Residencial Salema** is the big (many say too big) hotel in town (Db-6,500$ to 12,000$; CC; all rooms have balconies and side sea views, tel. 082-695328, fax 082-695329).

SOUTHERN SPAIN'S PUEBLOS BLANCOS: ANDALUSIA'S
ROUTE OF THE WHITE VILLAGES (CH. 37)
(140 ptas = about $1)

Arcos (zip code: 11630): **Hotel Restaurant El Convento**, deep in the old town, is the best deal, cozier and cheaper than Los Olivos (see below). Run by a hard-working family, several of its 10 rooms have balconies with incredible views (Db-7,500 ptas; CC; Maldonado 2, tel. & fax 956-70-23-33). **Parador de Arcos de la Frontera** is royally located, and for all its elegance, reasonably priced. If you're going to experience a parador (and you can't get into the convent), this might be the one (Db-16,500 ptas; CC; Plaza de España, tel. 956-70-05-00, fax 956-70-11-16). **Hotel Los Olivos**, a "poor man's parador," is bright, cool, and airy with a fine courtyard, roof garden, bar, view, friendly English-speaking folks, and easy parking (Db-7,000 ptas to 9,000 ptas; CC; San Miguel 2, tel. 956-70-08-11, fax 956-70-20-18). **Hostal Callejon de las Monjas** offers decent but frayed rooms (D-3,500 ptas, Db with terrace-4,500 ptas; CC; on noisy street next to Santa Maria Church, Dean Espinosa 4, tel. 956-70-23-02). **Hotel Marques de**

Torresoto is a restored 17th-century palace with classy rooms and a peaceful courtyard (Db-8,800 ptas to 9,000 ptas; CC; Marques de Torresoto 4, tel. 956-70-07-17, fax 956-70-42-05).

ALSACE AND COLMAR (CH. 38)
(5.5F = about $1)
Colmar (zip code: 68000): **Hôtel Le Rapp**, with 40 simple rooms and a small basement pool, is beautifully located and well-run (Db-390F; CC; 1 rue Berthe-Molley; good attached restaurant; tel. 03 89 41 62 10, fax 03 89 24 13 58, e-mail: rapp-hot@rmcnet.fr). **Hôtel Turenne**, a fine historic hotel in a great location, offers bright pastel and modern rooms with all the comforts (Db-310F to 375F; CC; 10 route du Bale, tel. 03 89 41 12 26, fax 03 89 41 27 64). For a fine private room downtown, try the funky and flowery **Maison Jund** (D-160F, Db-200F; 12 rue de l'Ange; open April to mid-September; tel. 03 89 41 58 72, fax 03 89 23 15 83).

 Eguisheim (zip code: 68420): **Madame Dirringer's** fine rooms are *très* Alsatian, clean, and spacious (D-160F to180F; 11 rue Riesling, tel. 03 89 41 71 87). If it's a hotel you want, try the comfortable **L'Auberge Alsacienne** (Db-270F to 310F; 12 Grand Rue, tel. 03 89 41 50 20, fax 03 89 23 89 32).

FROM FRANCE TO ITALY OVER MT. BLANC (CH. 39)
*(5.5F = about $1, * = French hotel rating, from zero to four stars)*
Chamonix (zip code: 74400): **Hôtel de l'Arve**** has a slick modern Alpine feel, with fine view rooms right on the Arve River overlooking Mont Blanc or cheaper rooms sans the view (Db-250F to 440F; CC; tel. 04 50 53 02 31, fax 04 50 53 56 92; friendly Isabelle and Bertrice speak English). **Hotel Savoyarde*****, with elegant chalet ambience, is a worthwhile splurge (Db-600F to 700F; CC; a 10-minute walk above the TI overlooking Chamonix at 28 rue des Moussoux, tel. 04 50 53 00 77, fax 04 50 55 86 82). **Hôtel de Clocher**** is a tidy family-run little place offering eight cozy rooms (Db-280F to 330F; CC; l'Impasse de l'Androsace, tel. 04 50 53 30 27, fax 04 50 53 73 19). **Hôtel Au Bon Coin**** has great views and a balcony for each room (Db-340F to 370F; 80 avenue L'Aiguille du Midi, tel. 04 50 53 15 67, fax 04 50 53 51 51; closed mid-April to June 30; and October to mid-December). **Hôtel Touring****, with large and well-worn rooms (many with four beds), is ideal for families. It's English-run by Dolly and Nick, so you'll have no trouble communicating (Db-285F to 350F; 95 rue Joseph Vallot, tel. 04 50 53 59 18, fax 04 50 53 67 25). Chamonix's **Chalet Beauregard** is friendly and peaceful with a private garden (Db-330F to 460F, breakfast included; above the TI toward Le Brévent lift, 182 montée La Mollard, tel. & fax 04 50 55 86 30; English spoken).

 Dorms: **Les Grands Charmoz** has 75F dorm beds and 200F doubles (468 chemin des Cristalliers, tel. & fax 04 50 53 45 57). The **Chalet Ski Station** also has bunks but no doubles (65F for a bed next to the Brévent *téléphérique*, a 10-minute hike up from the TI, tel. 04 50 53 20 25). Chamonix's classy **youth hostel** is well run, cheap, and almost luxurious (72F dorm bed, D-200F; tel. 04 50 53 14 52).

 For those trying to choose between the Gimmelwald/Jungfrau region and the Chamonix/Mont Blanc region, I'd choose Gimmelwald because it is less touristy, offers more diverse activities, and is more fun if the weather turns bad. With limited time in Chamonix, skip the Mer de Glace (unless you're dying to see a dirty old glacier).

ROTHENBURG AND THE ROMANTIC ROAD: FROM THE RHINE TO BAVARIA THROUGH GERMANY'S MEDIEVAL HEARTLAND (CH. 40)
(1.7 DM = about $1)

Rothenburg (zip code: 91541): I stay in **Hotel Goldener Rose** (D-65 DM, Db-87 in classy annex behind the garden; CC; Spitalgasse 28, tel. 09861-4638, fax 09861-86417). For the best real, with-a-local-family, comfortable, and homey experience, stay with **Herr und Frau Moser** (D-65 DM; Spitalgasse 12, tel. 09861-5971). **Pension Pöschel** has seven bright rooms (D-60 DM, small kids free; Wenggasse 22, tel. 09861-3430). **Hotel Gerberhaus**, a classy establishment in a 500-year-old building, is warmly run by Inge and Kurt, who mix modern comforts into bright and airy rooms while maintaining the half-timbered elegance (Db-100 DM to 150 DM; Spitalgasse 25, tel. 09861-94900, fax 09861-86555). Even classier and my best Rothenburg splurge, **Hotel Klosterstuble** is deep in the old town near the castle garden (Db-120 DM to 140 DM; Heringsbronnengasse 5, tel. 09861-6774, fax 09861-6474). Rothenburg's fine **Rossmühle Youth Hostel** takes reservations (open only to those under age 27; bed-and-breakfast-22 DM, sheets-6 DM, Db-54 DM, dinners-9 DM; tel. 09861-94160, fax 09861-941620).

HALLSTATT, IN AUSTRIA'S COMMUNE-WITH-NATURE LAKES DISTRICT (CH. 41)
(12 AS = about $1)

Hallstatt (zip code: 4830): Best beds are at **Gasthof Simony**, right on the square with a lake view, balconies, creaky wood floors, slip-slidey rag rugs, antique furniture, and a huge breakfast (Db-850 AS; Markt 105, tel. 06134-8231). **Pension Sarstein** has charming rooms in a modern building, a few minutes' walk along the lake from the center, run by friendly Frau Fisher (D-420 AS, Db-600 AS; Gosaumuhlstrasse 83, tel. 06134-8217). Her sister, **Frau Zimmermann**, runs a small Zimmer just down the street in a 500-year-old ramshackle house with low beams, time-polished wood, and fine lake views (200 AS per person; Gosaumuhlstrasse 69, tel. 06134-8309). **Gasthaus Muhle Naturfreunde-Herberge** is a good value with three- to six-bed rooms and hearty food (145 AS per bed in coed dorms, cheaper with a hostel sheet; Kirchenweg 36, just below the tunnel car park, tel. & fax 06134-8318). The manager, Ferdinand, runs a pizzeria in the Gasthaus, providing the cheapest dinners in town.

HALL, IN THE SHADOW OF INNSBRUCK (CH. 42)
(12 AS = about $1)

Hall (zip code: A-6060): **Gasthof Badl** is a big, comfortable, friendly place run by sunny Frau Steiner and her daughter, Sonja. It's easy to find, immediately off the Hall-in-Tirol freeway exit with an orange-lit "Bed" sign (Db-730 AS; CC; Innsbruck 4, tel. 05223-56784, fax 05223-567843). For a cheaper room in a private home, **Frieda Tollinger** rents out three rooms and accepts one-nighters (220 AS per person; follow Untere Lend, which becomes Schopperweg, to Schopperweg 8, tel. 05223-41366). **Alpenhotel Speckbacherhof**, a grand rustic hotel with all the comforts, is set between a peaceful forest and a meadow, across the street from the Hinterhornalm toll road (Db-840 AS to 880 AS, ask for discount with this book; CC; Gnadenwald-Tirol, tel. 05223-52511, fax 05223-525-1155; family Mayr).

THE BERNER OBERLAND: THE ALPS IN YOUR LAP (CH. 43)
(1.5 SF = about $1)

Gimmelwald (elevation 4,500 feet, zip code: CH-3826): The **Mountain Hostel** is goat-simple, as clean as its guests, cheap, and very friendly (15 SF per bed in six- to 15-bed rooms; 50 yards from the lift station, tel. & fax 033-855-1704). **Pension Gimmelwald**, next door, offers pleasant rooms (D-90 SF, Db-110 SF, dorm beds-20 SF to 25 SF; closed in November; tel. 033-855-1730). **Maria and Olle Eggimann** rent out three rooms in their Alpine-sleek chalet (D-100 SF, Db with kitchenette-60 SF a piece for two to three people; on "Main Street" 100 yards beyond the town's only intersection, tel. 033-855-3575, e-mail: oeggimann@bluewin.ch). **Hotel Mittaghorn**, the treasure of Gimmelwald, is run by Walter Mittler, a perfect Swiss gentleman. This is a classic, creaky, Alpine-style place with memorable beds, down comforters (short and fat, wear socks and drape the blanket over your feet), and a million-dollar view of the Jungfrau Alps. The loft has a dozen real beds on either side of a divider, with several sinks, down comforters, and a fire ladder out the back window. The hotel has one shower for 10 rooms (1 SF for five minutes). To some, Hotel Mittaghorn is a fire waiting to happen, with a kitchen that would never pass code, lumpy beds, teeny towels, and nowhere near enough plumbing, run by an eccentric grouch. These people enjoy Interlaken, Wengen, or Mürren, and that's where they should sleep. Be warned, you may meet more of my readers than you hoped for, but it's a fun crowd—an extended family (D-60 SF to 70 SF, loft beds-25 SF; reserve by telephone only, and then you must reconfirm by telephone the day before your arrival, tel. 033-855-1658).

LONDON: A WARM LOOK AT A COLD CITY (CH. 45)
(£1 = about $1.70)

London's Victoria Station Neighborhood: Woodville House offers small, tidy rooms and small-town warmth in downtown London (D-£58; 107 Ebury Street, SW1W 9QU, tel. 0171-730-1048, fax 0171-730-2574; Rachel Joplin). **Lime Tree Hotel**, enthusiastically run, has spacious rooms (£85–£100, Db-£65, David will deal in slow times; CC; 135 Ebury Street, SW1W 9RA, tel. 0171-730-8191, fax 0171-730-7865). **Cherry Court Hotel** offers small rooms and good prices on a quiet street close to the station (Db-£40; CC; 23 Hugh Street, SW1V 1QJ, tel. 0171-828-2840).

    London's Notting Hill Gate Neighborhood: Vicarage Private Hotel is family-run and elegantly British in a quiet, classy neighborhood with 19 rooms furnished with taste and quality (D-£62; a six-minute walk from the Notting Hill Gate tube station, near Kensington Palace, 10 Vicarage Gate, Kensington W8 4AG, tel. 0171-229-4030, fax 0171-792-5989). **Hotel Ravna Gora**, formerly the mansion of 18th-century architect Henry Holland, is now a large Slavic-run B&B—eccentric and well-worn (D-£50, Db-£60; CC; 50 yards from Holland Park tube station, 29 Holland Park Avenue, W11 3RW, tel. 0171-727-7725, fax 0171-221-4282). The **Norwegian YWCA** (Norsk K.F.U.K.) is for women under 30 only (and men with Norwegian passports). An incredible value, it's smoke-free with a Norwegian atmosphere on a quiet, stately street (July through August: bed in shared double-£25, shared quad-£18, with breakfast; September through June: same prices but with dinner included; 52 Holland Park, W11 3R5, tel. & fax 0171-727-9897). With each visit I wonder, "Which is easier—getting a sex change or getting a Norwegian passport?"

BATH: ENGLAND AT ITS ELEGANT AND FRIVOLOUS BEST (CH. 46)
(£1 = about $1.70)

Brock's Guest House will put bubbles in your Bath experience. Marion Dodd runs this charming 1765 Georgian townhouse located just off the Royal Crescent (Db-£55 to £65; 32 Brock Street, BA1 2LN, tel. 01225-338-374, fax 01225-334-245, e-mail: marion@brocks.force9.net). In the tidy **Woodville House**, Anne and Tom Toalster offer Bath's best cheap beds (D-£33, minimum two nights; smokers are not welcome; 4 Marlborough Lane, BA1 2NQ, tel. 01225-319-335). **Elgin Villa** is also a fine value (Db-£40, two nights minimum; 6 Marlborough Lane, BA1 2NQ Bath, tel. 01225-424-557, fax 01225-425-633). **Holly Villa Guest House**, with a cheery garden and a cozy TV lounge, an eight-minute walk from the station and center, is thoughtfully run by Jill McGarrigle (D-£35, Db-£46; no smoking; 14 Pulteney Gardens, BA2 4HG, tel. 01225-310-331, fax 01225-339-334). The **Henry Guest House** is a clean, bright, and vertical little eight-room, family-run place two blocks in front of the train station on a quiet side street (D-£34; 6 Henry Street, BA1 1JT, tel. 01225-424-052; Mrs. Cox).

YORK: VIKINGS TO DICKENS (CH. 47)
(£1 = about $1.70)

These small bed-and-breakfast places are a short walk from the train station, tourist information office, and town center, and charge around £20 per person with a huge breakfast. **Airden House** has spacious rooms, a grandfather clock–cozy TV lounge, and brightness and warmth throughout (D-£38, Db-£46; no smoking; 1 St. Mary's, Y03 7DD, tel. 01904-638-915). The **Sycamore** is a fine value with cozy rooms and piles of personal touches (D-£32, Db-£40; 19 Sycamore Place off Bootham Terrace, YO3 7DW, tel. 01904-624-712). The **Hazelwood** is my most hotelesque listing (Db-£50 to £53, Db with four-poster-£5 extra; CC; nonsmoking, 24 Portland Street, Gillygate, YO3 7EH, tel. 01904-626-548, fax 01904-628-032). The friendly **Claremont Guest House** offers two rooms and thoughtful touches (D-£32, Db-£42; no smoking; 18 Claremont Terrace off Gillygate, YO3 7EJ, tel. 01904-625-158).

BLACKPOOL: BRITAIN'S CONEY ISLAND (CH. 48)
(£1 = about $1.70)

The **Robin Hood Hotel** is a super place, cheery, family-run, with a big, welcoming living room and 12 newly and tastefully refurbished rooms (Db-£36; CC; entirely nonsmoking; trolley stop: St. Stevens Avenue, 1½ miles north of the Tower across from a peaceful stretch of beach, 100 Queens Promenade, North Shore, FY2 9NS, tel. 01253-351-599; Pam and Colin Webster). **Beechcliffe Private Hotel** is family-run with more charm than average (D-£33; trolley stop: Uncle Tom's, a block away from the beach, 16 Shaftesbury Ave., North Shore, FY2 9QQ, tel. 01253-353-075; David and Brenda) The **Prefect Hotel** is all smiles and pink-flamingo pretty: shabby but spacious-for-Blackpool, with all the appropriately tacky touches (Db-£34; ask for view room; trolley to Bispham, two miles north of the Tower at 204 Queens Promenade, FY2 9JS, tel. 01253-352-699; Bill and Pauline Acton). The current hot bar is Funny Girls, just a block from the North Pier. Every night they put on a "glam bam thank you ma'am" burlesque-in-drag show that delights footballers and grannies alike.

THE COTSWOLD VILLAGES: INVENTORS OF QUAINT (CH. 49)
(£1 = about $1.70)

Stow-on-the-Wold: The cozy **West Deyne B&B**, run by Mrs. Joan Cave, has a peaceful garden overlooking the countryside (D-£34 with evening tea and biscuits; Lower Swell Road, GL54 1LD, tel. 01451-831-011). The **Pound** is the comfy, quaint, restored 500-year-old, low-ceilinged, heavy-beamed home of Patricia Whitehead. She offers two spacious, bright rooms with good, strong twin beds and a classic old fireplace lounge (D-£34; nonsmoking; right downtown on Sheep Street, GL54 1AU, tel. 01451-830-229). The **Stow-on-the-Wold Youth Hostel**, on Stow's main square in a historic old building, has a friendly atmosphere, good hot meals, and a do-it-yourself members' kitchen. It's popular in summer, so call ahead (£8 per bed with sheets; CC; eight to18 beds per room; closed 10:00 a.m. to 5:00 p.m.; no lockers; tel. 01451-830-497).

Chipping Campden: Sandalwood House B&B is a big, comfy, modern home with a royal lounge and a sprawling backyard in a quiet woodsy/pastoral setting, well-run by gracious Diana Bendall (D-£40 to £44, evening tea and biscuits included; nonsmoking; left off Lower High Street on Hoo Lane, right on Back Ends, GL55 6AU, tel. 01386-840-091).

Moreton-in-Marsh: The Cottage, was built in 1620 with low ceilings, an inglenooky lounge, and lots of character with no loss of comfort. The twin is quieter and more spacious than the front double. I'd pay extra to sleep with Peter Rabbit in the garden (D-£36; the charming pastel open-beamed "annex cottage" in the garden is £45; nonsmoking; near station on Oxford Street, GL56 0LA, tel. 01608-651-740; Lorraine and Richard Carter).

DINGLE PENINSULA: IRELAND AT ITS SEDUCTIVE BEST (CH. 51)
(£1 = about $1.70)

Dingle Town (mail: Dingle, Co. Kerry): **Sraid Eoin B&B**, on the quiet end of town with four spacious pastel rooms and giant bathrooms, is warmly run by Kathleen and Morris O'Connor (Db-£32, family deals; CC; John Street, tel. 066-51409, fax 066-52156). **Kellihers Ballyegan House** is next door, run by friendly Mrs. Hannah Kelliher (£17 per person, Upper John Street, tel. 066-51702). **Greenmount House**, at the top of town, a three-minute walk from the town center, is one of Ireland's classiest B&Bs, with six standard rooms (Db-£40 per person) and six sprawling suites (Db-£60) in a modern building with lavish public areas and breakfast in a solarium. No singles, children under eight or burping (CC; up John Street to Gortonora, tel. 066-51414, fax 066-51974; book ahead). **Corner House B&B** is my long-time Dingle home. It's a simple, traditional place with five rooms run with a twinkle and a smile by Kathleen Farrell (D-£30; plenty of plumbing but it's down the hall; reserve with a phone call and reconfirm a day or two ahead or risk losing your bed; central as can be on Dykegate Street, tel. 066-51516). **Captain's House B&B** is a salty-feeling place with a stay-awhile garden and eight classy rooms in the town center (Db-£44; CC; the Mall, tel. 066-51531, fax 066-51079; Jim and Mary Milhench). **Ballintaggert Hostel**, a backpacker's complex, is in a stylish old manor house which was used by Protestants during the famine as a soup kitchen (for those hungry enough to renounce their Catholicism). It comes complete with horse riding, bike rental, laundry service, kitchen, café, classy study, fireplace, family room, a shuttle into town, and a resident ghost (166 beds; £7 in eight- to 12-bed dorms, £10 in quads,

£13 in singles and doubles, breakfast extra; one mile east of town on the Tralee Road, tel. 066-51454, fax 066-52207).

Dingle Peninsula Tours: Sciuird Archeology tours are run by the Sciuirds, a family that has Dingle history—and a knack for sharing it—in its blood. They offer serious 2.5 hour £6.50 minibus tours one, two, or three times a day depending upon demand. Drop by the Kirrary B&B (Dykegate and Grey's Lane in Dingle Town) or call 066-51937 early to put your name on the list. Tours fill quickly in summer. **Moran's Tour** does three-hour guided minibus trips around the peninsula with a more touristic slant (£6; departures normally at 10:30 a.m. and 2:00 p.m. from the Esso station near the roundabout in Dingle Town; tel. 066-51155). The **Mountain Man**, in Dingle Town on Strand Strret, also offers three-hour, minibus tours of the peninsula (tel. 066-51868).

NORTHERN IRELAND (CH. 52)
(£1 = about $1.70)

Belfast: The best budget beds cluster in a comfortable area just south of the university and Ulster Museum. Two train stations (Botanic and Adelaide) are nearby, and every few minutes buses zip down Malone Road (#70 and #71). Taxis, cheap in Belfast, will take you downtown for £2.50 (your host can call one). Belfast is more of a business town than a tourist town, so business-class room rates are lower or soft on weekends. **Queen's Elms Halls of Residence** is a big brick Queen's University dorm renting more than 300 rooms to travelers during summer break (mid-June through mid-September; D-£21, cheaper for students; 78 Malone Road, tel. 01232-381608). The **Ulster People's College Residential Centre** rents 30 beds in 10 cheery undormlike rooms year-round (D-£30; free laundry, 30 Adelaide Park, tel. 01232-665161, fax 01232-668111). **Malone Lodge Hotel** provides slick, modern, business-class comfort on a quiet leafy street (Db-£88 weekdays, £56 weekends; CC; elevator, 60 Eglantine Avenue, Belfast BT9 6DY, tel. 01232-382409, fax 01232-382706). **Camera House Guest House** is newly renovated with large smoke-free rooms and an airy, hardwood feeling throughout (Db-£45 to £52; CC; 44 Wellington Park, Belfast BT9 6DP, tel. 01232-660026, fax 01232/667856). **Jurys Inn**, the latest in this popular chain, is now in downtown Belfast. A copy of its sisters in Galway and Dublin, this huge American-style place rents its several hundred identical modern rooms for one simple price (up to three adults or two adults and two kids for about £55; two blocks from City Hall on Spires Mall, Dublin reservation board tel. 01-454 3363).

Bangor (mail: Bangor, Co. Down): For a laid-back seaside hometown—and more comfort per pound—sleep half an hour south of Belfast by commuter train in Bangor. **Pierview House B&B** is a chandeliered winner, with three of its five spacious rooms overlooking the sea (D-£30, grand Db-£32; family room; CC; 28 Seacliff Road, tel. 01247-463381; Mr. and Mrs. Watts). **Sea Crest B&B** is homey and friendly with no lounge but four fine rooms (D-£30; CC; 98 Seacliff Road, tel. 01247-461935; Irene Marsden).

OSLO (CH. 53)
(7 kr = about $1)

In Oslo the season dictates the best deals. In low season (July through mid-August, and Friday, Saturday, and Sunday the rest of the year), fancy hotels are the best value for softies, with 600 kr for a double with breakfast. In high season (business days outside of summer), your affordable choices are dumpy-for-Scandinavia (but still nice by European standards) doubles for around 500 kr in hotels and 350 kr in private homes. **City Hotel** has clean, basic, and homey rooms (D-550 kr, Db-680 kr; CC; depending on season, Skippergata 19, tel. 22 41 36 10, fax 22 42 24 29). **Rainbow Hotel Astoria** is a modern, comfortable place (cheaper Db twins-540 kr to 695 kr, Db-640 kr to 795 kr; CC; three blocks in front of the station, 50 yards from Karl Johans Gate, Dronningensgate 21, 0154 Oslo, tel. 22 42 00 10, fax 22 42 57 65). For maximum culture and economy, try a room in a private home: **Mr. Naess** offers big, homey old rooms overlooking a park and the use of a fully-loaded kitchen (D-250 kr; walk 20 minutes from the station or take bus #27 five stops to Olaf Ryes Plass, Toftegate 45, tel. & fax 22 37 58 94). The **Albertine Hostel** feels like a bomb shelter but offers clean, simple, spacious rooms (Db-300 kr, dorm bed-95 kr to 125 kr; catch tram 11, 12, 15, 17, bus 27 or 30 from the station, Storgata 55, tel. 22 99 72 00, fax 22 99 72 20). Summer vagabonds sleep cheap (100 kr) at the downtown **YMCA Sleep-In Oslo** (Møllergata 1, tel. 22 20 83 97).

STALKING STOCKHOLM (CH. 54)
(7 kr = about $1)

Peak season for Stockholm's expensive hotels is business workdays outside of summer. Rates drop by 30 to 50 percent in the summer or on weekends. The tourist office sorts through all of this for you. Their Stockholm Package offers business-class doubles with buffet breakfasts for 790 kr, includes two free Stockholm Cards, and lets children up to age 18 sleep for free. This is limited to mid-June through mid-August, and Friday and Saturday throughout the year. Assuming you'll be getting two Stockholm Cards anyway (370 kr), this gives you a $200 hotel double for about $50. This is for real (summertime is that dead for business hotels). Arriving without reservations in July is never a problem. It gets tight during the Water Festival (10 days in early August) and during a convention stretch for a few days in late June.

    Queen's Hotel, cheery, clean, and just a 10-minute walk from the station, is probably the best cheap hotel in town (summer rates: D-550 kr, Db-695 kr to 895 kr; CC; Drottninggatan 71A, 11160 Stockholm, tel. 08-249-460, fax 08-217-620). **Bentley's Hotel** is an interesting option with an old English flair and renovated rooms (summer rates include winter Sundays: small Db-490 kr, Db-690 kr; CC; one block up the street from Queen's at Drottninggatan 77, tel. 08-141-395, fax 08-212-492). The *af Chapman* (IYHF), Europe's most famous youth hostel, is a permanently moored cutter ship. It's just a five-minute walk from downtown, with 140 beds—two to eight per stateroom (110 kr per bed, Skeppsholmen, 11149 Stockholm, tel. 08-679-5015). **Zinken Hostel** is a big, basic hostel with plenty of doubles, a launderette, and kitchen facilities. If you want a cheap double, sleep here (D-355 kr, dorm bed-120 kr, extra for sheets and nonmembers; T-bana: Zinkensdamm, Zinkens Vag 20, tel. 08-616-8100 or 08/616-8188 in evenings).

ÆRØ, DENMARK'S SHIP-IN-A-BOTTLE ISLAND (CH. 55)
(7 kr = about $1)

Ærøskøbing (zip code: 5970): **Pension Vestergade** is a quirky 200-year-old home run by Susanna Greve (D-300 kr, Vestergade 44, tel. 62 52 22 98). **Det**

Lille Hotel is a friendly and shipshape 19th-century captain's home (D-465 kr; CC; Smedegade 33, tel. & fax 62 52 23 00). The **Ærøskøbing Youth Hostel** is a glorious place with a fine living room, members' kitchen, and rooms for families (dorm bed-80 kr, D-200 kr; closed October through March; Smedevejen 15, tel. 62 52 10 44, fax 62 52 16 44).

THE BALTICS AND ST. PETERSBURG (CH. 56)

St. Petersburg: If calling from the U.S., dial 011-7-812, then the local number. The **St. Petersburg International Hostel** is a normal hostel like those in Western Europe, with friendly English-speaking staff and 60 beds in clean three- to five-bed rooms ($17 per person, $19 for nonmembers). They're busy in summer, so reserve ahead (tel. 329-8018, fax 329-8019, e-mail ryh@ryh. spb.su). They'll also help you get your Russian visa.

Tallinn, Estonia (14 kr = about $1): If you're calling from the U.S., dial 011-372, then the local number. **Hotell Mihkli**, offering respectability at the best rates in town, has new furniture, functioning bathrooms, locked parking, a TV, phone, and nice writing desk in every room, and a welcoming reception desk (Db-820 kr; Endla 23; it's past the National Library, walk or take bus #2, #3, or #6 to the "Koidu" stop, tel. 245-3704, fax 245-1767).

Riga, Latvia (.58 lats = about $1): If you're calling from the U.S., dial 011-371, then the local number. The **Radi un Draugi** is an excellent small hotel right in the Old Town, with modern renovated rooms and bathrooms (Db-29.50 Ls, Mārstaļu iela 1, LV-1050 Riga, tel. 722-0372, fax 724-2239; reserve ahead).

Vilnius, Lithuania (4 Lt = about $1): If you're calling from the U.S., dial 011-370-2, then the local number. **Hotel Naujasis Vilnius** is a big hotel just across the river from the Old Town with an excellent restaurant, comfortable remodeled rooms (Db-330 Lt), and acceptable unremodeled rooms (Db-230 Lt to 250 Lt; CC; Ukmėrgės gatve 14, tel. 721-342, fax 723-161).

PELOPONNESIAN HIGHLIGHTS: OVERLOOKED GREECE (CH. 57)
(260 drx = about $1)

Finikoundas: Korakakis Beach Hotel is the best inexpensive hotel in town, with fine rooms and beach views, (Db-11,000 drx, 6,000 drx off-season tel. 0723/71221). For cheap rooms (6,000 drx) in private homes, try **Dhomatia Anastasios Tomaras** (tel. 0723/71378), **Dhomatia Athanios and Jiota Tsonis** (tel. 0723/71316), and **Dhomatia Alexis Tomaras** (tel. 0723/71306).

DUNGEONS AND DRAGONS: EUROPE'S NINE MOST MEDIEVAL CASTLE EXPERIENCES (CH. 59)

Carcassonne, France (5.5F = about $1, zip code: 11000): Right in the old center, **Hôtel des Remparts** is best, with a 12th-century staircase leading to modern, comfortable rooms (Db-300F to 330F; CC; 5 place de Grands-Puits, tel. 04 68 71 27 72, fax 04 68 72 73 26). **Hôtel Montmorency** is also good (Db-260F to 300F; CC; 2 rue Camille St. Saens, tel. 04 68 25 19 92). The **Auberge de Jeunesse** (youth hostel) is clean and well-run (dorm bed-70F, 20F extra for nonmembers; rue de Vicomte Trencavel, tel. 04 68 25 23 16, fax 04 68 71 14 84).

Reutte, Austria (12 AS = about $1, zip code: A-6600): **Hotel Maximilian**, up the river a mile or so, is a fine splurge (Db-840 AS to 880 AS; far from the train station in the next village, Ehenbichl-Reutte, tel. 05672/62585, fax 05672/625-

8554). **Gutshof zum Schluxen**, which gets the "remote old hotel in an idyllic setting" award, is a working farm offering good food and modern rustic elegance draped in goosedown and pastels, with a chance to pet the rabbit (Db-920 AS to 1,080 AS; between Reutte and Füssen in the village of Unterpinswang, tel. 05677/8903, fax 05677/890-323). These four *Zimmer* are comfortable, quiet, kid-friendly, about $20 a bed, have few stairs, speak some English, and are within two blocks of the Breitenwang church steeple in Reutte: **Maria Auer** (minimum two nights; Kaiser Lothar Strasse 25, tel. 05672/629-195), **Inge Hosp** (a more old-fashioned place; one night OK; Kaiser Lothar Strasse 36, tel. 05672/62401), her cousins **Walter and Emilie Hosp** (Kaiser Lothar Strasse 29, tel. 05672/65377), and **Helene Haissl** (humbler rooms; Planseestrasse 63, tel. 05672/67913). Reutte's homey and newly renovated **Jugendgastehaus Graben** (youth hostel) has two to six beds per room and includes breakfast, shower, and sheets (dorm bed-140 AS; Reutte-Höfen, Postfach 3, Graben 1; two miles from the station, tel. 05672/62644, fax 05672/626-444). Frau Reyman keeps the place traditional, clean, and friendly and serves a great 80-AS dinner. This is a super value.

Füssen, Germany (1.7 DM = about $1): Close to Ludwig's castles, you might stay in the modern, pricey **Hotel Kurcafé** (Db-119 DM to 189 DM; Bahnhofstrasse 4, 87620 Füssen, tel. 08362/6369, fax 08362/39424), in a private room at **Haus Peters** (D-86 DM; near station, Augustenstrasse 5, tel. 08362/7171), or, if you're under 27, at the fine, Germanly run **Füssen Youth Hostel** (dorm bed-20 DM; Mariahilferstrasse 5, tel. 08632/7754).

Bacharach on the Rhine, Germany (zip code: 55422): Bacharach's youth hostel, **Jugendherberge Stahleck**, is a 12th-century castle on the hilltop, 500 steps above Bacharach, with a royal Rhine view. This newly redone gem with eight beds and a bathroom in each room is warmly and energetically run by Evelyn and Bernhard Falke, who serve hearty, 9-DM buffet dinners (24-DM dorm beds with breakfast; 6 DM extra if over 26, without a card, for sheets, and in a double; normally rooms are available but call and leave your name, tel. 06743/1266). **Hotel Kranenturm** gives you the feeling of a castle (without the hostel-ity or the climb), mixing comfort and hotel privacy with zimmer warmth, a central location, and a medieval atmosphere. Its rooms with Rhine views come with train noise; the back side is quieter (Db-90 to 95 DM with this book, CC; Langstrasse 30, tel. 06743/1308, fax 06743/1021). **Frau Feldhege** rents two rooms in her quiet, homey, traditional place. Guests get a cushy living room, a self-serve kitchen, and the free use of bikes (Db-55 DM, no breakfast; Oberstrasse 13 in the old center, tel. 06743/1271). **Ursula Orth** rents out three small cheery rooms in the town center (Db-60 DM for one night, less for two; Spurgasse 3, tel. 06743/1557).

St. Goar on the Rhine, Germany (zip code: 56329): **Hotel Montag** is friendly, laid-back, and comfortable (Db-130 DM, price can drop if you arrive late or it's a slow time; CC; Heerstrasse 128, tel. 06741/1629, fax 06741/2086). **Hotel Hauser**, very central and newly redone, is warmly run by Frau Velich (D-88 DM, Db-98 DM, Db with Rhine view balconies-110 DM, show this book to get these prices, cheaper in off-season; CC; Heerstrasse 77, tel. 06741/333, fax 06741/1464). **Frau Kurz** offers all the comforts of a hotel at B&B prices (D-60 DM, Db-70 DM, showers-5 DM, minimum two nights; Ulmenhof 11, 5401 St. Goar/Rhein, tel. & fax 06741/459). The Germanly run **St. Goar Hostel** is a good value, with two to 12 beds per rooms, a 10:00 p.m. curfew, and hearty 9-DM dinners (20-DM beds with breakfast, 5-DM sleep sacks; Bismarckweg 17, tel. 06741/388).

EUROPE'S BEST-PRESERVED LITTLE TOWNS (CH. 61)

Óbidos, Portugal (170$ = about $1, zip code: 2510): If you spend the night, you'll enjoy the town without tourists. Two good values in this sterilized and overpriced touristic toy of a town are the hotelesque **Albergaria Rainha Santa Isabel** (Db-9,000$ to 12,000$ with breakfast, add 1,500$ in August; CC; on the main one-lane drag, Rua Direita, tel. 062/959-323, fax 062/959-115) and **Casa do Poço**, with four dim, clean rooms around a bright courtyard (Db-9,000$ with breakfast; on Travessa da Mouraria, in the old center near the castle, tel. 062/959-358).

Toledo, Spain (140 ptas = about $1): **Hotel Maravilla** is wonderfully central, quiet, and convenient. Despite its dark, narrow halls and slightly run-down rooms, it offers the best middle-range value in the old center (Db-6,700 ptas, includes breakfast and 7 percent IVA tax; CC; just behind Plaza Zodocover, at Plaza de Barrio Rey 7, 45001 Toledo, tel. 925-22-83-17, fax 925-22-81-55; some English spoken). **Hotel Carlos V** suffers from the obligatory stuffiness of a correct hotel but has bright, pleasant rooms and elegant bathrooms (Db-12,500 ptas, breakfast-900 ptas; air conditioning, elevator; CC; Plaza Horno Magdalena 3, 45001 Toledo, tel. 925-22-21-00, fax 925-22-21-05; English spoken). **Hostal Nuevo Labrador** is just as nice for half the price (Db-6,400 ptas; Juan Labrador 10, 45001 Toledo, tel. 925-22-26-20, fax 925-22-93-99). Down the same street, the smaller, family-run **Pension Lumbreras** has a tranquil courtyard and 12 simple rooms (D-2,850 ptas, breakfast-225 ptas; Juan Labrador 9, 45001 Toledo, tel. 925-22-15-71; no English spoken). **Hotel Santa Isabel**, in a 15th-century building, has clean, comfortable rooms (Db-6,200 ptas, breakfast-450 ptas, 7 percent IVA tax included; parking-810 ptas; air conditioning, elevator; CC; Calle Santa Isabel 24, 45002 Toledo, tel. 925-25-31-20, fax 925-25-31-36). **Pension Segovia** is old, rickety, and dingy, with firm beds and memorable balconies (D-2,600 ptas, shower-200 ptas; Calle de Recoletos 2, 45001 Toledo, tel. 925-21-11-24). The best splurge in town is the **Hostal de Cardenal**, a 17th-century cardinal's palace (Db-11,500 ptas; CC; near Puerta Bisagra, Paseo de Recaredo 24, 45004 Toledo, tel. 925-22-49-00; fax 925-22-29-91; the stuffy staff speaks English).

Collioure, France (5.5F = about $1, zip code: 66190): Stay in the old city, tucked behind the castle. You'll find several *chambres d'hôtes* (the TI has a list), the best of which must be the clean and spacious rooms at Monsieur and Madame Peroneille's **Chambres** (Db-250F; 20 rue Pasteur, tel. 04 68 82 15 31). The Spanish-feeling **Hôtel Templiers** rents thoughtfully appointed rooms (some with views) with wall-to-wall art and an easygoing staff (Db-325F to 410F; 12 avenue l'Amiraute, tel. 04 68 98 31 10, fax 04 68 98 01 24). The **Hôtel Triton**, just off the main drag across from the old city but still on the bay, offers just-remodeled rooms at fair rates (Db-300F; rue Jean Bart, tel. 04 68 82 06 52, fax 04 68 98 39 39).

Bruges, Belgium (35BF = about $1, zip code: 8000): **Hansa Hotel** is bright and tastefully decorated in elegant pastels, and each of the rooms has all the hotelesque comforts (Db-3,000BF to 3,950BF, best prices Sunday through Thursday nights; CC; a block north of Market, Niklaas Desparsstraat 11, tel. 050/338-444, fax 050/334-205, e-mail: information@hansa.be; run by Johan and Isabelle). **Hotel t'Keizershof** is a dollhouse of a hotel that lives by its motto, "Spend a night, not a fortune" (D-1,350BF; easy parking; one block in front of the station, Oostmeers 126, tel. 050/338-728; run by Stefaan and Hilda). Bed-and-breakfast places are really the best value of all. Each of these places are central, run by people who enjoy their work: **Yvonne De Vriese** (D-1,500BF, Db-1,800BF; CC; Predikherenstraat 40, tel. 050/334-224), **Koen and Annemie Dieltiens** (D-1,500BF, Db-1,800BF; nonsmoking; Sint-Walburgastraat 14, tel. 050/334-294, fax 050/335-230, e-mail: koen.dieltien@skynet.be), and **Paul and Roos Gheeraert**: (Db-1,600BF to 1,800BF; Ridderstraat 9, tel. 050/335-627, fax 050/345-201, e-mail: paul.gheeraert@skynet.be).

　　Cotswold Hills: See listing for Chapter 49.

　　Staithes, England (£1 = about $1.70, zip code: TS13 5BH): Each of these three- or four-bedroom places is cramped with old carpets, bad wallpaper, lumpy beds, and tangled floorplans that make you feel like a stowaway. The **Harborside Guest House** provides basic beds, sea-view rooms, breakfast in a fish and chips shop, and the sound of waves to lull you to sleep (D-£39; four rooms, tel. 01947/841296). Also check out **Toffee Crackle House** (two £32 twins and a family room; nonsmoking; tel. 01947/841401; Kay Lanny), **Endeavour Restaurant B&B** (D-£38, Db-£42; tel. 01947/840825; Lisa Chapman), and **Salmon Cottage** (a £32 twin and a family room; tel. 01947/841193; Geoff and Isabel Elliott).

TURKEY'S HOT (CH. 64)

Samos, Greece: Hotel Samos has spacious rooms with bayfront balconies (Db-$30; across from the dock, 11 Th. Sofoulis, Samos, tel. 0273/28377, fax 0273/23771). **Hotel Helen**, around the corner, has attractive, airy rooms (Db-$35, $5 breakfast; tel. 0273/28215), and the nearby **Hotel Bonis** is also good (Db-$30, $5 breakfast; tel. 0273/28790).

　　Kusadasi, Turkey: For clean, quiet rooms, try **Golden Bed Pansiyon** (Db-$25; Ugurlu I. Cikmazi #4, tel. 256/614-8708) or **Ozhan Pansiyon** (Db-$25; a couple of blocks from the tourist information office, Kibris Caddesi 5, tel. 256/614-2932). For a splurge, try **Hotel Stella** for its spectacular harbor views and warmly decorated rooms with balconies (Db-$60; steep hike up to Bezirgan Sokak #44, tel. 256/614-1632, fax 256/614-5338). Varan and Ulusoy are the best bus companies for overnight rides from Kusadasi to Istanbul.

European Weather

Here is a list of average temperatures and days of no rain. This can be helpful in planning your itinerary, but I have never found European weather to be particularly predictable.

1st line, avg. daily low; 2nd line, avg. daily high; 3rd line, days of no rain

	J	F	M	A	M	J	J	A	S	O	N	D
AUSTRIA	26°	28°	34°	41°	50°	56°	59°	58°	52°	44°	36°	30°
Vienna	34°	38°	47°	57°	66°	71°	75°	73°	66°	55°	44°	37°
	23	21	24	21	22	21	22	21	23	23	22	22
BELGIUM	31°	31°	35°	39°	46°	50°	54°	54°	50°	44°	36°	33°
Brussels	42°	43°	49°	56°	65°	70°	73°	72°	67°	58°	47°	42°
	19	18	20	18	21	19	20	20	19	19	18	18
DENMARK	29°	28°	31°	37°	44°	51°	55°	54°	49°	42°	35°	32°
Copenhagen	36°	36°	41°	50°	61°	67°	72°	69°	63°	53°	43°	38°
	22	21	23	21	23	22	22	19	22	22	20	20
EGYPT	42°	44°	50°	59°	69°	70°	73°	73°	71°	65°	54°	45°
Luxor	74°	79°	86°	95°	104°	106°	107°	106°	103°	98°	87°[b]	78°
	31	28	31	30	31	30	31	31	30	31	30	31
FINLAND	17°	15°	22°	31°	41°	49°	58°	55°	46°	37°	30°	22°
Helsinki	27°	26°	32°	43°	55°	63°	71°	66°	57°	45°	37°	31°
	20	20	23	22	23	21	23	19	19	19	19	20
FRANCE	32°	34°	36°	41°	47°	52°	55°	55°	50°	44°	38°	33°
Paris	42°	45°	52°	60°	67°	73°	76°	75°	69°	59°	49°	43°
	16	15	16	16	18	19	19	19	19	17	15	14
	40°	41°	45°	49°	56°	62°	66°	66°	62°	55°	48°	43°
Nice	56°	56°	59°	64°	69°	76°	81°	81°	77°	70°	62°	58°
	23	20	23	23	23	25	29	26	24	22	23	23
GERMANY	29°	31°	35°	41°	48°	53°	56°	55°	51°	43°	36°	31°
Frankfurt	37°	42°	49°	58°	67°	72°	75°	74°	67°	56°	45°	39°
	22	19	22	21	22	21	21	21	21	22	21	20
GREAT BRITAIN	35°	35°	37°	40°	45°	51°	55°	54°	51°	44°	39°	36°
London	44°	45°	51°	56°	63°	69°	73°	72°	67°	58°	49°	45°
	14	15	20	16	18	19	18	18	17	17	14	15
GREECE	42°	43°	46°	52°	60°	67°	72°	72°	66°	60°	52°	46°
Athens	54°	55°	60°	67°	77°	85°	90°	90°	83°	74°	64°	57°
	24	22	26	27	28	28	30	30	28	27	24	24
IRELAND	35°	35°	36°	38°	42°	48°	51°	51°	47°	43°	38°	36°
Dublin	47°	47°	51°	54°	59°	65°	67°	67°	63°	57°	51°	47°
	18	17	21	19	20	19	18	18	18	19	18	18
ITALY	39°	39°	42°	46°	55°	60°	64°	64°	61°	53°	46°	41°
Rome	54°	56°	62°	68°	74°	82°	88°	88°	83°	73°	63°	56°
	23	17	26	24	25	28	29	28	24	22	22	22
PORTUGAL	47°	57°	50°	52°	56°	60°	64°	65°	62°	58°	52°	48°
(Lagos/Algarve)	61°	61°	63°	67°	73°	77°	83°	84°	80°	73°	66°	62°
	22	19	20	24	27	29	31	31	28	26	22	22
	46°	47°	49°	52°	56°	60°	63°	64°	62°	57°	52°	47°
Lisbon	56°	58°	61°	64°	69°	75°	79°	80°	76°	69°	62°	57°
	22	20	21	23	25	28	30	30	26	24	20	21

1st line, avg. daily low; 2nd line, avg. daily high; 3rd line, days of no rain

	J	F	M	A	M	J	J	A	S	O	N	D
MOROCCO Marrakesh	40°	43°	48°	52°	57°	62°	67°	68°	63°	57°	49°	52°
	65°	68°	74°	79°	84°	92°	101°	100°	92°	83°	3°	66°
	24	23	25	24	29	29	30	30	27	27	27	24
Tangiers	47°	48°	50°	51°	56°	60°	64°	65°	63°	59°	52°	48°
	60°	61°	63°	65°	71°	76°	80°	82°	78°	72°	65°	61°
	21	18	21	22	26	27	31	31	27	23	20	21
NETHERLANDS Amsterdam	34°	34°	37°	43°	50°	55°	59°	59°	56°	48°	41°	35°
	40°	41°	46°	52°	60°	65°	69°	68°	64°	56°	47°	41°
	12	13	18	16	19	18	17	17	15	13	11	12
NORWAY Oslo	20°	20°	25°	34°	43°	51°	56°	53°	45°	37°	29°	24°
	30°	32°	40°	50°	62°	69°	73°	69°	60°	49°	37°	31°
	23	21	24	23	24	22	21	20	22	21	21	21
SPAIN Madrid	33°	35°	40°	44°	50°	57°	62°	52°	56°	48°	40°	35°
	47°	51°	57°	64°	71°	80°	87°	86°	77°	66°	54°	48°
	22	19	20	21	22	24	28	29	24	23	20	22
Barcelona	42°	44°	47°	51°	57°	63°	69°	69°	65°	58°	50°	44°
	56°	57°	61°	64°	71°	77°	81°	82°	67°	61°	62°	57°
	26	21	24	22	23	25	27	26	23	23	23	25
Malaga	47°	48°	51°	55°	60°	66°	70°	72°	68°	61°	53°	48°
	61°	62°	64°	69°	74°	80°	84°	85°	81°	74°	67°	62°
	25	22	23	25	28	29	31	30	28	27	22	25
SWEDEN Stockholm	23°	22°	26°	32°	41°	49°	55°	53°	46°	39°	31°	26°
	31°	31°	37°	45°	57°	65°	70°	66°	58°	48°	38°	33°
	23	21	24	24	23	23	22	21	22	22	21	22
SWITZERLAND Geneva	29°	30°	35°	41°	48°	55°	58°	57°	52°	44°	37°	31°
	39°	43°	51°	58°	66°	73°	77°	76°	69°	58°	47°	40°
	20	19	21	19	19	19	22	21	20	20	19	21
TURKEY Antakya area	39°	41°	45°	51°	59°	66°	71°	72°	66°	58°	51°	43°
	57°	59°	66°	74°	83°	89°	93°	94°	91°	84°	73°	61°
	23	21	25	25	27	28	30	30	29	28	25	24

Metric Conversion Table

1 inch	=	25 millimeters	1 ounce	=	28 grams
1 foot	=	0.3 meter	1 pound	=	0.45 kilogram
1 yard	=	0.9 meter	temp. (°F)	=	9/5 °C + 32
1 mile	=	1.6 kilometers	1 kilogram	=	2.2 pounds
1 sq. yd.	=	0.8 square meter	1 kilometer	=	62 mile
1 acre	=	0.4 hectare	1 centimeter	=	0.4 inch
1 quart	=	0.95 liter	1 meter	=	39.4 inches

RICK STEVES' BACK DOOR GUIDE TO
European
Railpasses

How to find the railpass that best fits your trip — and your budget.

When I started traveling in the 70s, the Eurailpass was king...cheap, simple, and the obvious best deal. My choices were kindergarten-simple: one month or two? Now, 25 years later, travelers have an exciting array of railpasses to choose from: Eurailpasses, Europasses, regional, country, and Rail & Drive passes. Most passes are available for purchase only outside of Europe, while others can be bought only after you arrive in Europe. Depending on your trip, it may be cheaper to buy tickets as-you-go. Budget travelers need to be more informed than ever in order to make the best choice.

This rail guide will help you decide which railpass, if any, is best for your trip to Europe. It covers Eurailpasses, Europasses, country and regional passes, tickets (purchased as you travel), rail & drive passes, and even car rental. The first section will help you learn how to make an informed choice — then you'll be ready to dive into the dizzying array of European railpass prices and features.

COMPARING COSTS: RAILPASSES VS. TICKETS

You can ride the rails in Europe with a railpass, or with tickets you purchase at train stations as you travel. With this guide, you can figure out which is more economical for your trip.

Throughout this guide, you'll find maps that list the prices for tickets (also called "point-to-point tickets"). Once you have a rough itinerary, use these maps to add up the cost of your journey. Compare the cost of tickets with the price of the railpass that best fits your trip. If the costs are close, it makes sense to buy the pass, unless you enjoy standing in lines at ticket windows.

CHOO-CHOOSING A RAILPASS

Consecutive-day or Flexipass?

You'll often need to choose between consecutive-day and flexipass versions of a pass. The major exception is the Europass, which comes only in a flexi-version.

Consecutive-day pass: If you plan to travel nearly daily and cover a lot of ground, a consecutive-day pass is the right choice for you. You get unlimited train travel for the duration of the pass. If you have a 15-day pass, for example, you can travel 15 consecutive days, hopping on and off trains many times each day.

Flexipass: If you like to stay for a few days or so at various places, a flexipass is the better choice. You have a certain number of travel days to use within a longer period of time (for example, any 10 days within a 2-month period). You can sprinkle these travel days throughout your trip or use them all in a row. You can take as many separate trips as you like within each travel day. A travel day runs from midnight to midnight, but luckily, an overnight train or boat ride uses only one travel day. For details, see "Using Your Pass" later in this guide.

First-class, Second-class, and Youth Passes

Wrestling with the choice between first and second class? Remember that nearly every train has both first and second class cars, each going precisely the same speed.

If you're considering a Eurailpass or Europass: The choice is made for you if you're age 26 or older—you must buy a first-class railpass. Those under age 26 have the choice of buying either a second- or a first-class pass.

If you're considering a country pass: Most country passes are available in second-class versions for travelers of any age.

If you're under 26: Some passes are discounted for youth traveling second class. To be eligible, you must be under 26 (according to your passport) the day you validate the pass in Europe. Generally, children from 4 to 11 get passes for half the cost of the adult first-class pass and those under 4 travel free. These ages vary a bit among different country passes.

Differences between first and second class: In train cars with compart-

---

Note: Eurail/Europass prices listed in this guide are good for 1999, but all other railpass prices are good through the end of 1998 (expect 1999 prices to be 3% higher). After 12/15/98 you can get a free 64-page revision of this guide with 1999 prices for all passes by calling (425) 771-8303 -- or go to www.ricksteves.com. Railpass prices and features are subject to change.

ments, first-class is configured with six seats (three facing three) while second-class sometimes has eight seats (four facing four). With open-style seating, first-class has three plush seats per row (two on one side and a single on the other) and second-class has four skinnier seats.

Choosing first class: If you have the extra money, riding first class is less crowded and more comfortable. First-class railpasses can be a good value: While individual first-class tickets cost 50% more than second-class, first-class railpasses generally bump your price up only 25% to 40%.

Choosing second class: If you're rugged and on a budget, go second class. In much of Europe, the new second-class cars are quite nice. And Back Door travelers know that nuns and soldiers are partying in second class. First class is filled with Eurail and Europass travelers age 26+ who had no choice, and business travelers who paid 50% extra in hopes that they wouldn't have to sit with the likes of you and me.

Switching classes: Those with first-class passes may travel in second-class compartments (although the conductor may give you a puzzled look). Those with second-class passes must pay the 50% difference in ticket price to upgrade to first.

Rail & Drive Passes
Most passes include a Rail & Drive option, offering a certain number of rail days and car days. For more information, see "Rail & Drive Passes" later in this chapter.

Longer or Shorter Pass: Some Money-Saving Tips
Both consecutive-day and flexi railpasses offer a varying number of travel days. Your first step in chosing a railpass should be to figure out how many travel days you'll need for your trip.

With some thoughtful juggling, a shorter consecutive-day pass can cover a longer trip. For example, you can take a one-month trip with a 21-day Eurailpass ($172 cheaper than a one-month pass) by starting and/or ending your trip...

...in a city where you'd like to stay for several days or more. On, say, a Copenhagen-Rome trip, spend a few days in Copenhagen, validate your pass upon departure, and arrive in Rome as your pass expires.

...in a country not covered by your pass. For example, a Eurailpass does not cover Britain. On a London-Amsterdam trip, start with a couple of days in London, pay for the $60 train trip from the border of France to Paris (to save your railpass), sightsee in Paris for several days, and validate your consecutive-day pass when you leave Paris. Plan for your pass to expire in Amsterdam, where you can easily spend a few days making short, cheap day trips that don't merit the use of a railpass.

✈ Travel tip: Where to turn when you are rail-ly confused.

Europe Through the Back Door: Sells all European and British passes.
Free rail video, guidebook and advice with every Euro/Eurailpass 425/771-8303

Rail Europe/BritRail: Sells most passes, Britain and France specialists 800/438-7245

DER: Sells most European (no French) passes, Germany specialists 800/782-2424

Depending on your trip, it can make sense to get a longer consecutive-day pass to cover a shorter trip. One long train ride (for example, $210 first class from Paris-Munich) at the end of a 25-day trip can justify jumping from a 21-day consecutive-day railpass to a one-month pass.

Stretch a flexipass by paying out of pocket for shorter trips. Save your flexipass to use for days that involve long hauls or several trips. To determine if a trip is a good use of a travel day, divide the cost of your pass by the number of travel days. For example, a 15-day Europass for $728 costs about $50 per travel day. If a particular trip costs significantly less than $50, pay out of pocket.

Flexipasses can be cheaper than consecutive-day passes, but before buying a flexipass, consider the number of days you'll go without train travel. Let's say you're planning a 21-day trip and choosing between a $718 Eurailpass for 21 consecutive days and a cheaper $654 Eurail Flexipass for 10 days in 2 months. For $64 more, the consecutive-day pass gives you the option to travel for 11 extra days, and you can just hop on the train without wondering if a particular trip justifies the use of a travel day. Of course, if you're sure you don't need any extra days, go with the cheaper flexipass.

More travel days on a pass = cheaper cost per day. Compared to shorter passes, longer railpasses are cheaper per travel day. For example, for a 15-day consecutive-day Eurailpass at $554, you're paying $37 a day. With a three-month Eurailpass for $1558, you're paying only $17 a day. Most one-hour train rides cost more than that. Consider the difference between a one-month Eurailpass for $890 and a two-month pass for $1260. You get an extra month of train travel for just $370, or just $12 a day. When you ponder getting a longer pass, remember to consider the cheaper cost per travel day. To cover a multiple-country trip, it's usually cheaper to buy one Europass or Eurailpass with lots of travel days than to buy several country passes with a few high-cost travel days per pass.

BUYING YOUR PASS

Most railpasses must be purchased in the USA and are not available in Europe. There are some exceptions: Eurailpasses are sold at some of Europe's major railway stations for about 10% more than the USA price. And some local passes (explained in each country's section of this guide) are available only in Europe.

Your neighborhood travel agent can sell you most of the passes listed in this guide. (A $10 "handling fee" is common.) Agents that don't do a lot of independent European travel may need your help to understand what's available. When you find a good travel agent, be loyal. If you don't have an agent, call Europe Through the Back Door (425/771-8303) or anyone else who specializes in budget Europe.

Save money by planning ahead: Since passes usually go up in price each January, those traveling in the first three months of a year can travel on last year's prices by buying before January 1. (After you buy a pass, you have three months to validate it; see "Validating Your Pass.")

✈ Travel tip: Pack light pack light pack light.
You'll never meet anyone who, after five trips, brags "every year I pack heavier." I pack the same amount for two weeks or three months. A 9x22x14-inch bag fits under the airplane seat, and that's my self-imposed limitation. In Europe there are two kinds of travelers — those who packed light and those who wish they had.

VALIDATING YOUR PASS

You must get your pass validated in Europe before you use it and within three months of the issue date (usually the day you bought it). For example, if May 24 is stamped on your pass as the issue date, you must validate—or start—the pass by August 23. *Never write anything on your pass before it's been validated.*

Validate your pass at any station: It's easy. At any European train station, present your railpass and passport to a railway official at a ticket window, who (for no charge) will write in the first and last dates of your travel period. All trips and bonuses must be started and finished within the valid life of your pass. If you have a group pass, all members must be present when the pass is validated.

You do not need to validate your country pass in the country it covers. Let's say you're in Amsterdam with a French railpass, you're heading to Paris, and you want the French portion of your route to be covered by your French railpass. At the Amsterdam train station, buy a ticket to the French border. Validate your French pass either on the train, or at the Amsterdam station. *Note: In some cases you may be charged a penalty of $5 to $12 (in local currency) if you wait till you're on a train to validate a pass.*

USING YOUR PASS

Unless you're taking a train that requires a reservation (see below), just hop on the train with your pass. After the train starts, the conductor will head down the train, checking for tickets and passes. Simply show the conductor your pass. He or she may ask to see your passport, too.

Using a flexipass: On your flexipass, you'll see a string of blank boxes, one for each travel day available to you. You can take as many trips as you like within each travel day. A travel day runs from midnight to midnight.

Before boarding the train (or bus or boat covered by your pass), you simply fill in that day's date in ink in one of the blank boxes on your pass. A railpass day normally runs from midnight to midnight. But an overnight train or boat journey uses up only one of your travel days if you board after 7 p.m. Then, you just write in the *next day's date* on your pass. If the very first use of your flexipass is for an overnight ride, you still write in the next day's date, though your pass will be validated for the actual date you board. The overnight trip uses up two days of your pass' total validity period, but just one travel day. All rides must be started and completed within the pass' validity period. A railpass month runs, for example, from April 26 through May 25. One-month passes last longest when started in a 31-day month.

TRAIN RESERVATIONS AND SUPPLEMENTS

A railpass doesn't cover any required train reservations, but does cover most supplements.

Reservations: Reservations are required for some of Europe's super trains (e.g., TGV), for any train marked with an $\boxed{R}$ in the schedule, on long rides in Spain and Norway, and for couchettes and sleepers (see "Sleeping on Trains," below). For many trains, reservations are not necessary and not worth the trouble and expense, unless you're traveling during a busy holiday period.

Seat reservations, which cost from $3 to $10 ($10 from the USA), can be made as long as 2 months in advance or as short as a few hours in advance (the same goes for special high-speed trains requiring seat reservations for railpass travelers). You can get reservations in Europe at a ticket window in any train station.

In 24 years of European train travel, I've never made or needed a reservation before I arrived in Europe. But if an advance reservation for a specific train will help you relax, call RailEurope at 800/438-7245 or DER at 800/782-2424. (While you're at it, ask for a window seat facing forward.)

Supplements. A few "super trains" charge a supplement, usually $10 to $25. These trains are usually identified in schedules. If you don't pay before boarding, the conductor will be happy to charge you a small penalty to collect for the supplement en route.

SLEEPING ON TRAINS

Taking long train trips at night makes sense. Every night spent riding the rails gives you an extra day to sightsee, saves you the cost of a hotel, and allows you to arrive early before the cheaper hotels fill up. The scenery missed is usually insignificant when you consider the time you gain — a day to bike in Holland, hike in the Alps, or sunbathe on an Italian beach.

You can sleep for free on the trains, or rent a couchette (berth) or sleeper (bed). Whether you have a ticket or a railpass, you must pay extra for a couchette or sleeper.

Sleeping for free: If you're in an open-style car (with airline-type seats) or in a crowded compartment, you'll sit up miserably all night. If you're in an uncrowded compartment, pull out the seats to make a free bed. Expect frequent interruptions and clip your bags to the luggage rack for security.

Couchette: One of Europe's great bargains is the $20 couchette (pronounced koo-SHET). It's a bed in a usually lockable compartment with two triple bunks (co-ed, with a blanket, pillow, clean linen, and up to five compartment mates). An car attendant monitors the compartments and also deals with conductors, thieves, and customs officials on your behalf as you sleep uninterrupted in relative safety.

Book your couchette a few days in advance, either through a European travel agent or at train stations ($20 in

IF SOMETHING GOES WRONG...

Insurance: *Unless you have railpass insurance, lost or stolen passes are non-refundable.* If you decide to get pass insurance, which is offered by most railpass retailers for $10 per pass, it must be purchased at the same time you buy your pass. Personally, I keep my pass in my moneybelt and take my chances.

Exchanges: Some unvalidated passes can be exchanged for a more expensive pass for a small fee. There is a 15% penalty for downgrading from a longer pass to a shorter, cheaper pass.

Refunds: Unused and unvalidated passes are 85% refundable if returned to the place of purchase within six months; or within one year for Eurailpasses, Europasses, French, Portuguese, Spanish, and Swiss passes. Most refunds take 6 to 8 weeks.

Europe, $29 if you buy it through your stateside travel agent). When space is available, unreserved couchettes or sleepers can be rented on the train from train attendants. Some countries offer roomier 4-person couchettes for about $30 per bunk.

Sleeper: A sleeper offers more privacy and comfort than a couchette. You'll pay from $40 to $100 on top of your ticket price for a berth in a still-crowded two- or three-bed sleeper with a tiny sink.

BUYING POINT-TO-POINT TICKETS IN EUROPE

Probably ten percent of railpass travelers would have traveled smarter and cheaper by simply buying tickets as they went. While point-to-point tickets are sold by travel agents in the USA, I'd keep my options open and maybe even save a little money by buying tickets on my own in Europe.

Railpass shoppers should consider the ticket option by using the fare maps scattered throughout this guide to add up the cost of their journey, and then compare it with the cost of a railpass.

Connecting the dots:
Point-to-point 1-way 2nd class rail fares in $US.

The "Time and Cost" map in Chapter 10 of this book shows the fares for international rides, and the country maps (listed per country pass) show the prices of domestic trips. These fares are listed in US dollars for one-way trips in second-class; for first class, add 50%. For example, if you're taking the train from Amsterdam to Paris, it'll cost you about $95 in second class or $145 for first class. While travelers age 26 and older who choose Eurail must buy a first-class pass, anyone can buy second-class tickets.

The point-to-point prices used in this rail guide are based on the "Eurail Tariff" fares which US travel agents charge for point-to-point tickets. After checking with station ticket offices in many European countries, I've concluded that these fares are generally accurate enough for the comparison purposes of this guide. Those willing to shop around in Europe and avoid the fast supplement-required trains will find some cheaper special point-to-point deals in Europe.

Local fares are based on kilometers traveled. Each country has its own "schillings per kilometer" type of formula (although some — like France — charge more during peak-use times). Rules vary with most tickets, allowing anywhere from one day to two months to complete a journey with unlimited stop-overs along the route.

Rail Europe has a new train schedule and fare information service. Call 800/4EURAIL to get times, costs and even a free fax.

Point-to-Point Ticket Deals for Youths and Seniors

For Youths: In Europe, travelers under 26 can buy discounted tickets (30% off) at over 6,000 travel agencies, or at any of Wasteels' 200 offices (tel. 407/351-2537 in USA, or www.welcomeusa.com). *Let's Go* guidebooks list budget travel offices in each city, usually located in or near major train stations. These cheap tickets, often called "BIGE" or "BIJ," are good for about 90% of international departures, except for a few exclusively first-class and express trains. The tickets generally, but not always, allow unlimited stop-overs along the route within a 2-month window. Here are some sample one-way BIGE/ BIJ fares: London-Rome, £99 ($160, 33% off the regular $240 fare); London-Amsterdam, £35 ($55, 45% off the regular $100 fare); and London-Paris, £50 ($78, 40% off the regular $130).

For Seniors: These often require you to buy a special senior ID card. In Britain, all over 60 get 30% off. In Austria, men over 64 and women over 59 get 50% off. Scandinavian countries give those over 65 (67 in Norway) 50% off, no card needed.

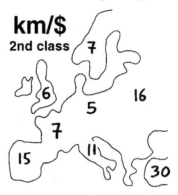

Point-to-point tickets: How many kilometers you can cover by rail for $1 depends on where you are in Europe.

Point-to-Point Prices of International Boat Crossings

Some boat crossings are covered by railpasses, but if you're buying point-to-point tickets, it helps to get an idea of the costs. Price ranges are listed, because fees vary with the season and who-knows-what-reason.

▼ Brindisi, Italy to Patras, Greece: 21 hrs, $50 to $100, free with Eurailpass, except for a peak-season surcharge of $15 from mid-June to September.

▼ Wales to Ireland: 4 hrs, $30 to $50 (free if you can talk your way into a car, which is allowed four free passengers).

▼ Ireland to France: 17 hrs, most days, $140 (half price with Eurailpass).

▼ Newcastle, England to Bergen, Norway: 21 hrs, $70 to $150.

▼ Calais, France to Dover, England: 1-2 hrs, daily, $30-$40.

▼ The sleek Eurostar "Chunnel" train cuts the London-Paris train trip from 6 hours to just over 3 hours. From downtown to downtown, the Eurostar train is actually faster than flying, and costs about the same ($100-$140).

Note: Eurail/Europass prices listed in this guide are good for 1999, but all other railpass prices are good through the end of 1998 (expect 1999 prices to be 3% higher). After 12/15/98 you can get a free 64-page revision of this guide with 1999 prices for all passes by calling (425) 771-8303 -- or go to www.ricksteves.com. Railpass prices and features are subject to change.

✈ Travel tip: Surf the Web.

The Web is overflowing with travel information. For a good start, go to my Web site at www.ricksteves.com, where you'll find this Rail Guide online, lots of travel tips from my readers, and much more. If you'd like to look up a specific European rail timetable, go to mercurio.iet.unipi.it.

RAILPASS PLANNING WORKSHEET

As the following pages are about to show you, with so many passes and prices to consider, choosing the right railpass can be downright intimidating. Use this worksheet to follow a logical, step-by-step process for finding the railpass that best suits your trip.

Arriving at start of trip in (city) _____ on (date) _____

Departing at end of trip from (city) _____ on (date) _____

Amount of time you'll be in Europe:_____

Where do you want to go? List places you want to visit in order of importance:

1_____   6_____
2_____   7_____
3_____   8_____
4_____   9_____
5_____   10_____

Now plot your destinations on the "Time and Cost" map in "Train and Railpass Skills" (Chapter 10 of this book), and connect the dots in a logical route. You'll find more detailed maps like this scattered throughout the following pages.

How do you plan to travel? Check your preferred method of travel and number of travel days below (for example, staying 3 days in one city counts as no travel days, but a day spent connecting cities does). This will help you determine whether a consecutive day, flexi, Euro or Rail & Drive pass is best for your trip.

❏ RAIL days____   ❏ CAR days____

How much will it all cost? Using the "Time and Cost" map, add up what your individual fares would cost (the individual country maps on the following pages offer more detail), and compare your total to the price of the various passes. **The Europass will offer the best value for most rail travelers**, so look at it first, especially if you are traveling with a companion.

INDIVIDUAL FARES:		RAILPASS OPTION A:	
_____	$ ____	_____	$ ____
_____	____	_____	____
_____	____	_____	____
_____	____	Total	$ ____
_____	____		
_____	____	RAILPASS OPTION B:	
_____	____	_____	$ ____
_____	____	_____	____
_____	____	_____	____
Total	$ ____	Total	$ ____

EURAILPASSES &

...are the two most popular types of passes. They offer the same basic benefits: discounts for two or more traveling together; cheaper second-class versions for youths; Rail & Drive versions; the same non-rail bonuses (such as free or discounted boat rides); and a pricing scheme that lowers your per-day travel cost as you add travel days. The main difference between the two is coverage: The

The EURAILpass, the grandaddy of all passes covers 17 countries, ranging from Portugal to Finland to Greece (see map). Eurailpasses are valid for a set number of days depending on which of the two types you choose: **Consecutive day** passes are valid for 15 days, 21 days, 1 month, 2 months, or 3 months. **Flexipasses** allow 10 or 15 travel days within a two-month period. Two or more people traveling together can save 15% by getting a **Saverpass.** The Eurailpass is all-encompassing and convenient, but for some travelers it's overkill. If you don't plan to travel through many of the 17 countries, consider a Europass.

EURAILPASSES

1999 prices!

	First Class Eurailpass	First Class Saverpass	Second Class Youthpass
10 days in 2 months flexi	$654	$556	$458
15 days in 2 months flexi	862	732	599
15 consecutive days	554	470	388
21 consecutive days	718	610	499
1 month consec. days	890	756	623
2 months consec. days	1260	1072	882
3 months consec. days	1558	1324	1089

These passes cover all 17 Eurail countries. Youthpasses are for travelers under age 26 only, no discounts for companions. Children 4-11 pay half, under 4 travel free. Saverpass prices are per person for 2 or more traveling together at all times. Because this is a "shared" pass, members of the entire traveling group must be identified and paid for at the time of purchase.

EURAILPASS COUNTRIES

✔ Austria
✔ Belgium
✔ Denmark
✔ Finland
✔ France
✔ Germany
✔ Greece
✔ Hungary
✔ Ireland
✔ Italy
✔ Luxembourg
✔ Netherlands
✔ Norway
✔ Portugal
✔ Spain
✔ Sweden
✔ Switzerland

✔ 15% OFF SAVERPASS DEAL: Looking to save money? When 2 or more adults travel together at all times, they can each save $84 to $234 by sharing a First Class Saverpass, compared to buying separate First Class Eurailpasses.

EURAILDRIVE PASS

4 first class rail days + 3 car days in a 2 month period.

Car categories	2 adults	1 adult	extra car day	extra rail day
A-Economy	$350	$435	$58	$55
B-Compact	380	495	78	55
C-Intermediate	395	525	88	55

Good in all 17 Eurail countries. **Prices listed are for 1998** (expect 1999 prices to be 3% higher). Third and fourth persons sharing car get a 4-day out of 2-month railpass for approx. $268 (kids 4-11 $134). You can add up to 5 extra rail and unlimited car days. Choose Avis or Hertz car.

Note: Eurail/Europass prices listed in this guide are good for 1999, but all other railpass prices are good through the end of 1998 (expect 1999 prices to be 3% higher). Railpass prices and features are subject to change.

EUROPASSES

Eurailpass is valid in 17 countries, while the cheaper Europass is valid in 5 countries (a few more can be added for an extra cost).

So which pass is best for you? In general, a whirlwind type trip covering many countries warrants a Eurailpass, while a trip focusing on the 5 core countries is best served by a Europass (see maps below). Read on to see which fits your needs best.

The **EUROpass** is a slimmed down version of the Eurailpass — think of it as Eurail Lite. The basic Europass is valid in Germany, France, Switzerland, Italy and Spain. For additional fees you can add adjacent countries (called zones) to your pass.

By figuring out the exact number of travel days and/or extra countries you need, you can custom-design your own pass. But if you want more than 15 days of travel, or want to add more than two zones to your Europass, a Eurailpass makes more sense.

EUROPASSES

1999 prices! All Europasses include France, Germany, Switzerland, Italy and Spain. No more than two of the following extra "zones" may be added: ▼ Austria/Hungary; ▼Belgium/Netherlands/Luxembourg; ▼Portugal; ▼Greece.

FIRST CLASS EUROPASS	5 standard countries	1 extra zone	2 extra zones
5 days in 2 months	$348	$408	$448
6 days in 2 months	368	428	468
8 days in 2 months	448	508	548
10 days in 2 months	528	588	628
15 days in 2 months	728	788	828

FIRST CLASS SAVERPASS	5 standard countries	1 extra zone	2 extra zones
5 days in 2 months	$296	$348	$382
6 days in 2 months	314	366	400
8 days in 2 months	382	434	468
10 days in 2 months	450	502	536
15 days in 2 months	620	672	706

Prices are per person, based on 2-5 traveling together. Kids 4-11 pay 1/2 adult Saverpass fare. Under 4 travel free.

SECOND CLASS YOUTHPASS	5 standard countries	1 extra zone	2 extra zones
5 days in 2 months	$233	$278	$311
6 days in 2 months	253	298	331
8 days in 2 months	313	358	391
10 days in 2 months	363	408	441
15 days in 2 months	513	558	591

You must be under 26 on your first day of railpass travel.

EUROPASS COUNTRIES

Included with all Europasses:

- ✔ France
- ✔ Germany
- ✔ Switzerland
- ✔ Italy
- ✔ Spain

Europass extra-cost add-on zones:

- ✔ Austria/Hungary
- ✔ Belgium/Neth/Lux
- ✔ Portugal
- ✔ Greece

✔ 15% OFF EURO SAVERPASS DEAL:
Looking to save money? When 2 or more adults travel together at all times, they can each save $52 to $122 by sharing a First Class Saverpass, compared to buying separate First Class Europasses.

EUROPASS DRIVE

3 first class rail days + 2 car days in 2 months.

Car categories	2 adults	1 adult
A-Economy	$265	$315
B-Compact	280	355
C-Intermediate	290	370
D-Compact Automatic	310	415

Good only in France, Germany, Switzerland, Italy, and Spain. **Prices listed are for 1998** (expect 1999 prices to be 3% higher). You can add rail days (max. 12, $42 per rail day) and car days (no limit, $55 to $105 per car day, depending on type of car). Choose Avis or Hertz car.

Choosing the Eurail or Europass That's Right for Your Trip

Here are a few factors to keep in mind regarding Eurail and Europasses:

✓ Neither the Eurailpass or Europass is valid in the United Kingdom (England, Scotland, Wales and Northern Ireland).

✓ Europasses and Eurailpasses pay for themselves more quickly in the north where rail travel costs are higher.

✓ A one month Eurailpass ($890 first class, $623 second class youth) pays for itself with a trip from Amsterdam to Rome to Madrid to Paris.

✓ One Europass is usually a better deal than buying several single-country railpasses.

Comparing Europasses, Eurail Flexipasses, and Saverpasses

Here is a basic comparison for single travelers and traveling two-somes:

Flexi Days in 2 months	EUROPASS for 1 person, incl. 5 countries	SAVERPASS per person 2 traveling together, incl. 5 countries	EURAIL FLEXIPASS for 1 person, incl. 17 countries	SAVERPASS per person 2 traveling together, incl. 17 countries
5 days	$348 ($70/day)	$296 ($60/day)	NA	NA
10 days	$528 ($53/day)	$450 ($45/day)	$654 ($65/day)	$556 ($56/day)
15 days	$728 ($49/day)	$620 ($41/day)	$862 ($58/day)	$732 ($49/day)

The per-day price difference between the 5-country Europass and the 17-country Eurailpass averages only about $10 per day (less if Euro add-on zones are included). If you like to cover a lot of ground and keep your itinerary options open, you may be better off buying the full-blown Eurailpass. With either pass, the more you travel, the more you save compared to buying tickets as-you-go. And with Euro/Eurail Saverpasses, two can always travel together more cheaply than one. Consider the sample trips listed below.

Sample trips

1. Mike and Peggy have 20 days to make the loop trip shown below. Their best bet is option **B**. Even though option D gives them more flexibility for taking sidetrips, the extra cost is more than $100/person.

Frankfurt → Paris → Madrid → Rome → Vienna → Berlin → Frankfurt

A: First class **Europass** plus Austria/Hungary, 10 days in 2 months (includes 7 countries, 6 night trips): $528

B: Same as A with 2 traveling together using the **Europass Saverpass**, per person: $450

C: First class **Eurail Flexipass**, 10 days in 2 months (includes 17 countries) : $654

D: Same as C with 2 traveling together (First class 17-country **Eurail Saverpass**) per person: $556

E: First class **tickets** purchased as-you-go in Europe: $1050

F: Second class **tickets** purchased as-you-go in Europe: $700

2. Janice is taking 7 weeks to do an open-jaws trip shown below. Her best bet is option **A**, a Europass.

Munich → Paris → Geneva → Nice → Venice → Rome

A: First class **Europass**, 5 days in 2 months (includes 5 countries, 3 overnight trips): $348

B: Same as A with 2 traveling together (per person): $296

C: First class **tickets** purchased as-you-go in Europe: $570

D: Second class **tickets** purchased as-you-go in Europe: $390

Europass Restrictions

Europasses are good for use only in the countries listed. Beware of your route — if a train you are on passes through a country not on your pass, you must buy a separate ticket for that stretch in advance, or pay a hefty fine. Adding zones does not increase your number of rail days. Adding days does not increase your 2 month "window." The Greece add-on zone includes the boat running between Brindisi, Italy and Patras, Greece. Saverpass users need to purchase their passes at the same time, and must travel together at all times.

Adding days: To determine if adding a day is worth it, compare that cost to buying an individual point-to-point ticket. For solo travelers, adding a day costs $40 first class ($30 second class). For example, if you are based in Paris, it doesn't make sense to add a day just to include the $10 side trip to Versailles, but it would pay off for an $80 side trip to the Loire Valley.

Adding zones: The Europass allows you to add no more than two of the following extra-cost zones: Austria/Hungary, Belgium/Netherlands/Luxembourg, Portugal, and Greece. The first zone you add costs $60, the second just $40. The chart below will help you to determine whether it's worth it.

Add-on zone	Sample 2nd class tickets for trips in that zone
Austria/Hungary	Salzburg-Vienna, $30; north-south border, $25 (e.g., fare through Austria from Munich to Italy via Innsbruck); German border (near Salzburg)-Budapest, $70.
Benelux	Amsterdam to French border, $65; Amsterdam to German border, $20; Brussels to any border, $20.
Portugal	Lisbon to Algarve or Spanish border, $20.
Greece	Covers Italy boat crossing (worth $50 - $100). Patras to Athens train $35.

Pass Coverage of Supplements and Special Trains

Eurail and Europasses cover 95% of all the state-run trains in Europe. They also include the supplements on all European EC and IC trains, France's TGV, Germany's ICE and Spain's Talgo. Exceptions are: International routes for TGV and Cisalpino ($25), Thalys between Amsterdam or Brussels and Paris ($25 extra), the ETR from Milan to Rome ($50 extra, includes a meal), and the AVE train between Madrid and Sevilla (about $50 extra). Both passes give a discount of about 33% on the Eurostar train crossing the English Channel. Some private Swiss trains are not covered -- see the Switzerland section later on for specifics.

Eurail/Europass Bonuses

The following European boat and bus rides are free for Eurail and Europass holders (but use up a "flexi" day). A number of other non-rail rides are discounted (e.g., France - Ireland boat is half-price). The map which accompanies each pass explains these bonuses and their restrictions in detail.

▼ German Romantic Road Bus
▼ German Castle Road Bus
▼ German Rhine Boats
▼ Swiss Lake Boats

International Boat Crossings:
  ▼ Italy - Greece
  ▼ Sweden - Finland
  ▼ Sweden - Germany
  ▼ Sweden - Denmark

COUNTRY RAILPASSES: GREAT BRITAIN

Britain's BritRail Pass gives you free run of the British train system: 15,000 train departures from over 2,500 stations daily in England, Scotland and Wales. It does not cover Northern Ireland or the Republic of Ireland (although the "BritRail Plus Ireland" pass does). Since Great Britain is not covered on the Eurailpass, and Britain's pay-as-you-go train fares are the highest in Europe, BritRail is a big seller.

Britain & Ireland:
Point-to-point 1-way 2nd class fares in $US by rail (solid line) and bus (dashed line).
Add up fares for your itinerary to see whether a railpass will save you money.

BRITRAIL CLASSIC PASS

	Adult first class	Adult standard	Over 60 first class	16-25 youth standard
8 consec. days	$375	$259	$319	$205
15 consec. days	575	395	489	318
22 consec. days	740	510	630	410
1 month	860	590	730	475

"Standard" is polite British for "second" class. No senior 2nd class pass discount.

BRITRAIL FLEXIPASS

	Adult first class	Adult standard	Over 60 first class	16-25 youth standard
4 days in 1 month	$315	$219	$269	$175
8 days in 1 month	459	315	390	253
15 days in 1 month	699	480	590	----
15 days in 2 months	----	----	----	385

Note: overnight journeys begun on your BritRail pass or Flexipass's final night can be completed the day after your pass expires--only BritRail allows this trick. A bunk in a twin sleeper costs $40.

BRITRAIL PLUS CAR PASS

	First class	First class over 60	Standard class
Any 3 days by rail + 3 days by car in 1 month:	$393	$360	$325
Any 6 days by rail + 7 days by car in 1 month:	$740	$689	$634

BritRail Plus Car gives you rail travel throughout England, Scotland and Wales and use of a Hertz car. Prices listed are per person for a manual shift 2-door economy car. An additional adult pays $221 (1st cl)/$153 (2nd cl) for a 3+3 pass, or $340/$234 for a 6+7 pass. Add about $50 per person for a compact car, and another $40 for an intermediate car. Possible to add car days, but no rail days. Drivers must be 25+. No senior discounts for standard class.

✔ **PARTY PASS:** Groups of 3 or 4 traveling together can now get a 20% to 25% "party" discount on many BritRail passes. See your travel agent for exact party pass prices.

✔ **KIDS PASS:** For each adult pass you buy, one child (5-15) gets a pass of the same type free (specify when you order). Additional kids pay the normal half-adult rate. The Kids Pass is available with BritRail Classic, Flexi, Senior, Plus Car and Plus Ireland passes.

LONDON TRAVELCARD AND LOCAL TUBE PASS ALTERNATIVES

Many travelers save money by buying cheaper alternatives to Travelcards once they are in London. Remember that most sightseeing occurs within or near the Central Zone (much less than 650 square miles!). Weekend passes offer 2 days at a 25% discount. Families also get a discount. Passes are easy to buy at any major London tube station, and include (with rough dollar costs):

▼ 1 day Central Zone, good for most of down-town, everything within and including the Circle Line, all day, but not before 9:30 a.m. on work days: £3.20 ($5).

▼ Same pass, but for all zones: £4.30 ($7).

▼ 7 Day Central Zone Pass with no 9:30 a.m. limit: £13 ($20) and a photo.

▼ LT Card, one day of tube and bus travel in any two zones, all hours: £4 ($6).

SCOTRAIL FLEXIPASS

4 days out of 8 flexi $110
8 days out of 15 flexi 160
12 days out of 15 flexi . 210
Good on all trains, standard class only, and covers Caledonian MacBrayne ferry service to Scotland's most popular islands. The Scots give no discounts for wee kiddies.

LONDON VISITOR TRAVELCARD

3 consec. days for $29; 4 consec. days for $39; 7 consec. days for $59.

These cover you on all 650 square miles of London's bus and subway (tube) system, including the tube (but not the "Airbus") trip from Heathrow airport and can be used any time during the day. Your travel agent will give you a voucher which you will exchange for your pass at any major underground or transport office, including Heathrow airport. Children 5 to 15 pay $12, $15, and $22.

BRITRAIL SOUTHEAST PASS

	First cl.	Standard cl.
3 out of 8 days:	$94	$69
4 out of 8 days:	126	94
7 out of 15 days:	166	126

Covers sidetrips from London to all of southeast England including Oxford, Cambridge, Salisbury, and Exeter. Kids 5-15 pay $27 (1st cl) or $18 (2nd cl) flat fare per pass.

BRITISH RAIL DEALS NOT SOLD IN THE USA

In Britain, round-trip "same-day-return" tickets can cost as little as 10% more than the one-way fares. Britain also offers **Super Advance Return** tickets at a savings of a few pounds — purchase before 2 p.m. the day before your trip. For more savings, consider **Apex** fares (buy at least 1 week in advance for trips of 100+ miles) or **Super Apex** fares (buy at least 2 weeks ahead for trips of 250+ miles). Apex deals get snapped up fast in summer, can be booked up to 8 weeks ahead, are non-refundable, and can be ordered from the USA by credit card (call to Britain 011-44-345-484950 for 24 hour information). For a London-Edinburgh round-trip, the regular fare is £73.50 ($118), Super Advance Return is £60 ($96), Apex is £48 ($77), Super Apex is £34 ($54). Blimey!

Britain's **Young Person's Railcard** costs £18 ($29) and offers a 34% discount on any British train trips and boat rides to Europe for those between 16-25. The **Family Rail Card**, available in Britain for £20 ($32), gives parents traveling with kids a 25% discount, and lets kids under 16 travel along for only £2 per trip. **Seniors** over 60 can get 30% off the price of point-to-point tickets.

Note: Regional/country railpass prices listed in this guide are good through the end of 1998 (expect 1999 prices to be 3% higher). After 12/15/98 you can get a free 64-page revision of this guide with 1999 prices for all passes by calling (425) 771-8303 -- or go to www.ricksteves.com. Railpass prices and features are subject to change.

BRITRAIL ANALYSIS:

At only 5 kilometers per dollar, Great Britain has Europe's most expensive train system. BritRail passes are no steal, but they still pay for themselves quickly if you travel at least from London to Scotland. The "unrestricted" direct one-way London-Edinburgh fare (one-way $157 1st class, $105 second class; round-trip $105 2nd class) costs about half of what you'll pay for BritRail's 4-day Flexipass. Those on a tight budget will find that standard class (British for second class) is fine, and first class passes are not worth the extra 40% (in fact, many "milk run" trains have only standard class cars). If you're traveling with wee ones under 16, the BritRail Kids Pass is a jolly good deal.

Bus travel will save you money. Before buying a BritRail pass, consider the good rail and bus deals available locally. As explained below, equivalent 8- and 15-day bus passes are 50% less than their second class rail counterparts.

BRITRAIL OR BRITBUS...

While many small towns and rural areas of Britain are simply not served by trains, travelers can go anywhere just about any time by coach. ("Bus" means city bus. "Coach" is British for any long distance bus). British coach travel is cheaper but slower than rail travel. While some argue you get a closer look at Great Britain through a bus rather than a train window, I'd bus Britain only to save money and to fill gaps in the train system.

Many buses are ideal for daytrips from London. People over 59 or un-

BRITISH TOURIST TRAIL FLEXI BUS PASS

3 consec. days	£50 ($80)
3 days in 5 flexi (sold in US by BTA only)	$79
5 days in 10 flexi	£80 ($128)
5 days in 30 flexi (sold in US by BTA only)	$139
8 days in 16 flexi	£120 ($192)
15 days in 30 flexi	£180 ($288)
15 days in 30 flexi (as sold in US)	$289
15 days in 60 flexi (sold in US only)	$299

Allows unlimited bus travel in England, Scotland and Wales on the extensive National Express bus service. (The prices in parentheses are the approximate $ cost to buy the passes in Great Britain.) Special youth and senior passes save about 30% for those over 59 or under 26.

der 26 can buy a £7 ($13) discount card in Great Britain (for up to 30% off on all National Express coaches). For more information on British coach travel passes, contact **BTA** (British Travel Associates), Box 299, Elkton, VA 22827, tel. 540/298-1395, or **National Express** (call Britain 011-44-990-808080).

There are several super cheap hop-on-and-hop-off bus circuits that take mostly youth hostelers around the country cheap and easy. For instance, **Slow Coach** does a 1,600-kilometer circle connecting London, Bath, Stratford, the Lakes, Edinburgh, York, Cambridge, and London youth hostels (open-ended pass £99, tel. 01249/891959).

Comparing train and "coach" travel in Britain

From London to:	miles	by train	by coach
Bath	107	25 per day / 1.25hr / $44	9 per day / 3 hr / £10 ($16)
Cambridge	56	31 per day / 1hr / $25	13 per day / 1.75hr / £ 5 ($8)
Cardiff, Wales	145	21 per day / 1.75 hr/ $60	9 per day / 3.25hr / £21 ($36)
Edinburgh	390	17 per day / 4hr / $105	2 per day / 8hr / £15 ($24)
Oxford	60	35 per day / 1hr / $20	46 per day / 1.75hr / £6 ($10)
Stratford	110	4 per day / 2hr / $30	3 per day / 3hr / £6 ($10)
York	188	27 per day / 2hr / $80	4 per day/ 4.25hr / £15 ($24)

THE ENGLISH CHANNEL TUNNEL

The fastest and most convenient way to get from Big Ben to the Eiffel Tower is no longer by plane — it's through the "Chunnel" on the Eurostar train. Go from downtown London to Paris (11/day, 3 hrs) or Brussels (6/day, 3 hrs) without all the advance check-in, luggage carousel, or airport-to-city taxi hassles. The train goes 100 mph in England and 186 mph on the

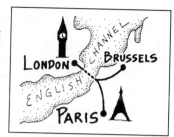

Continent. The actual tunnel crossing is a 20-minute black, silent, 100 mph non-event.

For the latest fares, call 800/EUROSTAR. When you're ready to commit to a date and time, call one of these numbers in the USA to book an "instant reservation" with your credit card, or contact your travel agent. Add $10 for handling and 2-day delivery. If your travel dates are uncertain, you can also book Chunnel tickets at any major European train station.

Eurostar "Chunnel" fares between London and Paris or Brussels

Category	Class	One-way	Round-trip
Full fare (includes a classy meal)	1st cl	$199	$398
Full fare (no grub)	2nd cl	139	278
Leisure (restrictions on refundability)	1st/2nd	159/99	318/198
Youth (under 26)	2nd cl	75	150
Eurail, Euro, BritRail, France or Benelux passholder	1st cl	139	278
Eurail, Euro, BritRail, France or Benelux passholder	2nd cl	85	170

Seniors 60+ save 20%, kids 4-11 approx. half price, under 4 ride free, no pre-purchase required. Call for current fares. Eurostar does not take a day off your railpass, but to qualify for the discount your trip must take place during your pass' validity period.

LONDON TO PARIS OR AMSTERDAM BY TRAIN, BUS AND BOAT

The old-fashioned way of crossing the channel is twice as romantic (when channel waters are calm), but twice as complicated and time-consuming, and just a little less expensive. You'll get better prices in London than from the USA (get latest fares there). Taking the bus is cheapest, and round-trips are a bargain. By bus/boat: £40 one-way, £50 round-trip, 10 hours, day or overnight, on Eurolines (tel. in Britain 0171/730-8235) or CitySprint (tel. 01304/240241). By train/boat: £40 one-way overnight, £57 by day, 7 hours. By plane: £90 regular, £40 student stand-by.

English ports of Dover, Folkestone, Ramsgate, or Harwich to:

Calais	31 trips/day	takes 1 hr	$35 ferry only
Oostende	3 trips/day	takes 2-4 hrs	$35 ferry only
Hoek van Holland	2 trips/day	takes 7 hrs	$100 ferry only

Train connections: London-Dover/Folkestone (2 hrs, $30), London-Harwich (1.5 hrs, $30), Calais-Paris (3.5 hrs, $65), Oostende-Brussels (1.5 hrs, $20), Hoek to Amsterdam (2 hrs, $20).

Note: Regional/country railpass prices listed in this guide are good through the end of 1998 (expect 1999 prices to be 3% higher). After 12/15/98 you can get a free 64-page revision of this guide with 1999 prices for all passes by calling (425) 771-8303 -- or go to www.ricksteves.com. Railpass prices and features are subject to change.

REPUBLIC OF IRELAND

Ireland's trains fan out from Dublin but neglect much of the countryside. The bus system is better and much cheaper (e.g. $15 Dublin-Galway, $20 Dublin-Cork). Your Eurailpass covers the boat from Ireland to France. Here's a taste of special Irish travel deals:

▼ The **Emerald Isle Card** is Ireland's best transportation pass deal. It gives train and long distance coach (Bus Eireann and Ulster Bus) service throughout all of Ireland (the Republic and the North) including city bus service in major cities: 8 days in 15 for $174, any 15 days in 30 for about $300. It's sold at train stations and CIE Tours in Dublin or Limerick, Ulster Bus in Belfast, or at CIE Tours/ Irish Rail in the USA (100 Hanover Ave, Box 501, Cedar Knolls, NJ, 07927, 800-243-8687). The USA number is helpful for information, but you can purchase your passes cheaper and faster at any major station in Ireland. Kids' passes are half price.

▼ The all-Ireland rail-only **Irish Rover** pass gives you 5 rail days in a 15 day period for $124.

▼ The combo **Irish Explorer** flexipass gives any 8 days of bus or rail travel out of 15 (in the Republic of Ireland only) for $150, or a rail-only version with 5 out of 15 days for $100.

▼ For bus travel only, the **Road Rambler**, offering 8 out of 15 days for about $110, is available only in Ireland.

▼ Any student can get discounts on rail and bus travel with a **Travelsave Stamp** (take your ISIC student I.D. card and $10 to any USIT student travel office in Ireland).

Ireland: Point-to-point 1-way 2nd class fares in $US by rail (solid line) and bus (dashed line). Add up fares for your itinerary to see whether a railpass will save you money.

BRITRAIL PLUS IRELAND PASS

	1st class	Standard
5 days out of 1 month	$473	$359
10 days out of 1 month	698	511

This pass covers the entire British Isles (England, Wales, Scotland, Northern Ireland and the Republic of Ireland) including a round-trip Sealink ferry crossing between Wales or Scotland and the Emerald Isle during the pass's validity (okay to leave via one port and return via another). Reserve boat crossings a day or so in advance -- sooner for holidays. One child (5-15) travels along free with each pass. Extra kiddies pay half fare.

SEALINK FERRIES AND CATAMARANS CONNECTING BRITAIN AND IRELAND

British port to...	Irish port	crossings daily	ferry/cat. hrs	ferry/cat. cost
Holyhead	Dun Laoghaire [1]	8	3.5 / 1.5	$35 / $40
Fishguard	Rosslare	6	3.5 / 1.5	$35 / $40
Stranraer	Larne	9	2.25 / 1.5	$35 / $40
London (RR + boat) [2]	Dublin	2	10 / 7	$85 / $90

Call 800/677 8585 in the USA for the latest details on ferry connections.

[1] Dun Laoghaire is a short bus or train ride from Dublin.

[2] Travelers from London to Dublin may find it worthwhile to catch a quick shuttle flight. Prices start at $80. National Express (Britain's Greyhound) offers great London-Dublin bus+ferry tickets for as low as £15 ($24).

FRANCE

France's SNCF, Europe's super train system, offers over 16,000 departures a day around this Texas-sized country. Unlike most countries, point-to-point French ticket prices go up in peak times. Local schedules show blue (quiet), and white (normal) times.

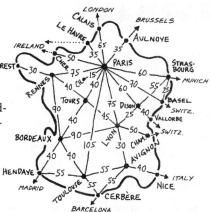

> **France:** Point-to-point 1-way 2nd class rail fares in $US. Add up fares for your itinerary to see whether a railpass will save you money.

FRANCE FLEXIPASS

	1st class	2nd class	Extra days
Any 3 days in a month*	$195	$165	$30 (6 max)
Flexi Companion**	156	132	30 (6 max)
Any 4 days in 2 months Youth (2nd cl)***	$150		25 (6 max)

*Kids 4-11 pay half fare.
**3 days in a month, price per person for 2 people traveling together on all journeys, no kids discounts.
***Must be under age 26.

> **Note:** *Regional/country railpass prices listed in this guide are good through the end of 1998 (expect 1999 prices to be 3% higher). After 12/15/98 you can get a free 64-page revision of this guide with 1999 prices for all passes by calling (425) 771-8303 -- or go to www.ricksteves.com.*

FRANCE RAIL & DRIVE PASS

Any 3 days of rail and 2 days of car in a month.

car category	1st class	2nd class	extra car day
A-Economy car	$189	$174	$45
B-Compact car	209	194	65
C-Intermediate car	229	214	85
D-Compact automatic	239	224	95

Price is per person, two traveling together. Solo travelers pay about $100 extra, third and fourth members of a group need only buy the equivalent flexi railpass. Extra rail days (6 max) cost $30 first class or $30 second class per day. You can add up to 6 extra car days.

✈ Travel tip: Don't be intimidated by French.

If you don't speak French yet, forget it. Rather than learning a few more verbs before you depart, sit down and think about communicating in what the Voice of America calls "simple English." Speak clear as a robot, choose easy words, make educated guesses, and you'll hurdle the language barrier. Your attitude will win more friends than your fluency. Use your phrasebook to smooth the way for routine transactions, and to give the locals an ice-breaking conversation piece.

FRANCE RAIL & DRIVE ANALYSIS:

Like all rail & drive passes, this is a good deal for two or more people traveling together. For not much more than the cost of two France Flexipasses, the France Rail & Drive pass tosses in two days of Avis car rental for $40 per day ($20 per person per day). This is much less than a typical daily car rental rate. Figure on spending an additional $30 per day to cover gas, tolls and CDW insurance. Many places in rural France are great for a day in a car. If having a car for a longer period appeals to you, consider the money-saving option of leasing. In France, you can lease a small car for as few as 17 days for around $549 (available through Europe by Car, call 800/223-1516 for details and insurance options).

GERMANY

GERMAN RAILPASS

	1st class	1st cl twin	2nd class	2nd cl twin	Junior
5 days in a month	$276	$138	$188	$94	$146
10 days in a month	434	217	304	152	200
15 days in a month	562	281	410	205	252

Discounted "twin" pass is for the companion of anyone who buys a full price pass in the same class (must travel together at all times). "Junior" passes are for those under 26. Covers all the Eurail bonuses in Germany (boats on Rhine and Mosel, Romantic Road bus tour, etc).

GERMAN RAIL & DRIVE PASS

4 days of rail and 3 days of Hertz car rental in a month. Add up to 4 extra 1st class rail days for $39/day ($29/day, 2nd class). Prices (except for extra car days) are per person for two traveling together. Solo travelers pay about $100 extra, 3rd and 4th persons pay $189 1st class, $129 2nd class. Another version is available with 5 rail days and 3 car days for $50 more. For specifics, call DER at 800/782-2424 or ETBD at 425/771-8303.

	1st cl	2nd cl	extra car day (no max.)
A: Economy car	$288	$218	$50
B: Compact car	308	248	65
C: Intermediate car	318	258	75
D: Compact automatic	318	258	75

SOLD ONLY IN GERMANY...

The 240DM **BahnCard** gives a 50% discount on 2nd class tickets for a year. Those over 59, under 23, students under 27, and spouses (traveling with someone with the 240 DM card) get the same card for 110 DM (children under 18, 50 DM). BahnCards are sold at German train stations. The **Guten Abend** ticket lets night owls go anywhere in Germany between 7 p.m. (2 p.m. Saturdays) and 2 a.m. the next day for about 60 DM (2nd class, buy at train stations).

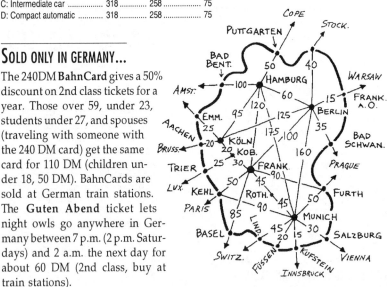

Germany: Point-to-point 1-way 2nd class rail fares in $US. Add up fares for your itinerary to see whether a railpass will save you money.

Note: Regional/country railpass prices listed in this guide are good through the end of 1998 (expect 1999 prices to be 3% higher). After 12/15/98 you can get a free 64-page revision of this guide with 1999 prices for all passes by calling (425) 771-8303 -- or go to www.ricksteves.com. Railpass prices and features are subject to change.

AUSTRIA

When considering the 3 days in 15 Austrian Flexipass for $145, remember there is a first class "European East Pass" which gives you any 5 days in a month for $199 and covers Austria with the Czech Republic, Slovakia, Hungary and Poland to boot. If you're going to Prague or Budapest, this may actually beat the Austrian pass. Austria's one-month **Bundesnetzkarte** (Network Pass) costs about AS 4,300 ($440) second class or AS 5,900 ($600) first class at

Austria: Point-to-point 1-way 2nd class rail fares in $US. Add up fares for your itinerary to see whether a railpass will save you money.

AUSTRIAN FLEXIPASS

	1st cl	2nd cl
Any 3 days out of 15 days ...	$145	.... $98
Add-on days (max 5):	 21	 15

Children 4-12 half price. Bonuses include 50% off some Danube boats, 10% off Lake Constance boats.

Austrian train stations. It offers unlimited travel on Austrian railways, and a 50% discount on boat trips. Groups of up to six travelers can buy and share a discount mileage pass called a **Kilometer-bank** which is good on any train trip of at least 44 miles. Sold only in Austria, 2,000 second class kilometers (1240 miles) cost AS 2,400 ($250), 3,000 second class kilometers cost AS 3,600, and 5,000 second class kilometers cost AS 5,850. First class costs 50% more, children 6-15 go for half price.

SWITZERLAND

We don't usually recommend railpasses for small countries, but Switzerland is a small *expensive* country where a railpass can save you money. For a few days in Switzerland, your Europass or Eurailpass is fine. It can get you discounts on some lifts and mountain trains (ask at local stations) and free boat trips on Swiss lakes. If you plan to take lots of trains, lifts, and boats, Swiss railpasses are usually a better value. You may pur-

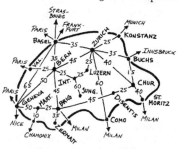

Switzerland: Point-to-point 1-way 2nd class rail fares in $US. Add up fares for your itinerary to see whether a railpass will save you money.

chase a second-class pass at any age, and "twin" passes are available in consecutive and flexi versions.

SWISS CARD

Sold in America, the Swiss Card gives you a round-trip train ride (each direction completed in one day) from any Swiss airport or border point to any point in Switzerland, plus 40-50% discounts on all Swiss railways, lake steamers, postal buses and most mountain lifts for a month ($166 first class or $128 second class). A Swiss Card is basically a one-month Half-Fare Travel Card with a round-trip train fare into and out of the country. Kids under 16 travel free with a parent using a Swiss Family Card.

SWISS FAMILY CARD

The Swiss Family
Card allows children
under 16 to travel free
with their parents.
Based on the validity
of the parent's ticket
or pass, this works
even on the high
mountain routes. The

SWISS PASS AND SWISS FLEXIPASS

	1st class	1st cl twin	2nd class	2nd cl twin
4 consec. days	$264	$158	$188	$112
8 consec. days	316	190	238	142
15 consec. days	368	220	288	172
21 consec. days	403	241	320	192
1 month	508	304	400	240
3 days in 1 month flexi	264	158	176	106
Add'l rail days (6 max)	30	18	24	14

Covers all trains, boats and buses with 25% off on the high mountain rides.
Discounted "twin" pass is for the companion of anyone who buys a full price pass
in the same class (must travel together at all times).

Swiss Family Card is available for 20 SF at major Swiss train stations, but you can
request a free Swiss Family Card when you order an adult Swiss Pass or Swiss Card
in the USA.

DEALS AVAILABLE ONCE YOU GET TO SWITZERLAND

The **Half-Fare Travel Card** gives you 50% off on all national and private trains,
postal buses, lifts, and steamers for 90 SF a month (sold at Swiss train stations).

The **Berner Oberland Pass**, allowing any 5 days of free second class travel
and 10 days at 50% off in a 15 day period for 190 SF ($170, 20% less if you have a
Swiss Pass or Card), is the most useful of Switzerland's regional passes. This pass
gives you free use of virtually all the trains, boats and lifts in the Bern, Interlaken,
and Luzern area. The highest mountain lifts (such as to the Jungfrau from Kleine
Scheidegg or to the Schilthorn from Murren) are 25-50% off with this pass during
the five "free travel" days. The 3-days-in-7 version of this pass (with 4 half price
days available) costs 150 SF.

SWISS TRAINS AND LIFTS COVERED — AND NOT COVERED — BY EURAILPASSES

The best scenic rides that **are covered** by Eurail/Europasses and Swiss passes:

▼ Geneva to Brig.

▼ Montreux to Spiez "Golden Pass"
(locally-made reservation required).

▼ Interlaken to Luzern (Lucerne).

▼ Chur, Switzerland to Tirano, Italy
"Bernina Express" (reservation required, through Rail Europe in USA,
or locally).

The following private trains are **not covered** by Eurail/Europasses — they **are
covered** by Swiss railpasses. The most important are:

▼ All the trains in the Jungfrau region south of Interlaken ($7 from Interlaken to
Grindelwald; $10 to Gimmelwald; $100 round-trip to Jungfraujoch). Note: If
you have a validated Eurail/Europass you can get a 25% discount on most
Jungfrau area trains and lifts, without using up a pass day. Ask at local ticket
offices for specifics.

▼ The $30 Brig-Disentis segment of the Glacier Express that scenically crosses
Alp-filled southern Switzerland from Martigny to Chur (reservation required;
in the USA, call Rail Europe at 800/438-7245).

▼ The private train to see the Matterhorn (Brig-Zermatt 37SF, $25).

ITALY

Traveling with point-to-point tickets in Italy is cheap, but often frustrating because of the long lines, confusing system of supplements (charged for just about any train other than the milk runs), and the predictable language problem when dealing with people in Italian train stations. The Kilometric Ticket sounds like a good deal to begin with, but it doesn't cover supplements, and requires a visit to the ticket window for validation every time you travel. The Italy Rail Card is worth a lot more than its point-to-point value for the fact that it covers all the supplements and lets you travel freely without dealing with train station lines and personnel.

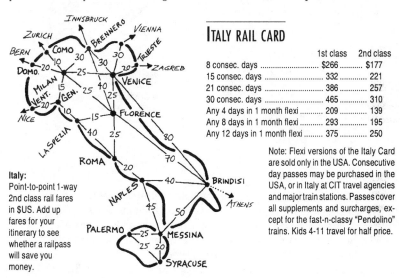

Italy:
Point-to-point 1-way 2nd class rail fares in $US. Add up fares for your itinerary to see whether a railpass will save you money.

ITALY RAIL CARD

	1st class	2nd class
8 consec. days	$266	$177
15 consec. days	332	221
21 consec. days	386	257
30 consec. days	465	310
Any 4 days in 1 month flexi	209	139
Any 8 days in 1 month flexi	293	195
Any 12 days in 1 month flexi	375	250

Note: Flexi versions of the Italy Card are sold only in the USA. Consecutive day passes may be purchased in the USA, or in Italy at CIT travel agencies and major train stations. Passes cover all supplements and surcharges, except for the fast-n-classy "Pendolino" trains. Kids 4-11 travel for half price.

ITALIAN KILOMETRIC TICKET

Also known as the "Biglietto Chilometrico," this features coupons for up to 20 trips totaling up to 3,000 kilometers that can be split by up to 5 people for $264 first class and $156 second class (e.g., a group of five could go the 570 km from Venice to Rome on a Kilometric Ticket for $32 each vs. the normal $50 regular ticket price). You must validate your ticket at the train station each time you travel. Supplements charged for fast intercity trains. The Kilometric Ticket is sold in the USA only by CIT (800/248-7245), or in Italy at CIT travel agencies and major train stations.

Note: Regional/country railpass prices listed in this guide are good through the end of 1998 (expect 1999 prices to be 3% higher). After 12/15/98 you can get a free 64-page revision of this guide with 1999 prices for all passes by calling (425) 771-8303 -- or go to www.ricksteves.com. Railpass prices and features are subject to change.

➤ Travel tip: Wear a moneybelt.

All your essential documents should be tied to your body under your clothes in a money belt...on you as thoughtlessly and securely as your underpants. Any street thief targets Americans. It's common knowledge among Europe's artful dodgers that it's the Americans who keep all their goodies in easy-to-grab purses and wallets. If I was a thief, my card would say "Yanks R Us."

BENELUX COUNTRIES

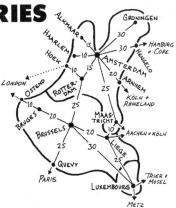

Most visits to Belgium, Luxembourg or the Netherlands don't cover enough miles to justify a railpass. This region has more than its share of special local deals. For example, the Amsterdam station offers many round-trip fares for only 25% over the regular one-way fare. For day-tripping sightseers there are some discounted train/museum deals; ask about Rail Idée.

BENELUX TOURRAIL PASS

	1st cl	2nd cl	Jr 5-25 2nd cl
5 days in 1 month flexi	$217	$155	$104
Same pass for "partner"	$109	$78	N/A

Covers trains in Belgium, Luxembourg and the Netherlands. Pass holders get discounts on Eurostar "Chunnel" train. You can buy this pass in Belgium for $10 to $20 less.

Benelux countries:
Point-to-point 1-way 2nd class rail fares in $US. Add up fares for your itinerary to see whether a railpass will save you money.

FOR SALE IN BELGIUM ONLY

Available at train stations in Belgium, the **Belgian TourRail** pass is a 5 day out of 30 day flexipass offering second class travel in Belgium for 2000 BF ($57) and first class travel for 3000 BF ($86). The **Go Pass** gives youths under 26 any ten 2nd class trips in Belgium for 1360 BF ($39). The **Multipass** (sold at any station ticket window) lets a group of 3 to 5 people (at least one must be 26 or older) take any two 1-way second class trips in Belgium for bargain prices: 3 pay 1230 BF ($35); 4 pay 1390 BF ($40); 5 pay 1450 BF ($42). The **Golden Railpass** gives seniors (60+) any 6 rides for 1230 BF ($35) 2nd class, or 1890 BF ($54) 1st class.

HOLLAND RAILPASS

	1st cl	2nd cl	2nd cl. Jr 12-26 yrs
Any 3 days in a month	$88	$68	$56
Any 5 days in a month	140	104	73

You can buy these passes through Rail Europe in the USA, or for 25% less at train stations (including Schiphol airport) in the Netherlands. There is also a 2nd class **One-Day Rail Pass** sold at Dutch train stations for 66 guilders ($41).

Note: Regional/country rail-pass prices listed in this guide are good through the end of 1998 (expect 1999 prices to be 3% higher). After 12/15/98 you can get a free 64-page revision of this guide with 1999 prices for all passes by calling (425) 771-8303 -- or go to www. ricksteves.com.

✈ Travel tip: Share a shower.

Cheap hotels have a shower down the hall — a radical and frightening concept for the average American traveler. "A whole hallway sharing one shower? I'm not going to waste precious time in Europe waiting for my shower every morning!" Remember, only Americans need a shower every morning...there are no Americans in these hotels...so you've got a private shower, down the hall. I travel 100 days a year in Europe, probably take 80 showers, and wait my turn 5 or 6 times...a small price to pay to enjoy Europe's vast array of small, simple, affordable hotels, guesthouses and pensions.

SCANDINAVIA

Train travel is expensive in Scandinavia, making the ScanRail Pass work considering. The ScanRail & Drive option is handy for those interested in Norwegian joyriding through mountainous fjord country not well served by the train. Both kinds of passes go very easy on the first class mark-up. Although second class is plenty comfortable, for $5 to $10 a day extra I'd probably spring for first class. Here are some Scandinavian country specifics (figure about 7 kroner to the dollar):

Norway: All express trains require a 20NOK ($3) reservation. Sleeping cars have 3 berths and cost 100NOK ($15), about the same as a 6-bed couchette elsewhere in Europe. Those wanting more privacy will pay 250NOK for a 2 berth room, 500NOK for a single. The scenic Myrdal to Flam trip now costs 60NOK, even for railpass holders. Norway offers point-to-point ticket discounts for certain "green departures" at off-peak times. Special "green departure mini-price tickets" take travelers from Oslo to any major Norwegian city for about 370NOK. These are sold at any station, one day in advance. Seniors over 67 who ask get a 50% discount on tickets purchased in Norway. Students can often fly in Norway for about the price of a train ticket.

Sweden: The **Reslust Card**, which costs about 150 kr, or 50 kr if you're over 65, gives travelers 50% off on trains booked 7 days in advance, 30% on others. SAS offers a standby fare to those under 26 for about 250 kr ($36) per flight.

International ferry connections: When the train actually goes on the ferry (e.g., Denmark to Germany, Norway or Sweden), the crossing is usually free if you have a railpass that covers both countries. Stockholm to Finland on the Silja Line is free with Eurail and about half price with Scanrail. Other ferry rides are discounted anywhere from 20-100%. Check with ferry companies or travel agents for specifics once you're in Scandinavia.

Scandinavia: Point-to-point 1-way 2nd class rail fares in $US. Add up fares for your itinerary to see whether a railpass will save you money.

SCANRAIL PASS

	1st class	1st class under 26	1st class over 54	2nd class	2nd class under 26	2nd class over 54
Any 5 out of 15 days	$228	$171	$203	$182	$137	$162
Any 10 days out of 1 month	364	273	324	292	219	260
21 consecutive days	422	317	376	338	254	301
1 month consecutive days	532	399	473	426	320	379

Trolls 4-11 half price. Most of these passes are available in Scandinavia at higher prices.

Scanrail & Drive Pass

Any 5 rail days and 3 Hertz car days in a 15 day period.

	2 adults 1st class	2 adults 2nd class	1 adult 1st class	1 adult 2nd class	extra car days (maximum 5)
A-Economy car	$300	$265	$385	$345	$58
B-Compact car	330	285	445	395	78
C-Intermediate car	350	305	475	435	88

Prices are approximate. No additional rail days available.

Norway railpass

	1st class	2nd class
3 days in a month	$175	$135
7 consecutive days	250	195
14 consecutive days	335	255

Few Norwegian trains offer 1st class, so save money and go with a 2nd class pass. Prices are about 20% less between October and April. Kids 4-16 half price, under 4 free.

Sweden railpass

	1st class	2nd class
3 days within a 7 day period	$170	$130

Two kids under age 15 can ride along for free.

Finnrail Pass

	1st class	2nd class
3 days in a month	$169	$109

Children 6-17 half price, under 6 free.

SPAIN/PORTUGAL

Considering the high cost of Spain and Portugal's railpasses and the cheap point-to-point bus and train fares, their passes are generally not a very good deal. Reservations are required on most long runs. Iberia is a good and reasonable place to rent a car (good rates, sparse traffic), but distances can be long, boring, and easily sleepable by train. Buses are cheap and efficient for short hops.

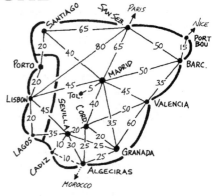

Iberia: Point-to-point 1-way 2nd class rail fares in $US. Add up fares for your itinerary to see whether a railpass will save you money.

Spain Flexipass

	1st class	2nd class
Any 3 days in 2 months	$190	$150
Extra rail days (max 7)	40	32

You'll need to pay a supplement (15%) on the Talgo 200 and AVE trains. Kids 4 - 11 half fare, under 4 cooked and sold as roast suckling pigs. For just $41 to $73 extra, your pass can get you from Madrid or Barcelona to Paris, Zurich, or Milan on a "Night Talgo" sleeper train.

Portuguese Flexipass

1st class: Any 4 days out of 15 .... $99
Kids 4-11 half fare, under 4 free.

Spain Rail & Drive Pass

Any 3 rail days and 2 Avis car days in 2 months.

	1st class	extra car day
A-Economy car	$239	$55
B-Small car	249	75
C-Medium car	259	85
E-Small automatic	289	105

Prices are per person for two traveling together. Solo travelers pay about $80 extra. The 3rd and 4th persons sharing the car buy only the railpass. Extra rail days (2 max) $40 each.

EASTERN EUROPE

Point-to-point tickets are very cheap throughout eastern Europe and the Balkans. The only reason to buy a country railpass is to avoid the need to change money and the hassle of buying tickets as you go. The European East Pass pays for itself with a Vienna-Prague-Warsaw-Budapest-Vienna loop.

EUROPEAN EAST PASS

Any 5 days in 1 month (first class) $199
Covers Austria, Czech Republic, Slovakia, Hungary and Poland. Add up to 5 extra days for $22/day.

PRAGUE EXCURSION PASS

First class only: $49 adults, $39 youth, $25 kids 4-11. Good for two train rides within a 7 day period: from any Czech border into Prague, and then from Prague to any border crossing. Since most travelers to the Czech Republic just do Prague, this is a convenient way to add Prague access to a Eurailpass. For info call EurAide in the USA at 630/420-2343, or in Munich at 089/593889. On the Web, go to www.cube.net/kmu/euraide.html.

CZECH FLEXIPASS

Any 5 days in 15 (first class) $69

HUNGARY PASS

Any 5 days out of 15 (first class) $64
Any 10 days in a month (first class) 80
First class, kids 5-14 half fare, Huns go free.

BULGARIA FLEXIPASS

Any 3 days in a month (first class) $70

ROMANIAN FLEXIPASS

Any 3 days in 15 (first class) $60

Eastern Europe:
Point-to-point 1-way 2nd class rail fares in $US. Add up fares for your itinerary to see whether a railpass will save you money.

BALKAN FLEXIPASS

Includes Bulgaria, Greece, Macedonia, Romania, Yugoslavia (Serbia + Montenegro), and Turkey.

	Adult	Youth
Any 5 days in 1 month	$152	$90
Any 10 days in 1 month	264	156
Any 15 days in 1 month	317	190

GREEK FLEXI RAIL & FLY PASS

3 days of 1st class rail plus 2 flights within Greece in 1 month, $202 adults, $108 kids. Choose your flights well and you might save a little money. But Greece's few rail connections and cheap, plentiful buses limit this pass' value. Make flight reservations only through Olympic Airways in Athens.

Note: Regional/country railpass prices listed in this guide are good through the end of 1998 (expect 1999 prices to be 3% higher). After 12/15/98 you can get a free 64-page revision of this guide with 1999 prices for all passes by calling (425) 771-8303 -- or go to www.ricksteves.com. Railpass prices and features are subject to change.

TRANSPORTATION OPTIONS FOR SEVEN GREAT THREE-WEEK TRIPS

Intimidated by all the data in this guide? Looking for a place to start? Here is a quick analysis of transportation options for my seven favorite three-week itineraries as described in my guidebook for that country or region. My preferred choices, if any, are checked and in bold:

3 WEEKS IN EUROPE

Route: Amsterdam → Rhineland → Romantic Road → Tirol → Venice → Florence → Rome → Italian Riviera → Swiss Alps → Beaune → Paris. For this plan, let your dreams rather than the cost dictate your choice:

$600   second class point-to-point tickets
$718   21 day Eurailpass
$654   10 days in 2 months Eurail flexipass
$628   10 days in 2 months Europass with Benelux and Austria add-ons.
$536   Average cost per person for 2 traveling together with 10 days Europass Saverpass with Benelux and Austria add-ons.
$670   EurailDrive split by 2 ($350) + 5 extra rail days ($275 apiece) for 9 rail days and 3 car days + $45 per person for gas and CDW (good for two buddies with an interest in driving a little, in a small manual transmission car).
$600   Three weeks in a leased car (split by 2, including gas, CDW, tolls and parking in Italy)

3 WEEKS IN GREAT BRITAIN

Route: London → Bath → Cardiff → Cotswolds → North Wales → Windermere → Oban → Edinburgh → Durham → York → Cambridge → London.

$400   second class point-to-point tickets
$288   15 days in 30 flexi bus pass
$510   22 days 2nd class BritRail pass
$480   15 days in a month 2nd class BritRail flexipass
$500   ✓ 3 weeks in a leased car ($1000 split by 2)

3 WEEKS IN FRANCE

Route: Paris → Normandy → Brittany → Loire → Carcassonne → Provence → Alps → Burgundy → Alsace → Paris.

$400   second class point-to-point tickets
$444   ✓ France Rail & Drive Pass (9 second class rail days and 3 car days, two people), $399+$45 for gas/CDW.
$718   21 day Eurailpass

3 WEEKS IN SCANDINAVIA

Route: Copenhagen → Kalmar → Stockholm → Helsinki → Stockholm → Oslo → Fjords → Bergen → Aarhus → Aero → Copenhagen.

$718   21 day first class Eurailpass
$422   ✓ 21 day first class ScanRail Pass
$500   2nd class point-to-point tickets
$292   Scanrail 10 days in 1 month 2nd class flexipass
$700   3 weeks in a leased car (split by 2) plus a round-trip boat to Finland

3 WEEKS IN ITALY

Route: Milan → Cinque Terre → Florence → Siena → Rome → Naples → Paestum → Venice → Dolomites → Como → Milan.

$210   2nd class point-to-point tickets
$375   12 days in a month first class Italy Rail Card
$250   12 days in a month 2nd class Italy Rail Card
$386   ✓ 21 days first class Italy Rail Card (worth it)
$257   21 days 2nd class Italy Rail Card
$718   21 days Eurailpass
$600   3 weeks in a leased car (including Italian extras: theft insurance, extra-strength Tylenol, city parking and autostrada tolls, split by 2)

3 WEEKS IN GERMANY, AUSTRIA & SWITZERLAND

Route: Frankfurt → Romantic Road → Reutte → Munich → Salzburg → Hallstatt → Vienna → Innsbruck → Appenzell → Interlaken → Bern → Lausanne → Baden → Baden → Mosel → Rhine → Bonn → Frankfurt.

$600   second class point-to-point tickets
$718   21 day Eurailpass
$806   15 day Europass with Austria add-on
$570   German 4 rail days and 2 car days ($178+$20 gas+$20 CDW), 3 days in 15 Austrian Flexipass ($98), Swiss Rail & Drive pass with 3 rail days and 3 car days ($205+$50 gas and CDW), best for couples who don't mind second class train and want to do some driving.
$500   ✓ 3 weeks in a leased car ($1000 split by 2).

3 WEEKS IN SPAIN & PORTUGAL

Route: Madrid → Salamanca → Coimbra → Lisbon → Algarve → Seville → Gibraltar → Nerja → Granada → Toledo → Madrid.

$220   ✓ 2nd class point-to-point tickets (best for tight budgets)
$500   ✓ 3 weeks in a leased car split by two (a great car trip)
$369   5 days in a month Spain 1st class flexipass and 4 days in 15 days Portugal flexipass
$500   Spain Rail & Drive split by 2 people with 3 rail days and 4 car days ($294+$60 gas and CDW) plus 4 days in 15 days Portugal flexipass and some extra joyrides.

✓ These itineraries and destinations are given detailed coverage in Rick Steves' country guidebooks.

EUROPEAN COUNTRY RAILPASSES

Pass	1st cl	2nd cl	youth 2nd
BritRail Pass			
8 days	$375	$259	$205
15 days	575	395	318
22 days	740	510	410
One month	860	590	475
4 days in 1 month	315	219	175
8 days in 1 month	459	315	253
15 days in 1 month	699	480	N/A
15 days in 2 months	N/A	N/A	385

See text for specifics on:
BritRail Party Passes
BritRail Plus Car Pass
BritRail Southeast Pass
BritRail Kids Pass
BritRail senior discounts
London Visitor TravelCard

Pass	1st cl	2nd cl	youth 2nd
ScotRail Flexipass			
4 days in 15 flexi	N/A	$110	N/A
8 days in 15 flexi	N/A	160	N/A
12 days in 15 flexi	N/A	210	N/A

BritRail Plus Ireland Pass			
5 days in 1 month	$473	$359	N/A
10 days in 1 month	698	511	N/A

France Flexipass			
3 days in 1 month	$195	$165	N/A
Same pass for 2 traveling together:			
(price per person)	156	132	N/A
Additional days	30	30	N/A
4 days in 2 months	N/A	N/A	$150

See text for specifics on:
France Rail & Drive Pass

Swiss Pass and Swiss Flexipass			
4 days	$264	$188	N/A
8 days	316	238	N/A
15 days	368	288	N/A
1 month	508	400	N/A
3 days in 15 flexi	264	176	N/A

See text for specifics on:
Swiss Pass partner deals
Swiss Rail & Drive Pass
Swiss Card
Swiss Family Card

Italy Rail Card			
8 days	$266	$177	N/A
15 days	332	221	N/A
21 days	386	257	N/A
30 days	465	310	N/A
4 days in 1 month	209	139	N/A
8 days in 1 month	293	195	N/A
12 days in 1 month	375	250	N/A

Pass	1st cl	2nd cl	youth 2nd
German Flexipass			
5 days in 1 month	$276	$188	$146
2nd Person/Twinpass	138	94	N/A
10 days in 1 month	434	304	200
2nd Person/Twinpass	217	152	N/A
15 days in 1 month	562	410	252
2nd Person/Twinpass	281	205	N/A

See text for specifics on:
German Rail & Drive Pass

Austrian Flexipass			
3 days in 15	$145	$98	N/A

Benelux TourRail Pass			
5 days in 1 month	$217	$155	$104

Spain Flexipass			
3 days in 2 months	$190	$150	N/A

See text for specifics on:
Spain Rail & Drive Pass

Portuguese Flexipass			
4 days in 15	$99	N/A	N/A

ScanRail Pass			
5 days in 15	$228	$182	$137
10 days in 1 month	364	292	219
21 days	422	338	254
1 month	532	426	320

Norway Rail Pass			
7 days	$250	$195	N/A
14 days	355	255	N/A
3 days in 1 month	175	135	N/A

See text for specifics on:
Scandinavian senior discounts
ScanRail & Drive Pass
Sweden Pass
Finnrail Pass

European East Pass			
5 days in 1 month	$199	N/A	N/A

Hungary Pass			
5 days in 15	$64	N/A	N/A
10 days in 1 month	80	N/A	N/A

Czech Flexipass			
5 days in 15	$69	N/A	N/A

See text for specifics on:
Prague Excursion Pass
Balkan Flexipass
Bulgaria Flexipass
Romanian Flexipass
Greek Flexi Rail & Fly Pass

Note: Eurail/Europass prices listed in this guide are good for 1999, but all other railpass prices are good through the end of 1998 (expect 1999 prices to be 3% higher). After 12/15/98 you can get a free 64-page revision of this guide with 1999 prices for all passes by calling (425) 771-8303 -- or go to www.ricksteves.com. Railpass prices and features are subject to change.

INDEX

You'll Feel like a Local When You Travel with Guides from John Muir Publications

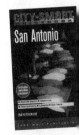

CiTY-SMaRT™ GUIDEBOOKS

Pick one for your favorite city: *Albuquerque, Anchorage, Austin, Calgary, Cincinnati, Cleveland, Denver, Indianapolis, Kansas City, Memphis, Milwaukee, Minneapolis/St. Paul, Nashville, Portland, Richmond, San Antonio, St. Louis, Tampa/St. Petersburg, Tucson*

Guides for kids 6 to 10 years old about what to do, where to go, and how to have fun in: *Atlanta, Austin, Boston, Chicago, Cleveland, Denver, Indianapolis, Kansas City, Miami, Milwaukee, Minneapolis/St. Paul, Nashville, Portland, San Francisco, Seattle, Washington D.C.*

TRAVEL ✦ SMART®

Trip planners with select recommendations to: *Alaska, American Southwest, Carolinas, Colorado, Deep South, Eastern Canada, Florida Gulf Coast, Hawaii, Kentucky/Tennessee, Michigan, Minnesota/Wisconsin, Montana/Wyoming/Idaho, New England, New York State, Northern California, Ohio, Pacific Northwest, South Florida and the Keys, Southern California, Texas, Western Canada*

Rick Steves' GUIDES

See *Europe Through the Back Door* and take along country guides to: *France, Belgium & the Netherlands; Germany, Austria & Switzerland; Great Britain & Ireland; Italy; Russia & the Baltics; Scandinavia; Spain & Portugal;* or the *Best of Europe*

ADVENTURES IN NATURE

Plan your next adventure in: *Alaska, Belize, Costa Rica, Guatemala, Honduras, Mexico*

JMP travel guides are available at your favorite bookstores. For a FREE catalog or to place a mail order, call: 800-888-7504.

John Muir Publications ✦ P.O. Box 613 ✦ Santa Fe, NM 875